www.wadsworth.com

www.wadsworth.com is the World Wide Web site for Thomson Wadsworth and is your direct source to dozens of online resources.

At *www.wadsworth.com* you can find out about supplements, demonstration software, and student resources. You can also send e-mail to many of our authors and preview new publications and exciting new technologies.

www.wadsworth.com
Changing the way the world learns®

EMOTION

James W. Kalat
NORTH CAROLINA STATE UNIVERSITY

Michelle N. Shiota
UNIVERSITY OF CALIFORNIA, BERKELEY

THOMSON
WADSWORTH™

Australia • Brazil • Canada • Mexico • Singapore • Spain
United Kingdom • United States

To our families

THOMSON
WADSWORTH

Publisher: *Vicki Knight*
Editorial Assistant: *Juliet Case*
Managing Technology Project Manager: *Darin Derstine*
Marketing Manager: *Raghu Reddy*
Senior Marketing Communications Manager:
    Kelley McAllister
Project Manager, Editorial Production: *Karol Jurado*
Creative Director: *Rob Hugel*
Senior Art Director: *Vernon Boes*
Senior Print Buyer: *Karen Hunt*
Senior Permissions Editor: *Joohee Lee*

Production Service: *G&S Book Services*
Text Designer: *Anne Draus, Scratchgravel Publishing
    Services*
Photo Researcher: *Roman A. Barnes*
Copy Editor: *Pat Tompkins*
Illustrator: *G&S Book Services*
Cover Designer: *Bill Stanton*
Cover Image: *Photodisc*
Cover Printer: *Transcontinental/Louiseville*
Compositor: *Scratchgravel Publishing Services*
Printer: *Transcontinental/Louiseville*

Printed in Canada

 2   3   4   5   6   7   09   08   07

Library of Congress Control Number: 2005936431

Student Edition: ISBN 13: 978-0-534-61218-4
            ISBN 10: 0-534-61218-0

Thomson Higher Education
10 Davis Drive
Belmont, CA 94002-3098
USA

For more information about our products,
contact us at:
Thomson Learning Academic Resource Center
1-800-423-0563

For permission to use material from this text
or product, submit a request online at
http://www.thomsonrights.com.
Any additional questions about permissions can be
submitted by e-mail to **thomsonrights@thomson.com.**

Brief Contents

Contents

3 Culture and Emotion   49

6 Anger   124

9 Love   187

10 Disgust and Contempt   212

11 The Self-Conscious Emotions: Embarrassment, Shame, Guilt, and Pride   226

Preface

After decades as a near-taboo subject for empirical psychologists, emotion has recently emerged as a major area of research. During the middle of the twentieth century, when behaviorism completely dominated American experimental psychology, research on emotions was sparse. Clinicians discussed emotion, of course, but laboratory research was mostly limited to the "conditioned emotional response," which researchers used as a way to study classical conditioning, not emotion itself. Behaviorists considered emotion private, unobservable, and therefore barely fit for serious conversation. Introductory psychology texts included an obligatory section on emotion, but if we compare the textbooks of one decade after another, progress in understanding emotion was unimpressive—until recently.

Since the 1970s, for a number of reasons, research on emotion has increased dramatically in both quantity and quality. Researchers in fields ranging from social psychology to developmental psychology to neuroscience have "discovered" emotion and now have interesting stories to tell. This is not to say that the behaviorists were wrong. To a large extent, they were right: Emotion *is* fundamentally internal and difficult to measure. (You will find us belaboring that point throughout this text.) We hope that students start with a healthy skepticism that a scientific study of emotion is even possible. However, despite the difficulties and challenges, researchers have been devising clever ways to manipulate and measure emotion, and their results say a great deal about why we have emotions, when we have emotions, and how emotions affect our lives. Many of those results do not find their way into standard texts on social psychology, cognitive psychology, and so forth. The time is ripe, we believe, for the growth of college courses on emotion and thus for textbooks to serve those courses.

In the fall of 2001, as one of us (Kalat) was finishing the sixth edition of his introductory psychology textbook, he contemplated how interesting and challenging it might be to try writing a textbook on emotion, but he knew he had major gaps in his knowledge of the field. Alas, if only he could find the right co-author. At just that time his editor, Vicki Knight, sent him the latest batch of anonymous reviewers' comments, including one that was unusually insightful and well written, by someone who happened to mention being a specialist in emotion! A series of phone calls and emails revealed that this anonymous reviewer was Michelle Shiota, a graduate student at the University of California, Berkeley, and that she was indeed interested in co-authoring a text on emotion. Every chapter in this text is the product of multiple drafts passed back and forth by email between the two authors. (For example, the copy submitted for Chapter 1 was marked "version 13.")

Our emphasis here has been on empirical research studies of emotion, including social, cognitive, biological, and clinical aspects. Because there is no fixed tradition of how to organize a text on emotion, we faced the challenge and opportunity of starting from scratch on the table of contents. Should the structure emphasize processes that generalize across emotions, or research on particular emotions? One of the major theoretical disputes in the field is whether people have a few discrete "basic" emotions (such as those listed in the table of contents) or a couple of continuous dimensions of emotion, such as positive–negative and active–inactive. Some study results are best explained in terms of processes, and others in terms of specific emotions, depending on the approach favored by a given researcher. In this text we have tried to honor both perspectives. Although we have organized much of the text around specific emotions, we did so without any theoretical commitment to the idea of basic emotions. Our rationale was that many studies address specific emotions, rather than processes general to all emotions. If we had discussed emotion strictly in terms of dimensions and processes, we almost certainly would have omitted conceptually important topics such as love, embarrassment, disgust, and amusement. However, we have also included chapters on more general emotion processes, such as the development of emotion, the effect of culture on emotion, and the role of emotion in cognition.

College courses on emotion are few today, and the ones that do exist are diverse. No text is equally appropriate for all purposes. We have aimed this text at undergraduate students who have had an introductory psychology course and who remember the essentials about research design, classical conditioning, what a "neuron" is, and so forth. However, we assume no additional background, and we believe the text should be suitable for a course that enrolls mainly sophomores and juniors. We know that many of the professors currently teaching a course on emotion ask their students to read a collection of original articles. Anyone who supplements this text with such articles could certainly raise the level of sophistication and make it suitable for more advanced students. We have included at the end of each chapter a few suggestions of our own for additional reading. The course could also be supplemented with student projects. Again, we have listed at the end of each chapter one or more suggestions for simple data-collection projects that do not require expensive equipment.

Many people deserve our thanks. Our heartiest thanks go to our editor, Vicki Knight, for encouraging and supporting a specialized text in a field without an established "market." We thank Joohee Lee for managing permissions for the illustrations, Anne Draus for the design, Bill Stanton for the cover illustration, Pat Tompkins for copyediting, and Scratchgravel Publishing Services for overseeing the production.

A large number of reviewers, anonymous to us until now, contributed substantially. When we began this project we fantasized that it would not take long. The few instructors who teach a course on emotion, we imagined, would be so starved for a new text that they would thank us for whatever we did and make only a few suggestions for improvements. Wow, were we wrong! Instructors were eager not just for a text, but for a text that gets it right, and virtually every reviewer provided lengthy, detailed, extremely helpful comments and suggestions. We could not accommodate all the suggestions, especially those asking for a much longer book or one organized in an entirely different way. Nevertheless, the reviewers' comments led to many changes that, we believe, strengthened this text greatly. The reviewers are: William Arsenio, Wesleyan University; Linda Bastone, Purchase College, SUNY; Jennifer Beer, University of California, Davis; Marc Brackett, Yale University; Rebecca Compton, Haverford College; Elaine Hatfield, University of Hawaii; Timothy Ketelaar, New Mexico State University; Gretchen Lovas, Sesquehanna University; Fayneese Miller, Brown University; Albert Porterfield, Oberlin College; Geoffrey Potts, Rice University; Susan Rivers, Yale University; and Louis Schmidt, McMaster University.

Finally, we thank our family and friends for their support, encouragement, and patience. Michelle Shiota especially thanks her mentors Dacher Keltner and Robert Levenson, two leaders in the field of emotion, who made it easy to become fascinated with this area of research and supported her development at every step. James Kalat belatedly thanks Paul Rozin, his graduate school adviser, for encouragement and inspiration over the years. Back in 1971, when Kalat received his Ph.D. from the University of Pennsylvania, neither Kalat nor Rozin had any particular interest in emotion, but Rozin encouraged his students to develop broad interests. By the time Kalat developed an interest in emotion, Rozin had become a key contributor to the field, especially in the field of disgust.

We welcome comments from our readers, both students and faculty. Eventually we hope to write a second edition, and your comments can help. Please send your suggestions via email to james_kalat@ncsu.edu and lshiota@socrates.berkeley.edu.

James W. Kalat
Michelle N. Shiota

PART ONE
General Principles and Issues

1

The Nature of Emotion

Many textbooks begin by explaining why you should care about their subject. Do you need to be convinced that emotions are important and interesting? Probably not. We constantly express our interest in emotions. We routinely ask one another, "How are you feeling today?" The biggest news stories are those likely to arouse fear, sadness, anger, joy, or other emotions. After a sports event, one of the first questions asked of the winners and losers is how they feel. We seek movies, books, music, and television shows that provide a window into other people's feelings in a wide range of situations. We care about other people's emotions and we want to share their feelings. Indeed, it is hard to imagine what "want" or "good" would mean if we had no emotions. As Antonio Damasio (1999, p. 55) has written, "Inevitably, emotions are inseparable from the idea of good and evil."

Emotion is central to many areas of psychology. Clinical psychologists spend much, probably most, of their time trying to help people control their harmful or dysfunctional emotions. Cognitive psychologists have to consider emotions to explain why people make the decisions they do. Much of social psychology and personality theory deals with the impact of emotions on our relationships with other people.

Furthermore, emotion is an important and challenging issue for theory and research. We hope you are starting this book with healthy skepticism about whether a productive study of emotion is even possible. For decades, experimental psychologists virtually ignored emotion, and even today, anyone with behaviorist inclinations has misgivings about scientific research into private, subjective experiences. Scientific progress almost always depends on good measurement, and as we shall emphasize repeatedly throughout this book, accurate measurement is difficult for emotions. As Nobel Prize–winner Sidney Brenner has said, "Progress in science depends on new techniques, new discoveries, and new ideas, probably in that order" (McElheny, 2004, p. 71). The challenge to emotion researchers, therefore, is to find better techniques to measure emotion and ways to make the best use of the measurements currently available.

In this chapter, we begin with several attempts to define emotion and to distinguish it from motivation and other psychological processes. Then we discuss general strategies for measuring emotion.

(More detailed techniques will emerge in later chapters.) We discuss the classical theories of how emotion relates to physiological arousal and motor activity. Finally, we discuss research on the relationships among cognitive, feeling, and action aspects of emotion.

◻ What Is Emotion?

In 1884, William James, the founder of American psychology, wrote an important article titled "What Is an Emotion?" Well over a century later, psychologists continue to ask that question. As with several other important concepts, emotion is difficult to define with any precision. St. Augustine (397/1955,* Book 11, Chapter 14) once wrote, "What, then, is time? If no one asks me, I know what it is. If I wish to explain it to him who asks me, I do not know." William James (1892/1961, p. 19) said about consciousness, "Its meaning we know so long as no one asks us to define it." Joseph LeDoux (1996, p. 23) has said much the same about emotion: "Unfortunately, one of the most significant things ever said about emotion may be that everyone knows what it is until they are asked to define it."

The term *emotion* literally reflects a kind of motion (e-motion), a motion outward. When it first came into common use, the term *emotion* meant disturbance or turbulence, and people spoke of a thunderstorm as an "emotion" of the atmosphere. Today we limit the word's meaning to turbulent experiences felt by humans and perhaps other animals.

Because it is difficult to measure private feelings, Antonio Damasio (1999) has recommended that we define emotion entirely in terms of observable behaviors such as attack and escape, leaving feelings out of the picture, at least for scientific purposes. The problem is that if emotion means nothing more than attack, escape, and other observable behaviors, then we don't need the word *emotion* at

---

*When two dates appear in a citation, the earlier year indicates first publication, and the later year refers to a reprint.

all, and we may as well talk simply about the behaviors. Ordinarily, when we talk about emotions, we refer to feelings as well as behaviors, and we often invoke feelings as explanations for behaviors ("Don't mind her, she's just cranky today"). In some cases we actually care more about people's feelings than about their behaviors, don't we?

People studying emotion disagree about how to define it, and some doubt even that it refers to any natural category. James Russell (2003) has suggested that *emotion* is merely a convenient category to discuss some interesting experiences that seem to us to have something in common, much as the categories *art* and *music* include many dissimilar items. We can argue about whether a particular experience is or is not emotional, just as we can argue about whether a child's scribbling is "really" art or whether an elephant banging on a drum is "really" making music, but according to Russell, this argument is pointless. The border between emotion and not-emotion is as arbitrary as the border between art and not-art or music and not-music. People draw those borders; nature doesn't. In this book, we adopt a "don't know" stance on this issue. Perhaps emotion is a natural category, or perhaps it is not. The only way to resolve that question is through further research. (Incidentally, we shall have to say "don't know" or "not sure" on many important questions. If you insist on definite conclusions, you should study geometry, not the psychology of emotions.)

Let's consider a typical definition of emotion, so that we can consider its limitations as well as its strengths. Robert Plutchik's description captures many elements generally considered central to emotion: "[Emotion is] an inferred complex sequence of reactions to a stimulus [including] cognitive evaluations, subjective changes, autonomic and neural arousal, impulses to action, and behavior designed to have an effect upon the stimulus that initiated the complex sequence" (Plutchik, 1982, p. 551).

Note a few points about that definition:

1. Emotion is inferred, not observed. You feel your own emotions, but you can only infer

someone else's. Inferences are perfectly respectable in science. After all, physicists study electrons, quarks, black holes, and all sorts of other things they cannot observe directly. However, anyone who makes inferences needs to state clearly the evidence behind the inferences. In some cases, especially when we are inferring emotions of infants, brain-damaged people, or nonhuman animals, the evidence may be quite indirect.

2. According to Plutchik's definition, every emotion is a reaction to a stimulus. Ordinarily our experiences support that idea: We are happy about something, we are angry at something, or we are afraid of something. However, this point is controversial. Some psychologists argue that just being very uncomfortable can make you angry, even if you are not angry at anyone or about anything. You're just angry in general (Berkowitz & Harmon-Jones, 2004). We shall return to this issue in more detail in the chapter on anger. Furthermore, sometimes people seem to be happy or sad for long periods of time for no apparent reason. One resolution to this seeming contradiction is that a long-term tendency is *not* an emotion. Instead we might call it a mood, global affect, or temperament. Moods have much in common with emotion, but when we say *emotion,* we want to limit our meaning to temporary experiences that arise in response to specific events (or the imagination of possible events). (How long is "temporary"? you might ask. All right, we admit there is no sharp dividing line between emotions and moods or affects.)

3. According to this definition, every emotion includes three aspects: cognition, feeling, and action. Cognition includes appraisal—the way someone interprets a situation or event, such as "I perceive a danger." Feeling is . . . well, how the experience *feels*! It is a kind of sensation. An action tendency is the impulse to behave in a certain way, even though you might inhibit that impulse. Cognitions, feelings, and action

tendencies ordinarily happen at the same time, and it is sometimes difficult to distinguish among them, but feelings really are different from thoughts, and the distinction is worth maintaining (Panksepp, 2003).

Defining emotion in terms of three aspects is also controversial because cognitions, feelings, and action tendencies do not always hang together (Russell, 2003). To define emotion as having those three aspects implies that an event produces "the emotion" (such as fear), and when that happens, we necessarily develop all three aspects—a cognition, a feeling, and an action tendency. An alternative possibility is that various events can provoke a cognition, a feeling, or an action tendency, but a given event does not necessarily produce all three. When all three occur together, we call it a prototype for that emotion, but sometimes events produce only certain aspects instead of the full emotion. For example, sometimes when you are hot and uncomfortable you might start to feel angry, without any cognition of why you are angry. Some brain-damaged people, to be described later, recognize when a situation calls for fear or anger, but they don't really *feel* the anger, or at least they don't feel it much. Also, you might sometimes have both a cognition and a feeling but no action tendency. That combination is common for joy and sadness, but it can happen with other emotions, too.

For the purposes of this book, we shall indeed define emotion as including cognitions, feelings, and action tendencies. However, we have to recognize that "partial" emotions, including just one or two of those components, may also arise.

4. Emotions are functional—that is, useful (Ekman, 1972; Keltner & Gross, 1999; Lazarus, 1991; Levenson, 1999; Plutchik, 1982). Almost all theorists agree that emotion includes either an actual or a potential response to a situation. Many philosophers, including Aristotle and Buddha, have considered emotional behaviors

to be disruptive or dangerous. Extremely emotional behaviors—as in a panic, for example—are undeniably disruptive. However, under many circumstances, emotions guide us to quick, effective actions. For example, when we feel fear, we try to escape. When someone commits an injustice against us, we strike back. When people take care of us, we stay close to them. If doing something "just feels wrong," chances are it really is a bad idea.

We do not need to settle on a final or perfect definition of emotion. Presumably as future research clarifies our understanding, we can also improve our definition. However, in any given discussion, we do need to make clear what definition we are using. When different people use different definitions, confusion is likely to result. For example, psychologists have sometimes argued about whether certain cognitions—such as blame—lead to anger. If cognition is one aspect of an emotion, as in Plutchik's definition, then asking whether cognitions cause emotions makes about as much sense as asking whether eggs cause omelets (Clore & Centerbar, 2004). Asking whether the cognitive *aspect* of emotion leads to the feeling and action *aspects* is reasonable, but keeping the terminology straight will improve the discussion.

Can We Recognize an Emotion When We See One?

Even if we cannot define emotion precisely, can we agree about which states are emotions? Not always. Nearly all psychologists regard joy, sadness, fear, and anger as good examples of emotions. Many also include disgust, contempt, and surprise as emotions. Some list additional possibilities, such as hope, embarrassment, shame, pride, love, hate, jealousy, interest, confusion, concentration, worry, contentment, and awe (Ekman, 1994a; Fredrickson, 2001; Hejmadi, Davidson, & Rozin, 2000; Keltner & Buswell, 1997; Rozin & Cohen, 2003; Shaver, Morgan, & Wu, 1996). Is interest an emotion or a cognitive state? The same

question applies to surprise, confusion, concentration, and awe. Is contentment an emotion or the absence of emotion? Some languages do not even have a word for "emotion" (Hupka, Lenton, & Hutchison, 1999), and those that do have such a word vary in their boundaries of what it includes (Niedenthal et al., 2004). However, we can make the boundaries of emotion into an empirical question—that is, one that the evidence decides. The question is, "Which of these various states have enough in common to justify treating them as a single category?" In other words, what definition of the category *emotion* helps us organize our investigations better than we would if we had no such category?

Distinction Between Emotions and Motivations

Let's re-examine the definition we considered a few paragraphs ago: Emotion is an inferred complex sequence of reactions to a stimulus including cognitive evaluations, subjective changes, autonomic and neural arousal, impulses to action, and behavior designed to have an effect upon the stimulus that initiated the complex sequence. Suppose we agree that this definition applies reasonably well to anger, fear, joy, and other emotions. Here is the problem: Read it again to see whether it rules out hunger or thirst. It doesn't! Are hunger and thirst emotions? Most people think of them as "drives" or "motivations." How can we rephrase our definition so it distinguishes emotions from other concepts?

Emotions and motivations do, in fact, overlap substantially. Remember, one part of the definition of emotion is "an impulse to do something"—a good definition of motivation. In other words, whenever you have an emotion, you also have a motivation. For the clearest examples, fear entails a motivation to escape, and anger implies a motivation to attack. "Drives" such as hunger and thirst also involve motivations, impulses to eat or drink. Still, even if emotions, drives, and motivations overlap, we find it useful to distinguish among them, because fear and anger (two prototypical emotions) seem to have more in common with each other than either does with hunger or thirst.

One difference is that emotions generally weaken over time, sometimes rapidly (Robinson & Clore, 2002), whereas drives persist until accomplishment of the goal. For example, when someone compliments you, you feel great at that moment, but your smile probably won't last long. If someone insults you, your anger gradually diminishes, as in the saying, "Time heals all wounds." Extreme fear also fades because your body is not capable of maintaining a permanent panic. In contrast, when you feel hungry, thirsty, or cold, or when you have a thorn in your skin, your drive to action persists until you remedy the situation.

Another distinction between emotions and drives is that drives reflect the needs of the body. For example, you become hungry or thirsty because you need food or water; you add or remove clothing when you are feeling too cold or too warm. Emotions are usually reactions to something outside the body, probably in the social environment, and therefore require processing complex information. Drives are modified by external stimuli, such as the sight and smell of good food, but those stimuli are relatively simple. In contrast, emotions respond to a cognitive appraisal of some event in the world—at least according to many psychologists who study emotion. Psychologists disagree about whether purely internal events (in the absence of any cognition) can provoke, say, the feelings and actions of anger (Berkowitz & Harmon-Jones, 2004).

To more clearly differentiate emotions from drives, consider this alternative definition, which modifies Plutchik's definition that we considered earlier : "An emotion is a universal, functional reaction to an external stimulus event, temporarily integrating physiological, cognitive, phenomenological, and behavioral channels to facilitate a fitness-enhancing, environment-shaping response to the current situation" (Keltner & Shiota, 2003, p. 89). One key advantage to this definition is that it specifies that emotion is a response to an *external* stimulus, such as a threat or an insult (although that threat or insult could be remembered or imag-

ined), not an internal, physical stimulus such as hunger or thirst. The definition strongly implies that emotion depends on a cognitive appraisal of that external stimulus. For example, if you hear that someone was badly injured, your reaction varies depending on whether that person is a close friend, a remote acquaintance, or someone you never heard of before (Lazarus, 2001). Seeing people smile or frown also can make you happy or sad, but the intensity of your response depends on why you think they are smiling or frowning. In short, emotions depend on fairly complex evaluations of events and their meaning. No wonder emotions vary so much from person to person, situation to situation, and culture to culture.

In this definition, also note the term "fitness-enhancing." That expression refers to the evolutionary meaning of "fitness," which includes both survival and reproduction. To say that an emotion enhances fitness is to imply that emotions have generally been helpful throughout our evolution as a species. We evolved a tendency to feel emotions because in past generations, those who experienced emotions were more likely to survive, reproduce, and become our ancestors.

That definition works to a large extent, but it leaves a few questions hanging. For example, what about the sex drive? Sexual desire has a strong internal component, like hunger or thirst, but also depends on your cognitive appraisal of a situation, as with happiness or sadness. Perhaps we should classify sexual desire as both an emotion and a drive. Further research should help to clarify the distinction between emotions and drives.

◻ **Measuring Emotion**

Whatever exists at all exists in some amount. (Edward Thorndike, 1918, p. 16)

Anything that exists in amount can be measured. (W. A. McCall, 1939, p. 15)

Anything which exists can be measured incorrectly. (Douglas Detterman, 1979, p. 167)

If emotions exist, we should be able to measure them. Unfortunately, it is also easy to measure them incorrectly.

You don't need to understand something thoroughly to measure it. For example, you might not understand temperature at a theoretical level, but you can measure it with a thermometer. You could also measure magnetism, electrical resistance, and many other physical variables without deeply understanding them. Similarly, psychologists do their best to measure intelligence, motivation, memory, and many other processes that they cannot clearly define or explain. Psychologists who study emotion rely mainly on the following methods:

Self-reports: descriptions of how you feel today using your own words, or rating your feelings on a scale from "the unhappiest I have ever been" to "the happiest I have ever been."

Physiological measurements: measures of blood pressure, heart rate, sweating, and other variables that fluctuate during emotional arousal. Researchers also measure brain activity or chemicals in the blood.

Behaviors: facial and vocal expressions, as well as running away, attacking, and other actions. Behaviors include anything we could observe. We also include potential actions, or a readiness for action. For example, when you watch a frightening film, your body might become prepared to run away, even though under the circumstances you don't carry out that impulse.

Each of these methods has its strengths and weaknesses, as we shall discuss repeatedly throughout this book. For each method, and indeed for any kind of measurement, researchers want to know whether a measure is reliable and valid before they are willing to use it, or to trust research that used that measure. The **reliability** of a measure reflects the consistency or repeatability of its scores. If a test is reliable, then people who are tested repeatedly *under the same conditions* get approximately the same score each time. If the reliability is close to zero, meaning that people get completely different scores

every time they complete the measure, even under the same conditions, then the test is not really measuring *anything* consistently. For example, a questionnaire might have low reliability if the items were worded in a confusing way.

In addition to reliability, **validity** is an assessment of whether the scores on some measure represent what they claim to represent. A questionnaire that gives the same score each time a person takes it is reliable, but it might not be valid if it is measuring something other than what it claims to measure. For example, in a questionnaire that is supposed to measure dispositional anger, an item such as "I feel hurt when people leave me out of plans and activities" would not be very valid—it could measure feeling hurt or rejected, not angry. A questionnaire could also be invalid if people tended to answer it untruthfully.

There are several kinds of validity, and researchers often try to make sure a new measure is valid in all of these ways. To determine face validity, researchers just ask whether a measure appears to make sense, or if it is clearly measuring something other than what was intended. The invalid anger questionnaire item we just described is a good example of a failure of face validity. To determine the predictive validity of some test, researchers find the correlation between the test scores and some other, theoretically expected measure. For example, scores on a valid test of anger should accurately predict who will get into fights and arguments. To determine the discriminant validity of a test, researchers ask whether the test also *fails* to predict things to which it should *not* be related. For example, there is no reason to think that scores on a measure of anger will predict how tidy people are. If they do, either there is evidence for a new and remarkable relationship between anger and cleanliness, or something is wrong with the anger measure.

Self-Reports

Self-reports are easy data to collect although not necessarily to interpret. In this method, researchers simply ask people to describe their current, past, or

FIGURE 1.1   It is possible to cry for extreme joy. However, if we don't know the reasons for someone's crying, we assume sadness, even if the person denies it.

typical emotions. For instance, participants might rate their nervousness, happiness, or level of some other emotion on a scale such as this:

Not at All Nervous		Somewhat Nervous				Very Nervous
1	2	3	4	5	6	7

Self-reports cannot be precise, simply because each person's standard differs from anyone else's. Many centuries ago, people measured distances in cubits and spans. A cubit is the distance from the elbow to the tip of the middle finger; a span is the distance from the end of the thumb to the end of the little finger when extended. The obvious problem is that your cubit or span is different from someone else's. Self-reports of emotions have the same problem; if you rate your nervousness "5," your 5 may be different from someone else's, or even from your own 5 at some other time. In fact, psychological self-reports are worse than cubits. With cubits, at least it is possible to compare the length of one person's cubit to another's. How can we determine whether your nervousness rating of "5" is larger or smaller than someone else's?

Suppose you ask a crying person, "Why are you sad?" and the person replies, "I'm not sad. I'm fine." Do you believe that report? It might be true. People sometimes cry from happiness, amusement, or relief. (See Figure 1.1.) People also cry while peeling an onion, or while acting in a play. However, when in doubt, we assume that a crying person is probably sad. That is, when we have reason to doubt the validity of a self-report, we rely on behavioral observations.

A further limitation of self-reports is that we sometimes want to study emotions in infants, brain-damaged people, nonhuman animals, or others who cannot speak. With people who speak different languages, translation is sometimes uncertain, especially for fine distinctions.

In spite of these serious problems, self-reports are useful for many purposes, especially when we have no good alternative method of measurement. For example, if you rate your nervousness 5 today and 2 tomorrow, the change presumably means your nervousness has decreased, even if your 5 means something different from someone else's. If you rate your current nervousness as "4" but your current sadness as "2," presumably you are more nervous than sad. If a researcher is interested in *changes* in emotion over time, or in *relative* experience of different emotions, self-reports can be effective.

Physiological Measurements

Consider the statement "17 + 33 = 50." When you contemplate that thought, do you feel anything emotionally? Do you get any body sensations at all? Probably not. It is a purely factual statement. In contrast, most of our experiences in life and probably all of our choices include an emotional component. Antonio Damasio (1994) in his book *Descartes' Error* argued that the main mistake of the great philosopher René Descartes was in trying to describe thinking independently of the body. When we think, especially when we think emotionally, we ready the whole body for action, and we receive feedback from it. The consequence for researchers is that they can measure certain aspects of emotion from body activities.

Any emotional state includes a readiness for action, or "action tendency." For example, anger implies readiness to attack and fear implies readiness to flee. During a period of overwhelming joy, you might want to jump and yell, perhaps hug everyone in sight. Many emotional conditions are states of intense arousal. The intensity relates to the activity of the autonomic nervous system, which has two branches, as Figure C.1 on the inside cover shows. The **sympathetic nervous system (SNS)** readies the body for "fight or flight" emergency actions. Activation of the sympathetic nervous system increases heart rate, breathing rate, sweating, and adrenaline secretions. It decreases digestive activity (which would take energy away from skeletal muscle contractions) and sexual arousal. (While you are fighting for your life, sexual arousal would be a pointless distraction!) The sympathetic nervous system is controlled by a chain of ganglia (neuron cell clusters) located to the left and right of the middle areas of the spinal cord. The ganglia of the sympathetic nervous system tend—with many exceptions—to become active together, as a group. (Action together is what "sympathetic" means.) Their activity is partly—but only partly—independent of the central nervous system. (Independence is what "autonomic" means.) However, the sympathetic nervous system also receives input from adjacent cells in the spinal cord, which in turn receive input from the brain.

The **parasympathetic nervous system (PNS)** increases maintenance functions that conserve energy for later use and facilitates growth and development. For example, activation in the parasympathetic system increases digestion and decreases heart rate and breathing rate. The parasympathetic nervous system is controlled by neurons in the pons and medulla (the parts of the brain just above the spinal cord) and by neurons in the sacral portion (the lowest end) of the spinal cord.

Both the sympathetic and parasympathetic systems are always active, although the balance may shift from mostly one to mostly the other. Many physiological processes involve a distinct combination of sympathetic and parasympathetic responses (Wolf, 1995). For example, nausea increases the sympathetic stimulation to the stomach, producing a tendency to vomit, and the parasympathetic stimulation to the intestines, speeding the excretion of wastes. Sexual arousal requires parasympathetic activity (relaxation) at first, but sympathetic activity (excitement) at the stage of orgasm.

Researchers often measure sympathetic nervous system arousal as an indicator of emotion (e.g., Levenson, Carstensen, & Gottman, 1994a; Mauss et al., 2005). Is this a good idea? Only if people really do become more aroused when they are feeling a strong emotion, right? Initial studies of **emotional response coherence,** or the extent to which self-reports of emotion predict physiological changes and simple behaviors, such as facial expressions, actually offered weak evidence for this claim (Bradley

& Lang, 2000). In these studies, researchers measured people's sympathetic nervous system arousal while they performed some task, such as watching an emotional film, and then asked them how much emotion they felt during the task. They would then ask whether the people who had the strongest sympathetic nervous system reactions were the same people who reported feeling the strongest emotion. Many studies found that this was not the case—self-report and sympathetic arousal only weakly predicted each other.

Think about this for a minute. Let's say that Iris, for example, reported feeling very strong emotion while watching the film, relative to all of the other participants, but only relatively weak increases in arousal. Is that the same as saying that her arousal did not go up *at the same time that her own self-report of emotion increased?* Not at all! Here we run into one of the big problems in emotion research—self-reports are one of the "gold standards" we use for other measures, but we know they are very subjective. Iris's idea of "strong" feelings may be different from other participants, but as long as her self-report of emotion and her arousal seem to "hang together" over time, the "coherence hypothesis" is in good shape.

A recent study tested this "within-subject" approach to emotional response coherence (Mauss et al., 2005). A within-subject approach is helpful because it avoids comparing your self-rating to someone else's; instead it compares yours at one time to yours at another time. In this study, participants watched a five-minute film clip, which went from funny to sad and back to funny again, three times. For each viewing, their sympathetic nervous system arousal was measured. Once they just watched the film; another time they used a handheld rating dial to indicate, continuously, how amused they felt throughout the film; another time they used the same dial to indicate, again continuously, how sad they felt throughout the film. Afterward, the researchers asked whether people's sympathetic arousal and self-reports of emotion tended to "hang together," or travel consistently at the same time,

over the course of the film. They found much better evidence of coherence, in this way, than researchers had found before. That is, when participants felt more sad, they tended to be more aroused, and when they felt more amused, their arousal tended to go down.

The polygraph (or lie-detector test) is based on the partly true, partly false assumption that people are more nervous when they lie than when they tell the truth. Nervousness increases sympathetic nervous system activity, which in turn increases heart rate, breathing rate, and sweating. However, your heart rate, breathing rate, and so forth depend not only on your emotions but also on your activity level, your health, any medications you are taking, and many other non-emotional influences. They also vary from individual to individual, so what is an "elevated" heart rate for one person may be just average for another. Measurements of sympathetic nervous system arousal are good enough for certain research purposes but inadequate for making important decisions about individuals, such as who should go to jail or who should lose a job.

Most studies of emotion physiology have focused on the sympathetic nervous system, rather than the parasympathetic branch. The emphasis on the sympathetic branch tends to favor study of negative emotions—hence the term "fight or flight" to describe the SNS. Happiness is generally associated with less intense SNS activity and often with the increased relaxation that accompanies parasympathetic activity (Levenson, Ekman, & Friesen, 1990). In the chapter on love and other social bonding emotions, we will talk about some new measures of parasympathetic nervous system activity that may be more promising for the study of positive emotions.

Because bodily changes differ from emotion to emotion, one cannot use any physiological indicator to measure emotionality in general. Might it be possible to use physiological measures to gauge the *type* of emotion? For example, disgust, which is associated with nausea, may include slowing of the heart rate, instead of speeding it up as anger does (Levenson, 1992). However, it may not be possible to distinguish physiologically between fear and anger because those states produce strongly overlapping patterns of arousal.

Beginning in the 1990s, measurements of brain activity have become increasingly popular measures of emotion (e.g., Damasio, 1999). One common technique for measuring brain activity is **electroencephalography (EEG),** a procedure in which the researcher pastes electrodes on someone's scalp to measure momentary changes in the electrical activity under each electrode. An EEG is quick and inexpensive and provides millisecond-by-millisecond information about the activity of cells in the brain area closest to each electrode. However, an EEG records activity only from the brain cells nearest the electrodes on the scalp, not from any areas deeper in the brain, and some of the deep-brain areas are especially important for emotion. Another limitation is that each electrode summates activity over a fairly large area, so an EEG supplies precise information about the time of brain activity but not its location. A closely related method is magnetoencephalography (MEG), which records momentary changes in brain cells' magnetic activity instead of electrical activity. (The passage of an electrical current generates a magnetic field.)

One advantage of EEG is that it can provide precise information about timing. When people give a self-report of fear, anger, or any other emotion, they usually summarize how they have been feeling over some period of time. In contrast, researchers can present photographs, sounds, smells, or other stimuli and record EEG changes over fractions of a second. (Whether those fluctuations actually represent emotional changes is a difficult question, however.)

Another method has become increasingly popular: **functional magnetic resonance imaging (fMRI),** which measures brain activity based on changes in oxygen uptake (Detre & Floyd, 2001). When a brain area increases its activity, it uses more oxygen, and therefore the hemoglobin molecules in the nearby blood vessels release their oxygen. Hemoglobin molecules with oxygen respond differently to a magnetic field than do hemoglobin molecules without oxygen, and an fMRI scanner surrounding the head can detect changes in magnetic responses from various areas. An fMRI image can detect changes happening in a little less than a second—not on the order of milliseconds as with an EEG, but good enough for many purposes. It can determine the location of the change to an accuracy of 1 or 2 mm, even deep in the brain—far greater accuracy than an EEG (Figure 1.2). The procedure poses no known risks. In fact, most people who undergo one particular type of fMRI (echo-planar

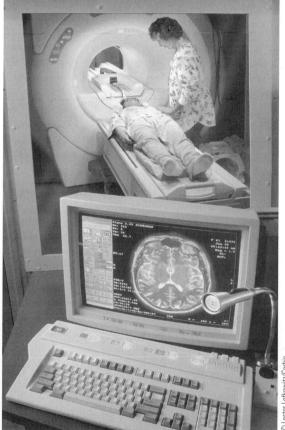

© Lester Lefkowitz/Corbis

FIGURE 1.2 An fMRI scanner records activity from all areas of the brain, revealing changes that happen in less than a second. However, the person must lie motionless in a tight, noisy device.

magnetic resonance spectroscopic imaging) say it improves their mood, and some researchers have begun testing this procedure as an antidepressant (Rohan et al., 2004).

An fMRI does have a few practical disadvantages, however. The person must lie motionless in a very noisy device that tightly surrounds the head. Most young children are unable or unwilling to do so, as are people with claustrophobia (fear of closed-in places). Also, fMRI technology is expensive, and few researchers outside hospitals or major research centers have access to it. Furthermore, the procedures restrict the kinds of experiences an investigator can test. Most of our everyday emotional experiences occur while we are walking around and interacting with other people, not while lying motionless in a noisy machine, looking through a small window at pictures on a monitor. As with so many areas of research, we sometimes have to sacrifice the **ecological validity** of a study—the extent to which what happens in the study reflects what really happens in everyday life—for more precise measurement. We will encounter this issue again and again as we travel through the emotion literature.

Brain scans help to identify the brain areas that contribute to emotions in various ways. For example, much evidence indicates that activity in the amygdala (Figure 1.3), an almond-shaped structure in the temporal lobe of the brain, is associated with learning what situations are dangerous and with processing emotional information in general (LeDoux, 1996; Whalen, 1998). People with damage to the amygdala report weakened emotions under many circumstances, as we shall discuss in the chapter on fear and anxiety.

Brain scans can also contribute to psychological understanding. For example, when people deal with difficult moral issues—such as whether and under what circumstances they might intentionally kill one person to save several others—they hesitate longer than with easy questions, and their brain shows heightened activity in the areas known to be important for problem solving and those critical for emotions (Greene, Nystrom, Engell, Darley, &

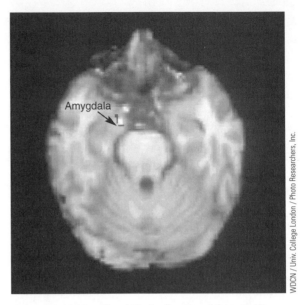

FIGURE 1.3   Neural activity in the amygdala, a small structure in the temporal lobe of the brain, has been associated with the experience of fear in humans and other animals.

Cohen, 2004). That is, the brain recordings support the interpretation that people are weighing the relative importance of competing arguments.

The results of any brain scan study must be interpreted cautiously. For example, increased activity of the amygdala during fear could mean that it is necessary for the experience of fear, for the information processing that leads to fear, or for some other process that accompanies the experience (Baxter & Murray, 2002). At this point, we cannot look at a brain scan and identify what someone is experiencing. Authors of an extensive review compared many studies of brain activation during emotional experiences. Figure C.2 on the inside cover shows their results (Phan, Wager, Taylor, & Liberzon, 2002). Certain areas tended to be activated more frequently than others, and the results depended somewhat on the type of emotion studied in a given experiment. However, much of the variance in results stemmed from the procedures. For example, studies that aroused emotions by showing pictures activated the visual cortex, whereas studies that relied on the spoken word activated the auditory cortex. Ultimately, researchers might be able to use brain scans to determine the type or intensity of someone's emotion, but all such results must be interpreted cautiously.

Behavioral Observations

If you were frightened of something, you might tremble and run away. Therefore, when you see other people tremble and run away, you might reasonably infer that they are frightened. Your parents used this manner to teach you the words for emotions. When they saw you running away from something and screaming loudly, they probably inferred that you were frightened and told you that you were "afraid."

Similarly, we infer anger, happiness, disgust, and other emotions from people's behavior. Researchers studying emotion often use facial expressions, or contractions of particular sets of muscles in the face, as measures of the emotions people feel during a study. For example, when people are angry, they often lower their eyebrows, scrunch them together, and tighten their lips (Figure 1.4).

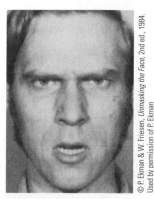

Image credit (vertical): © P. Ekman & W. Friesen, Unmasking the Face, 2nd ed., 1984. Used by permission of P. Ekman

Using a behavioral coding system called EM-FACS (Ekman & Friesen, 1984), researchers can identify which muscles are contracted on a person's face at any given moment and can record how long and how intensely those muscles contract. Certain patterns of muscle contraction, such as the one Figure 1.4 illustrates, are observed reliably when people

FIGURE 1.4   Researchers often use facial expressions to measure the emotions people feel during a study. This is a "prototypical" expression of anger.

say they are feeling a particular emotion and when they are in a situation that you would expect to elicit a certain emotion. For example, people reliably make the face shown in Figure 1.4 (or a close approximation of it) when dealing with an injustice or insult, even if they do not say they are angry. For this reason, researchers can use the patterns of muscle contraction as a nonverbal measure of people's emotions.

As with the other measures of emotion, coded facial expressions have their limitations. First, people can try to fake or conceal their emotions, although certain facial muscles are very difficult to move deliberately, and when people try to hide their emotions, a careful observer can often detect "micro expressions" leaking through (Ekman, 2001). Second, coding facial expressions is extremely time intensive. The muscle movements can be subtle, and it takes a lot of training and patience to distinguish "emotional" movements from all of the other facial movements people make. Also, a typical emotional expression lasts only one or two seconds, so to catch every instance, you have to watch videotapes of a person's behavior many times, slowing down to catch the exact start and stop of each movement. It typically takes 30 to 60 minutes to code a single minute of videotape! Third, although many researchers agree that some facial expressions indicate a particular emotion, many expressions are less certain; some people think they indicate an emotion, others don't, and the research does not yet give a solid answer. Still, with time and effort, facial expressions do avoid many of the problems of self-report, and they are especially useful for researchers studying the effects of emotion on social interaction.

Sometimes researchers use bigger, more obvious measures of behavior to measure emotion. For example, when people jump or yell at the sight of a spider, you can reasonably infer that they are afraid. In fact, if we want to study emotion in animals, behavioral observation is nearly the only option. However, inferences based on behavior have limitations, too. Do nonhuman animals experience emotions at all? Many psychologists dismiss the question because we cannot ask for verbal reports. (We're back to that problem of self-report as the gold standard.) However, remember that your parents taught you the words for emotions by inferring your emotions from your actions and then telling you "you are afraid" or "you are sad." If we could not infer emotions from behavior, we could not learn the words to make self-reports. With nonhumans, our inferences about emotion are admittedly uncertain, but the brain structures known to be important for human emotions operate in largely similar ways for other vertebrates, especially mammals. One problem with inferring nonhuman emotions is that some emotions have more visible signs than others. An animal that attacks may be angry, and one that runs away may be frightened, but most animal species give no clear signals of happiness, sadness, or surprise.

If a bee attacks you, does it feel anger? Does it feel anything? In this case, we are quite at a loss. A bee cannot give us a self-report, and its physiology is so different from ours that we cannot rely on any of the usual measures, such as sweating, heart rate, pupil dilation, or brain activity. The more remote a species is from humans, the less confidently we can infer that species' emotions (if any).

Remember: An emotion has three aspects—cognition, feeling, and action. We observe the action, and we mostly rely on self-reports about the cognition, but for the feeling aspect we are necessarily making an inference. The more kinds of evidence we have, the better. For example, if we can examine both self-report measures and physiological measures, we can note areas of agreement or disagreement. In any case, measurement is an essential aspect of any study of emotion, and the strength of any conclusion is no better than the quality of measurement that led to it.

◻ Theories of Emotion

In the previous section, we described three central aspects of emotion: appraisals, feelings, and action tendencies. Some of the most fundamental questions about emotion concern the relationships among these three aspects. Do the three aspects arise separately, or does one of them lead to the other two? If so, which one is primary? Let us consider the most famous theories.

The James-Lange Theory

The scientific approach to psychology began in Germany in 1879 when Wilhelm Wundt established the first laboratory to investigate issues of the mind. A few years later, the founder of American psychology, William James (Figure 1.5), put forth the first major theory of emotions, indeed one of the first

FIGURE 1.5 William James, founder of American psychology. He theorized that emotion requires sensations, usually from the muscles or internal organs.

general theories in all of psychology. The Danish psychologist Carl Lange ("LAHNG-uh") (1885/1922) proposed a similar idea at about the same time, so the theory came to be known as the **James-Lange theory.** According to the James-Lange theory, emotions are the labels we give to the way the body reacts to certain situations (James, 1884, 1894). In James's words, "The bodily changes follow directly the perception of the exciting fact, and . . . our feeling of the same changes as they occur IS the emotion" (James, 1884, p. 190). That idea contradicts the common-sense view that you feel angry and *therefore* you attack, or you feel frightened and *therefore* you try to escape. The James-Lange theory reverses the direction of cause and effect: You notice yourself attacking and therefore you feel angry. You notice yourself trying to escape and therefore you feel frightened.

Common sense view:
Event → Emotional feeling → Action

James-Lange theory:
Event → Action → Emotional feeling (which is the perception of the action)

More specifically, according to the James-Lange theory, some sort of sensation from the muscles or the internal organs is necessary for the full experience of emotion. Any decrease in the sensation decreases the emotion. One example Carl Lange offered in support of this theory was the common observation that wine decreases anxiety. The wine decreases your body's response to a stressor, and as you feel your body become calmer, you feel less emotion.

The James-Lange theory is easily misunderstood, partly because William James's original statement was less precise than it could have been (Ellsworth, 1994). James used the example of someone's fear of a bear: He said that you don't run away because you are afraid of the bear; rather, the sight of the bear itself causes you to run away, and you feel fear because you run away. Critics pointed out that this statement is obviously wrong: You do not automatically run away from a bear. For example, you would not run away from a caged bear, a trained

bear in a circus, or even a sleeping bear. True, James (1894) conceded: The cause of your running away is not really the bear itself, but your perception or appraisal of the entire situation (e.g., untamed, uncaged bear coming toward you). Still, he argued, you assess that situation as one calling for escape. As you start trying to escape, your perception of your body's escape activities is your fear. James did not clearly distinguish between the various aspects of emotion, but using the terminology of today, we would say that James's theory applies to the feeling aspect of emotions, not to the cognitive appraisal. So, the proper statement of the James-Lange theory is that the *feeling aspect* of an emotion is the perception of the body's actions and physiological arousal:

James-Lange theory, clarified:

Event → Appraisal → Action → Emotional feeling

| | the cognitive aspect | the behavioral aspect, including physiology | the feeling aspect |

The Cannon-Bard Theory

Walter Cannon, a physiologist of the early 1900s, was famous for discovering that the sympathetic nervous system is responsible for fight-or-flight responses. He and another leading physiologist, Philip Bard, proposed an alternative to the James-Lange theory (Bard, 1934; Cannon, 1927). According to the **Cannon-Bard theory,** the cognitive experience of emotion, occurring in the cerebral cortex, is independent of the arousal and other actions of the muscles and glands, even though the cognitive experience occurs at the same time as the actions. Restated in modern terms, the cognitive, behavioral, and action aspects of an emotion arise independently:

Cannon-Bard theory:

Event → { Appraisal
Action (behavior and physiology)
Feelings

For example, the sight of a mad killer approaching you with a chainsaw would cause you to decide that you were frightened and independently cause feelings of fear and the action of running away. Note that the assumed independence of emotions and actions has two aspects: Your fear does not cause you to run away, and the fact that you are running away does not increase your fear. Cannon argued, for example, that the responses of the muscles and organs are too slow to contribute to the feeling of an emotion.

This theory is even further from common sense than the James-Lange theory, and much evidence argues against it. For example, a sudden loud noise can evoke muscle tension, increased heart rate, and increased sweating in a fraction of a second, surely fast enough to contribute to the feeling of an emotion. Furthermore, it is hard to believe that actions and feelings are completely independent of each other. When some event moves you to action—such as attacking or fleeing—your sensations of those actions become a major part of how you feel at the time. Even altering someone's facial expression into a smile or frown can facilitate positive or negative emotions, as we shall discuss later in this chapter. The Cannon-Bard theory was the forerunner to many modern theories that emphasize the cognitive aspects of emotion. However, virtually no one in recent decades has defended this theory in anything close to its original form. We include it here for historical completeness.

The Schachter-Singer Theory

According to the **Schachter-Singer theory** (proposed by Stanley Schachter and Jerome Singer), the arousal and other actions that are part of any emotion are essential for determining how strong the emotional feeling will be, but they do not identify the emotion. You identify which emotion you feel on the basis of all the information you have about a situation (Schachter & Singer, 1962). Figure 1.6 contrasts the James-Lange, Cannon-Bard, and Schachter-Singer theories.

The Schachter-Singer theory is often described as an alternative to the James-Lange theory, but it

FIGURE 1.6 According to the James-Lange theory, physiological arousal defines the emotion. According to the Cannon-Bard theory, it is separate from the emotions. According to the Schachter-Singer theory, arousal determines the strength of the emotion but does not identify the emotion.

does not contradict James's later clarification of his theory. Remember, the James-Lange theory says that the *feeling aspect* of an emotion depends on your arousal and other actions. Many people have read James's writings to imply that the feeling aspect tells you which emotion you are experiencing, but James did not say so. He was noncommittal on whether one emotion feels different from another, and indeed he was skeptical of whether different emotions are fully distinct from one another. That is, the James-Lange theory does not explicitly address how you determine which emotion you feel (Russell, 2003).

The Schachter-Singer theory, unlike the James-Lange theory, deals mainly with how you distinguish one emotion from another. The Schachter-Singer theory assumes that all emotions evoke such similar physiological responses that you cannot recognize which emotion you are feeling just by observing your body's reactions. Instead, you have to examine what you know about the situation. In other words, the difference between one emotion and another is in the cognitive appraisal aspect, not the feeling aspect.

Could you, in fact, recognize one emotion from another, based only on feedback from your heart rate, breathing rate, sweating, and so forth? The emotions do produce somewhat different physiological changes. For example, hand temperature increases more during anger than during other emotions. Heart rate rises greatly during fear or anger; it seldom increases much during happiness, and often it even decreases. And so forth. However, the differences among anger, fear, disgust, and surprise are small, and it seems doubtful that anyone could identify his or her emotion just from the pattern of physiological arousal (Ekman, Levenson, & Friesen, 1983; Lang, 1994).

To test this possibility further, consider this imaginary experiment: Suppose a researcher puts you in one room and your friend in another. The researcher attaches wires to devices that record your friend's heart rate, breathing rate, and other physiological responses and connects those wires to a machine attached to you. Whenever your friend's heart rate increases or decreases, the machine will cause your heart rate to increase or decrease by the same amount at the same time. It does the same to your breathing rate, sweating, and so forth. Now your friend watches an emotionally gripping movie. You experience exactly the same changes in heart rate, breathing rate, and so forth at exactly the same times as your friend, even though you are not watching the movie. Will you experience the same emotion?

The James-Lange theory makes no clear prediction. It says you will have the same emotional *feeling* as your friend, but it does not necessarily claim that you can identify your type of emotion from your feeling. The Cannon-Bard theory says your physiological changes are irrelevant to your emotional feelings. According to the Schachter-Singer view, the physiological changes determine only the strength of the emotion, not which emotion you experience. This view presumes that all emotions produce sufficiently similar changes that the differences are uninformative. You identify your emotion by appraising the situation, not by attending to your breathing, sweating, or other activities. According to this theory, if you are just sitting alone in a room, you have no event to which you can attribute your arousal. Therefore you would simply report the arousal without calling it an emotion.

The experiment just described is not feasible, but Schachter and Singer did something else that they thought might answer the question: They induced physiological arousal in participants and then put them into different situations. If arousal itself is the whole basis for emotion, the participants should all feel the same emotion. However, if people interpret the arousal differently depending on the situation, then people in different situations should experience different emotions, even though they have the same arousal.

Because this experiment has been so influential, let's examine it in some detail. It is an interesting study, but it also has some serious flaws. Schachter and Singer (1962) gave one group of participants an injection of epinephrine (otherwise known as adrenaline), a hormone that increases the activity of the sympathetic nervous system. Another group received a placebo injection—that is, one with no pharmacological effects. Of those receiving the epinephrine injection, half were told what to expect. They were told that the injection would increase their heart rate, make them sweat, cause a sensation of butterflies in the stomach, and so forth. The other participants receiving epinephrine were not told about its effects.

At that point, some participants were put into a "euphoria" situation and the others into an "anger" situation. In the euphoria situation, intended to elicit happiness, the experimenters had each participant wait with a young man who was supposedly also a participant, but who was in fact paid to play the role of "happy, playful person." He flipped wads of paper into a trash can, sailed paper airplanes, built a tower with manila folders, played with a hula hoop, and tried to get the other participant to join in his play.

The "anger" situation is a classic and diabolically clever. The experimenters simply asked participants to fill out a lengthy questionnaire, which was full of personal, insulting, and downright rude questions. Examples:

1. What is your father's average annual income?
2. Which member of your immediate family does not bathe or wash regularly?
3. Which member of your immediate family needs psychiatric care?
4. With how many men (other than your father) has your mother had extramarital relationships? 4 or fewer? 5–9? 10 or more?

Again, each participant in this condition had a partner posing as another participant, who was in fact paid by the experimenters to play a role. In this case, he muttered in annoyance at the questions and ultimately ripped up the questionnaire and stormed out of the room.

The results: The participants who were given epinephrine and told what to expect showed little emotional response. They found their playful partner mildly amusing or they considered the questionnaire mildly annoying. Those who were given epinephrine without instructions on what to expect showed stronger emotions. People in the euphoria condition often joined in the play. Of those in the anger condition, not many told the experimenter that they were angry, but some muttered angry comments and a few refused to complete the questionnaire.

These results are difficult to interpret because of the results for the placebo group, who had not received the epinephrine injection. People in the placebo group behaved about the same as those in the epinephrine group who were uninformed about the injection. They showed playfulness in the euphoria condition and anger in the anger condition. In other words, the epinephrine injections apparently had nothing to do with the results.

The main finding from the study seems to be that telling people to expect arousal actually decreases their emotional experience in a situation. It may be that, contrary to Schachter and Singer's hypothesis, people will attribute arousal to emotion *unless* they already have another explanation for a racing heart and sweating palms. This is consistent with the findings of two later studies by Maslach (1979) and Marshall and Zimbardo (1979). In these studies, participants experiencing unexplained sympathetic arousal tended to report negative affect (that is, unpleasant mood) more often than control participants who received placebo injections or who were told to expect the injection to have "physiological side effects."

One difficulty with this study is the assumption that "euphoria" is associated with physiological arousal at all. Unpleasant emotions are associated with sympathetic arousal, but there is little evidence that the same is true of pleasant emotions. Perhaps Schachter and Singer were only partly right, in that certain emotions can be confused with each other more easily than others can. Here's a later experiment based on the Schachter and Singer theory: The idea was that if one aspect of a situation triggers intense arousal, you might be more likely to associate that arousal with other aspects of the situation as well. In this experiment, young men were asked to participate in a study of "the effects of scenic attractions on creative expression." The men were taken to a bridge and asked to cross it; halfway along the bridge, they were stopped by an attractive young female "experimenter." Participants looked at pictures on some cards and told short stories about the pictures. At the end of the questions, the experimenter gave each man her telephone number in case he wanted to find out more about the experiment.

The critical variable was the type of bridge the men crossed. Some men talked with the experimenter while standing on a wide, sturdy bridge 10 feet (3 meters) above a river. The other interviews took place on a narrow, wobbly wooden bridge 230 feet (70 meters) above a canyon. Presumably those on the wobbly bridge felt greater arousal due to their precarious situation, and the research question was whether these men might interpret their arousal as attraction toward the experimenter. Evidently many of them did. Of those on the wobbly bridge, 39 percent called the experimenter after the study, compared with only 9 percent of those on the sturdier bridge (Dutton & Aron, 1974).

In a related, more recent study, young heterosexual men examined the women in the *Sports Illustrated* swimsuit issue and rated the attractiveness of each one (in the name of science, of course). Meanwhile, they heard sounds, which were in fact random. Some were told that they were random sounds, but others were told that the sounds were playbacks of their own heartbeat. Men who thought they were hearing their own heartbeat gave high ratings to whichever photograph they were examining while their heartbeat seemed to be increasing (Crucian et al., 2000). Presumably, they thought, "Wow! Listen to my heart racing! What a beautiful, exciting woman!" Curiously, this effect was weak in men with right-hemisphere brain damage, and actually increased in men with left-hemisphere brain damage. We shall return to this point repeatedly in later chapters: The right hemisphere seems to be specialized for interpreting emotions (others' expressions as well as one's own).

These experiments on people misattributing their arousal to sexual excitement are entertaining, to say the least. Unfortunately, the effect is not easy to replicate. Sometimes people misattribute their arousal and sometimes they do not, depending on many details of the research procedure, and we can't always predict what will happen (Reisenzein, 1983).

◻ Relationships Among Cognition, Feeling, and Action

Let's return to the question of how the three components of emotion relate to one another. According to the James-Lange theory, you first appraise a situation cognitively, then produce motor and autonomic responses, and finally experience the feeling aspect, which is the sensation from those responses. Many

other theorists, collectively known as appraisal theorists, differ in their views on various issues but agree that cognitive appraisal comes first and is essential to any emotion. That is, how you react emotionally to an event depends on what that event means to you (Lazarus, 2001). You might be terrified at the sight of a snake or calm if you recognize it as a harmless species. Receiving a compliment might make you happy if you think it is sincere, but angry if you think that the person giving the compliment is just getting ready to ask you for a favor.

The relationships among cognition, feeling, and action relate to several research questions: How fast is the cognitive appraisal? Is sensation from your responses necessary for emotional feelings? Is it sufficient?

The Speed of Emotional Appraisals

When you experience some event, how quickly do you identify it as good, bad, or neutral? According to the James-Lange theory and other theories that emphasize appraisal, your emotional response begins with your assessing the overall situation and classifying it as calling for escape, attack, some other kind of action, or no action at all. The terms *appraisal* and *assessment* here are used in a very broad sense. You don't necessarily analyze the situation well enough to put it into words. What is necessary is that something in your brain identifies broad, simple qualities of the object, such as "safe" or "dangerous" or "likely to give me food." Theorists expect this appraisal to be quick, and from an evolutionary standpoint, it should be. Certainly in the presence of danger, the faster you react, the greater your chance of survival.

As predicted, the brain shows signs of identifying the emotional quality of a stimulus extremely fast. In one study, physicians studied a man who was undergoing brain surgery for severe epilepsy. As is often the case, the surgery was conducted with just local anesthesia to the scalp, so the man was awake and alert throughout the procedure. (Keeping the patient awake is helpful. As surgeons probe one brain area after another, eventually the patient says, "That makes me feel the way I do when I'm about to have a seizure." The surgeons then know they are close to the area causing the seizures.) In this particular study, while they had the patient's brain exposed, the physicians inserted electrodes into his prefrontal cortex, an area important for certain aspects of both memory and emotion. Then they asked him to look at some pictures of pleasant and unpleasant scenes, as well as happy and frightened faces. Cells in the prefrontal cortex responded within as few as 120 milliseconds to each picture, and they responded with a different pattern of activity to happy faces and pleasant pictures than to frightened faces and unpleasant pictures (Kawasaki et al., 2001). This very fast response is consistent with the idea that cognitive appraisal precedes and presumably determines the reactions of muscles and glands.

In another study, college students looked at photographs of faces with happy, angry, or neutral expressions while the investigators recorded brain activity with an EEG. (Remember, an EEG records an average of the electrical activity for all cells under a certain area of the scalp.) Looking at an angry, threatening face evoked a strong response 200 to 300 milliseconds after the onset of the photograph, whereas seeing a happy or neutral face did not evoke that response (Schupp et al., 2004). Again, the evidence indicates that the brain categorizes the emotional quality of a scene quickly and automatically, at least for certain kinds of emotions (Robinson, 1998). (Not much research has dealt with how quickly we process material relating to more complex emotions such as pride or embarrassment. Presumably they take longer, because they require a more elaborate processing of information.)

In still another study, researchers recorded movements of facial muscles while participants looked at photos of people with various facial expressions. Looking at a smiling face slightly activated the muscles responsible for smiling, and looking at an angry face activated the muscles responsible for frowning. The muscles reacted within less than half a second after onset of a photo, although the reactions were brief (Dimberg & Thunberg, 1998). (The results are "micro expressions," a term

we shall discuss in more detail in later chapters.) That is, people slightly imitate facial expressions quickly, unintentionally, and automatically. Another experiment found that looking at a photo of a fearful face caused slight sweating and trembling, even if the photo was presented so briefly that people did not report consciously seeing it at all (Kubota et al., 2000; Vuilleumier, Armony, Driver, & Dolan, 2001). These results imply that the brain classifies and responds rapidly to the emotional quality of a photo. They do not mean that classifying something as happy is the same thing as feeling happy.

When you think about it, these results are stunning, even hard to believe. They say that before your brain has figured out what it is seeing, in fact before it can even say for sure that it has seen anything at all, it has already begun to classify what it sees as good or bad, threatening or harmless.

The research just described indicates that classification as good versus bad is very fast in some situations and that it usually precedes and probably guides the emotional actions and feelings. However, we are not in a position to say that emotional appraisal is always fast or that it always precedes feelings and actions. Suppose you are in a bad mood because of something that happened half an hour ago. Now your roommate or someone else says or does something that isn't quite what you wanted and you yell angrily. After the emotional outburst, you have to find an explanation—a cognition—to explain your anger. You say, "You're always so inconsiderate!" or something similar. (Have you ever reacted that way? If not, have you ever seen anyone else do so?) In such cases, the cognition apparently comes after the feeling and action. If so, we will need a complicated description of emotion: Cognition leads to actions and feelings *usually*, but sometimes the actions and feelings help cognitions along too.

Are Body Sensations Necessary for Emotional Feeling?

If you had no sensations from your organs or muscles, would you still feel emotions? According to the James-Lange theory, you could appraise the situation cognitively (for example, "this situation calls for anger"), but you would not *feel* an emotion. Furthermore, if sensations are critical for emotional feelings, then people with weak feedback from their organs would experience only weak emotions, and people who are especially sensitive to feedback from their organs might experience especially intense emotions. We can examine these issues by comparing various kinds of people.

In one study, people were asked to report whether they thought their heart rate was increasing or decreasing, while researchers measured the actual heart rate. The participants also reported how sensitive they thought they were to visceral (gut) sensations in general and how intensely they felt moments of fear and sadness. The people who were in fact the most accurate at judging their heart rate tended to be those who reported high sensitivity to visceral sensations and great intensity of unpleasant emotions (Critchley, Wiens, Rotshtein, Öhman, & Dolan, 2004). That is, the more you notice your own arousal level, the more intensely you feel emotions, especially the negative ones.

At the opposite extreme are people with diminished responses or who for some reason do not feel their responses. Several researchers have focused on people who have become paralyzed by spinal cord injuries. Because they have no body movements, they have fewer body sensations than normal, although they still have changes in heart rate and other responses by internal organs. The results vary depending on how one phrases the question, but most people with spinal cord injuries report that they experience their emotions as strongly as before, especially fear and sadness (Chwalisz, Diener, & Gallagher, 1988; Cobos, Sánchez, García, Vera, & Vila, 2002; Lowe & Carroll, 1985). Viewing unpleasant pictures has a normal, or nearly normal, effect on their muscle tension, as indicated by responses to sudden noises (Cobos et al., 2002). Also, one young woman with total paralysis of her facial muscles reported that she, too, felt normal emotions (Keillor, Barrett, Crucian, Kortenkamp, & Heilman, 2002).

Although certain psychologists regard these results as contradictory to the James-Lange theory, it would be better to say they put constraints on the theory. People with spinal cord injuries or facial paralysis lack many or most muscular responses (depending on the location of the damage), but they retain many of the responses controlled by the autonomic nervous system. (Recall that the autonomic nervous system is the set of nerves controlling heart rate, breathing rate, sweating, digestion, and so forth, as Figure C.1 on the inside cover illustrates.) So, given that these people continue to report more or less normal emotional feelings, we can conclude that the feeling aspect of emotions does not require muscle movements—including those of running away, which was William James's primary example. It remains possible, however, that their emotional feelings depend on autonomic sensations, such as heart rate and sweating.

To test that possibility, we need to examine people who lack autonomic responses. **Pure autonomic failure** is a medical condition in which the autonomic nervous system ceases to influence the body. The causes of this uncommon, incurable condition are unknown. Usually its onset occurs when people are middle aged. One prominent symptom occurs when people stand up: The blood sinks rapidly from the head to the trunk, and the person faints. (The medical term for this symptom is "orthostatic hypotension.") The same thing would happen to everyone except for the actions of the sympathetic nervous system. When we stand up, we reflexively trigger mechanisms that increase heart rate and constrict (tighten) the veins leading from the head. People with pure autonomic failure lose this reflex and therefore have to stand up very slowly to prevent the blood from sinking out of the head. A further symptom is that physical or mental stresses of any kind have no effect on their heart rate, breathing rate, sweating, and other autonomic responses. What about their emotions? They report feeling the same emotions as anyone else, under the same conditions, but less intensely (Critchley, Mathias, & Dolan, 2001). Presumably the appraisal part of their emotion is intact but the feeling part is weakened. Even someone with few or no emotional feelings can say, "I recognize this as a situation that calls for fear" (or anger or whatever). But without autonomic changes, they have nothing to *feel*.

Locked-in syndrome is an even more extreme condition in which people lose almost all output from the brain to both the muscles and the autonomic nervous system, although they continue to receive sensations. The cause is a stroke or other damage to the part of the brainstem (see Figure 1.7). Most people with spinal cord damage retain control of some of their muscles, depending on the location of the damage. Even those who are paralyzed from the neck down have output to the heart and other organs because the nerves of the parasympathetic nervous system originate in the pons and medulla, not the spinal cord. In locked-in syndrome, however, key areas of the pons and medulla themselves are damaged. In these areas axons travel from the brain to the spinal cord. The pons and medulla also include neuron clusters that control the parasympathetic nervous system. However, a few clusters of neurons above the damaged area control eye movements, so the person retains the ability for eye movements. Otherwise, the person is totally paralyzed while remaining intellectually alert and capable of surviving for many years.

What happens to their emotions? They can tell us, although not easily. First, someone has to teach them to spell out words by a code in which different patterns of eye movements or blinks represent different letters of the alphabet. When they give their first message, you might expect a message of terror or despair. After all, the person is permanently paralyzed except for the eye muscles, and most of us imagine that we would feel overwhelming distress at that prospect. The James-Lange theory, however, would predict greatly weakened emotion, because of the virtual lack of feedback from the body.

Unfortunately, the results are sparse and unclear on this point. Communication with these people is slow and laborious. Most of what they say is remarkably unemotional, certainly without any expression of panic or despair. One woman's first message after learning an eye-blinking code was, "Why do I wear such an ugly shirt?" (Kübler, Kotchoubey,

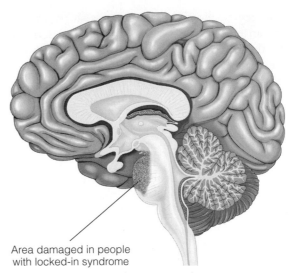

Area damaged in people
with locked-in syndrome

FIGURE 1.7 The stippled area shows the location of brain damage in people with locked-in syndrome. Axons in this area provide the communication between the brain and nearly all the nerves controlling muscles. The only muscular control these people retain is of their eye movements, controlled by cells above the area of damage.

Kaiser, Wolpaw, & Birbaumer, 2001). Many of the reports by locked-in patients are described as "tranquil"—that is, calm (Damasio, 1999). A likely interpretation is that they do not experience fidgeting, heart palpitations, stomach churning, or any of the other bodily responses that ordinarily accompany emotions.

However, an autobiography by a locked-in patient (dictated by blinks of one eyelid) does refer to sadness, disappointment, frustration, and similar emotional terms (Bauby, 1997). Two websites by or about locked-in patients also assert that they feel emotions, including at least sadness and frustration. (See http://www.strokesafe.org/resources/locked-in_syndrome.html.) We would like to know more: Do they really *feel* emotions, and do they feel them as intensely as before, or are they talking about a cognitive appraisal of emotions? This distinction is theoretically important to psychologists studying emotions although somewhat obscure to anyone else. Furthermore, remember that the patients continue to have normal control of the eyes. That control includes the ability to cry, so the patients do receive feedback relevant at least to the emotion of sadness. The few research studies currently available simply do not provide enough information to answer our questions about emotional feelings.

Are Body Sensations Sufficient for Emotional Feeling?

Remember William James's example of running away from a bear as a cause of feeling fear. The studies on people with spinal cord damage indicate that muscle responses are not necessary for emotions. Might they, however, be sufficient? That is, if you make the muscle movements associated with some emotion, or if you have the appropriate autonomic responses, would you then start to feel that emotion? Would the muscle movements at least strengthen your emotional feeling?

For example, does smiling make you feel happy or amused, and does frowning make you feel annoyed? To test these hypotheses, researchers can't simply tell people to smile or frown and then ask them how they feel. Well, they could, but it wouldn't be a good idea. If you were in that study, you would probably guess what hypothesis the experimenters were testing, and you might give an answer just because it was what you thought they wanted you to say. Psychological researchers call problems such as this "demand characteristics," meaning the cues that tell participants what the experimenter hopes to see.

To avoid demand characteristics, researchers use methods that disguise the intention of the study. Here is one clever procedure they have used, which you could try yourself, or ask a friend to try: Hold a pen with your lips, as Figure 1.8 illustrates. Later repeat the procedure holding the pen with your teeth. In each case go through a stack of newspaper comic strips, using the pen to rate each one as funny (+), somewhat funny (÷), or not funny (-). When holding the pen with your teeth, you are virtually forced to smile; when holding it with your lips, you press your lips together in a way that people do when they are angry or annoyed. In one study, participants holding the pen in a "smiling" position rated cartoons slightly

Kathleen Olson

FIGURE 1.8   Holding a pen with your teeth forces a smile; holding it with your lips prevents one. A smiling position tends to enhance reports of amusement.

FIGURE 1.9   We express emotions with body posture as well as facial expression.

funnier than did those who held it in the "annoyed" position (Strack, Martin, & Stepper, 1988). That is, the sensation of smiling apparently increases amusement. Another study found similar results using ratings of movies instead of cartoons (Soussignan, 2002).

Parenthetically, we need to explain that this experiment is more complex than it might seem. Changes in facial expression induce additional changes in heart rate, breathing, and so forth, so it is not clear that the facial expressions by themselves were responsible for people's emotional responses (Levenson, Ekman, & Friesen, 1990). Also, not everyone is convinced that this procedure completely avoids demand characteristics. Might an occasional participant in this study guess what the experimenters were hoping to find? Given that we cannot read people's minds, it is hard to be sure.

In a follow-up study on frowning, researchers told their participants they wanted to study "divided attention." The participants were to do two things at once: One was to rate the pleasantness or unpleasantness of various photos. The other task depended on golf tees that the experimenters attached near their eyebrows, just above the inside of each eye. The participants were to try to touch together the tips of the two golf tees. The only way to do that was to frown; so the instructions sneakily got them to frown without in fact saying anything about frowning. While

participants were touching the two golf tees together (and therefore frowning), they rated most photos less pleasant than at other times when they were not supposed to touch the golf tees together (Larsen, Kasimatis, & Frey, 1992). Several other studies have also found that facial expressions can elicit or at least strengthen the corresponding emotional feelings, although the effectiveness varies considerably from one person to another (Duclos & Laird, 2001; Hess, Kappas, McHugo, Lanzetta, & Kleck, 1992).

When you feel fear, anger, or sadness, you express it not only with your facial expression but also with your body posture. (See Figure 1.9.) If you adopted both the facial expression and the posture, would you start to feel that emotion? To find out, researchers asked 54 college students to adopt certain postures and facial movements. They concealed the point of the experiment by saying it was a study on how people's movements affected their thinking. They went on to say that sometimes feelings influence the relationship between movements and thinking, so they would have to ask about emotional feelings as well as thoughts. Then they gave detailed instructions about what muscles to move and postures to adopt (Flack, Laird, & Cavallaro, 1999).

Their instructions follow. Try each of them and see whether you start to feel any emotion. Unfortunately, unlike the participants in the experiment, you know the hypothesis, so your results are contaminated by your expectations. However, you could try reading these procedures to some friends without telling the hypothesis. After you have tried each of these procedures, read further to see what emotion the instructions were intended to induce and what results occurred in the experiment.

1. Push your eyebrows together and down. Clench your teeth tightly and push your lips together. Put your feet flat on the floor directly below your knees, and put your forearms and elbows on the arms of the chair. Now clench your fists tightly, and lean your upper body slightly forward.

2. Lower your eyebrows down toward your cheeks. With your mouth closed, push up lightly with your lower lip. While sitting, rest your back comfortably against the back of the chair, and draw your feet loosely in under the chair. You should feel no tension in your legs or feet. Now fold your hands in your lap, just loosely cupping one hand in the other. Drop your head, letting your rib cage fall and letting the rest of your body go limp. You should feel just a slight tension up the back of your neck and across your shoulder blades.

3. Raise your eyebrows, and open your eyes wide. Move your whole head back, so that your chin is tucked in a little, and let your mouth relax and hang open a little. Scoot to the front edge of your chair, and draw your feet together and underneath the chair. Now turn your upper body toward the right, twisting a little at the waist, but keeping your head facing forward. Now dip your right shoulder a bit, and lean your upper body slightly backward. Raise your hands to about mouth level, arms bent at the elbow, and palms facing forward.

4. Push the corners of your mouth up and back, letting your mouth open a little. Sit up as straight as you can in your chair. Put your hands at the ends of the armrests, and make sure that your legs are straight in front of you, with your knees bent and feet directly below your knees.

The results were these: Instruction #1 was intended to induce anger. On the average, participants did report higher than usual anger levels and also somewhat elevated levels of disgust. The latter result is not too surprising because disgust is somewhat similar to anger.

Instruction #2 was intended to induce sadness, and it did, without elevating any other emotion. Instruction #3 was meant for fear. Here the results were less clear. People reported an elevated fear level but an even more elevated feeling of surprise. This result actually makes sense, because the behaviors associated with fear and surprise are similar. Finally, instruction #4 was intended for happiness, and people following this instruction did increase reports of happiness, on the average.

Figure 1.10 shows all the results. The graph may look more complicated than it really is. It shows the results for four sets of instructions, arranged left to right: anger, sadness, fear, and happiness. For each set of instructions, people reported their degree of six emotional feelings: anger, sadness, fear, happiness, disgust, and surprise. Note that each set of instructions aroused the intended emotion and sometimes aroused a related emotion also. Unfortunately, the researchers did not report a baseline of

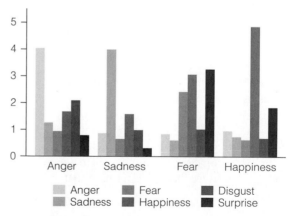

FIGURE 1.10 The instructions intended to arouse anger, sadness, fear, and happiness did indeed arouse those feelings, but in some cases they aroused a closely related feeling also. Source: Based on data of Flack, Laird, and Cavallaro (1999).

how much of each emotion people might feel when given no particular instructions about facial expression or posture. Oops.

In addition to facial expressions and postures, breathing patterns are also associated with emotions. Researchers first determined the breathing patterns associated with various emotions. For example, angry or frightened people take many rapid, irregular breaths with occasional tremors. Sad people sigh frequently. Joyful people breathe deeply, but slowly. Then researchers asked other people to follow certain instructions for breathing while filling out questionnaires about physical and mental sensations. When they got people to breathe the way sad people generally do, people reported feeling sad. People who were breathing like joyful people said they felt happy, and those who breathed like angry or frightened people reported feeling angry or frightened (Philippot, Chapelle, & Blairy, 2002).

In summary, the results indicate that the facial expressions, postures, breathing patterns, and other actions associated with a given emotion tend to elicit the feeling of that emotion. That is, as the James-Lange theory predicts, feedback from your muscles and glands is sufficient for at least the start of an emotional feeling. However, all of these effects are small. When a researcher takes the average across a large number of participants, people's induced smiles, frowns, postures, and so forth appear to facilitate emotions congruent with their expressions, but we certainly can't rely on that result for every person every time. The fact that these effects occur at all is theoretically important, but the feedback from your facial expression, posture, or breathing is just one small influence among many other determinants of your emotion. So to someone deeply depressed, don't say, "Smile; it will make you feel better!" Facial feedback doesn't have that strong an effect.

Overall Evaluation

Here we are, about a century and a quarter after William James proposed one of the first general theories of psychology. Isn't it about time we decided whether it is right or wrong?

We contend here that the theory is more or less correct, if described in modern terms and understood in the limited and revised form of James's later writings. It is *not* a general theory of emotion. For most questions about emotion, it has no clear implication. It is, rather, a theory of the order in which three elements of emotion occur. We describe it thus: The appraisal comes first, then actions (including autonomic responses), and the feeling aspect is the sensation arising from the actions. The data indicate that emotional appraisal is quick, preceding actions. Feedback from actions is sufficient to produce at least a mild emotional feeling. In the absence of all feedback from actions, would someone have a complete absence of emotional feelings? On this key point, the answer is "probably," based on data from pure autonomic failure and locked-in syndrome. Exactly how much emotional feeling these patients have is hard to say, and no patient has a complete absence of feedback, but people with very limited feedback seem to have a low intensity of emotional feeling.

Feedback from one's actions probably does not identify which emotion is present, however, and the James-Lange theory did not unambiguously claim that it did. Fear and anger, in particular, are very similar physiologically, and we may distinguish them by cognitive appraisal, rather than physiological sensations.

In closing, we shall suggest a modification of the James-Lange theory, to which we believe both James and Lange would have agreed: The chain of events does not go entirely in one direction. That is, after appraisal leads to actions and actions to feelings, the actions and feelings alter the appraisal, and the whole process can continue to change again and again. For example, if something makes you angry, your anger changes your interpretation of new events, so that a new event that might otherwise seem unimportant now seems like additional cause for anger (Lerner & Keltner, 2000). Much work remains to be done before we fully understand the emotion process.

◻ Summary

What have we learned so far? Emotion is complex, elusive, and hard to define, and sometimes researchers disagree about what causes emotion mainly because they have different ideas of what the term emotion means. We have tentatively defined emotion as including three major elements—cognition (appraisal), feelings, and actions. The full experience of emotion includes all three, but some events arouse just one or two aspects. Ordinarily, an emotion-producing event rapidly triggers a cognitive appraisal, which directs a series of autonomic responses and a readiness for muscular actions. The feeling aspect of emotion is closely related to feedback from the muscles and glands. However, in some cases the feelings and actions may come first, with a cognition added later to try to explain the actions that already occurred.

Scientific study always requires accurate measurement, and measurement is especially difficult for emotional feelings. For that reason, researchers seek a variety of methods and they try to be cautious in their conclusions. Throughout this book, we shall return repeatedly to the theme of careful measurement and cautious interpretation of results.

◻ Key Terms

Cannon-Bard theory: view that the cognitive experience of emotion, occurring in the cerebral cortex, is independent of the arousal and other actions of the muscles and glands, even though the cognitive experience occurs at the same time as the actions (p. 15)

ecological validity: extent to which what happens in a study reflects what really happens in everyday life (p. 12)

electroencephalography (EEG): procedure in which the researcher pastes electrodes on someone's scalp to measure momentary changes in the electrical activity under each electrode (p. 11)

emotional response coherence: extent to which self-reports of emotion, physiological changes, and simple behaviors (such as facial expressions) predict each other (p. 9)

functional magnetic resonance imaging (fMRI): procedure that measures brain activity based on changes in oxygen uptake (p. 11)

James-Lange theory: view that emotions (especially the feeling aspects of emotions) are the labels we give to the way the body reacts to certain situations (p. 15)

locked-in syndrome: condition in which people lose almost all output from the brain to both the muscles and the autonomic nervous system, although they continue to receive sensations (p. 22)

parasympathetic nervous system (PNS): branch of the nervous system that increases maintenance functions that conserve energy for later use and facilitates growth and development (p. 9)

pure autonomic failure: medical condition in which the autonomic nervous system ceases to influence the body (p. 21)

reliability: the repeatability of the results of some measurement, expressed as a correlation between one score and another (p. 7)

Schachter-Singer theory: view that the arousal and other actions that are part of any emotion are essential for determining how strong the emotional feeling will be, but they do not identify the emotion; you identify which emotion you feel on the basis of all the information you have about a situation (p. 16)

sympathetic nervous system (SNS): branch of the nervous system that readies the body for "fight-or-flight" emergency actions (p. 9)

validity: an assessment of whether some procedure measures what it claims to measure (p. 7)

◻ Thought Questions

Each chapter will offer a small number of "thought questions," designed for you to contemplate and perhaps discuss in class. In each case, we do not believe the evidence to date offers a "right" answer. We hope you will consider not only what would be a good answer, but also what research would help improve our ability to answer each question.

1. We have proposed two slightly different definitions of emotion. Can you offer any way to improve on them?
2. Suppose we discover some animals on another planet. They have an entirely different physiology from ours, but their behavior seems similar to ours in various ways. Would it be possible to determine whether or not they have emotions, based on the definitions and criteria outlined in this chapter? If so, how? If not, why not?
3. It is possible that initially we need feedback from our actions and autonomic responses for the feeling aspect of emotions (as proposed by the James-Lange theory), but that eventually we learn how to feel the emotions even with weak or absent feedback. What evidence would we need to evaluate this hypothesis?

◻ Suggestions for Research Projects

At the end of most chapters, we shall suggest possible research projects that a student could conduct in a limited amount of time, with little or no equip-ment and no major ethical limitations. In this chapter, we have already mentioned two possibilities:

1. Measure people's ratings of the funniness of cartoons while they hold a pen between their teeth or between their lips, as described on page 23.
2. Ask people to adopt the postures described on page 25 and then describe what emotion, if any, they feel.

◻ Suggestions for Further Reading

Damasio, A. R. (1994). *Descartes' error: Emotion, reason, and the human brain.* New York: G. P. Putnam.

Damasio, A. R. (1999). *The feeling of what happens.* New York: Harcourt Brace.

Damasio, A. R. (2003). *Looking for Spinoza.* Orlando, FL: Harcourt.

All three of these books are well-written, thought-provoking discussions by a neurologist who has studied patients with brain damage that affects their emotions.

2

Classification of Emotions

Dmitry Mendeleyev's periodic table of the chemical elements was one of humanity's great intellectual achievements. Not only did it list all the naturally occurring elements known at the time, but it systematized them as well. It predicted the properties of other elements yet to be discovered or created in laboratories. It also paved the way for research on atomic structure that established why the elements on the table are the only elements that could exist.

Psychological researchers understandably envy that accomplishment. In the earliest decades of psychology (the late 1800s and early 1900s), psychologists called the "structuralists" tried to identify elements of the human mind, such as ideas or sensations. They presumed that the elements of psychology would be the building blocks that combine to form all of human behavior and experience. The search for the elements of the mind proved frustrating, however, and psychologists eventually abandoned that goal.

However, even if the mind in general does not have elements, perhaps certain aspects of psychology have elements. For several decades, psychological researchers tried to list all the naturally occurring, or primary, motivations or drives (e.g., Madsen, 1959;

McDougall, 1932; Murray, 1938; Young, 1936). A few are obvious: hunger, thirst, sex, comfortable temperature, and avoidance of pain. Urination, defecation, and sleep are less obvious, but reasonable choices after we think about them. But psychologists' lists continued to grow, and different psychologists offered different choices. Breathing certainly belongs on the list, but is it just one motivation, or should we count inhaling and exhaling separately? Is activity a drive? How about curiosity? Infant care? Aggression? Laughter? Listening to music? Eventually psychologists gave up trying to list all the drives, because deciding what should go on the list seemed more trouble than it was worth.

One area in which many psychologists continue to seek the "elements" is emotion. Many consider it feasible to list a limited set of **"basic" emotions**—emotions that are fundamentally distinct from one another, as chemical elements are from one another. Researchers working from this perspective refer to certain emotions as "basic" or "primary." If such "emotional elements" do exist, then other emotion experiences would be compounds or "blends" of the basic emotions.

Not everything in nature comes in elements, though. In fact, other than the chemical elements, most of the categories we use to think about the world reflect somewhat arbitrary conceptual divisions, rather than absolute, "real" divisions. So the question is, do people have a set number of discrete, irreducible emotions with natural boundaries, or do we have a continuous gradation of possible emotions that we divide up in an arbitrary way? Chemists established through centuries of research that no tinkering or blending could turn lead into gold—they are fundamentally different. Psychologists also need research to establish whether sadness and anger, for example, are also fundamentally different or just reflect different proportions of the same ingredients. Chemists have also established that the elements sodium and chlorine combine to form table salt. In a similar way, psychologists ask whether all emotional experience involves combinations of a few, discrete units. In fact, although much current research presumes that such elements exist, the whole idea of "basic emotions" has been called "an article of faith" rather than a conclusion based on empirical evidence (Ortony & Turner, 1990, p. 315). Some of the research needed to answer these questions has been done, but there's still a long way to go before we can reach a confident consensus.

Resolving this issue would have huge implications for how we study emotions and how we link emotions to the rest of human behavior and experience. However, what is at stake here goes well beyond the study of emotions. To say that certain emotions are natural elements of our experience seems to affirm the idea of "human nature." It implies that we are "born that way." For example, if anger is a naturally occurring elemental emotion, then we might draw three conclusions. First, except for the effects of brain damage, genetic mutations, or other abnormalities, everyone probably experiences anger in a similar way—it's just a normal part of life. Second, the emotion anger is probably an evolved characteristic, such as upright walking and language, which means that experiencing anger in certain kinds of situations helped our ancestors survive and reproduce long ago. Third, the eliciting events, bodily feelings, facial expressions, and be-

haviors associated with anger should be the same in all cultures—they "hang together" wherever you go.

An alternative view is that our emotions, as with much of the rest of our experience, are "socially constructed." That is, the way we describe our emotions and even how we perceive them are based on the "narratives" (stories) that our culture tells about human feelings (Neimeyer, 1995). A social constructivist perspective presumes that emotion words represent arbitrary categories of experience, rather than "real" ones. Thus, the English word *anger* may represent a combination of feeling offended, having high blood pressure and a certain facial expression, and wanting to hurt or yell at somebody, but another language may lack a word for this combination or may have a word that reflects a somewhat different combination of features. Just as we learn from our culture what to consider a food, beauty, and so forth, we may learn from our culture exactly what (if anything) constitutes anger, fear, and sadness.

Some psychologists have argued that even the colors we see are socially constructed; that is, the reason we see the world in terms of red, yellow, green, and blue is that our language has words for those colors. Some other culture might have divided up the colors in a different way, so that they would see some other colors as "primary." Doing good research on that question is much more complicated than it might sound (Roberson, Davies, & Davidoff, 2000), but most researchers now believe that what we regard as the best examples of *red* or *green* stand out as "central" or "primary" colors for people in other cultures also.

Applying the social-construction idea to emotions suggests that we learn from people around us what emotions to feel, how to express them, and how to interpret other people's expressions. By this view, emotions are not human nature—we have to learn them. If, however, expressions and their meanings are similar across cultures, then certain aspects of our emotions are "given." We have certain inborn categories of emotions, or at least certain fixed dimensions along which emotional experience varies. You may be wondering, "Do I really have to choose one perspective or the other?" Probably not, although psychologists studying emotion often make it seem like we do. As is so often the case, both perspectives may be right, in different ways. In this chapter, we'll discuss research that deals with the "basic emotion" question.

◻ Criteria for "Basic Emotions"

Chemists established that gold is an element by failing in repeated attempts to make it from other kinds of metal. They demonstrated that water is a compound because one can make it by combining oxygen with hydrogen. Psychologists cannot literally combine one part of anger with one part of fear in a test tube. How can we identify elemental, or basic emotions, or even decide whether such a concept is meaningful?

Psychologists don't just fail to agree on which emotions, if any, are basic. They also disagree on what evidence would be decisive. We consider five popular criteria here, but remember that not everyone accepts these criteria (e.g., Ekman, 1992; Johnson-Laird & Oatley, 1989; Lazarus, 1991; Shaver, Schwartz, Kirson, & O'Connor, 1987; Tooby & Cosmides, 1990).

The least controversial criterion is that *a basic emotion should be universal* within our species. That is, if an emotion is basic, it should occur in all societies in nearly all people, except perhaps infants or those with brain damage or genetic mutations. Finding some emotion in all societies is no guarantee of its being basic, but finding it in some societies and not others would imply that it is socially constructed and not a built-in aspect of human nature.

For example, nearly every culture and every language has words that translate approximately as happiness, sadness, and fear, so those are at least good candidates to be basic emotions. A few societies report that they never experience anger or don't have a word for anger. Does that mean they feel no anger at all, or just that they control it effec-

tively? (Or maybe they just don't want to talk about it.) Some psychologists have argued that certain societies have "culture-specific" emotions. This might seem like an easy question to address—just look through foreign-language dictionaries and see which English emotion words map onto words in other languages—but it's more complicated than that. For example, the German word *Schadenfreude* refers to the pleasure one feels at seeing someone else get hurt, especially one's enemy. The English language doesn't have a corresponding word, but be honest, have you never felt that way? Perhaps German-speakers are just more honest about admitting it.

There are many other examples as well. We will introduce them here and discuss them in more detail in Chapter 3 and in later chapters on specific emotions. The Japanese call one emotion *amae*, variously defined as "the pleasant feeling of depending on someone else" or "the feeling of comfort in another person's acceptance." That emotion may seem unfamiliar to you, but researchers who study amae deny that it is culture specific; rather, they believe people in other cultures feel it, but don't always encourage it or talk about it (Doi, 1973; Lambie & Marcel, 2002; Morsbach & Tyler, 1986). People of the Ifaluk culture (in the Micronesian islands of the Pacific) report an emotion called *fago*, which does not translate as any single English word. It corresponds to a combination of compassion, love, and sadness (Lambie & Marcel, 2002). Whereas an Ifaluk psychologist might regard fago as a basic emotion, English speakers regard it as a blend of other emotions. As you see, it is difficult to determine the cross-cultural universality of an emotion just from language or self-report data. However, researchers have looked for evidence of universality in other aspects of emotion. Later we will discuss the evidence on facial expressions of emotion—a line of research that has been especially important.

A second criterion is a bit more complex. According to many theorists, *a basic emotion must facilitate a functional response to a specific, prototypical life event, or "antecedent."* The idea is that if we all share an emotion, we must have evolved the ability to feel it, and if we evolved the tendency to feel it, it must be useful for dealing with some common problem. For example, in every culture that we know about, sadness is experienced in response to a loss, such as the death of a loved one, and it is functional because it elicits social and practical support from other people. Fear, a response to danger, facilitates escaping from a threat. With a little effort, you can describe the events that lead to surprise, anger, happiness, and several other emotions.

However, once an emotional mechanism has evolved for certain situations, a similar situation may trigger it even where the emotion is not evidently useful. For example, a child is sad after separation from a parent (for good reasons, because parents provide nurturance and protection from danger) and also sad when separated from a stuffed animal (where the sadness has no apparent function). Parents feel a rush of tenderness and compassion when picking up an infant (where the evolutionary function is obvious—if you don't take care of your infant, it probably won't pass on your genes), and many people, including one of us (M.S.), also feel tenderness and compassion when picking up a pet cat. In each of these cases, the capacity to feel the emotion is functional, even if the emotion also occurs in some less useful situations.

A third criterion is that *a basic emotion should be evident early in life.* Newborn infants cry when they hear a sudden, loud noise or if they hear another baby crying. If we were to label this expression with a single emotion term, that term would be "distress." During early infancy, the infant's facial expressions do not distinguish among distress, fear, anger, and sadness (Messinger, 2002). So, by this criterion, distress qualifies as a basic emotion. In contrast, we would not think of nostalgia as a basic emotion, because it emerges much later in life (if at all) and depends on many kinds of experience.

The problem is, how early in life must an emotion occur to qualify as basic? Newborns do not smile or laugh, although they do respond to a par-

ent's happy tone of voice by opening their eyes wider (Mastropieri & Turkewitz, 1999). Perhaps that means they experience happiness, perhaps not. Smiling and frowning emerge gradually within two or three months (Izard, 1994). Expressions of fear (as opposed to distress) develop by about six months. Expressions of anger develop gradually over a longer period. We can easily see anger in an 18-month-old, but for a 6-month-old infant, the boundary between anger and distress is still not certain. The onset of disgust is also difficult to specify. Even newborns spit out bitter or sour food, but children must be several years old before they begin to show disgust at anything other than bad-tasting food. When do children first show surprise? If you cover a toy and then remove the cover and the child sees a different toy, not the one that was hidden, even infants well under a year old stare at the new toy longer than usual. But they do not show a facial expression that resembles the adult "surprise" expression (Camras et al., 2002). Again, it is a matter of definition whether we say infants less than a year old show surprise.

Children don't show evidence of embarrassment or shame until they are about a year and a half old, and because of that delay, most psychologists regard shame and embarrassment as "social emotions," different from the primary emotions that develop earlier. But that conclusion is hardly rock solid. Most expressions, after all, are not present in newborns, and all take time to approach their mature form. Besides, nearly everyone accepts the idea that the capacity for language is part of human nature, even though language capacity does not emerge until children are more than a year old. In short, the "present from infancy" criterion is problematic.

A fourth criterion, also widely used, is the basis for much of the emotion research since the 1970s. Many psychologists assume that *if an emotion is basic, people should have a built-in way of expressing it, such as through facial expressions or tone of voice.* Furthermore, in accordance with the first criterion (similarity across cultures), it is important to demonstrate that people in all cultures can recognize the same facial expressions and interpret them in approximately the same way. A great deal of research (and controversy) deals with facial expressions, and we shall consider this topic in some detail later in this chapter.

If the evidence were strong enough, a fifth criterion would probably be the most persuasive: that *each primary emotion should have its own physiological basis,* presumably a certain kind of activity in the brain or the autonomic nervous system. For example, suppose that some kind of brain damage, drug treatment, or genetic mutation caused someone never to feel anger, while leaving other emotions unimpaired. That evidence would strongly implicate anger as a primary, independent emotion. If some other brain damage or mutation impaired fear, and still another impaired happiness, then we could identify those as primary emotions also. On the other hand, if some other emotion—shame, for example—could not be impaired without altering the others, we might conclude that it was "not basic." Although researchers have conducted studies of the physiology of the emotions, the current evidence does not conclusively demonstrate that any emotion is physiologically distinct from the others.

◻ Facial Expressions of Emotion

One of the most important aspects of the basic-emotions controversy is the question of how similar the emotions are across cultures. Any emotion that seems similar across cultures is at least a reasonable candidate as a "basic" emotion. Evidence of significant variation across cultures would support the idea of social construction.

Much of the research evidence relevant to the universality question has involved facial expressions of emotion (e.g., Ekman, 1972; Russell, 1994), and many studies have focused on the ways in which people around the world decode such expressions. Because this research has been so influential, these classic studies deserve extra attention.

Darwin's Theory of Emotional Expression

After Charles Darwin developed his theory of evolution by natural selection, he became curious about the expression of emotional states (Darwin, 1872/1998). He had noticed strong similarities in the physical behaviors that animals of a great many species exhibited when they were threatened, angry, sad, or excited. For example, many species react to a threat by changing posture to appear larger; birds raise their feathers and spread their wings, cats arch their backs and their hair stands on end, and primates stand on their hind legs and lift their arms. Darwin also noted that some of the most common human expressions of emotion occur in monkeys and apes as well, including the expressions of fear and anger (see Figure 2.1).

In his classic book *The Expression of the Emotions in Man and Animals,* Darwin (1872/1998) argued that expressions of emotion probably evolved because they conferred some kind of survival or reproductive advantage on individuals who displayed them. For instance, animals that react to threats by making themselves look larger increase their chance of surviving that threat because the change in appearance might scare off the attacker. In much of the book, Darwin argues that human expressions of emotion are also the result of evolutionary processes that link us to our closest primate relatives.

How might emotional expressions have evolved? Darwin (1872/1998) suggested three mechanisms that might lead to species-typical expressions: action of the nervous system, serviceable associated habits, and the principle of antithesis. Those hypotheses remain our most prominent explanations today.

Action of the nervous system refers to changes that occur as a result of overall sympathetic arousal. When you become highly aroused with any emotion, you breathe rapidly and perspire. An intense emotion prepares you for vigorous action, but if the circumstances do not permit you to do anything,

FIGURE 2.1   Nonhuman primates have some facial expressions that clearly resemble those of humans and use them in similar situations.

your hands may tremble. Trembling is a common sign of fear, but people also sometimes tremble with anger or joy. The expressions that occur as by-products of arousal signal the intensity of an emotion, although they do not distinguish well between one type of emotion and another.

Serviceable associated habits are movements that become associated with particular situations because they usually help in that kind of situation. For example, when you are disgusted by something and want to avoid looking at it, you close your eyes. Darwin thought that this kind of movement was repeated so often that it became habitual—you do it without even thinking about it in that general sort of situation. This idea would explain why certain expressions are automatic, even when they don't make immediate sense. For example, first imagine watching someone do an everyday task, like reading the newspaper. Then imagine watching someone vomit. Did you close your eyes? Many people close their eyes when imagining something disgusting, even though closing your eyes doesn't actually prevent

you from "seeing" (in this case, imagining) the disgusting event.

Darwin also believed that habits developed by parents were passed on to offspring without the offspring having to learn them. It turns out that he was wrong on this point. "Acquired" or learned traits are not, in fact, passed on genetically. However, the mechanism of serviceable associated habits still goes a long way toward explaining many expressive behaviors. Behaviors can confer enough fitness advantage to spread through a species if they are frequently useful. The whole point of emotional expressions is to prompt a very rapid reaction without your having to think too hard about it. Imagine having to "decide" whether or not to pull back from a snake when it strikes! If pulling back automatically helps you stay alive when the snake would bite you, it's not a problem when you do the same thing while watching a snake strike in a movie or television show.

Finally, the *principle of antithesis* is the idea that if an expression means one thing, an opposite ex-

FIGURE 2.2   A posture indicating threat (left), and an opposite posture indicating complete submission. Source: Darwin, Charles, *The Expression of the Emotions in Man and Animals* (1872/1998), with permission from Oxford University Press.

pression means the opposite. For example, if you shake your head from side to side to indicate "no," then nodding it up and down means "yes." Darwin gave the example of a dog that takes an attack posture to indicate threat. It takes an opposite posture to indicate submission, as Figure 2.2 shows. If your pet dog barks loudly, and then suddenly discovers that you, not some intruder, is behind the front door, it may take this exaggerated submissive posture to indicate the opposite of threat and anger.

Darwin recognized that if facial expressions were inherited from primate ancestors, they should be the same in all human cultures. He lived in an era, the mid 1800s, when photography was awkward and expensive, so he had to test his hypothesis by relying on written reports from missionaries and others who had traveled to other continents. Darwin wrote to anybody he knew of living in another part of the world, described "typical" facial expressions of particular emotions, and asked his correspondents if natives of that culture expressed each emotion in the same way. He, of course, had no way of checking the accuracy of their answers.

Darwin's correspondents replied that people throughout the world show similar expressions of many feelings. When surprised or astonished, they open their eyes widely and sometimes their mouths as well. When puzzled or perplexed, they frown.

When determined, they frown and close their mouths tightly. When they feel helpless, they shrug their shoulders. Even some people who were born deaf or blind show these same expressions. When embarrassed, people use their hands to cover their face. Again, even people born blind do the same—although they have never experienced what it means to see or be seen. People throughout the world also pout, mostly in childhood. (When was the last time you saw an adult pout?) The similarity of all these expressions across cultures, and their presence in people born blind and/or deaf, suggests that they are not learned, but a product of our genetic heritage.

About a hundred years later, the Austrian biologist Irenäus Eibl-Eibesfeldt (1973) made extensive visits to remote cultures, photographing people's facial expressions. He too reported remarkable similarities in expressions across cultures. Eibl-Eibesfeldt recorded one expression that Darwin had not considered: People often exchange a friendly greeting by raising their eyebrows and slightly opening their mouths (Figure 2.3). Symbolically, the gesture says, "I am glad to see you. I open my eyes wide to see you better." The expression is constant in both meaning and duration. Throughout the world, the average duration of the expression, from eyelids relaxed to raised position to down again, lasts about a third of a second.

FIGURE 2.3   People throughout the world greet one another by raising their eyebrows, sometimes also slightly opening their mouths. Source: Eibl-Eibesfeldt (1973).

Cultural Differences in Gestures and Expressions

Darwin documented important similarities in the nonverbal gestures and expressions people use around the world. There were, however, some problems with his research strategy. First, consider the nature of the questions he asked his far-flung assistants. A question was not: "How do people's faces typically look when they are astonished?" A typical question read more like: "Is astonishment expressed by the eyes and mouth being opened wide and by the eyebrows being raised?" Darwin's correspondents simply said yes or no. Today, most researchers would avoid such a suggestive question and let the correspondents describe expressions in their own words. Alternatively, they might offer a series of choices without implying one over another. People sometimes say yes even if the description is not quite accurate, or if they are not sure, especially when it is clear what hypothesis the researcher is testing. Also, Darwin's question required that the correspondents infer people's emotions by some other means than facial expressions, and it's not clear how.

In the early twentieth century, the prevailing theories in psychology and anthropology favored strong environmental influences, and Darwin's conclusions about emotion fell into disregard. Several influential anthropologists described cultural differences in the expression of emotions (Birdwhistell, 1970; LaBarre, 1947). For example, whereas clapping the hands usually indicates joy or delight in the United States, it often suggests worry or disappointment in Chinese culture (Klineberg, 1938). In most cultures, people indicate "no" by shaking their heads back and forth, and "yes" by nodding it up and down. In Greece and Turkey, however, people typically indicate "yes" by tilting their heads back, and in Sri Lanka, they express approval by shaking their heads back and forth.

In the United States, a common gesture joins the tip of the thumb with the tip of the index finger to make a circle, as shown here, to indicate "we're in agreement," or "everything is going well." In many other cultures, however, that gesture is meaningless, and in some it is considered a rude invitation to have sex!

Other ethnographic work documented expressive reactions that made no sense to Westerners. For example, people in some parts of Southeast Asia bite their tongues when they feel shame, and according to some reports, Japanese wives of Samurai warriors smiled when they learned their husbands had died in battle.

By the middle of the twentieth century, ethnographic reports of differences in emotion expression had persuaded most social scientists that the whole concept of emotion must be socially constructed. Beginning in the 1960s, however, new research focusing on facial expressions rather than hand gestures revolutionized the field of emotion and revived the search for universal, innate, basic emotions.

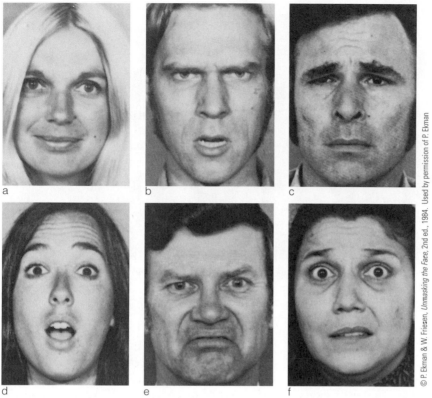

The image credit reads vertically along the right side: © P. Ekman & W. Friesen, *Unmasking the Face*, 2nd ed., 1984. Used by permission of P. Ekman

FIGURE 2.4   People in many cultures have been asked to identify which face goes with which emotion: anger, disgust, fear, happiness, sadness, and surprise. Source: Ekman and Friesen (1984).

Interpreting Facial Expressions

Recall that two major criteria for a basic human emotion is that it should occur in all cultures and should have its own facial expression. Darwin and Eibl-Eibesfeldt reported that the same facial expressions occur throughout the world, but what they meant was that the expressions looked the same to them and seemed to be occurring in the same situations. Do people in other cultures agree about the meaning of facial expressions? If they see a smile, do they assume the person smiling is happy? If they see wide eyes and an open mouth, do they infer surprise? In the 1960s, Paul Ekman and Carroll Izard both hypothesized that yes, people from different cultures should agree on the interpretations of a

few, simple facial expressions of emotion, and they went out to test this hypothesis.

The basic test was this. Imagine that you are one of the research participants. Someone shows you the six photos shown in Figure 2.4 and asks you to identify which one represents each of the following emotions: anger, disgust, fear, happiness, sadness, and surprise (Ekman & Friesen, 1984). If you speak a language other than English, then the researchers would first get someone to translate those six words into your language.

Versions of this basic study have been conducted dozens of times, in countries all over the world. In some of the studies, participants lived in small, isolated agricultural villages where they seldom

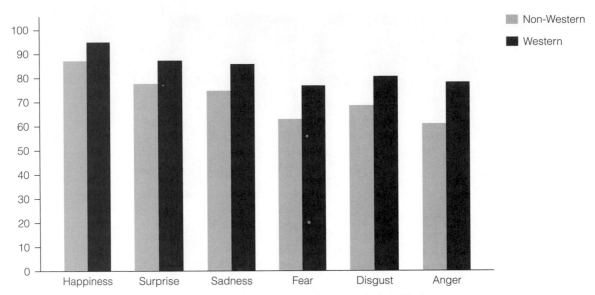

FIGURE 2.5   Mean accuracies for pairing the expressions in Figure 2.4 with their labels.
Source: Based on data of Russell (1994).

encountered people from the Western world and did not watch television or movies. In one case, the participants had never even seen Caucasians before the researchers arrived in their village. Figure 2.5 shows the results, averaged across several studies and almost two thousand people (Russell, 1994). In the graph, one bar represents how often non-Western observers matched the facial expression of an emotion to the "correct" emotion word. Another bar represents the corresponding statistic for Western participants. Random guessing would produce one sixth to one third correct for each emotion (depending upon the exact version of the study), and clearly people did better than that. Even though the photographs were of Caucasians (people of European ancestry), people from other societies throughout the world identified most of the expressions correctly. So, from the standpoint of our original question about basic emotions, one major question is answered: Yes, certain emotions do have facial expressions that people throughout the world can recognize.

In general, Western participants have been a little more accurate than non-Western ones. How can we explain this difference? Given that the people in

the photos were Caucasian, the difference in accuracy could mean that it is easier to recognize expressions posed by someone from your own culture, just as it is easier to understand someone who speaks with your accent or dialect (Elfenbein & Ambady, 2003). However, the following alternative explanations are possible as well (Matsumoto, 2002):

- Perhaps when the researchers attempted to translate words such as anger, surprise, or disgust into other languages, something got lost along the way. This discrepancy would make the matching task more difficult.
- The Americans and Europeans were probably more experienced at looking at displays on a piece of paper and answering a researcher's questions about them. People in some non-Western cultures become nervous when talking to outsiders.
- Americans and Europeans might be better at recognizing facial expressions in general, not just those from their own culture. This hypothesis seems less likely, but we can test it only by collecting data.

The best way to get around these problems is to use more than one set of photos (Matsumoto, 2002). For example, researchers might show photos of Americans and Africans to both American and African observers. If Americans identify the American photos better, and Africans identify the African photos better, then we could conclude that it is easier to recognize expressions from your own culture. The limited research done so far of this type has shown a small tendency for people to recognize emotions better for their own culture. Also, if people look at faces from other cultures, it is easier to recognize expressions from a familiar culture, one with which the observers have had some contact (Elfenbein & Ambady, 2002a, 2002b).

An additional problem with all these studies is that the matching procedure could overestimate people's accuracy (Russell, 1994). For example, when you look at Figure 2.4, presumably you identify face (a) as happy. Almost everyone does. Now you are left with five faces to pair with five labels. Suppose you are unsure whether face (d) represents surprise or fear. If you decide that face (f) is a better expression of fear, you choose (d) for surprise. Suppose you have no idea what to call face (e). If you identify (b) as anger and (c) as sadness, you label (e) as disgust just by process of elimination.

One way to get around this limitation is to present photos one at a time and ask which emotion (if any) it expresses. The difficulty of this method is that people sometimes give answers that are not exactly what the researchers expect (Ekman, 1994a). For face (f), the intended answer is "fear." Various people call this expression terror, horror, panic, or "she looks like she just saw a ghost." Presumably, we would count all those answers as correct, treating them as synonyms for fear. But what if someone called the expression distress or worry? Are those answers close enough to fear that we should consider them correct? Indeed, what if someone called

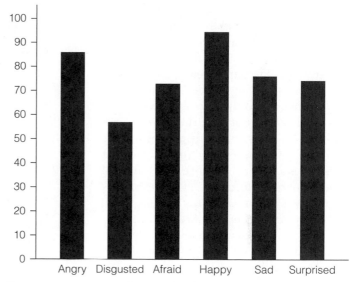

FIGURE 2.6   Accuracy of one group of college students in correctly labeling six emotional expressions. The students were not given the labels or any other suggestions about their answers. Source: Based on data of Ekman (1994a).

the expression surprise? We probably would count that answer wrong, because a different expression was intended to represent surprise, but fear and surprise often go together, so this "wrong" answer is not entirely incorrect.

A similar problem arises with the anger expression: Is the description "frustrated" right or wrong? Frustration strongly overlaps anger, although the terms are not synonyms. When observers name facial expressions, researchers do their best about assessing the answers. (Assessment is especially difficult when researchers and participants speak different languages.) Researchers find that people are reasonably accurate at recognizing facial expressions, even of faces from other cultures, but they can match faces to given labels more accurately and more confidently (Frank & Stennett, 2001). Figure 2.6 shows the accuracy of one group of college students in labeling the emotions portrayed by six faces (Ekman, 1994a).

In real life, of course, we do not try to read someone's emotions entirely from static facial expressions. We notice changes over time, such as eyeblinks, trembling, and direction of gaze. Notice that the researchers posed all the faces in Figure 2.4 to look directly at the viewer. In real life, happy people look straight at you and so do angry people, especially if they are angry at *you*. However, sad people seldom look straight at you; they mostly gaze down and to the side, and you recognize the expression of sadness partly from the fact that someone is looking down. (We sometimes call a sad expression "downcast.") Frightened people look at whatever is frightening them. Unless you are personally threatening someone, you would be puzzled to see the person looking at you with an expression of fear. Although people recognize an angry expression about equally well for a face looking at them or looking away, most people identify a fearful expression more easily for a face looking to the side, as Figure 2.7 shows (Adams & Kleck, 2003).

We also notice body movements outside the face, such as shoulder shrugging, head turns, slouching, standing erect, speed and direction of walking, and hand gestures (Edwards, 1998). You might not recognize an expression of "pride" from facial expression alone, but with the addition of body posture, most people can (Tracy & Robins, 2004). We also consider tone of voice, including laughs and shrieks. People can assess someone's emotion moderately well from just hearing the tone of voice (Adolphs, Damasio, & Tranel, 2002), and they gauge emotions much faster and more accurately if they see and hear the person than if they only see or only hear (de Gelder, 2000). Even when people listen to someone speaking an unfamiliar foreign language, they are quite accurate at identifying anger or sadness in the voice and moderately accurate at detecting happiness, fear, and tenderness (Juslin & Laukka, 2003). Our ability to detect emotions from tone of voice may even be what enables music to convey emotion (Scherer & Zentner, 2001).

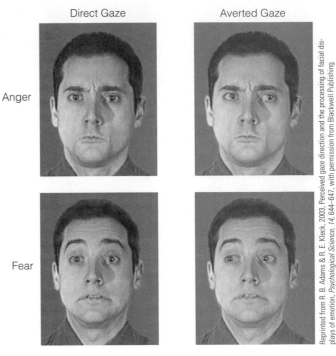

Reprinted from R. B. Adams & R. E. Kleck, 2003. Perceived gaze direction and the processing of facial displays of emotion, *Psychological Science, 14,* 644–647, with permission from Blackwell Publishing

FIGURE 2.7   How quickly can you identify these expressions? Most people identify fearful expressions more easily when the person is looking away than straight ahead. However, people recognize expressions of anger about equally well in either direction.

We also infer emotions from people's posture and speed of walking. Sometimes even smells influence our perceptions of someone's emotion. For example, the presence of an unpleasant smell interferes with our ability to recognize that other people are smiling and happy (Leppänen & Hietanen, 2003). (It's as if we were thinking, "How could anyone be happy in a room that stinks like this one?") In summary, people in everyday life recognize emotional expressions from a wide variety of cues that go beyond what photographs provide. Therefore, the results that Figures 2.6 and 2.7 present probably *underestimate* people's true abilities to recognize emotions.

However, despite the difficulties of accurately measuring people's ability to interpret emotional expressions, the research to date does make a persuasive case that several facial expressions convey roughly the same meaning from culture to culture. How does this conclusion address the question of basic emotions? Many psychologists conclude that universal human nature includes an "affect program," consisting of innate emotional reactions to some situations, standard displays of those emotions, and the ability to recognize displays by other people. In sum, they regard the emotions in question as "basic emotions."

We can identify these six emotions by facial expression, but are these the only emotions we can recognize and therefore the only basic emotions? In addition to the six emotions depicted in Figure 2.4, many psychologists list contempt as a seventh basic emotion. (See Figure 2.8.) Pride is another candidate, as are guilt, interest, hope, relief, frustration, love, awe, boredom, jealousy, regret, and embarrassment (Ekman, 1992; Fredrickson, 2001; Keltner & Buswell, 1997; Shaver, Morgan, & Wu, 1996). Hindus regard heroism, amusement, peace, and wonder as additional emotions (Hejmadi, Davidson, & Rozin, 2000). Although none of us could reliably recognize all of these emotions from still photographs, most people do fairly well when watching videotapes, which are closer to what we experience in everyday life (Hejmadi et al., 2000).

Photo courtesy of Dr. Paul Rozin

FIGURE 2.8   An expression of contempt. Many psychologists regard contempt as an additional basic emotion.

Finally, one of the easiest facial expressions to identify is sleepiness. Should we therefore count sleepiness as an emotion? If not, then we concede that having a recognizable facial expression for something does not necessarily make it an emotion. What about surprise? Is surprise really an emotion, or is it a cognitive state? The fact that we recognize its facial expression does not necessarily make it an emotion. Before we can decide what is and is not an emotion, we need more evidence than just facial expressions.

Physiological Studies

Where has all this research on facial expression led us so far? Most psychologists conclude that at least a few facial expressions are universal, in the sense that they convey approximately the same information to people of all cultures. People in any culture recognize a smile as a sign of pleasure. Frowns are also universal signals of displeasure, although they do not distinguish one kind of displeasure from another.

However, the research on facial expressions has not answered the question of how many basic emotions we have or indeed whether there is such a thing as a basic emotion. Potentially more decisive evidence comes from physiological studies. Does any emotion produce a pattern of brain activity that sets it apart from all others? Could any kind of brain damage impair one emotion without affecting others?

Several studies have measured brain activity while people examined emotion-generating photos or recalled highly emotional personal experiences (Damasio et al., 2000; Kawasaki et al., 2001; Royet et al., 2000). Although these studies usually were not designed to distinguish one emotion from another, they did show that happy emotions excite different patterns of brain activity than do sad, angry, or frightened emotions. In fact, one study found that sadness increased activity in several brain areas whereas happiness *decreased* activity in many of those same areas (George et al., 1995).

As discussed in Chapter 1 (see Figure 1.5), the patterns of brain activity elicited by different emotions apparently overlap more than they differ. Much of the difference in brain activity from one study to another depends on the experimental procedures rather than on the type of emotion studied. However, many of these studies have concentrated on activity in the cerebral cortex. As Panksepp (2003) has noted, focusing on the cerebral cortex

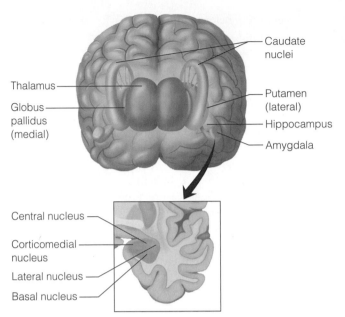

Caudate nuclei

Thalamus

Globus pallidus (medial)

Putamen (lateral)

Hippocampus

Amygdala

Central nucleus

Corticomedial nucleus

Lateral nucleus

Basal nucleus

FIGURE 2.9   The amygdala, a small structure in the temporal lobe of the cortex, is important for emotions, perhaps especially for fear. The top view shows positions of the amygdala and several other internal brain structures as if the outer surface were transparent. The bottom view shows part of a cross-section through the brain, parallel to the plane of the forehead.

overlooks the subcortical areas, which may respond more specifically to one emotion or another.

Several kinds of evidence at one time suggested a specific physiological basis for fear, linking it to a brain area called the amygdala, which Figure 2.9 depicts. A later chapter will review this research in more detail, but here let's consider a few highlights.

Many studies on rats and other laboratory animals reported that damage to the amygdala impairs the ability to learn new fears. An animal with this damage would still give a startle response to a loud noise, showing a built-in fear, but it would not readily learn that some other event (such as a blinking light) predicted an electrical shock. As a result, it would not learn to fear the blinking light (Hitchcock & Davis, 1991).

A rare genetic disorder called Urbach-Wiethe disease causes skin lesions and sometimes also causes a gradual loss of neurons in the amygdala because of calcium accumulation. People with this disease have trouble recognizing other people's emotions, especially expressions of fear, from their facial expressions (Anderson & Phelps, 2000) or tone of voice (Scott et al., 1997). When they need assistance, they approach people on the street haphazardly, instead of looking for people who look friendly or trustworthy (Adolphs, Tranel, & Damasio, 1998). However, that behavioral oddity does not necessarily indicate lack of fear; it might be better described as difficulty interpreting other people's expressions. One man with extensive damage to the amygdala and surrounding areas could not recognize any expression other than happiness from photos, but he could identify almost any emotion from a story about events that would elicit emotions (Adolphs, Tranel, & Damasio, 2003). So amygdala damage does not necessarily impair emotions themselves; indeed, most people with amygdala damage report that they continue to experience both pleasant and unpleasant emotions (Anderson & Phelps, 2002). Rather, amygdala damage impairs attention to certain kinds of emotional information or the processing of information related to emotions (Whalen, 1998). For example, when words are flashed briefly on a screen under conditions that make them difficult to read, most people report seeing more of the emotionally loaded words (such as RAPE) than neutral words (such as RAKE). People with amygdala damage see and remember as many of the neutral words as the emotional words (Anderson & Phelps, 2001).

Furthermore, the problem is not limited entirely to fear. People with amygdala damage also have difficulty recognizing expressions of anger, disgust, and surprise. Brain scan studies have found that when people look at photographs of facial expressions, the amygdala responds most strongly to fearful and unhappy faces, but it also responds somewhat to other faces, including happy faces

Insula (primary taste cortex)

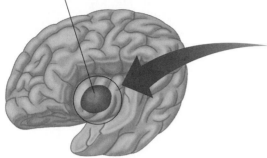

FIGURE 2.10 The insula (or insular cortex) is the primary area of the cortex for taste information and apparently also critical for the emotion of disgust.

(Hamann, Ely, Hoffman, & Kilts, 2002; Iidaka et al., 2001). Damage to the amygdala impairs the processing of information about reward as well as information about fear (Baxter & Murray, 2002). In short, the amygdala is not specifically a fear center.

Another emotion with possible neurological specificity is disgust. One study using brain scans found that when people looked at disgusting photos (such as mutilated bodies), they showed increased activity in a brain area called the anterior insular cortex (M. L. Phillips et al., 1997). That finding is especially interesting because this brain area is also critical for the sense of taste. (See Figure 2.10.) Disgust is literally bad-taste, and disgust is essentially a sense of wanting to spit something out. Damage to just the insular cortex is uncommon, but it does sometimes occur. Two patients with damage to the insular cortex could recognize expressions of other emotions but not disgust, either from facial expressions or retching sounds (Adolphs et al., 2003; Calder, Keane, Manes, Antoun, & Young, 2000). One of these patients heard a story about someone vomiting and then was asked how the person must have felt. He replied that the person would feel "hungry" and "delighted" (Adolphs et al., 2003). The other patient did describe a filthy toilet as disgusting, but it is possible to "know" that something is disgusting (because one has been told so) without actually feeling the disgust. In short, disgust may indeed depend on the insular cortex.

Other emotional states have not been linked to any specific physiology, although so far no one has tried very hard. Future research may identify different physiologies for different emotions.

◻ Alternatives to the "Basic Emotions" Approach

The case for "basic" or primary emotions is growing but hardly overwhelming. At the very least, we should consider alternatives. Several related theories describe emotions as points on a continuous plane, rather than a few discrete units; another theory describes emotion as compounds made up of even smaller units (analogous to protons, neutrons, and electrons). Let's consider these views.

Dimensional Approaches to Emotional Feelings

Instead of listing items separately, an alternative is to arrange them along dimensions. For example, if you were displaying diamonds at a store, you might arrange them in columns from largest to smallest and in rows from most to least sparkling. You could describe brightness in terms of a continuous dimension from white to dark.

Perhaps we could also describe emotions in some similar way, as positions along some small number of continuous dimensions (Russell, 1980, 1997, 2003). One way to derive these dimensions is to start with a theory. For example, we might propose that all emotional experiences vary along a continuum from pleasant to unpleasant or from approach to avoidance. Another way is to collect results and then analyze them with a method called multidimensional scaling that allows us to see what dimensions emerge from peoples' ratings of their experience.

Without discussing the mathematics of multidimensional scaling, let's illustrate the idea with an

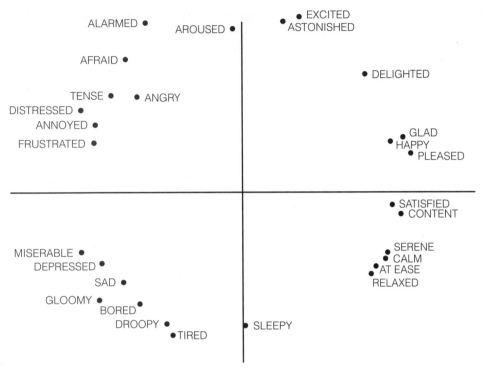

FIGURE 2.11   The terms that people rated as similar to each other appear close together, whereas those rated as dissimilar appear far apart. Source: From "A Circumplex Model of an Affect" by James A. Russell in *Journal of Personality and Social Psychology, 39,* pp. 1161–1178. © 1980 American Psychological Association. Reprinted with permission from the author.

example. Consider color. Suppose we show people various pairs of colors and ask them to rate how similar or different they look. For example, someone might rate two shades of purple as very similar, purple and blue as somewhat similar, but purple and green as less similar. A mathematical model would therefore put the first two colors close together, the second pair intermediate, and the third pair far apart. After collecting ratings on many pairs of colors, we might present the results graphically, putting purple near blue, then bluish green, then green, and so forth.

Applying this approach to emotion, researchers offer people various emotion-related words and ask them to rate the degree of similarity among various pairs. Or they ask people to report how strong their emotions are at various moments and then note which pairs of emotions tend to occur together. For

example, when people report they are afraid, they usually also report they are tense, whereas they virtually never report being excited and bored at the same time. So *afraid* and *tense* should be represented close together, whereas *excited* and *bored* should be far apart.

Using this method, Russell (1980) reported the arrangement of emotional terms shown in Figure 2.11. Studies in other countries, using other languages, have produced reasonably similar outcomes (Yik & Russell, 2003). From such results, James Russell proposed what he called a **circumplex model** (Figure 2.12), in which the emotions form a circle. Emotions close to each other on the circle are very similar and are likely to be confused with each other or experienced at the same time. Emotions on opposite sides of the circle are likely to be perceived as opposites or at least as very different. In this model,

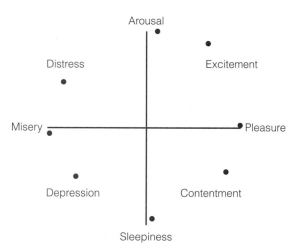

FIGURE 2.12 According to Russell's circumplex model of emotions, emotional experiences depend on two major dimensions, the degree of arousal and the degree of pleasure. Source: From "A Circumplex Model of an Affect" by James A. Russell in *Journal of Personality and Social Psychology, 39,* pp. 1161–1178. © 1980 American Psychological Association. Reprinted with permission from the author.

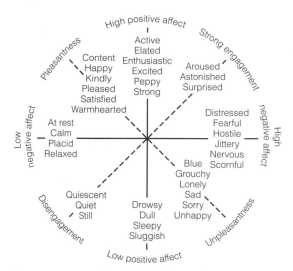

FIGURE 2.13 In this model, the main dimensions are positive affect (arousal) and negative affect (fear and hostility). Source: From "Toward a Consensual Structure of Mood," by D. Watson and A. Tellegen, *Psychological Bulletin, 98,* pp. 219–235. © 1985 American Psychological Association. Reprinted by permission of D. Watson.

one major dimension ranges from arousal to lack of arousal (sleepiness), and the other ranges from pleasure to displeasure (or misery). Using this model, we can describe excitement as a combination of pleasure and arousal, contentment as a combination of pleasure and inactivity, and so forth.

Other researchers, starting from a different theoretical basis and using slightly different procedures, have proposed a somewhat different arrangement. Examine Watson and Tellegen's (1985) model in Figure 2.13. At first glance, this model looks much like Russell's circumplex model, but the dimensions are described in different terms. In Russell's model, you might feel neutral, but you could not feel strong positive emotion and strong negative emotion at the same time. Watson and Tellegen's model allows for this possibility. The vertical axis, called positive affect, asks how much positive emotion someone is feeling; the horizontal dimension, called negative affect, reflects distress (fear and hostility) versus lack of distress. However, "pos-

itive affect" in their sense is not the same as happiness; it is closer to the concept of arousal.

The most controversial point about this model is its claim that positive affect and negative affect are independent. (Their lines cross at a right angle.) Because of a variety of complicated measurement problems, different sets of researchers get different results on the relationship between positive affect and negative affect. Some find them to be nearly independent of each other, meaning that it should be possible to feel both positive and negative affect at the same time (Tellegen, Watson, & Clark, 1999; Watson, Clark, & Tellegen, 1984, 1988). Other researchers have found that positive and negative affect are polar opposites—you can only feel one or the other but not both (Remington, Fabrigar, & Visser, 2000; Russell, 1980). A few researchers have even found a positive correlation; that is, Negative Affect (fear/hostility) overlaps with Positive Affect in the sense of excitement (Green & Salovey, 1999). Still other researchers have found multiple kinds of relationships between positive and negative affect. According to one study, positive and negative affect are opposites in most situations, but in a few bitter-sweet situations (such as graduating from college), people do feel a lot of both (Larsen, McGraw, & Cacioppo, 2001).

Let's not get too embroiled in that controversy. For the purposes of this discussion on classifying emotions, what's most important is what these different approaches have in common. Here are three major points of agreement among the theories that describe emotions as points on a few continuous dimensions:

1. It is possible to describe emotional experience in terms of a small number of dimensions, such as arousal and pleasantness, or positive and negative affect.
2. These models characterize the feeling aspect of emotions, not the cognitive aspect. Several emotions might *feel* nearly the same, even though we distinguish among them in other ways. For example, disgust, guilt, and embarrassment arise in different situations with different cognitions and different associated behaviors, but they might feel about equally unpleasant and produce about equal degrees of arousal.
3. Because these models describe only the feeling aspect of emotion, they are not necessarily an alternative to the idea of basic emotions. For example, someone could accept one of these models and nevertheless maintain that fear and anger are separate, primary emotions that happen to have very similar feelings. However, the dimensions models do contradict any theory that requires each basic emotion to have a distinct feeling.

Emotions as Compounds of Underlying Processes

Another view unambiguously denies the existence of basic emotions. Recall from Chapter 1 the idea that it is possible to experience just parts of an emo-

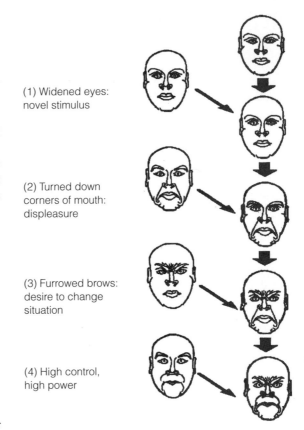

(1) Widened eyes: novel stimulus

(2) Turned down corners of mouth: displeasure

(3) Furrowed brows: desire to change situation

(4) High control, high power

FIGURE 2.14 The expression we describe as anger could be a compound of several elements. Source: Reprinted from K. R. Scherer (1992), What does facial expression express? In K. T. Strongman (Ed.), *International Review of Studies on Emotion,* Vol. 2 (pp. 139–165). Chichester: Wiley.

tion—for example, cognition and feeling without action tendency, or feeling and action tendency without cognition. **Component Process Theory** takes this idea a step further, holding that what we typically consider to be an emotion consists of underlying, more elementary units. Consider, for example, the display of anger in the last face in Figure 2.14. Instead of calling this a single expression, we could analyze it as a combination of at least four components (Ortony & Turner, 1990; Scherer, 1992). First, the widened eyes could indicate that the stimulus is novel or unexpected. This part of the anger expression is also a component of surprise and fear.

A second element is turning down the corners of the mouth. According to component process theorists, this expression indicates displeasure, which also occurs in sadness and disgust.

Third, the furrowed brows might indicate a desire to change the situation. People often furrow their brows when they are frustrated or concentrating, as well as when they're angry.

Fourth, the compressed lips are a sign that one feels powerful or in control.

In many cases of anger, though not particularly in Figure 2.14, angry people have compressed lips. Component process theorists of emotion have proposed that this is a sign that one feels powerful in the situation or in control. Compressed lips might be associated with determination as well. Recent research suggests that compressed lips are also part of the display of pride—another emotion that involves feelings of power and control (Shiota, Campos, & Keltner, 2003).

The key point is that what we call anger could be described as a compound of several components, each a reaction to a different aspect of the situation. A given situation might arouse just one or two of these units or all of them. When all occur, we recognize a clear example of anger, but "parts" of anger can arise without the full expression. For example, anger at your neighbor, anger at your dog, anger at your government, and anger at yourself differ in many ways and not just as a matter of degree. Furthermore, some of the components of anger could combine with other components to make different emotions, which we might describe as frustration, determination, surprise, and so forth. Similarly, we could describe fear as a compound of several components and describe any of the other emotions similarly.

The "component" approach to emotion may seem unfamiliar because we are in the habit of thinking about prototypical examples of fear or anger, where all the components are present. However, from a research standpoint, the component approach has

much potential. For example, instead of studying what causes "anger" in general, we could analyze the causes of different components: What causes the element of novelty? What leads to the feeling of displeasure? What influences the desire to change the situation? What controls the probability of threatening to strike? If different components of anger have different causes, we will understand them better by studying them separately.

◻ Summary

At this point you should feel a little confused. "So, what is the answer? Are there basic emotions or not?"

Emotion researchers are far from agreement on this point, and as you can see, the evidence is inconclusive. We can identify a few emotions that have well-defined facial expressions with approximately the same meaning in all human cultures, so those expressions are evidently part of human nature and not something arbitrary or culture specific. However, they may or may not be the "basic" units out of which every other emotional experience is built.

If we do have a large number of distinct emotions, the differences among them may not be in the feelings they generate. Researchers have argued persuasively that emotional feelings can be described in terms of continuous dimensions such as arousal. So the feelings associated with one emotion may largely overlap those of another. The overlap is particularly strong for fear and anger.

An alternative to basic emotions is smaller behavioral components, such as those described for anger. This approach certainly deserves more research and consideration. Give the matter some thought. What kinds of additional evidence would be more decisive? If you had the opportunity, what research would you do? What would be convincing evidence that sadness and fear are biologically distinct, fundamental units of emotion?

In the meantime, however, psychologists continue to find it useful to use terms such as sadness, anger, and fear, at least until we have something better to take their place. Whether they are actually "basic" is undecided, but studying them separately is at least a productive way to organize research. You might think of the basic-emotion idea as the dominant hypothesis or the working hypothesis, the one that guides most researchers until and unless they settle on a better hypothesis.

Emotion researchers often describe the "basic emotion" and "social construction" perspectives as though they were mutually exclusive. Surely, though, it is possible that emotional experience is determined partly by evolution and partly by culture. In this chapter, you have seen that cross-cultural studies are theoretically essential to establishing any conclusion about human nature. It may also be that ideas regarding the evolutionary functions of emotions can help us to understand differences in the ways cultures experience emotions. We shall return repeatedly to issues of how cultural influences combine with biology to influence our behavior and experience, and the role of culture in emotion is the focus of the next chapter.

◻ Key Terms

basic emotions: emotions that are fundamentally distinct from one another, as chemical elements are from one another (p. 29)

circumplex model: theory that arranges the emotions to form a circle; emotions close to each other on the circle are very similar and are likely to be confused with each other or experienced at the same time (p. 44)

Component Process Theory: view that what we typically consider an emotion consists of underlying, more elementary units (p. 46)

◻ Thought Questions

1. If people's "basic" emotions are analogous to chemical elements, there must be "compound" emotions that combine two or more of the basics. If so, what would you propose as a "compound" emotion?
2. According to the "components" view, a situation can evoke certain emotional components without evoking fear, anger, or any other identifiable emotion as a whole. Do you, and if so how often do you, recognize yourself as experiencing just one or two components or aspects of some emotion?

◻ Suggestions for Research Projects

1. Here is an idea for a simple observational study: Watch people unobtrusively while they are eating, walking across campus, or engaged in other activities. How many people who are in groups are smiling or frowning? How many who are by themselves are smiling or frowning?
2. It would also be interesting to measure how long smiles and frowns typically last. Might the durations of the expressions relate to how long someone would want to advertise a happy, frightened, or aggressive tendency? (For example, a person might want to show anger for a longer time to make sure an opponent gets the message.)
3. To test people's ability to recognize emotional displays across cultures, rent a film from a different culture, in a language you do not speak (preferably without subtitles). Then ask several people to watch it and record what emotion, if any, they detect at particular times. How closely do they agree? Does someone from that culture, who speaks the language, also agree?

◻ Suggestion for Further Reading

Ekman, P., & Davidson, R. J. (1994). *The nature of emotion: Fundamental questions*. New York: Oxford University Press. In this book, the editors ask several fundamental questions about emotion—including questions about how to classify emotions—and many of the top emotion researchers in the world provide their answers.

3

Culture and Emotion

Emotions are the products of evolution, or at least so we argued in Chapter 1. Evolution equipped us with emotions to prepare us to deal with universal problems and situations, such as competing for resources and escaping attackers. In later chapters, especially those on fear and anger, we shall discuss research on rats, monkeys, and other nonhumans, implying some similarity of emotions even across species. Yet for decades, anthropologists claimed that people in various human societies differed enormously in how they experienced, expressed, and understood emotion. The anthropologists' emphasis on cultural differences led to the idea of the **social construction of emotion,** or the ways in which societies create culture-specific ways of thinking about, experiencing, and expressing emotion. As discussed in Chapter 2, this idea implies that such English words as *fear* and *anger* are arbitrary categories that we happen to treat as meaningful because they fit the narratives that our culture uses to make sense of our experience.

Something is wrong here. If emotion is largely similar from one species to another, it should not vary that much between one human society and another. There is, however, a way to resolve the contradiction: Some aspects of emotion are evolved, innate, and universal, whereas other aspects are socially constructed in different ways by different cultures. As already argued in Chapter 2, the underlying mechanisms of emotion are indeed consistent across cultures and presumably the products of our evolutionary history. If you feel your needs have been met, you are happy. If you feel you have lost something you cared about, you feel sad, and if you feel you have been insulted, you feel angry. Happy people smile, whereas sad or angry people frown, and again the expressions are similar for almost all people, even blind people who have never seen other people display these expressions.

Remember, however, that an emotion typically arises because we interpreted or "appraised" a given situation in a particular way, rather than some other way. For example, if a large dog barks loudly at you and appears angry, you could have one of several reactions based upon how you interpret the situation. If you think dogs are dangerous and you feel unable to protect yourself, you could be frightened. If you think you can protect yourself, but that the owner should be making a better attempt to control the dog, you might feel angry. If you like dogs and don't feel threatened by them, you might even feel amused.

This is where culture comes in. Culture has a tremendous influence on the ways in which we interpret different situations. If situations can be interpreted in many ways, a given culture will probably encourage some interpretations and discourage others. Thus, the same event may typically elicit amusement in one culture, but anger or fear in another. Culture also sets standards for how openly you can display your emotions—for example, whether it is acceptable to cry in public, or how much pride you can show before it seems like rude bragging. In this chapter, we discuss what it means to talk about "culture," ask how culture can have such a powerful influence on our understanding of the world, and consider the implications for human emotion.

◻ What Is Culture?

If you look up *culture* in a dictionary, you may find 5 to 10 distinct meanings. Clifford Geertz (1973) complained that one article had offered 11 definitions of human culture within 27 pages! To be fair, those 11 definitions did not contradict one another. Still, it helps to focus on a single definition.

A Definition and Its Implications

Here is a suitable definition, offered by the anthropologist Richard Shweder (1993, p. 417): **Culture** consists of "meanings, conceptions, and interpretive schemes that are activated, constructed, or brought 'on-line' through participation in normative social institutions and practices (including linguistic practices) . . . giving shape to the psychological processes in individuals in a society." Yes, we know, that's a mouthful. Let's break it down a bit and highlight key points.

First, cultures are *systems of meaning*—ways of interpreting, understanding, and explaining what is going on in the world around us. Specific units of meaning are often represented in words—the labels we use to symbolize some category of experience or combination of features. Some categories are natu-ral, or nearly so, and we would expect almost all cultures to define them the same way. For example, the term *cat* refers to a particular species, and even though a particular cat may be odd or atypical in some way, virtually everything in the universe either is or isn't a cat. (A hybrid with some other species could be a borderline case.) Other categories are more arbitrary, less clearly defined, and therefore culture specific. For example, the English language distinguishes among bottles, jars, jugs, flasks, canisters, and other kinds of containers, but other languages draw more, fewer, or different distinctions (Malt, Sloman, Gennari, Shi, & Wang, 1999). Language distinctions are just one example of how a culture defines the meaning of objects and events. Think also about religious rituals, holidays, birthday parties, funerals, and marriage ceremonies. Consider several objects: the national flag, an autograph by a famous person, or a monument commemorating a historical event. In each case, something has a certain meaning or significance because the culture says that it does.

Second, culture activates or constructs meanings *through social participation*. For example, in one class you might sit quietly throughout the lecture, while in another you discuss your own ideas and argue with others. How did you know to behave differently in the two classes? You might sit quietly during a symphony but much less quietly during a rock concert. Again, why? In each instance, you learn largely by imitation. You watch what other people do, and you do the same.

Third, cultures *give shape to the psychological processes in individuals*. Shweder means that how we think about the world and behave in it depend on the concepts we have learned. For example, most Americans think of a cat as a "pet." Many less wealthy cultures have no such concept. They treat animals as food, workers, or a source of danger, and they might be baffled by the idea of buying cat food. At best, it would make no sense; at worst, it would seem immoral to give food to the cat instead of a needy person. Still other cultures have classified cats as holy beings, worshipped them, and offered them the choicest food and shelter. To many Americans, this degree of care would seem wasteful or even sacrilegious. In short, differences in concepts and meanings can translate into substantial differences in behavior.

◻ Cultural Differences in Concepts of Emotion

Cultural differences in the ways people think about, classify, and find meaning in emotion can be dramatic. If you and your classmates try to define "emotion" or list some typical emotional experiences, you will probably find that you agree, for the most part, on what the term means. If we ask people from another culture for a definition, they may have quite a different answer; you may not even be able to ask the question in some cultures because not every language has a word corresponding to "emotion" (Russell, 1991).

Even when a language does have a word that translates as "emotion," it might not refer to the same set of concepts that the English term covers. For example, the Japanese term *jodo* includes "angry," "happy," "sad," and "ashamed," which are states that most American psychologists readily identify as emotions (Matsuyama, Hama, Kawamura, & Mine, 1978). However, it also includes states that translate as "considerate," "motivated," and "lucky," which would not classify as emotions in English. Keep in mind that these terms are inexact translations as well. What the Japanese mean by "lucky" may not be what Americans mean by "lucky," so it is hard to say whether "lucky" in Japanese is really an "emotion" in English.

Other languages have words that seem to correspond to the English word *emotion*, except that they refer to the situation, not the internal feeling that the situation produces. For example, the Fulani word *semteende* (from a culture of West Africa) denotes a social situation in which an American would probably feel embarrassment or shame. The term is often translated as "embarrassment," but it actually refers to the situation and not how the person feels

(Riesman, 1977). A better translation might be "embarrassing." The Ifaluk of the South Pacific also tend to emphasize social situations over internal states in their emotion lexicon (Lutz, 1982).

In Chapter 1, we described a study in which participants held a pencil with either their teeth or their lips; those holding it with their teeth, forcing a smile, rated cartoons as funnier than people holding it with their lips. Robert Levenson and colleagues asked participants to perform a similar task, but used subtle, muscle-by-muscle instructions to produce expressions of anger, fear, sadness, happiness, surprise, and disgust (Levenson, Ekman, Heider, & Freisen, 1992). When Americans performed this task, their autonomic nervous system physiology mimicked that of people feeling the corresponding emotion, and they said they felt the emotion. But Levenson and colleagues found somewhat different results with members of the Minangkabau, an Indonesian tribe. The posed facial expressions triggered the same physiological changes as with the Americans. But unlike the Americans, the Minangkabau did not interpret those experiences as emotions, and they reported little emotion during the task. For the Americans, an emotional face and physiology equaled "having" an emotion. The Minangkabau, in contrast, would not report feeling an emotion if they were not in the appropriate social situation.

Here's another kind of example. You go to a friend's house because no one has seen him in a couple of days and you wonder how he's doing. He seems droopy and lethargic, sighs frequently, and lowers his eyes. He says he doesn't really feel like doing anything. He also tells you that his wife and children recently left town for a long trip, and he won't see them for a while.

In a word, how would you describe him? An anthropologist studying life in Tahiti found himself in roughly this situation (allowing for a bit of literary license) and drew the conclusion most Americans would draw—the man was sad because he missed his family (Levy, 1973). The man himself, however, did not describe his state as an emotion, and Tahitians

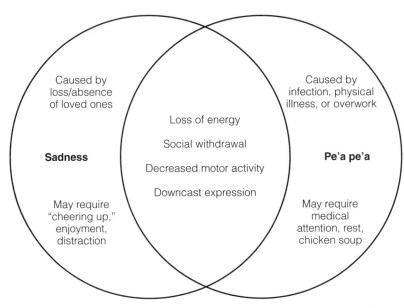

FIGURE 3.1   The conceptual territory of "sadness" in English corresponds closely, though not exactly, with the conceptual territory of illness or fatigue in Tahitian.

don't have a word for what we call "sadness." Instead, he described himself as *pe'a pe'a*, which means sick, fatigued, or troubled. He described his condition as an illness, not an emotion. Here we see the differences and similarities between the concept of illness in Tahitian and sadness in English. They have much in common, but belong in different categories. See Figure 3.1 for a visual diagram of the relationship between these words. In China, also, people often describe their reaction to a situation in body terms— "sick"—rather than emotional terms—"sad" (Tsai, Simeonova, & Watanabe, 2004). In other words, the emotional feelings may be universal for nearly all people (as we would expect if emotions are a product of human evolution), but how we describe them is a product of our culture.

Let's also consider how culture defines love, and some possible consequences of that definition. When you think about love, what images come to mind, what stories, what memories? According to Ann Swidler (2001), people's answers reflect their culture: their network of meanings, ideas, and beliefs about intimate relationships. In her study,

Swidler interviewed 88 middle-class Californian men and women of many ages. She asked what "real love" means, what their experiences with love had been, where their ideas of love came from, what makes a romantic relationship good or bad, and so forth.

Swidler found that American culture promotes two distinct concepts of romantic love, and that individuals even within a single culture often struggle to reconcile them. One concept is the Hollywood, bolt-of-lightning kind of love that turns your world over in an instant and lasts a lifetime. As Swidler summarizes it, "They met, and it was love at first sight. There would never be another girl (boy) for him (her). No one could come between them. They overcame obstacles and lived happily ever after" (Swidler, 2001, p. 114). In this image of love, the beloved is "the one," there is a feeling of destiny, of being meant for each other, and the beloved is completely irreplaceable.

The other concept of love is more prosaic. This kind of love, often espoused by people who are skeptical of the Hollywood version, grows slowly over time rather than happening in an instant. The couple's story revolves around compatibility of personality, social connections, and activities, rather than obstacles to overcome. This type of love does not require you to find your one perfect mate; you might find many people with whom this kind of love would have the potential to develop, given the opportunity. People who advocate this image of love say it is slow to grow, but deep and sure, whereas "Hollywood" love is flashy and shallow.

The important point, to Swidler, is that neither of these versions of romantic love is objectively more "real" or valid than the other. Both are socially constructed narratives, stories we tell about how ro-

FIGURE 3.2   Two versions of "love" in middle-class American culture.

mantic relationships are supposed to work and what experiences and feelings should be involved. Many American movies emphasize the "love at first sight" version, but in societies where arranged marriages are the norm, and among Western couples who have been together for many years, people tend to talk more about the slow-growing, deep, and steady kind of love. We will discuss love in more detail in Chapter 9. The key point now is that each of these ways of thinking about love is a cultural creation.

▢ Do All Cultures Have the Same "Basic" Emotions?

Recall that one criterion for a "basic" emotion is that it should occur among people everywhere. At least a few emotions seem to meet that criterion, so far as we can tell: In all cultures studied so far, people recognize the expressions of joy, sadness, fear, anger, disgust, and surprise; furthermore, the expressions occur under similar circumstances. Are there, however, any additional emotions that occur in some cultures but not others? If so, they would limit the idea of universal emotions that developed through evolution.

The English language offers more than 2,000 emotion words, although most of them are seldom used (Wallace & Carson, 1973). (When was the last time you said you were chagrined, tantalized, enthralled, flabbergasted, or vexed?) Taiwanese includes about 750 emotion words (Boucher, 1979). The Chewong language of Malaysia only includes 7 words that could be translated into English emotion words (Howell, 1981). However, the number of words in a language is not the same as the number of emotions. English has many synonyms or near-synonyms and far more emotion words than emotions. (English dictionaries have accumulated more words than other languages for almost everything.) A culture with fewer words could recognize and even discuss an emotion without having a word for it; for example, someone with no word for "embarrassment" could say, "the way you feel when you have made a mistake and others are staring at you." Still, to study cultural differences, one place to begin is to examine the emotions identified by one language and not another.

James Russell (1991) reviewed dozens of ethnographies that explicitly described the emotional lives of different cultures. He identified English emotion

TABLE 3.1   English emotion words "missing" in other languages (summarized from Russell, 1991)

Sadness	Surprise	Guilt	Love	Anxiety	Depression
Chewong (Malaysia)	Chewong (Malaysia)	Chewong (Malaysia)	Nyinba (Nepal)	Eskimo	Chewong (Malaysia)
Tahitian	Ifaluk (Micronesia)	Ifaluk (Micronesia)		Machiguenga (Peru)	Eskimo
		Ilongot (Philippines)		Yoruba (Nigeria)	Fulani (West Africa)
		Pintupi (Australia)			Kaluli (New Guinea)
		Quichua (Ecuador)			Malay
		Samoan			Mandarin
		Sinhalese (Sri Lanka)			Xhosa (South Africa)
		Tahitian			Yoruba (Nigeria)

concepts that various other languages lack and emotion terms in other languages that English lacks. (See Table 3.1.) We already mentioned one example: The Tahitian language has no word for sadness, so the Tahitian man whose family was away described himself as ill or fatigued instead.

Many languages also contain emotion words that have no English counterpart. Consider the description of *litost* offered by Milan Kundera (1979/1980) in the *Book of Laughter and Forgetting* (pp. 121–122; edited version from Russell, 1991):

Litost is a Czech word with no exact translation into any other language. It designates a feeling as infinite as an open accordion, a feeling that is the synthesis of many others: grief, sympathy, remorse, and an indefinable longing. . . . Under certain circumstances, however, it can have a very narrow meaning, a meaning as definite, precise, and sharp as a well-honed cutting edge. I have never found an equivalent in other languages for this sense of the word either, though I do not see how anyone can understand the human soul without it. . . . *Litost* is a state of torment caused by a sudden insight into one's own miserable self. . . . *Litost* works like a two-stroke motor. First comes a feeling of torment, then the desire for revenge.

Litost is hardly the only example. English also has no equivalent to the German word *Schadenfreude*, meaning the enjoyment of another person's suffering (Leach, Spears, Branscombe, & Doosje, 2003). The Ilongot speak of the emotion *liget,* which, like anger, can be a response to insult or injury (Rosaldo, 1980). However, unlike anger, *liget* can also be evoked by mass celebrations, by a successful hunt, or by the death of a loved one. Also unlike anger, *liget* is considered a positive force that contributes to society.

What, if anything, do these language differences mean for emotional experience? Not much, perhaps. For example, even without having an English word for *Schadenfreude*, don't you sometimes enjoy seeing someone suffer? Never? Not even when some rich celebrity gets arrested for illegal dealings? Not even when a brutal criminal gets punished? Maybe you are a saint and never feel this way, but most people do.

Another emotion that researchers often describe as culture specific is the Japanese emotion *amae*, described as a feeling of pleasurable dependence on another person, such as the feeling an infant has toward his or her mother (Doi, 1973). In Japan, one feels amae when one receives a gift, or is cared for, or is allowed to be dependent and childlike (even childish), without any obligation to reciprocate. It is a core characteristic of relationships between spouses and among family and close friends. In his description of amae, Doi (1973) says it is a foundation of the Japanese social structure and that Japanese individuals expect this unconditional nurturance from their close and potentially close relationships. It shows up in many situations. Japanese people rely on social support for getting through a stressful experience more than Americans do (Morling, Kitayama, & Miyamoto, 2003). Japanese mothers talk with their infants more about relatedness than American mothers do (Dennis, Cole, Zahn-Waxler, & Mizuta, 2002). Japanese people define happiness and success in terms of interpersonal relationships, not in terms of individual accomplishments; that is, happiness relates more to intimacy than it does to pride or self-esteem (Kitayama, Markus, & Kurokawa, 2000; Uchida, Norasakkunkit, & Kitayama, 2004).

To many Americans, however, the concept of enjoying dependence on other people seems alien. Americans expect adults to take care of themselves without depending on others. For example, imagine yourself as a guest in an American home. Your host says there are snacks in the refrigerator and invites you to "help yourself." An American might like that message, interpreting it as an invitation to treat the host's home as your own; a Japanese might take it as the slightly insulting message, "No one is going to help you."

Is *amae* really a culture-specific emotion? Or perhaps a culturally defined situation for feeling a pleasant, loving emotion? Not necessarily. According to Doi, amae is a basic, universal emotion but one that Americans refuse to acknowledge and Japanese may encourage too much.

The Sapir-Whorf Hypothesis

Let's consider a broad, related issue: To what extent does emotion vocabulary reflect or limit the emotions we feel? Edward Sapir (1921) and Benjamin Whorf (1956) each proposed what came to be known as the Whorf hypothesis or **Sapir-Whorf hypothesis**: Humans require language to think, and

therefore we have only those experiences, thoughts, and perceptions for which we have words. In the emotion domain, the consequence would be that people couldn't experience an emotion for which they have no word. Or, according to a weaker form of the hypothesis, people might more readily experience or express an emotion for which they have a word than one for which they lack a word.

Researchers have tested the Sapir-Whorf hypothesis in many ways over the past 50 years, but have found little evidence for the strong version. For example, this hypothesis implies that people whose languages lack a word for the color green would be unable to see that color, or to distinguish it from, say, blue. This prediction is simply false. People do discriminate among colors even if they have no words for the differences (Ludwig, Goetz, Balgemann, & Roschke, 1972). Language may have a subtler effect: Perhaps the color words of a language influence how easily we remember colors or what boundaries we draw between one area of the color spectrum and another (Özgen, 2004). This research raises complex methodological issues, however, and researchers do not yet agree on the exact relationship between language and thought and perception (Heider, 1972; Roberson, Davies, & Davidoff, 2000).

A more subtle influence of language on perception, memory, or reasoning is consistent with Shweder's definition of culture, as discussed earlier in this chapter: Culture (including language) helps define the categories of experience we use to make sense of the world around us, and it influences the ways in which we communicate our experience to others. But we should not assume that people whose language lacks a word for a certain emotion cannot feel it. After all, nonhuman animals and preverbal infants sometimes appear to be afraid, and they have no words at all.

A study by Jonathan Haidt and Dacher Keltner (1999) offers evidence to this effect. Haidt and Keltner showed photographs of several emotional facial expressions to participants in the United States and in Eastern India, where people speak the Oriya language. The posed expressions included an embarrassment display (which includes a smile with the lips pressed together, averted glance, and touching the face) and a photo of a person covering her face with one hand, suggesting shame. Researchers then asked participants to tell a story about what event caused the person to make each face. As expected, American participants labeled one expression embarrassment and the other one shame, and they described somewhat different situations in which each would be felt. But Oriya has only a single word—"ladja"—that combines the meanings of both embarrassment and shame. Accordingly, most Indian participants labeled both of the facial expressions *ladja*. Nevertheless, they typically said the person covering her face (in what Americans would call shame) had probably done something wrong or had failed at something. They said the person making the averted glance (in what Americans call the embarrassment display) had done nothing wrong but had suddenly been the focus of awkward social attention, such as being publicly praised or winning an award. The implication is that even though the Indian participants did not have separate words for embarrassment and shame, they still recognized the different situations that prompted different expressions. They "knew the difference" and could describe it, even if that distinction was not explicit in the Oriya vocabulary.

Hyper- Versus Hypocognized Emotions

If emotion vocabulary does not actually define or constrain our emotional experience, what does it do? In addressing this question, Levy (1984) invoked his extensive field research on Tahitian life and language (not exactly the worst job one could imagine). The Tahitian language has 46 words for anger, yet not a single word for what we call sadness (Levy, 1973). Instead, someone like the man whose family was away would describe himself as *pe'a pe'a*, sick or tired. Levy concluded, after really getting to know this culture, that Tahitians do experience sadness. How then did he account for the absence of a word for this emotion in Tahitian vocabulary?

Levy proposed that cultures **hypercognize** some emotions, creating an elaborate network of associations and distinctions that lead to an increase in the vocabulary for those emotions. For example, the 46

Tahitian words for anger probably distinguish among different degrees of anger, specific anger versus general irritability, anger against the fish that got away from you versus anger at the jerk who bumped into you while you were trying to catch the fish, anger that makes you storm home in silence with no fish versus anger that makes you yell at the guy who bumped into you, and so on. You get the idea. Other emotions in a culture might be **hypocognized**, lacking much cognitive elaboration or detail. In Tahiti, sadness may be a "real" emotion in the biological sense but of so little social interest that it is lumped linguistically with illness and lack of energy. (The Tahitians are partly correct on this point. As we shall discuss in Chapter 7, sadness has much in common with illness.)

How can researchers study emotions in different cultures, if the emotion words of one language don't translate exactly into the other language? One solution is to move away from vocabulary and to try to understand the concepts beneath the words. For example, if we wanted to study sadness in Tahiti, we might ask the following questions. When does one feel *pe'a pe'a*? How does one behave? What does one's face look like? The more these features of *pe'a pe'a* resemble those of sadness, the more confident we might be that the two words refer to approximately the same state. The more differences we find, the more we might suspect that *pe'a pe'a* does not really refer to sadness. Even if sadness and *pe'a pe'a* showed serious differences, however, if we found that Tahitians reliably look sad, sound sad, have sad nervous system physiology, and act sad when a loved one dies, we might conclude that Tahitians experience a universal form of sadness, whether they have a word for it or not. Such research might also help us to understand which aspects of emotion are universal and which more influenced by culture. We turn now to some studies of this sort.

◘ Culture and Emotional Appraisals

Recall from Chapter 1 the idea that emotions may depend on certain kinds of cognitive appraisals—interpretations about events that might trigger an emotional response. For example, the appraisal of "threat" is expected to lead to the emotion fear, and the appraisal of "loss" is expected to lead to sadness. Researchers conducting cross-cultural research on emotional appraisals have typically asked two kinds of questions. First, do particular emotions accompany the same appraisals, or different ones, from culture to culture? Second, do people in different cultures apply certain appraisals to the same situations or different ones? Said another way, do emotional responses to the same event differ across cultures mainly because we *interpret* that event differently?

The first question has been most strongly addressed by Klaus Scherer (1997), with the help of dozens of colleagues around the world. In this study, participants in 37 countries on 5 continents were asked to think of a time they felt each of the following emotions: joy, anger, fear, sadness, disgust, shame, and guilt. (Words were translated and back-translated to try to get the best word possible in each language. For back-translation, one person translates something from language A to B, and then someone else translates it from B to A, to see how closely it matches the original.) Then participants were asked to describe a situation in which they felt the emotion and to rate that situation on several appraisal dimensions, or how they interpreted the situation: novelty/expectedness, pleasantness, goal conduciveness, fairness, responsible agent (self versus someone else), coping potential (how much control the participant felt in the situation), morality, and relevance for self-concept. Scherer then examined whether participants around the world associated the same patterns of appraisals with each emotion.

Figure 3.3 shows the average appraisal pattern associated with each emotion by people on each of the five continents studied. Across continents, similarities were much greater than differences regarding which appraisal pattern fits a given emotion. For example, in nearly every culture, people said they felt happy in response to an event that was somewhat expected, very pleasant, consistent with their goals, fair, and that made them feel good about themselves. We will go into greater detail regarding the specific appraisal patterns associated with each emotion in later chapters.

For now, let's focus on the few cultural differences. One of the few striking cultural differences was in the role of fairness and appraisals of morality. African participants were likely to describe any sadness-eliciting event as unfair and immoral—an idea that sounds odd to most Americans, Europeans, and Asians. Think of it this way: You are sad when your 14-year-old dog dies, but how does fairness come into it? In what way is the event morally wrong? By contrast, Latin American participants typically rated events that elicited negative emotions as *less* immoral than participants from other continents. African participants also perceived events eliciting negative emotions as more externally caused.

Interpreting the differences among cultures is difficult because we can imagine many plausible explanations. One hypothesis is that the Africans equated negative emotions with a sense of immorality or injustice, and the Latin Americans had to feel a sense of moral rightness or justice to feel certain negative emotions. Keep in mind, however, that Scherer and colleagues did not measure appraisals of unemotional situations. Another possibility is that African cultures emphasize the immorality and unfairness of all situations, emotion producing or not, whereas Latin American cultures are generally more likely to think of the world as morally right.

Overall, this study suggests that certain appraisal patterns are associated with the same emotions essentially everywhere in the world. This does not mean, however, that culture does not shape emotional experience. Think back to the example of being a guest in someone's home and being invited to "help yourself" at the refrigerator. An American would probably interpret this as pleasant (an invitation to feel at home), fair (courteous gesture by the host), goal conducive (allowing you to eat), and controllable (you can choose whatever you want). Thus, an American might feel happy in this situation. By contrast, a Japanese might interpret the event as unpleasant (the host has just told you he will not take care of you), unfair (what did you do to be treated in this rude way?), uncontrollable (surely there are things in the refrigerator the host does not

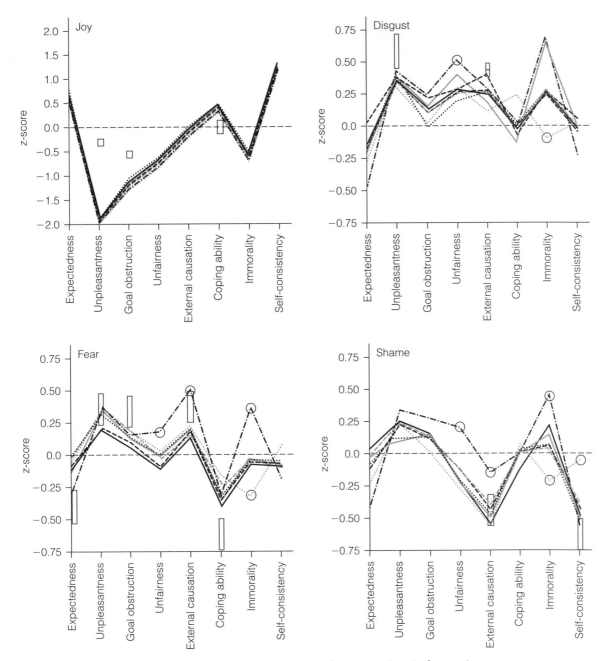

FIGURE 3.3   Appraisal patterns associated with the experience of seven emotions in five continents around the world. Source: From K. S. Scherer, "The Role of Culture in Emotion-Antecedent Appraisal," *Journal of Personality and Social Psychology, 73*, pp. 902–922. © 1997 American Psychological Association.

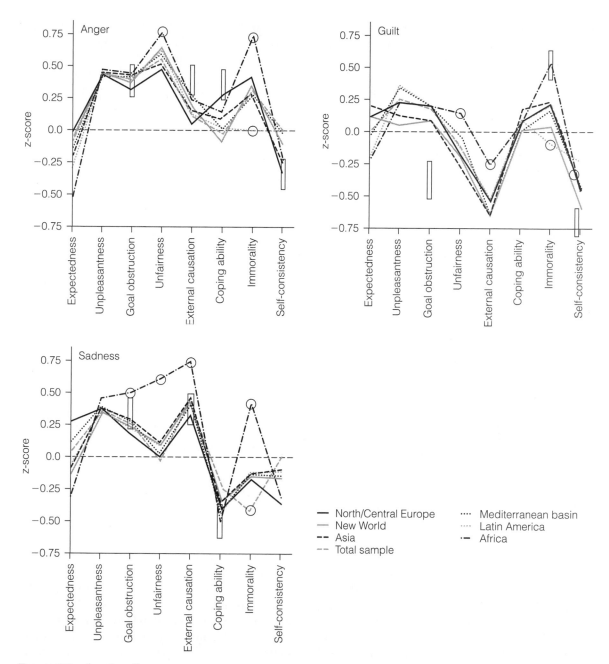

FIGURE 3.3 *(continued)*

wish you to eat—how are you supposed to know what they are?), and goal obstructing (now you cannot eat anything). Thus, using the same calculus for converting appraisals but appraising the same event in a different way, a Japanese might experience sadness or anger.

◘ Cultural Differences in Displaying Emotions

So far we have found that, although the relationship between appraisals and emotions is similar across cultures, the ways people appraise the same event can be very different, leading to a different emotion. A similar distinction seems to be important for understanding the role of culture in emotional expression. The facial expressions themselves appear to be "built in," at least for a few emotions. That is, they emerge in early childhood for people throughout the world, even blind children. However, although the expressions themselves are fixed, they can vary in intensity, and some people tend to express their emotions more strongly than others do, even in the same situation.

Some researchers have suggested that differences in the intensity of expression are due to differences in intensity of autonomic nervous system arousal. When young adults in the United States are exposed to a brief stressful experience, on the average those of African ancestry show the greatest changes in blood pressure, those of Asian ancestry show the least, and those of European ancestry are intermediate (Jackson, Treiber, Turner, Davis, & Strong, 1999; Shen, Stroud, & Niaura, 2004). (These are, of course, differences *on the average.* When we examine individuals, we find much overlap between one group and another.) An explanation of expressions in terms of intensity of arousal would be consistent with Darwin's "action of the nervous system" hypothesis of emotional expression, discussed in Chapter 2. Keep in mind, however, that correlations do not always indicate causal relationships—if people with bigger changes in blood pressure also show the strongest expressions, it does not necessarily fol-

low that the blood pressure *causes* the expressions. However, it is one possible explanation.

Another explanation is that people learn from their culture to vary their emotional expressions in subtle ways. Just as people in different parts of any given country pronounce the same words somewhat differently, people who live in different cultures "accent" their facial expressions in slightly different ways. In one study, Japanese people (living in Japan) and Japanese-Americans (living in the United States) posed a variety of emotions, including "neutral." Americans of several ethnic groups examined the photos and tried to guess which of the posers were native Japanese and which were Japanese-Americans. Most were able to identify more than half of the posers correctly, and their accuracy was higher for posers showing emotional expressions than for neutral expressions (Marsh, Elfenbein, & Ambady, 2003). In short, people of different cultural backgrounds have slightly different facial expressions, even if they come from the same ethnic group.

How might culture influence people's emotional expressions and why? The main purpose of emotional expression is communication. Just as you do not always want to say in words everything that you are thinking, you sometimes feel emotions without wanting to display them fully. Cultures differ somewhat in their rules for which emotions should be displayed and which hidden and under what circumstances. These cultural **display rules**—rules about when and with whom it is appropriate to display certain kinds of emotional expressions—are an important tool for any society. We learn at an early age when and where we can express our emotions freely and when it is best to hide them. For example, when you are in a job interview, you try not to act nervous. If a guest spills something on your carpet, you try not to show anger. If a friend says something stupid, you try not to laugh. If you are proud of some accomplishment, you might hide your feelings, lest others think you are bragging. Other display rules require us to express emotions even if we do not feel them. Have you ever laughed politely at a joke that wasn't especially funny or dis-

FIGURE 3.4   Cultures differ in how much display of sadness is expected at funerals.

played more sorrow than you really felt over someone else's loss?

We learn all of these rules from the people around us, and cultures vary somewhat in their rules and expectations. For example, European and American adults, especially men, are discouraged from crying in public (see Figure 3.4), and the pro-

hibition is even stronger in other cultures, such as Chinese. Public laughter is generally acceptable in Europe and America, although customs vary from one locale to another. One of us (J.W.K.) recalls having dinner at a restaurant in Spain when the people at another table broke into uproarious laughter. One of the Spanish people said, "They must be

Americans. No Spanish person would laugh that loudly in public." Some cultures discourage emotional expression in general. One study of Hmong immigrants to the United States found that the immigrants who were more assimilated into U.S. culture expressed emotions such as happiness and disgust more visibly than did those who were more traditional (Tsai, Chentsova-Dutton, Freire-Bebeau, & Przymus, 2002).

Wallace Friesen (1972) conducted a classic study of display rules as his doctoral dissertation. In his study, Friesen compared the behavior of Japanese and American participants while they watched disgusting videos of surgical procedures. Undergraduate participants first watched the videos alone and then watched them again in the presence of an experimenter, introduced as a graduate student and wearing a lab coat. Although participants from both countries showed considerable disgust when they watched the video alone, Japanese participants masked this disgust with a polite smile when the experimenter was in the room (Friesen, 1972). Japan emphasizes the social hierarchy much more than the United States does, and the Japanese consider it inappropriate to show negative emotion to a high-status person. American participants were evidently less intimidated by the experimenter and saw no reason to hide their feelings.

A number of other display rules also distinguish American and Japanese culture. One study found that Americans expressed their emotions more visibly than either Japanese or Russian people. Japanese and Russians were more likely than Americans to "qualify" their display of negative emotions. That is, when displaying fear, anger, or sadness, Japanese and Russian people often add a slight smile to soften the impression, indicating that "although I am distressed, it isn't really that bad" (Matsumoto, Yoo, Hirayama, & Petrova, 2005). In the United States, moderate displays of anger are fairly common. In Japan, a high-status person can display anger toward subordinates, but almost any other display of anger is considered uncouth and shockingly inappropriate (Matsumoto, 1996). In ad-

dition, the Japanese consider it more appropriate to show sadness and other negative emotions to acquaintances than to close friends and family, whereas the reverse is true for Americans (Matsumoto, 1990).

Display rules raise particular difficulties for **bicultural** people, those who alternate between membership in one culture and membership in another (Harrison, Wilson, Pine, Chan, & Buriel, 1990; LaFramboise, Coleman, & Gerton, 1993). Many immigrants and their children are bicultural. To a small degree, almost all people are: The culture of your school differs from that of your workplace, your place of worship, or the friends with whom you share some other activity. One group of friends or relatives may like you to express your feelings openly, but another may prefer that you restrain your expressions or express them in different ways.

You might get the impression from these examples that only other cultures have display rules, whereas Americans show exactly what they feel. Arlie Hochschild (2002) offers a powerful challenge to this myth in her book *The Managed Heart*, describing the wide range of display rules that govern American interpersonal behavior, especially in commercial settings. For example, in her research on the U. S. airline industry, Hochschild found that companies make explicit demands for employees' emotional behavior, especially that of flight attendants. As the "front line" of customer service in this extremely competitive industry, flight attendants are expected to communicate pleasure, warmth, concern, enthusiasm, and sometimes even sexual attraction as part of their daily work. Those applying for flight attendant positions may actually be put through an explicit test of their sociability and perkiness, asked to chat lightly with other applicants while recruiters evaluate their social interaction style. Any failure to express the appropriate feelings on the job typically leads to miscommunication with passengers and disapproval from supervisors.

Worse yet, the ups and downs of that industry have led to some mixed messages. Flight attendants are supposed to be friendly but should not start personal relationships with customers. They should talk with customers but not enough to slow down the performance of their duties. They should act friendly, but their expressions should be "genuine" (as if they could, as a matter of policy, *actually* like each customer).

As we have seen, display rules are a common aspect of culture. However, the American combination of professional demands with cultural values regarding emotion puts flight attendants in a particular bind. It is easier to pose an appropriate facial expression of emotion when required than it is to generate an actual emotional experience, although a combination of reappraisal and solid acting make the latter possible. As we have seen, a number of cultures (such as Japanese) encourage the posing of appropriate emotional displays, without demanding that individuals actually feel what they display. In the United States, however, people put a high premium on authenticity and emotional genuineness. If flight attendants take the less demanding route, feigning positive emotion displays rather than actually generating emotions, they run the risk of feeling "fake" and questioning their own integrity, even losing touch with their own emotional experience. What we see here is a complex network of rules about feelings as well as emotional expressions.

◻ Cultural Differences in Interpreting Facial Displays

Because cultures differ somewhat in how strongly they express emotions, we should expect that they also would differ in how they interpret emotional displays. For example, if you and those around you ordinarily restrain your public displays of emotion, and now you see someone showing a fairly strong expression, it may seem to you even more extreme than it is and more extreme than it would to someone who was accustomed to seeing such displays.

As discussed in Chapter 2, people from cultures throughout the world assign similar labels to a few "basic" expressions (Ekman et al., 1987). Results are

FIGURE 3.5   When people examine faces showing relatively low-intensity emotional displays, as in this one, Japanese observers tend to infer slightly higher emotional feelings than do Americans. Source: Matsumoto et al. (2002).

less consistent when people are asked to look at pictures of facial expressions and estimate the *intensity* of the emotions. In one study, David Matsumoto and Paul Ekman (1989) showed photos of several prototypical emotion expressions, using Caucasian and Japanese posers, to participants in the United States and Japan. Regardless of the poser's ethnicity, Japanese raters tended to rate both the negative emotions and happiness expressed by the posers as less intense. In another study, when people looked at photographs of relatively *weak* expressions, as in Figure 3.5, Japanese people estimated a *stronger* underlying emotion than Americans did (Matsumoto et al., 2002).

Several factors enter into these confusing and contradictory findings. One possibility is this: Japanese people are accustomed to trying to inhibit public emotional displays, so when they see a weak emotional expression, they may infer that the person felt the emotion strongly and partly inhibited it. With expressions of average or strong intensity, Americans may be more inclined to trust the authenticity of the display, whereas Japanese guess that such exaggerated displays are probably feigned to some degree. Also, as a general rule, when Japanese people fill out rating scales, they tend to answer toward the middle of the scale, whereas Americans are more apt to give extreme (either high or low) ratings. Perhaps the most important point here is that it is difficult to explain cultural differences, especially subtle ones, because we cannot experimentally assign people to one culture or another.

◻ Summarizing Cultural Differences in Emotion

The various cultural differences in emotional appraisal, display, and interpretation can be difficult to keep track of and even more so to explain. Many early studies of cultural differences in emotion (and in other domains as well) simply noted a difference between the United States and some other culture and left it at that. Frustrated with the hodgepodge of findings produced in this way, several researchers suggested a new approach. They argued that, although every culture is unique, cultures can nevertheless be compared to one another along a few dimensions that have strong implications for how people relate to each other. These dimensions also are relevant to people's experience and expression as well, helping to make sense of many otherwise confusing cultural differences. As examples, we will discuss the two cultural dimensions that have been most important for emotion researchers interested in culture.

Individualism Versus Collectivism

First, cultures have been described as varying along a continuum from individualism to collectivism (Markus & Kitayama, 1991). According to many cultural psychologists, people in Western cultures (especially Americans) tend to be high on **individualism**, which emphasizes individual uniqueness, personal rights, being true to one's self, and independence from others. For example, compared to other industrialized nations, the United States has

an unusually high crime rate, an unusually high divorce rate, but also very high rates of volunteerism and contributions to charities. It has never had a socialist government, and its citizens take pride in the idea that anyone can rise to the top in business or government. People high in individualism generally agree with statements such as the following:

- *I take pride in accomplishing what no one else can accomplish.*
- *I am unique—different from others in many respects.*

In contrast, many other cultures, including most South and East Asian cultures, emphasize **collectivism**, or prioritizing the group over the individual, valuing group identification, deference, social harmony, and interdependence. Each person has a role, knows that role, and tries to fulfill duties rather than compete with others. People who have a collectivist attitude tend to agree with these statements:

- *To understand who I am, you must see me with members of my group.*
- *Before making a decision, I always consult with others.*

China is generally taken as an example of a collectivist culture, and one indication is that Chinese people talk more about their friends and family whereas Americans talk more about themselves. A natural question about that tendency is whether it really reflects the way people think or just some difference between the Chinese and English languages. In one study, investigators studied young Chinese-American adults whose parents had been born in China, Hong Kong, or Taiwan. All the participants were fluent in English, but some were more acculturated (Americanized) than others in terms of their activities, attitudes, food, and social life. The investigators conducted systematic interviews with each, always in English, and found that the less acculturated Chinese-Americans spoke significantly more than the others did about friends, family, receiving advice, and other social or collective activities (Tsai, Simeonova, & Watanabe, 2004).

In another study, when people were asked to describe experiences from memory, North Americans usually described how *they* felt, whereas Asians described how they thought the people around them felt (D. Cohen & Gunz, 2002). In one classic study, Chinese and American participants were simply asked to complete the phrase "I am . . ." 20 times, in any way they wanted (Triandis, McCusker, & Hui, 1990). The researchers found that Chinese participants were three times more likely than Americans to list group membership as part of their identity. Whereas Americans tended to list things that made them different from others, Chinese participants listed similarities. Obviously, these differences pertain to averages across many people. Americans do list group memberships, and Chinese participants describe unusual aspects about themselves.

In another study, researchers asked people to describe the behavior of the fish on the right in Figure 3.6. Most Americans say this fish is leading the others. Among Chinese people, a common answer is that the other fish are chasing this one (Hong et al., 2000). That is, the Chinese emphasize group influences and context in interpreting ambiguous situations. As we saw earlier, such differences in appraisal can lead to differences in emotional experience. Someone who thinks the fish is a leader would probably think the fish is happy, whereas someone who thinks the fish is being chased would probably infer that it is afraid.

However, it is an oversimplification to equate "Western" cultures with individualism and "Eastern" cultures with "collectivism." Even within a culture, individualist and collectivist attitudes vary from region to region and person to person (Fiske, 2002) and even from one situation to another (Bond, 2002). Furthermore, several studies have used Chinese participants to represent "Eastern" cultures, but Eastern cultures are not all equally collectivist. Researchers find that the Japanese people of today are about as individually competitive as Americans and in some ways more so (Bond, 2002; Oyserman, Coon, & Kemmelmeier, 2002; Takano & Osaka, 1999). Japanese culture was described as highly collectivist

FIGURE 3.6   Chinese people are more likely than Americans to say the group to the left is chasing the fish on the right; most Americans say the fish on the right is leading the others.

shortly after World War II, but indeed almost any country develops collectivist attitudes in the face of danger or after a disastrous loss (Takano & Osaka, 1999). (People in the United States seemed strongly united shortly after the terrorist attacks of September 11, 2001.) Japan today has vastly different customs and attitudes from those of the late 1940s and vastly different from those of today's China.

How might cultural differences in individualism versus collectivism affect emotional life? Such differences might explain many of the differences in displaying and interpreting facial expressions we discussed earlier in the chapter. For example, if Japan is a collectivist society, then the Japanese may inhibit expressions of negative emotion as a way of preserving group harmony and prioritizing group needs over one's own. Some researchers have proposed that collectivism also facilitates the *experience* of certain kinds of emotion, whereas individualism discourages such emotions. One striking example occurs in what situations arouse the **"self-conscious" emotions** such as pride, shame, and guilt that require an appraisal of one's self as good or bad. Research in the United States suggests that people experience pride when they have accomplished something and their social status is on the rise (Seidner, Stipek, & Feshbach, 1988; Tiedens, Ellsworth, & Mesquita, 2000). Americans experience shame and guilt after doing something wrong, when others are likely to express disapproval (Tangney, Miller, Flicker, & Barlow, 1996). Thus, pride, shame, and guilt all appear to require an interpretation of whether the self is good or bad. However, "self" means different things to people in different cultures. In individualistic cultures, my "self" is something unique, distinct from the people around me. In collectivistic cultures, "self" is more closely tied to group memberships and relationships with friends and family (Triandis, McCusker, & Hui, 1990). Therefore, we might predict that people in collectivist cultures would experience pride and shame in response to their friends' and relatives' actions, not just their own.

Deborah Stipek (1998) tested this hypothesis in a study of American and Chinese university students. She asked participants in each culture to read several scenarios and to rate how proud, guilty, and ashamed they would feel in each situation. In two of the scenarios, someone was accepted to a prestigious university, but in one scenario it was the participant and in the other it was the participant's child. In two other scenarios a person is caught cheating, either the participant or the participant's brother. Americans reported that they would be equally proud if they or their child were accepted to a prestigious university, but Chinese participants reported that they would actually be prouder to have their child accepted. Chinese participants reported that they would feel more guilt and shame than Americans in the cheating scenario regardless of who did it, and participants in both cultures said they would feel more guilt and shame if they were caught than if the brother were caught. However, Chinese participants reported that they would feel more guilt and shame in the "brother cheated" scenario than did Americans.

Note that this study suggests both similarities and differences between Chinese and American culture. In both cultures, participants expected to feel pride if they accomplished something and guilt and shame if they did something morally wrong. The difference is that Americans felt the emotions more strongly if they did these things themselves, whereas in China, the activities of one's family reflect strongly enough on one's own identity that those activities can produce strong self-conscious emotion. In fact, participants in China said that it is *more* appropriate to feel pride for other people's accomplishments than for one's own (Stipek, 1998).

Vertical Versus Horizontal Societies

Another major difference among cultures is the degree to which they emphasize power distance, or social hierarchy. David Matsumoto (1996) defines a **vertical society** as one that emphasizes the social hierarchy and encourages emotions and behaviors that advertise and reinforce status differences. By contrast, a **horizontal society** is one in which people typically minimize attention to status differences and seldom acknowledge those differences publicly. For illustration, contrast various nonhuman species: Most monkey troops have a rigid vertical structure in which one monkey, usually a large male, dominates the others. Deer and cattle have a more horizontal structure, in which all members of the herd have approximately the same status.

Nancy Much (1997) contrasts the social structure she observed in Hindu Indian households with typical American social interaction. Traditional Indian society is a prototypical vertical society, with a firm class structure and detailed rules for how people interact with others within and between classes. Even within a family, people observe rules of hierarchy, often addressing one another by title (such as "older brother") rather than by name. Younger family members are expected to prostrate themselves (touching their head to the feet of a higher-ranking, older family member) as a standard display of respect. Failure to use the proper title or gesture of respect is a breach of propriety, reflecting badly on both parties. Your father's friend would never invite you to call him by his first name, and you would never agree to do so.

American culture is more horizontal, although no human society is completely horizontal. Americans recognize status differences and acknowledge the authority of parents, bosses, elected leaders, and such, but this authority is limited to certain domains. A worker acknowledges the boss's right to give orders at the office but not to command what meal to order at a restaurant or how to interact with one's spouse. The lower status of children is temporary, according to Much (1997), and when children reach adulthood, they are considered their parents' equals. Status differences in wealth or education are seldom made explicit. The United States has no hereditary aristocracy, and Americans treasure the idea that someone born poor can ascend to a position of power and success. Canada is similar in this regard.

The difference between vertical and horizontal social structures sometimes leads to misunderstandings or confusion. In English, you might at first address an adult acquaintance by his or her last name, such as "Dr. Johnson." When you became friendlier, you would shift to the first name, such as "Jennifer." Russian and several other Eastern European languages distinguish multiple levels of intimacy. In some novels, when two people shift from one level of intimacy to the next—the equivalent of shifting from "Robert" to "Bob" or from "Bob" to "Bobby"— the shift means a change in their social relationship. That plot point gets lost in English translation. When two Polish visitors meet in an English-speaking country and speak to each other in English, they may be on first-name terms. If they meet again when back in Poland, they have a moment of awkwardness: They were on first-name terms in English, but on which of several levels are they in Polish?

The vertical versus horizontal dimension can influence emotional experience in several ways. As with individualism/collectivism, power distance can facilitate or discourage the experience of certain kinds of emotion. For example, some vertical societies encourage an emotion that the English language does not even recognize—an emotion that combines shame, embarrassment, gratitude, shyness, and respect (e.g., Abu-Lughod, 1986; Menon & Shweder, 1994; Russell, 1991). In the Orissa language in India, for example, this is called *ladja*, and

among the Bedouin it is called *hasham*. People feel this emotion in the presence of a higher-status person and show their respect by displaying it.

In the United States and Canada, most people typically think of shame as an unpleasant experience that they try to avoid because it threatens their self-esteem. (Exceptions do occur. For example, some religions stress the value of confessing your sins.) In contrast, people in more vertical societies are likely to think of shame as a virtuous, constructive experience. In one study, Japanese and Canadian students were given a series of creative-thinking items. Half received easy items and half received difficult items, so that when they graded their own papers against the key and then compared their scores to the supposed average, people in the first group were almost certain to conclude that they had done very well, whereas those in the other group were almost certain to see their scores as a failure. Afterward, they were asked to rate themselves on various scales, including creativity, sense of humor, attractiveness, athletic skills, and so forth. Most Canadian students rated themselves above average on every scale, regardless of whether they had done well or poorly on the creative-thinking test. That is, those who had just failed didn't let that experience lower their self-esteem. Japanese students who had done well rated themselves merely average. (Japanese seldom describe themselves as "above average" at anything, no matter how skillful they actually are.) Those Japanese students who had been given a failure experience on the creative-thinking items evidently felt ashamed, and they rated themselves well below average on *every* scale, including those such as athleticism and attractiveness that had nothing to do with creativity (Heine, Kitayama, & Lehman, 2001). Evidently the Japanese felt no resistance to the emotion of shame.

The emphasis on power distance in a society can also predict who displays what emotions. In Japan, for example, it is appropriate for a high-status person (such as a coach of a sports team) to express anger at a player, but deeply offensive for the player to show anger to the coach (Matsumoto,

1996). Anger implies high status, and for the player to show anger to the coach would be a direct threat to the hierarchy (Matsumoto, 1990). By contrast, group leaders are expected not to show sadness or fear, which might convey weakness. Note that this is a prescription for emotional *display*, not necessarily for emotional *experience*. Inevitably, players will sometimes feel angry toward their coaches, and group leaders will sometimes feel sad or afraid. They can, however, stifle expression of these feelings to maintain the harmony of the group.

Similarly, investigators found differences among Nepali children in their willingness to express anger, based partly on status. In rural Nepal, Brahman Hindu children have relatively high status compared to Tamang children, who follow Tibetan Buddhism. When psychologists interviewed children about how they would feel and act in various difficult situations, the Brahman children said they would feel and express anger in many situations; the Tamang children almost never said they would feel anger. In contrast, the Tamang children were far more likely to say they would feel shame or "just okay." These contrasts relate partly to status and partly to religion; Buddhism praises a calm "okay" attitude as highly desirable (Cole, Bruschi, & Tamang, 2002; Cole & Tamang, 1998).

Note that this difference among cultures is relative, not absolute. The United States is certainly not a purely horizontal culture, and a coach is more likely to yell at a player than a player to yell at a coach. Similarly, an employer will show anger toward an employee, and a professor toward a student, more often than the reverse.

❑ Methodological Issues in Studying Culture

In this chapter, we have asked how culture molds our emotions, in terms of language, experience, and expression. Because it is impossible to contrast how you would have developed with culture versus without it (because without some sort of culture you

couldn't develop at all), researchers ordinarily contrast people who grew up in one country versus those in another. The studies presented in this chapter all took that approach, looking at differences (or similarities) between people in two or more countries. There are, however, several limitations to this strategy and to the way it has been applied so far.

The first is a practical one: The vast majority of psychological and anthropological researchers come from prosperous, first-world countries, and when they study culture it usually involves going someplace else and comparing that place with home. They might choose the other culture because of its theoretical significance, but they also consider how easily they can gain access. A great many cross-cultural studies contrast Japan versus the United States, Japan versus Canada, Japan versus Australia, and so forth. The reason is that Japan is a prosperous, modern country with many psychological researchers of its own. It is by far the easiest to study of all "non-Western" cultures. As a result, many other cultures are largely overlooked. This tendency makes it difficult to understand "culture" as something distinct from "how North America and Japan are different."

A second problem is that cultures do not follow national boundaries. In the United States, cultures differ between people of different ethnic backgrounds, religions, and sections of the country. Cultures differ also between people living in large cities versus small towns or rural areas. People moving from one part of the United States to another often experience "culture shock" as if they had moved to another country. Beliefs, attitudes, and behaviors also depend on birth cohort; being an American child today differs nearly as much from being a child 50 years ago as it does from growing up in a different country (Twenge, 2002). Even within one city during one time—Minneapolis, Minnesota—researchers found that young adults of Scandinavian ancestry expressed their emotions with more restraint than those of Irish ancestry (Tsai & Chentsova-Dutton, 2003). And that result represents a difference between two types of European-Americans, in the same city, at the same time.

Cultural or subcultural differences are probably even greater within many other countries, where transportation and communication are more difficult. For example, the constitution of India recognizes 18 official languages.

A few researchers have examined culture more directly, comparing people who speak different languages, or who have different ethnic backgrounds, but even these may be crude ways to measure culture. The typical study of culture and emotion compares a sample of Japanese college students to a sample of U.S. college students, as if each were a suitable representation of a whole culture. Researchers know, of course, that this is an incorrect assumption, but they hope that the relationship between country and culture is strong enough that the results are still meaningful. Ideally, we would prefer to see studies that measure culture more directly, but first researchers need to agree upon how to measure culture—a step that will take some time.

Odd though it sounds, culture itself is the third major difficulty in interpreting differences between two countries: Suppose researchers collect self-report measurements, as emotion researchers typically do. They ask people of various cultures, for example, to rate themselves on a 1-to-7 scale for how happy they are, or how nervous, or how open in expressing their emotions. Rating yourself on such a scale implies a comparison of how happy (or whatever) you are *in comparison to others.* So if you rate your happiness "4" (average), you mean average with respect to the other people you know, presumably of your own culture. Suppose the mean happiness rating for people in your culture is 4 (as it should be, theoretically) and the mean rating in some other culture is also 4. Can we conclude that people in the two cultures are equally happy? Of course not. Suppose people in one culture rate their happiness *higher* than those of another country. Even then we cannot compare the results with confidence; perhaps people in the two cultures differ not in happiness, but in how they use the rating scales. In short, cultural comparisons based on self-ratings are shaky evidence (Heine, Lehman, Peng, & Greenholtz, 2002).

Comparing people in different countries is the best approach we have at this point, while researchers are looking for better ways to define and measure culture. But look back at the definition of culture offered at the beginning of the chapter. Is studying differences between people in two countries the same as studying the effect of culture on emotion? Not really. When we study differences between, say, China and the United States, we study an outcome in each country and have to infer the cultural process that explains it. Ideally, researchers studying culture and emotion would look directly at the process by which different cultures construct emotion concepts, display rules, and so on, but that will be a difficult task. The proper response to all these problems is not to give up in despair but to proceed with caution and to use a variety of research methods. We can at least determine some of the ways in which culture can influence our emotions and some of the ways in which emotions are similar across cultures.

◻ Integrating Evolutionary and Cultural Approaches

On one hand, certain aspects of emotion appear to be universal, or nearly so, but on the other hand, culture influences how we appraise situations and how we express emotions. Although research supports both of these aspects, some researchers mainly emphasize the universal aspect while others stress the cultural differences. Is there any way to integrate both aspects in one theory? Three major proposals have been offered to meet this goal.

Ekman (1972): Neuro-Cultural Theory of Emotion

Paul Ekman's (1972) Neuro-Cultural Theory was the first explicit attempt to articulate where and how culture might influence universal emotion processes. In this model (see Figure 3.7), events in the environment (as well as fantasies and memories) may elicit

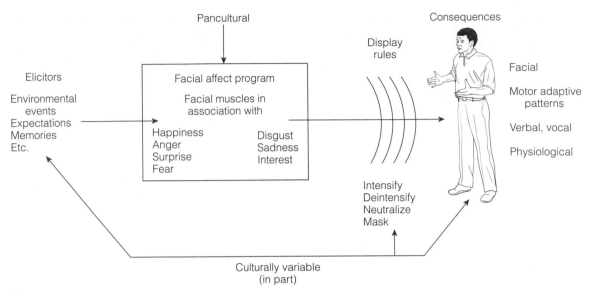

FIGURE 3.7   Paul Ekman's Neuro-Cultural Theory of facial expressions of emotion.
Source: © 1972 by Paul Ekman.

particular appraisals or interpretations that then lead to an emotion. That emotion involves several biological features, including autonomic nervous system changes, cognitive biases, and automatic facial expressions generated by an innate and universal "facial action program." If conditions are right, then these biological features, as well as consciously felt motivations, lead to prototypical emotional behavior.

The Neuro-Cultural Theory was primarily intended to explain universality and cultural variation in facial expressions of emotion. According to Ekman, it is possible, with deliberate effort, to override the expressions triggered by the facial action program. Over time, when one has negated the "natural" expression enough times in the same kind of situation, this overriding can even become habitual. Thus, the Japanese participants in Friesen's study of display rules need not have been thinking "uh oh, high-status person present, can't display negative emotion, must fake smile to cover real feelings." They had probably just learned over countless situations with high-status people what was and was not appropriate emotional behavior, and they enacted

the appropriate behavior without much thought, just like riding a bicycle or driving a car. Sometimes these display rules are specific to a particular family or other group. For example, although we noted earlier that display rules generally prevent laughing when a friend says something stupid, one of us (M.N.S.) shares with a group of college friends a display rule of laughing at each other whenever possible. Display rules are also, however, prominent parts of the cultural system, helping to guide a consistent pattern of social interaction.

Figure 3.7 also suggests, however, that cultures provide feeling rules as well as display rules. Culture has an impact on how different situations are interpreted, so that a given emotion can be elicited by different kinds of situations in different cultures. We saw an example of this in Deborah Stipek's (1998) work on the events that might elicit self-conscious emotions such as pride and shame in China and the United States. Because behavior is so subject to conscious control, the actions that follow upon the experience of an emotion can vary a great deal from culture to culture as well.

Keltner and Haidt (1999): Levels of Analysis

Dacher Keltner and Jonathan Haidt (1999) built upon Ekman's Neuro-Cultural Theory by specifying the levels of analysis at which one might expect universality versus cultural variation in emotion. The term "levels of analysis" refers to whether one looks at the "big picture," the details that compose it, or the details within the details, and so forth. For example, one might study human respiration through research on breathing rates during exercise, research on the structure of the lungs, or studies of how hemoglobin molecules absorb oxygen. Each of these lines of research is valid and important, but people doing one kind of research may not know the other lines especially well, and one may have a somewhat different understanding of what "respiration" means, depending on one's level of analysis.

According to Keltner and Haidt, the whole universality/social construction conflict reflects confusion over levels of analysis. Much of this argument has centered on the "real" function of various emotions, with some researchers arguing in favor of evolutionary functions that aid survival and reproductive fitness and others emphasizing the role of emotion in social and cultural life. Keltner and Haidt propose that emotions need not have a single function, and that the emotion literature makes the most sense if you think about function at four different levels of analysis.

The first of these is the intra-individual level—how does an emotion help the individual survive and reproduce? An example is fear, which makes you hide or run from a predator, thereby saving your own hide. The second is the dyadic level—how do emotions help two people form and maintain a relationship in a way that benefits them both? An example is compassion, which motivates parents to nurture their offspring, thereby preserving the life of the latter and the reproductive success of the former. A third level is that of small groups, where emotions are used to negotiate everybody's social roles. Examples of this were discussed earlier, where

emotions were used to express and reinforce the social hierarchy in vertical societies. Fourth, emotions are functional at the level of the culture, in that we use stories, legends, gossip, and other narratives, intended to evoke emotion, as ways of teaching a society's values.

Keltner and Haidt propose that functions at the first two levels—individual and dyad—are largely innate and universal, but that the group and culture levels allow much room for variation. This idea implies that all cultures should have similar relationships among appraisals, biological changes, and behavioral urges (which constitute evolutionary functionality, as we discussed it in earlier chapters). By contrast, groups and cultures will encourage those emotions that support the overall social structure (including individualism/collectivism and power distance) and will discourage experience and display of those emotions that interfere with the social structure. Within a culture, emotions may be experienced and/or expressed only by certain people or in certain situations, again in ways that support the social structure.

Russell (1991): Emotion Episodes as Scripts

James Russell (1991) has proposed a third way to integrate universal and cultural aspects of emotion. To understand his explanation, think back to the definition of emotion we tentatively proposed in Chapter 1. This definition included a sequence of events: Person X perceives some event in the environment and interprets it in a certain way; X's autonomic nervous system changes, perhaps with increased heart rate and blood pressure; X reports having a certain feeling; X displays a particular facial expression; X wants a certain outcome in the situation; X takes action to bring about that outcome. We called this series of events an emotion, as have many researchers.

Researchers working from the assumption that emotions are evolved responses to the environment think of sequences such as these as innate and universal. Russell has offered a somewhat different interpretation—that such sequences are actually culturally identified scripts, or beliefs about what events, thoughts, feelings, and behaviors "go together." Some combinations are inherently more common than others, thereby forming a "natural" pattern that is likely to receive universal recognition. However, there is plenty of room for cultures to tinker with individual components of the scripts, defining and encouraging less common combinations. According to Russell, emotion scripts can be broad or precise and can emphasize some components over others, and any given components or combination of components may be culture specific or universal.

As do Keltner and Haidt (1999), Russell proposes that it is possible to identify aspects of emotion scripts that are more likely to be universal and those more likely to be culture specific. The former include such components as prototypical antecedents or eliciting situations, facial expressions, physiological changes, and action tendencies. Russell proposes, however, that the perceived cause of the emotion, or the thing that is believed to kick off the script, may vary tremendously from one culture to another. In some societies, the "cause" may be an interpersonal event; in others, it may be a physical illness or supernatural events such as curses, possession, or ghosts. Note the difference between the "eliciting event" or abstract appraisal, as discussed in Chapter 1, and the "cause" embedded in the meaning system of the person in some culture. Russell says they may be very different.

Also, the expected and endorsed consequences of emotion in the script may vary considerably. This statement takes Ekman's concept of display rules and says that they are incorporated into the emotion concepts that a society recognizes. As an example of these differences, we can take *litost*, the Czech emotion described by Milan Kundera earlier in this chapter. *Litost* is caused by a sudden insight into one's own misery—a completely internal event that may or may not reflect some universally recognizable or objective event in the environment. The outcome of litost is a desire for revenge—a consequence that might manifest very differently in another society with another set of feeling and display rules.

▣ Summary

Some aspects of emotion seem to be universal, or nearly so, but cultures differ in what emotions they encourage or discourage, in who is expected to express what emotions in what situations, and in the typical causes and effects of emotions. Furthermore, cultures vary in how they *talk* about emotion, carving up emotion space in ways that make the most sense for a particular society, and assigning labels to each slice. According to all three proposals for integrating the universalist and social-construction approaches to emotion, culture influences emotion because emotion is inherently social, and different cultures endorse very different patterns of social interaction.

Which of the three proposals—Ekman's, Keltner and Haidt's, or Russell's—is right? A good deal of research is yet to be done before we can answer this question, but it helps to focus on the things the three proposals have in common. Each suggests that once an emotion-eliciting appraisal has taken place, the corresponding emotional experience and nervous system changes are likely to follow no matter what culture you grew up in, and the emotional experience and physiology make some behaviors more likely than others. This idea is consistent with the research we have seen so far. But each proposal also says that the frequency of various appraisals can differ substantially from culture to culture, so that a given emotion may be experienced often in one culture but not much in another. Also, behavior is under considerable conscious control, so cultures can have rules about how people should act when they experience a given emotion, depending on the exact situation.

We hope we have convinced you that the universalist and social-construction approaches to emotion are fully compatible. We still have much to learn about the effects of culture and evolution, but clearly both make massive contributions to our emotional lives.

▢ Key Terms

amae: Japanese term describing the feeling of pleasurable dependence on another person, like the feeling an infant has toward its mother (p. 54)

biculturalism: the ability to alternate between membership in one culture and membership in another (p. 62)

collectivism: prioritizing the group over the individual, valuing group identification, deference, social harmony, and interdependence (p. 64)

culture: the meanings, conceptions, and interpretive schemes that are activated by participation in social practices (including language) (p. 50)

display rules: policies about when and with whom it is appropriate to display certain kinds of emotional expressions (p. 60)

horizontal society: one in which people typically minimize attention to status differences and seldom acknowledge those differences publicly (p. 66)

hypercognize: to create an elaborate network of associations and distinctions that lead to an increase in the vocabulary for some emotion (p. 56)

hypocognize: to fail to give some emotion much cognitive elaboration or detail (p. 56)

individualism: emphasis on individual uniqueness, personal rights, being true to one's self, and independence from others (p. 64)

Sapir-Whorf hypothesis: proposal that humans require language to think, and therefore we have only those experiences, thoughts, and perceptions for which we have words (p. 55)

self-conscious emotions: experiences such as pride, shame, and guilt that require an appraisal of one's self as good or bad (p. 65)

social construction of emotion: process by which societies create culture-specific ways of thinking about, experiencing, and expressing emotion (p. 49)

vertical society: one that pays particular attention to the social hierarchy and encourages emotions and behaviors that respect status differences (p. 66)

Thought Questions

1. As described in this chapter, the Minangkabau apparently define emotion differently from the way most English speakers do, and certainly differently from the way we have defined it. Would the James-Lange theory apply just as well under their definition of emotion or better or worse than it does under that of English speakers?

2. How many words can you think of relating to anger? (Angry, livid, peeved. . . .) How many can you think of relating to sadness? Embarrassment? Other emotions? Can you conclude which emotions are hypercognized or hypocognized in English?

3. Of the various subcultures and sub-subcultures in which you participate, such as clubs and organizations, do some have a more horizontal social structure and others a more vertical structure?

4. Much research has focused on how cultures differ in individualism versus collectivism and horizontal versus vertical structure. Surely those are not the only important dimensions of culture. In what other crucial ways might one culture differ from another?

▢ Suggestions for Research Projects

1. The text discussed airlines' rules on how flight attendants should display friendly emotions toward customers. Observe and describe the emotional displays of employees in stores and restaurants. Do they show similar tendencies?

2. Keep a record of times when you inhibit an emotional display or express one more strongly than you felt it. What display rules are in action?

◻ Suggestions for Further Reading

Matsumoto, D. (1997). *Culture and modern life.* Pacific Grove, CA: Brooks/Cole. An excellent review of how culture relates to all aspects of psychology.

Shweder, R. A. (2003). *Why do men barbecue? Recipes for cultural psychology.* Cambridge, MA: Harvard University Press. An insightful and sympathetic discussion of cultural differences, combining psychological and anthropological perspectives.

4

Development of Emotion

If you watch infants and toddlers, you will quickly notice a great deal of emotion. Infants cry from the start; within a couple of months, they start smiling and laughing, sometimes long and loud. In many ways infants' and children's emotional expressions are more frequent and less restrained than those of adults. On the other hand, infants do not know embarrassment, shame, or pride. At first, newborns show only distress, not separate emotions such as fear and anger. They reject bad-tasting foods, but otherwise they don't show anything resembling adult disgust. During the course of maturation, different emotions appear to emerge at different times, until by about 3 years of age children express a wide range and variety of emotions. By this time they seem fairly savvy in understanding their own emotions; they also usually understand other people's emotional expressions, although they still need years of practice to pick up on some of the subtler cues. The process of learning to regulate their emotional displays takes still longer. The cultural rules we described in Chapter 3 for when and how to display emotions do not apply at all to infants and barely to toddlers. As children grow older, we expect gradual improvement in their ability to

regulate their displays, but the task is difficult and never ending. Presumably, even your parents and grandparents are still working on it.

As described in Chapter 2, one proposed criterion for calling any emotion "basic" is that it emerges early, as a built-in, evolved mechanism. However, the idea of a built-in capacity for emotion does not contradict a role for learning. Consider, for example, that we are also born with the capacity for language, but we still have to learn to talk. As with speech, some aspects of emotion are more variable than others. (Spoken languages vary in their words and word order, but not much in the sound frequencies they use. A few aspects of grammar may also be universal.)

To discuss the development of emotions, it helps to distinguish among several aspects of emotion, and the model diagrammed in Figure 4.1 offers one way to do so (Halberstadt, Denham, & Densmore, 2001). According to this model, we develop the capacities to *experience* emotions, *send* messages about our emotions, and *receive* emotional messages from others. The model is shaped like a pinwheel to emphasize the fact that it spins around: One aspect leads to the next, which leads to the next.

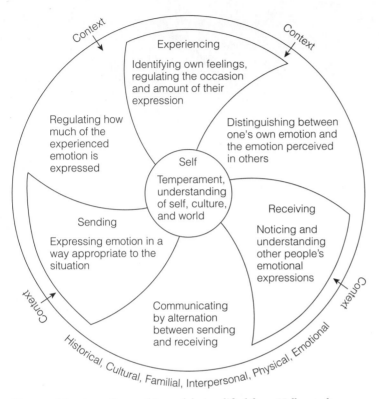

FIGURE 4.1 According to this model, simplified from Halberstadt, Denham, & Densmore (2001), emotion includes experiencing emotions, sending messages about them, and receiving other people's emotional messages. Each of these three aspects affects the others.

For example, if you (rightly or wrongly) interpret someone else's behavior as hostile, you feel either hostile or afraid, therefore express that emotion, and your expression modifies the other person's behavior (Crick & Dodge, 1994). Then the cycle continues. Furthermore, any way in which a child matures in one aspect of this cycle facilitates development in other aspects also.

In this chapter, we shall explore the ways in which emotional experience, display, and reception develop during infancy and early childhood. In the final section, we discuss the emotional changes that continue through adolescence and adulthood and into old age.

Development of Emotional Experience

The behavioral repertoire of a human newborn is limited. "Eat, sleep, and poop" largely summarizes the first weeks. What emotions, if any, do newborns have?

Unfortunately, infants are notoriously difficult to study. Even after they begin to talk, we can hardly expect them to provide accurate self-reports of their emotions. In fact, we adults have to guess the infants' emotions before we can even teach them the words they would use for self-reports. That is, a parent has to tell a child, "Oh, you're scared," or "I see you're angry," before the child can learn those words. If we couldn't infer emotions from children's actions, we couldn't teach the words.

Even ignoring self-reports, many of the other methods we use for measuring emotions in adults are inappropriate with infants and young children. Infants' facial expressions are limited, compared to the rich variety that adults show. We certainly can't ask infants or toddlers to examine photos, watch films, or sit motionless in a brain-scan device. For the most part, researchers observe infants' spontaneous behaviors or their reactions to simple situations, such as the mother leaving the room. Even then, researchers have to be creative in finding appropriate measures.

Crying

The one emotional expression readily apparent from birth is crying (see Figure 4.2), so a study of newborn emotions is essentially a study of crying. Newborns cry when they are hungry, sleepy, gassy,

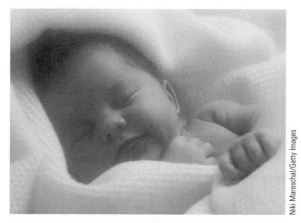
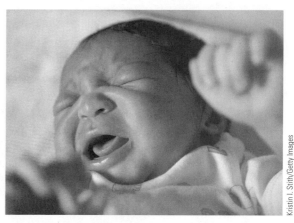

FIGURE 4.2   At the very least, newborn infants show emotional displays of comfort and distress.

or uncomfortable in any other way. A newborn's cry expresses **distress**—an undifferentiated protest against anything unpleasant or aversive. Crying has an immediate and powerful effect on people nearby, especially the baby's parents: Suddenly everybody wants to know why this thing is howling and how to make it stop. The advantage to the infant is clear: Crying is at first its only way of communicating and therefore of getting attention and care. Later, the addition of smiling and laughter offers a second message: "Keep doing that." (We can speculate: Did humans evolve crying and laughter primarily as a way for infants to communicate with their parents?)

Newborns also exhibit **sympathetic crying**, or crying in response to the sound of another newborn's cry. It is as if they are thinking, "I don't know what it is, but something is happening that's bad for babies!" Sympathetic crying is surprising because, until they are about a year old, babies show no evidence—and even then, only limited evidence—of knowing or caring about how others are feeling (Blackford & Walden, 1998). One hypothesis about the function of sympathetic crying comes from observations of nonhumans: In a nest of baby birds, the chick that peeps loudest gets fed the most. So, if you're a baby, it may be risky to keep quiet while another baby is demanding attention. Researchers

aren't sure what function sympathetic crying serves, but babies are very picky about when they do it. Tape-recorded cries of older children, monkeys, or the infants themselves usually fail to provoke this reaction. Only the cry of another newborn will suffice (Dondi, Simion, & Caltran, 1999; Martin & Clark, 1982). Sympathetic crying typically stops by about age 6 months (Hay, Nash, & Pedersen, 1981).

Smiling

The closest newborns come to displaying positive emotion is when they relax. Sometimes they curl up the corners of the mouth, but that expression is unconnected to the social situation, so it doesn't really count as a smile. It's more like exercising the mouth muscles. By about age 3 weeks, their eyelids begin to crinkle as well, and infants may open their mouths into a full grin (Emde & Koenig, 1969; Wolff, 1987). At this age babies smile mostly while they are asleep, especially during REM (rapid eye movement) sleep. A few weeks later, infants may start to smile indiscriminately at any new experience. A simple game of peekaboo may elicit smile after smile. With increasing age and cognitive maturity comes the ability to smile at more symbolic or abstract kinds of information. For example, an adult might smile after

© Blend Images / Alamy

FIGURE 4.3   Social smiling, which emerges in the second or third month of life, makes it more rewarding for adults to interact with babies. This interaction is critical for babies' continued cognitive development.

hearing about improved living conditions in some other country, or a breakthrough in treatment for some disease, or something else that would be of no consequence to an infant and not even any direct benefit to the adult.

At about age 6 to 8 weeks, infants begin **social smiling**—exchanging smiles with another person (Wolff, 1987). Suddenly the infant responds to other people's smiles by grinning in return (see Figure 4.3). This behavior is incredibly rewarding for parents and other people interacting with the infant. Parents find it more pleasurable to interact with infants who reciprocate their smiles, so they are more likely to play with infants who have reached this stage of development. This increased social interaction is crucial for the infant's further cognitive and social development (Bower, 1977). The reward value of the social smile become clear in studies of parents whose babies show deficits in this behavior, such as babies with Down's syndrome (Emde, Katz, & Thorpe, 1978). Parents of Down's babies often report feeling less rewarded by interaction with their infants than do parents of

healthy babies, an effect that may lead to decreased investment of time and energy.

Why does the social smile emerge at this time? Many researchers relate the transition to the development of visual acuity and to changes in the way the infant looks at people's faces. For the first few weeks of life, infants have only blurry vision, and they tend to look toward the top of the face (the eyes) rather than the bottom, including the mouth (Cassia, Turati, & Simion, 2004). At about 6 to 8 weeks, infants begin to look more closely at people's features and have a chance of detecting a smile when they see one. However, improved vision alone does not explain social smiling. To study the role of visual development in this transition, Selma Fraiberg (1974) studied the emergence of social smiling in blind babies. She worried that parent–child relationships might suffer because blind babies could not respond to parents' smiles with smiles of their own. She noticed, however, that many parents of blind children played physically with their babies (tickling, bouncing, and so on) more than parents of sighted children, and that the blind babies often smiled in response to this play. Fraiberg developed a training program for parents of blind babies, showing them how to maximize the opportunity for their babies to develop social smiles.

Other researchers since then also have confirmed that blind babies smile in response to tactile and auditory social cues (Rogers & Puchalski, 1986). Indeed, tactile cues, especially skin contact, are an important basis for bonding in all babies, regardless of their visual abilities or lack of them (Klaus & Kennell, 1976). Even for teenagers and adults, a good hug is a powerful way of calming tension (Hertenstein, 2002).

Responses to Danger

Besides crying and smiling, one other infant behavior that we might think of as an emotional expression is the **Moro reflex**—a sequence in which the infant flings out its arms and spreads its fingers, then contracts quickly into a fetal position with fingers bent. The Moro reflex has been described as an "infant startle," and the second part of it does look somewhat like the adult startle response (see Chapter 5). Babies display the Moro reflex in situations that suggest danger, such as being dropped, hearing a sudden loud noise, or seeing a large figure moving quickly toward them. Infants need not understand that these signals mean danger, and they probably don't, any more than a duck understands why it sits on eggs or why it feels an urge to fly south for the winter. Rather, the human nervous system has developed to produce a startle response in situations that, during our evolutionary history, have usually been dangerous.

The utility of the Moro reflex is clear. In a potentially dangerous situation, an infant reaches out and grabs onto whatever it can, pulling in tightly. Grabbing something might prevent an infant from falling. Grabbing an adult might mean that the adult will carry the infant away from danger.

Does the Moro reflex indicate that newborns feel fear? Possibly, but there are reasons for doubt. Fear and startle are closely related but not quite the same thing. The Moro reflex looks different from the prototypical fear expression shown in Chapter 2 (Figure 2.4). Also, the adult experience of fear depends on a cognitive appraisal of the situation. If a loud noise or sudden flash of light startles us, we might flinch, but if we appraise the situation and find no danger, the startle might give way to an expression of amusement, anger, or indifference, rather than one of fear. Young infants seem unable to perform the cognitive appraisals that lead to this flexible "secondary" response in many adults—they just start crying regardless of what else is in the environment. So if they start to cry at the sound of fireworks, for example, their crying will continue despite the lack of any other sign of danger. However, they fail to show fear of many situations adults find dangerous. Infants are not afraid of heights until they begin to crawl and have a few experiences of falling (Adolph, 2000; Campos, Bertenthal, & Kermoian, 1992). Even toddlers 2 or 3

years old approach snakes, play with loaded guns, stick their fingers into electric outlets, and so forth. In short, the newborn's Moro reflex is related to fear, but it does not seem to include all the same processes as adult fear.

One consistent trend emerges from these lines of research. In newborns, expressions such as crying, smiling, and startle are responses to simple biological states. Newborns cry because they are in pain, not because someone has hurt their feelings or because they miss their stuffed animals. They smile because their bodies feel good and their tummies are full, not because they see a friend coming. They exhibit the Moro reflex, or startle, only in response to sudden bright lights or loud noises or when they are dropped. Emotions in response to cognitive appraisals of social events come later.

Do Infants Experience Discrete Emotions?

Crying is newborns' only emotional expression, so at that point we see evidence for only one kind of emotion—distress. Two or three months later, they begin to smile. Over the succeeding months and years, they gradually develop a full range of emotional expressions. What accounts for that change?

One hypothesis is that even newborns possess the full range of basic emotions, or at least the potential for them. By this reasoning, newborns do not display anger partly because they lack the cognitive capacity to assign "blame" and partly because they lack the motor capacity to make an angry expression. A second hypothesis is that newborns' distress is a mixture of anger, fear, sadness, disgust, and so forth. As the infant matures, these emotions separate from one another, as if you took a mixed pile of objects and sorted them into different stacks. A third hypothesis is that some of the emotions are simply absent at birth. For example, according to this hypothesis, a newborn is no more capable of experiencing anger than of seeing ultraviolet light. The capacities for anger, disgust, and so forth develop later, either through brain maturation,

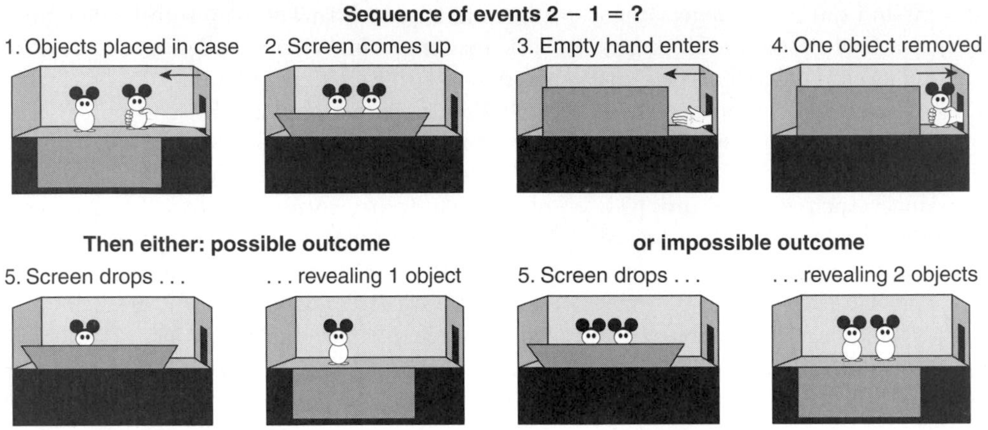

Sequence of events 2 − 1 = ?

| 1. Objects placed in case | 2. Screen comes up | 3. Empty hand enters | 4. One object removed |

| **Then either: possible outcome** | | **or impossible outcome** | |

| 5. Screen drops . . . | . . . revealing 1 object | 5. Screen drops . . . | . . . revealing 2 objects |

FIGURE 4.4   Experimenters show infants a possible or impossible outcome of removing one doll. The question is whether the infants stare longer at the "impossible" and therefore "surprising" outcome.

learning, or a combination of both. Presumably, different emotions emerge at the age when they first become useful. (Anger is useless at an early age. Who would be intimidated by a newborn's threats?)

At first glance, these distinctions may seem like splitting hairs. After all, does it really matter whether a crying baby is feeling anger, fear, sadness, or just distress? In either case, aren't you going to check its diaper, try feeding it, and rock it in your arms? The importance of the distinction is theoretical. Someone who thinks that emotions are socially constructed might find support in the idea that infants are not born with specific emotions. A defender of the idea of evolved, built-in emotions might want to find evidence of those emotions in infants as young as possible. Also recall the debate about whether people have a few "basic" emotions or continuous dimensions of emotional experience, such as pleasant/unpleasant, and active/inactive. If we have continuous dimensions, then it is unsurprising that infants fail to show specific emotions such as anger. However, if you accept the idea of discrete, basic emotions, then you have to explain why newborns don't show them.

Unfortunately for theoreticians, the evidence is often ambiguous as to the age at which some kind of emotion first appears. Consider "surprise," for example. In research on several aspects of cognitive development, psychologists have proposed that infants can feel surprise. For example, experimenters show an infant two objects, then cover them with a screen and retrieve one of the objects from behind the screen, as shown in Figure 4.4. Then they remove the screen to show either one object (the "possible" outcome) or two objects (the "impossible" outcome). Even infants just a few months old sometimes, but not always, stare longer at the impossible outcome (Wakely, Rivera, & Langer, 2000; Wynn & Chiang, 1998). When they do, experimenters infer that the infants were "surprised" by the impossible outcome, suggesting a primitive understanding of number. However, the infants don't *look* surprised. Yes, they stare (sometimes), but they don't show the facial expression of surprise (which includes lifted eyebrows and widened eyes).

Follow-up studies examined infants' and toddlers' reactions when an experimenter's voice suddenly changed to a squeaky, metallic sound (because the experimenter was speaking into a microphone connected to a sound distorter). Even up to age 14 months, the children almost never made any vocal or facial expressions resembling adult surprise. They did, however, stop whatever else they were doing and stare at the experimenter (Scherer, Zentner, & Stern, 2004). So do infants feel "real" surprise, or not? We might say they are showing "interest," rather than surprise, but that raises a debate over whether interest is an emotion or not, and so forth. The point is that it is difficult to conclude whether infants do or do not experience surprise. In some ways they do and in some ways they don't; it's not a yes-or-no question. Infants show a distinct response in situations where we would expect them to feel surprise, but it doesn't actually look like surprise (at least, as adults display it). Whether you consider these studies evidence of emotion depends, in part, on how you define "emotion"—and the difficulty of this issue is why we spent so much time on that debate in Chapters 1 and 2. Similarly, the presence of other emotions in infancy is not exactly a yes-or-no question.

Research on Infant Emotions

Psychologists have several hypotheses about how infants progress from just one or two emotions to many. The first is that infants already do feel many distinct emotions, but they can't express them (e.g., Sroufe, 1996; Witherington, Campos, & Hertenstein, 2001). For example, researchers in one study examined the emergence of anger in infants of 1, 4, and 7 months of age (Sternberg & Campos, 1990). To elicit anger, the researchers gently held down the infant's arm to prevent its movement, and videotaped the infant's reactions. Later they carefully coded all the facial expressions and changes in gaze direction.

Sternberg and Campos found that their tiny participants' expressions started out resembling mild annoyance, but looked increasingly distinct in older groups. The 1-month-old infants did not show a prototypical anger display, but they did lower their brows and raise their cheeks in an expression somewhat different from the standard distress display. Their expressions differed from a prototypical anger display in that their eyes were closed, and their tongues stuck out of their mouths. At 4 months, infants showed a

more characteristic anger expression, narrowing their eyes, pulling back their lips, frowning, and raising their cheeks. At this age they looked primarily at the arm that was being restrained during their protest. At 7 months, infants again showed a prototypical anger expression and looked at the face of the experimenter doing the restraining—and at their mothers, who were in the room. In short, the anger expression emerged gradually.

According to Sternberg and Campos, this sequence reflects development from a fuzzy sense of frustration to prototypical anger, directed specifically at the experimenter. At 1 month, the infant can't move its arm and presumably doesn't understand why. By 4 months, the infant can localize this frustration to the arm restraint but still cannot attribute the event to the actions of another person. By 7 months, the infant appears to blame the experimenter (and maybe Mom) for the situation. By this interpretation, infants are beginning to feel different kinds of distress even in the first month of life, but they become more prototypically angry as they develop the cognitive ability to attribute their frustration to a particular cause, especially another person. They also develop the motor capacity to display their anger.

The other hypotheses suggest that newborns experience only comfort or distress and not a variety of separate emotions. By this view, a single general emotion becomes differentiated into more specific types later (e.g., Camras, 1992; Messinger, 2002; Spitz, 1965). Again, most of the evidence relies on analyses of infants' facial expressions. One can examine expressions by infants and be impressed by slight differences between anger situations and fear situations—or be impressed with the considerable similarity.

In one of the largest studies, researchers obtained photographs of strong facial expressions by dozens of infants ranging in age from 2 hours to 21 months (Oster, Hegley, & Nagel, 1992). The researchers first wanted to know whether untrained adult participants would label negative facial expressions with discrete emotion terms, or whether they would tend to refer to all of the displays as global "distress." Second, they wanted to know whether two separate coding systems, used to classify infant facial expressions of emotion, would interpret the displays in the same way.

The researchers found little evidence that very small infants (especially those less than 3 months old) displayed discrete emotions that adults could recognize. Untrained coders were in agreement about happy and sad expressions, but they tended to label most negative expressions as distress rather than assigning a specific negative emotion word. The two facial coding systems also failed to agree in most cases. Both systems identified expressions of happiness and surprise. However, only 3 of the 19 expressions coded by the first system as displays of a particular negative emotion were coded the same way by the other system.

Several studies have indicated that infants sometimes make adult-like emotional expressions, but not necessarily in the "right" situations. Consider, for example, disgust. Even very young infants sometimes respond to sour or bitter tastes by opening their mouths and puckering their lips as if to spit it out (Oster et al., 1992; Rosenstein & Oster, 1988). These expressions look somewhat like adult disgust responses, except that an adult also wrinkles the nose and retracts the lips (shown in Figure 2.4). Also, infants show this expression only in response to bad tastes, not to blood and gore, dirty toilets, or any of the other items adults consider disgusting. In short, it is hard to be sure whether infants experience "real" disgust.

Do infants have distinct emotions or not? We recommend caution on this point. Adults, especially parents, are tempted to overinterpret infants' expressions: "Oh, look, our baby is happy! Ooh . . . now she's angry." Well, maybe so, but maybe not. Psychologists sometimes overinterpret expressions also. We cannot get "inside the infant's head" to know what an infant feels. However, we also should beware of drawing conclusions from the *absence* of facial expressions. For example, an adult with paralyzed facial muscles would have no emotional expressions, but we would be wrong to infer the absence of emotions. Similarly, infants' lack of clear facial expressions could reflect motor limitations rather than a lack of distinct emotions.

How Do Emotions Develop?

Regardless of whether young infants have the capacity for discrete emotions, it is clear that emotional experience and expression change enormously over the first couple of years of life. By age 1 year or so, infants show clear expressions of happiness, sadness, anger, and fear (Lewis, 2000). To what extent does this development rely on learning and to what extent on physical growth and other maturational processes?

PHYSICAL MATURATION

The capacity to display emotions requires a certain degree of physical maturation. For example, newborn infants have poor vision, especially in the center of the eye, where adults' visual acuity is best (Abramov et al., 1982). For the first six months, they have trouble shifting visual attention from one object to another; a bright or moving object will capture their attention so thoroughly that they literally cannot look away from it (Clohessy, Posner, Rothbart, & Veccra, 1991; M. H. Johnson, Posner, & Rothbart, 1991). Their immature vision does not limit their emotions, but it does limit their ability to respond to visual stimuli.

Similarly, developing abilities to crawl and walk introduce new situations with implications for emotion. An infant who is newly able to crawl also has to face a new risk of getting lost or of encountering danger. An infant who is newly able to stand and walk suddenly has to cope with the risk of falling. These changes in motor ability may trigger the development of new emotion systems, or they may activate emotion systems that were present but dormant.

More important, increasing motor maturation enables the infant to express emotions more clearly. A newborn human cannot make a fist in anger or run away in fright, cannot yet laugh, and in many ways resembles a computer that is not attached to a screen or printer. That is, much may be going on inside, but no one knows about it. Muscle control increases greatly in the first year or two of life, and with it comes a great increase in the capacity for emotional and other communication.

COGNITIVE MATURATION

Recall from the definition in Chapter 1 that one important element of emotion is an appraisal, or cognitive interpretation of some event. Without an adequate appraisal, an emotion is either absent or incomplete. For example, in the Sternberg and Campos (1990) arm restraint study, the 1-month-olds and 7-month-olds differed in many ways, and presumably one of them was that the older infants looked for a cause of their distress, whereas the younger ones could not.

Cognitive development is hardly limited to infancy. The frontal cortex of the brain, closely associated with planning and logic, doesn't reach maturity until the late teens (Sowell, Thompson, Holmes, Jernigan, & Toga, 1999; Sowell, Thompson, Tessner, & Toga, 2001), and learning continues throughout life. The first few years of life, however, see the most dramatic transitions in cognitive ability. During this time, humans develop an ability to understand events from another person's perspective, an awareness of how one looks to other people, and many other cognitive abilities that we, as adults, typically take for granted. After all, we can't remember a time when we did *not* have them. However, they do have to develop, and the infant's emotional life is limited without them.

The importance of cognitive development is particularly salient with regard to the self-conscious emotions of pride, shame, and guilt, which require comparing yourself to an internally held standard of behavior. Younger infants clearly do not compare themselves to a set of expectations (Mahler, Pine, & Bergman, 1975), and most psychologists believe that infants lack a clear sense of "self." Lewis and Brooks-Gunn (1979) designed a clever study to determine when children can recognize themselves. They asked the mothers of 9- to 24-month-old children to put a

FIGURE 4.5   A child younger than age 1½ to 2 years sees the red dot on the nose or forehead and points at it in the mirror. An older child points to his or her own head, indicating recognition that the child in the mirror is himself or herself.

spot of rouge on the children's noses, while pretending to wipe off their faces. The mothers then held the children up to a large mirror. Infants younger than about 16 months of age typically reached out to the mirror, as though it were another child. By contrast, children 18 to 24 months of age consistently did what adults would do—reach up to their own noses to wipe off the spot. (See Figure 4.5.) That is, they recognized, "The child I see in the mirror is me."

Self-awareness and self-recognition open the door to new emotions based on self-evaluation. For example, before age 2 years, children react to their failures with sadness; after that, they react with shame or guilt (Lewis, 1992; Lewis, Sullivan, Stanger, & Weiss, 1989). These emotions continue to develop over at least the next few years. Around the fourth year of life, children begin to show **theory of**

mind, the understanding that other people have minds too and the ability to discern what other people know or think (Astington & Gopnik, 1991). Once you have "theory of mind," you understand that other people are sometimes watching you, thinking about you, and evaluating you. This awareness of other people's judgments is important for pride, shame, and guilt. For this reason, some researchers refer to these as "other-conscious" emotions, rather than self-conscious emotions (e.g., Witherington, Campos, & Hertenstein, 2001).

SOCIAL INTERACTION

Finally, as social constructivists have pointed out, humans learn a great deal about emotion from their social environment. Infants begin looking to trusted caregivers to find out how they should feel about novel objects or events sometime late in the first year of life (Klinnert, Emde, Butterfield, & Campos, 1986; Mumme, Fernald, & Herrera, 1996; Sorce, Emde, Campos, & Klinnert, 1985; Walden & Baxter, 1989). From that point on, social interaction has tremendous implications for the person's emotional life (Keltner & Haidt, 1999). Different cultures have different expectations about emotions and different rules for displaying them. Infants begin learning these expectations very early from day-to-day interactions with family and other people (Much, 1997).

☐ Development of Emotional Communication: Perceiving, Sharing, and Talking About Emotions

We noted earlier that, aside from the sympathetic cry, newborn infants do not show signs of perceiving or caring about other people's emotions. Clearly this is something that changes with development—even preschool children are savvy at "reading" other people's feelings and understanding what caused them. Emotional communication is crucial for human survival, partly because your perception of

someone else's emotion can powerfully influence your own emotions and vice versa. Imagine you are visiting somewhere far from home. You go walking through the wilderness, accompanied by people who live in the area, when suddenly you see an animal that you don't recognize at all. Is it dangerous or harmless? You don't know. If the other people smile and keep walking, you do too. But if they shriek and start running away, so do you. Psychologists refer to this process as **social referencing** (Klinnert et al., 1986; Walden & Baxter, 1989): You based your own emotional reaction to the ambiguous situation on your perception of other people's emotions.

Infants and young children gradually develop the capacity for social referencing, and as they do, they mature in the appropriateness of their own emotions. The age at which it begins to emerge depends on the type of test or situation. The earliest sign of social referencing appears at about 9 months, in the visual cliff: Researchers place an infant on a table with plates of clear glass on either side. On the "shallow" side, the infant sees a floor that is just a short step down. On the "deep" side the floor appears to be much farther (see Figure 4.6). Infants who have had some experience with crawling, and therefore some experience with falling down, usually turn toward the shallow side, indicating the ability to detect depth (and a preference for avoiding injury).

In one study, researchers placed infants on the safe (shallow) side and asked mothers to stand on the other side of the table, beyond the deep end. Mothers were then instructed either to look frightened or to smile and encourage the infant to cross. Starting at about 9 months of age, the infants appeared to use their mothers' cues to decide whether to cross: Infants stayed put when their mothers looked frightened but tested the glass and then crossed when mothers looked happy and encouraging (Sorce, Emde, Campos, & Klinnert, 1985).

Other kinds of research show social referencing beginning at a later age. For example, imagine an infant who is suddenly confronted with one or more unfamiliar toys, such as a remote-controlled robot

FIGURE 4.6 Infants late in their first year of life will look to caregivers to decide how to respond to novel situations, such as the visual cliff.

that makes odd sounds. The toy captures the infant's attention, but the infant is not sure how to react. If the child's mother says, "Oh, that toy scares me," making a facial expression of fear, children as young as 11 months also act afraid of the toy, with girls generally more responsive to the mother's expression than boys are (Blackford & Walden, 1998). (Note that children this young have little language comprehension, so they are probably reacting to the facial expression or tone of voice, not to the word "scared.") Similarly, if an infant sees two new toys, and someone—even a stranger—reacts to one of them with pleasure and the other one with disgust, the infant becomes more likely to play with the "pleasant" toy and to avoid the "disgusting" toy (Moses, Baldwin, Rosicky, & Tidball, 2001; Mumme, Fernald, & Herrera, 1996; Walden & Baxter, 1989). An 11-month-old avoids the "disgusting" toy only if

tested within a few minutes; a 14-month-old avoids it even an hour later, suggesting that the older child remembers the emotional association learned from the other person (Hertenstein & Campos, 2004).

Infants also use social referencing to decide how to approach new people. As a general rule, children respond more positively to people with whom they see parents interacting warmly (Lewis & Feiring, 1981).

Intersubjectivity

Social referencing is really part of a larger phenomenon, known as intersubjectivity. Social smiling and shared affect are called primary intersubjectivity—the sharing of experience. Parents often make a deliberate effort to share an infant's emotions and let the infant know about the sharing (Jonsson et al., 2001). For example, an infant reaches out to grab a toy, and the parent says, "Ohhh!" In the process, the parent communicates, "I understand what you feel," and the infant gets some idea of what the parent is feeling. Observers have found that mother and infant usually match each other's change of emotions within seconds (Beebe, 2003). Beginning when infants are very young, they and their parents—usually mothers—learn to coordinate their responses. Infants more or less match their rhythms of babbling and glancing at the mother with the mother's rhythm of talking and glancing at the infant (Beebe et al., 2000; Crown, Feldstein, Jasnow, Beebe, & Jaffe, 2002). In effect, they maintain nonverbal "conversations" long before the infant learns any words. All these processes contribute to a sense of shared experience, which is a major step toward understanding each other and knowing what to expect from each other (Rochat & Striano, 1999).

Secondary intersubjectivity occurs when the infant and the caregiver share their experience of an object or a third person (Trevarthen & Hubley, 1978). For example, when a child sees a puppy, gets a parent's attention, and points to the puppy, the two of them are engaging in secondary intersubjectivity. The parent and child jointly attend to the

© LWA-Dann Tardif/Corbis

FIGURE 4.7   Young children and their parents often have the same emotional expression at the same time because they are reacting to the same event. This synchrony provides one opportunity for infants to learn what different expressions mean.

puppy and share their feelings regarding that object. When the third object or situation in question is unfamiliar, infants use social referencing to decide how to act. That is, they wait to see someone else's reaction before deciding to enjoy the object or avoid it. When the third object or situation is more familiar, infants may still engage in secondary intersubjectivity to share their experience with caregivers.

Interpreting Facial Expressions of Emotion

Most research on the development of emotional perception concerns what children can do at different ages; how children learn their skills has received less attention. When young children see a smile, how do they know that it means "happy"? How do they know what frowns mean or anything else? Answers here are speculative. One possibility is that an infant who sees smiles and frowns automatically knows what they mean, based on inherited mechanisms. That hypothesis is plausible, but some opportunities for learning occur also. Infants and their parents (or others near them) tend to have similar emotional experiences and expressions at the same time. (See Figure 4.7.) One reason is that they react to the same events at the same time (Kokkinaki, 2003); another is that they sometimes copy each other's expressions. Parents often imitate their infants' expressions, and infants more than 9 months old also imitate their parents (Feldman, Greenbaum, & Yirmiya, 1999). An infant who smiles, feels happy, and sees someone else smile at the same time has the opportunity to associate a happy feeling with the sight of a smiling face.

Facial **mimicry**, copying other people's facial expressions, has also been reported in the first days of life, although its significance is unclear (Field, Woodson, Greenberg, & Cohen, 1982; Meltzoff & Moore, 1977, 2002). (See Figure 4.8.) How does an

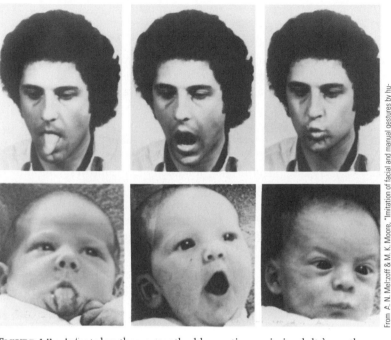

From A. N. Meltzoff & M. K. Moore, "Imitation of facial and manual gestures by human neonates" *Science, 198* (1977), pp. 75–78.

FIGURE 4.8   Infants less than a month old sometimes mimic adults' mouth expressions. Source: Meltzoff and Moore (1977).

infant know which facial muscles to contract to produce the expression it sees? Why does it imitate? Why does this mimicry sometimes occur in newborns but then become rare for the next several months? Perhaps the newborn's mimicry is closer to being an automatic reflex than a motivated behavior. Although researchers know this behavior exists at a remarkably young age, no one is sure *why* or what significance the mimicry has for other aspects of emotion.

Emotion Language

Another way of studying young children's development of emotional perception is to analyze their language. Almost as soon as children start to talk (around age 1½ to 2), their emotion vocabulary grows rapidly, and they talk often about both their own and other people's emotions. However, the fact that they use words like "angry" or "sad" does not tell us how thoroughly they understand those terms. For example, a child might have learned to label a frowning face as "angry" without necessarily understanding what internal feelings constitute anger. To test how well toddlers understand emotions as internal experiences, Judy Dunn and colleagues (1987) examined the situations in which preschool children use emotion words. The researchers found that even 2-year-old children use emotion words in fairly accurate ways. In play, they attribute emotions to dolls and stuffed animals in appropriate situations. Toddlers also talk about what they and others have felt in the past and what they expect to feel in the future, not just in the present (Wellman, Harris, Banerjee, & Sinclair, 1995). This emotion talk is a good predictor of healthy social development. In one study, 3-year-old children who talked more with their families about emotional experiences showed better ability to figure out other people's emotions when they reached first grade (Dunn, Brown, & Maguire, 1995).

Even as young as age 2 years, children are so good at understanding emotion, and so aware of the effects of their emotions on other people, that they may begin faking emotion to get what they want (Bretherton, Fritz, Zahn-Waxler, & Ridgeway, 1986). For example, they might pretend to be sad or frightened to get attention. At this young age, children use emotion to "train" their parents just as much as parents use emotion to train their children.

By 3 years of age, children's understanding of emotion is even more sophisticated. In one study, researchers watched children while they played at their day-care centers, and noted each time a child displayed happiness, sadness, distress, or anger (Fabes, Eisenberg, Nyman, & Michaelieu, 1991).

After each expression, the researcher approached another child, who had seen the expression but was not the cause of it, and asked what the target child was feeling and what event had caused that emotion. In the meantime, an adult observer recorded what he or she thought the target child felt and why. Even the 3-year-old children, the youngest group studied, agreed about two thirds of the time with the adult observer's interpretation of the event. By this stage of development, children seem to have acquired the basics of most emotion skills.

▢ Development of Emotional Bonds: Attachment

As we have seen, infants develop their ability to communicate emotions about objects and events in the world. At around the same time, infants develop the capacity to form selective emotional bonds with a few special people. At first, an infant who has just developed social smiling reacts with a smile to any smile it sees. Beginning at about 6 to 9 months, the infant becomes more discriminating. Not anyone can elicit a shared smile now; social smiling must be earned, as the baby grows to know and trust certain individuals. A baby who would lie contently in anyone's arms just a few weeks earlier suddenly becomes hysterical when Mom leaves the room. Rather than playing with every new object or person it encounters, the infant checks in frequently with a few people, to see if they're around and paying attention. Developmental psychologists refer to this new pattern of behavior as **attachment**—a long-lasting emotional bond between the infant and a few regular caregivers, producing distress upon separation, joy upon reunion, and much emotional sharing.

Attachment in infants and toddlers is usually observed in a research paradigm called the **Strange Situation** (Ainsworth, 1989): An infant and parent enter a toy-filled room and the infant is allowed to play. A stranger then enters the room. After a couple of minutes the parent leaves the room, and then returns. Next both the stranger and the parent leave the room, the stranger returns alone, and finally the

parent returns. All this tedious coming and going creates a good scenario for observing attachment-related emotional behavior. A "securely attached" infant more than about 6 months old will typically protest when the parent leaves the room, show joy when the parent returns, and "check in" with the parent frequently while playing.

Why does attachment begin specifically at 6 months? Several theories have been proposed, and as usual, they probably all have some element of truth. First, infants' vision improves substantially from birth to age 6 months (Banks & Salapatek, 1983). Some researchers have suggested that this is the first time infants can see parents and other caregivers well enough to recognize them as individuals; as a result the infants can now notice when someone has gone. If taken as an absolute, the idea that infants do not recognize other individuals until age 6 months is certainly overstated. Even newborns show signs of recognizing their mother's voice (DeCasper & Fifer, 1980). However, recognizing by voice and recognizing by sight are different, and vision has obvious advantages for monitoring people's movements at a distance.

Another explanation relates to cognitive maturation. During Jean Piaget's sensorimotor stage of development (from birth until almost two years), infants respond mostly to what they see and hear right now instead of anything they remember. Piaget argued that infants less than 9 months old lack **object permanence**—the understanding that objects continue to exist even when we do not see or hear them. For example, infants less than 9 months old will reach for objects they see, but not for objects that have been covered or hidden (Piaget, 1937/1954). Later researchers using different research methods have found indications of object permanence much earlier, even at ages 4 to 6 months (Baillargeon, 1986, 1987; Wynn & Chiang, 1998). Still, the tendency by the youngest infants to respond mainly to what they see at the moment would decrease their response to someone leaving the room (Schaffer, 1971).

The final explanation is probably the most commonly accepted. At about 6 to 8 months of age, most babies begin to crawl, and they begin their rush to explore the world. This new skill opens doors to all sorts of new experiences including, unfortunately, such possibilities as getting lost, tumbling down the stairs, touching something sharp or hot, and encountering less-than-gentle animals. Before the baby could crawl, it could rely on caregivers to keep the immediate environment safe. Now the baby must balance the thrill of exploration with the risk of wandering away and getting into serious trouble. According to John Bowlby (1969), a biological attachment behavior system develops at about the time a baby starts to crawl, to help regulate these two competing needs. As long as a trusted caregiver is nearby and in regular contact, a child will play happily; as soon as the caregiver is out of sight, the child will do something to repair the breach. The emotions and behaviors necessary for this regulation constitute attachment.

Note that this last explanation means that attachment behavior—especially the protest when a caregiver leaves—has the specific purpose of keeping caregivers close enough to help when needed, but distant enough for the infant to explore on its own. That strategy is valuable for children of a particular age. Before 6 months it is unimportant, because the infants are not yet crawling. It gradually becomes less important again as the child grows old enough and competent enough to explore without constant supervision. In the Strange Situation, children continue protesting the caregiver's departure up to age 18 months and beyond, but their protests become less and less intense (Izard & Abe, 2004).

Because the caregiver is an agent in this equation too, an infant's most effective attachment behavior depends on both the infant's age and on how the caregiver responds to the infant (Isabella & Belsky, 1991). Not all infants show a "secure" attachment. If a caregiver is smothering, ignoring the infant's need to explore on its own, the infant may become especially uncomfortable with being alone, yet need to push away to gain some space. These infants, with an "anxious" attachment style, become extremely upset when the caregiver leaves and simultaneously cling to the caregiver and push her away when she returns. With a distant, rejecting caregiver, an infant may not show much distress when the caregiver leaves or returns. Infants with this "avoidant" attachment style pay little attention to the caregiver when present, show little apparent reaction when he or she leaves, and do not go for comfort when the caregiver returns. Thus, intrusive, pushy caregivers are more likely to have anxiously attached infants, and unresponsive caregivers to have avoidant infants (Isabella & Belsky, 1991). There are three possible explanations for this, which may all be true to some degree: First, infants develop an attachment style that corresponds to their caregivers' typical behavior. Second, the caregivers' behavior may depend to some degree on the infants' personality and inherent emotional style. Third, most studies pertain to children and their biological parents, so many of the same genes may control their behavior tendencies.

Hand in hand with attachment comes **stranger anxiety**—a fear of unfamiliar people (Sroufe, 1977). Not all children experience this sudden increase in fear of strangers, and in most children this fear declines over time (Greenberg & Marvin, 1982). Developmental psychologists relate the fear of strangers partly to advances in memory—a newfound ability to recognize familiar people and therefore to notice when that familiarity is absent. Fear of strangers may also relate to maturation of the capacity for fear in general. A similar trend is common in the animal kingdom: Baby mammals and birds curiously explore the world, and as they grow older, they become more cautious and more likely to flee from unfamiliar objects or situations.

❑ Socialization of Emotional Expression

Emotional expressions such as smiles and frowns develop naturally as a child's muscle control matures. The more interesting aspect of emotional development, from the standpoint of most psychologists, is how children learn when, where, and how strongly to express their emotions.

Expectations about emotional expression vary somewhat according to culture. For example, parents in America and much of Europe encourage their children to be independent and assertive and to express their feelings openly. In contrast, the parents of the Gusii culture of Kenya consider the ideal child to be quiet, respectful, and obedient (LeVine, 1997). In general, however, the differences across cultures are small. A survey of 48 countries found that parents in all locations wanted their children to be happy, not too fearful, and capable of controlling their anger. The cultures differed in how much they emphasized happiness, fearlessness, or anger control, but the goals were largely similar (M. L. Diener & Lucas, 2004). Collectivist cultures such as the Javanese society of Indonesia put enormous stress on harmonious relationships and restraint of emotional displays. However, in both the Javanese society and the more individualist society of the United States, children who openly express anger get into frequent trouble with adults and tend to be rejected, sometimes even ostracized, by their peers (Eisenberg, Liew, & Pidada, 2001; Eisenberg, Pidada, & Liew, 2001; Hanish et al., 2004).

Expectations for emotional expression also vary by gender, although again the differences are not huge. Across cultures, most parents stress control of fear and anger more for their sons than for their daughters and encourage the expression of happiness more for their daughters than for their sons (M. L. Diener & Lucas, 2004). According to observations of preschool children, parents tend to discuss emotions with their daughters more than with their sons, possibly because the girls initiated such conversations more often (Fivush, Brotman, Buckner, & Goodman, 2000). Parents, especially fathers, pay more attention to angry outbursts by their sons than by their daughters (Chaplin, Cole, & Zahn-Waxler, 2005). Perhaps parents are less worried that their daughters' anger will get out of control.

When do children learn the "display rules" of their culture, and when do the skills needed to comply with those rules emerge? By age 3 years, many children are beginning to learn to hide their feel-

ings. One study demonstrated this by instructing children not to look at a hidden toy, filming their behavior while the experimenter left the room, and then asking the children whether or not they had disobeyed (Lewis, Stanger, & Sullivan, 1989). Naturally, many of the children did look at the toy and then lied about it. Although careful behavioral coding revealed that the lying children showed subtle hints of shame and guilt, such as nervous smiles and self-touches, untrained adults could not distinguish liars from the children who really did not look at the toy. Thus, the children in this study seemed to succeed at hiding their guilty emotions from adults.

Another study found substantial individual differences among children in their ability to conceal their emotions. In the United States, one rule of polite behavior is to express thanks for any gift and never to react with disappointment. Preschool children were asked to rank-order five small presents from best to worst, and experimenters promised to give them one of the presents later, after the children performed a task. When the time came, the experimenters at first gave each child his or her least preferred gift, waited a few seconds, and then apologized and gave the most preferred gift. During those few seconds' delay, the experimenter recorded the children's reactions. Some children cried, threw the unwanted present, and demanded a better one. Others politely accepted it and hid their disappointment. As you might guess, those who vigorously displayed their frustration were rated by their teachers and others as "lacking social skills," whereas those who hid their disappointment were considered good at controlling their emotions in a variety of situations (Liew, Eisenberg, & Reiser, 2004). On the average, boys lag behind girls in their ability to regulate their emotional displays (Weinberg, Tronick, Cohn, & Olson, 1999).

How do children learn the rules for displaying or concealing emotions? According to anthropologists, much of this training happens through day-to-day interactions in the home, beginning early (Much, 1997). Most mothers of 6- to 12-month-old infants in the United States express much joy, interest, and surprise during their interactions with their babies and respond strongly to their infants' displays of interest or surprise (Malatesta, Grigoryev, Lamb, Albin, & Culver, 1986; Malatesta & Haviland, 1982). As a rule, parents who express mostly positive emotions have children who also express positive emotions; parents who express much negative emotion have children who also vigorously express their fears and anger (Cole, Teti, & Zahn-Waxler, 2003; Denham et al., 2000; Valiente et al., 2004). It is tempting to assume that the children react to their parents' displays and copy them. No doubt that is true to some extent; however, these studies are correlational and we cannot draw cause-and-effect conclusions. Perhaps the parents are reacting to their children's emotional outbursts. Perhaps parent and child show similar emotional displays because of their genetic similarity. Studies on parents of adopted children would help to unravel this problem, but few such studies have been conducted.

In one study, researchers asked Japanese and American mothers to yell angrily while their 11-month-old infants crawled toward a toy (Miyake, Campos, Kagan, & Bradshaw, 1986). The American babies typically paused briefly but then kept approaching the toy, whereas Japanese babies paused far longer. According to the researchers, the American babies had heard their mothers yell so often that they did not take them seriously. ("Mom's yelling at me again. Oh well.") For Japanese babies, however, an angry voice was a rare occurrence and therefore worth their attention. Even in the first year of life, infants are learning cultural rules about how to interpret other people's emotions; American babies might also be learning that anger is acceptable and normal, whereas Japanese infants might be learning that anger is rare and generally inappropriate.

Children also learn cultural rules when parents and other caregivers reinforce or discourage emotion displays. We noted above that the type of attachment an infant displays depends, in part, on caregiver reactions to the infant's signals—responsive but unintrusive caregivers tend to have securely attached toddlers, unresponsive, distant caregivers tend to have

avoidant toddlers, and intrusive, always-in-your-face caregivers tend to have anxiously attached toddlers. One can think about these parenting styles as examples of good versus bad parenting, but one can also think of them as reflections of emotional style, which differs from culture to culture. For example, in one study of the Strange Situation in Germany, nearly half of the infants were classified as attachment-avoidant, compared with an average 23 percent of American infants (Grossman, Grossman, Spangler, Suess, & Unzer, 1985). Many infants did not seem terribly worried about their mother's absence. When researchers observed the mothers' behavior, they did not find that German Moms were neglectful or unresponsive. Rather, the mothers expressed a value for interpersonal distance and a belief that parents should encourage independence in their children.

In Japanese samples, high proportions of toddlers are typically classified as attachment-anxious by U.S. standards (e.g., Miyake, Chen, & Campos, 1985; Rothbaum, Weisz, Pott, Miyake, & Morelli, 2000). Mothers in traditional Japanese families rarely leave their infants, and they intentionally encourage dependence on others in their children. The Strange Situation is thus a great deal "stranger" for Japanese toddlers than it is for American toddlers. Sometimes experimenters have trouble even persuading Japanese mothers to leave their infants briefly in the presence of a stranger to conduct the research. As a result, cultural differences in infants' emotional responses to this situation are to be expected. As cultures change, so do the emotional lessons conveyed by parents. Studies of attachment in Japanese families where the mother has a career find attachment type proportions similar to those observed in the United States (Durrett, Otaki, & Richards, 1984).

Not all emotion lessons are this explicit. Sometimes parents give lessons in emotional regulation without even realizing what they are doing. In one study, researchers asked Japanese and American mothers of 3- and 4-year-olds how they would respond to various kinds of misbehavior, such as drawing with crayons on the wall or knocking products off the shelves at the supermarket (Conroy, Hess, Azuma, & Kashiwagi, 1980). Mothers in the United States often said they would demand that the child stop the behavior, or that they would physically force the child to stop. These strategies trigger a clash of wills between parent and child, encouraging the child to argue and become angry. If the parent then gives in to a child's tantrum, the emotional behavior is reinforced—if you don't get what you want, get angry, fight, and you will win.

By contrast, Japanese mothers said they were more likely to explain why the misbehaviors hurt other people, appealing to their children's desire to please and cooperate. In training children to reinterpret such situations from other people's perspectives, Japanese mothers encourage the development of positive social emotions and discourage self-focused appraisals that may lead to anger.

▢ Emotion in Adolescence

When you think of emotion during adolescence (loosely defined as ages 10 to 21 years), what comes to mind? Many people think of this period of life as incredibly turbulent, with emotions causing all kinds of "storm and stress" that calm down as one reaches adulthood. Certainly parents think of adolescence as an emotionally difficult time because they face increased conflict with their teenagers. Is there any truth to this image? Studies suggest that there is, although the turbulence may be limited to specific kinds of emotions, may be more noticeable in some relationships than others, and is definitely more dramatic for some individuals than others (Arnett, 1999). To complicate matters further, the whole concept of extended adolescence is relatively new in world history and still does not exist in many cultures (Arnett, 2000). Instead, a formal ceremony around the age of puberty marks the transition from childhood to full adult responsibility, including an obligation to provide for oneself economically and the opportunity to begin having children. As a result, what we know about emotion during adolescence is limited to the developed Western world.

Compared with younger children and adults, Western adolescents do report more frequent and intense mood swings (Larson & Lampman-Petraitis, 1989), but we must approach data based entirely on self-report with our usual caution. One consistent finding in self-report and observational studies is that the risk of clinical depression and depressive symptoms rises substantially throughout early and late adolescence (Magnusson, 1988; Petersen, Kennedy, & Sullivan, 1991; Rutter, 1986). This rise in depressive symptoms is much greater among girls than among boys. During childhood, boys are slightly more likely than girls to show signs of depression, but beginning at about 14 years of age, girls are three times more likely to show such symptoms (Ge, Conger, & Elder, 2001; Gjerde & Block, 1991). This gender difference continues throughout adulthood, and we shall discuss it in more detail in Chapter 7.

For now an important question is, *Why* does the gender difference emerge in adolescence, specifically? What about adolescence makes depression more likely, and why is this so much more true for girls than for boys? One explanation is that just about every aspect of life changes during this period—demands at school change (and for many, the school itself changes), responsibilities at home increase, one is likely to have a first job, and relationships are changing in many ways as well (Graber & Brooks-Gunn, 1996). These changes can be very stressful, and the more stressors an adolescent faces in different life domains at the same time, the more vulnerable he or she is to depression (Compas, Ey, & Grant, 1993).

Some studies suggest that the hormonal changes associated with puberty may increase risk for depression, especially for girls, although other studies have failed to find this effect (Flannery, Torquati, & Lindemeier, 1994). Some studies suggest that for girls, the hormonal changes of puberty may not themselves be as important in predicting depression as *when* puberty takes place. Girls who mature early, start menstruation, and develop breasts earlier than most of their peers may face yet another dramatic life transition in an especially lonely way;

early maturing girls are at particular risk for depression, are more likely to engage in risky behaviors, and have more conflict with their parents (Angold, Costello, & Worthman, 1998; Ge et al., 2001).

Aside from this, the claims of turbulent adolescence may be a bit exaggerated. Many teenagers go through adolescence without major distress or extreme conflict, although a moderate increase in negative emotion is the norm (Arnett, 1999). During this time, emotions become more negative at home, but they actually become more positive with friends and in activities outside the home (Larson & Richards, 1991). This disparity may explain why teenagers have such a reputation for volatility—parents see many outbursts, but peers and others mostly see happiness and calm. There is still a great deal to learn about how emotions develop during adolescence and about what causes the changes that are observed.

◻ Emotional Development in Adulthood

Until now, we have focused on how emotion develops in early life. What happens later? Although most research has focused on childhood emotional development, a few researchers have examined emotional development throughout people's adult lives.

Individual Consistency Across the Lifespan

By about age 3, children clearly express most of the same emotions as adults. They can detect other people' emotions, understand what events probably caused them, and comprehend how their own emotions influence others. We might therefore suppose that further emotional development consists merely of fine-tuning these basic elements. Unfortunately, few researchers have explored the development of emotion during the school years, when this process would be expected to take place.

We do know that an individual's emotional characteristics tend to be consistent throughout life.

For example, studies of twins and adopted children have demonstrated genetic contributions to anxiety levels (Gross & Hen, 2004), extraversion (Carver & White, 1994; Gray, 1970; Loehlin, 1992), neuroticism (Lake, Eaves, Maes, Heath, & Martin, 2000), shyness (Kagan, 1984; Kagan, Reznick, & Snidman, 1988), and degree of arousal of the autonomic nervous system while people watch emotionally charged films (Lensvelt-Mulders & Hettema, 2001). In one study of emotional continuity across the lifespan, investigators observed hundreds of 7-year-olds and later followed up on them when they reached age 35. "Proneness to distress" in childhood correlated .24 with adult measures of anger, indicating a moderate relationship (Kubzhansky, Martin, & Buka, 2004). In another study, researchers coded the quality ("felt" versus "polite") and intensity of smiles posed by young women in their college yearbooks and then asked whether these single expressions of emotion could predict the outcome of these women's lives decades later (Harker & Keltner, 2001). They found that women who had displayed stronger and more "felt" smiles (Duchenne smiles) in the college photographs were more likely to have married and less likely to have divorced. They described themselves as more competent, more emotionally stable, and more agreeable with other people than women with less intense or genuine smiles in their college photographs. In this case, the expression of emotion in a single instant reflected an enduring emotional disposition, one that predicted the women's interpersonal experiences throughout their lives.

Age Trends in Emotional Intensity

The studies we have just described examined whether people who are above average (or below average) in warmth or some other characteristic remain above average (or below average) years later. These studies did not consider what happens to the average itself. For example, if you are warmer than average for people your age, you could become less and less affectionate over the years and still remain "above average" if other people your age declined as fast or faster than you did.

Therefore, a different question is how people's emotions change, on average, between young adulthood and old age. Laura Carstensen and her colleagues have conducted some excellent research on this question, finding that emotional experience, the importance of emotion, and people's ability to regulate or control their emotions do change substantially over the course of adulthood.

First, as people grow older, they pay more attention to emotional matters in general. Carstensen asked participants in their 20s through their 80s to read a two-page excerpt from a novel and then to spend the next hour doing various other tasks (Carstensen & Turk-Charles, 1994). At the end of the hour, participants were asked to remember as much as they could from the story. The researchers then compared the amount of emotional material older and younger subjects included in their descriptions. Although memory for most kinds of material gets worse as people age (Smith, 1996), the older participants showed a greater memory for the emotional aspects of the story (see Figure 4.9)

However, although older adults pay attention to emotional material in general, they report fewer negative events. Carstensen and Charles (1998) distributed pagers to people ranging from 18 to 94 years of age, paged them several times a day over the course of a week, and asked them each time to rate and describe their current emotional experience. Older and younger adults in the sample reported about the same frequency of positive emotions, but older adults reported feeling negative emotions considerably less often. Older adults also reported more complex emotional experiences than did younger adults, in that they were more likely to report feeling positive and negative emotions at the same time (Carstensen, Pasupathi, Mayr, & Nesselroade, 2000).

Why do older adults report less negative emotion? Perhaps, as a result of financial security, lack of job pressure, and so forth, they actually have fewer unpleasant experiences. Another possibility (which does not contradict the first) is that they shift their attention away from unpleasant events. In one study, researchers displayed pleasant and unpleasant

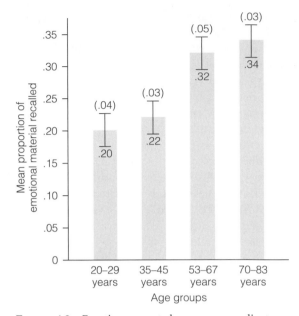

FIGURE 4.9 Emotion seems to become more salient, or important, to people as they age. This graph shows the amount of emotional material participants of different ages remembered from a two-page story. Source: From "The salience of emotion across the life-span" by L. L. Carstensen and S. Turk-Charles in *Psychology and Aging*, 9, pp. 259–264. © 1994 American Psychological Association. Reprinted with permission from the authors.

photos while using fMRI techniques to record activity of the amygdala, a brain area known to be highly responsive to emotional stimuli. In young adults, the amygdala responded more strongly to the unpleasant photos. For people over age 70, the amygdala responded more strongly to the pleasant than the unpleasant photos (Mather et al., 2004).

A related study used a more complex procedure to measure attention to emotional stimuli. People stared at a point in the center of a computer screen, and then two faces appeared, to the left and right of the fixation point, for one second. One face had a neutral expression while the other had either a pleasant or unpleasant emotional expression. Then the faces disappeared and a small dot appeared on either the left or right side. The participant's task was to indicate the position of the dot, as quickly as

1. Participant fixates vision on a marker in the center of the screen.

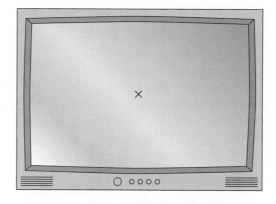

2. An emotional and a neutral face appear for one second.

(left) © Patrik Giardino/Corbis; (right) Jonathan Kim/Getty Images

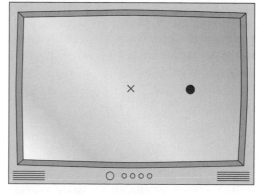

3. A dot appears on one side or the other. The participant is to indicate as quickly as possible the location of the dot.

FIGURE 4.10 People viewed a screen that displayed a pleasant or unpleasant emotional face and a neutral face. Then they were to indicate as quickly as possible the position of a dot, which appeared in the location of either the neutral or the emotional face.

possible. Figure 4.10 outlines this procedure. Whereas young adults responded to the dot about equally rapidly regardless of its location, older adults (mean age 74) responded more slowly if the dot appeared where a sad or angry face had been (Mather & Carstensen, 2003). Evidently they had been focusing their attention away from the unpleasant face.

Emotional Salience

What might explain the drop in attention to negative events that these studies have reported? Carstensen and her colleagues (1999) proposed that people often have to trade off two potentially conflicting goals. Simply put, sometimes you have to choose between having a good time now and doing something stressful or unpleasant to build resources that will help you or protect you in the future (Carstensen, Fung, & Charles, 2003). According to **Socioemotional Selectivity Theory**, midlife triggers an increase in adults' motivation to make the most of their remaining time, and consequently older adults put a high priority on emotional quality of life in social interaction and other activities. Most young adults seek to gain information that will help them build resources for the future, even at the cost of experiences that could be stressful or unpleasant. Older adults, by contrast, are less motivated to build resources for the future and more motivated to seek maximum emotional enjoyment from their social lives.

Studies of older and younger adults' behavior in social situations support Socioemotional Selectivity Theory. For example, would you prefer to spend this weekend meeting interesting new people, strengthening relationships with people you know at work, or getting together with friends and family members you have known for most of your life? Younger people are more likely to prefer the new relationships, whereas older people prefer to be with family and long-term friends (Carstensen, 1992; Carstensen & Charles, 1998). Older adults also behave differently when interacting with loved ones. For example, when talking about an area of conflict in their marriage, older adults are less likely to quarrel (Levenson, Carstensen, & Gottman, 1994a), and more likely to express affection during the discussion (Carstensen, Gottman, & Levenson, 1995).

The message so far is that as people grow older, they try to maximize their pleasant emotions and minimize their unpleasant emotions. But when they have emotional experiences, especially the unpleasant ones, do they *feel* them as strongly as when they were young? This is not an easy question. Older and younger adults rate the intensity of their emotions about equally (Carstensen, Pasupathi, Mayr, & Nesselroade, 2000), but we do not know whether they are using the rating scale the same way. That is, a "5" on a 1-to-7 scale of some emotion may mean something different to an 80-year-old than to a 20-year-old. As people grow older, even though their ratings of the emotional experience remain about the same, their heart rate and other physiological responses to an emotional event decline (LaBar, Cook, Torpey, & Welsh-Bohmer, 2004; Labouvie-Vief, Lumley, Jain, & Heinze, 2003; Lawton, 2001). That is, a given emotional rating corresponds to a much less intense physiological feeling for an older person than for a younger one.

Emotional Regulation

You've probably heard the expression "older but wiser." Is it true? One aspect of wisdom is managing one's emotions effectively—entering rewarding situations and avoiding unpleasant ones, thinking about events in ways that facilitate a more positive emotional experience, and maintaining emotional balance in difficult situations. When James Gross and his colleagues (1997) asked American and Norwegian participants about their emotional experience and behavior, he found that older adults rated themselves as less emotionally expressive, less impulsive, and better able to control their emotions than younger adults. These measures rely on self-reports, which may not be fully accurate, but at least older adults believe that they have gained some emotional wisdom over the course of their lives.

In another study, adults of various ages named up to six people they knew well and then described a recent occasion when they had some irritation or difficulty with each person. Finally, they described how they handled each situation. On the average, older people described their conflicts as less intense than those of younger people, and the older people were much less likely to react with anger (Birditt & Fingerman, 2003). In short, emotion may be one aspect of life that significantly improves in old age.

▢ Summary

Emotions change considerably throughout the life-span, from early infancy through late adulthood. The emotions of infancy are theoretically interesting because of the hope that they might shed light on the question of "basic" emotions. If infants have a set of discrete emotions, then those emotions would satisfy one major criterion for being basic. However, as you have seen, the results on this point have been indecisive. Infants' ability to display particular emotions develops gradually over a year or more. Research to date does not tell us conclusively whether the youngest infants lack certain emotions altogether, have them but don't distinguish one emotion from another, or have discrete emotions without being able to express them. Even if newborns do lack discrete emotions, that lack does not contradict the idea of basic emotions; after all, language also matures at a later age, and psychologists widely agree that language is a built-in feature of human nature.

Even if the capacity for emotions is evolutionarily built in, many important aspects of emotional development depend on the environment, too. For example, you were born with the capacity to develop language, but whether you speak English, Chinese, or Swahili depends on social and cultural influences. Similarly, your biological nature gave you the capacity to feel emotions, and your genes probably even influence how intensely you feel them, but you have learned from your culture the appropriate ways to express them and the situations in which you should suppress or modify them.

We hope that you have seen in this chapter that the topic of emotional development raises deep, important, hard-to-answer psychological issues. To review a few: How much emotion can infants experience, despite their limited cognition? Why do newborns imitate the facial expressions they see? How do infants learn what various emotional expressions mean? What accounts for the changes in emotion observed between young adults and older adults? These and other issues will continue to pose huge challenges to researchers for decades to come.

▢ Key Terms

attachment: a long-lasting emotional bond between an infant and a caregiver, indicated by distress upon separation, joy upon reunion, and much emotional sharing (p. 88)

distress: an undifferentiated protest against anything that is unpleasant or aversive (p. 77)

mimicry: copying (such as other people's facial expressions) (p. 86)

Moro reflex: a sequence in which the infant flings out its arms and spreads its fingers, then contracts quickly into a fetal position with fingers bent (p. 78)

object permanence: the understanding that objects continue to exist even when we do not see or hear them (p. 88)

secondary intersubjectivity: process by which the infant and the caregiver share their experience of an object or a third person (p. 85)

social referencing: looking at the emotional expressions of trusted caregivers before responding to novel objects, people, or situations (p. 84)

social smiling: exchanging smiles with another person (p. 78)

Socioemotional Selectivity Theory: view that midlife triggers an increase in adults' motivation to make the most of their remaining time and that, consequently, older adults put a high priority on emotional quality of life (p. 96)

Strange Situation: procedure in which an infant and parent enter a toy-filled room and the infant is allowed to play. A stranger then enters the room; after a few minutes, the parent leaves the room, then returns; next both the stranger and the parent leave the room, the stranger returns alone, and finally the parent returns (p. 88)

stranger anxiety: a fear of unfamiliar people (p. 89)

sympathetic crying: crying in response to the sound of another newborn's cry (p. 77)

theory of mind: the understanding that other people have minds too and the ability to discern what other people know or think (p. 83)

▢ Thought Questions

1. Early in this chapter, we noted that crying is an infant's way of getting care and attention from adults. If so, why doesn't it cry all the time, to get even more care and attention?

2. Infants less than 2 months old respond to the sight of a smiling face by giving a smile of their own. What does this observation imply about an infant? Does the infant respond reflexively without understanding the meaning of a smile? Or does an infant understand that someone else's smile means happiness? What research might help answer such questions?

3. What kind of research evidence would convince you that 6-month-old infants feel surprise? What kind of evidence would convince you that 6-month-old infants are *not* capable of feeling surprise?

4. In what ways have your emotions changed since your early childhood? How could you design a study that would test whether these changes are true for most other people as well?

▢ Suggestions for Research Projects

1. Ask several people to describe their earliest emotional memories. Examine when these memories took place, what kinds of emotions people felt, what kinds of situations led to the emotions, and what other people's responses were to these early emotional displays. If possible, ask the same questions of children, whose memories of their earliest emotional experiences should be fresher.

2. Look for examples of intersubjectivity in your own experience. How often do adults use other people's reactions to guide their own emotional responses?

▢ Suggestion for Further Reading

Erikson, E. H. (1963). *Childhood and society* (2nd ed.). New York: Norton. An influential classic that discusses the social and emotional crises people face at each stage of life.

PART TWO
Individual Emotions

5

Fear and Anxiety

With this chapter, we begin describing the research on several specific emotions. In Chapter 2, we took no firm position on whether emotion consists of several basic emotions or a couple of continuous dimensions. Regardless of the answer to that theoretical question, discussing one emotion at a time has practical advantages. Just as it is often useful to discuss Europe separately from Asia, even though the border between them is arbitrary, it can be useful to distinguish between fear and anger, even if we cannot precisely place the line between the two. For example, psychologists often want to understand how to reduce someone's fearfulness, how to control someone's outbursts of anger, or what to do when someone is extremely sad, when one of these emotions is causing particular problems in a person's life. Fearfulness has characteristics that distinguish it from sadness and anger. If a person has a particular phobia (for example), then treating that phobia requires an understanding of those special features. Cross-cultural research suggests that a few distinct emotions are recognized by most societies. Even if the exact borders between "basic" emotions turn out to be somewhat arbitrary, these constructs have been useful in guiding research. Sometimes this research has supported the discrete emotion approach; at other times, it has challenged it. We present this re-

search in the next several chapters; after reading them, you can decide for yourself whether a "discrete emotion" or "dimensional" approach makes the most sense to you.

Why start with unpleasant experiences such as fear and (in the next chapter) anger? Many researchers consider fear and anger the most prototypical emotions—the best examples of what we mean by "emotion." In Chapter 1, we defined emotion as including cognition, feeling, and action; fear and anger have clear cognitions, intense feelings, and clear-cut actions (escape or attack). Joy and sadness, in contrast, produce less clear actions and sometimes none at all.

Furthermore, fear is relatively well understood. We easily define it as a reaction to danger. Whereas psychologists sometimes get bogged down in arguments about what disgust means or what is or is not a good example of embarrassment (as we shall see in later chapters), many examples of fear are uncontroversial. This is even true for nonhuman animals. Researchers often disagree about what animal behaviors (if any) indicate other emotions, but many agree that a rat freezing when it hears a cat's meow is a sign of fear. Because we can measure fear with laboratory animals, we have had more opportunities to study the biology of fear than, say, the biology of happiness. Finally, because fear and anxiety are central features of certain clinical disorders, they attract much research by psychiatrists and clinical psychologists as well as academics.

Fear and anxiety are similar experiences, characterized by feelings of danger or dread and a sense of being threatened. Their differences have to do with the experiences that trigger them, and with how long each feeling lasts. We speak of **fear** when the dread is directed toward a specific object or event, such as an airplane flight, a snake, or a gunshot. Fear is a response to a perceived danger, either to oneself or to a loved one, and it subsides quickly when the threat is gone.

By contrast, the term **anxiety** refers to a more general expectation that "something bad might happen," without identifying any particular danger (Lazarus, 1991). For example, a rabbit might develop anxiety after seeing or smelling a cat or fox. Because a predator no longer seen or smelled might still be present, the anxiety fades very slowly. Similarly, if you have anxiety about a vague possible danger to yourself or your loved ones, you can never be sure the unidentified danger has passed. If you have anxiety about being in public places, or about meeting new people, again you cannot relax for long because the situation arises repeatedly. Many people have anxiety about the whole idea of death, and death can only be postponed, not avoided altogether. When anxiety is persistent and intense, it becomes a such problem that people may seek help from clinical psychologists.

We usually experience fear as unpleasant and disturbing—something to be avoided whenever possible. It is nevertheless advantageous, up to a point. In Chapter 1, we argued that emotions evolved because individuals who experience emotions survive longer or reproduce more successfully than those who don't. Nowhere is the advantage of an emotion more evident than in the case of fear. A totally fearless person would walk right into one dangerous situation after another and would almost certainly die young. Fear presumably evolved to help animals attend to and escape from predators. People in modern, industrialized countries seldom need to escape from lions or tigers, but we do face dangers from mosquitoes, ultraviolet radiation, air pollution, sexually transmitted diseases, automobile accidents, and a host of other modern hazards. A moderate fear of real dangers leads to intelligent precautions (Rosen & Schulkin, 1998). Moderate fear may even be enjoyable—consider the popularity of horror movies or the amount of money people spend to be dropped and thrown around on rides at amusement parks. On the other hand, someone with excessive fear avoids even safe actions and misses useful opportunities.

◻ What Elicits Fear?

Are we born with any fears? At least one is certain: Sudden, loud noises frighten virtually everyone, from birth through old age. Even a fetus in the womb sometimes startles at a sufficiently loud noise. That fear is present in other species, too, from elephants to insects. To some extent we also react with automatic fears, or at least heightened caution, to other abrupt stimuli, such as a sudden bright light. Separation from loved ones may be another cause of automatic fear. In many mammalian species, an infant separated from its mother reacts with distress calls (Shair, Brunelli, Masmela, Boone, & Hofer, 2003). Many old fairy tales, such as "Hansel and Gretel," described the fear of young children lost in the woods. Today's children are more likely to get lost in a shopping mall or an amusement park, but the idea of separation from one's parents is still frightening.

However, the vast majority of our fears are learned. A few fears, such as those of snakes and spiders, are learned so readily as to suggest a built-in predisposition to learn them (Öhman, Eriksson, & Olofsson, 1975). In contrast, we certainly have no inborn predisposition to fear guns, because they have been around for only a few hundred years—an evolutionary eyeblink for a slow-breeding species like humans.

Most fears arise not just from an object by itself, such as a snake or a gun, but also from an appraisal of the overall situation. For example, your fear of a snake depends on the type of snake and its distance from you. Your fear of a gun depends on your own experience with guns, whether the gun is loaded, who is holding it, and how that person is acting. Exactly what appraisal leads to fear? To specify the appraisals that arouse various emotions, Klaus Scherer (Scherer, 1997; Scherer & Wallbott, 1994) asked people in 37 countries on 5 continents to describe in detail a time when they felt sadness, fear, anger, or disgust. He then asked them to rate each of the situations they had described along the dimensions of expectedness, unpleasantness, goal obstruction, unfairness, external cause, coping ability, and immorality. Cultures differed in a few subtle ways, but overall people throughout the world described remarkably similar appraisal patterns for each emotion. In the case of fear, people described situations that they rated as unexpected, unpleasant, externally caused, and uncontrollable (Scherer, 1997). Those features applied to sad situations also; the difference between sadness and fear was that fear situations included uncertainty (Mauro, Sato, & Tucker, 1992). You feel fear if something bad might happen, but hasn't happened yet. If something bad has already happened or is sure to happen, you feel sad. Sadness provokes little activity. (It's too late for any action to do much good.) Fear, however, leads either to an intense action, such as running away, or to remaining very still and hoping the threat doesn't find you.

Many of the situations calling for fear also overlap those calling for anger. If someone has harmed you or is about to harm you, you react with a mixture of anger and fear. A major difference between anger and fear is the sense of power. How would you react if someone insults you in a particularly nasty way for no good reason? First imagine that the offender is a child. Then imagine the same insult from someone bigger and stronger than you are, carrying a gun. The insult provokes anger when you are in a position of power, but fear when you are powerless (Keltner, Gruenfeld, & Anderson, 2003). In all countries for which we have data, men report more anger than women do, whereas women report more fear and sadness (Fischer, Mosquera, van Vianen, & Manstead, 2004). Why? A simple hypothesis is that anger is associated with power, and fear with lack of

power; in most places, men tend to have more power, more ability to back up their anger with physical force and/or economic control.

◻ Behaviors Associated With Fear

By definition, every emotion gives rise to a behavioral tendency. What do you do when you are afraid? You run away, right? Sometimes, but your response depends on the circumstances. Imagine you are home alone when you think you hear a noise in the house. Although you are frightened, you won't run . . . after all, where would you run *to*? Instead, you might cautiously walk *toward* the noise to investigate. Alternatively, you might stay where you are, highly attentive but "frozen with fear."

The Behavioral Inhibition System

How can the *lack* of movement be a behavioral tendency? Jeffrey Gray (1982) has argued that fear elicits two responses. One is the flight response (as in fight or flight), and the other is activation of a neurological system called the Behavioral Inhibition System (BIS). BIS activation increases arousal and attention while inhibiting action. Behavioral inhibition differs from flight in several regards, the obvious one being that flight increases activity whereas BIS decreases it. Also, tranquilizers weaken the BIS response (thereby increasing activity and possible approach to the threatening object), but they have little effect on the tendency to flee from an actual attack or pain (McNaughton & Corr, 2004). The BIS response does prepare the body for flight, however, by increasing heart rate and muscle tension, just in case. Think of it this way—if you are in the forest and you see a lion, plan A is to freeze and hope it neither sees nor hears you. If it does, though, plan B is to run, fast. BIS activation makes you freeze, while still getting your body ready to escape if necessary.

Chronic BIS activation may be responsible for "trait anxiety"—that is, a tendency to experience anxiety and nervous arousal easily and frequently

(Knyazev, Slobodskaya, & Wilson, 2002). People high in this trait tend to react strongly to possible threats and dangers. For example, they are likely to become nervous if a boyfriend or girlfriend shows even a slight interest in someone else (Meyer, Olivier, & Roth, 2005).

Effects on Attention and Information Processing

One of the most important aspects of fear may be that it focuses your attention on nearby threats. In one clever study, investigators asked young adults to focus on a central spot on a computer screen and then displayed slides like the one in Figure 5.1. On each trial, a participant was instructed to attend either to the top and bottom pictures, or to the left and right pictures, and indicate whether the pictures were the same or different. On each trial, one of the pairs showed houses and the other pair showed faces, which had either a fearful or a neutral expression. So, on a given trial the participant was supposed to attend to either the houses or the faces and ignore the other pair. People who reported on a questionnaire that they were feeling low fear and anxiety at the time had no trouble focusing their

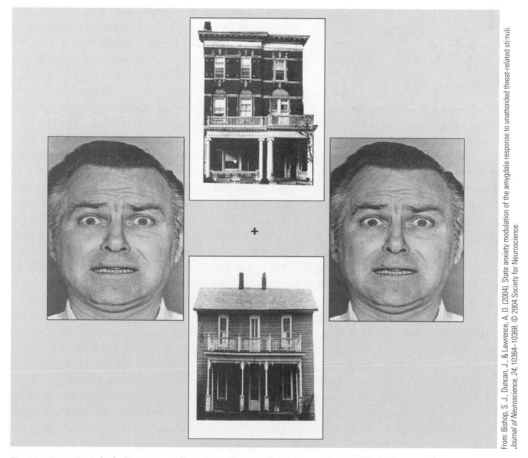

From: Bishop, S. J., Duncan, J., & Lawrence, A. D. (2004). State anxiety modulation of the amygdala response to unattended threat-related stimuli. *Journal of Neuroscience, 24,* 10364–10368. © 2004 Society for Neuroscience.

FIGURE 5.1 People feeling strong fear showed strong brain responses to frightened expressions, even when the instructions were to ignore the faces and attend to the houses. Source: Bishop et al. (2004).

attention according to instructions. However, those who reported strong fear and anxiety attended strongly to fearful faces even when instructed to focus on the houses. The increased attention was measured by fMRI brain scans of activity in the amygdala, a brain area strongly linked to emotional responses (Bishop, Duncan, & Lawrence, 2004).

For another example, consider the following task. Two words are displayed simultaneously on a screen for one second, one above the other, and then a dot is presented in either the up or down position:

The observer's task is to press a computer key to indicate whether the dot appeared in the upper or lower position. When one of the words is related to anxiety, such as *worry, blush,* or *nervous,* people who report strong fears respond faster if the dot was in the same location as the fear-related word than if it was in the other position (Egloff, Wilhelm, Neubauer, Mauss, & Gross, 2002). Presumably, the reason is that highly fearful people direct their attention toward the fear-related words, whereas less fearful people attend equally to the fear-related and neutral words. However, the difference among people shows up only as an average over many people and many trials. It is not a reliable way to measure the fearfulness of a given individual at a given moment (Egloff et al., 2002).

Fear influences responses even when a stimulus is so vague that we cannot identify it consciously. Imagine yourself in this study: You see pictures flashed on a screen for just 10 milliseconds, followed by a masking image. Under these conditions, no one can identify any of the pictures consciously. If asked, people insist they saw nothing or at most a blur. Some of the photos shown to you—let's say photos of snakes—are followed by shocks, whereas photos

of spiders would not be followed by shocks. (For half of the research participants, it would be the other way around.) This procedure continues for a while. All you know is that sometimes you get shocks and sometimes you don't. You certainly don't know the snake pictures predict shock because you don't consciously see any pictures at all.

However, part of your brain does note the difference between the spiders and the snakes, and you gradually develop a conditioned response. When they flash a spider picture, you sit there calmly, but when it is a snake picture, your heart rate and breathing rate suddenly increase (Katkin, Wiens, & Öhman, 2001). This response takes place even when you cannot consciously recognize the snakes. You might think of this as "unconscious" learning, although most psychological researchers prefer the term "implicit" learning to avoid the unwanted Freudian implications of "unconscious."

Would you notice your occasional surges of quicker heart rate and breathing? Some people do and some don't. The experimenters asked participants to report any changes they perceived in their heart rate and also to predict when they thought they were about to get a shock. All of them said they were just guessing about the shocks. (Remember, they didn't consciously see the snake or spider pictures.) The fascinating result was that the people who were the best at reporting sudden increases in their heart rate were also the best at "guessing" when they were about to get a shock (Katkin et al., 2001).

The implications of this study are still speculative but potentially important. One implication is that parts of your brain respond to fear-related information, even when the stimuli are so weak that you cannot identify them consciously. Remember that fear makes you more attentive to threats that you *can* identify consciously—it's as though the automatic fear prompts you to look around carefully for any sources of danger, so you can take more specific actions to avoid them.

Another implication pertains to what people call "gut feelings": Suppose you are very sensitive to your own internal changes. Not just in laboratory experiments but also in everyday life, you occasionally notice changes in your heart rate and breathing rate. Those changes may be for some irrelevant reason, but it is also possible that you were reacting to some danger that you detected "implicitly." If so, then you may not be consciously aware of a cause for worry, but your autonomic responses are telling you something. It's possible that people who are "sensitive" or "intuitive" are picking up on cues of danger that are real but so subtle even they are not consciously aware of them. (Of course, not everyone who claims to be sensitive or intuitive really is.)

On the other hand, this kind of sensitivity can backfire. People who are hypersensitive to their internal state, and look for a threat every time their heart rate goes up, can drive themselves into a spiral of constant and increasing anxiety. The result could be a clinical condition including pathological experience of fear.

◻ Measuring Fear and Anxiety

Most scientific advances depend on measuring something more accurately than it has been measured before. Emotion research that relies on self-reports can answer some questions but not others. For example, you can report whether you feel more fearful today than yesterday, but less accurately whether you feel more fearful than other people. (Most color-blind people, until they are tested for color vision, have no suspicion that other people see colors better. Presumably, people with extremely strong or weak emotions don't recognize their own distinctiveness, either.)

In the case of fear, however, researchers can use an array of behavioral and physiological measures to measure the emotion, as well as self-reports. Running away and shrieking usually indicate fear. In some cases, remaining tense but utterly motionless is another indicator. Frightened people sweat and tremble and their faces flush. People can lie about being frightened, but it's hard to fake sweating, trembling, and flushing and almost as hard to prevent these signs. Because researchers can use multiple measures to check their conclusions in different ways, we know more about fear than about other emotions.

Facial Expression of Fear

As with other animals faced with danger, humans can freeze, attack, or run away. People also react with facial expressions. We can divide expressions of fear roughly into two categories, without claiming that the categories are entirely distinct. One category is the familiar, overt facial expressions that we can inhibit or pretend, when we want to. Second, we also show brief expressions even when we do our best to inhibit them.

Let's start with the overt expressions. In their work with human emotional expression around the world, Paul Ekman and his colleagues found that every culture they studied recognized the same facial display of fear (see Figure 5.2). This display includes lifting the inner and outer eyebrows, pulling them together; widening the eyes; and contracting the muscles below the corners of the lips, pulling the skin of the lower cheeks down and to the side (Ekman et al., 1987). Typically, the mouth opens slightly. It is easy to see how this expression might

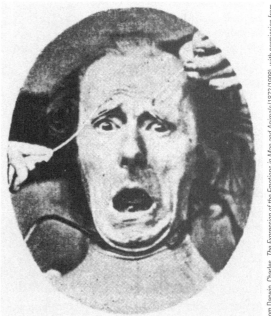

From Darwin, Charles, *The Expression of the Emotions in Man and Animals* (1872/1998), with permission from Oxford University Press.

FIGURE 5.2   A typical facial expression of fear.

have grown out of natural responses to a frightening situation. Lifting the eyebrows and widening the eyes enable the individual to see better and, therefore, to appraise the danger and any possible defenses to it. Opening the mouth may be a preparation for screaming a warning or yelling for help; it is also helpful for taking a deep breath.

This expression is similar to the face people make when they are surprised, and participants often confuse the two expressions when asked to look at a photo and guess how someone is feeling (Ekman et al., 1987). However, fear and surprise expressions differ in a couple of important ways. When people are surprised, their eyebrows go up and their eyes get wider, as in fear, but only the "fear face" includes the contraction of the eyebrows and lower cheek movement that Figure 5.2 shows.

In addition to the overt facial expressions, people also have very brief expressions even when they are trying to suppress or hide their emotions. These involuntary, momentary expressions that contradict the intended impression of calmness are called **micro expressions.** We usually overlook micro expressions, but with effort we can learn to notice them. Paul Ekman (2001) found that micro expressions are the most valid guide currently available to discerning people's hidden feelings, especially nervousness.

In addition to facial expressions caused by muscle movement, frightened people also have increased blood flow to the head, presumably to "wake up" the brain as much as possible so it can choose the best emergency response. Blood flow increases to the face as well. In extreme cases of fear, you may notice someone's face turning red. In milder cases, a researcher can use a thermal camera, which measures heat radiated from the face. Figure C.3 on the inside cover of this book shows one

example. One preliminary study indicated that most people's blood flow to the face increases when they are nervous about telling a lie (Pavlidis, Eberhardt, & Levine, 2002). Thermal photography has some interesting potential; researchers could even use this technique without telling someone (although ethically the researchers would be required to tell the person afterward). So, for example, interrogators might use thermal photography while interviewing suspected terrorists or even while observing people speaking in public places. The accuracy is probably not high enough for confident judgments, but the procedure could provide an approximate guide as to which lines of questioning seem to be making someone more nervous than others.

Facilitation of the Startle Reflex

As already mentioned, a wide variety of animals, including humans of all ages, show a built-in fear of sudden, loud noises. That reaction is called the **startle response** (Figure 5.3). The muscles tense rapidly, especially the neck muscles; the eyes close tightly;

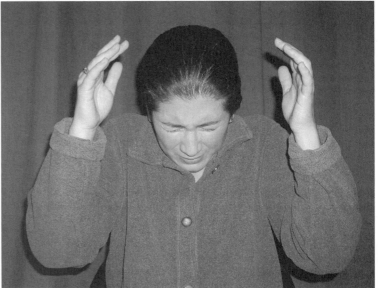

Michelle Shiota

FIGURE 5.3 A sudden, loud noise evokes a startle reflex, marked by tense neck muscles, closure of the eyes, and raising of the shoulders.

the shoulders shrug quickly, pulling close to the neck; and the arms may pull up toward the head. All these movements are apparently geared toward protecting the neck, which is an extremely vulnerable area. Information about the loud noise goes from your ears to a brain area called the *pons* in less than 10 milliseconds and from there to cells in the medulla and spinal cord that control your muscles (Figure 5.4). The full startle reflex occurs in less than one-fifth of a second (Yeomans & Frankland, 1996).

Although the startle response itself is automatic, input from the rest of the nervous system can modify its intensity, and researchers use that modification as a measure of fear or anxiety. When psychological researchers try to infer any internal process—such as some kind of motivation or emotion—they use an **operational definition**—that is, a definition in terms of a way to measure the process. For example, an operational definition of hunger might be "the length of time since the most recent meal." A possible operational definition of love is

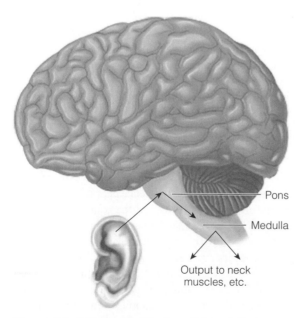

FIGURE 5.4   The startle reflex depends on a reflexive connection from the ears to the pons to cells in the medulla and spinal cord that control the muscles.

Pons

Medulla

Output to neck muscles, etc.

"the amount of time and effort you will spend with someone who needs your help." An operational definition does not tell us what something *is* at a theoretical level, or what it feels like, but just how to measure it. A good operational definition leads to useful results that other laboratories can replicate.

Facilitation of the startle reflex is a good operational definition of fear. For example, suppose a rat receives training in which a tone always precedes an electric shock, and later the rat hears that tone followed by a sudden loud noise. It then gives a larger-than-usual startle response. However, if it hears some other tone that was previously associated with pleasant events, then a loud noise after the "safe" stimulus produces a smaller-than-usual response (Schmid, Koch, & Schnitzler, 1995). Similarly, people show a stronger startle reflex when in the presence of unpleasant stimuli than in the presence of pleasant ones (Lang, Bradley, & Cuthbert, 2002). The similarity of startle behavior in humans and other animals allows us to study the brain mechanisms of fear in laboratory animals.

Fear-related information strongly modifies the startle reflex (Lang et al., 2002). Imagine, for example, that you are walking alone at night through a dangerous neighborhood, or perhaps a graveyard, when you suddenly hear a loud sound. Then imagine that you are sitting among friends in your own home in the middle of the afternoon when you hear the same loud sound. You will startle in both cases, but much more in the frightening place than in the familiar, safe place. Emotion researchers use this **startle potentiation** effect as a behavioral measure of fear.

Your startle is also modified by your personal history. Some people have endured truly terrible experiences—kidnapping, rape, war attacks, near-fatal automobile accidents, watching someone die, or discovering the dead body of a loved one. For months or years after an experience of this type, a sudden noise or an unexpected tap on the shoulder can yield a sharp startle and a shriek of horror. Severe and long-lasting cases are known as *post-traumatic stress disorder,* which we shall consider in more detail later. People with post-traumatic stress disorder show a stronger startle response than do other people (Morgan, Grillon, Southwick, Davis, & Charney, 1995, 1996; Shalev et al., 2000).

Other Behavioral Measures of Anxiety

One simple behavioral measure of fear is suppression of movement—the behavioral inhibition we discussed earlier. This method is especially popular for research with nonhuman animals. In the presence of a smell, sound, or other indicator of danger, most small animals simply "freeze" (Bolles, 1970). When rats are put into an unfamiliar enclosure, some explore freely while others stay motionless in a corner or against a wall; the failure to explore is generally interpreted as an indication of fear. (Motionlessness is a good defense for a small animal because predators readily detect anything that moves.) Researchers interested in human emotions seldom use this measure, although researchers interested in childhood temperament do use it, and emotions are closely related to temperaments. Children with an "inhibited" temperament tend to be fearful and shy, remaining in the background instead of exploring their environment (Kagan, Reznick, & Snidman, 1988). Even when they reach adulthood, they show signs of more easily aroused fears compared to other people (Schwartz, Wright, Shin, Kagan, & Rauch, 2003). In short, shyness is closely related to inactivity in a threatening environment, and both are closely related to fear.

Another behavioral measurement relies on our knowledge that the more frightened a person is, the more threatening information will capture his or her attention. In this procedure, people read a variety of short passages, some of them containing threatening content, such as, "The child went running after his new ball, but while he was crossing the road, a van suddenly appeared without brakes. The van swerved around the child instantly." While people are reading, a device monitors their eye movements. On the average, people with high fear levels have more regressive (backward) eye movements

than others do on the threatening sentences. That is, they are more likely than others are to stop, go back, and reread the fear-provoking sentences (Calvo & Avero, 2002). Presumably, the threatening content heightens their tension and makes them want to double-check their understanding. Similarly, people tend to focus more on emotional pictures than neutral pictures, especially in the first several seconds of their presentation (Calvo & Avero, 2005).

Another method takes advantage of the fact that the English language includes many pairs of words with the same sound, but different spellings and meanings. Imagine yourself in this experiment: On each trial, you see a word on a computer screen while hearing a different word, and your task is to write the word you heard, ignoring—so far as you can—the word you see. In each case, the sound you hear could be either of two words, and you are to write the one you think of first. Although you don't need to do anything about the word on the screen, it suggests a context that might influence your interpretation of what you hear. For example, you might see the word *agony* while hearing a word that could be either "pane" or "pain." Or you might see *fruit* while hearing a word that could be either "bury" or "berry." If you were randomly assigned to the "high anxiety" condition, you have a video camera placed right in front of your face, reportedly to record your facial expressions, but actually as a means of making you nervous. Are you more likely to report anxiety words such as "pain" or neutral words such as "pane"?

The results of one study were that a camera right in front of the face did influence people's perceptions of the ambiguous words, but the results were somewhat complicated (Blanchette & Richards, 2003). You might expect that people in the high-anxiety condition would simply report more fear-related words than others would. Instead, they became more dependent on the context. If the word on the screen suggested distress (e.g., *agony*), then people in the high-anxiety condition were more likely to report the fear-related meaning ("pain" instead of "pane"). However, if they saw an unemotional word (e.g., *fruit*), they were more likely than others to report hearing the emotionally neutral word ("berry" instead of "bury"). These results suggest the possibility of using people's interpretation of ambiguous words as a subtle, implicit measurement of fear or anxiety. They also tell us something of theoretical interest: Fear doesn't simply bias someone toward perceiving everything as dangerous. Rather, it heightens people's attention to the context, so that they increase their response to whatever cues are present, including both emotional and unemotional cues.

▢ The Biology of Fear and Anxiety

Researchers also measure emotions by physiological measures such as heart rate and brain activity. However, these methods provide information about overall emotional arousal and not specifically the difference between fear and any other emotion. The similarity of startle behavior in humans and other animals allows us to study emotion-related neurology in lab mammals; as a result, we know more about the biology of fear and anxiety than any other emotion and can address more complex questions.

The Autonomic Nervous System and "Fight or Flight" Response

As discussed in Chapter 1, strong emotional arousal, such as that from fear or anger, activates the sympathetic nervous system, which readies the body's organs for a brief, vigorous burst of fight-or-flight activity—increased heart rate; rapid and irregular breathing; increased sweating (as indicated by increased electrical conductance of the skin); louder, faster, and higher-pitched speech; sometimes increased blinking of the eyes; and so forth. Two points are worth stressing: (1) Many nonemotional factors also influence sympathetic activity. For example, when you run up a flight of stairs you will also breathe faster, your heart rate will increase, and

you will start to sweat. These responses are not specific to emotion. (2) Even if the person is feeling an emotion, the physiological response may not reliably indicate which emotion someone is feeling. Rapid breathing, high heart rate, and sweating could indicate fear, but they could also indicate anger or other emotional states.

Researchers have, however, identified a pattern of autonomic nervous system activity that seems more characteristic of people experiencing a "threat" than of people experiencing "challenges" over which they believe they have some control (Tomaka, Blascovich, Kibler, & Ernst, 1997). In one study of how situational appraisals affect cardiovascular physiology, researchers told participants they would have to spend four minutes in a "serial subtraction" task: The person would start with a high number, such as 1,528, and then subtract a small number like 7 over and over again (1,521, 1,514, 1,507, . .), aloud and as fast as possible. Right after describing the task, researchers either emphasized how important it was to do the task well, and said that participants' speed and accuracy would be measured, or they suggested that participants just do their best and "think of the task as a challenge to be met and overcome." Participants receiving the first set of instructions tended to be more threatened by the task—they rated the task as highly threatening and their ability to cope with it relatively low. By contrast, participants hearing the second set of instructions were more likely to interpret the task as a challenge—their ratings of their own ability to cope outweighed their rating of the task as threatening.

How did the physiological responses of participants in the "challenge" versus "threat" conditions differ? The researchers used specific measures of cardiovascular activity to answer this question. Heart rate increased in both the challenge and threat groups, but it increased more for the challenge group. Among participants given the "challenge" instructions, the heart filled with blood for a longer period of time before pumping ("pre-ejection period"), and pumped more blood when it did contract ("cardiac output") than was true for participants given the "threat" instructions. Also, total peripheral resistance (a ratio of blood pressure to cardiac output, which indicates how much pressure is being placed on the blood vessels throughout the body) increased slightly in threat participants and decreased in challenge participants. In short, the challenge participants mobilized their cardiovascular system in the way that is most efficient in delivering more blood throughout the body—the heart pumped faster, pumped more blood per heartbeat, and blood met less resistance from vessels as it moved through the body. Although threat participants' hearts also beat faster, each beat delivered less blood to the body than was true for challenge participants.

This finding has been replicated frequently—it is what we call a "robust" effect. However, we should consider three questions. First, is "threat" the same as fear? Certainly the pattern of appraisals reported by participants in the threat condition correspond to the ones we described at the beginning of the chapter—an unpleasant event that has not happened yet, but is about to, and over which one feels little or no control. But it seems unfair to assume people in the threat condition felt fear, without asking them or observing facial expressions or using some additional measure of fear.

Second, is the cardiovascular response to threat specific to that situation, or might angry people show the same response? When people are angry, they tend to think they have more control over the situation, suggesting that they should show a "challenge" cardiovascular profile instead. If this were the case, it would suggest a striking difference between the biology of fear and the biology of anger. In these studies, however, the "challenge" participants felt good, not angry. A study looking at challenge and threat responses in experimentally elicited anger and fear might answer this question.

Third, what function, if any, does the cardiovascular "threat" response serve? The researchers who performed these studies have described the threat response as an inadequate or faulty attempt to mo-bilize physical resources. Is it actually an ineffective attempt to deliver fuel to the body, or does it produce benefits we have not yet identified?

Application: Anxiety and Lie Detection

Although exercise, pain, and other factors influence sympathetic nervous system arousal, a sudden increase in arousal may suggest strong emotions, if we have no reason to attribute the changes to something else. The **polygraph,** literally a "many-measures" test, popularly known as the lie-detector test, is based on the assumption that people get nervous when they lie and, therefore, show increased heart rate and blood pressure, rapid and irregular breathing patterns, increased skin conductance, or increases in other sympathetic nervous system activities, as Figure 5.5 illustrates.

Is that assumption correct? Well, partly but not entirely. In the "control-question" version of the polygraph test, the examiner asks *relevant questions* such as "Did you steal $500 from the convenience store last night?" and *control questions* such as "Have you ever taken anything that was not yours?" The underlying assumption is that someone who did not rob the convenience store will be at least as nervous about saying no to the control question as they are about saying no to the relevant question. However, if you know you have been strapped into a polygraph machine because the police are investigating a robbery at a convenience store, you could still become more nervous about the relevant question, even if you are innocent. On the other hand, a habitual liar might not be nervous about either question and might show the polygraph profile of an innocent person.

Figure 5.6 shows hypothetical results for two groups of people, some innocent and some guilty. Note that some of the innocent people appear more nervous when telling the truth than some of the guilty ones do while lying. The amount of overlap between the two groups depends on the people involved, the wording of the question, and so forth.

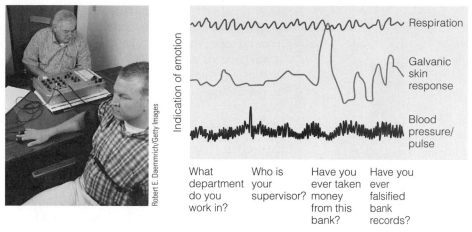

FIGURE 5.5 A polygraph examiner compares answers to control questions and relevant questions. Greater nervousness on relevant questions is taken as evidence of lying. The galvanic skin response is a measure of slight sweating, which in turn indicates sympathetic nervous system arousal.

The examiner in effect sets a cutoff score, such that anyone who shows more than a certain amount of nervousness is considered to be lying. Note that wherever you set that cutoff, you will call some liars innocent ("misses") and call some honest people liars ("false alarms"). The more you reduce one kind of error, the more you increase the other.

You may be surprised to learn how few good studies have been done on the accuracy of polygraph tests. Research has not adequately tested how often the test correctly identifies liars, how often it misiden-

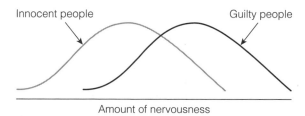

FIGURE 5.6 On a polygraph test, some innocent people are more nervous than some guilty people. The exact amount of overlap varies.

tifies innocent people as lying, or what advantages and disadvantages it might have compared to other possible methods (Fiedler, Schmid, & Stahl, 2002; Iacono & Patrick, 1999). What would seem an obvious design is to examine results for people known to be guilty or innocent of serious crimes. However, we seldom know for sure who is guilty. An alternative is to examine people in laboratory conditions, some of whom have been instructed to tell the truth and others to lie. In that case, people have little at stake, so they may not be as nervous about their lies as accused suspects would be in a serious situation.

One of the few good studies of lie detection dealt with 50 criminal cases in which two suspects in a crime were given polygraph tests and one of them later confessed (Kleinmuntz & Szucko, 1984). That is, at the time of the interrogation, the examiners presumably treated every suspect about equally, and later it was possible to determine how accurately they categorized each suspect. Figure 5.7 shows the results. The examiners correctly identified 76 percent of the guilty people as lying, but also identified 37 percent of the innocent suspects as lying.

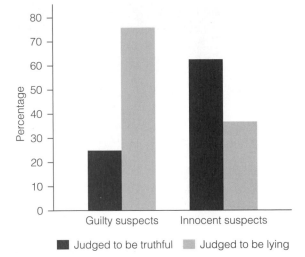

FIGURE 5.7   Results from one study of polygraph accuracy. Note how many innocent suspects were judged to be lying. (Based on data of Kleinmuntz & Szucko, 1984.)

In other words, polygraph results are neither highly accurate nor utterly worthless. They are more accurate than most people's unaided judgments. Most people greatly overestimate their ability to judge who is lying (Ekman & O'Sullivan, 1991; Ekman, O'Sullivan, & Frank, 1999; Etcoff, Ekman, Magee, & Frank, 2000; Wiseman, 1995). However, most authorities agree that polygraphs are not accurate enough for making important decisions. Therefore, American and European courts almost never permit polygraph results to be entered as evidence (Fiedler et al., 2002; Saxe & Ben-Shakhar, 1999). In the United States, it is illegal for an employer to ask employees or job applicants to take a polygraph test, except under special circumstances (Camara, 1988).

Hand and body gestures can also reveal people's fear, nervousness, or other emotions. Each culture has certain gestures, called **emblems,** with specific meanings. For example, in the United States and most of Europe, head nodding means *yes* and head shaking means *no*. A fist or an upraised middle finger indicates anger or contempt, and a shrug of the shoulders means, "I don't know. I'm helpless. What

does it matter?" When people intend to make these gestures, they display them openly. In addition, people who are concealing an emotion sometimes make a brief, partial emblem. Paul Ekman (2001) found that many people make a brief, partial shrug when they are lying.

The Amygdala and Fear in Laboratory Animals

Emotions activate not only the autonomic nervous system but several brain areas as well. Much of the research on this point begins with laboratory animals and the brain areas responsible for modifying their startle reflex.

In order for one's perception of danger or safety to modify the startle response, the **amygdala** ("uh-MIG-duh-luh"), an area within the brain's temporal lobe (Figure 5.8), has to process the information. (The amygdala is shaped somewhat like an almond, if you use a little imagination, and *amygdala* is the Greek word for almond.) As with nearly all brain areas, the amygdala is a bilateral structure; that is, each hemisphere contains an amygdala. The amygdala receives input representing vision, hearing, other senses, and pain, so it is in a position to associate various stimuli with dangerous outcomes that follow them (Uwano, Nishijo, Ono, & Tamura, 1995). It sends information to the pons and other areas controlling the startle reflex (Fendt, Koch, & Schnitzler, 1996), as well as to the prefrontal cortex (Garcia, Vouimba, Baudry, & Thompson, 1999) and a variety of other brain areas (Gifkins, Greba, & Kokkinidis, 2002).

Consider the effect described earlier, where rats show a facilitated startle after hearing a tone associated with electric shock and a dampened startle after hearing a tone predicting a safe period. If an animal has damage to the amygdala, especially damage to the amygdala on both sides, the startle response is nearly constant at all times, no greater after a shock signal than after a safety signal (Heldt, Sundin, Willott, & Falls, 2000; Hitchcock & Davis, 1991; Phillips & LeDoux, 1992).

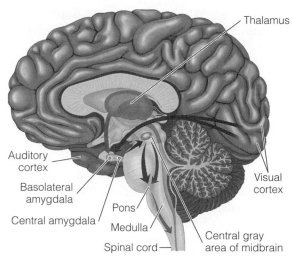

Auditory cortex

Basolateral amygdala

Central amygdala

Pons

Medulla

Spinal cord

Thalamus

Visual cortex

Central gray area of midbrain

FIGURE 5.8 Although the startle response itself depends just on a reflexive connection through the pons, it can be facilitated or diminished by input from the amygdala. The amygdala processes the emotional content of information, such as "dangerous" or "safe."

In addition, the amygdala seems to play a role in learning new fears. For example, after chemical injections have temporarily disabled rats' amygdalas, they fail to learn signs of danger in classical conditioning studies. Rats with amygdala damage, for example, do not learn that a particular tone signals an electric shock a few seconds later. Even after many repetitions of the tone-shock pattern, these rats do not tense up as normal rats would (Schafe et al., 2000). Rats with damage to the amygdala also lose the fears they had learned from this kind of training before the brain damage (Gale et al., 2004). One study reported greater deficits after damage to the right amygdala than the left amygdala (Baker & Kim, 2004); damage to both produces a still stronger effect.

Normal rats and mice stop whatever they are doing if they smell a cat. Frequently they stand on their hind legs to look around and sniff. (They can't run away until they know which way to run.) After a tranquilizer has decreased activity in the amygdala, rats become almost indifferent to a cat's odor (McGregor, Hargreaves, Apfelbach, & Hunt, 2004).

After destruction of the amygdala, some rats and mice fearlessly approach a cat (Berdoy, Webster, & Macdonald, 2000).

Monkeys with damage to the amygdala show similar behavior patterns. In the 1930s, two researchers who were studying monkeys with brain damage identified what came to be known as the **Klüver-Bucy Syndrome (KBS)**, a pattern of emotional changes accompanying removal of the anterior temporal lobe (including the amygdala) on each side of the brain. Animals with such damage seem not to recognize the emotional implications of objects. For example, they approach snakes, try to pick up lighted matches, and put feces into their mouths (Klüver & Bucy, 1939). Monkeys with damage to the amygdala also fearlessly approach more aggressive monkeys and unfamiliar humans (Kalin, Shelton, & Davidson, 2004). In a sense, they become "friendlier" (Emery et al., 2001). Think about it: Why do you sometimes hesitate to approach someone you don't know? Isn't it because you are afraid of being rejected? A monkey (or human) with no fear has no hesitation about approaching others. Unfortunately, the monkeys that fearlessly approach the large, aggressive monkeys sometimes get injured (Rosvold, Mirsky, & Pribram, 1954). (A certain degree of shyness isn't always a bad idea.)

These results apparently suggested that the amygdala might be responsible for feeling fear. In the strongest form of this hypothesis, amygdala activity *is* fear, and any person or animal lacking an amygdala has no fear. However, a rat that approaches a cat, or a monkey that approaches a snake, might not have lost its capacity for fear. Perhaps it simply fails to perceive the danger; it has trouble interpreting the emotional aspects of the situation.

The Amygdala and People's Responses to Faces

Studies of laboratory animals are helpful for many questions, but now we get to some subtler issues that are difficult to address with rats and monkeys. In fact, they are difficult even with humans. Is the amygdala responsive to the feeling aspect, the cognitive aspect, or some other aspect of emotions? Is it specialized for fear or for all emotions?

One approach has been to show people pictures likely to arouse their emotions and then examine their amygdala activity using fMRI or similar procedures. The amygdala becomes active when people see or hear signals of danger (Phelps et al., 2001) or look at faces with emotional expressions (Rotshtein, Malach, Hadar, Graif, & Hendler, 2001), especially expressions of fear. The response is strongest to a new photo and weakens after repeated presentations (Breiter et al., 1996; Büchel, Morris, Dolan, & Friston, 1998). You could note the same tendency even without using a brain scan: The more times you look at the same unpleasant photo, the less distressing it becomes.

The amygdala also responds strongly to faces expressing sadness (Wang, McCarthy, Song, & LaBar, 2005), disgust, and anger. People with **social phobia** (a fear of social interactions) show a particularly strong amygdala response to the sight of an angry or contemptuous face (Stein, Goldin, Sareen, Zorrilla, & Brown, 2002). In one fascinating study, seeing an angry expression facing the viewer produced a stronger amygdala response, and greater self-reports of emotion, than seeing an angry face looking to the side (Sato, Yoshikawa, Kochiyama, & Matsumura, 2004). As reported in Chapter 2, people recognize an angry expression about equally well in either direction, but seeing it facing you tends to be more upsetting.

The amygdala's response to happy expressions has been more controversial. Some studies have found a clear response to happy faces, whereas others have not. Part of the problem is that most studies report the average for a small group of people, and individuals differ rather widely on this task, so a group with a few highly reactive people can differ substantially from another group. (Researchers call this problem "sampling error.") One study found a strong amygdala response to happy faces only in viewers who had an extraverted personality—that is, a strong tendency to enjoy meeting new people

(Canli, Sivers, Whitfield, Gotlib, & Gabrieli, 2002). Presumably these people are more excited than others are by the sight of a stranger's smiling face.

Furthermore, the usual procedure is to measure responses to several kinds of faces, including neutral faces, and report a response to happy faces only if it exceeds the response to neutral faces. Some viewers, especially those with elevated anxiety levels, have strong emotional responses to the sight of a neutral face (Somerville, Kim, Johnstone, Alexander, & Whalen, 2004). They evidently react to the ambiguous, neutral face as being rather ominous. In short, the amygdala probably does respond to happy faces, although not very strongly as a rule. What conclusion should we draw from the fact that the amygdala seems to respond more strongly to fearful faces than to faces with other expressions? One possibility is that the amygdala is specialized for attending to fear. Another possibility is that fear responses tend to be stronger and quicker than other emotional reactions, so a brain area responsive to emotion in general will show an especially strong reaction to fear.

The amygdala responds to emotional stimuli even when someone cannot identify them consciously. For example, if a frightened face is flashed on a screen very briefly and followed by an interfering stimulus, a viewer does not report seeing a face at all, but the picture nevertheless activates the amygdala, which evokes changes in sweating and other autonomic responses (Kubota et al., 2000; Vuilleumier, Armony, Driver, & Dolan, 2001). The same picture under the same circumstances evokes no autonomic responses from someone with amygdala damage (Gläscher & Adolphs, 2003).

In another type of experiment, researchers displayed items like those in Figure C.4 for a half second each (see the inside cover of this book). Note that each picture has a face in one color superimposed on a house in a different color. People wore glasses with a red filter over one eye and a green filter over the other. Under these conditions people see the house in one eye and the face in the other, but when the brain gets this kind of conflict, it attends to just one eye or the other. With prolonged exposure, it switches back and forth between the two eyes, but with a half-second exposure, almost any viewer reports just one image. Some people nearly always report the green image whereas others almost always report the red image. (The difference presumably relates to how many medium-wavelength and long-wavelength cones they have in the retina.) The key finding is that even when people were conscious of only the house, the amygdala responded to the emotion of the face, with an especially big response to a fearful face (M. A. Williams, Morris, McGlone, Abbott, & Mattingley, 2004). Evidently the cerebral cortex (which does most conscious processing) attends to one stimulus or the other, but the amygdala gets enough visual input to make an independent assessment of its emotional content.

Effects of Damage to the Human Amygdala

People with damage to the amygdala are rare but important to researchers. Many stroke patients have damage to the amygdala and surrounding areas in at least one hemisphere, but virtually never is stroke damage limited to just the amygdala. In a rare condition called Urbach-Wiethe disease, calcium accumulates in the amygdala and damages it, generally without much damage to surrounding tissues. Much of our understanding of the human amygdala depends on these few patients.

People with amygdala damage have some of the same symptoms as monkeys with Klüver-Bucy syndrome described earlier, such as putting inedible or disgusting substances into their mouth. Much like the monkeys that fearlessly approached larger, more aggressive monkeys, people with amygdala damage, when they need help on the street, approach strangers virtually at random, instead of trying to choose someone who looks friendly or trustworthy. In fact, if asked to look at faces and rate which ones look friendliest or most trustworthy, they rate all faces as almost equal (Adolphs, Tranel, & Damasio, 1998).

Ordinarily, nearly everyone pays more attention to emotionally charged words than to other words. If you watched a screen that displayed many words each for less than a tenth of a second under conditions of distraction, you would be more likely to notice a word like *bitch* than one like *birch*. People with amygdala damage report the emotionally charged words and the everyday words about equally (Anderson & Phelps, 2001). If you heard a story that included some boring details plus a gruesome description of a child's injury, you would remember the emotionally upsetting part far more than the rest. People with amygdala damage do not (LaBar & Phelps, 1998). For most people, looking at a gruesome photo temporarily increases the startle response to a loud noise, but people with damage in and around the amygdala fail to show this enhancement of startle (Funayama, Grillon, Davis, & Phelps, 2001). In short, people with amygdala damage barely respond to events that arouse strong emotions for other people.

People with amygdala damage have trouble naming the expression in a face or even determining whether two faces are expressing the same or different emotions (Boucsein, Weniger, Mursch, Steinhoff, & Irle, 2001). One woman with Urbach-Wiethe disease was asked to examine photos and rate the amount of emotional expression in each. On the faces showing fear, anger, or surprise, she gave lower ratings than anyone with an intact brain did. When asked to draw faces showing various expressions, she drew good representations of happy, sad, surprised, disgusted, and angry faces, but then said she didn't know what a frightened face looked like (Adolphs, Tranel, Damasio, & Damasio, 1995). Several studies reported that people with amygdala damage are particularly impaired at recognizing facial expressions of fear (Adolphs, Tranel, Damasio, & Damasio, 1994; Hayman, Rexer, Pavol, Strite, & Meyers, 1998; Lilly et al., 1983).

But then the interesting question arose of why. One simple explanation could be that these patients just don't feel fear themselves and, therefore, don't understand it in others. However, they report that

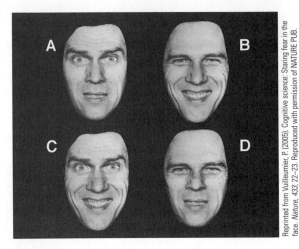

Reprinted from Vuilleumier, P. (2005). Cognitive science: Staring fear in the face. *Nature, 433,* 22–23. Reproduced with permission of NATURE PUB. GROUP via Copyright Clearance Center.

FIGURE 5.9   Parts A and B show normal expressions of fear and happiness. Parts C and D combine the eyes of one expression with the mouth of the other. Source: Vuilleumier (2005).

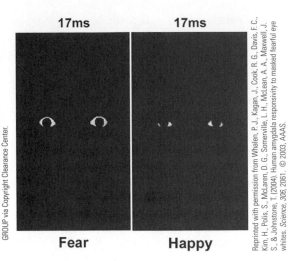

Reprinted with permission from Whalen, P. J., Kagan, J., Cook, R. G., Davis, F. C., Kim, H., Polis, S., McLaren, D. G., Somerville, L. H., McLean, A. A., Maxwell, J. S. & Johnstone, T. (2004). Human amygdala responsivity to masked fearful eye whites. *Science, 306,* 2061. © 2003, AAAS.

FIGURE 5.10   The eye whites alone are enough to identify fear (left), although not to identify happiness (right). Source: Whalen et al. (2004).

they continue to feel fear and other emotions more or less normally in their everyday lives (A. K. Anderson & Phelps, 2002). We can question whether they feel it as strongly, as quickly, or under all the same circumstances as other people, but they do not seem to be totally lacking in fear. Researchers found a different explanation for why people with amygdala damage have trouble recognizing facial expressions of fear: When they look at a face, they focus almost entirely on the nose and mouth, unlike normal people, who spend much of their time looking at the eyes (Adolphs et al., 2005). The reason for that attentional focus is unknown, but the consequences are enormous for recognizing fear. More than any other emotion, fear is expressed with the eyes. Frightened eyes with a neutral mouth still look frightened. A slightly open mouth adds a little to the impression of fear, but it isn't necessary, provided that the eyes look frightened (Morris, deBonis, & Dolan, 2002). Even a combination of frightened eyes and a happy smile gives some impression of fear. Examine Figure 5.9 (Vuilleumier, 2005). Part A shows an expression of fear; part B shows happiness. In part D, with the eyes of happiness and the mouth

of fear, most people perceive little emotion. However, contrast that reaction to part C, which shows fear in the eyes and happiness in the mouth. If you focus on the eyes, you perceive fear; if you focus on the mouth, you perceive happiness. Overall, fear is probably the dominant impression.

As another illustration of the importance of the eyes for fear expressions, examine Figure 5.10. Here the entire face has been removed except for the whites of the eyes. Although the face on the right (happy) is not identifiable with any confidence, most people react to the one on the left as indicating fear (Whalen et al., 2004).

Researchers found that if they instructed a patient with amygdala damage to focus on the eyes, she could indeed identify the expression of fear (Adolphs et al., 2005). This result contradicts the idea that the amygdala is necessary for fear. Most researchers now favor the idea that the amygdala's main contribution is for quick processing of information that leads to emotions (Whalen, 1998). When people with amygdala damage fail to show strong emotions, perhaps it is because they don't yet understand the situation well enough to feel the emotion (Baxter & Murray, 2002). They can eventually process the information, relying on prefrontal areas of the cortex (Lacroix, Spinelli, Heidbreder, & Feldon, 2000; Pezze, Bast, & Feldon, 2003), so the deficit shows up in some situations and tests, but not others.

Neurochemistry: Tranquilizers and Their Mechanisms

One way to learn about the neurochemistry of emotion is to find out what chemicals turn that emotion "off." People have known since prehistoric times that alcohol, for example, can help people relax. More recently, researchers have found many other drugs that decrease anxiety. Drugs that relieve anxiety are known as **tranquilizers**. The most common ones fall into a biochemical class known as the *benzodiazepines* (BEN-zo-di-AZ-uh-peens). Examples include diazepam (trademark Valium), chlordiazepoxide (Librium), and alprazolam (Xanax). These drugs can be given as injections but are more commonly taken as pills. Their effects last for hours, and the duration varies from one drug to another.

Tranquilizers act by facilitating the effectiveness of a neurotransmitter known as GABA (gamma-aninobutyric acid). GABA is the main inhibitory neurotransmitter throughout the nervous system, including the amygdala. Therefore, tranquilizers suppress activity in the amygdala, decreasing the response to threatening or otherwise emotional stimuli. However, they also suppress activity in much of the rest of the brain, producing drowsiness and memory impairment. Tranquilizers temporarily produce some of the same emotional effects that amygdala damage produces permanently. For example, people on tranquilizers have trouble identifying other people's facial expressions of emotion, such as anger or fear (Zangara, Blair, & Curran, 2002). It's important to recognize, therefore, that GABA is not exclusively an "anti-fear" neurotransmitter—it is the main inhibitory neurotransmitter throughout the brain, for a huge variety of functions.

Other chemicals modify amygdala activity also. The neurotransmitter cholecystokinin (CCK) has excitatory effects on the amygdala, acting about the opposite of GABA (Becker et al., 2001; Frankland, Josselyn, Bradwejn, Vaccarino, & Yeomans, 1997; Strzelczuk & Romaniuk, 1996). Cortisol and other stress-related hormones increase the responsiveness of the amygdala, whereas alcohol decreases it (Nie et al., 2004). In that regard, alcohol resembles tranquilizers, decreasing anxiety and, therefore, reducing the social inhibitions that deter people from approaching strangers. Decreased fear may also be the reason why people are more likely to become violent after consuming alcohol. As we have seen, however, amygdala activation is not the same thing as fear, so these chemicals are probably not fear-specific either.

▢ What We Learn From Anxiety Disorders

The study of emotions can shed light on many psychological disorders. Conversely, studies of psychological disorders can add to our understanding of emotions. In learning to treat disorders of the emotions, we often learn a great deal about the biological, cognitive, and social aspects of normal emotion. Some people are simply more prone than others to strong fears. For example, children who show excessive anxieties are more likely than others to become adults with anxiety disorders (Otto et al., 2001). The question is, why? Let's quickly survey the common anxiety disorders and then consider the research on their causes.

Types of Anxiety Disorders

Anxiety disorders are defined in terms of "excessive" fear and avoidance. What is the "right" amount? The answer, of course, is, "It depends." Do you live in a friendly, safe neighborhood or a war-torn country? If you have had some horrible experiences, it makes sense to increase your level of fear and caution; your world really *is* a dangerous place (Rosen & Schulkin, 2004). So we need to define "excessive" fear in terms of what seems appropriate under someone's circumstances.

The *Diagnostic and Statistical Manual of Mental Disorders*, 4th edition (*DSM-IV*), of the American Psychiatric Association (1994) lists more than a dozen psychological disorders in which the main symptom is excessive fear or anxiety. The simplest example, **generalized anxiety disorder (GAD),** is characterized by almost constant nervousness and a wide range of worries. People with GAD worry intensely about their health, finances, job, and even minor matters such as household chores or car repairs. Sometimes they are not even sure what they are worried about. Their worries make them irritable, restless, and fatigued, and consequently they have trouble doing their jobs and getting along with their families. About 5 percent of all people qualify for a diagnosis of generalized anxiety disorder at some point in life (Wittchen, Zhao, Kessler, & Eaton, 1994). However, because anxiety is a symptom of many other disorders, few people have GAD alone; most people with GAD qualify for one or more additional diagnoses (Bruce, Machan, Dyck, & Keller, 2001).

Panic disorder is characterized by repeated attacks of physical panic, with sharply increased heart rate, rapid breathing, noticeable sweating, trembling, and chest pains. About 1 to 3 percent of people experience panic disorder at some time during their lives, with greater frequency in women than men (Weissman et al., 1997). People having a panic attack often fear they are having a heart attack. Most panic attacks last only a few minutes, although some last longer.

Not everyone who has a panic attack develops panic disorder. Some people have one or more panic attacks, shrug them off, and go on with life (K. A. Wilson & Hayward, 2005). Ironically, the problem escalates when people worry too much about their panic attacks. Their fear of fear itself, or of anxiety-provoking situations, increases their anxiety level and thereby increases the probability and severity of future panic attacks (McNally, 2002). After having a few panic attacks, people begin to associate them with the events and circumstances that accompanied them. Later, similar circumstances evoke new panic attacks

as a conditioned response (Bouton, Mineka, & Barlow, 2001). Also, whenever they begin to notice rapid breathing or other signs of arousal, people with panic disorder tend to interpret them as the start of a panic attack; the resulting anxiety then triggers an actual panic attack (Battaglia, Bertella, Ogliari, Bellodi, & Smeraldi, 2001; Gorman et al., 2001).

Many people with panic disorder also develop a condition called *agoraphobia*. Because agoraphobia is uncommon in people without panic disorder (Wittchen, Reed, & Kessler, 1998), we can regard it as linked to panic disorder. The term **agoraphobia,** based on the Greek words *agora* (marketplace), and *phobia* (fear), literally means excessive fear of open, public places. However, it now refers to an excessive fear of situations that would be difficult to escape in the event of a panic attack. Those situations include open, public places, as well as tunnels, buses, and so forth. Agoraphobia develops because people with panic disorder fear that they could be embarrassed by a panic attack in public. It once was common to give all phobias Greek names, such as acrophobia (fear of heights), claustrophobia (fear of confinement), triskaidekaphobia (fear of the number 13), and ophidiophobia (fear of snakes). Translating words into Greek accomplished little, however, except providing more terms to memorize. Some of these terms are still in common use, but most are not.

Phobia is an extreme fear that interferes with everyday life. It should not be defined as an unrealistic fear. For example, many people are afraid to fly in an airplane, which is a demonstrably unrealistic fear. The statistics say that airplane travel is so much safer than automobile travel that, depending on how close you live to the nearest airport, you may be more likely to die in an automobile accident on the way to the airport than you are to die in the airplane itself (Sivak & Flannagan, 2003). However, an unrealistic fear of airplanes usually does not qualify as a phobia, simply because it does not interfere with your everyday life, unless your life requires frequent long-distance travel. On the other hand, fear of snakes and spiders is realistic, but when this fear is so intense that it interferes with daily life, it qualifies as a phobia. Phobias

TABLE 5.1   Common objects of phobias
(Cox et al., 2003)

Open, public places (*agoraphobia*)
Public speaking
Heights (including elevators, being on a high floor of a building)
Not being on solid ground (being in the air or on the water)
Being with or being observed by strangers (*social phobia*)
Being alone
Threats or reminders of threats (snakes, spiders, other animals, blood, injections, storms, etc.)

usually begin in the teens or young adulthood and are more common among women than men (Burke, Burke, Regier, & Rae, 1990).

Whereas generalized anxiety disorder is almost constant fear and panic disorder is extreme anxiety at largely unpredictable times and places, a **specific phobia** (sometimes also known as a *simple phobia*) is characterized by excessive fear of a particular object or situation. Table 5.1 lists some common objects of phobias (Cox, McWilliams, Clara, & Stein, 2003). The presence of that object or situation can provoke extreme fear, as can a film depiction (Sarlo, Palomba, Angrilli, & Stegagno, 2002) and sometimes even a thought about the object.

One of the key characteristics of phobia is the ability of the feared object to dominate attention. Recall the research cited earlier in this chapter that for anyone, fear increases attention to fear-related objects. That tendency is simply magnified in people with a phobia. In one study, people were asked to try to find the one picture of a mushroom among many pictures of flowers or to find the one mushroom among many pictures of flowers and one picture of a spider. People with a phobia of spiders had no trouble finding the mushroom in the case without a spider, but they had much trouble, relative to other people, if one spider picture was present (Miltner, Krieschel, Hecht, Trippe, & Weiss, 2004). Evidently the spider picture grabbed their attention strongly.

Finally, in **post-traumatic stress disorder (PTSD)**, someone who has experienced a traumatic event has frequent distressing recollections (flashbacks) and nightmares about the traumatic event, avoidance of reminders of it, and an exaggerated startle reflex. PTSD victims also report outbursts of anger, guilt, and sadness. PTSD lasts for months and sometimes years (Pitman, van der Kolk, Orr, & Greenberg, 1990).

The various anxiety disorders have much in common, but they also differ in important ways. In one study, researchers recorded people's sympathetic nervous system responses and frowning expressions when they heard brief reminders of their fears. People with specific phobias showed the strongest responses. For example, if someone is deathly afraid of snakes, even the slightest reminder of snakes provokes severe distress. People with generalized anxiety disorder showed the weakest responses. They are a little afraid of almost everything, but not much afraid of any one item, so no brief reminder elicits much response. People with panic disorder were intermediate (Cuthbert et al., 2003). That is, anxiety disorders vary from being intensely aroused by a few items to being mildly aroused by many items.

Causes of Anxiety Disorders

Even when people are in the same dangerous situation, and even when they seem to be equally powerless, some seem more frightened than others. Of people exposed to virtually the same traumatic experience, some develop problems such as post-traumatic stress disorder and some do not. Why?

LEARNING

Many people develop fears after painful experiences. For example, sexually abused children are, on the average, more likely than others to develop both anxiety disorders (Friedman et al., 2002) and depression (E. C. Nelson et al., 2002). John B. Watson, one of the pioneers of American psychology, was the first to try to demonstrate learned fears experimentally, although by today's standards his research was flawed both scientifically and ethically. He first demonstrated that a young orphan named "Little Albert" was not afraid of white rats. From then on, every time Little Albert saw a white rat, Watson struck a loud gong nearby. After a few such pairings, Albert reacted to the sight of a white rat by crying, trembling, and moving away (Watson & Rayner, 1920).

However, a fear is not the same as a phobia. If Watson had conducted long-term follow-up studies, it is unlikely he would have found that Albert planned his day to avoid reminders of white rats. A more general problem: People acquire phobias of some objects much more readily than others. For example, snake phobias are common whereas automobile phobias are almost unheard of, although automobile accidents are common and snakebites are rare.

Why are phobias of snakes more common than those of automobiles? One theory is that people are born "prepared" to learn certain fears, such as those of spiders, snakes, and heights (Seligman, 1971). The reasoning is that snakes have been dangerous to people throughout their evolutionary history. Most of your ancestors stayed away from snakes, and many ancient people who were slow to learn a fear of snakes did not survive long enough to pass on their genes. Evidence for this *preparedness* idea includes several studies with monkeys, which might share that same preparedness. Ordinarily, laboratory-reared monkeys show inhibition and withdrawal from snakes the very first time they see one. If nothing bad happens, their fear habituates (declines), but this initial wariness suggests a predisposition toward fear (Nelson, Shelton, & Kalin, 2003). If a monkey sees another monkey show fear of snakes, it acquires the fear too, even though the observer has never been bitten or even seen any other monkey bitten (Mineka, 1987; Mineka, Davidson, Cook, & Keir, 1984). If it watches a movie of a monkey running away from a snake, it develops a fear of snakes, but if it watches an edited movie showing a monkey apparently running away from flowers, it develops no fear (Mineka, 1987).

Humans also learn fears of snakes relatively easily. People who get shocks paired with pictures of snakes quickly show a conditioned response (increased heart rate and breathing rate), whereas those who get shocks paired with pictures of houses develop weaker responses (Öhman, Eriksson, & Olofsson, 1975).

All of these results suggest something general and profound about fears: that we may have been born with a predisposition to learn to fear certain objects. However, other interpretations are possible. For example, other things being equal, unpredictable, uncontrollable events are more stressful than ones we think we can control. Snakes and spiders pose unpredictable dangers; cars and tools are unlikely to attack you by surprise. Also, an object becomes less frightening if we have safe experiences with it. You may not have had a personal bad experience with snakes or spiders, but you also probably lack many safe experiences with them. In short, people typically develop phobias toward objects that are unpredictable, uncontrollable, and seldom experienced in a safe context.

PREDISPOSITIONS

A few people can trace the onset of their phobias to a personal experience—such as one person who found a dead body in a lake and thereafter had a phobia of water (Kendler et al., 1995)—but most people do not recall any experience that led to their phobias. Investigators in one study identified people with a phobia, each of whom had a twin. (The twin might or might not also have a phobia.) Some individuals with a phobia could trace their phobia to a frightening experience; others could not. If the frightening experience *caused* the phobia, then presumably genetic factors were more important for people who could not recall a precipitating experience. Contrary to this prediction, researchers found the same elevated risk of phobia in twins of those who could and those who could not recall an experience that started their phobia (Kendler, Myers, & Prescott, 2002). In other words, there was no evidence that having a shocking experience increased the risk of phobia beyond whatever risk already was present, based on genetic factors. Although it is hard to believe the environment has no influence on phobias—and we should always be wary of drawing conclusions from any single study—the implication nevertheless is that genetic predispositions are important.

Both panic disorder and phobias are more common among people who have relatives with similar disorders, especially if those with the disorders are close relatives such as identical twins (Hettema, Neale, & Kendler, 2001; Kendler, Myers, Prescott, & Neale, 2001; Skre, Onstad, Torgerson, Lygren, & Kringlen, 2000). Those results imply a genetic predisposition. But how might such a predisposition act? One of the neurotransmitters found in the amygdala (as well as elsewhere in the brain) is serotonin. After a neuron releases serotonin, serotonin activates receptors on a neighboring neuron, then detaches from its membrane, and finally is reabsorbed into the first cell by a protein called the serotonin transporter. People vary in the structure of a gene that controls production of the transporter protein. Several studies found that people with the "short" form of the gene were more likely to develop various anxiety disorders than were people with the "long" form of the gene. One study used fMRI to measure amygdala responses as people examined photographs showing expressions of anger or fear. Those with the "short" form of the gene showed stronger responses in the amygdala (Hariri et al., 2002). Presumably, this alteration in serotonin activity led to an over-responsive amygdala, which is related to anxiety disorders (Rosen & Schulkin, 1998). However, not everyone with this gene develops a disorder, and some people without it do. This is presumably not the only gene that influences disposition to experience fear, and its influence by itself is limited.

At one time, post-traumatic stress disorder seemed like a perfect example of a disorder caused purely by an experience, but now PTSD too appears to be influenced by genetic predispositions. Long-term studies of people who were severely injured in automobile accidents have found that the intensity of anxiety and stress soon after the accident has almost no relationship to the probability of developing PTSD later (Harvey & Bryant, 2002; Shalev et al., 2000). That is, even if two people have the same experience and react about the same way to it immediately, one might develop PTSD while the other one does not.

One reason for the difference relates to brain anatomy. On the average, people with PTSD have a smaller than average hippocampus, a brain area responsible for control of stress hormones in addition to its more widely known role in memory (Stein, Hanna, Koverola, Torchia, & McClarty, 1997). To determine whether that brain difference developed as a result of PTSD or prior to it, investigators examined pairs of identical male twins. One member of each pair had developed PTSD during war, whereas the other had not been in battle and had thus not developed PTSD. The investigators found that *both* twins had a smaller than average hippocampus (Gilbertson et al., 2002). That is, the hippocampus must have been smaller than average before development of PTSD; it was a predisposing factor, not a result of PTSD.

So, what do clinical conditions tell us about fears and anxiety? First, although a moderate amount of anxiety is natural and a good brake against foolish actions, excessive anxiety permeates life and interferes with its enjoyment. Second, fear is most common in situations where we feel unable to predict or control the outcomes. Third, people vary in their predisposition to fears, and some of that variation is traceable to genetic influences on specific brain structures, including the amygdala.

◻ Summary

Fear is like so many other things in life: A little is good for you, but too much is harmful. Of all the emotions we shall study, fear and sadness are the ones you are most likely to have too much of.

Although fear is a reaction to an event or object in the immediate environment, the tendency to feel fearful or anxious is a long-term predisposition, based at least partly on genetics. We hope this theme is already familiar to you as a psychology student: Almost any aspect of behavior has both hereditary and environmental contributions.

Another clear point is that fear is often an intense feeling. When you are confronted by imminent, serious danger, fear readies the body for quick, vigorous action. Joy and sadness seldom require such emergency action, and even anger usually does not have the same urgency as fear. Fear activates the sympathetic nervous system strongly and quickly, and we can observe fearful behavior easily in laboratory animals as well as humans. We will rarely have this luxury with other emotions.

We can, however, find reasons to be optimistic about controlling fear. Researchers have more and stronger ways of measuring fear than any other emotion, and progress has been encouraging. Certainly, we do not know nearly as much as we would like to know, but at least the research is enabling us to answer some questions and pose new ones clearly.

▢ Key Terms

agoraphobia: excessive fear of situations that would be difficult to escape in the event of a panic attack (p. 118)

amygdala: an area within the brain's temporal lobe (p. 112)

anxiety: a general expectation that "something bad might happen," without identifying any particular danger (p. 101)

emblems: hand and body gestures that have specific meanings within a given culture (p. 112)

fear: experience in which the dread is directed toward a specific object or event (p. 101)

generalized anxiety disorder (GAD): condition characterized by almost constant nervousness and a wide range of worries (p. 118)

Klüver-Bucy Syndrome (KBS): a pattern of emotional changes accompanying removal of both anterior temporal lobes (p. 113)

micro expressions: involuntary, momentary emotional expressions that contradict the intended impression of calmness (p. 106)

operational definition: defining something in terms of a way to measure it (p. 107)

panic disorder: condition characterized by repeated attacks of panic, with sharply increased heart rate, rapid breathing, noticeable sweating, trembling, and chest pains (p. 118)

phobia: extreme fear that interferes with everyday life (p. 118)

polygraph: set of measurements based on the assumption that people get nervous when they lie and, therefore, show increased heart rate and blood pressure, rapid and irregular breathing patterns, increased skin conductance, or increases in other sympathetic nervous system activities (p. 110)

post-traumatic stress disorder (PTSD): frequent distressing recollections (flashbacks) and nightmares about a traumatic event, avoidance of reminders of it, and an exaggerated startle reflex (p. 119)

social phobia: marked, persistent fear and avoidance of situations in which one might be embarrassed (p. 114)

specific phobia: excessive fear of a particular object or situation (p. 119)

startle potentiation: enhancement of the startle response in a frightening situation as compared to a safe one (p. 107)

startle response: reaction to a sudden loud noise or other strong stimulus in which the muscles tense rapidly, especially the neck muscles, the eyes close tightly, the shoulders quickly pull close to the neck, and the arms pull up toward the head (p. 106)

tranquilizers: drugs that relieve anxiety (p. 117)

▣ Thought Questions

1. Observations on PTSD and other disorders suggest that an experience can reset our anxiety to a higher level and that we can increase our anxiety level more easily and more quickly than we can decrease it. Why might we have evolved this tendency?

2. Facial expressions of emotion communicate our needs and tendencies to other people. What good does it do us to communicate our fear? (And are there times when it is best to hide our fear instead of expressing it?)

▣ Suggestions for Research Projects

1. Try measuring the startle reflex under various conditions. To elicit the startle reflex, you could use a noisemaker of some sort, perhaps from a toy store. Test people at different times of day, different lighting conditions, or after they have listened to different kinds of music or heard different kinds of stories. You might also measure the startle reflex at various delays after watching a scary movie, to see how fast the anxiety decreases. You will, of course, need to find a good way to measure the startle reflex.

2. Observe, or ask someone else who has already observed, facial expressions of fear in blind people. If they are the same as those of sighted people, we could infer that the expressions are built in, and people do not need to learn them. If the expressions are similar but not quite the same, we could conclude that people learn to refine the expressions.

▣ Suggestions for Further Reading

Elliott, C. H., & Smith, L. L. (2002). *Overcoming anxiety for dummies.* New York: Wiley. Written by two practicing clinical psychologists, this is a great introduction to the topic of clinical anxiety.

Glassner, B. (2000). *The culture of fear: Why Americans are afraid of the wrong things.* New York: Basic Books. Well-documented critique of the role mass media play in constructing targets of fear.

6

Anger

From the standpoint of someone feeling fear or anger, the similarities between the two emotions are strong. From the standpoint of a researcher, the contrasts are striking. Eliciting fear is easy: a sudden, loud noise will do or the threat of an electric shock. But imagine trying to elicit anger in a research laboratory without severely overstepping ethical limits. Researchers often elicit emotions such as fear, sadness, disgust, and amusement by showing people film clips, but they have yet to find a film clip that reliably makes people angry. If you were the researcher, what would you do? A sharp insult angers most people, but it produces some combination of fear, sadness, and embarrassment as well. Also, some people fail to notice insults or simply shrug them off, assuming the rude person is just having a bad day. You might promise a nice reward and then refuse to give it; again you manage to anger some participants, but not all. Although fear is an almost universal reaction to certain situations, anger is more idiosyncratic—people are angered by very different kinds of events.

Still, it helps to start with a tentative definition, one that emphasizes what most anger seems to have in common. A reasonable definition is that **anger** is the emotional state associated with a desire to hurt someone or drive that individual away. The term *desire* in that definition can be problematical, and explains why few researchers have studied anger in infants or lab animals. (We can observe what a mouse or infant *does*, but not what it *desires*.) However, regardless of how we rephrase the definition, we will almost certainly include something that implies a motivation or drive. As with fear, anger is an emotion strongly linked with a drive to do something about whatever caused it.

Note one other point about this definition: Because anger is linked to the desire to hurt or drive away, it sometimes leads to aggressive, harmful behavior. Many researchers even use aggression as a primary measure of anger. However, not all aggressive behaviors begin with anger. Psychologists distinguish between hostile and instrumental aggression. **Hostile aggression** is harmful behavior motivated by anger and the events that preceded it. **Instrumental aggression** is harmful or threatening behavior used purely as a way to obtain something or to achieve some end. Examples include bullying, theft, and killing prey. This is another reason why it is difficult to study anger in laboratory animals. A mouse may attack another mouse, but how can you tell whether it is angry or just wants the sunflower seed the other mouse happens to be eating? Unlike humans, the mouse can't tell you.

Recall that according to the definition of emotion, any emotion serves a function. Although most people think of anger as destructive, it can have positive effects. A quick, mild "constructive" display of anger on your part tells your friend or romantic partner, "Hey, that hurt! Don't do it again." Someone who is reasonably perceptive will detect your irritation, apologize, understand you better, and avoid similar acts in the future. The interchange can improve your relationship (Kassinove, Sudholdolsky, Tsytsarev, & Solovyova, 1997; Tafrate, Kassinove, & Dundin, 2002). People confer power and status to people who express moderate amounts of anger (Tiedens, 2001), and people who express mild anger in negotiations tend to get more of what they want (Van Kleef, De Dreu, & Manstead, 2004). Anger lets people know your limits and demands. Under appropriate circumstances, small displays of anger can sometimes improve a social interaction.

However, a stronger display may drive someone away, either temporarily or permanently. The old saying, "Once bitten, twice shy" captures the idea that a brief flare-up of anger produces emotional scars that heal slowly. Strong anger is also associated with harm to the person feeling it. For example, people who feel frequent anger tend to dislike other people and feel dissatisfied with their own lives (Robinson, Vargas, Tamir, & Solberg, 2004). They have trouble maintaining close friendships. At the physical level, intense and frequent anger has been associated with increased risk of cardiovascular disease. For all of these reasons, therapists may try to help people avoid or restrain frequent, extreme anger.

◻ What Elicits Anger?

Back in Chapter 1, when we defined emotion in terms of a response to a stimulus or event, we mentioned a controversy and promised to return to it in the chapter on anger. Well, now is the time to keep that promise. The controversy concerns whether anger ever arises without a stimulus or event. Can you just feel cranky for no good reason?

According to one view, anger is a fairly specific response to an event or condition that is unpleasant, unfair, and potentially changeable (if you tackle the person or thing causing the problem). This view stresses the importance of appraisal: A stimulus or event angers you only if you think someone caused your displeasure, through malice, negligence, or lack of consideration. Many, probably most, of our experiences of anger fit that description. The question is whether they all do. The competing view is that anger sometimes arises directly from some unpleasant, uncomfortable feeling, without any appraisal of blame. Let's begin by considering the roles of situation, appraisal, and blame. Then we shall consider the hypothesis that people can also feel anger without blame.

Prototypical Elicitors of Anger

As mentioned in Chapter 5, Klaus Scherer and Harold Wallbott (1994) asked thousands of university students on five continents to describe a time when they felt each of several emotions and then to rate characteristics of the situation, what their body felt like, and how they behaved. People said they usually felt angry in unpleasant, unfair situations deliberately caused by someone else. Participants also described the situations as potentially changeable. (An uncontrollable bad situation elicits more sadness than anger.)

Consistent with this idea, many studies have found that anger arises mostly when someone has caused harm intentionally or through thoughtlessness. For example, if someone steps in front of you and knocks you off balance, your degree of anger depends on *why* you think the person stepped in front of you. You probably would not feel angry with a toddler or a blind person. You might become angry with people who had no apparent excuse for their carelessness. You would become even angrier if you thought someone stepped in front of you intentionally. In one study, American, European, and Asian students reported anger most strongly in situations where someone treated them unfairly on an individual basis and somewhat less anger when they saw someone violate the laws of society (Ohbuchi et al., 2004). Because of observations like these, Lazarus (1991) described the typical elicitor of anger as a "demeaning offense against me and mine."

The tendency to attribute hostile intentions also helps explain why some people become angry more often than others do. In one study, highly aggressive and unaggressive boys were shown videotapes of events that could be either accidental or deliberate, such as one child knocking down another's blocks or bumping into the other in the lunch line (Dodge & Coie, 1987). In some cases, the offender's facial expression and verbal cues suggested the offense was intentional; in some cases, it appeared to be accidental; and in some cases, the intent was left ambiguous. The aggressive boys usually thought the offense was deliberate, even when the facial expressions and verbal cues indicated an accident. Several later studies replicated the finding that children who attribute hostile intentions to others are more likely than other children to start fights, especially in response to teasing (Crick & Dodge, 1994, 1996). That is, they evidently regard the teasing as hostile, not as playful, and they react accordingly.

In another study, researchers first employed a questionnaire to measure people's usual tendency toward anger (anger-proneness as a personality trait). Then they showed each participant a videotape of a person taking someone else's change in a bar and another videotape of someone driving in front of another car to take a parking spot. Each videotape had two versions, of which each participant saw only one. In one version, the antagonist clearly intended harm. The other version was ambiguous as to whether the person acted intentionally or absent mindedly. The researchers found that the most anger-prone people were more likely than others to attribute malicious intent to the antagonists, even in the ambiguous situations (Hazebroek, Howells, & Day, 2000).

In yet another study, people reported recent events in which someone or something frustrated their wishes. They reported feeling angry only on those occasions when they had someone to blame for their frustration (Kuppens, Van Mechelen, Smits, & De Boeck, 2003).

One point about scientific inference is important here. In each of these studies, the results suggest that blame and anger go together. However, did the blame *cause* the feelings of anger, or did the experience of anger make people look for someone to blame? Because these are correlational studies, not experiments, the answer is not obvious.

Another factor that seems important in eliciting prototypical anger is a sense of control. As mentioned in the previous chapter, you might react to an insult with either fear or anger, depending on who insulted you (Keltner, Gruenfeld, & Anderson, 2003). If you feel more powerful than the other person, you are angry; if you feel powerless, you are frightened. Surveys have found that people who seldom perceive situations as dangerous are predisposed to become angry, whereas people who see many situations as risky are prone to frequent fear and less anger (Lerner & Keltner, 2001).

In the United States, anger often arises when people are driving (Figure 6.1). Why? One obvious reason is that driving elicits frustration. You are trying to get somewhere in a hurry and some *$#@%^&* slows down, straddles two lanes, or makes a sudden turn without signaling. But you feel frustrated elsewhere, too. People show more anger in their cars than they would in face-to-face situations, such as a grocery store. One reason why we get so angry while driving is that we can get away with it. In the safety of your car, you can honk, yell, or make a fist without much fear of retaliation (unless you are on a Los Angeles freeway, in which case it's really a bad idea).

So you get angry or threaten a fight when you think you are safe. If you are not sure, you vacillate, alternating between attack and escape. The same is true for other species. Have you ever watched a cat approach a mouse? If the cat is an experienced mouser and the mouse is small and not very active, the cat makes a quick kill. But suppose the cat is less accomplished and the mouse is large. The mouse hisses and bares its teeth. Under these conditions, the cat may well retreat. In an intermediate case, with a moderately experienced cat and a medium-size, slightly threatening mouse, the cat approaches cautiously. It bats at the mouse with its paws again and again until it weakens the mouse enough to bite it easily. Observers sometimes think the cat is "playing" with the mouse, but the behavior is in deadly earnest. Substitute a weaker mouse and the cat will strike quickly; substitute a stronger mouse and the cat will retreat. Give the cat a mild tranquilizer to reduce its fears, and a cat that would have "played" with the mouse goes for a quicker attack (Adamec, Stark-Adamec, & Livingston, 1980; Biben, 1979; Pellis et al., 1988). Something similar is true in humans: People who have drunk alcohol or taken tranquilizers sometimes get into fights because they have suppressed their fear of injury. Of course, much larger doses calm them enough to become inactive and cease fighting (Valzelli, 1979).

FIGURE 6.1   Anger and aggressive behavior are common while people are driving.

Sean Murphy/Getty Images

The Frustration-Aggression Hypothesis

As just described, many researchers emphasize the importance of blame and a sense of injustice as causes of anger. A different tradition arose among the behaviorists who dominated experimental psychology in the mid-1900s. With their emphasis on observable behaviors and animal models, they did not resonate to concepts such as "blame" and instead looked for situational determinants of aggressive acts. In particular, they and their followers have emphasized the possibility of aggressive behavior, and possibly anger, without any cognitive appraisal of the situation.

To illustrate, think about the last time you found yourself stuck in horrible traffic, wasting time, needing to use the toilet, and crawling along at a few miles an hour. Besides that, it's hot out, and your car's air conditioner is broken. If you appraise the situation objectively, you can't logically blame anyone for your distress, but you might start to feel angry anyway. In a situation like this, many people honk their horns, make angry faces, and yell. For another example, have you ever found yourself furious with a broken copy machine? It's no one's fault, and the copy machine isn't deliberately trying to annoy you, but you feel an overwhelming desire to kick it until it makes your darn copies.

What these situations have in common is goal blockage, or frustration. According to the **frustration-aggression hypothesis,** anything that interferes with one's ability to obtain some expected gratification leads to aggressive behavior (Dollard, Miller, Doob, Mowrer, & Sears, 1939). If you want something, or you want to do something, anything that gets in your way will tend to instigate anger and aggression. It doesn't matter whether that barrier is specific or vague, living or inanimate, accidental or deliberately trying to get in your way—as long as you are not getting what you want, you will be angry and you will want to attack (figuratively if not literally). Note that the frustration-aggression hypothesis applies to hostile aggression, not instrumental aggression. Note also that it implies the possibility of anger and aggression without any appraisal that blames anyone.

Examples fitting this description are abundant, from nonhumans as well as humans. If two rats or mice are together when they both get a foot shock, they attack each other. If a rat gets a foot shock and then sees something unusual, like a plastic hedgehog, it attacks the apparent intruder (Keith-Lucas & Guttman, 1975). We can observe something similar in human infants. In one study, also discussed in Chapter 3, researchers placed 7-month-olds on a table and restrained their arms and legs, so that they could not move (Sternberg, Campos, & Emde, 1983). The babies displayed facial expressions resembling the prototypical anger expression shown later in this chapter (Figure 6.2). In another study, small infants learned to "call up" a picture of a smiling baby by moving their arms; when researchers turned off the effect so that the babies could no longer make the picture appear, most of them showed an angry face (Lewis, 1993). Most psychologists doubt that infants that young can analyze the situation well enough to blame anyone for their discomfort; the anger—if we can call it that—may result from the discomfort or frustration itself.

But is their experience really anger? Some researchers have contended that an angry expression by itself does not necessarily imply a feeling of anger (e.g., Clore, Ortony, Dienes, & Fujita, 1993). Similarly, the aggressive behavior of rats after a foot shock may or may not indicate anger, unless one equates anger with aggression. Unable to get inside the infant's head, we cannot really resolve this issue.

The Cognitive-Neoassociationistic Model: Anger Without Attribution?

The frustration-aggression hypothesis ran into a few significant problems. First, it became clear that not all instances of frustration lead to aggression or anger. Imagine wanting some ice cream after a movie but reaching your favorite vendor and finding it closed. Your goal has been blocked, but you would probably call yourself "disappointed," not angry. Second, the frustration-aggression hypothesis omits many circumstances that do lead to aggression. For example, acts of violence are most common when the weather is hot (Preti, Miotto, De Coppi, Petretto, & Carmelo, 2002), or when the aggressors themselves feel hot (Anderson, 2001).

To broaden the frustration-aggression hypothesis, Leonard Berkowitz (1990) proposed the **Cognitive-Neoassociationistic (CNA) Model of Anger Generation,** which states that anger and hostile aggression are facilitated by any unpleasant event or aversive condition. That event/condition might be frustration, but it could also be danger, pain, heat, an unpleasant odor, or almost anything else. Any unpleasant event activates the autonomic nervous system's fight-or-flight response, which readies the individual to take some action to change the situation. The emotion accompanying fight is anger and the emotion accompanying flight is fear. According to Berkowitz, it's possible to feel both fear and anger, but fear will tend to dominate when the environment holds cues of immediate danger, whereas anger will dominate when no signs of physical danger are present.

Note that this proposal contradicts the idea that anger requires an attribution. Berkowitz suggests that being too hot, feeling crowded, having a headache, being in pain, smelling something foul, or otherwise being uncomfortable can *by itself* provoke a feeling of anger even if you have no one to feel angry at. In fact, blame may be something we invent after the fact of anger to justify it: You feel angry, you yell at someone, and then you quickly rationalize, "I was angry at that person because. . . ."

Berkowitz's suggestion goes to the heart of what we mean by emotion. Remember the definitions offered in Chapter 1: Emotion is a "complex sequence of reactions to a stimulus" (Plutchik, 1982), or it is a "functional reaction to an external stimulus event" (Keltner & Shiota, 2003). Berkowitz suggests that an emotion can arise directly from a bodily feeling, without any cognition about a stimulus (Berkowitz & Harmon-Jones, 2004).

What evidence supports Berkowitz's theory? To give just a few examples, study participants who were subjected to physical pain (Berkowitz, Cochran, & Embree, 1981), trapped with an extremely unpleasant noise (Geen, 1978), or exposed to secondhand cigarette smoke (Zillmann, Baron, & Tamborini, 1981) all tended to behave more aggressively toward convenient target people, even though the targets were not responsible for the conditions and had no control over them. These findings are not well explained by either the prototypical descriptions of anger, or by the original frustration-aggression hypothesis, but are consistent with the CNA model.

Putting It All Together: What Causes Anger?

None of these theories has achieved a consensus among researchers studying emotion. On one hand, the appraisal prototype theory fails to explain why people become hostile when they are in an unpleasant situation that is no one's fault. On the other hand, if an emotion, by definition, includes three components—cognition, feeling, and action—then an emotion without cognition (for instance, anger without blame) is impossible, or at least incomplete (Clore & Centerbar, 2004; C. A. Smith & Kirby, 2004). However, that definition of emotion assumes

that cognition, feeling, and action hang together as a unit. If one or two of them frequently arise independently of the others, as Berkowitz has suggested, then perhaps we should revise our definition of emotion.

Part of the issue is the relationship between anger and aggressiveness. In the Cognitive-Neoassociationistic Model of Anger, Berkowitz assumes that pain or other discomfort elicits anger, which leads to hostile aggression. Maybe so, or maybe Berkowitz's theory applies to aggressive behavior without applying to anger. Here are the two possibilities:

Berkowitz's CNA approach

Appraisal approach

Clearly, the two theories have much in common. Everyone apparently agrees that an appraisal of hostile intent magnifies anger and that discomfort tends to magnify aggressive behavior. The dispute concerns whether appraisal of hostile intent is necessary for anger and whether anger is necessary for aggressive behavior.

Conceivably, both theories might be right but for different ages. Remember that some of the evidence for the frustration-aggression hypothesis came from studies of infants. In another study of the causes of anger, mothers recorded events that had made them or their children angry. Mothers reported feeling anger mostly when their children were inconsiderate, failed to say where they were going or when they were coming home, or did not do their household chores. In short, the mothers were angry when the children hurt their feelings or failed to live up to expectations. Events that angered their children were mostly "goal blockages": They got angry because their parents didn't buy them something they wanted, didn't let them spend their own money as they wanted, or disciplined them by taking something away (Carpenter & Halberstadt, 2000). Could it be that the very nature of anger somehow changes as we age or that the frustrated anger of childhood exists side by side with adult anger, with its more complex attributions and appraisals?

Indeed, it is possible that anger has two forms, analogous to fear and anxiety. Fear is related to a specific object and anxiety is more diffuse. One type of anger might be a response to a particular kind of event, and another might be more diffuse and apt to be directed toward whomever happens to be around. The latter "irritability" or "crankiness" is something we can all relate to, but it deserves more research attention by emotion scientists.

In sum, each of these theories has its merits. It will probably be some time before these perspectives are resolved satisfactorily.

◻ Measuring Anger and Aggression

As with any other emotion, research on anger can be only as good as our methods of measuring it. Much of the research on anger has focused on physical aggression for two good reasons: (1) Anger does often imply at least a mild desire to hurt someone, and (2) aggression is observable, even in laboratory animals and young children, whereas anger is not. However, the relationship between anger and physical aggression is far from perfect. How often do you feel angry? How often do you actually hit someone? Across all the cultures that have been studied, people report feeling angry far more often than they even consider turning to violence (Ramirez, Santisteban, Fujihara, & Van Goozen, 2002). Equating anger with aggressive behavior has been useful in some ways but misleading in others. For example, we know less about

women's anger than about men's, precisely because women more often express their anger indirectly or verbally, instead of resorting to physical violence (DiGiuseppe & Tafrate, in press).

Furthermore, people sometimes engage in instrumental (benefit-seeking) aggression without anger. Unrestrained cruelty sometimes occurs in the name of following orders. Consider killing and torture during a war. Social psychologists have found that normal, healthy, well-intentioned people sometimes will inflict pain and suffering on someone they've never met, possibly even endanger that person's life, if an authority figure tells them to (Milgram, 1974). Aggression and anger are certainly related, but it would be a tremendous mistake to assume that they are synonymous.

Self-Report Measures of Anger

Given our definition of emotion as including cognitions, feelings, and actions, a good measure of anger should assess cognitions (appraisals that lead to anger), angry feelings, and the resulting behavior (Martin, Watson, & Wan, 2000). Researchers often rely on self-reports to gauge cognitions and feelings. Sometimes that approach works fine, but it has its limitations. First, as with all self-reports, accuracy is questionable. Second, people sometimes hesitate to admit their anger. In one experiment, Stanley Schachter and Jerome Singer (1962) did everything they could think of, within the bounds of ethics, to make one group of students angry, but when they asked them about their feelings, very few said they were angry. Maybe they really weren't, but the other possibility is that they didn't want to tell their professors how irritated they were.

For many purposes, researchers want to know more than just "how angry" you are. Anger varies along several dimensions, and the Multidimensional Anger Inventory (Siegel, 1986) measures several of them. Some questions relate to how angry you generally become. Another set measures the variety of situations in which you become angry—for example, being delayed, not getting credit for the work you have done, or having to take orders from someone less qualified than you. A third set deals with hostile attitude—for example, whether you sometimes find people's mere presence to be annoying. A final set asks how you deal with anger: Do you let the other person know, or do you just keep quiet and let your anger continue to bother you?

The most widely used paper-and-pencil measure of anger is the Spielberger State-Trait Anger Expression Inventory, or STAXI (Spielberger, 1991; Spielberger, Jacobs, Russell, & Crane, 1983). The idea behind this questionnaire is that anger is both a **state** (a temporary condition related to recent events) and a **trait** (a long-term aspect of personality). Therefore, the STAXI includes items such as the following:

How do you feel right now?

I feel like yelling at someone.

(1) Not at all   (2) Somewhat
(3) Moderately so   (4) Very much so

How do you generally feel?

I am quick-tempered.

(1) Almost never   (2) Sometimes   (3) Often
(4) Almost always

The first of these examples measures anger as a current state; the second measures it as a trait. (As an analogy, a state is like the current weather in some region, and a trait is like the usual climate.) Certainly that distinction is useful for many purposes. If we want to know how someone will behave in the next few minutes, we care about his or her current anger (state), whereas for predicting behavior next week, the important information is the long-term tendency (trait).

As with many other measures, the STAXI tends to emphasize intense, somewhat destructive kinds of anger. Another instrument concentrates on people's ability to handle anger in helpful ways. The Constructive Anger Behavior-Verbal Style Scale (CAB-V) consists of items that can be filled out either as a self-report or by an observer or interviewer,

who provides a presumably less biased account (Davidson, MacGregor, Stuhr, Dixon, & MacLean, 2000). Sample items include:

Person discusses his/her anger to see if others can help him/her to come up with constructive solutions.

(1) Almost never   (2) Sometimes   (3) Often
(4) Almost always

Person finds that after discussing his/her anger things don't look as bad as she/he thought they did.

(1) Almost never   (2) Sometimes   (3) Often
(4) Almost always

Generally, people with high scores on this inventory handle stressful situations well and keep their anger under control. The value of having different anger questionnaires is that each serves a different purpose, and researchers can choose the one most appropriate for the issue they are investigating.

Facial Expression of Anger

Anger is one of the six "basic" emotions that Paul Ekman and colleagues studied in their original cross-cultural work, and indeed, Ekman found that people throughout the world recognize a prototypical "angry face" (Ekman et al., 1987). Although angry expressions range from mild to very intense, the prototype is clear. Decidedly angry people open their eyes wide and force their eyebrows down and toward the middle of their forehead. Their lower eyelids pull up and toward the inner corner of the eyes, and their lips tighten. Figure 6.2 shows a few examples. Some of these movements are difficult to make voluntarily, but try them while looking in a mirror. If you can't quite get it, think of the last time you were really angry with someone, and watch how your face changes. In addition to facial changes, body posture shifts, as does the tone of voice. Even in a telephone conversation, you can sense when someone is angry.

People usually look angry while they report feeling angry, but not always (Bonanno & Keltner,

FIGURE 6.2   Facial expressions of anger.

2004). For example, someone might turn red in the face, frown, and shout while insisting, "I'm not angry!" Or someone might say quite calmly, "I'm angry," without any facial expression. When various measures disagree, an investigator attempts to determine why. Should we trust the person's words or what the face and voice indicate?

Aggressive Behaviors

Researchers can also observe aggressive behavior. That approach is really the only option for studying nonhuman animals. Researchers simply watch a group of animals and record attacks, their circumstances, and how each fight ends. As we have seen, however, these attacks may or may not indicate what most of us mean by "anger." Observing human aggressive behavior faces a different obstacle: Even in a place where fighting seems most likely, such as a bar, a prison, or an unsupervised playground, an observer might have to wait through long intervals between one fight and the next. War zones have a great deal of fighting, but most soldiers are just carrying

out orders, so observing them is not a fruitful way to study anger.

Researchers sometimes stage artificial situations to try to increase aggression, but ethical considerations constrain what they can do. Suppose you have a theory of what causes someone to become a serial killer. You would like to test your theory on a group of people to see how many of them become serial killers. . . . Oh, never mind. Maybe that research isn't such a hot idea after all.

One clever way researchers get around this problem is to set up a situation in which people *think* they are attacking someone although, in fact, they are not. For example, imagine yourself participating in this experiment: You have a discussion with someone you never met before and don't expect to meet again; this person repeatedly belittles and insults you. Then the two of you are put into separate rooms, and you are told to teach the other person something. You should periodically test that person's performance and signal an error by pressing a button to deliver an electric shock. You get to choose among buttons to determine the intensity of that shock. At least, you think you are delivering shocks; in fact, there are none, and the other person isn't really mean but was paid to pretend to be. The whole point of the experiment is to find out how intense a shock you would choose (e.g., Berman, Gladue, & Taylor, 1993). That is, your button presses measure your tendency toward aggressive behavior without allowing any actual attack.

In a related task, people press a button to subtract points or money from another person. (Ordinarily there is no other person, but each person thinks he or she is competing against someone in another room.) For example, in one study the instruction was to press either button A or button B. For every 100 A presses, you will gain 10 cents. Any B response gets you nothing, but it subtracts winnings from the other person (without giving them to you) and temporarily blocks the other person from pressing B to hurt you. Here the (supposed) consequence is to hurt someone financially, not physically, but the result is the same: People who have a history of violent experiences tend to press B more often than others do (Moe, King, & Bailly, 2004).

Psychologists have developed many variations of these tasks, but all of the common versions are subject to certain criticisms or limitations, including these:

• The rules authorize, even encourage, people to commit the aggressive act.
• The participants are strangers to each other, with no previous social relationship and no expectation of a future one.
• The target of the aggressive act is distant, usually in another room.
• In some cases, the target of the aggression has no opportunity to retaliate.
• The two people have no way to interact with each other *except* for the designated aggressive act.
• The aggressive act could be described as competitive rather than hostile. Ordinarily, the researchers do not attempt to ascertain participants' actual motivations or emotions.

In all these ways, the methods of producing and measuring aggressive behavior are unlike typical aggressive acts (Ritter & Eslea, 2005). Often psychologists learn a great deal from laboratory procedures that seem distant from the events of the real world, so we should not dismiss this type of research as irrelevant. Still, we should be aware of its limitations; we don't know how well the laboratory results generalize to other cases of anger and aggression. Regardless of how aggression was elicited, or where it was observed, it can be difficult to distinguish hostile from instrumental aggression. Still, researchers have devoted far more attention to physical aggression than to other measures of anger, partly because it has such serious consequences for society.

Implicit Measures of Anger and Aggression

Implicit measures infer an emotion (or a memory or whatever) from related behaviors instead of attempting to measure them directly. Here are some examples of implicit measures of anger and aggression.

In one study, people read brief, incomplete stories, some of which included aggressive events. Their task was to write a couple of sentences to finish the story. Researchers then recorded the amount of aggressive content that each person wrote. On the average, men included more aggression than women did, and people who reported much anger on standard questionnaires tended to include more aggression than did people who reported less anger (A. J. Bond, Bauer, & Wingrove, 2004). Note the importance of blind observers in such a study. The observers judging the amount of aggressive content must not know which people have already reported being angry or aggressive.

Another measure is called the **themed dot-probe task:** Two words (one of which might be aggressive) flash briefly on the screen, one above the other. Then a dot appears in the same position as one of them, and the person must press a key as quickly as possible to indicate whether the dot appeared in the upper or lower position.

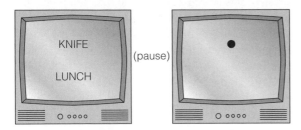

The idea is that a violent word might distract attention and slow the response if the dot appears in the same location where the violent word had been. People with a history of violence, such as prisoners convicted of violent crimes, respond slightly more slowly than other people do when the dot is in the same location where a violent word had been (P. Smith & Waterman, 2004). (You may recall a similar task as a measure of fear in Chapter 5.)

In the **visual search task,** a target word appears briefly in the center of the screen, surrounded by three other words. Then the target word and three new words appear, and the task is to identify the location of the target word. The screens would look something like this:

In cases where the target word is surrounded by violent words, as in the example here, people with a history of violence tend to respond more slowly in finding the target word on the second screen (P. Smith & Waterman, 2004). Again, the apparent reason is that violent words distract attention for some people more than others.

Implicit measures are clever and theoretically interesting, and they confirm the idea that aggressive words capture attention more thoroughly for people who are prone to anger and aggression than for other people. However, the difference in response times between highly aggressive and unaggressive people is just a small fraction of a second, on the average, so these tests are not useful for such practical purposes as identifying dangerous individuals.

❑ The Biology of Anger and Aggression

Wouldn't it be nice if researchers found that excessive aggressiveness had a simple physiological basis, such as overactivity of one kind of synapse in the brain? Then we could find a medication that suppressed that activity, prescribe doses that are enough but not too much, close down the prisons, and live happily ever after. Right?

The reality is that researchers have found no single mechanism responsible for either anger or aggression. However, they have found that some people have a *decrease* in mechanisms that ordinarily *inhibit* aggression. In that sense, the physiological research meshes nicely with our understanding of anger: Aggression occurs in part when there is not enough inhibition against it. That is, we commit aggression when we are not thinking about the consequences.

The Neurology of Anger and Aggression

Aggressive behavior is often impulsive, and one basis for impulsivity is damage to the prefrontal cortex (Figure 6.3). People with known damage to certain parts of the prefrontal cortex are impaired at suppressing their emotional expressions after such instructions as "Try not to act startled after the sudden sound you're about to hear." They also are more likely to lose money by making bad gambling decisions and to choose a smaller reward now over a larger reward later. People with a history of explosive outbursts of anger, including impulsive murderers, show these same behavioral patterns, even though they have no

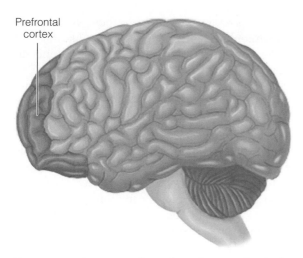

Prefrontal cortex

FIGURE 6.3 Damage to the prefrontal cortex often leads to impulsive behavior, including outbursts of aggression.

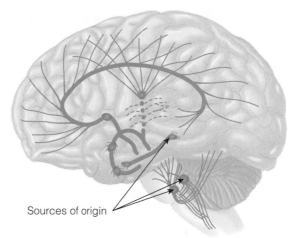

Sources of origin

FIGURE 6.4 Just a few clusters of neurons in the brainstem manufacture serotonin, but their axons influence activity in widespread areas. Source: Based on Valzelli (1980).

demonstrated brain damage (Best, Williams, & Coccaro, 2002; Davidson, Putnam, & Larson, 2000). The implication is that their prefrontal cortex is intact but may be less than normally active.

Neurochemistry: Serotonin and Testosterone

A behavioral similarity between brain-damaged people and impulsively aggressive people is only a suggestion, of course, and not solid evidence that violent people have any brain abnormality. If the prefrontal cortex is less responsive than normal, that unresponsiveness could be the result of a disorder in the activity of some neurotransmitter, and one particular candidate is **serotonin**. Serotonin is produced by only a few clusters of neurons in the brainstem (the central core of the brain), but their axons spread widely, influencing activity throughout most of the brain, as Figure 6.4 shows.

Laboratory research since the 1970s has demonstrated that rats and mice with low levels of serotonin release are more likely to fight with one another (Saudou et al., 1994; Valzelli, 1973; Valzelli &

Bernasconi, 1979). (Serotonin release is generally inferred from measurements of serotonin metabolites in the blood or other body fluids. The assumption is that the less serotonin released, the less its metabolite shows up in body fluids.) Long-term observations of young monkeys included a blood test to measure serotonin metabolites. Monkeys with the lowest levels were the most likely to start fights and to be victims of attacks (Higley et al., 1996; Westergaard, Cleveland, Trenkle, Lussier, & Higley, 2003). Many of these low-serotonin monkeys sustained repeated injuries and died within the first few years of life. However, highly aggressive monkeys that survived—at least the males—had a high probability of achieving a dominant status within the troop (Fairbanks et al., 2004). That is, low serotonin seems to be linked to a high-risk, high-payoff strategy.

Instigated by these results, other researchers have examined serotonin release in humans. Low levels have been found in people convicted of arson and other violent crimes (Virkkunen, Nuutila, Goodwin, & Linnoila, 1987). Studies of inmates being let out of prison found that those with low serotonin levels are the most likely to be convicted of additional violent crimes within the next few years (Virkkunen, DeJong, Bartko, Goodwin, & Linnoila, 1989; Virkkunen, Eggert, Rawlings, & Linnoila, 1996). Similarly, of children and adolescents being counseled because of aggressive behavior, those with the lowest serotonin levels are the most likely to commit additional violent acts (Kruesi et al., 1992). Of people who survive violent attempts at suicide, those with the lowest serotonin release are the most likely to attempt suicide again within the next five years (Roy, DeJong, & Linnoila, 1989).

A thorough review of the available human literature found that the relationship between decreased serotonin and increased violent behavior was consistent but only moderate in size (Moore, Scarpa, & Raine, 2002). That is, if we examined two large groups of people differing in their serotonin levels, we could confidently predict which group will show more violence, but a serotonin measurement on a given individual would not tell us what to expect about that person. Consider two reasons: First, blood measurements give only an approximate measure of actual processes in the brain. Second, the effects of serotonin depend on other circumstances in the person's brain chemistry, previous experiences, and present life. Low serotonin has been linked not only to increased violence but also to depression, obsessive-compulsive disorder, and other conditions not generally associated with violence. It is as if low serotonin release removes inhibitions against various impulses, but different people have different impulses. When researchers have used drugs or other methods to lower people's serotonin levels suddenly, the people with a previous history of violence became violent, those with a history of depression became depressed, and those with a history of substance abuse reported a sudden craving for drugs (Van der Does, 2001).

Furthermore, the exact role of serotonin in aggression remains unclear. Neurons actually release serotonin *during* aggressive behavior, not while the individual is preparing for or refraining from aggression (van der Vegt et al., 2003). According to one hypothesis, those who usually have low levels of serotonin release react more strongly than usual to events causing its release, and therefore, those with the lowest serotonin turnover have the highest likelihood of violence. In any case, drugs that elevate serotonin do not reliably decrease aggressive behavior.

Another possibility is that **testosterone**, a hormone more common in males than females, may predispose people to aggression. The literature on this point is also not entirely clear. On one hand, violence is most common among males in the age range 15 to25, which is also the time of highest testosterone levels. Also, in a variety of animal species, aggression is most common in males when their testosterone levels are highest. If you watch birds in the mating season (spring), when the males' testosterone levels are high, you can see repeated threat displays. In the fall, when breeding is over and testosterone levels drop, birds cluster in large, peaceful flocks. On the other hand, for a single group and at any particular moment, some males are more aggressive than others, and the correlation between testosterone levels and aggression is weak (Bernhardt, 1997; Brooks & Reddon, 1996). In short, testosterone fluctuations from one time to another for a given individual may predict aggressiveness, but differences between one individual and another do not mean as much.

An interesting way to study the effects of testosterone is to examine aggressiveness in women. One study found significant positive correlations between women's testosterone levels and measures of their anger and verbal aggression (von der Pahlen, Lindman, Sarkola, Mäkisalo, & Eriksson, 2002). In another study, researchers injected women with testosterone and observed a temporary increase in their heart rate acceleration after looking at photographs of angry faces (van Honk et al., 2001). The interpretation was that testosterone increases attention to stimuli that suggest aggression and conflict.

Anger and the Autonomic Nervous System

Yet another way to measure anger is physiological arousal, such as heart rate and breathing rate. The physiological state that accompanies anger closely resembles that for fear. One special feature of anger is its relationship with the adrenal gland. At the start of an aggressive attack, part of the hypothalamus (at the base of the brain) sends messages that activate the adrenal gland to increase its release of cortisol and related stress hormones. Those hormones feed back to increase the activity in the hypothalamus. Thus, at the start of a fight, the arousal is self-sustaining and self-magnifying (Kruk, Halász, Meelis, & Haller, 2004). The arousal cannot keep building forever, of course, but a common result is that when something makes you angry, you quickly become angrier and angrier.

The relationship between anger and autonomic nervous system activity has often been cited as an explanation for the association between high dispositional hostility and cardiovascular disease (Davidson et al., 2000). However, some research has suggested that how anger is expressed, rather than the experience of anger itself, predicts health problems. For example, Siegman (1994) reviewed the literature and concluded that hostile people who express anger frequently and explosively are more vulnerable to cardiovascular problems, whereas people who experience anger often but express it differently are at less risk. Another study found that people who express their anger verbally while trying to understand the other person's point of view had lower resting blood pressure than people who were less articulate when angry (Davidson et al., 2000). This effect continued to be significant after the researchers controlled for other variables known to predict hypertension, such as sex, weight, and smoking. Although we cannot draw cause-and-effect conclusions from these correlational studies, it is possible that the risk of heart disease depends on how people handle and express their anger, not on anger per se.

◻ Individual and Situational Differences

One of the most striking observations about anger is that it varies so much. Have you noticed that some of the people you know get angry more often than

others? Do you go through moods of your own when you get angry easily? Certainly some people are more prone to violence than others. These variations call out for investigation and explanation.

Who Becomes Aggressive?

For practical purposes, predicting violence is easy: The more violent acts someone has committed in the past, the more likely that person is to commit further violent acts. That statement is a special case of one of the strongest generalizations we can make in psychology: The best predictor of future behavior is past behavior. You will soon note that much of this research addresses individual differences in aggressive behavior, rather than in anger per se. Keep in mind, as you read through this section, the limitations of using aggression to measure anger. Which studies do you think truly help us to understand anger, and which reflect other motives for aggression?

From a theoretical standpoint, of course, predicting future violence from past violence is unsatisfactory because it does not explain why some people were more violent in the past. Let's first dispense with a couple of popular explanations that the data do not support. One is that violent behavior is a product of low self-esteem. According to this view, people who see themselves as failures try to raise their own status by attacking someone else. The attraction of this hypothesis comes from observations that many highly violent people are poorly educated, have trouble keeping a job, and in general seem to be the kind of people who *should* have low self-esteem. However, the results do not consistently support the hypothesis if we use standard measurements of self-esteem. Those measurements rely on questions such as these (Blascovich & Tomaka, 1991):

T F At times I think I'm no good at all.

T F I'm a failure.

T F There are lots of things about myself I'd change if I could.

T F I'm often sorry for the things I do.

As you could guess, a "false" on any of these four items counts as a point toward high self-esteem. As measured in this way, most studies find at best a weak relationship between self-esteem and violent behavior (Donnellan, Trzesniewski, Robins, Moffitt, & Caspi, 2005). People who are consistent *victims* of violence report low self-esteem, but many perpetrators of violence are self-confident, self-centered, and arrogant. In one study of elementary-school children, the most aggressive children tended to be those who overestimated how much the other children liked them (David & Kistner, 2000). That is, they tended to have unrealistically high self-esteem. Of course, not everyone with high self-esteem becomes violent. It may be that some people react violently when other people threaten their arrogant self-esteem. However, most researchers find no evidence that violent people suffer from overall low self-esteem (Baumeister, Smart, & Boden, 1996).

Another unsatisfactory hypothesis is that violence results from mental illness. You will sometimes hear reports about a mental patient who commits multiple acts of violence against haphazardly chosen strangers. Such cases are frightening and difficult for the police to solve because the killer does not know the victims and has no apparent motive. However, violent mental patients are a rarity, except for those who abuse alcohol and other drugs. Mental patients who are not alcoholics or substance abusers have about the same crime rate as the rest of the population (Hodgins, Mednick, Brennan, Schulsinger, & Engberg, 1996).

Genetics

As with any other behavior, one hypothesis concerning individual differences is that they result from genetics. Estimates of the heritability of human behaviors rely mostly on studies of twins and adopted children. Studies of aggressive, delinquent, and criminal behaviors have consistently found greater similarities between monozygotic (identical) twins than dizygotic (fraternal) twins. Studies have also found that adopted children tend to resemble their biological parents in these regards. The degree of resemblance, according to one review of the literature, implies that genetic factors account for about 40 percent of the variance in aggressive and criminal behavior, whereas environmental factors account for the rest (Rhee & Waldman, 2002). Various attempts have been made to tie aggressive behavior to a particular gene. Researchers have identified several genes that are somewhat more common among people with a history of violence than in the general population, such as 66 percent versus 57 percent or 51 percent versus 34 percent (Abbar et al., 2001; Manuck et al., 1999; Rujescu et al., 2002). These effects are strong enough to suggest that some people are more predisposed than others to violence, but they are hardly strong enough to identify any gene as a "cause" of violence.

In one study, pairs of dizygotic twins and monozygotic twins showed equal resemblances in juvenile offenses, but monozygotic twins showed much stronger resemblances in adult crimes (Lyons et al., 1995). Those results imply that the effects of heredity *increase* as people grow older. A possible explanation is that adults can choose their own environment. For example, someone predisposed to impulsive violence may choose friends, a neighborhood, and a way of life consistent with antisocial behavior. Children have less control over their environment, and both members of any twin pair will live in the same neighborhood and have mostly the same friends and activities. This **interaction between personality and environment**—where your disposition motivates you to select an environment that reinforces the personality disposition you had in the first place—could explain why the effects of genetics seem to become stronger over time.

Sex Differences

Who is angry more often, men or women? The common stereotype is that men get angry more often, but the research does not support that view. When people keep records of when and where they become angry, men and women record about the same frequency of events (Averill, 1983; DiGiuseppe & Tafrate, in press).

The difference is in what people do when they are angry. One of the biggest and best-documented differences between males and females is that males engage in more physically aggressive behavior. Little boys get into fistfights far more often than little girls do, men get into barroom brawls vastly more often than women do, and men commit most of the violent crimes in every culture for which we have data, throughout the world.

This does not mean that women are not aggressive when angry. Although girls and women seldom get into physical fights with one another, they may be aggressive indirectly, such as by refusing to talk to someone, spreading unkind rumors, or manipulating one person to hurt another (Xie, Cairns, & Cairns, 2002). Sometimes men behave that way too, but women are more likely than men to rely heavily on indirect aggression (Salmivalli & Kaukiainen, 2004). Some researchers have argued that both men and women handle anger poorly: Men are more likely to be violent, and women are more likely to express their anger passively, such as by ignoring someone (Thomas, 1993). One problem with passive aggression is that people can't easily make up after the fight is over, because they aren't sure when it's over. Expressing anger "constructively" can be helpful, but learning to do so takes much work.

Even with regard to physical aggression, the sex difference depends on circumstances. The tendency for males to be more aggressive than females virtually disappears under conditions of extreme provocation. That is, when people have very strong reasons to be angry, women get just as angry as men and are as likely to lash out in one way or another. The difference between sexes occurs under conditions of mild provocation. Men—or, at least, some men—pick fights when they have only slight reasons to be offended, whereas nearly all women would find some other way to handle the situation (Knight, Guthrie, Page, & Fabes, 2002).

The sex difference in physical aggression also depends on what we count as violence. Most fights occur between people who know each other well, not between strangers (Averill, 1983), and much violence occurs between spouses or romantic partners. According to an extensive review of the literature, women commit more than half of this violence (Archer, 2000). Almost everyone finds that statistic surprising because we often hear about battered wives and seldom about battered husbands. The explanation is that most researchers defined aggression to include a wide range of minor acts, so that a woman slapping a man counts as an act of aggression, just as much as a man injuring a woman. If we limit attention to acts that could produce serious injury, men clearly commit most of them.

Evolutionary Explanations

Given that males of so many species tend to fight more than females, it is natural to suggest that evolution has genetically predisposed males to be more aggressive. Traditionally, evolutionary theorists have pointed out that a male gains in two ways by winning a fight: He forces a competing male out of the way, and he impresses the females. A highly dominant male has the potential to impregnate many females and thus spread his genes.

Anne Campbell (2002) has suggested a different evolutionary explanation by changing the question to why women are *less* aggressive. She begins with the fact that men are more risk taking than women under a wide variety of circumstances, including walking through a dangerous neighborhood alone at night—an act that has little chance of impressing females because they are probably not around to watch. Campbell's interpretation is that women are predisposed to value their own lives more than men do. Evolutionarily, that tendency makes sense: If a woman dies before her children are mature, they probably will not survive and she does not pass on her genes. A man, however, has a reasonable chance that his children can survive even if he does not.

Some degree or type of aggressive behavior by females makes sense, evolutionarily. As Campbell (2002) points out, males of almost all species compete for the chance to copulate with females,

© Mike Lane/Alamy

FIGURE 6.5 Great reed warblers breed in continental Europe. In good territories, satellite females set up nests near the primary nest and, if they get an opportunity, attack the primary female's eggs.

whereas almost any female who wants to copulate can find a willing partner. Females do compete, however, to protect or advance themselves and their children. Few animals can be more ferocious than a mother bear defending her cubs. For another illustration, consider this observation of great reed warblers, European birds (Figure 6.5): A male and female share nesting and infant-care duties, while the male defends the territory against other males. If the male has a particularly good territory, one or more other females set up "satellite" nests nearby. The male fertilizes their eggs, but otherwise devotes his attention to the nest and young of the primary female. However, if her eggs fail to hatch, he moves to help one of the satellite females. In fact, the eggs of the primary female frequently fail to hatch, because when they are unguarded, one of the satellite females pecks at them and kills them (Hansson, Bensch, & Hasselquist, 1997). (You might remember that story the next time someone says that females are naturally unaggressive.)

You should note that all of these examples suggest instrumental motives for aggression, rather than hostile motives, so it's not clear whether evolutionary explanations make much sense with regard to individual differences in anger. Still, the correlation between anger and aggression makes this a potentially interesting line of research.

Family Environment

Violence is most common in people whose parents physically abused them, frequently fought with each other, got into trouble with the law, and abused alcohol and other substances (Malinosky-Rummell & Hansen, 1993). Violence is also widespread among those who grew up in a violent neighborhood. (Hardly surprising.) It might seem obvious that growing up in such circumstances leads to violence by making the child dispositionally angry and by setting an example of violence. However, we need to consider the alternative possibility that violent and impulsive parents have violent and impulsive children because of genetics. The best evidence comes from studies of adopted children. Adoption agencies seldom place children with violent or alcoholic parents, but when they do, those children tend to show increased violence. However, that increase in violence is often smaller than you might expect. The greatest incidence of violence occurs in adopted children who had *both* a history of violence in their biological parents *and* exposure to violence by their adoptive parents (Cadoret, Yates, Troughton, Woodworth, & Stewart, 1995).

One of the most remarkable and least understood aspects of human development is **resilience,** the ability of people to overcome the effects of extremely unfavorable environments. For example, only about one third of abused children become abusive parents (Widom, 1989). In some cases, abused children are helped by a relationship with another person; in other cases, they resist harmful influences anyway, without any obvious explanation. Much more work is needed to understand the protective factors that help children to thrive in spite of threatening environments.

One parenthetical point worth mentioning: The fact that so many people are resilient in the face of abusive or painful experiences does not mean that we should be indifferent to those experiences. One review article (Rind, Tromovitch, & Bauserman, 1998) found that most children subjected to sexual abuse (broadly defined to include such things as seeing a "flasher") recovered reasonably well. That article became the focus of a heated controversy because many critics assumed the authors were implying that childhood sexual abuse is acceptable. They meant no such thing, of course. It is also true that most children who fall on their heads recover, but no one concludes that it is okay to drop children on their heads.

Effects of Watching Media Violence

Do children who grow up frequently watching violent movies, television, and video games become more violent than those who seldom watch them? This argument has been around for a long time. The ancient Greeks debated whether people who told violent stories had a bad influence on the young (J. P. Murray, 1998), and people in the early twentieth century worried about whether violent radio programs increased the crime rate (Dennis, 1998). Today the issue is more important because of the quantitative increase in exposure. According to surveys in the United States, the average child spends an average of 40 hours per week watching television, movies, or video games, and most of the programs contain violence. Authorities in this field estimate that by the time a child leaves elementary school, he or she will have watched depictions of 8,000 murders and perhaps a hundred thousand other acts of violence (Bushman & Anderson, 2001). Many television and movie executives have defended these programs by saying that watching televised violence does not affect people's behavior. Bushman and Anderson (2001) reply to this claim with the question, "If watching television does not affect behavior, why are so many companies willing to pay for commercials?"

Studies routinely find that people who watch more television or movie violence, or who play more violent video games, also engage in more aggressive behaviors, on the average. (Obviously,

group averages do not apply to every individual.) One of the stronger studies examined 707 families, determined how much violent television the children watched, and measured the children's aggressive behavior. Then, over the next 16 to 18 years, the researchers repeatedly retested the children. They found that, regardless of how aggressive the children were at the start of the study, those who watched more violent programs tended to become more aggressive over the years. They found similar trends when they compared children from homes that resembled one another in parental education, parental income, parental supervision of the children, and type of neighborhood: Even then, the children who watched the most violent programs increased their aggressive behavior more than children who watched it less (Johnson, Cohen, Smailes, Kasen, & Brook, 2002).

However, the interpretation of such correlational results is problematical. Does watching violence lead to violence, or is it just that people who tend toward violent behavior also like to watch violence? The fact that watching violent programs correlates better with future violent behavior than with past violent behavior is strongly suggestive, but not conclusive. To examine cause and effect, we need experimental research. For example, one study randomly assigned different groups of college students to watch nonviolent or extremely violent movies for four nights. On the fifth night, they participated in what they thought was a separate study. As part of this study, the graduate student experimenter insulted some of the students, calling their performance on the task "terrible." Later they were asked to evaluate this graduate student and recommend whether he or she should receive financial support for the next year. Naturally, those who had been insulted gave low ratings, but the interesting result was that among those who were insulted, those who had been watching violent movies gave even lower ratings than the others (Zillman & Weaver, 1999).

Similarly, children who are randomly assigned to watch television episodes containing even mild violence show more aggressive playground behavior a while later than do children who watched television episodes without any aggression (Boyatzis, Matillo, & Nesbitt, 1995; Steuer, Applefield, & Smith, 1971). These effects are stronger when the show is human rather than cartoon, when the aggressor is the "good guy" rather than the "bad guy," and when the aggressor is similar to the person watching on variables such as sex, age, and ethnicity.

Research on violent video games has shown a similar disturbing result: Playing violent video games increases physiological arousal, increases aggressive thoughts and actions, and decreases cooperative behaviors in both males and females from early childhood through adulthood. The average effect across 33 studies was rather small, but the change in behavior was quick (C. A. Anderson & Bushman, 2001). Unfortunately, we do not yet have information about long-term effects. Does repeatedly pretending to shoot people on a video screen increase the probability of actually shooting someone? No one knows, but whether we like it or not, all of us are participants in a very big study as society gradually learns the answer.

A strong body of research now supports the claim that mass media violence encourages aggressive behavior, at least in some people under some circumstances. An important question remains, however—what mechanism explains this effect? When we see violence on television and in video games, are we more likely to see the world as a dangerous place where people are trying to hurt us? If so, the effect of media violence on aggression may indeed involve increased tendency toward anger. Alternatively, does media violence simply desensitize us to the idea of aggression, so that hitting or shooting another person does not seem like such a big deal? Do media presentations of violence teach us that aggression is a good way to get what we want? These mechanisms have fewer implications for our understanding of individual differences in anger, although of course they are important in their own right.

To summarize the factors predisposing to anger and aggressiveness: People may vary in their predisposition to anger and aggression because of genetic factors and prenatal environment, but even the influence of those factors depends on the environment. The greatest probability of violence occurs in people from a troubled family in a violent neighborhood who also had a biological predisposition. Exposure to violence in the media increases the risk of aggressive behavior; again, the influence is probably greater in those who were already predisposed for other reasons.

◻ Application: Violence Prevention

As human technology has developed the ability to make stronger and stronger weapons, the need for violence control has increased accordingly. Many treaties among nations deal with preventing war: "We promise we won't attack you if you promise you won't attack us." "We won't build any more nuclear weapons if you won't either." Unfortunately, many of these treaties are broken. Within a country, a major focus of laws is to deter or punish violent acts. As with international treaties, laws are not always effective, in part because anger is behind so much of the violence. The importance of finding better ways to control anger and violence could hardly be overstated.

Reconciliation

People who have been quarreling often make an effort to heal the rift afterward. **Reconciliation** is an attempt to restore friendship after a fight (physical or verbal) and to prevent further hostility. For decades, psychologists overlooked reconciliation because so much of the research on aggression examined birds and rodents (which are cheap and easy to observe). Most species of birds and rodents live alone or in families, and they have little to lose by driving a competitor out of their territory. Once a relationship is damaged, it is damaged permanently. Behavior is different among highly social animals such as chimpanzees: After a fight, they have to remain in a troop together, and neither they nor the other chimpanzees can afford to tolerate continual fighting. After a fight, they spend much time together, hug, hold hands, and so forth. If they don't do so at first, the other troop members push them together. A pair of chimpanzees who have gone through this reconciliation ceremony become less likely to fight in the future (de Waal, 2000).

People certainly do the same. You might quarrel and never reconcile with a stranger you meet on a trip, but with relatives or coworkers or anyone else you need to deal with repeatedly, you can't afford constant hostility. After a fight, you look for ways to restore harmony.

Childhood Aggressive Behavior

Most adults who get angry find a way to handle the situation without actually hitting each other. Children, especially little boys, fight somewhat frequently, as you may remember from your own childhood. Still, most childhood squabbles are minor. A few shootings in schools have been widely publicized, but in general, schools are relatively safe places (Mulvey & Cauffman, 2001).

However, although very few of the fights in school are lethal, many are demoralizing and degrading to the victims. Some children bully others mercilessly. One of the strongest predictors of bullying is being larger and stronger than others in early childhood. Apparently some children learn that they can push others around, and they get in the habit of doing so. Bullying at age 11 depends more on how large a boy was at age 3 than how large he is at 11 (Raine, Reynolds, Venables, Mednick, & Farrington, 1998). Most children are consistent over the years in whether they are bullies, victims, or a bit of both (Camodeca, Goossens, Terwogt, & Schuengel, 2002).

Bullies are seldom venting anger; more often, they are using their power for gain or entertainment. Researchers who interviewed young bullies found that the bullies simply enjoyed tormenting other children. They took another child's money or food, forced him or her to eat grass, and did whatever else amused them. The best way to stop the bullying was to increase adult supervision and enforce rules—that is, to make sure the child did not get away with it (Olweus, 1995).

Controlling Anger in Adulthood

Anger management training refers to a whole set of methods therapists use to try to help people control their anger. Any therapy is most effective for people who are sincerely trying to change, and that statement is especially true for anger control. Getting people committed to controlling their anger is a major first step.

Effective progress is likely by means of the following procedures, which are classed as cognitive-behavioral therapy (Dahlen & Deffenbacher, 2001). Well-controlled experimental studies have demonstrated significant benefits (Ireland, 2004).

Cognitive Restructuring. The person is taught to reinterpret events as less threatening or hostile, to replace anger-evoking thoughts with calmer ones. For example, if another driver pulls into your lane without signaling, the driver may have been thoughtless rather than deliberately insulting you. A cashier who gives you incorrect change may have miscounted rather than trying to cheat you. Cognitive restructuring is based on the research suggesting that anger is more likely when a person interprets an offense as intentional rather than accidental.

Social Skills Training. Conflict with other people is probably the major cause of anger, and one reason for conflict is poor communication. Therapists try to teach people to identify when they are starting to get angry, relax themselves, and calm down before speaking. They also try to get people to communicate their needs more clearly to others, so that the others can meet those needs and therefore provoke less anger. They also help people practice social skills in real-life situations (Conduct Problems Prevention Research Group, 2002; Farmer, Compton, Burns, & Robertson, 2002).

Distraction. When someone is starting to get angry, a good strategy is to think about something else, such as something pleasant or amusing (Wilde, 2001). In one experiment, people first were asked to recall an emotionally painful experience of feeling rejected. Those who were asked to focus on remembering how they felt reacted with hostility; those who were asked to focus on what they remembered of the setting (such as the room's appearance) were much less upset (Ayduk, Mischel, & Downey, 2002). So the idea is to get people to focus on the facts of the situation, not their own distress.

Exposure Therapy. A common treatment for phobia is called systematic desensitization: Someone with a fear of something is gradually exposed to that object while remaining relaxed. The same procedure can be applied to someone with extreme anger. The person is told to relax and then is gradually exposed to the kinds of events or insults that would usually provoke anger. The person practices remaining calm in the presence of these insults (Grodnitzky & Tafrate, 2000).

Problem Solving. Here the idea is very simple: People who can find a way to solve their problems have less cause to be angry. For example, children with anger problems benefit from academic tutoring.

Other Kinds of Therapy. Discussing problems of chronic aggression can help, but not always. In particular, group therapy sometimes backfires. People with anxiety problems or substance-abuse problems often profit by meeting with other people with similar problems. However, bringing together a group of violent individuals sometimes aggravates the problem. In one study, groups of seven or eight adolescents with a history of aggression and delinquency were brought together for 12 weekly meetings, in which they discussed their problems and set goals for prosocial behaviors. Over the next year, these participants showed an *increase* in delinquent behaviors, compared to a no-treatment control group (Poulin, Dishion, & Burraston, 2001).

Evidently, associating with an all-delinquent group provided bad role models and did more harm than good.

▫ What We Learn From Conduct Disorder and Antisocial Personality Disorder

Psychology has many diagnostic categories for people with excessive anxiety, such as phobia, panic disorder, and generalized anxiety disorder. In contrast, despite the fact that excessive anger can lead to serious life disruption, psychology recognizes no specific disorder for which intense anger is the primary symptom (Deffenbacher, in press).

However, two psychological disorders classed as *personality disorders* include excessive aggression as a major symptom: conduct disorder and antisocial personality disorder. **Personality disorders** are maladaptive, inflexible ways of dealing with the environment and other people. In most cases, they last a lifetime or close to it. They are not exactly something you "get" but more like something that you "are." Whereas most people with depression or anxiety disorders want to get rid of their problems, people with personality disorders are less likely to want to change. When they do seek help, it is often because *other* people want them to change.

Conduct disorder is diagnosed predominantly in children and adolescents. Someone with conduct disorder engages in some combination of the following: frequent bullying or fighting, using a weapon against people, cruelty to people or animals, theft, using force to get sex, destroying property, lying, and violation of parents' and school's rules (American Psychiatric Association, 1994). The diagnosis requires a judgment that the inappropriate behavior is more severe and persistent than ordinary youthful mischief or rebelliousness. Most people with conduct disorder have additional problems as well, especially attention deficit disorder, mood disorder, anxiety, substance abuse, poor social relationships, and academic difficulties (C. Clark, Prior, & Kinsella, 2002). Conduct disorder is more common in boys than girls. For both boys and girls, it reaches its peak prevalence in the teenage years and then declines (Maughan, Pickles, Rowe, Costello, & Angold, 2000). That is, someone who has gone through the teenage years without ever getting into trouble is unlikely to become impulsively violent later.

The criteria for **antisocial personality disorder** are similar except that the person is at least 18 years old: repeated illegal behaviors, dishonesty, impulsive behavior, repeated fighting, reckless disregard for other people's safety, consistent failure to keep a job or pay debts, and lack of guilt feelings for misbehavior (American Psychiatric Association, 1994). It is common for an adolescent with conduct disorder to "graduate" to a diagnosis of antisocial personality disorder after reaching age 18, although it is possible for adults to continue to be diagnosed with conduct disorder.

The underlying causes of conduct disorder and antisocial personality disorder are not well understood. The data support several possibilities, including genetic predispositions; growing up in a poor, crime-ridden neighborhood; physical abuse; and lack of parental supervision (Burke, Loeber, & Birmaher, 2002; Jewell & Stark, 2003; Loeber, Burke, Lahey, Winters, & Zera, 2000). Note the overlap of these factors with the causes of aggressive behavior in general.

You might imagine that excessive aggressive behavior stems from excessive anger, but most research does not support that view. People with conduct disorder or antisocial personality disorder tend to have somewhat lower than average sympathetic nervous system arousal (such as resting heart rate) at most times, although their arousal may increase more than average during periods of excitement (Burke et al., 2002; Lorber, 2004). These trends are, however, small and not entirely consistent. To the extent that they hold, one interpretation is that most of us are inhibited from antisocial behavior because we feel anxiety or guilt. People with less arousal experience less of these inhibiting emotions because

their sympathetic nervous system is less quickly aroused. Excessive aggressive behavior reflects a lack of inhibition, a lack of fear of the consequences.

◻ Summary

As you have seen, emotion researchers have not yet reached a consensus on some basic issues regarding anger and, therefore, emotion in general: Is a cognitive appraisal (such as attributing hostile intention to someone) necessary for anger? Or can anger sometimes arise just from bodily discomfort? Indeed, how closely linked are emotional cognitions and emotional feelings? We sympathize if you feel frustrated by uncertainty, but we also take this opportunity to remind you that the uncertainty makes emotion an exciting field for new research.

A couple of themes have emerged in this chapter that closely resemble points made in the previous chapter and that will emerge again in later chapters: One theme is that research requires good measurement, and measurement is best when we use a variety of methods. For example, if self-reports, behaviors, and physiological measures all indicate anger, we can be more confident than if we used just one of those types of measure. A second theme is that we need to distinguish among different kinds of emotion at different time scales. Just as we distinguish between short-term fear and long-term anxiety, it helps to distinguish among anger over some event, longer-term "crankiness," and proneness to anger or aggression as a lifelong personality trait. Similarly, in later chapters, we need to distinguish immediate joy from a happy disposition and immediate sadness from chronic depression. A third theme is that the consequences of any emotion depend on other emotions that might be present at the same time. In particular, whether anger leads to aggressive behavior depends largely on how much fear someone feels about the possible consequences.

Anger stands out from other emotions because of its social impact. If you are sad or fearful, your emotions are a problem for you and your family and friends but not of great concern to most other people. Angry people, however, can harm people they hardly know, and we need to learn how to predict and control violent behavior. Anger leads to violence mostly when inhibitions are low, when people think they can attack without much risk of harm. To control violence, we can look to decreasing the causes of people's anger, but we need also to strengthen inhibitions against violence.

◻ Key Terms

anger: the emotional state associated with a desire to hurt someone or drive that individual away (p. 124)

anger management training: methods therapists use to try to help people control their anger (p. 143)

antisocial personality disorder; condition in which people at least age 18 display repeated illegal behaviors, dishonesty, impulsive behavior, repeated fighting, reckless disregard for other people's safety, consistent failure to keep a job or pay debts, and lack of guilt feelings for misbehavior (p. 145)

Cognitive-Neoassociationistic (CNA) Model of Anger Generation: theory that anger and reactive aggression are enhanced by any unpleasant event or aversive condition (p. 128)

conduct disorder: condition diagnosed predominantly in children and adolescents, characterized by some combination of the following: frequent bullying or fighting, using a weapon against people, cruelty to people or animals, theft, using force to get sex, destroying property, lying, and violation of parents' and school's rules (p. 144)

frustration-aggression hypothesis: proposal that anything that interferes with one's ability to obtain some expected gratification leads to aggressive behavior (p. 128)

hostile aggression: an aggressive reaction to anger and the events that preceded it (p. 124)

instrumental aggression: an aggressive act the individual starts not as a reaction to anyone else's act but simply as a way to achieve some end (p. 124)

interaction between personality and environment: tendency for the effect of environment to depend on personality; for example, someone's disposition motivates him or her to select an environment that reinforces that personality disposition (p. 138)

personality disorders: long-lasting, maladaptive, inflexible ways of dealing with the environment and other people (p. 124)

reconciliation: an attempt to restore friendship after a fight (physical or verbal), and to prevent further hostility (p. 142)

resilience: the ability of people to overcome the effects of extremely unfavorable environments (p. 140)

serotonin: a neurotransmitter with many behavioral effects (p. 135)

state: a temporary condition related to recent events (p. 131)

testosterone: steroid hormone more common in males than females, important for male sex-related behaviors (p. 136)

themed dot-probe task: Task in which two words (one of which might be aggressive) flash briefly on the screen, one above the other. Then a dot appears in the same position as one of them, and the person must press a key as quickly as possible to indicate whether the dot appeared in the upper or lower position. (p. 133)

trait: a long-term aspect of personality (p. 131)

visual search task: Task in which a target word appears briefly in the center of the screen, surrounded by three other words. Then the target word and three new words appear, and the task is to locate the target word. (p. 134)

◻ Thought Questions

1. Researchers have found that people express anger more often at home than when they are at work (Bongard & al'Absi, 2003). Can you suggest an explanation?

2. Compare the Cognitive-Neoassociationistic Model to the James-Lange theory presented in Chapter 1. Are they compatible or contradictory?

3. If anger is most intense when we attribute hostile intention to someone, what are the implications concerning anger in children and non-human animals (which presumably are less likely to attribute intentions at all)?

◻ Suggestion for Research Projects

Keep an anger diary over a week or more. What kinds of events make you angry and what do you do about them?

◻ Suggestions for Further Reading

Beck, A. T. (1999). *Prisoners of hate: The cognitive basis of anger, hostility, and violence.* New York: Harper Collins. Aaron Beck is best known for his research on the cognitive factors in depression. In this book he applies principles of cognitive appraisal to research on anger and violence.

Goldstein, J. H. (Ed.). (1998). *Why we watch: The attractions of violent entertainment.* New York: Oxford University Press. In this collection of essays, several mass media researchers offer their thoughts on why violence and aggression are so prominent in human entertainment.

7

Sadness

Sadness is the opposite of happiness, right? If so, there is something peculiar about this pair of opposites. You can't be old and young at the same time, or tall and short, but you can be happy and sad at the same time. If you compete against your best friend for an award, then when the award is announced—regardless of which one of you wins—you will feel simultaneously happy and sad, an experience some call *bittersweet.* People also report bittersweet feelings during major transitions in their life, such as graduating from college or watching their children get married, and sometimes after watching a sad but inspiring film (Larsen, McGraw, & Cacioppo, 2001).

In fact, not everyone agrees that sadness is the opposite of happiness. According to surveys in the United States, most people who say they frequently feel happy also say that they seldom feel sad (Russell & Carroll, 1999). That conclusion may seem so obvious that you would wonder why psychologists would waste their time doing the research. However, people in many Asian cultures, influenced heavily by the teachings of Buddhism, Hinduism, and Confucianism, believe that happiness and sadness are compatible with each other. Surveys in those countries—such as Japan, China, Thailand,

and Korea—find that people who say they frequently feel happy are neither more nor less likely than other people to say they frequently feel sad (Schimmack, Oishi, & Diener, 2002).

◻ Sadness, Depression, and the Events Behind Them

Recall from Chapter 1 the distinction between emotion and mood. Sadness is an emotion provoked by an event, whereas depression is a long-lasting mood. **Sadness** is the emotional reaction to a sense of loss. You feel sad when you lose money, lose a job, get a bad grade on a test, or end a friendship or romance. **Bereavement** is a special kind of sadness in reaction to the loss of a loved one. In contrast, **depression** is an unhappy mood that persists for a long time, without any clear precipitating event that would be sufficient to merit such a severe reaction. For example, someone grieving over the recent death of a loved one should not be diagnosed as depressed.

Major depression is defined as a loss of pleasure, interest, and productive activity lasting most of each day for at least two weeks, severe enough to interfere with life (American Psychiatric Association,

1994). For example, major depression often leads to loss of a job, a breakup of friendships, or alienation from family. People who have experienced severe depression say that you cannot really imagine how bad it is unless you have lived through it yourself. Depression is classed as a mood or affect, rather than an emotion. Of course, the distinction is not an absolute one. When people suffer a loss, such as the loss of a job or the breakup of a romance, they vary in the severity and duration of their reactions. Any line separating "normal sadness" from "depression" is arbitrary. As we shall see, scientists have produced much research on depression and little on garden-variety sadness. For now, consider sadness and depression as categories that overlap in a fuzzy way but have some important although poorly understood distinctions. You will get a sense throughout the chapter of where the overlap is and where questions remain.

Although depression lasts at least two weeks by definition (and usually more), sadness can also last a long time, and bereavement can last a year or more. When you are bereaved, you are sad *no matter what* good event happens. You can still react with brief pleasure to a bit of good news, but that momentary pleasure does not take away from your deep grief. Remember, it is possible to feel joy and sadness at the same time. You won't get back to a genuinely happy mood until time starts to heal the pain. The emotional reaction is greatest shortly after hearing the bad news, and it does gradually dissipate over time, although people vary greatly in how fast they recover. Many people say they never fully recover after the death of a close loved one.

One study examined 94 Iraqi children who were in a shelter when it was bombed during the 1991 Gulf War, killing more than 750 people. Those children continued to show fear and sadness, intensely at first, rather severely for the first year, and then a little less intensely two years later (Dyregrov, Gjestad, & Raundalen, 2002). This result is typical of traumatic events and grief in general, with intense emotional experience at first and a gradual fading of response over months or years.

◻ What Causes Sadness and Depression?

Recall the study, discussed in the previous two chapters, in which Klaus Scherer (1997) collected data from 37 countries, asking people to describe situations in which they felt various emotions. Scherer found that people throughout the world become sad in situations that are unpleasant and therefore undesirable (not a huge surprise). Also, a sadness-producing event is incompatible with our goals and something external to ourselves causes it. (That is, most events that make you sad are not your fault. You can also feel sad about something that is your fault, but in that case you feel a mixture of sadness, guilt, and embarrassment.) Finally, consistent with much other research, Scherer found that people thought they could do little to remedy the sad outcome. That is, the losses that make us saddest are *irrevocable* losses—ones where nothing can change the outcome or bring back what we lost (Lazarus, 1991). We feel helpless in these situations, and the sense of helplessness is part of sadness. Sometimes we feel sad because we mistakenly think we are helpless, or we feel hopeful because we mistakenly think we are in control. That is, our emotions depend more on our perception of control than on actual control. In sum, a sadness-producing situation is unpleasant, probably caused externally, and apparently uncontrollable.

Sadness and depression share many features in common, such as inactivity, and research using brain scans has found that depressed people show larger than normal responses when they see a picture of a sad face (C. H. Y. Fu et al., 2004). However, Richard Davidson has argued persuasively that for most depressed people, the main symptom is not extreme sadness but a lack of pleasure. For example, in one study, depressed and undepressed people watched several kinds of films and reported their responses. The two groups responded about equally to the sad and frightening films, but the depressed people reported much less amusement from the comedies. In fact, they sometimes reported mild sadness during the comedies (Rottenberg, Kasch, Gross, & Gotlib, 2002).

In another study, people with major depression and healthy comparison people carried a device that beeped at random throughout the day. Whenever it beeped, they were to describe what was happening at the time, as well as their emotional reactions to it. The depressed people described the same number of unpleasant events as the other people, but far fewer pleasant events (Peters, Nicolson, Berkhof, Delespaul, & deVries, 2003).

For another study, depressed and undepressed women viewed a series of pictures and reported their emotional responses while researchers observed their facial expressions. The depressed and undepressed women reacted about equally to the sad pictures, but the depressed women showed significantly less response to the pleasant pictures. (See Figure 7.1.) In the same study, the participants were asked to rate how well 12 pleasant words and 12 unpleasant words applied to themselves. Afterward, they were asked (to their surprise) to recall the 24 words. The depressed women recalled fewer of the pleasant words than the nondepressed women did; the two groups recalled equal numbers of the unpleasant words (Sloan, Strauss, & Wisner, 2001).

In yet another study, depressed and undepressed participants viewed words on a computer screen and then completed a second task as a distraction. Then the researchers presented a longer list of words and asked participants to identify which ones had been on the original list. There were two types of trials, however. On some trials, participants were simply told to answer as accurately as possible, without any opportunity for rewards. On a different set of trials, all "hits" (correct identifications of previously viewed words) gained the participant 10 cents, with no penalty for saying "yes" incorrectly. If you were a participant, what would you do? Presumably, on the no-reward trials, you would do your best to answer correctly. On the rewarded trials, you would change your strategy: "When in doubt, say yes." After all, you have something to gain and nothing to lose. Most undepressed participants showed just this pattern. Depressives, by contrast, failed to change their strat-

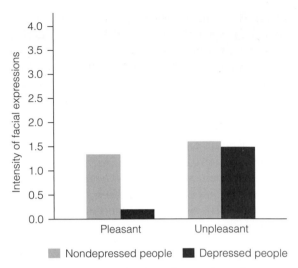

FIGURE 7.1   Depressed and nondepressed people showed about equal intensity of facial expressions when viewing unpleasant slides, but the depressed people showed much less response to the pleasant slides. Source: From "Diminished Response to Pleasant Stimuli by Depressed Women," *Journal of Abnormal Psychology, 10,* pp. 488–493. © 2001 American Psychological Association. Reprinted with permission from Dr. D. Sloan.

egy. That is, they did not increase their yes answers when those answers had a chance of being rewarded. Evidently they were less responsive than other people to the potential rewards in the situation (Henriques & Davidson, 2000).

Each of these studies points to the same conclusion: The main emotional characteristics of major depression are a loss of pleasure and attention to pleasure, rather than excessive sadness. Many seriously depressed people say they not only don't feel happy but also can't imagine anything that would make them happy.

◘ The Functions of Sadness

Recall from the definition in Chapter 1 that emotion is functional; that is, it serves some purpose. The functions of fear and anger are clear, but those of sadness are not. Imagine that someone develops a treatment that could prevent you from ever feeling sad again, no matter what happens. Would you take it? Should you? Of course, we all want to minimize the events that make us sad. And certainly we would like to avoid feeling excessively sad without good reason. But would we be better off if we lost all capacity for feeling sad? If not, sadness must be good for something. But what?

In the long run, a happy, optimistic disposition is linked with a variety of benefits in social life, physical health, and mental health. Unhappiness and depression lead to inactivity and social withdrawal, which are certainly disadvantageous for most people most of the time. Can we identify any circumstance in which inactivity and social withdrawal might be helpful?

Yes, at least one: When you are sick or in pain, your body reacts with increased sleep, decreased activity, decreased appetite, and decreased sex drive. Those reactions help you conserve energy and resist behaviors (like foraging for food) that would risk further harm. The body reacts in much the same way to highly stressful events as to pain. For example, a series of unavoidable electric shocks produces fever, sleepiness, loss of appetite, and other symptoms resembling illness. Some people react this way even to the stress of having to give a public speech (Maier & Watkins, 1998). That is, the body treats stressful events like an illness. (Is the body confusing stress with illness? Or is the body's reaction appropriate? That is, do fever, sleepiness, and inactivity help us deal with stress? This question is at present unanswered.)

Sadness is closely linked to stress, pain, and illness, and so it is possible that sadness is just one more manifestation of the body's way of dealing with such events. In fact, prolonged pain strongly increases the probability of feeling depressed (Bair, Robinson, Katon, & Kroenke, 2003). So, one hypothesis is that we evolved a tendency to become inactive and withdrawn when we are ill or in pain; we now react the same way to defeats and losses of many kinds. Let's call this idea the "sadness = pain or illness" hypothesis. (You might recall from Chapter 3 the Tahitians who use the term *pe'a pe'a*, meaning sick, when English-speaking people would say "sad." Given the relationship between sickness and sadness, the Tahitian point of view makes sense.)

According to another hypothesis, sadness evolved specifically for one social function: to lead you to withdraw from social contact at times when other people would be likely to exclude you anyway (N. B. Allen & Badcock, 2003). That is, sometimes you perceive that your presence would be unwelcome to others, maybe because you have failed at some important task. Under those circumstances, perhaps you should avoid risks, withdraw from other people, conserve your energy, and avoid opportunities for other people to reject you publicly. With the passage of time, you may be in a better position to return to social activities. We'll call this idea the "sadness = I'll stay out of your way" hypothesis. According to this viewpoint, sadness is useful in its proper time and place, but only for social animals like ourselves.

A third hypothesis is that sad behavior serves the opposite function: Sad behavior calls attention to your distress, shows you to be vulnerable like a child or infant, and therefore increases the chance that other people will tend to you and offer help. We can call this proposal the "sadness = help me" hypothesis. Again, note the assumption that sad behaviors have a social function, although this hypothesis suggests that sadness increases social attention instead of decreasing it.

So far, little research has been done to evaluate these hypotheses. Here are a few ideas that we consider testable; we invite you to think of additional suggestions:

- The "sadness = pain" hypothesis suggests that people in pain should feel sad (as we know that they do). It also implies that procedures that decrease pain (such as pain-killing drugs) should decrease sadness. The strongest form of this prediction would be that painkillers might decrease sadness regardless of its cause, even if it originated from social experiences.
- Both the "sadness = I'll leave you alone" and the "sadness = help me" hypotheses link sadness to social relationships. They imply that

sadness should be most clearly expressed by people with strong social relationships.

- Similarly, both of these hypotheses imply that sadness should occur more clearly in highly social species—such as humans, dogs, monkeys, or elephants—than in less social species, such as bears or house cats. Of course, the challenge is to determine when some nonhuman species is sad. We might take prolonged inactivity as one measure, but that measure is far from perfect.

- The "sadness = I'll leave you alone" hypothesis implies that anyone who fails to act sad after suffering a defeat should encounter long-term social rejection. It also implies that other people should welcome back to society someone who withdrew temporarily because of sadness.

- The "sadness = help me" hypothesis implies that people who act sad should get more social support than those who don't act sad, other things being equal.

It is also possible that some combination of these hypotheses is correct. For example, sadness might cause you to withdraw from the company of most people, while getting increased attention and help from your family and closest friends. Sadness could be closely related to pain and illness, as well as serving social functions. In any case, the topic needs more research.

Psychologists have also considered the possibility that depression is an adaptive mechanism. Note that this question is separate from the function of sadness: A brief reaction of sadness could be advantageous even if long-term depression is not. The **Social Navigation Hypothesis** proposes that depression serves two functions similar to the "I'll leave you alone" hypothesis and the "help me" hypothesis. According to this view, depression causes someone to withdraw from society long enough to ruminate—that is, to rethink one's lifestyle and change social behaviors. It also attracts other people's attention and solicits their help (P. J. Watson & Andrews, 2002). However, critics of this view argue that prolonged depression is almost always disadvantageous. For example, if you act sad briefly, your friends and

family come to your aid, but if you remain depressed for months, they start avoiding you (Nettle, 2004). Therefore, depression may not have a function at all; it may be just the disadvantageous tail end of the normal distribution (Nettle, 2004).

◻ Measuring Sadness: Feelings, Behaviors, and Physiology

Because people express sadness in so many ways, we might imagine that it would be easy to measure. The apparent simplicity may be deceptive, however, as even the classic expression of sadness—crying—can mean many different things. As with other emotions, in the process of trying to measure sadness, we learn much about it.

Self-Report Measures

Research on sadness almost always begins with self-reports. Researchers observe behavior or physiology to determine how it is associated with sadness; rarely do they use the behavior or physiology to determine whether someone is sad. Because of this heavy reliance on self-reports, most research on sadness is restricted to humans.

You might imagine that such a common feeling as sadness would be studied so often that psychologists would have carefully standardized and extensively researched some highly valid questionnaires. However, because most of the focus in this area deals with psychological patients rather than healthy individuals, most of the questionnaires deal with depression, not with sadness.

The most widely used depression questionnaire is the **Beck Depression Inventory—II,** a multiple-choice questionnaire about sadness, guilt, self-blame, suicidal thoughts, loss of interest, sleep problems, fatigue, and so forth. People answer in terms of how they have felt over the previous two weeks. A score above 15 on this scale indicates moderate depression and a score above 30 indicates severe depression. This questionnaire is highly regarded for its ability to identify depressed people and measure changes in their level of depression. However, because it is aimed at clinical depression, it does not distinguish among various degrees of temporary or mild sadness.

One questionnaire that is labeled as a depression scale actually does a reasonably good job of measuring sadness. Recall Spielberger's State-Trait Anger Expression Inventory, discussed in Chapter 6. The **State-Trait Depression Scales**, also devised by Charles Spielberger and his colleagues, is similar. It asks you about your current depressive state (approximately equal to sadness) and your usual level of depression (depression as a trait). The "state" items deal with sad feelings, lack of energy, and hopelessness. The "trait" items deal with longer-lasting conditions, such as sleeplessness. The State-Trait Depression Scales, which have been translated into several languages and used in many countries, show fairly high reliability (Krohne, Schmukle, Spaderna, & Spielberger, 2002).

Although research on sadness relies mostly on self-reports, behavioral studies provide a helpful way of double-checking. People usually look and act sad when they say they are feeling sad, but not always (Bonanno & Keltner, 2004). When we find a discrepancy—such as someone acting sad while denying sadness—psychologists search for a reason. For example, is the person trying to hide a problem?

Behavioral Measures

The most characteristic behavior associated with sadness is inactivity. However, people can be inactive for many reasons other than sadness. Illness is one obvious possibility. Consequently, it is problematic to use what people are *not* doing to infer what they are feeling.

FACIAL EXPRESSION

Sadness does have a characteristic facial expression. Darwin (1872/1998) first described the face and posture of sadness, and his description has received a great deal of support since then. In cross-cultural studies of facial expressions, Paul Ekman and his colleagues confirmed that people around the world recognize a facial display of sadness (Ekman et al., 1987). In this display, the inner eyebrows but *not* the outer eyebrows are raised, and the brows may be scrunched together somewhat as well. The corners of the lips are turned down, and the chin may be raised and wrinkled. People usually look down and seldom maintain eye contact for long (Adams & Kleck, 2005). The cheeks are raised and the muscles around the eyes are tightened, as they are in smiles also. But the rest of the expression readily distinguishes the sad expression from smiles. (See Figure 7.2.)

Darwin, Charles, *The Expression of the Emotions in Man and Animals* (1872/1998), with permission from Oxford University Press.

FIGURE 7.2 Typical facial expressions of sadness.

© David Young-Wolff/PhotoEdit

FIGURE 7.3   Depression is usually apparent in people's facial expression, posture, and actions.

Figure 7.3 shows a depressed person. Some depressed people hide their feelings from others, but most don't. Depressed people often look sad, although perhaps the more characteristic description is that they almost never look happy. Their posture, tone of voice, sighs, and inactivity are further indications of their distressed mood.

CRYING

The other behavioral sign of sadness is crying. Crying is highly characteristic of sadness, but not of depression. One study found that depressed people cried no more than average while watching a sad movie (Rottenberg, Gross, Wilhelm, Najmi, & Gotlib, 2002). In fact, the patients who had been depressed for the longest time cried the least, supporting the notion that depression is more strongly linked to lack of pleasure than to excessive sadness.

Infant birds and mammals of many species wail when hungry or when separated from their mother. For example, the vocalizations of a baby rat separated from its mother (which are ultrasonic as far as humans are concerned, although other rats can hear them) clearly differ from those that rats make during sex or other pleasant activities, and other rats respond to the distress calls as an indication of danger (Knutson, Burgdorf, & Panksepp, 2002). Adult rats also howl or yelp in pain or distress. In other words, crying in distress is a common form of communication in many species. However, human crying is special in two ways:

- Infants of other species, including chimpanzees, almost always stop crying when they get fed or when the mother returns to them (Bard, 2000). Human infants sometimes keep on crying, despite every attention the parents can provide.
- Humans often shed tears when they cry. No other species is known to accompany its wailing sounds with watery eyes, at least not frequently.

It seems obvious why infants cry; they have no other means of communicating their distress and need for attention. But why do adults cry? Adults have speech, so it might seem that crying is unnecessary. To some extent the answer is that crying is simply left over from early childhood, just as our belly buttons are left over from prenatal life. We humans do remain childlike in some ways throughout adulthood. Consider playfulness: The young of many animal species engage in actions we might call "play," but adult nonhumans are seldom if ever playful,—with the exception of dogs, which humans have selectively bred for such behaviors. By contrast, human adults play all the time, from card games to Frisbee to crossword puzzles.

Another reason for adult crying is that it elicits a much stronger reaction from other people than any verbal statement would, just as laughter elicits a greater reaction than would the words "that's funny." When we see someone cry, we react with sympathy and care, much as we would toward an infant or young child who had been hurt.

To try to understand adult crying, researchers collected self-reports from 1,680 men and 2,323 women in 30 countries (Becht & Vingerhoets, 2002). As always with self-reports, we can question how accurately people report the frequency of their crying. Still, some of the trends were large enough to take seriously, even if the figures were not exact. Certain cultures tolerate adult crying far more than others do. For example, U.S. men reported crying an average of 1.9 times per month and women 3.5 times, as compared to China where the means were 0.4 for men and 1.4 for women. Obviously, individual differences are enormous within any culture. Some people cry frequently and others almost never. Women reported crying more than men within any given culture, although the men of some cultures cried more than the women of others. A study across ages found that during childhood, boys and girls cry about equally. As they grow older, both boys and girls decrease their crying, but boys decrease more, so that from the teenage years and beyond, women cry more than men (Van Tilburg, Unterberg, & Vingerhoets, 2002).

In another survey, researchers explored *why* people cry. They asked 164 medical students to keep track of all the occasions when they cried over two weeks. Nearly all instances fell into two categories—requesting help and offering help. That is, we cry when we are suffering or when we sympathize with someone else's suffering (Murube, Murube, & Murube, 1999). In some cases, people also cry from intense joy, such as when attending a wedding. Researchers have not had much to say about that kind of crying.

Although we interpret crying as a plea for help, people don't always react with sympathy when they see someone else cry. You probably have heard the expression, "Laugh and the world laughs with you. Cry and you cry alone." Laughter is so contagious that if you laugh long enough and hard enough, the world—or at least part of it—will laugh with you, even if they have no idea why you are laughing

(Provine, 2000). If you cry, people do not automatically cry with you. They try to see *why* you are crying. If they see that you are in great pain or that you have just suffered a personal tragedy, your tears will evoke a powerful emotional response, and some people will cry in sympathy with you and possibly try to help you. Even if they don't cry, observing your pain produces brain responses typical of very unpleasant emotional experiences (Singer et al., 2004). However, if people believe you are crying about something unimportant, or if they decide you have used tears to manipulate them, their response will be less sympathetic (Kottler, 1996).

One reason why you are more likely to cry alone than to laugh alone is that ordinarily people *want* to cry alone. Most adults are embarrassed to cry in front of other people, especially people they do not know well, except in special situations such as funerals. However, some people say that crying together with someone led them to become intimate friends (Kottler, 1996). So the social aspect of crying is important and needs to be explored more fully.

Why did we evolve the tendency to cry? Most people report that crying makes them feel better (Becht & Vingerhoets, 2002), and one hypothesis is that crying relieves tension. However, several kinds of evidence argue against that hypothesis. Crying is associated with a marked *increase* in heart rate and other signs of arousal (J. J. Gross, Fredrickson, & Levenson, 1994). The tension subsides only after the crying ends. Also, consider this experiment: People in one group were encouraged to cry while they watched a very sad film, while those in another were instructed to hold back the tears. The instructions succeeded and those encouraged to cry did cry on the average almost 10 times as much as the others. The criers' tension increased greatly while they were crying and subsided afterward, but by the time the movie ended their tension was merely equal to that of those who inhibited crying. That is, criers would notice a relief of tension, but mainly because the crying itself had increased their tension, and they felt relief when it stopped. According to questionnaire results, the criers actually felt a bit worse

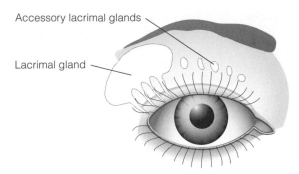

FIGURE 7.4 The lacrimal gland is the source of tears. Other smaller glands in the eyelids provide a steady supply of moisture that covers the eyes, but they do not produce sudden bursts like the lacrimal gland does.

(more depressed) after the film than did the noncriers (Kraemer & Hastrup, 1988). In short, the results showed no physiological or psychological benefits from crying. This result is especially striking because, in most other studies of how people regulate their emotions, the people who expressed their feelings have shown *less* cardiovascular arousal than people who tried to hold them back.

Why do people shed tears when they cry? Remember, many species make howling sounds when they are in pain or other distress, but only humans frequently shed tears to accompany their wails. One hypothesis is that shedding tears is beneficial because it excretes some toxin that builds up during times of sadness. Chemically, tears are mostly salt water, very similar to sweat. They come from the **lacrimal gland,** a structure controlled by the trigeminal nerve, one of the cranial nerves. (See Figure 7.4.) Tears do contain a small amount of proteins and more when we cry from sadness than when we cry from peeling an onion (Frey, DeSota-Johnson, Hoffman, & McCall, 1981). Still, it seems far fetched to imagine that we weep to excrete a tiny amount of proteins. Perhaps the tears themselves have no physiological function except to call more attention to the crying and therefore attract help (Murube, Murube, & Murube, 1999).

The Biology of Sadness

We are somewhat limited in describing the biology of sadness because it is difficult to elicit intense sadness in laboratory situations where neurological activation and cardiovascular physiology can be measured. If you were going to try to make someone sad in a small room hooked up to recording leads or a brain scanner, how would you do it? Some researchers use video clips. That procedure works to some extent, but it has a couple of limitations. First, people know they're watching a movie instead of reality, and although some people are very moved by films, others are not. Second, most films elicit several different emotions, varying from one person to another. Film clips portraying a death are a fairly reliable way to elicit sadness, but they often elicit fear or anger as well.

Yet another approach is to ask people to remember a sad event, such as when someone close to them died or when they broke up with a romantic partner. This method can be effective, but it too has limitations. Obviously, some people have had more recent and more intense sad memories than others, so the recollection task is not the same for all participants. Also, if the experimenter asks people to talk about the sad event, instead of just imagining it silently, talking produces physiological responses of its own. It is possible to compensate by asking a control group to describe some unemotional experience and then comparing the two groups.

Another method is to play sad music, such as Bartok's "Divertimento for String Orchestra." The ability of music to elicit an emotional response is quite amazing. It will not make people as intensely sad as an actual tragic event, but for many research purposes, brief, mild sadness is quite adequate and raises fewer ethical problems.

Studies of these types have revealed some of the neurological and cardiovascular correlates of sadness. However, much more research has dealt with depressed people because of the clinical importance of this disorder. As already discussed, depression is not the same as sadness.

AUTONOMIC NERVOUS SYSTEM ACTIVITY

When you think about what sadness feels like, you think of having very little energy and of being passive. Therefore, you might suspect that the cardiovascular physiology of sadness would be sluggish as well. Surprisingly, researchers have found that when people adopt sad expressions, their physiology shows arousal. In the "directed facial action" task, participants were asked to pose the sadness displays shown in Figure 7.2, responding to such instructions as "lift the inner parts of your eyebrows, but not the outer parts." Participants who followed the instructions well showed *increased* heart rate and faster breathing relative to baseline—both signs of arousal (Levenson, Ekman, & Friesen, 1990). As we saw in the section on crying, shedding tears is also associated with sympathetic nervous system arousal. Furthermore, sadness is associated with increased release of cortisol from the adrenal gland (Buss et al., 2003). That hormone, often called a "stress hormone," also accompanies fear. Because the physiological response of sadness overlaps that of fear and anger, researchers cannot use peripheral physiology to distinguish among these emotions.

BRAIN ACTIVITY

As we shall see in the next chapter, increased activity of the frontal cortex of the left hemisphere is associated with happiness and a tendency to approach. Increased activity in the frontal cortex of the right hemisphere is associated with sadness and a tendency to withdraw. For example, temperamentally shy children show increased activity in the right frontal cortex during social activities they would like to avoid, such as speaking in public about embarrassing topics (L. A. Schmidt, Fox, Schulkin, & Gold, 1999). The same tendencies appear to hold throughout life. Shy college students show more right than left frontal activity (Schmidt, 1999). Even among 6-month-old babies, those with greater activity in the right frontal cortex tend to show more fear and sadness under a variety of circumstances (Buss et al., 2003).

Figure C.2 (see inside cover) showed that any given emotion activates a wide variety of areas within either hemisphere, varying with details of procedure. Viewing a sad film tends to activate several areas in the frontal cortex, the temporal cortex, and the midbrain (Lévesque et al., 2003). The nature of contributions by each of those areas remains to be determined; the key point is simply that sadness, like any other emotion, depends on a wide circuit of brain areas.

NEUROTRANSMITTERS

Several neurotransmitters show a strong relationship, either positive or negative, with sadness and depression. One of the strongest relationships is with **beta endorphin**, a naturally produced neurotransmitter that serves as the body's natural painkiller. The term *endorphin* is a contraction of "endogenous morphine" because it acts like a self-produced morphine. Pain does not always release endorphins, but when it does, the endorphins help to curb the pain. Social loss and grief decrease endorphin release, thereby magnifying the unpleasant feeling associated with pain. That result has been measured in both humans and laboratory animals. For example, in one study, young women were asked to describe various life events, including some that were sad and some that were neutral. PET scans indicated decreased endorphin release in several brain areas while the women were describing sad events (Zubieta et al., 2003).

In another study, infant guinea pigs cried when separated from their mothers (presumably indicating distress and low endorphin release), but if they were given a mild dose of morphine (replacing the decreased endorphins), they stopped crying. If given naloxone, a drug that blocks endorphin activity, they cried even harder than usual (Herman & Panksepp, 1978).

In short, the emotional distress that accompanies a sad event resembles pain or magnifies pain. In one study, researchers used fMRI to measure brain responses while young adults played a computer game in which the player tossed a virtual ball back and forth with two other players, supposedly in other rooms. In fact, there were no other players, and a computer controlled everything to make it appear that two others were playing. At first, all three apparent participants passed the ball back and forth about equally, but then the other two passed it between themselves, completely excluding the actual, live participant. Being excluded caused people to report feeling distressed; moreover, this experience activated a brain area called the anterior cingulate cortex, which also responds strongly to physical pain (Eisenberger, Lieberman, & Williams, 2003). (See Figure C.5 on the inside cover of this book.) So when we talk about a "painful" emotional experience, we are correct in a more than metaphorical way.

Chronic depression is associated with a class of neurotransmitters known as the catecholamines, specifically the neurotransmitters dopamine and norepinephrine. In general, frontal lobe dopamine and norepinephrine activity are associated with responsiveness to reward (Henriques & Davidson, 2000). Dopamine is released in certain brain areas, especially the nucleus accumbens, during a wide variety of reinforcing activities, including sex, drug abuse, and videogame playing. Some investigators have reported decreased levels of dopamine metabolites in people with depression (Reddy, Khanna, Subhash, Channabasavanna, & Rao, 1992). People with bipolar disorder (which used to be called "manic depressive disorder") may have unusually large fluctuations in dopamine, with higher levels of release during their manic episodes and decreased levels during their depressive phases.

However, people with depression vary in both their symptoms and their body chemistry, so one explanation may not fit all. James Maas (1975) proposed distinguishing two types of depression. Type "A" depression, he suggested, was associated with a deficiency of dopamine and norepinephrine, whereas Type "B" was characterized by serotonin deficiency. These two neurochemical patterns may correspond to different behavioral symptoms. *DSM-IV*, the standard reference work on diagnosing mental disorders, also identifies two types of depression: **Typical or melancholic depression** (possibly corresponding to Maas's Type B?) is characterized by decreased appetite and weight loss, insomnia, and psychomotor agitation—such as wringing one's hands or pacing back and forth. **Atypical depression** (possibly Maas's Type A?) is characterized by increased appetite and weight gain, sleeping too much, and psychomotor retardation (Posternak & Zimmerman, 2002). This distinction offers at least a hypothesis to guide research and a possible way to reconcile some of the conflicting results on depression.

Most antidepressant drugs increase the availability of serotonin and dopamine at their synapses. One of the most popular antidepressants, fluoxetine (trademark Prozac) is fairly specific to serotonin, with little effect on other neurotransmitters. After serotonin is released at a synapse, it attaches to its receptors, activates them, breaks away, and then in most cases becomes reabsorbed by the cell that released it, through a membrane protein called the serotonin transporter. Fluoxetine blocks the serotonin transporter and, therefore, causes released serotonin to remain longer in the synapse, where it can reattach to its receptors. Many antidepressant drugs block the dopamine transporter as well as the serotonin transporter, thereby prolonging the effects of both neurotransmitters. A few antidepressants, such as buproprion (Wellbutrin), act on just dopamine synapses. Different people respond to different drugs, as we should expect if depression comes in several types.

The fact that most antidepressant drugs increase serotonin activity suggests that depression is associated with, perhaps even caused by, a deficit in serotonin. However, other kinds of evidence offer only mixed support for this hypothesis. For example, we might predict that depressed patients would show low levels of serotonin or its metabolites in their blood and other body fluids. Multiple tests of that hypothesis have found only inconsistent results (Leonard, 2000). Low levels of serotonin metabolites in the blood generally correlate better with aggressiveness and suicidal tendencies than with depression

(Mann, McBride, Anderson, & Mieczkowski, 1992; Spreux-Varoquaux et al., 2001). However, the research has been more consistent in finding that depressed people have abnormalities of the serotonin transporter proteins (Leonard, 2000).

Another relevant type of research tests the effects of decreasing or increasing someone's serotonin levels. One way to deplete the brain of serotonin, quickly and temporarily, is by a diet that is rich in most amino acids but lacking in tryptophan, the amino acid that the brain converts into serotonin. That procedure can trigger a bout of depression, aggressive behavior, or neither (Neumeister et al., 2004; S. N. Young & Leyton, 2002). We do not know why different people react differently. Procedures that increase serotonin levels tend to increase social, gregarious behaviors in species as different as humans (Tse & Bond, 2002), monkeys (Raleigh, McGuire, Brammer, Pollack, & Yuwiler, 1991), and lobsters (Huber, Orzeszyna, Pokorny, & Kravitz, 1997). So that effect seems surprisingly robust, although the behaviors tested in lobsters aren't much like those of extraverted humans.

As a further complication, the effects of the antidepressant drugs themselves are problematic. They increase serotonin activity quickly (generally within an hour or so), but a depressed person has to take the drugs for at least two weeks before feeling any benefit. So the drugs are probably producing their benefits by some other mechanism besides increasing serotonin activity. In short, don't think of serotonin as the "antidepression" transmitter.

Note also that the research on dopamine and serotonin pertains just to depression. To date, researchers have seldom tested any link between these neurotransmitters and everyday sadness.

◻ Sad and Depressed Thinking

Your mood affects your whole approach to life. When you are cheerful, the world seems a good place, and you feel capable of great things. For every cloud, you find a silver lining. When your spirits are low, you don't like anything, including yourself. For every silver lining, you find a cloud.

People feel sad when they believe they are helpless in some situation; they become depressed if they feel helpless or hopeless in general (Lazarus, 1991). One consistent feature of depression is a tendency toward a pessimistic explanatory style for negative events. An **explanatory style** is a characteristic way of making attributions (explanations) for success or failure. Generally, people recognize that their successes depend on varying combinations of luck, skill, and hard work. In contrast, people tend to be more consistent in how they explain their failures. Some tend to blame their failures on themselves, some generally blame bad luck, some blame other people, and so forth. A person's explanatory style for failures tends to be consistent across situations and over a long time, even decades (Burns & Seligman, 1989). Blaming failure on your lack of effort is a somewhat optimistic style; it implies that you have the skill to succeed and next time, with more effort, you will. Blaming failure on your lack of ability ("I'm stupid") is the most pessimistic style. It implies that the reason for failure is within yourself, stable (that is, consistent over time), and global (consistent over situations). Most depressed people have a pessimistic explanatory style (Alloy et al., 1999).

In addition to a pessimistic explanatory style, most depressed people have dysfunctional attitudes, which are unrealistic beliefs about what they "must" become or what they "must" accomplish to be satisfied. One example of a dysfunctional attitude is, "Failing at something means I am less worthy as a person." Aaron Beck (1973, 1987) has reported that depressed people find failures in the most ordinary events because of their dysfunctional attitudes. Every minor defeat seems further evidence of their weakness or stupidity. If someone walks by without smiling or talking, they take it as further evidence of their unpopularity. People who interpret almost every event as a failure quickly become discouraged, as you can imagine, and one of the main hallmarks of depression is a lack of motivation and activity.

The dysfunctional attitudes of depression are clearly related to the pessimistic explanatory style, but dysfunctional attitudes appear to be the better predictor. That is, dysfunctional attitudes correlate more strongly with depression than the pessimistic explanatory style does (Spangler & Burns, 1999).

◻ Predispositions

Who becomes sad or depressed? To the first question, the answer seems obvious: "Everyone becomes sad." Yes, but why do some people become sad more often than others? Again the answer might seem obvious: Isn't it because more unpleasant events happened to them? Not necessarily. In the face of similar life events, some people become sadder than others or remain sad longer. Researchers have documented that a tendency toward frequent sad experiences correlates about .6 with the personality trait "neuroticism" (Stewart, Ebmeier, & Deary, 2005). (Reminder: A zero correlation means no linear relationship; a correlation of 1 indicates a perfect relationship.) In a sense, a fairly high correlation between sadness and neuroticism seems almost trivial because neuroticism is defined as a tendency to feel negative emotions easily. So, of course, someone who frequently feels negative emotions also feels sad more often than others. But the point is simply that consistent individual differences do occur. Some people do feel sad more often than others, as part of a personality trait, and not entirely as a result of events beyond their control. Exactly how this personality trait originates is another question, but several studies have indicated that it is partly under genetic control (Heath, Neale, Kessler, Eaves, & Kendler, 1992; Loehlin, 1992; Viken, Rose, Kaprio, & Koskenvuo, 1994).

People also vary in their tendency to become depressed. After any terrible experience, some become more depressed than others. Some of this variation relates to people's "default" mood. One study took advantage of the fact that a group of college students had filled out personality questionnaires shortly before a major earthquake struck their city in California. Researchers found that virtually everyone felt sad or depressed in the first weeks after the damage, but those who already had been mildly depressed before the earthquake reacted more strongly to it and remained strongly depressed longer than the other students (Nolen-Hoeksema & Morrow, 1991).

Yet the questions remain: Why do people have different default moods? And why do some react more strongly than others to a given event? One hypothesis is genetics. Depression tends to run in families (Erlenmeyer-Kimling et al., 1997). That evidence by itself is inconclusive, but better evidence is that when an adopted child develops depression (after reaching adulthood), depression is generally more common among that person's biological relatives than among the adoptive relatives (Wender et al., 1986). The risk of depression is highest for people whose relatives became depressed early in life, and higher for those with depressed female relatives than those with depressed male relatives (Bierut et al., 1999; Kendler, Gardner, & Prescott, 1999; Lyons et al., 1998). The apparent interpretation is that many people who become depressed early in life have genes predisposing them to depression.

However, the genes are probably not specific to depression. Major depression runs in the same families with alcohol dependence, other substance dependence, antisocial personality disorder, bulimia, panic disorder, migraine headaches, attention-deficit disorder, and a variety of other problems (Dawson & Grant, 1998; Q. Fu et al., 2002; Hudson et al., 2003; Kendler et al., 1995). That is, if you have a relative with any of these disorders, your risk is above average for developing the same disorder or any of the others. The predisposition interacts with other factors, including gender. Within a given family, on the average, more men will have alcohol problems and more women will have depression (Dawson & Grant, 1998). The underlying genetic predisposition may be the same.

Gender is, in fact, another correlate of depression. In studies throughout the world, women are more likely to be diagnosed with depression than men. One theory relates this difference to women's tendency to "ruminate" (think repeatedly about negative events) more than men do. Studies find that men are less likely to ruminate and tend toward higher senses of mastery, and only those women who ruminate extensively and have lower mastery scores show greater susceptibility to depression (Nolen-Hoeksema, Larson, & Grayson, 1999). If, as we said before, a pessimistic explanatory style predicts depression, it may be that women are more likely to have learned this explanatory style than men. An alternative interpretation is that rumination does not cause later depression; it just precedes it as an early symptom. That is, those who ruminate extensively are already a little depressed. However, teaching people not to ruminate does help prevent depression, so rumination does appear to be a factor leading to depression (Morrow & Nolen-Hoeksema, 1990).

Another hypothesis about the causes of depression is that having gone through previous bad experiences may predispose people to react more strongly to new ones and therefore become depressed. Some of these experiences are more likely to happen to women than men. For example, several studies have found that women who were sexually abused during childhood are at increased risk for adult depression and suicide (Brent et al., 2002; Davidson, Hughes, George, & Blazer, 1996). One difficulty in interpreting those results is that many of those growing up with sexual abuse may also have been exposed to poverty, various kinds of nonsexual abuse, and other problems. To control for these other influences, researchers examined people who reported childhood sexual abuse and among them identified those with a twin who did not report childhood sexual abuse. As a rule, the twin reporting sexual abuse had the greater risk of depression and suicide attempts, although the other twin also had more than the average for the rest of the

population (E. C. Nelson et al., 2002). The implication is that the overall family life predisposed somewhat to depression (as seen in both twins), but sexual abuse significantly added to that predisposition.

◻ Limiting Sadness and Preventing Depression

The only way to avoid sadness is to avoid having anything bad happen in your life. Good luck with that. However, you can take steps to prevent sadness from overwhelming you or developing into depression.

Much of the advice is the same as that for coping with stress. A later chapter will cover that topic in more detail, so we will emphasize just a few points here. One recommendation is to reinterpret negative events to make them less catastrophic. In one study, college students who were at risk for depression because of their attitudes and pessimistic attributional style were randomly assigned to receive no treatment or a series of eight workshops on how to combat negative thoughts about themselves. For example, if you fail a test, it doesn't mean that you should give up on yourself academically. It might be a message to rethink your educational plans and take different types of courses. If you lose a job, you should not conclude that you will never keep a good job. Maybe it wasn't the right kind of job for you, and when you find the right job, maybe everything will work out for the best. In any situation, the idea is to interpret unfavorable events in a way that avoids excessive discouragement and self-blame. The students who received this kind of training reported significantly fewer episodes of anxiety and depression over the next three years (Seligman, Schulman, DeRubeis, & Hollon, 1999).

Another recommendation is to try to get onto a more regular sleep schedule. Sleeplessness is closely related to depression, and getting to bed at a more consistent time can help reduce the risk of depression (Wehr et al., 1998). Also try to get some exercise on a regular basis. Moderate aerobic exercise such as jogging, brisk walking, or dancing—enough to speed up the blood flow—is one of the most reliable ways to combat mild depression (Leppämäki, Partonen, & Lönnqvist, 2002). Of course, that advice is impractical for severely depressed people, who hardly want to get out of bed, much less go jogging.

Many studies suggest that the prevalence of depression has been rising over the decades, especially in the United States (Murphy, Laird, Monson, Sobol, & Leighton, 2000). Why? No one knows, but presumably it is related to some change in our lifestyle. One obvious change is that people today are more sedentary. People sit at desks instead of working in factories or farms. They drive instead of walking and take elevators instead of climbing the stairs. We don't want to suggest anything so simplistic as that a little more exercise will prevent depression, but it would probably help somewhat, and it can't hurt.

▢ Summary

The universe has a strange kind of asymmetry: In many situations, a little bit of bad seems more powerful than a little bit of good. Psychologist Paul Rozin quotes a Nebraska mechanic who said that if you add a spoonful of sewage to a vat of fine wine, you ruin it, but if you add a spoonful of fine wine to a vat of sewage, you don't do any good at all. Likewise, it is easier for one person to do a great deal of harm than for one person to do a great deal of good. Good government can improve people's lives a little bit at a time, but bad government can wreak misery rapidly. If you hear many good things about someone but one bad thing (like "he cheats" or "she is cold and uncaring"), the bad usually outweighs the good in your evaluation of that person (Ito, Larsen, Smith, & Cacioppo, 2002). And one event can make a person permanently sad, but it is unusual for one event to make anyone happy for long.

In short, sadness and depression often last a long time and sometimes too long. We discussed the possible functions of sadness and depression: Maybe under some circumstances, social withdrawal and inactivity help conserve energy and enable you to prepare for a better life later. Maybe a sad expression elicits help from some friends and relatives. At best, the benefits of sadness and depression are temporary. Long-term withdrawal and inactivity, beyond what is needed to recover one's energies, becomes part of the problem, not the solution. Long-term expressions of sadness no longer elicit help from your friends; if you act sad long enough, you start losing your friends. Why do these reactions last so long and what we can do about them? Clearly, depressed people dislike feeling depressed and would welcome relief. In spite of all the research, we don't understand why depression sometimes lasts so long. We still have much to learn about how to control our emotions and moods.

▢ Key Terms

atypical depression: condition characterized by depressed mood, increased appetite and weight gain, sleeping too much, and psychomotor retardation (p. 158)

Beck Depression Inventory—II: multiple-choice questionnaire about sadness, guilt, self-blame, suicidal thoughts, loss of interest, sleep problems, fatigue, and so forth (p. 152)

bereavement: sadness in reaction to the loss of a loved one (p. 148)

beta endorphin: a naturally produced neurotransmitter that serves as the body's natural painkiller (p. 157)

depression: unhappy mood that persists for a long time, without any clear precipitating event that would be sufficient to merit such a severe reaction (p. 148)

explanatory style: characteristic way of making attributions (explanations) for success or failure (p. 159)

lacrimal gland: structure responsible for the tears shed during crying, controlled by the trigeminal nerve, which is one of the cranial nerves (p. 156)

major depression: loss of pleasure, interest, and productive activity lasting most of each day for at least two weeks, severe enough to interfere with life (p. 148)

sadness: emotional reaction to a sense of loss (p. 148)

Social Navigation Hypothesis: view that depression serves functions of withdrawing a person from society long enough to change social behaviors and of attracting people's help (p. 152)

State-Trait Depression Scales: questionnaire concerning a person's current and usual levels of depression (p. 153)

typical or melancholic depression: condition characterized by depressed mood, decreased appetite and weight loss, insomnia, and psychomotor agitation (p. 158)

◻ Thought Questions

1. Many psychologists group fear, anger, and sadness as the "negative" emotions. What, if anything, do they have in common?
2. You have read about three theories of the function of sadness. What research could help to evaluate them or decide among them?

3. What explanation could you propose (speculatively, of course) for why extreme joy and extreme sadness both lead to crying?

◻ Suggestion for Research Project

Play some sad music, such as Bartok's "Divertimento for String Orchestra" or Barber's "Adagio for Strings," and ask listeners to describe their mood at various times during it or afterward. How fast does the sad mood develop? How long does it last?

◻ Suggestions for Further Reading

Bowlby, J. (1982). *Loss: Sadness and depression (attachment and loss)*. New York: Basic Books. The third volume in John Bowlby's original treatise on childhood attachment (see Chapter 9), this book has strongly influenced modern researchers' ideas about the causes and functions of sadness.

Smith, L. L., & Elliott, C. H. (2003). *Depression for dummies*. New York: Wiley. Written by two practicing clinical psychologists, this is a great introduction to the topic of clinical depression.

8

The Positive Emotions: Happiness, Joy, Hope, and Amusement

What is your primary, overall goal in life? Many people in the United States and other Western societies would reply in three words: "to be happy." The statement "I just want you to be happy" is considered a powerful expression of interpersonal support, and the phrase "whatever makes you happy" seems to justify many behaviors. The Western philosophy of utilitarianism is based on the moral superiority of whatever course of action results in happiness: "The greatest happiness of all those whose interest is in question [is] the right and proper, and only right and proper and universally desirable, end of human action" (Bentham, 1780/1970, p. 11). The United States' Declaration of Independence includes these famous words: "We hold these truths to be self-evident, that all men are created equal, that they are endowed by their Creator with certain unalienable Rights, that among these are Life, Liberty and the pursuit of Happiness."

Does anybody *not* agree that the pursuit of happiness is a primary goal, right up there with life itself? In some cultures, including many Asian cultures, people report that doing their duty to family and community is more important than personal happiness. However, with a wide enough definition of happiness, one could argue that doing one's duty also provides a kind of happiness or satisfaction.

A few of the research questions about happiness are obvious: What makes people happy? Why does happiness sometimes last so long and sometimes so briefly? What can we do to make ourselves happier? Are happy people more productive and more successful than unhappy people? What *is* happiness, anyway? What purpose does it serve?

Given people's interest in living happy, fulfilling lives, you might suppose that researchers would have devoted enormous efforts to these questions. However, research on the **positive emotions**—feelings that enrich life, such as happiness, love, amusement, hope, compassion, pride, gratitude, and awe—began receiving serious attention in the 1990s, remarkably late relative to research on anger, fear, and depression (Seligman & Csikszentmihalyi, 2000). One reason for this delay is that clinical psychologists spend most of their time trying to help people overcome or control their anger, fear, and depression. True, people would like to be happier, but generally their reason for seeking help is to *stop* being so *unhappy!* The other reason for the research delay is that happiness is remarkably difficult to define and measure, even more so than other emotions. In this chapter, we will discuss positive emotions such as joy, hope, and amusement; in the following chapter, we consider the positive emotions involved in important relationships, such as love and compassion.

◘ Happiness and Joy

Chapters 5 and 6 dealt with fear and anger, which are clear and typical examples of emotions. Happiness fits the definition of emotion much less clearly. Recalling the definition we proposed in Chapter 1, let's try applying its criteria to happiness and contrasting the results with fear and anger:

1. *Emotions are reactions to a stimulus.* When we feel fear or anger, we usually have a reason. We are worried about something that may hurt us or we are angry at someone for a particular offense. Happiness can also be a reaction to an event, like winning a game or receiving a compliment, but often people are happy for no particular reason (unless you count "being happy to be alive.") Also, fear and anger usually fade after some eliciting event. They might fade slowly, but they do fade. (The body isn't capable of maintaining permanent panic.) When people feel happy *about* some event, like winning a prize, their emotion fades over time as well, but people who are happy for no particular reason tend to remain happy most of the time, day after day. Happiness or satisfaction is more persistent than typical emotions; in some ways, it is closer to being a personality trait.

2. *Emotion is a complex sequence of physiological, behavioral, and subjective changes.* Fear and anger evoke clear physiological changes—the fight-or-flight response. Sudden elation elicits a mild increase in heart rate, but general happiness or contentment often entails a slight decrease. In either case, the autonomic changes are unimpressive compared to anger or fear. Fear leads to fleeing and anger to fighting or at least threatening. What behavior does happiness evoke? It usually evokes only a smile and perhaps some changes in social responses.

3. *An emotion is a functional response to the situation.* Here "functional" means "beneficial." We can easily describe how fear or anger leads to life-protecting behaviors. In what way does happiness help you survive? If happiness does have a benefit, it is indirect.

In short, happiness—in the sense of contentment or general satisfaction with life—does not fit the standard definitions of emotion. Remember from Chapter 1 the distinction between emotions and mood or affect. Emotions are temporary reactions to events, whereas mood or affect is a general long-lasting predisposition not dependent on any single event. By this distinction, happiness qualifies as a mood or affect. When we talk about "angry" or "frightened" people, we refer to people in a temporary state of anger or fear. However, when we talk about "happy" people, we can refer to people who are habitually happy, as a personality trait. People with a happy personality have been described as emotionally stable, conscientious, trusting, and either in control of the situation or trying to be in control (DeNeve, 1999; DeNeve & Cooper, 1998). Another description is that happy or satisfied people have autonomy, mastery of their situation, personal growth, positive relations with others, purpose in life, and self-acceptance (Ryff & Singer, 2003). Happy people are not ecstatic all the time. They have their bad moods, too, but they snap back relatively quickly (Diener & Seligman, 2002).

Happiness in the sense of a personality trait is important, and we should discuss it in a textbook on emotions. But it is *not* an emotion in the usual sense. In contrast, sometimes we do have an intense pleasant emotional experience in response to a particular event—a surprising gain or success of some sort. We shall refer to that emotion as **joy**, to distinguish it from happiness. It may sound as if we are quibbling about words, but the distinction is important. Joy results temporarily from a wide variety of events, such as doing well on a test, seeing your team win a game, having a good meal, or going shopping (Arnold & Reynolds, 2003). But long-term happiness or life satisfaction is not just the sum of many events producing short-term joy.

◻ Measuring Happiness or Life Satisfaction

Although we classify happiness more as a mood than an emotion, we shall spend some time discussing it, partly because much research is available and partly because mood is clearly related to emotion. In Chapter 1, we discussed some basic measurement issues, but let's revisit them here. Researchers measure emotions—and mood or affect as well—in three ways—by behavioral observation, physiological recording, and self-report. All three offer opportunities and difficulties to researchers studying happiness.

Behavioral Observations

Anger and fear produce observable behaviors, and we can observe fighting or fleeing even in nonhuman animals. But what does a happy animal do? Dogs wag their tails at times when we assume they are happy and cats purr. According to one study, zookeepers agree with one another fairly consistently about which chimpanzees seem happiest or most satisfied with life (King & Landau, 2003). However, most animals give no particular signals at times when we assume that they might be happy. At best, evaluating nonhuman happiness is a difficult and uncertain inference.

Behavioral observations of happiness in humans are not much easier. What do people *do* when they are happy? For one thing, they act more optimistically. They approach other people more boldly than usual, they take more chances, and they react less strongly than usual to threats (C. Peterson,

2000). When a task appears to be impossible, they quit (appropriately) and go on to something else, but if they can't find anything else constructive to do, they persist on trying the apparently impossible task (Aspinwall & Richter, 1999). These complex behaviors are interesting and certainly have important implications for people's chances of success in their social and practical lives. They are also hard to measure, however, and none of them is an unambiguous sign of happiness.

The most easily measurable behavior associated with happiness is smiling. Yet even smiling poses measurement problems. Happy people don't always smile (especially when they are alone), and most smiles don't last long. Furthermore, people learn to smile politely in certain situations, and some cultures encourage public smiling more than others. On the average, women smile more than men. Should we conclude that women are happy more often than men? Perhaps, but women are also more likely than men to learn to smile even when they are not particularly happy (LaFrance, Hecht, & Paluck, 2003).

Fortunately, there is a fairly reliable way to tell whether a smiling person actually feels happy or is just being polite. Researchers studying facial expressions of emotion have identified a special kind of smile, the full **Duchenne smile** (named after the investigator who first described it), which includes raised cheeks and crow's feet at the corners of the eyes plus a smiling mouth, that usually communicates "real" positive emotion. Figure 8.1 supplies examples of Duchenne and non-Duchenne smiles. Because the eye muscles that contract in the Duchenne smile are difficult to control voluntarily, few people can "fake" a Duchenne smile. Try it yourself!

It is important to note (especially when seeing your relatives) that not all emotional smiles are Duchenne smiles. Observers have found that young children usually react to any pleasant event first with a non-Duchenne smile. If the pleasure is strong enough, the non-Duchenne smile gradually blends into a Duchenne smile (Messinger, 2002). Even with

© Paul Ekman

FIGURE 8.1   Very happy or amused people show a Duchenne smile, as in the photo on the left. Note the raised cheeks and the appearance around the eyes. Voluntary smiles usually look like the photo on the right. However, the smile on the right could also be an honest expression of moderate happiness or amusement.

adults, many sincere but unintense smiles fail to meet the Duchenne criteria. A good way to think of it is this: A Duchenne smile almost always indicates genuine happiness, but a non-Duchenne smile can also indicate happiness.

Using the Duchenne smile as an indicator of happiness is more difficult than it probably sounds. Participants must be videotaped during the session of interest, and then the facial behavior must be painstakingly coded for the presence, frequency, intensity, and duration of Duchenne smiles using a coding system that takes about 100 hours to learn. Once you learn the coding system, it takes about six minutes to code every minute of "real time," going back and forth over the videotape slowly. The problem is that the Duchenne smile is subtle. Ordinarily, we evaluate the happiness of someone's expression almost entirely by the mouth. Consider the several versions of the Mona Lisa painting in Figure C.6 (see the inside cover of this book). Nearly everyone regards B as happy and A as sad because of the differences in the mouth. Many insist that the eyes look happier in B also, even though the eye expressions are in fact the same for A and B. In contrast, the eye expressions differ for C and D, but most people don't notice, because the mouth expressions are the same (Kontsevich & Tyler, 2004).

Despite its drawbacks, the Duchenne smile has proved a very useful measure of happiness—one of the strongest and most reliable in research on positive emotion. For example, one remarkable study looked at the ways young women smiled in their college yearbook photos several decades ago and then asked whether the smiles predicted how the women's lives played out throughout adulthood (Harker & Keltner, 2001). In this study, women who showed stronger Duchenne smiles in this single photograph were happier in their marriages and less likely to divorce, and they described themselves as more competent and more socially active decades later than women with more "polite" smiles, or no smile at all. Clearly our smiles convey something important about the way we approach the world.

Physiological Measurements

Physiological measurements of happiness also have their limitations. However, although no physiological measure is distinct enough to identify when someone is happy, several measures correlate strongly enough with happiness to be useful for certain kinds of research.

Autonomic measures have not been particularly helpful in assessing positive emotions. A sudden moment of joy increases heart rate but not by much and not for long compared to fear or anger (Levenson, Ekman, & Friesen, 1990). Prolonged satisfaction or contentment is usually associated with a slight decrease in heart rate.

Brain scans find increased activity in some brain areas and decreased activity in others when people are happy (George et al., 1995). However, studies comparing the activity during happiness and sadness have had inconsistent results, which seem to depend as much on the details of procedure as they do on the difference between happiness and sadness (Esslen, Pascual-Marqui, Hell, Kochi, & Lehmann, 2004; Eugène et al., 2003; Murphy, Nimmo-Smith, & Lawrence, 2003).

A more robust phenomenon pertains to differences between the left and right hemispheres of the brain. Most (although not all) research has linked activation of the frontal cortex of the left hemisphere to approach tendencies (including both happiness and anger) while linking activity of the frontal cortex in the right hemisphere to withdrawal tendencies (including sadness and fear). This linkage apparently takes place in two ways (Coan &

Allen, 2004). One is as a predisposition: People who usually (when nothing much is happening) have greater left than right activity tend to respond more strongly than others do to pleasant events, such as comedy films; people who usually have greater activity on the right side tend to respond more strongly to events provoking fear or sadness. In one study, adults who reported greater subjective well-being (life satisfaction) had greater frontal lobe activity in the left hemisphere, whereas those who reported lower overall life satisfaction had greater right hemisphere activity (Urry et al., 2004).

The second aspect is as an outcome: Events that elicit approach tend to activate the left hemisphere more than the right hemisphere, whereas events that elicit withdrawal tend to activate the right hemisphere more strongly (R. J. Davidson & Fox, 1982; R. J. Davidson & Henriques, 2000; Reuter-Lorenz & Davidson, 1981). For example, researchers used electric sensors attached to the scalp to monitor brain activity while 10-month-old infants watched videotapes of someone smiling or looking sad (R. J. Davidson & Fox, 1982). While the babies viewed the happy faces, their left frontal lobes were more active than their right. When viewing the sad faces, the activity was about the same on both sides of the frontal lobes. In most similar studies, the right side was more active than the left in the sad condition (Henriques & Davidson, 2000).

Another study compared responses of the right and left hemispheres to happy and sad stimuli. This study is based on the fact that the right hemisphere processes information coming from the left side of the visual field (anything to the left of your focus), whereas the left hemisphere processes information coming from the right side of the visual field. With the proper equipment, researchers can show different images to your right and left hemispheres at the same time. Participants viewed pairs of images in this way, with either a happy or a sad face on one side and a neutral face on the other. The task was to say as quickly as possible which side had an emotional face. On the average, people responded faster if the right hemisphere was viewing a sad face or if the left hemisphere was viewing a happy face, rather than the other way around (Reuter-Lorenz & Davidson, 1981).

However, the difference between left and right hemispheres is not simply a matter of happiness versus sadness. The left frontal lobes seem to be specialized for processes associated with *approach*, including anger as well as happiness (Murphy, Nimmo-Smith, & Lawrence, 2003). So any researcher who uses brain recordings to infer emotions needs to guard against confusing one "approach emotion" with another.

Self-Reports

Because of the difficulties of observational and physiological measures, most researchers interested in happiness have relied on self-reports. As we noted in Chapter 1, self-reports have their limitations.

One of the most frequently used measures of happiness is the Satisfaction With Life Scale (Pavot & Diener, 1993). This measure asks people to rate how much they agree with each of the following statements on a scale from 1 (strongly disagree) to 7 (strongly agree):

____ In most ways my life is close to my ideal.

____ The conditions of my life are excellent.

____ I am satisfied with my life.

____ So far I have gotten the important things I want in life.

____ If I could live my life over, I would change almost nothing.

This measure has generated much important work, including many of the studies we shall discuss in the rest of this chapter. As a result, it deserves especially careful attention. Look closely at the items. Do you agree that these questions measure happiness? (If not, how would you measure it?)

Another often-used measure of overall happiness is the Positive Affect scale of the Positive and Negative Affect Schedule, or PANAS (Watson, Clark, & Tellegen, 1988). The PANAS has 20 items, each of which is a single word; a participant says, on a scale from 1 to 5, how well that word describes his or her feelings during a certain time (which could be a day, a week, a month, "in general," or any other unit of time). Ten of the 20 items are negative words such as "scared," "upset," "distressed," and "ashamed." The 10 Positive Affect items are "enthusiastic," "interested," "determined," "excited," "inspired," "alert," "active," "strong," "proud," and "attentive."

Does this instrument measure emotion? Words like "enthusiastic" and "proud" seem to correspond to emotions, but what about "strong," "alert," and "determined"? These are desirable qualities, and if you feel strong, determined, and alert, then you probably feel good. Many researchers have recently agreed that the Positive Affect scale is best thought of as measuring high energy and overall positive mood, rather than emotion as we defined the term in Chapter 1. Still, mood is an important concept in emotion research, and the Positive Affect scale has generated a tremendous amount of helpful research.

Another strategy for self-report research is to examine the emotions that people mention spontaneously. That is, instead of directly asking people how happy or satisfied they are, take samples of their speech or writing and count how many times they say something about feeling happy. In one study, researchers examined information about a homogeneous group over time. An order of Catholic nuns had asked young recruits in the 1930s and 1940s to "describe themselves" and had kept those autobiographical essays. Some had expressed a great deal of positive emotion, whereas others had expressed little positive emotion (and generally little emotion of any types). Here are two examples (Danner, Snowdon, & Friesen, 2001, p. 806):

> [High expression:] God started my life off well by bestowing upon me a grace of inestimable value.... The past year which I have spent as a candidate studying at Notre Dame College has been a very happy one. Now I look forward with eager joy to receiving the Holy Habit of Our Lady and to a life of union with Love Divine.

[Low expression:] I was born on September 26, 1909, the eldest of seven children, five girls and two boys. . . . My candidate year was spent in the Motherhouse, teaching chemistry and Second Year Latin at Notre Dame Institute. With God's grace, I intend to do my best for our Order, for the spread of religion and for my personal sanctification.

The researchers obtained data on what happened to those women over the rest of their lives. On the average, those who had expressed the most positive emotion survived the longest. This is a remarkable study in terms of having few interfering influences. That is, the nuns had similar life styles and socioeconomic status; none married or had children; and few engaged in risky behaviors that might endanger their health. The strong effect of reported positive emotion on later survival attests to the strong potential of this method of measuring emotions (Danner et al., 2001).

▣ What Makes People Happy?

Self-report measures such as the PANAS and the Satisfaction With Life Scale have been used extensively to measure happiness. According to these measures, a "happy" person is someone who reports high positive affect, low negative affect, and high life satisfaction. What makes some people happy and others not?

One striking finding is that most people in reasonably prosperous countries say they are generally happy overall—that is, above the middle on a scale from very unhappy to very happy (Diener & Diener, 1996). Some have argued that we evolved to make happiness our "default setting" (Buss, 2000). In general, happy people tend to be more productive than others and are more likely to compete successfully for reproductive opportunities. (After all, wouldn't you rather mate with a happy person than an unhappy one?) According to this reasoning, happy people are more likely than other people to pass on their genes (Buss, 2000). If so, most of us are descended from a long line of ancestors who tended to be reasonably happy most of the time, and we in-

herited genes that predispose us toward happiness. Still, even among people who call themselves happy, some report being happier than others, and it is interesting to see what predicts—and what *fails* to predict—these differences.

Self-Reported Causes of Happiness

If we want to know what makes people happy, the most obvious thing to do is to ask them. This method is far from perfect, but it is a reasonable way to start. You might try this yourself. Ask people you know about the causes of their happiness, but ask different people in two different ways: "What *makes* you happy?" versus "What *would* make you happier?" The different wordings of this question tend to give different results. One of us (J.W.K.) has informally surveyed his introductory psychology class using these questions several times. In each case, half of the students received a questionnaire with the first wording and half with the second. For those who were asked "What would make you happier," the most common answers fell into these categories:

- More money or possessions
- A good job and a secure future
- A new boyfriend or girlfriend or a better relationship with the current one
- Better grades in school
- More time with family and friends
- More sleep

Here are a few interesting individual answers:

- "To experience more of what life has to offer."
- "Being in a log cabin in the mountains where there's snow sitting in front of a large fire place on a comfy couch with a blanket."
- "Warm weather or 10 million dollars or both."
- "To understand myself and my reactions to others."
- "If I could know without a doubt that the career I choose is the best one for me so that 20 years from now I will not look back and regret the choice I made."

- "For my mother and father to be happy together like they were when I was small."
- "To be given enough money as to be never forced into a real job."
- "To have a ~~great~~ social life." (The individual crossed out "great.")

In contrast, here are the common answers to the question "What makes you happy?":

- Friends and family (by far the most common answer)
- My boyfriend or girlfriend
- A feeling of success or accomplishment
- Relaxing
- Playing sports, being active
- Enjoying nature
- Music and humor
- Religion
- Making others happy

Note the contrast: Most of the items people say *would* make them happy are things that could happen to them. However, most of what people say *does* make them happy are either their own actions or an appreciation of what is readily available (friends, family, nature).

A more systematic survey of middle-aged U.S. adults also found that most people said that their relationship with family and friends was their main source of satisfaction in life. Other common answers included physical health, financial security, self-development, a satisfactory job, faith, and simply enjoying the activities of life (Markus, Ryff, Curhan, & Palmersheim, 2004). Curiously, when people are asked about the sources of their happiness or satisfaction, few mention music, but if someone suggests that as a possible answer, almost everyone agrees it is a good one. People with different lifestyles tended to give different answers to what gave them satisfaction. In particular, many of those with a college education cited their accomplishments. Those with only a high-school education seldom mentioned accomplishments and were more likely to cite a "sense of autonomy"—that is, feeling in control of important events (Markus et al., 2004). A sense of control is important

to almost everyone, and people who feel a sense of control tend to be healthier as well as happier than others (Lachman & Firth, 2004). College-educated adults presumably did not mention it because they took it for granted. To less educated people, many of whom presumably got bossed around in their jobs, a sense of control was important wherever they could find it.

Happiness as Disposition or Reaction to Events?

A quote attributed to Abraham Lincoln is, "Most folks are about as happy as they make up their minds to be." Is that true? To what extent is happiness something we decide or create for ourselves, and to what extent is it a product of the events life has brought us?

This issue is sometimes phrased as "top down" versus "bottom up," where top down means that your personality or disposition controls your happiness and bottom up means life events do (Heller, Watson, & Ilies, 2004). Psychologists initially assumed the bottom-up hypothesis: Good life events make you happy and bad events make you unhappy. But then evidence gradually accumulated showing that events account for less of the variance in people's happiness than we might expect. For illustration, let's examine how well happiness relates to one kind of event (wealth) and one personality trait (extraversion).

Wealth and Happiness

When asked what would make them happier, many people answer "more money." If you think more money would make you happy, how much more money would you need? According to one newspaper survey, people earning $25,000 per year thought $50,000 would make them happy. People earning $50,000 said $100,000 would be enough. Those earning $100,000 thought they would need about $200,000. And so on (Csikszentmihalyi, 1999).

Let's ask the question a different way. When people gain wealth, do they become happier? Right after people have won a lottery, they rate their happiness very high, to no one's surprise. However, a few months later, their happiness ratings decline to about the same as average (Diener, Suh, Lucas, & Smith, 1999; Myers, 2000a). Unfortunately, the meaning of this result is not altogether certain. The obvious interpretation is that money doesn't buy happiness. That truism is especially likely for lottery winners, for whom the riches often bring problems as well as benefits. Some lottery winners, unaccustomed to such wealth, spend it all quickly. Some forget that they have to pay taxes on their new wealth and actually end up in debt. Many have conflicts with friends and relatives who expect a share of the lottery winnings.

However, these data do not enable us to conclude that money has nothing to do with happiness. First, people's interpretation of "very happy" may change after they have become accustomed to greater wealth. Also, studies of wealth have what scientists call a "restriction of range" problem: You won't find an influence of some variable if you have measured only a small range of its possible values. Think of it this way: If you wanted to know whether people get happier or sadder as they grow older, could you find out by studying typical high-school students? Of course not! The difference in age between, say, 14 and 18 is inconsequential compared to the full human life span. Now think about lottery winners: Most Americans are middle class, most people who buy many lottery tickets are also middle class, and the American middle class is wealthy compared to the standards of most of the rest of the world. Therefore, winning the lottery usually means a transition from "doing reasonably well" to "absurdly wealthy." Even if that difference has little to do with happiness, we don't know how increased wealth might affect an impoverished person.

One way to ask this question is to compare happiness ratings for people from different countries (Myers, 2000a). Figure 8.2 shows the mean results for many countries in the year 1991 (Inglehart, 1997). National averages fall into two clusters—one of prosperous countries and one of poorer countries. Clearly, people in the wealthier countries tend to report more happiness than those in the poorer

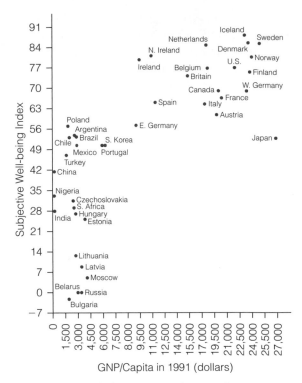

FIGURE 8.2   Each dot represents the mean for one country. The value along the *x*-axis shows the mean income per person in that country. The value along the *y*-axis shows the mean rating of Subjective Well-Being (that is, happiness). Source: From *Modernization and Postmodernization* by R. Inglehart, 1997. Copyright © 1997 by R. Inglehart. Reprinted by permission of Princeton University Press.

countries. However, if you examine differences in happiness *within* the cluster of prosperous countries (or the cluster of poorer countries), wealth and happiness are almost uncorrelated. One way to summarize these data, at the risk of oversimplification, is that wealth does not guarantee happiness, but poverty generally leads to unhappiness.

Within any given country, the wealthiest people also do not generally say they are happier than people of average or below-average wealth. However, most deeply impoverished people do report being very unhappy. Again, wealth beyond a certain point has little effect on happiness, but poverty has a big influence

(Myers, 2000a). Another study found that the effects of wealth interacted with those of health: Apparently many poor people are happy, and many sick people are happy, but it is difficult to be happy if you are both poor and sick (D. M. Smith, Langa, Kabeto, & Ubel, 2005). If you would like to check out the data on reported happiness for people in a variety of countries, try this website; you can also find information on many other aspects of happiness: www.eur.nl/fsw/research/happiness/index.htm.

The data across countries are somewhat difficult to interpret because richer countries differ from poorer ones in many ways besides wealth. For example, richer countries tend also to have better health care and more political freedom. According to one study, the mean happiness for people in various countries correlates strongly with life expectancy (+.63, where +1 is the highest possible correlation) and negatively with violations of human rights (−.57). That is, most people are unhappy when human rights violations are common. Happiness is also low in extremely traditional countries where men strongly dominate over women economically and politically (Basabe et al., 2002). Because so many of these variables correlate one way or the other with national wealth, it is difficult to factor out the effect of just one influence.

Overall, here are some tentative conclusions:

1. There is little evidence that wealthy people are much happier than those of average means. We cannot conclude that wealth *doesn't* make people happier. We just don't have evidence that it *does*. You should remember this cautious principle for evaluating evidence: If a comparison between two groups, such as wealthy versus average, shows no difference in some regard, maybe there really is no difference, but another possibility is that the study didn't measure the variables accurately enough.
2. Even if wealth doesn't bring happiness, poverty does bring unhappiness, especially for an impoverished person surrounded by people doing better, or an impoverished person who is also sick.

3. To the degree that wealth does bring happiness, it is the *change* in income that has the effect, not the total amount (outside of extreme poverty). People may experience a rush of happiness when they suddenly have more money than before, but once they get used to their new situation, happiness goes back to "normal." This is an important principle and one we'll return to later in the chapter.

Personality, Happiness, and Predispositions

If wealth has only a small influence for people above the poverty line, where does happiness come from? One strong determinant of happiness is, for want of a better term, people's natural disposition or personality, which tends to be consistent over long periods of life.

Two studies, each examining thousands of pairs of twins, found that monozygotic (identical) twins resemble each other in life satisfaction more strongly than do dizygotic (fraternal) twins, both in young adulthood and later in life (Lykken & Tellegen, 1996; Røysamb, Harris, Magnus, Vittersø, & Tambs, 2002). In other studies, monozygotic twins also resemble each other more strongly than dizygotic twins do in their degree of optimism (Schulman, Keith, & Seligman, 1993).

These results imply that subjective well-being (or happy disposition) is like a personality trait. Long-term life satisfaction correlates moderately well with the personality trait "extraversion" (Costa & McCrae, 1980). The term "extravert" literally means "turned out," and extraverted people are outgoing in two senses: They seek to interact with new people, and they like to stay busy. They like to be in large groups of people, and they enjoy stimulation and activity going on around them. A wide range of studies suggest they tend to be cheerful and show strong emotional responses to positive events (R. J. Larsen & Ketelaar, 1989).

(Time out for a point about research methods: Questionnaires for measuring extraversion typically ask how much you enjoy meeting people, how much you enjoy stimulation, how much you enjoy trying new activities, and so forth. We should hardly be surprised that people who score high on these scales also report enjoying life and being happy in general. That is, enjoying many specific aspects of life surely correlates with enjoying life itself.)

Still, if happiness relates to extraversion, what controls someone's extraversion? Twin studies suggest that extraversion as well as happiness depend partly on genetics (Eid, Riemann, Angleitner, & Borkenau, 2003; Loehlin, 1992). That is, identical twins correlate in extraversion more strongly than dizygotic twins do. Extraversion also depends partly on *birth cohort*—when you were born. People born in the United States in recent decades score higher on extraversion measures than previous generations did, when tested at the same ages (Twenge, 2002). (The reasons for that trend are unknown; one speculation focuses on the increased number of children in preschools, who therefore had earlier experience with other children.)

Do the results of the twin studies point to a "gene for happiness"? Probably not, but several genetic factors might play into how happy people tend to be. One neurotransmitter associated with positive emotionality is dopamine. (A *neurotransmitter* is a chemical released by one neuron to communicate with another.) Cocaine and amphetamine exert their effects by prolonging the activity of dopamine at the synapses, so dopamine is probably important for arousal, attention, or reward. Some researchers have proposed that people genetically predisposed to high levels of dopamine, or to highly reactive dopamine receptors, end up being both extraverted and happy (Depue & Iacono, 1989; Gray, 1970). However, research has found only a tenuous, inconsistent relationship between dopamine receptors and extraversion (Benjamin et al., 1996; Ebstein et al., 1996; Persson et al., 2000; Soyka, Preuss, Koller, Zill, & Bondy, 2002). The endorphin transmitters, which inhibit pain, also contribute to mood. Endorphin release increases during happiness and decreases during sadness (Zubieta et al., 2003). However, little is known about genetic variations in the endorphin sys-

tem or their possible relationship to personality. Many genes probably contribute to extraversion, but according to research so far, no single gene has been found to have a major influence.

Because life satisfaction tends to be consistent over time, how happy you are now is a fairly good predictor of how happy you will be in the future, across a range of life events (Pavot & Diener, 1993; D. Watson, 2002). In the quote we cited earlier, Lincoln captured an essential truth: Although it is unlikely that people "decide" how happy to be, some people manage to be happy most of the time while others are neutral or unhappy, and only part of that difference can be traced to life events. Happiness is in large part something we create and not something the world does for (or to) us.

Other Variables That Predict (or Don't Predict) Happiness

Wealth is not the only variable that has less influence on happiness than we might predict. Wouldn't you guess that young people would be happier than old people? Most young people are healthy, active, and good looking. They have a whole lifetime of exciting opportunities to anticipate. Perhaps they *are* happier than older people, but as a rule they don't *say* they are happier (Inglehart, 1997). In some studies, people age 65 or older report more positive affect, and less negative affect, than younger or middle-aged adults (Mroczek, 2004). Other studies find much variability among older people, with some showing sharp drops in happiness, especially in the year before they die, whereas others continue to report high levels of positive affect (Mroczek & Spiro, 2005). One study found that older men tend to report higher life satisfaction than older women (Ryff, Keyes, & Hughes, 2004).

Again we have a measurement problem: When a 20-year-old and a 70-year-old rate their happiness about the same, are they in fact equally happy? Perhaps they are comparing their current states to different standards. Nevertheless, the results from self-reports parallel those from other kinds of research. Recall a study mentioned in Chapter 4: When young adults and old adults looked at emotionally relevant photos, fMRI scans of brain activity showed that the amygdala of young adults responded more strongly to the unpleasant photos; in older adults it responded more strongly to pleasant photos (Mather et al., 2004). Exactly *why* older adults attend more to the positive events of life, and less to the negative events, is not obvious. Perhaps it is a biological process, or perhaps it is a learned strategy. In either case, it appears to be a real trend. That is, research supports the idea that most people "mellow" with age.

Who would you guess is happier, people who live in Michigan, with its long, cold winters, or people who live in sunny California? Most people guess that the weather would make a difference, but in fact young people in the two states rate themselves about equal in happiness (Schkade & Kahnemann, 1998). Warmer, sunnier weather during spring improves the mood of many people, but year-round climate has little demonstrable effect on mood (Keller et al., 2005).

Would you expect well-educated people to be happier than less-educated ones? Here the answer is a bit more complicated. Better educated people tend to have more challenging jobs, with higher pay but more stress. Higher pay is an advantage, but stress is a disadvantage. When researchers control for pay and stress, by comparing people with similar pay and stress but different education, they find virtually no difference in people's positive affect (Mroczek, 2004). That is, education by itself has little influence on happiness. It does, however, correlate significantly with "interest," which we could regard as a different kind of positive emotion (Consedine, Magai, & King, 2004). (Better educated people tend to have more diverse interests.)

A few other factors do correlate with reported happiness or life satisfaction, although each of these correlations is small. Because the investigator does not control either variable, we cannot draw cause-and-effect conclusions. For example, even if we found a very high (close to +1) correlation between height and weight, we could not conclude that increased height causes increased weight or that increased weight causes increased height. That point is important throughout the coming discussion.

In general, people with more close relationships (close family members and friends) say they are happier than those with fewer relationships. On average, married people describe themselves as happier than unmarried people (DeNeve, 1999), and among college undergraduates, people with strong romantic attachments and close friendships are happier than those without such attachments (Diener & Seligman, 2002). How shall we interpret this result? One obvious possibility is that strong friendships and romantic attachments are good for people. A before-and-after study found that young people reported decreased stress in their lives after getting married (Coombs & Fawzy, 1982). Another longitudinal study found that marriage produced long-term increases in happiness for some people, though certainly not for all (Lucas, Clark, Georgellis, & Diener, 2003). However, consider another plausible interpretation for the correlation between happiness and social relationships: Happy people are more likely than unhappy people to attract partners, develop lasting attachments, get married, and stay married. The reported correlation between marriage and happiness almost certainly reflects actions in both directions: Happiness promotes close relationships, and close relationships increase happiness.

In general, healthy people are happier than unhealthy people (DeNeve, 1999; Myers, 2000a). Here the explanation is less difficult because it is hard to doubt that being ill makes people unhappy. However, part of the correlation probably reflects an influence in the other direction: Being happy decreases the probability of becoming ill (e.g., Danner et al., 2001). Also, happy people are less likely than sad people to *say* they are ill and tend to report fewer symptoms, even when they are about equally ill (Salovey & Birnbaum, 1989).

People with religious faith tend to be happier than those without it (Myers, 2000a, b). The natural assumption here is that religion provides a sense of purpose, some assurance, comfort in difficult times, and a community of fellow worshipers and friends. However, we should also recognize the possibility that happy people may be more likely than unhappy people to accept religion. Religious faith is not the same as attending religious services, and at least among college students, formal religious observance does not differ between happy and less-happy individuals (Diener & Seligman, 2002).

Happy people are more likely than other people to have a clear goal in life (Csikszentmihalyi, 1999; Diener, Suh, Lucas, & Smith, 1999). Typical goals of happy people include making the world a better place in some way, such as improving the environment or advancing the cause of peace and justice for all.

The importance of a broad-reaching goal has been "rediscovered" by psychologists in one generation after another. The idea goes back at least to Alfred Adler (1927), a personality theorist and rival of Sigmund Freud. Adler proposed that people's primary motivation is "striving for superiority" and that different people seek that goal in different ways. The obvious way is to try to do something especially well, to win at some kind of competition. Another way is to find excuses for your failure, to find other people you can blame. According to Adler, the healthiest way to strive for superiority, and the way most likely to lead to a feeling of satisfaction, is to strive for the welfare of something greater than yourself, such as the betterment of society, world peace with justice, or the advancement of knowledge. Similar ideas were developed by the humanistic psychologists (e.g., Maslow, 1971), and again by researchers interested in self-esteem, who found that life satisfaction depended not on self-esteem itself, but on finding a good way to strive for life satisfaction—in other words, a worthy goal (Crocker & Park, 2004).

The one goal that does not consistently lead to happiness is that of making money. In one study, researchers asked more than 12,000 U.S. college students about their life goals and followed up on them later. On the average, those who had expressed the greatest interest in becoming rich were the least happy 19 years later. One major reason is that most of them did *not* become rich. Those who had achieved their goal of becoming rich were reasonably happy, but those who failed were aware of their failure and dissatisfied (Nickerson, Schwarz, Diener, & Kahneman, 2003). People whose goal was to make the world a better place usually felt that they were accomplishing that goal, at least to some extent. Also, of course, a goal of doing something for the greater good, and not just for yourself, gives life a greater sense of purpose.

Although a goal in life contributes to satisfaction, many other factors contribute only in rather small ways. Income, age, health, and marital status *combined* account for less than 20 percent of the variance in people's happiness (Heller et al., 2004). These contributions may increase if some variables are measured differently. For example, one reason why marriage has only a small correlation with happiness is that some couples are unhappily married. *Happily* married couples are, on the average, much happier with their lives than are unhappily married couples (Heller et al., 2004). But the question remains: How much does a good marriage lead to overall happiness and how much does a happy disposition lead to a good marriage?

Exceptions: Some Events Do Matter, After All

Sometimes psychologists get too carried away with a conclusion: "Wealth, health, and so forth don't control much of happiness. You're either born happy or you'll be miserable, no matter what!" Well, no, that's not true, either. No one has found any event that will greatly increase anyone's happiness for long, but some events do decrease it. One such event is losing a job. If you lose a job that you care about, one that you take pride in as your long-term career, it hurts badly. One study of more than 24,000 German workers found that their satisfaction dropped sharply when they lost a job, recovered somewhat over time, but on the average did not return to its

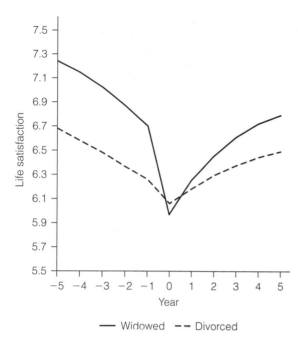

— Widowed - - Divorced

FIGURE 8.3 People reported gradually decreasing life satisfaction during the years prior to losing a spouse by death or divorce and gradually increasing satisfaction in the subsequent years, but on the average, satisfaction did not return to its original peak level. Source: From E. Diener & M. E. P. Seligman, "Beyond Money," *Psychological Science in the Public Interest, 5,* pp. 1–31. Copyright 2004 Blackwell Publishing. Reprinted with permission.

previous level even after 15 years, despite getting a new job (Lucas, Clark, Georgellis, & Diener, 2004).

Another powerful influence is loss of a spouse by either death or divorce. Figure 8.3 shows the results of one long-term study, in which people reported their satisfaction repeatedly over years (Diener & Seligman, 2004). The researchers isolated the data from those participants who lost a spouse and lined up their results so that year "0" was in each case the year of the loss. Several points are worth noting in the graph: Life satisfaction declined gradually over the years *before* the loss, presumably because the marriage was deteriorating for those couples who divorced and because health was deteriorating for those spouses who died. In general,

widows and widowers were happier than divorced people, both before and after the loss, though about equal at the time of loss. Life satisfaction recovered slowly after the loss, but on the average, it did not return to its previous peak. Obviously, these average results do not apply to every individual. Some people recover fully and some hardly at all.

Even for people who have not lost a job or a spouse, job satisfaction and marital satisfaction correlate strongly with life satisfaction. In both cases, the causes no doubt go both directions. That is, people who like their jobs like their lives, and people satisfied with life find something to like about their jobs; the same pattern applies for marriage. However, at least a moderate part of job satisfaction and marriage satisfaction depends on circumstances. For example, some employers treat their employees well and keep most of them satisfied, whereas others treat their employees disgracefully and leave nearly all of them dissatisfied. An unsatisfying job or a bad marriage occupies so much of a person's life that it inevitably takes a toll on someone's overall feelings, in spite of anyone's original disposition (Heller et al., 2004).

▢ Positive Emotion as a Contrast Effect

Happiness and unhappiness are inseparably linked concepts. We would not know the meaning of the word *happiness* except by contrast with unhappiness or know the meaning of unhappiness without having been happy (Lu, 2001). In other words, the emotional value of any event depends on a comparison with whatever was happening right before the event or with some alternative event we might have anticipated. For example, in one study people sometimes knew they were going to win something (without knowing how much) and sometimes knew they were going to lose (again without knowing how much). When they won smaller amounts than they hoped, they were sad. When they lost smaller amounts than they feared, they were happy (J. T. Larsen, McGraw, Mellers, & Cacioppo, 2004).

Al Bello/Getty Images

FIGURE 8.4 Finishing second is disappointing to someone who thinks, "Oh, how close I came to finishing first!"

In another study, researchers examined video-tapes and interviews from the 1992 Olympics (Medver, Madey, & Gilovich, 1995). They found that, on the average, bronze medal winners (third place) looked and acted happier than silver medal winners (second place). The researchers' interpretation was that the silver medalists were reacting, "Ouch! Just a little more and I might have won the gold medal!" The bronze medalists were thinking, "What a relief! I just barely missed finishing fourth and going home with no medal at all!" (See Figure 8.4.) Psychologists refer to this tendency as a **contrast effect,** the emotional influence of whether an outcome was better or worse than some other likely outcome.

Consider your grades. How would you feel about receiving a "B" in a course? If you had been expecting a C, the B would make you happy. If you had expected an A, then you would be sad and frustrated (Mellers & McGraw, 2001). (See Figure 8.5.) We have both noticed, in our own classes, that students who received a B+ are most likely to complain—much more likely than students who got Cs, or even Ds. It

seems that "almost A" makes people even more disappointed than a lower grade. In short, almost any event can be either a reward or a punishment, depending on what alternative seemed likely.

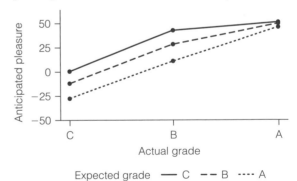

FIGURE 8.5 Students who received various grades rated how they felt about them. Their emotions depended on whether the grades were higher or lower than they had expected. Source: From Mellers & McGraw, "Anticipated Emotion as Guide to Choice," *Current Directions in Psychological Science,* Vol. 10, pp. 210–214. Copyright 2001 Blackwell Publishing. Reprinted with permission.

◘ Enthusiasm: The Anticipation of Reward

When we think we might get really good news, or look forward to an especially exciting experience, we experience **anticipatory enthusiasm**—pleasure from expecting a reward. For example, suppose we could arrange to provide you with a wonderful, romantic kiss from the movie star of your choice. Would you rather have it now or a week from now? Most people prefer to delay it (Loewenstein, 1987), presumably because they want to enjoy looking forward to it. Also consider this question: "I have some good news for you and some bad news. Which do you want to hear first?" Most people want the bad news immediately (Lovallo & Kahneman, 2000). They know they can't feel good until they recover from the bad news, and after all, they will feel relief if it's not as bad as they fear. The good news, however, can wait, and they can look forward to hearing it.

This kind of positive emotion has been associated with a particular brain pathway sometimes called the "reward circuit," including the ventral tegmental area (VTA) and the nucleus accumbens, as well as part of the frontal lobes. This circuit is activated by a signal that a reward is on the way. Researchers have found that these brain areas, especially the nucleus accumbens, show enhanced release of the neurotransmitter dopamine both during a reinforcing experience and during anticipation of the reinforcer. (See Figure 8.6.) The nucleus accumbens reacts to a wide range of reinforcers, including drugs (such as cocaine), sex, food, and video games (Giuliani & Ferrari, 1996; R. A. Harris, Brodie, & Dunwiddie, 1992; Hull et al., 1992; Koepp et al., 1998). It also responds in a gambling game when someone has been winning or appears likely to win. The amygdala (Figure 8.6) responds strongly, though in different ways, to both reinforcing and punishing events.

Studies of rats and other mammals have shown that cells in the nucleus accumbens and ventral tegmental area rapidly learn about the relationships between events that predict rewards and the rewards themselves. Activity in these cells then predicts be-

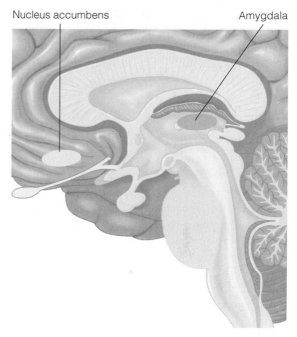

Nucleus accumbens   Amygdala

FIGURE 8.6   A wide variety of reinforcers increase the release of the neurotransmitter dopamine in a brain area called the nucleus accumbens. In turn, the nucleus accumbens sends impulses to widespread areas of the cerebral cortex. The amygdala responds to a variety of emotional stimuli, reacting differently to pleasant and unpleasant events.

havior involved in going to get the reward (such as moving toward a chute that will deliver a tasty snack). For this reason, researchers have called the pathway that includes these brain areas the "Behavioral Activation System" (Gray, 1970). In brain imaging studies with human participants, this system becomes active in all kinds of rewarding situations, from eating chocolate to eye contact with an attractive person, humor, and listening to one's favorite music (Blood & Zatorre, 2001; Kampe, Frith, Dolan, & Frith, 2002; Mobbs, Grecius, Abdel-Azim, Menon, & Reiss, 2003; Small, Zatorre, Dagher, Evans, & Jones-Gotman, 2001).

An important distinction here is between the positive emotion associated with *anticipating* something, versus the pleasure associated with actually *consuming* something (Berridge & Robinson, 1995). Brain activity in the Behavioral Activation System demonstrates the power of the contrast effect. The system becomes highly active if you see something that you want just within your reach. As soon as you consume the reward, however, the reward circuit quiets down again. In one study, researchers found that people's reward circuits were active when they were first offered pieces of chocolate, but over time, as they ate more and more chocolate and reported getting tired of it, their reward circuits "turned off" as the offers continued (Small et al., 2001).

In another study, investigators used functional magnetic resonance imaging to record brain activity while people were playing a game of chance, somewhat like a slot machine (Breiter, Aharon, Kahneman, Dale, & Shizgal, 2001). Each participant was given $50 to start and told that he or she would have to spin a dial a certain number of times to determine how much money would be added to or subtracted from that total. Different players had different dials, as diagrammed here:

Note that some participants could only win, some could win or lose, and some could only lose, but all had the possibility of a zero on a given spin. The researchers were specifically interested in activity in the nucleus accumbens and the amygdala (Hamann, Ely, Hoffman, & Kilts, 2002). Both the nucleus accumbens and amygdala reacted to an outcome of zero as a reward when the alternatives were −$1.50 and −$6, but they reacted to it as a punishment when the alternatives were +$2.50 and +$10 (Breiter et al., 2001).

We can apply this principle to the happiness rating studies previously described. Immediately after gaining wealth, such as winning a lottery, people's happiness should increase, as indeed it does, because their wealth is higher than usual and higher than expected. After people have become accustomed to their wealth, the contrast is no longer present and their happiness returns to its usual level. Their wealth may still be high, but they now *expect* it to be high.

◻ Hope and Optimism

Imagine that it is the night before you are to take an important exam, and a classmate calls you in terror to say that among previous classes, more than 60 percent of the students failed. You know things look bad, but you also prepared carefully for the exam, believe that if you approach the test the right way you'll do well, and are determined to put in another hour of study before getting a good night's sleep to refresh your mind. How would you describe the emotion you might be feeling? According to Snyder and colleagues, this is the essence of **hope**—high agency in a challenging situation combined with active generation of plans that can facilitate the desired outcome (Snyder, Sympson, Michael, & Cheavens, 2001). People who are hopeful also tend to be optimistic. **Optimism** is generally defined as an expectation that mostly good things will happen. In this sense, optimism is the type of appraisal that facilitates the emotion hope. Optimism is often measured by a questionnaire called the Life Orientation Test (Scheier, Carver, & Bridges, 1994). Here are some example items:

In uncertain times, I usually expect the best.

1	2	3	4	5
Strongly disagree				*Strongly agree*

If something can go wrong for me, it will.

1	2	3	4	5
Strongly disagree				*Strongly agree*

Overall, I expect more good things to happen to me than bad.

1	2	3	4	5
Strongly disagree				*Strongly agree*

As you might guess, an optimist is someone who strongly agrees with the first and third items but disagrees with the second. A pessimist, the opposite of an optimist, agrees with the second item but not the other two. Pessimism is related to but not synonymous with **neuroticism,** a tendency to experience fear, sadness, and anger relatively easily.

One common optimistic belief is that "better things will happen to me than to other people." That is, I am more likely than other people to succeed in life, more likely to survive to old age, less likely to have an automobile accident, less likely to get a dreaded disease, and so forth. That belief is often called "unrealistic optimism" because most people have no reason to believe their chance of success or of illness is any different from the average of other people (Nezlek & Zebrowski, 2001). A mild degree of unrealistic optimism is nevertheless widespread. Most U.S. adults think they are more likely than others to succeed on the job, and feel they are less likely than others to become seriously ill (Quadrel, Fischhoff, & Davis, 1993). They also overestimate the accuracy of their guesses on difficult questions (Plous, 1993), their probability of winning a lottery (Langer, 1975), and their ability to explain complex physical phenomena (Rozenblit & Keil, 2002).

We might assume that "unrealism" is a bad thing, and indeed it is when it leads someone to take foolish risks, ignoring the dangers. As a rule, however, a little unrealistic optimism helps people deal with bad news and muster up the energy to go on with life (Taylor & Brown, 1988; Taylor, Kemeny, Reed, Bower, & Gruenwald, 2000). When something goes wrong, people say, "This experience will just strengthen me," or "In the long run, it will work out for the best this way," or "The situation is bad but I can overcome it."

Another type of belief is that "everything will turn out all right no matter what I do, so I don't have to do anything." That is a calming attitude, but not a productive one. The more helpful type of optimism is the belief that "my problems are solvable, my actions make a difference, and I can control my future chances for success." Optimism in this sense differs from pessimism by the attributions people make for their successes and especially for their failures (Carver & Scheier, 2002; Peterson & Steen, 2002). Pessimists tend to feel that desirable outcomes are beyond their control, whereas optimists believe that their actions will make a difference and that effort will pay off.

People with an optimistic attitude have advantages in many aspects of life and no known disadvantages, unless their overconfidence leads to bad decisions. Optimistic people make friends more easily (Helweg-Larsen, Sadeghian, & Webb, 2002). In tense or trying situations, optimistic people experience less anxiety (Wilson, Raglin, & Pritchard, 2002) and less emotional exhaustion (Fry, 1995). They are less likely than other people to abuse drugs (Park, Moore, Turner, & Adler, 1997). After major surgery, they report less distress and better overall quality of life. One reason is that optimistic people try to take control of the situation, as well as circumstances permit. A pessimistic person believes "nothing I do will make any difference anyway" and makes no plans for recovery from the surgery. An optimistic person asks questions of the doctors and nurses, reads about the illness and its treatment, and makes plans for overcoming the problem (Carver et al., 1993; Scheier et al., 1989). Generally, a well-informed patient is more likely to follow medical advice, to get proper nutrition and exercise, and to take all the other steps that improve chances for recovery. So optimism provides its benefits in both direct and indirect ways.

◻ Laughter and Amusement

In the final part of this chapter, we explore one of the most understudied mysteries of human psychology—laughter and humor. Think how much we value humor. We gladly buy tickets, sometimes at high prices, for a show that promises to make us laugh. When people describe the characteristics they want in a dating partner or potential lifelong mate, "sense of humor" is usually near the top. However, few psychologists have done much research on humor or laughter, and many of the fundamental questions are unanswered.

The good news is that if you are interested in doing your own research, you can find questions that are easy to address with a minimum of equipment, and you won't have to compete with hundreds of other researchers trying to answer the same questions.

What Makes People Laugh?

Try to laugh, voluntarily, right now. Go ahead, do it. Was your laugh hearty, robust, and convincing? Probably not. Voluntary laughter is difficult. (Voluntary crying is even worse.) Laughter, along with other emotional expressions, occurs mostly in response to genuine emotional events.

Laughter is fundamentally a kind of communication. It is a way for even a preverbal child to tell a parent, "Yes, I'm enjoying what you're doing! Keep it up!" It is a way for one adult to tell another, "I'm happy and enjoying your company." As a method of communication, it occurs mostly in social settings (Provine, 2000). Recall the discussion from a previous chapter about smiling: People smile in a social setting much more than when they are alone. The same is true of laughter. If you sit alone while reading the comic pages or watching a humorous show on television, you won't laugh much. Watch a similar show with friends who are laughing, and you will laugh longer and louder. Many television shows include a "laugh track" of recorded laughter to prime you to laugh along.

Laughter is contagious, much like yawning. If you hear other people laughing vigorously, you may laugh along with them, even if you don't know why they are laughing. However, the contagion of laughter depends on how it sounds. Some laughs are "unvoiced": They consist of just a single noisy grunt or snort. Someone who makes an unvoiced laugh evokes little emotional response in the listener (Bachorowski & Owren, 2001). A "voiced" laugh includes several puffs of "ha," "ho," or "he." And you almost always continue with whichever sound you start with. You might laugh "ha ha ha ha ha" or "ho ho ho ho ho," but not "he ha ho ha ho." Each puff

lasts about 1/15 of a second, and the delay between one puff and the next is 1/5 of a second. Who would have guessed that the timing would be so constant? The figures are nearly the same for people of all ages and backgrounds, so they are probably part of our biological heritage (Provine, 2000). If you hear laughs that fit this pattern, you are likely to laugh along. However, if you hear "ha . . . ha . . . ha . . ." at a noticeably different speed, even if you recognize it as a laugh, you will feel little or no urge to imitate.

An unanswered question here: Is the contagiousness of laughter built in or learned? Newborn infants imitate one another's crying. One crying baby in a nursery can get all the others crying. But even when infants are old enough start laughing, at first they hardly react to other babies' laughs. Do they have to learn how their own laugh sounds before they recognize it in others? No one seems to have studied this issue. Similarly, we know next to nothing about imitation of laughter in hearing-impaired children, who see the laughing without hearing it.

When Robert Provine (2000) set out to observe laughter, he assumed, as most of us do, that people laugh mainly when they hear something funny. However, when he and his students spent many hours eavesdropping in malls and other hangouts, they found that people laughed mostly when they were talking, not in response to someone else. The great majority of laughs came right after saying something that would not strike a listener as amusing, such as, "I'll see you guys later. Ha! Ha! Ha!" or "I hope we all do well. Ha! Ha! Ha!" If you have any doubt about this observation, listen to laughs yourself at some social gathering. Do people laugh more after their own statements or those of others? And how many laughs follow truly witty or amusing statements?

Humor is difficult to define or characterize. We know it depends on surprise. A joke that seems hilarious the first time you hear it evokes little or no response the second time. Just seeing someone make a strange face, wear odd clothing, or yell "boo" can seem funny if it catches you by surprise. The same act is hardly amusing if you expected it.

However, not all surprises are funny, and it is difficult to describe exactly what constitutes humor.

One reason why it is so difficult is what strikes one person as funny may not amuse another. Consider for example puns, bathroom humor, dirty jokes, ethnic jokes, and slapstick. (See Figure 8.7.) In each case, some people laugh uproariously and others consider the joke rude, tasteless, stupid, or at least not very funny. Furthermore, few comic movies, plays, or books stand the test of time. Granted, *A Midsummer Night's Dream* still amuses audiences hundreds of years after it was written, but many comic movies of even 10 or 20 years ago miss the mark today. Even *A Midsummer Night's Dream* was no doubt funnier in Shakespeare's time than today. The humor of a different culture often fails completely in translation. By contrast, a well-done serious play or tragedy has a much better chance of deeply moving audiences in a different culture or a different point in time. Even old monster movies, such as *Frankenstein, Dracula,* or *Godzilla,* hold much of their appeal over time and place.

Amusement reactions also depend on who presents the humor. You probably won't laugh at a joke told by someone you dislike, regardless of the quality of the joke itself. Professors who liven their lectures with humor often find that their humor falls flat on days when they pass back test results. (The students who are disappointed with their scores are unhappy with the professor and therefore don't like the humor.) Ethnic humor is especially fragile in this way. A black person can make fun of other black people and a Jew can joke about

© Bettmann/Corbis

FIGURE 8.7   Tastes in humor vary by country, culture, gender, age, and historical era. Many films that your parents or grandparents considered hilarious or that were big hits in another country may not amuse you at all.

Jews, but an outsider should beware of telling the same jokes.

In general, however, one thing does seem to characterize events that are perceived as funny. George Orwell once said, "A thing is funny when—in some way that is not actually offensive or frightening—it upsets the established order. Every joke is a tiny revolution." According to one theory, people experience humor in response to a **cognitive shift** in the perception of some target—a transition from thinking about the target from one perspective to thinking about it from a completely different, but still appropriate, perspective (Latta, 1999). Consider the following joke:

Q: How do you stop a lawyer from drowning?
A: Shoot him before he hits the water.

If you think this is funny, why? According to the cognitive shift perspective, the humor lies in switching from the assumption that one is trying to save the lawyer's life to the idea that the goal is choosing the method of death. The implicit assumption set up in the premise of the joke is then shattered and replaced by the punch line, so you have to think about the situation in a whole new way. For the joke to work, you have to restructure the situation quickly. If someone has to explain the joke to you, the humor is lost. Note that the effectiveness of the joke depends on your having some contempt for lawyers. If you are a lawyer, or thinking about becoming a lawyer, or have close friends who are lawyers, this joke might not seem funny. Starting with the question "How do you stop a kindergarten teacher from drowning?" will presumably dampen the joke's value.

One implication of this definition is that humor is in the eye of the beholder, as we noted earlier. What makes something funny is not the content of the joke or event itself, but what happens as you think about it. Some jokes are constructed in such a way as to be funny to almost everybody. Other events, by contrast, may seem funny to some people and puzzling to others. But the cognitive shift approach allows for this difference, as long as the change in perspective is what drives the amusement. As we discussed in the first chapter, emotion is a reaction that follows from appraising or interpreting an event in a particular way. In this case, the cognitive shift may be the appraisal involved.

Gender Differences in Humor and Laughter

Men tell more jokes, but women laugh more (Provine, 2000). (See Figure 8.8.) In childhood, boys and girls laugh about equally. By adolescence, men tell more jokes, but women laugh and smile more (Hall & Halberstadt, 1986; Provine, 2000). The fact that women laugh more does not necessarily mean that women are on the average more amused than men. Both laughter and smiling make other people feel comfortable, understood, and appreciated (LaFrance, Hecht, & Paluck, 2003; Provine, 2000).

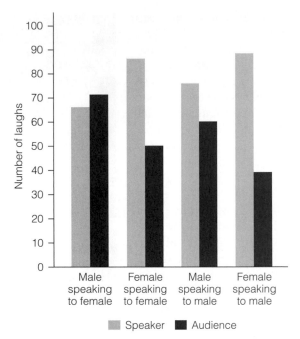

FIGURE 8.8   For each occasion in which at least one person laughed, the graphs show how often the speaker laughed and how often the audience laughed. Note that, in general, speakers laugh more often than audiences, and that women laugh more than men. Source: Based on Provine (2000).

Gender differences in laughter may reflect different social role expectations rather than, or in addition to, differences in emotional experience.

Functions of Laughter

What good is laughter? You may hear people claim that laughter is good medicine, that it reduces pain and cures illnesses. Much of the evidence for this idea is anecdotal, from people who used laughter when they felt ill and then recovered nicely. Anecdotes are weak evidence, though. Several studies have found that positive experiences in general, which can include humor, can enhance the activity of the immune system. Humor reportedly enables surgical patients to decrease their use of pain-killing drugs and to decrease their fear of death (Lefcourt, 2002). However, research on humor and health is sparse, and much of it has used only a few participants and questionable control groups. Humor may be good for you medically, and it can't hurt, but the scientific evidence regarding its health benefits is weak (R. A. Martin, 2001). In summary, humor shows many characteristics of an emotion, but we really don't yet know what its function might be.

▢ Summary

Happiness rises and falls with the events of the day, of course, but to a large extent it seems to be part of someone's disposition or personality, an enduring trait that we bring to the situation as much as it is something we take away from the situation. Optimistic people find something to be happy about or make something good happen.

On the other hand, when people are not happy, it doesn't make sense to say, "Well, too bad, I guess they just don't have happy dispositions." Disposition is part of life satisfaction, but not all of it. Events do matter. Many people remain cheerful despite unpleasant circumstances, but that doesn't mean we shouldn't try to change the circumstances. As we shall see in a later chapter, the way we think about situations is also part of our personality that affects our emotions, but it is a part we can actually change with practice and effort.

As a society, the United States (along with many other countries) strives for economic prosperity. Why? Presumably because it will make us happy. Why not strive for happiness itself? Most people say they have other goals besides wealth and some they consider far more important than wealth. Wealth gets more than its share of attention, possibly because it is easy to measure. Diener and Seligman (2004) have proposed that psychologists should try to measure life satisfaction and use that as a guide to public policy, just as economists advise the government based on economic measures. It is an idea worth pursuing and refining and a likely basis for much future research.

▢ Key Terms

anticipatory enthusiasm: pleasure from expecting a reward (p. 179)

cognitive shift: transition from thinking about some target from one perspective to thinking about it from a completely different, but still appropriate, perspective (p. 183)

contrast effect: emotional influence of whether an outcome was better or worse than some other likely outcome (p. 178)

Duchenne smile: expression that includes raised cheeks and crow's feet at the corners of the eyes as well as a smiling mouth (p. 166)

hope: high agency in a challenging situation, combined with active generation of plans that can facilitate the desired outcome (p. 180)

joy: intense pleasant emotional experience in response to a surprising gain or success (p. 165)

neuroticism: tendency to experience fear, sadness, and anger relatively easily (p. 181)

optimism: expectation that mostly good things will happen (p. 180)

positive emotions: feelings that enrich life, such as happiness, love, amusement, hope, compassion, pride, gratitude, and awe (p. 164)

▢ Thought Questions

1. You may sometimes hear people recommend increasing your right-hemisphere activity, on the theory that it will heighten creativity. Regardless of possible effects on creativity, what mood change would you predict?

2. In Chapter 2, we considered the controversy about what (if anything) constitutes a "basic" emotion. Here we have discussed joy, hope, optimism, and amusement. Should we consider each of them a separate (basic) emotion?

3. Presumably we smile when happy because we gain some advantage by communicating our happiness to others. Why is that communica-

tion helpful? Is it ever disadvantageous? (That is, are there times when we should inhibit our smiles?)

Suggestions for Research Projects

1. Observe infants in a nursery or day-care setting. At what age do they start laughing? At what age do they start laughing in response to hearing others laugh? Do the infants who laugh early also talk early? (These questions get at the issue of the role of whether we learn to imitate laughter.)

2. Observe children in a hearing-impaired school. Does the laughing of deaf children sound like that of hearing children? How do they respond when they see other children laugh? (Again, the issue is the role of learning in the imitation of laughter.)

3. Ask people to rate how happy they are just before, during, and after a positive event. This event could be going out to a nice dinner, going on a date, taking a vacation, or any other positive experience. When does happiness peak—during the anticipation, the event itself, or the memory of it?

Suggestions for Further Reading

Diener, E., & Suh, E. M. (Eds.). (2000). *Culture and subjective well-being.* Cambridge, MA: MIT Press. A review of cultural differences in life satisfaction.

Seligman, M. E. P. (1991). *Learned optimism.* New York: Knopf. A book by one of the leaders of the positive psychology movement.

9

Love

What is love? This question has proved notoriously difficult for emotion researchers (as well as everyone else), and for good reason. In the English language, the word *love* refers to the way you feel toward your romantic partner, parents, children, other family members, close friends, pets, chocolate, a day at the beach, television shows, music, great restaurants, a favorite sweater, and occasionally (we hope) your classes. Our use of the single word *love* for all these targets implies some important similarity among them. Yes, they do have similarities, but the differences are huge also. Certainly the love you feel toward your parents is not the same as love you feel toward a romantic partner, and neither of them is like love of really good Thai food.

To make things even more confusing, love felt for any one target may itself be complex. For example, over the course of a romantic relationship, you might feel concern, gratitude, dependence, physical attraction, warmth, and a whole range of other feelings toward your partner. Which of these are most prominent varies from person to person and from time to time. One couple may be overwhelmed by passion, whereas another emphasizes the trust and warmth they share. No wonder so many people ask,

"How will I know when I'm *really* in love?" And it is no wonder that the answers tend to be vague and unsatisfying.

In this chapter, we shall explore the wide body of research that social scientists have produced on love and other positive emotions in close relationships. We will discuss some of the ways researchers have talked about love, theories about different types of love, biological and behavioral aspects of love, and the role of love in marriage. We will also talk about the ways in which people in close relationships "read" each other's emotions. The goal is not to tell you how to recognize "true love." (We didn't set that goal because we knew we couldn't achieve it!) We do hope to convey a sense of the kinds of issues that emotion researchers wrestle with when they approach these important questions.

◻ Is Love an Emotion?

Before we start analyzing the emotion of love: Is it an emotion? If you ask people to write a list of emotions, one of their most common answers is "love" (Fehr & Russell, 1984; Shaver, Schwartz, Kirson, & O'Connor, 1987). However, when psychologists list the "basic" emotions, most do not include love. Love can be an emotional experience without being "an" emotion. In the same way, hate is an emotional experience, but it is a mixture of anger, contempt, and fear, not a single emotion on its own.

Instead of considering love an emotion, many psychologists consider it an **attitude**—a combination of beliefs, feelings, and behaviors directed toward a person, object or category (e.g., Rubin, 1970). Attitudes are similar to emotions in that they include cognition, feeling, and behavior aspects, but we distinguish between attitudes and emotions nevertheless. With attitudes, we tend to emphasize the cognitive aspect; with emotions, we stress the feeling aspect. Attitudes are presumably learned, whereas emotions may be innate. Also, emotions (or at least the capacity to feel emotions) are functional (useful), whereas an attitude may or may not be. To consider love as an attitude emphasizes that you wish the best for those whom you love, even when your emotional feelings are not intense.

Others have described love, especially romantic love, as a **script**, or culturally learned set of expectations about events, thoughts, feelings, and behaviors (e.g., Skolnick, 1978). As we noted in Chapter 3, a simple American script for romantic love goes something like, "They met, and it was love at first sight. There would never be another girl (boy) for him (her). No one could come between them. They overcame obstacles and lived happily ever after" (Swidler, 2001, p. 114). Even if you don't accept that script, you probably accept some other script—some set of assumptions about what happens when someone is in love.

Both the attitude approach and the script approach focus on romantic love and attempt to account for the complex feelings lovers experience over the course of a relationship. Both approaches conclude, quite reasonably, that the whole package of romantic love (at least in American terms) is too complex to reflect a single, biologically based and evolutionarily inherited emotion.

One oft-cited reason for skepticism in defining love as an emotion is function. After all, nearly everybody doing research on emotion agrees that emotions are functional. But what is the function of romantic love? In modern Western cultures, romantic love is often given as the motivation for marriage and reproduction, so it may be that romantic love serves the function of bringing (and keeping) reproductive partners together. We can find empirical support for this idea because people do associate love with commitment (Gonzaga, Keltner, Londahl, & Smith, 2001). And romantic love is a widespread, if not universal idea. One study of 166 cultures found that 89 percent showed evidence of romantic love (Jankowiak & Fischer, 1992).

On the other hand, romantic love is *not* considered a prerequisite for marriage and reproduction in all cultures, and it may even be seen as a threat to the extended family relationships that provide the foundation of many cultures' social structures (Dion & Dion, 1993). In many societies, parents arrange young people's marriages for economic or other practical considerations and virtually ignore romantic love. People in these societies manage to mate and rear their children successfully. "Yes," you might say, "but are those marriages happy?" Some are and some aren't. And in the United States, where partners choose each other based on love, some marriages are happy and some aren't. Studies have found that, on the average, parent-arranged marriages in India are happier than love-based marriages in the United States (Gupta & Singh, 1982), although parent-arranged marriages in China tend to be less happy (Xu & Whyte, 1990). So the role of love in a marriage is debatable.

The Prototype Approach to Love

If the properties of romantic love are learned, and depend largely on culture, then love does not qualify as a "basic" emotion as described in Chapter 2. Why, then, does love feel so emotional? Rather than focusing on romantic love, Beverly Fehr and James Russell (1991) used a different approach to untangling the web of relationships, thoughts, feelings, and behaviors associated with the word "love." They proposed that love (as with other emotions) is best thought of as a **prototype**—a set of characteristics that describes the ideal example of some category but that may not be held by every member of that category. Instead of asking what characteristics were necessary to call something love, Fehr and Russell thus asked what the "best examples" of love are, and what those examples have in common.

Fehr and Russell asked their participants to list as many types of love as they could think of, and then the researchers examined which types were listed most often. Although some participants did list love of food, country, music and art, and material things, the most commonly mentioned examples were close interpersonal relationships: love for parents, children, family members, romantic partners, and very close friends. When Fehr and Russell asked another set of participants to rate how "prototypical" 20 different kinds of love were, again people said the best examples were love for family, romantic partners, and close friends (see Table 9.1).

So what do these best examples of love have in common? Fehr and Russell asked a third group of participants to rate the prototypicality of each of the 20 types of love listed in Table 9.1, and then asked how natural 20 statements were in describing each type. For example, one statement was "_____ is very painful if not reciprocated." Participants had to rate different versions of each sentence, such as "maternal love is very painful if not reciprocated" and "romantic love is very painful if not reciprocated." People generally reported that the kinds of love they considered most prototypical—such as romantic love—were also the kinds that fit best with certain statements. For example, consider the statement "love is a giving process, understanding the other, and realizing the other's faults." Clearly, that statement fits romantic love, and to a large extent love between parent and child, but it fits only awkwardly with love of country and not at all with love of chocolate. Similarly, romantic love, parent–child love, and other prototypical examples of love fit well with such statements as, "commitment and caring are important components of love," and "love has to be worked at and strived for to truly be achieved."

This study has helped emotion researchers to narrow their focus. People may talk casually about loving material things, but prototypical love is

TABLE 9.1   Although the term *love* describes people's feelings toward many kinds of targets, American participants agree that some kinds of love are more "love-like" than others. This table shows how prototypically love-like Fehr and Russell's (1991) participants considered 20 different types of love.

Type of Love	Prototypicality
Maternal love	5.39
Parental love	5.22
Friendship	4.96
Sisterly love	4.84
Romantic love	4.76
Brotherly love	4.74
Familial love	4.74
Sibling love	4.73
Affection	4.60
Committed love	4.47
Love for humanity	4.42
Spiritual love	4.27
Passionate love	4.00
Platonic love	3.98
Self-love	3.79
Sexual love	3.76
Patriotic love	3.21
Love of work	3.14
Puppy love	2.98
Infatuation	2.42

Source: From "Concept of Emotion Viewed From a Prototype Perspective," by B. Fehr and J. A. Russell, in *Journal of Experimental Psychology; General 113*, pp. 464–486. Reprinted with permission of Dr. Beverley Fehr.

mainly experienced in the context of close relationships. Prototypical love involves a certain level of commitment to someone else, a willingness to give even under difficult circumstances. Love also includes knowing people for who they really are, accepting their faults as well as their strengths.

This approach suggests that, if love is an emotion or set of emotions, its function has to do with building and maintaining close relationships. When people talk about the function of emotions, they often refer to an emotion's **intrapersonal functions**, or the way an emotion coordinates the cognitive, physiological, and behavioral impulses within an individual (e.g., Levenson, 1999). That is, the intrapersonal functions of your emotions are what your emotions do for you in terms of directly helping you to pass on your genes. For example, fear and disgust help you avoid life-threatening harm.

However, humans are among the most social of all animals. Emotions also serve **interpersonal functions,** facilitating the development of relationships between people (Keltner & Haidt, 1999; Shiota, Campos, Keltner, & Hertenstein, 2004). The idea here is that we benefit greatly from our relationships with other people, so any emotion that helps us build and maintain those relationships will help pass along our genes in the long run. Sometimes we even have to decide whether to act in our own, immediate self-interest or to do something that benefits the people around us, earning their trust and commitment. For example, if you lived in prehistoric times and you brought back gazelle meat from a hunt, you could choose between eating it all yourself, or sharing with your children, or even sharing with non-relatives who might offer *you* a handout next time your hunt doesn't go so well. Love for your neighbors and relatives may help encourage commitment to the group so that our emotions make it natural to work together as a team.

◻ Bowlby and the "Affectional Bonds"

John Bowlby, who spent his career carefully observing infants and their parents, agreed that emotions in close relationships are an important part of our evolutionary heritage. Based on his observations, Bowlby (1979) described three distinct "behavioral programs" that he considered the biological foundations of social bonding within families: attachment, caregiving, and sex. He did not call these behavioral programs emotions but rather described them as complex social instincts. Bowlby was not an emotion researcher per se. He was a developmental psychologist interested in the evolutionary basis of specific characteristics of parent–child interactions. As

a result, much of the research described in the next section involves finding the correlates of certain kinds of behaviors (such as calling for a parent when left alone or comforting a crying child), rather than finding the correlates of emotional experience. According to Bowlby, however, each of these programs includes an important, and distinct, emotional component. As we shall see, Bowlby's typology of behavioral programs in close relationships suggests distinctions among three kinds of love (Shaver, Morgan, & Wu, 1996).

Love as Attachment to Parents and Other Caregivers

Most people's first experience of love is love for their parents—the people who care for and nurture us on a daily basis from the first moments of life. According to Bowlby, the behavioral program that facilitates this kind of love is also the first to emerge. Bowlby called this behavioral program the **"attachment" system**—the system that motivates infants and small children to stay near their parents or other caregivers. We have already encountered attachment in Chapter 4, where we discussed the development of emotion in small children. The attachment system comes into play as soon as infants can move around independently and thus risk getting separated from their caregivers. Emotions associated with the attachment system make it pleasurable for infants to be close to their parents and prompt cries of distress when caregivers leave or can't be found.

The English language does not really have a single emotion word that applies specifically to love for caregivers. However, the Japanese word *amae* comes close. Recall from Chapter 3 that *amae* describes the feeling of pleasurable dependence on another person, like the feeling an infant has toward its mother (Morsbach & Tyler, 1986). According to Takeo Doi (1973), one experiences *amae* when one feels passive acceptance of another's nurturance and concern, being able to rely on that person without a need to reciprocate. Imagine having a terrible case of the flu, being barely able to move from your bed, and having a friend or a romantic partner go to the store and get your medicine, bring you hot soup, make you tea, turn on your favorite television show, and pick up the facial tissues that are littering the floor. In this situation, you might feel *amae* toward your kindly caregiver.

According to Doi, the prototypical experience of *amae* is the emotion that a small child feels for his or her mother beginning around 6 months of age, when attachment begins. The emotion re-creates a sense of oneness with Mom, even as the child's developmental needs lead to increased levels of separation. Thus, although *amae* is often referred to as a "Japanese" emotion, Doi himself describes it as "a psychological phenomenon that is basically common to mankind" (Doi, 1973, p. 28).

If *amae* is universal, why has it received so much attention in Japan and so little in the United States? In Japan, says Doi, the mother–infant relationship is considered an ideal to which all other relationships aspire, even in adulthood. As a result, Japanese seek the opportunity to *amaeru* (the verb form of *amae*) in many of their close relationships throughout their lives. By contrast, in the United States, we place such a high value on individual independence that we may deliberately avoid situations that would elicit *amae*. Think back to the flu scenario we just described. How would you feel in that situation? Some people relax and enjoy letting someone care for them. But many Americans are annoyed with this helpless role and uncomfortable with giving another person so much trouble. According to Doi, both extremes are a problem. On one hand, the Japanese let *amae* interfere with their willingness to act as a self-sufficient adult; on the other hand, Americans may resist other people's care so strongly that they avoid true intimacy (Dion & Dion, 1993).

Perhaps as a result, positive emotion associated with attachment has received relatively little attention from Western scientists. Such scant empirical research addresses the subject that we are unprepared to say whether attachment love has the qualities of a distinct emotion or not. Researchers have devoted a great deal of energy to the study of adult attachment behavior, however, and the principles suggested by this research may help to guide future studies of love for attachment figures.

THE BIOLOGY OF ATTACHMENT: ENDOGENOUS OPIATES

One of the core features of attachment is distress at being separated from an attachment figure. Baby rats, chicks, kittens, puppies, and monkeys all cry in distinctive ways when separated from their mothers, much like human infants do. Researchers have found that these separation distress cries are associated with a sudden decrease in neurotransmitters called **endorphins**—naturally occurring brain chemicals with effects similar to those of heroin and morphine (E. E. Nelson & Panksepp, 1998).

When young rhesus monkeys, for example, are separated from their mothers, a small amount of morphine reduces their cries, and the drug *naloxone*, which blocks opiate receptors, increases their cries (Kalin, Shelton, & Barksdale, 1988). Endorphins are also known as the body's natural painkillers. Physicians prescribe opiates such as morphine to patients with injuries, or those recovering from surgery, because these chemicals quiet the brain's pain messages. The role of endorphins in separation distress helps to explain why people find loss of an attachment figure so literally "painful"— people who have lost or are separated from a loved one may actually experience something like physical pain. In humans, fMRI studies have found that brain areas associated with physical pain, such as the anterior cingulate cortex, become more active during an apparent social rejection as well (Eisenberger & Lieberman, 2004; Eisenberger, Lieberman, & Williams, 2003).

A study on infant mice provided strong evidence for the role of endorphins in attachment. Francesca D'Amato and her colleagues studied mice that lacked the gene for producing the μ (mu) type of endorphin receptor. The researchers reasoned that if endorphins are important for attachment, then animals insensitive to endorphins should develop only weak attachments. And, indeed, these mice made far fewer than the normal number of ultrasonic cries when they were separated from their mothers (Moles, Kieffer, & D'Amato, 2004). These behaviors suggest less separation distress and, therefore, support the idea that endorphins are important for attachment.

In addition to separation distress, normal mice also exhibit behaviors that suggest that they find their mother's presence rewarding. First, when they have been separated from their mothers for a while, see their mom briefly, and then are again separated, they will vocalize more often during the reunion and second separation than during the first separation—as though they had learned that their calls would be rewarded by the mother's return, as long as she is near. This effect is called "maternal potentiation" of the calls. Second, normal mice prefer to spend time in bedding that smells like their own mother than in bedding that smells like another female mouse—the mother's bedding seems to be comforting.

D'Amato and her colleagues found that the mice lacking the opiate receptor did not show the maternal potentiation effect on calls and were far less likely than normal mice to choose their mother's bedding over an unfamiliar mouse's bedding. The researchers concluded that the opiate system is important for the pleasurable aspects of attachment, as well as attachment-related distress. Mice lacking opiate responses seem to develop only weak pleasures of attachment.

One key difficulty in this area of research is measuring the positive emotions involved in attachment. It is easy to measure distress cries evoked by separation from the mother. But it is less clear what behaviors indicate positive feelings of attachment, especially in mice. Inferring animal emotions is always a tenuous matter, and especially when the behavioral signs are subtle, such as approaching one smell instead of another.

Thanks to a long series of studies, we now know a great deal about the role of attachment processes in relationships, but most studies still focus more on distress from separation than joy from attachment. With both humans and mice, it is easier to measure the negative emotions than the positive ones. However, researchers are well aware of the importance of attachment in close relationships, so we can hope for future research progress on this topic.

Compassionate Love and the Caregiving System

Bowlby called the second of his three behavioral programs the **"caregiving" system,** which motivates parents to nurture and protect their offspring, especially while they are young and almost helpless. Throughout the animal kingdom, a parent's devotion to offspring is remarkably dependable. Exceptions do occur, of course, but the strong repulsion that we feel toward neglectful parents attests to the power of the biological imperative to care for one's children. As with the attachment system, however, the caregiving system can be activated by a broader range of situations, such as those involving someone who is young, helpless, needy, or in distress.

Emotion researchers have described two states that could be associated with activation of a caregiving system—sympathy and compassion. **Sympathy** has been defined as concern, attention, and empathic sadness for another person who is suffering (Eisenberg et al., 1989). By comparison, **compassion** has been defined as an emotional desire to promote another's well-being (Shiota et al., 2004). Both sympathy and compassion lead to other-focused, nurturant behavior and thus may reflect the emotional components of the caregiving system.

Although emotion researchers sometimes seem to use the two terms interchangeably, or at least fail to distinguish clearly between them, the two concepts differ in a subtle but important way. Sympathy, by definition, is always a response to a distressed person, and it begins with feeling sad on that person's behalf. Compassion is not necessarily a response to distress. Because it can be evoked by something helpless or cute, it may not include the component of sadness. Both states can be contrasted with **personal distress,** or self-focused anxiety in the face of another's suffering.

Nancy Eisenberg and her colleagues have conducted a strong program of research comparing sympathy and personal distress experienced in response to another person's sadness. Earlier studies had found that participants who reported feeling the most sympathy to another's suffering were the most likely to try to help (e.g., Batson, O'Quin, Fultz, Vandeplas, & Isen, 1983; Fultz, Batson, Fortenbach, McCarthy, & Varney, 1986). Eisenberg and her colleagues noted one limitation of this research. In earlier studies, participants were either given instructions designed to elicit sympathy or personal distress or simply asked to report what they felt. In either case, participants were likely to say what they thought was the "right thing to say," or do what was expected of a good person. If so, people might be motivated by other people's opinions instead of their own sympathy.

To get around this problem, Eisenberg measured other signs of emotion as well, such as facial expressions and autonomic nervous system changes, to see if these could differentiate between sympathy and personal distress and predict helping behavior. She used a **multimethod approach:** If you think one measure of an emotion might have flaws, use several kinds of measures, and see if you get the same pattern of results with each. If so, you can feel more confident that the results were not the product of a particular measurement or an overlooked flaw in the design of an experiment.

Eisenberg and her colleagues brought elementary-school-aged children and college students into the lab and showed them a short local community news program (Eisenberg et al., 1989). Participants were told that the researchers were hired by a local television station to find out how people responded to some possible news stories. The program showed a single mother and her two children in a hospital room and described a car accident in which the two kids had been seriously injured. The woman talked about the kids' fears of falling behind in school and about her own feeling of stress trying to support the household and still spend time at the hospital. As participants watched this program, experimenters videotaped their facial expressions and measured their heart rates.

After the news program, the experimenter gave the participant an envelope from "the professor in charge of this study." In the envelope was a letter from the mother portrayed in the news clip, asking for the participant's assistance, along with a note from the professor saying she had encouraged the mother to write the letter. Adult participants were asked to spend some time helping the mother with housework; child participants were asked to help collect the injured children's homework assignments during their own recess breaks. Then the participants were left alone for a few minutes with a slip of paper. Adults could write the number of hours they were willing to help the mom; children could mark on a calendar the days they would collect homework.

As you've probably guessed, the "news story" was really designed by the researchers to see how people would respond to this opportunity to help. What did they find? Eisenberg and colleagues split participants into "low helper" and "high helper" groups to see whether their heart rates, facial expressions, and self-reports of emotion were different. They found that high helpers' heart rates dropped when the segment showing the hospital scene began, whereas low helpers' heart rates tended to speed up. Also, high helpers tended to show more sadness (see the photograph in Figure 2.4) and more concerned attention (leaning forward with the eyebrows contracted and lowered, as though concentrating) while watching the news story than low helpers did. Expressions of personal distress (a mild version of the fear expression shown in Figure 2.4) were not associated with helping. In an interesting twist, facial expressions of sadness were associated with *both* self-reported sympathy and self-reported personal distress. (That is, looking sad could mean "I'm sad for you," or "I'm sad that I have to watch this.") In later studies, Eisenberg and her colleagues have found that high helping is also predicted by greater variability in participants' heart rates, a sign of activity in the parasympathetic nervous system and of relaxation (Fabes, Eisenberg, & Eisenbud, 1993).

Is sympathy an emotion? On one hand, Eisenberg and colleagues' research has identified a facial display (concerned attention), physiological characteristics (decreased heart rate and increased heart rate variability), and behavior tendency (helping) that seem to cluster together in a way that sounds like an emotion. On the other hand, it is possible that both high helpers and low helpers experienced the same sad emotion but displayed their emotion differently and responded differently. In a follow-up study, the researchers also found that children high on dispositional sympathy were very good at regulating their emotions—that is, controlling their emotional feelings and behavior (Eisenberg et al., 1996). Further research is needed to tease apart the unique aspects of sympathy from those of sadness.

What about compassion? Although there is increasing theoretical interest in compassion (R. J. Davidson & Harrington, 2002), it has not been a popular topic for empirical research. The questions are many: Do sympathy and compassion elicit the same facial expressions and nervous systems patterns? Do sympathy and compassion feel different and, if so, how? Do people behave differently in situations eliciting sympathy versus compassion, or does the helping behavior look the same either way? Far more research is needed to address these issues.

Sexual Desire

Bowlby called the third behavioral program the **"sex" system**. As the name suggests, this system is designed to prompt sexual interest in people who are likely to be good reproductive partners. Who are these people? Well, what constitutes a "turn on" does vary considerably from person to person (Morse & Gruzen, 1976), but most people, even across cultures, agree on a few features that enhance sexual attractiveness (Buss, 1989; Cunningham, Roberts, Barbee, Druen, & Wu, 1995). One of the most consistent is health. Other things being equal, healthy people are sexier than unhealthy people. In women, features such as long, healthy hair and clear, flushed skin are considered attractive, perhaps because hair and skin are quick to show signs of malnutrition or illness (Rushton, 2002). A waist-to-hip ratio around .70, in which the waist is somewhat smaller than the hips, is also considered most attractive for women in many cultures (Singh, 1993; Streeter & McBurney, 2003). Researchers have proposed that these proportions are ideal for conception and childbearing, suggesting both a healthy level of nutrition and hips wide enough to bear children without extreme risk. Waist-to-hip ratio is not the same thing as thinness— one can have wider hips than waist while being either slim or plump. Preference for overall body weight does not seem to be as universal as preferences for certain proportions—some cultures consider very thin women to be the most attractive, whereas others prefer rather heavy women (Marlowe & Wetsman, 2001; Tassinary & Hansen, 1998; Yu & Shepard, 1998).

Statistically "average" features are also attractive. For example, if you photograph many people with their faces in the same position, and then get a computer to average the faces, most observers rate the resulting average as a very attractive face (Langlois & Roggman, 1990; Langlois, Roggman, & Musselman, 1994). Why? Average features are familiar, so they may make us feel comfortable. They also represent genes that have succeeded in past generations. A nose, mouth, or other feature noticeably larger or smaller than usual deviates from this successful pattern and may be a sign of something wrong. So the theory goes, anyway. Three studies have examined the relationship between attractiveness (rated from high-school or college photographs) and various measures of health, fertility, and longevity. Two found a small but statistically significant relationship; one did not (Henderson & Anglin, 2003; Kalick, Zebrowitz, Langlois, & Johnson, 1998; Shackelford & Larsen, 1999).

In addition to good looks, we are also attracted to people with certain personality characteristics, such as a happy disposition and kindness toward others (Cunningham et al., 1995; A. E. Gross & Crofton, 1977; Langlois & Roggman, 1990). Our opinion of someone's personality influences our regard of physical attractiveness. That is, after you come to like and respect someone, you find that person more attractive than before. You may find yourself repulsed by the appearance of someone you deeply dislike. Some people show this tendency much more strongly than others do (Kniffin & Wilson, 2004).

How do people behave when they feel sexual desire for another person? You probably have some ideas about this. (If you have gotten all the way to college without noticing how people flirt, you haven't been paying attention!) To explore and quantify some of the ways young people flirt, Monica Moore (1985) went to an ideal place to observe flirting—a bar near a college campus—and took careful notes recording women's behavior. Women seemed to display initial interest in a man through a "darting glance," looking at the man for a couple of seconds and then quickly looking away. A bolder approach involved gazing at the man for a longer period of time. Some women also tossed their heads and flipped their hair with their hands, tilted their heads, licked their lips, and caressed the objects around them.

Were these behaviors really flirting or just things young women do from time to time? To check, Moore compared women's behavior in another bar and at other locations where flirting was less appropriate (such as the campus cafeteria and the library). She found that women displayed the listed behaviors far more often in the bar than in the other locations. Also, in each location, women displaying more of these behaviors attracted more approaches from men.

Does anything strike you as odd about this study? Moore detailed how women flirt, but did not study men's flirting behavior at all! Some researchers have suggested that men actually display fewer nonverbal flirting behaviors than women because when they are interested they simply approach a woman and talk with her (Grammer, Kruck, Jutte, & Fink, 2000). Women may prefer a less direct way of expressing their interest. One rea-

FIGURE 9.1   Men and women often show their attraction to each other by matching each other's posture and movements.

son is to slow down courtship while they gather more information. Another is that even when women flirt in subtle ways, men tend to overestimate women's interest, so a more direct approach would certainly invite men to misunderstand (Abbey, 1982).

Studies of mixed-sex interaction suggest that men and women subtly match each other's nonverbal cues when they are attracted to each other (Figure 9.1). That is, one signals, the other copies, and so forth. Still, it is unclear whether the men, women, or both control this correspondence (Grammer, Kruck, & Magnusson, 1998). We still have much to learn about how men and women express attraction.

Physiologically, the experience of desire is associated with a complex interplay of relaxation and sympathetic nervous system arousal. People generally need to be relaxed to get sexually aroused in the first place. This makes considerable biological sense—after all, a situation that calls for fight or flight is probably not a great time to be mating. As sexual desire increases, however, sympathetic activity increases in the form of increased heart rate and blood pressure, flushing, and overall muscle tension (Masters & Johnson, 1966). This response prepares the body for the physical exertion of sex.

Bowlby, Revisited: Three Kinds of Love?

John Bowlby proposed that intimate human relationships reflect three universal behavioral programs, each with a strong emotional component. The prototypical example of the first behavioral program was the attachment of a young infant to its mother. The prototypical example of the second was the nurturant bonding of a mother to her baby. The prototypical example of the third behavioral program was a sexual relationship.

Although distinguishing among these programs is theoretically reasonable, not all examples of love fall neatly into one category or another. For example, a close friendship may include a mixture of attachment and caregiving. A romantic relationship generally includes all three behavioral programs at various times (e.g., Ainsworth, 1989; Fraley & Shaver, 2000). For example, a couple that initially united because of sexual attraction might later develop a relationship dominated by attachment and caregiving. Even over shorter times, you might depend on your partner for support one day and take a nurturant role the next. Which system is activated depends on events and needs in each partner's life.

It is also unclear whether Bowlby's three behavior patterns relate to similar or different emotions. Researchers have amassed evidence regarding appraisal themes, central and autonomic nervous sys-

tem physiology, behavioral displays, development, and universality concerning *amae*/attachment, sympathy/compassion, and sexual desire, but they have still not fully described all the differences. You might think of this research as a puzzle—there are enough pieces now to start fitting them together and make some guesses about what the puzzle will show, but we can't be sure until we find and put in the rest of the pieces.

◻ Oxytocin: The Love Transmitter?

An alternative to the three-types-of-love proposal is that there is really only one type of love, biologically speaking, which plays out in different ways under different circumstances. After all, different kinds of love do overlap. New mothers talk about "falling in love" with their babies in much the same way that they fell in love with the baby's Dad, and nursing a baby provides intensely pleasant physical sensations. In fact, many mothers while nursing a baby experience sexual arousal, which they may find distressing or embarrassing, especially if they had not been told to expect it. Conversely, one may feel a rush of tenderness toward a romantic partner that closely resembles tenderness toward a helpless baby. (Consider the affectionate use of the term "babe" or "baby" toward a romantic partner.)

Biologically, one major similarity among attachment, caregiving, and sex relates to the pituitary hormone **oxytocin**. Oxytocin stimulates the uterus to contract while a mother is giving birth. It also stimulates the mammary glands to produce and release milk, and the brain releases it as a transmitter to facilitate maternal behaviors. Skin-to-skin touch between mother and child also releases oxytocin, so it facilitates **maternal bonding**, the attachment behaviors of a mother toward her baby (Keverne & Kendrick, 1992; Klaus & Kennell, 1976). Because the hormone makes its way easily into breast milk, and from there into the infant, it may influence the infant's as well as the mother's behavior. Baby rats injected with a chemical that interferes with oxytocin fail to develop preference for their mother's smell (Nelson & Panksepp, 1996), suggesting that the hormone helps mediate infant attachment to the mother. In short, many kinds of evidence link oxytocin to the caregiving system.

Why does adult love depend on a hormone related to the mother–infant relationship? One theory is that over evolutionary time the attachment and sexual types of love "tapped into" this pre-existing caregiving system (Diamond, 2004). Both male and female brains release oxytocin and the closely related chemical *vasopressin* during the sex act. In many animal species, the brain also releases oxytocin or vasopressin as a function of attachment—that is, just being close to one's partner. For example, oxytocin and vasopressin increase social approaches and decrease anxiety (Uvnäs-Moberg, Johansson, Lupoli, & Svennersten-Sjaunja, 2001; Young, 2002). (A negative relationship between social behavior and anxiety makes sense, theoretically. Social contact decreases anxiety and anxiety decreases social contacts.)

Some fascinating studies comparing different animal species have emphasized the link between oxytocin and attachment. In most mammalian species, a male mates with a female and then virtually ignores her and her babies, but in some species, male and female form long-term pair bonds, and the male helps with infant care. Generally, species forming pair bonds show more oxytocin and vasopressin release in certain brain areas during the sex act than do species lacking pair bonds (Carter, 1998; Young, 2002). This result suggests that sexual activity may lead to attachment in mammals with high levels of these hormones.

In particular, consider voles, which are similar to mice. Prairie voles and meadow voles (Figure 9.2) are closely related species, but prairie voles develop long-term male–female pair bonds, whereas meadow voles

FIGURE 9.2   Prairie and meadow voles are closely related species, but their relationships after mating look very different. Researchers believe that the hormones oxytocin and vasopressin may facilitate the strong pair bonds formed by prairie voles after mating.

do not. If a male meadow vole is given a choice between the female he recently mated with and some other female, he shows a 50–50 preference, as if he did not even recognize one from the other. Prairie voles release much oxytocin during the sex act and during social encounters; meadow voles release little. Sue Carter and her colleagues found that injecting oxytocin directly into a female prairie vole's brain caused her to form an attachment to a nearby male, even without a mating experience. On the other hand, blocking oxytocin prevented formation of pair bonds, even after voles did mate (Williams, Insel, Harbaugh, & Carter, 1994).

Researchers genetically engineered some male meadow voles, which ordinarily do not form pair bonds, to produce more vasopressin receptors. The result: Each male developed a strong attachment to the female with which he mated. He spent as much time with her as possible and even helped take care of her babies (Lim et al., 2004).

You may have noticed that most of the research on oxytocin and bonding has used rodents as subjects. How much does this tell us about the biological processes associated with bonding in humans?

Surely our emotional relationships are deeper than those of prairie voles, and our parenting is far more complex, so why should we assume that the chemical systems associated with rat bonding work the same way in us? The truth is, we can't yet be sure of the role of these chemicals in human social behavior (Insel, O'Brien, & Leckman, 2002). There are reasons for caution in extrapolating from rodent research to humans. Whereas voles and most other mammals recognize one another by smell, humans and other primates recognize one another mostly by sight. One of the ways in which vasopressin and oxytocin promote social behavior is by improving olfactory sensitivity and, therefore, the ability to recognize familiar members of the species (Young, 2002).

There is, however, some initial evidence that oxytocin plays a role in human social behavior as well. Participants in one study received a nasal spray, containing either oxytocin or a placebo, and then engaged in an "investment" task (Kosfeld, Heinrichs, Zak, Fischbacher, & Fehr, 2005). Imagine yourself in this study: You are given 12 "units," each worth .25 Euro (about 32¢). You can keep it all, or invest any or all of it by giving it to another player, called the "trustee," whom you have never met before. Whatever amount you give the trustee immediately quadruples in value, and then the trustee decides how much to return to you. For example, if you invested all 12, they became 48. The trustee might, for example, return 30 to you, keeping 18 as a commission. If so, both of you profited. However, the rules permit the trustee to keep any amount, even all 48. The researchers found that participants who received the oxytocin spray invested more than participants given the placebo, suggesting that they were more willing to "trust" a stranger. It makes sense that a hormone linked to love should be linked to trust as well; love certainly requires trust.

Some evidence also links oxytocin to the relationship between social support and physiological health. Psychological stress interferes with the healing of physical wounds (Kiecolt-Glaser, McGuire, Robles, & Glaser, 2002). In studies of hamsters, both experimentally injected oxytocin and the presence of other hamsters blocked the effects of stress on wound healing, and hamsters given chemicals that interfere with oxytocin did not show the usual social facilitation of healing (Detillion, Craft, Glasper, Prendergast, & DeVries, 2004).

◻ Empathy

When people think of positive aspects of relationships, empathy often comes to mind. The term has a somewhat muddled history in psychology because people have used it in so many ways, but researchers are finally settling on useful definitions and distinctions. Rather than being a distinct emotion, **empathic accuracy** is the ability to figure out what another person is thinking and feeling (Ickes, Stinson, Bissonnette, & Garcia,1990; Levenson & Ruef, 1992). **Emotional empathy** is actually feeling what another person is feeling, usually including similar physiology and expression as well as subjective experience.

Are some people more empathically accurate than others? Researchers have identified some predictors of empathic accuracy, but they might surprise you. Take a guess now about what kind of person you think would be most accurate. We'll soon see whether you are right.

To study empathic accuracy, William Ickes and his colleagues (1990) brought men and women who had never met before into the lab, and (under the pretext that the experimenter needed to copy some forms) left them alone for several minutes. During this period the two participants were videotaped. Then the participants were taken to separate rooms, shown the videotape, and asked to stop the tape every time they remembered having a specific thought or feeling and to write down what the thought was and whether they were feeling positive, neutral, or negative. Each participant then watched the tape again, but this time the experimenter stopped the tape every time the other person reported having thought or felt something. The participant then had to guess what the other person was thinking and feeling.

Would you guess women were more accurate than men at guessing their partner's thoughts and feelings? If so, you are wrong. Actually, men and women were about equally accurate. This finding is a little difficult to interpret, however, because Ickes and colleagues studied only mixed-sex dyads and in only this one limited situation. It's possible that men and women are equally good decoders, but it's also possible that women are more expressive and that men had an easier task.

Unsurprisingly, people's accuracy scores were higher when their partners talked more, and specifically when the partners talked more about themselves. Somewhat more interesting was the finding that people were more accurate when rating a physically attractive partner than when rating a less attractive partner. Several explanations are possible: Participants may have spent more time looking at attractive partners or may have been more motivated to get to know attractive partners, or attractive people may have been somewhat more open in subtle ways that made them easier to read.

People with higher grade point averages tended to be more accurate, and interestingly, people who smiled more tended to be more accurate in evaluating their partners. In interpreting this last finding, the researchers asked whether the partners of smilers talked more about themselves, whether the partners of smilers were more physically attractive, and whether smilers spent more time looking at their partners than nonsmilers did. The data did not clearly support any of these explanations, so the researchers concluded that smilers were just more interested in their partners in a way not picked up by their other measures.

So is empathy always good for relationships? According to the research, "it depends." Research suggests that the effect of empathy on a relationship seems to depend on at least two things: (1) whether we are talking about empathic accuracy or emotional empathy and (2) what the "target" is thinking and feeling. Emotional empathy can sometimes become hazardous in situations where one or both partners might become upset (Levenson & Gottman, 1983). Several studies have found that people in happy relationships seldom express displeasure toward one another, and even when they do, the other person usually doesn't notice (Gable, Reis, & Downey, 2003; Simpson, Oriña, & Ickes, 2003).

So the effect of empathic accuracy depends on what the target partner is thinking and feeling. Let's put it this way. You are on a date and are watching a great new movie in the theater. During the date, your partner thinks, "Wow, that actor/actress is incredibly hot!" Do you want to know that your date has this feeling? Would that knowledge help your relationship? Here's another scenario. You are out grocery shopping with your partner, and your partner thinks about you, "She (or he) should think twice before buying so much ice cream—it's starting to show." Do you want to know this? Is it helpful for your relationship?

Maybe not. Researchers in one study brought young romantic couples into the lab and told them they were participating in a study of physical attractiveness. The couple was shown 12 photographs of men and women of varying attractiveness and told that in a follow-up study they might be asked to talk with the people they rated most attractive. The couples who were closest showed the *least* empathic accuracy in guessing what their partners were thinking and feeling when they later watched a videotape of the task, especially if the partners were rating very attractive people (Simpson, Ickes, & Blackstone, 1995). In another study, researchers found that empathic accuracy was associated with decreased relationship satisfaction when the target partner was thinking about something that threatened the relationship (Simpson, Oriña, & Ickes, 2003). By contrast, when the target partner's thoughts and feelings were unthreatening, empathic accuracy was associated with higher relationship satisfaction. In essence, when your partner is thinking something favorable to your relationship, you want to know about it. If he or she is thinking something that might annoy you, you might not want to pay close attention.

◻ Romantic Love and Marriage

So far we have discussed many different types of love, including love for parents, love for friends, and love for children. For young adults, however, the most salient kind of love is romantic love. Many people wonder, "How will I know when I'm in love?" or "How will I recognize the person who is right for me?" There is no easy answer to these questions. The fact that about half of all American marriages end in divorce suggests that many people either don't know how to choose the right partner or don't know how to maintain love once the sparks have died down and they have to figure out whose job it is to change the diapers or clean out the garage. Although we wish science had more well-tested advice to offer on this subject, psychologists studying emotion in marriages and other romantic relationships have found a few predictors of couples' happiness and stability. But first, what does a "typical" romantic relationship look like?

The discussion that follows applies mainly to Western cultures where young people date many partners, virtually unsupervised. Many Arab, Asian, and Latin American cultures consider it scandalous for an unmarried couple to spend time together without a chaperone, and in some cases, parents arrange a marriage between young people who are not even acquainted. So from the start, we must admit that a "typical" romantic relationship varies among cultures. Our discussion also focuses on heterosexual dating and marriage. The research on homosexual couples is relatively meager. The few available studies suggest that many of the important issues are similar for homosexual and heterosexual relationships. For example, in either case, people want a partner with similar attitudes, who will be honest, supportive, and trustworthy (Bāccman, Folkesson, & Norlander, 1999).

Although (as we noted earlier) love is unnecessary for marriage in many societies, in America it is considered essential. Storybooks offer tale after tale of love at first sight, but most real-life romances develop gradually, and the emotional intensity of the relationship changes over time (Levinger, 1980, 1983). Two people meet and find each other attractive. If initial contacts go well, they see each other more and more often. The early stages of a romantic relationship usually constitute **passionate love**, marked by frequent thoughts about the other person, intense desire to be together, and excitement from the partner's attention (Diamond, 2004; Hatfield & Rapson, 1993). At this stage, each person is likely to idealize the other—to be well aware of the other's positive qualities, but less aware of flaws and limitations.

Passionate love is intensely rewarding, even at the neurological level. One study examined 17 young adults who professed to be "deeply and madly in love." Each viewed photographs of friends and of the person he or she was in love with, while researchers used fMRI to measure brain activity. Viewing the loved person activated a variety of brain areas, including the dopamine-laden reward centers responsive to such drugs as cocaine and alcohol. During the stage of passionate love, the sight of the loved one produces euphoric excitement (Bartels & Zeki, 2000). Just as with cocaine and alcohol, however, people can become somewhat dependent on the rush of passionate love, and this need for emotional excitement may interfere with their ability to maintain relationships beyond this early stage.

Many people report that they changed dramatically when they fell in love. Some of this change is the emotional "rush" we just described, but some of the perceived change may be a change in behavior. In one study, Arthur Aron asked hundreds of college students five times over the course of a semester to answer the question "who are you today?" with as many simple words or phrases as they wanted (Aron, Paris, & Aron, 1995). Each time, Aron also asked whether the participant had fallen in love since the last report. People who said they had recently fallen in love described themselves in more diverse ways than they had prior to falling in love. They described more personality traits, more feelings, and more social roles. Why might this be? One possibility is that, when people become intimately involved with another person, they explore aspects of themselves that they had previously neglected. Aron also believes that when people fall in love, they begin to incorporate into themselves various aspects of the partner's personality, activities, and attitudes—a process he describes as "self-expansion."

If the relationship continues, partners typically begin to increase their commitment to the relationship and their integration into each other's lives. Lovers are introduced to each other's families, they may begin to share resources or live together, and they may decide to marry or make some other long-term commitment. Over the course of this process, relationships are characterized more by **companionate love**, with an emphasis on security and mutual care and protection (Diamond, 2004; Hatfield & Rapson, 1993). Each wishes the best for the other person and is confident that the other person wishes the best in return. A strong companionate love is usually related to high satisfaction with life, much more so than passionate love is. Passionate love, on the other hand, tends to be related to strong overall emotional feelings (Kim & Hatfield, 2004).

However, nobody can make a good impression all the time, hard as they may try during the passionate phase. Pretenses fade, idealization wanes, and each partner begins to see the other's weaknesses, quirky habits, and bad moods. Each starts to see how the other reacts to stressful and challenging circumstances. They will also find out about little or big incompatibilities, differences that they need to negotiate to get along. In general, people tend to be more satisfied with their relationship if they consider their partner's flaws specific to particular situations or if they see the flaws as related to virtues (S. L. Murray & Holmes, 1999). For instance, a woman may tolerate her boyfriend's occasional impulsiveness or shocking comments if she regards these behaviors as evidence of "spontaneity and honesty" instead of "bad judgment and disrespect."

Physical attraction is still present in companionate love, but each person feels less excitement from the other's presence and less insistence on being together constantly. Remember, joy comes mainly from surprises, from events that are better than expected. When things don't change much from one time to the next, it is hard to feel the same excitement (Berscheid, 1983). Just think how many stories—from fairy tales to Hollywood movies—deal with dating, overcoming obstacles, and eventually getting married. In contrast, think how few stories deal with the couple *while* they are living "happily ever after." Living happily ever after is great, but it's not an exciting story. The love is nevertheless deep, and if one partner becomes sick or dies, the depth of their relationship becomes very clear.

However, couples may be able to re-ignite the spark in their lives by doing novel and exciting activities together. Arthur Aron and his colleagues (2000) brought long-term romantic couples into the lab and assigned them to work together either on a somewhat boring task or on a novel and arousing task such as having two of their legs tied together and crossing a large room on "three" legs. Participants not only reported having more fun with the second task, but they also reported that their relationship improved afterward.

Predicting Romantic Attraction

It is often fascinating to see who finds whom attractive. Have you ever tried to pair two people who you think would be good for each other? Friends and family introduce single individuals they believe will find each other appealing, and dating services make phenomenal amounts of money helping people to find "that special someone." Sometimes these matches work well and sometimes they don't.

What predicts whether or not two people will fall in love? Although people have elaborate ideas about what makes a good match, research suggests that a few simple factors account for a great deal of romantic attraction. Earlier in the chapter, we discussed some of the physical and personality characteristics that most people find attractive, including a healthy body type, a happy outlook, intelligence, and kindness. One of the best additional predictors of a long-term stable relationship is similarity (Caspi & Herbener, 1990). Although "opposites attract" when we are talking about magnets, studies consistently find that relationships work best between people with similar values, lifestyles, favorite activities, and beliefs. This rule holds especially for people who like themselves in the first place— if you like yourself, you will probably like a partner who is similar (Klohnen & Mendelsohn, 1998). As a relationship continues, partners grow even more alike (C. Anderson, Keltner, & John, 2003; Davis & Rusbult, 2001). However, couples often overestimate their similarity in attitudes and preferences because they emphasize shared feelings over different ones and each projects his or her own feelings onto the partner (S. L. Murray, Holmes, Gellavia, Griffin, & Dolderman, 2002). One fascinating study found that the longer couples dated, their estimates about each other's attitudes and behaviors became more *confident* without becoming more *accurate* (Swann & Gill, 1997).

Similar behaviors, even in subtle nonverbal cues, enhance attraction. When people like each other, they often subconsciously mimic each other's little movements, such as nodding their heads, crossing their legs, or standing a certain way. Studies suggest that this mimicry creates an increased sense of rapport (Lakin & Chartrand, 2003). Although most people are not even aware of it, they feel more comfortable with others whose movements and gestures match their own.

The similarity principle also applies to what people are looking for from a relationship. Clyde and Susan Hendrick (1986) identified three major styles of romantic love, giving them Greek and Latin names. The *eros* style is based on passion and physical "chemistry." The *ludus* style is love as a kind of game playing, with relatively frequent changes of partners. The *storge* style is based mainly on friendship. Of course, most relationships straddle the borders instead of falling exclusively into one category or another. Still, most people identify with one of these styles more than the others, and a romance is most likely to succeed if both partners approach love with the same style.

Are people more likely to fall in love at some times than others? In the preceding section, we described a study that followed college students over a semester to see how falling in love changed their self-descriptions (Aron et al., 1995). The study was conducted at a university in Northern California, and a few weeks into the study, a devastating earthquake hit the Bay Area. (The news in 1989 showed many pictures of San Francisco on fire.) The study found no evidence that more people fell in love after than before the quake. However, people who did fall in love during the couple of weeks following the quake reported being much more upset than the average for other people immediately after the quake (before they fell in love) and significantly less upset 10 days later (after they had fallen in love).

What might explain this effect? First, increased overall arousal can enhance your sense of attraction to someone else, and nothing gets your sympathetic nervous system going like a good earthquake. It may be that the people who were more disturbed by the quake were also more likely to transfer those feelings of arousal to a potential romantic partner. Also, keep in mind that threatening situations activate our attachment needs—we actually start looking for someone to take care of us. The earthquake may also have prompted some highly distressed people to develop attachments to those who provided comfort during a time of great stress.

Attachment in Adult Romantic Relationships

Earlier in the chapter we distinguished among three kinds of love, each associated with one of Bowlby's behavioral programs. Which kinds are involved in romantic love? Although this area needs much more attention, initial research and most people's experience suggests: all of them! As you've probably already figured out for yourself, sexual desire is part of romantic love. Tenderness and commitment are typical among our feelings toward long-term partners, although, as we noted earlier, sympathy and compassion have received very little research attention.

One area of tremendous research interest is the role of attachment in adult romantic relationships. Although attachment was originally described as a set of behaviors observed in infants, attachment remains an important aspect of close relationships throughout people's adult lives (Ainsworth, 1989; Hazan & Shaver, 1987). **Adult attachments** are relationships in which one or both people (1) prefer to be in close contact, experiencing distress during extended separation, (2) turn to the partner for support in times of stress or danger, and (3) derive security and confidence from the partner, facilitating an open and engaged approach to the rest of the world (Fraley & Shaver, 2000). Among young children, parents are the primary attachment figures. As people enter their teen years, however, they form attachments to a few close friends and eventually to romantic partners.

Although few psychologists have studied attachment in close friendships, a strong body of research now documents the role of attachment in long-term romantic relationships (Fraley & Shaver, 2000). Many individuals do appear to rely on their romantic partners to provide a safe haven and a secure base, in much the same way that toddlers rely on their parents (Hazan & Shaver, 1987). How do researchers know that romantic relationships and adult friendships really activate the same attachment system as infant attachment? One of the key features of infant attachment is that any infant who feels threatened or stressed turns to the attachment figure for protection and comfort. Mario Mikulincer and colleagues (2000) wanted to know whether adults showed these same tendencies. People certainly report that they do. For example, if you have had a particularly difficult or troubling day, you probably turn to some loved one who will say something reassuring. But can we measure this tendency?

Measuring attachment with toddlers is relatively easy: The mother takes the toddler into an unfamiliar room and then leaves, and researchers measure how long the child cries. With an adult

couple, it wouldn't make sense to bring them into a room, have one leave, and record whether the other one cries. Mikulincer developed an indirect measurement by asking whether people are quicker to detect words of closeness or separation when they feel threatened. In an ingenious experiment, he asked participants to watch a computer screen. After they saw one word (called a "prime") flash on the screen for a second, they had to decide whether the next string of letters was a word or not. Sometimes the first word was "failure," and sometimes it was a neutral word. The following string of letters might be a proximity-related word like "closeness" or "love," a distance-related word like "rejection" or "abandonment," or a neutral word or a nonword string of letters.

The idea was that if certain kinds of thoughts are already in a person's mind, they should be able to identify words related to those thoughts faster than if they were thinking about something unrelated. Mikulincer found that, in general, people identified proximity-related words faster after seeing the word "failure" than after seeing a neutral word. It was as though the tiny threat of thinking about failure made people want to feel close to someone. In a later study, the same effect was found using the names of participants' particular attachment figures rather than generic proximity words (Mikulincer, Gillath, & Shaver, 2002).

Adults appear to have different "attachment styles," just as toddlers do, that influence their feelings and behavior in romantic relationships. Think about how you generally feel in romantic relationships. Then read the three paragraphs in Figure 9.3; which describes you best?

Cindy Hazan and Phil Shaver (1987) designed the three paragraphs in Figure 9.3 to represent what secure, anxious, and avoidant attachment styles—the three observed in infant attachment to parents—might feel like in the context of adult romantic relationships. Hazan and Shaver had these three paragraphs printed in a local newspaper, along with dozens of self-report items measuring beliefs about relationships, attitudes toward the respondent's most

Remember the descriptions of secure, anxious, and avoidant attachment styles in Chapter 3? The following paragraphs were written as descriptions of what those styles might be like in the context of people's attitudes toward adult romantic relationships. Which best describes you? Which paragraph do you think describes the "secure" style, which the "anxious" style, and which the "avoidant" style? The answers are printed upside-down at the bottom of the figure.

(1) I am somewhat uncomfortable being too close to others; I find it difficult to trust them completely, difficult to allow myself to depend on them. I am nervous when anyone gets too close, and often, love partners want me to be more intimate than I feel comfortable being.

(2) I find it relatively easy to get close to others and am comfortable depending on them and having them depend on me. I don't often worry about being abandoned or about someone getting too close to me.

(3) I find that others are reluctant to get as close as I would like. I often worry that my partner doesn't really love me or won't want to stay with me. I want to merge completely with the other person, and this desire sometimes scares people away.

Answers: (1) Avoidant, (2) Secure, (3) Anxious

FIGURE 9.3   Descriptions of secure, anxious, and avoidant attachment styles

important relationship partner, and characteristics of the respondent's relationships with parents and important romantic partners. Readers were asked to complete the whole questionnaire printed in the newspaper, cut it out, and mail it back to the researchers.

Hazan and Shaver found that adults classified themselves into attachment styles in about the same proportions observed in studies of infants: 56 percent of the sample said the secure paragraph described them best, 25 percent chose the avoidant paragraph, and 19 percent said the anxious paragraph described them best. (Of course, these labels were not printed in the actual newspaper questionnaire.) People endorsing different attachment styles also had different relationship histories and different beliefs about relationships and about them-

selves. Adults endorsing the secure paragraph tended to have had longer relationships than adults with other styles, were less likely to have been divorced, and typically described their most important love experience as happy, friendly, and trusting. They tended to endorse the belief that ups and downs are normal in relationships—sometimes the romance will cool down, but then it will flare up again. They were unlikely to say that it was easy to fall in love or that they fell in love frequently. In a follow-up study, participants with secure attachment styles described themselves as easy to get to know and likable and described other people as well intentioned and good hearted.

By contrast, people endorsing the anxious paragraph described themselves as obsessively preoccupied with their romantic partners, experiencing intense emotional highs and lows during relationships. They were more likely than secure and avoidant individuals to agree that their love experiences constituted "love at first sight" and that an intense feeling of oneness with their partner was important to them. They were most likely to say that they fell in love easily and often. They also agreed most strongly of the three groups that they experienced much self-doubt, were misunderstood or unappreciated, and were more able than most people to commit to a long-term relationship.

Finally, people endorsing the avoidant paragraph described being afraid of closeness in their most important relationships and unable to accept their partner's imperfections. They were more likely than secure and anxious participants to agree that intense romantic love does not last forever, and they were less likely to agree that romantic feelings grow and wane repeatedly over the course of a relationship. They were also most likely to endorse a statement that they were independent and able to get along by themselves.

How do the three adult styles relate to the attachment types observed in infants? According to Philip Shaver and his colleagues, adult styles reflect the same kinds of deeply ingrained expectations about caregiver/partner relationships that are the basis for infant styles (Fraley & Shaver, 2000). Securely attached infants expect that caregivers will be responsive, consistent, and warm; securely attached adults think of themselves as lovable and worthy and consider their lovers as kind, trustworthy, and dependable. Anxiously attached infants seem to expect inconsistency from caregivers and are highly dependent, yet terrified of separation. Attachment-anxious adults want to be in a deep, intense relationship and think such relationships are possible, but they don't really trust others, don't think of themselves as lovable, and are constantly afraid of being abandoned. Avoidant infants appear to have given up on their caregivers, playing on their own and showing little reaction when the caregiver leaves. Attachment-avoidant adults seem to have given up on committed, intimate relationships in a similar way.

But have they? Have attachment-avoidant people really turned off their attachment needs in the way their self-reports and surface behaviors suggest? In the Mikulincer, Birnbaum, Woddis, and Nachmias (2000) word-recognition study described earlier, researchers found that people with more anxious attachment styles were quick to detect proximity-related words regardless of whether the prime was "failure" or the neutral word. They seemed to be thinking about attachment needs at all times, stressed or not. Also, attachment-anxious people were quicker to recognize distance-related words after the "failure" prime, as though the stress made them worry about rejection.

Because attachment-avoidant people should also expect rejection from others, one might have expected them to show a similar pattern, but they did not. To find out whether avoidant people were just suppressing these attachment anxieties, Mikulincer and colleagues (2000) repeated their study, but this time participants had to complete the word-detection task while listening to a loud and annoying story over a set of headphones. This time, the stressful prime had an even bigger effect on the avoidant participants' distance word recognition than it did on the anxious participants' recognition.

It was as though avoidant participants usually put mental effort into suppressing their fears of rejection, but when they were overloaded, these fears were released.

You may be wondering at this point, "Do people really fall that neatly into one attachment style or another? Are adult feelings about romantic relationships that easy to categorize?" Those are good questions. Toddlers can't tell us in detail about their feelings, so we have to rely on their behavior in the Strange Situation to measure their attachment to caregivers. As described in Chapter 4, behavior in the Strange Situation is fairly easy to categorize, so the three-type model is the one used most often in studying small children. Adults, however, may describe themselves as "mostly secure, but kind of anxious," or "somewhat avoidant," or even "both anxious and avoidant." When reading the three newspaper paragraphs used by Hazan and Shaver (1987), you may have found yourself identifying with two or more paragraphs as well.

According to Kim Bartholomew (1990; Bartholomew & Horowitz, 1991), this is because attachment styles really represent the junction between two "working models," or implicit internal beliefs—one about the value of the self and one about the value of other people. As a result, adult attachment is best measured in terms of two dimensions, rather than three categories (Fraley & Waller, 1998). The anxiety dimension measures whether a person generally has positive or negative feelings of self-worth and desirability as a social partner. People who think of themselves as less worthy and desirable thus score higher on "attachment anxiety." The avoidance dimension measures whether a person generally has positive or negative beliefs about other people. People who think others are less trustworthy and who see less value in having close, intimate relationships score higher on "attachment avoidance." This way of thinking about attachment style really emphasizes internal beliefs, so it's not very helpful when working with toddlers. Unlike toddlers, however, adults can read questionnaire items measuring anxious and avoidant beliefs and tell you how strongly they agree with them. Attachment questionnaires based on the two-dimensional model have proved to be a reliable and useful way of measuring adults' attachment styles (e.g., Brennan, Clark, & Shaver, 1998; Griffin & Bartholomew, 1994).

The critical test of a questionnaire measure, of course, is whether it predicts people's thoughts, feelings and behavior in the way that it should. In an extremely creative study, Chris Fraley and Phil Shaver (1998) went to a local airport, asked couples in the gate areas to complete an attachment questionnaire, and then surreptitiously recorded their behavior toward each other until either both partners got on the plane or one got on the plane and the other left. (Obviously this study was done when you could still go to a gate without a ticket.) Because attachment styles should be activated only when a relationship is threatened (say, by one partner going on a trip and leaving the other behind), Fraley and Shaver expected that the attachment questionnaire would *not* predict couples' behavior if they were traveling together, and this is largely what they found. The picture was different for women who were expecting separation from their partners. Women who scored higher on attachment anxiety, as measured by the questionnaire, reported feeling more upset about the separation. Women who scored higher on avoidance showed fewer contact and caregiving behaviors (such as kissing, hugging, gently touching, and whispering to the partner) and more avoidance behaviors (such as looking away from the partner and breaking off physical contact).

One interesting feature of this study is that it demonstrated the independence of attachment anxiety and avoidance as separate dimensions, just as Bartholomew had suggested. Attachment anxiety most effectively predicted how women *felt* when facing a separation, with more anxious women feeling more distress. By contrast, attachment avoidance best predicted women's *behavior* in terms of avoiding contact or closeness when separation was imminent. Thus, a very anxious woman could be feeling very distressed at the idea of separation, but her avoidance score would predict whether she handled the distress by seeking or avoiding contact. Similarly, an avoidant woman might or might not feel particularly sad about the separation, but was likely to disengage from her partner either way.

The questionnaire measure of attachment did not predict men's behavior or feelings as well, and it's not clear why. Do men have different attachment systems than women? Are there different kinds of constraints on men's affectionate behavior in public than on women's behavior? There is still a great deal to learn about the role of attachment processes in adulthood, but Bowlby's original ideas have proved remarkably helpful in our understanding of romantic relationships.

Marital Stability and Satisfaction

Most love stories end with the couple getting married. What happens beyond that point? Although some marriages last "as long as we both shall live," the United States is the most divorce-prone country in the world. For the past 30 years or so, around half of all new marriages ended in divorce, most within a few years. What predicts whether a marriage will survive and flourish or end with the spouses parting ways?

First, marriage is not a good way to save or improve a troubled relationship. One study examined recently married couples and then followed up on them years later to see which marriages ended in divorce. The researchers found that most marriages that ended in divorce within seven years were shaky from the start. When a couple got married hoping they could fix the problems in their relationship, the problems only grew worse (Huston, Niehuis, & Smith, 2001).

Some predictors of marital stability involve simple demographic characteristics (Harker & Keltner, 2001; Howard & Dawes, 1976; Karney & Bradbury, 1995; Myers, 2000b; Thornton, 1977; Tzeng, 1992). First marriages are most likely to last if the spouses:

- Were over 20 when they married
- Grew up in two-parent homes

- Dated for a long time before marrying, and the wife was not pregnant at the time of marriage
- Have about the same level of education, especially a high level of education
- Have a good income
- Have a long-term happy disposition
- Live in a small town or a rural area
- Did not live together before marriage
- Are religious and of the same religious affiliation
- Are approximately the same age and have similar attitudes
- Have sexual relations often and arguments rarely

We could summarize most of the items on this list briefly: Marriages do best if the spouses are happy and similar. The similarity principle makes obvious sense: If people are similar in many ways, they have fewer conflicts.

Does this list mean that if you don't go to church you are doomed to divorce? Or that you should give up now on the partner you've been living with for a year? Should you move to a farm to keep your marriage alive? Of course not. Keep in mind that each of these factors *correlates* with, or tends to predict, whether a couple divorces or stays married. A correlation does not demonstrate a *causal* relationship. For example, how would living together before marriage *cause* divorce? Other things being equal, marriages do better when people have dated for a long time and already know each other's quirks and flaws; living together is certainly a way to learn about each other. Think of it this way: Who *doesn't* live together? Well, a number of religions specifically prohibit living together outside of marriage, and these same religions tend to prohibit (or at least seriously discourage) divorce.

That consideration suggests a related issue: Given that many religions prohibit or strongly discourage divorce, we should not be surprised that religious people are less likely than nonreligious people to divorce. Can we infer that religious people are more happily married? Or are they just more likely to remain married even if they are unhappy?

Because duration of a marriage is not the same thing as happiness of a marriage, researchers have turned more to studying the predictors of marital satisfaction.

One important factor relates to people's expectations for their relationship. On average, spouses' marital satisfaction takes something of a dive soon after the birth of their first child and increases over the next 20 years or so, so that they are pretty happy again after the kids leave home (Feeney, Peterson, & Noller, 1994). Some parents experience an "empty nest syndrome" (sadness when the last child leaves home), but frankly most are rather pleased. Children are wonderful but stressful as well. Many couples have trouble finding time for passion and romance while they are taking care of children . . . including teenagers. Couples who are prepared for these transitions, and know that changes in their feelings probably reflect the stresses of raising a family rather than anything inherent in the marriage, may find it easier to survive the challenging years with a young family.

People differ in the extent to which they think passionate love is crucial for a successful marriage, and cultures differ on this issue as well. In the early 1990s, 78 percent of American women agreed that "keeping romance alive" was important for a good marriage, compared with 29 percent of Japanese women (*American Enterprise*, 1992). Also, people whose motivation for commitment is very strong and who are willing to wait out the less happy periods of a relationship may be rewarded. One national survey in the United States found that, of the people who reported being unhappily married during the first wave of the study but did not divorce, 86 percent reported being happily married five years later (Popenoe, 2002). (Presumably one reason why they did not divorce is that their marriages improved.)

Another factor that predicts marital satisfaction is equity, especially in terms of what skills, effort, and resources each spouse brings to their shared life. People who feel, in general, that they get about as much as they give in their relationships tend to be happier, and people who feel like they are doing all the work are less satisfied (Van Yperen & Buunk,

1990). Individuals tend to feel more trust in a relationship if they perceive that the partner is willing to make some sacrifices for them (Wieselquist, Rusbult, Foster, & Agnew, 1999). That is, both should feel they are getting a "fair deal."

However, do not infer that couples should keep "scorecards" about who did what for whom. In fact, one sign of closeness in both friends and married couples is that they don't expect instant repayment for favors or explicit exchanges of one favor for another (Buunk & Van Yperen, 1991). They long ago lost track of who has done more for the other, and they continue doing nice things for the other just because they want to make the other happy. If necessary, one will nurse the other through a long illness, even knowing that the other will never be able to return the favor. In short, equity is important at the start of a loving relationship, but less important later.

Many other predictors of marital satisfaction (at least in the United States, where most of the research has been done) concern how spouses communicate with each other. Couples with happy relationships generally have high levels of **self-disclosure**, or the sharing of personal, intimate, and confidential information (Hendrick, Hendrick, & Adler, 1988; Sanderson & Cantor, 2001). In strong relationships, this process develops gradually over time. As a general rule, people like others who self-disclose to them (Aron, Melinat, Aron, Vallone, & Bator, 1997), although they feel uneasy if someone discloses deep secrets too early in a relationship. We also prefer the people to whom we have self-disclosed (Collins & Miller, 1994). Do not infer that you need to tell your partner *everything* about yourself. (For one thing, that would take a long time.) But anything that you think your partner should know about you, or is likely to find out anyway, you should tell. If your partner discovers that you have lied or have withheld important information, you will lose a great deal of trust.

Researcher John Gottman (1994; Gottman, Coan, Carrere, & Swanson, 1998) has spent decades studying the ways in which married couples interact with each other. To determine which relationships will succeed, he has observed couples at their worst—when they are arguing about some area of disagreement in their lives. Gottman and his colleagues first work with a couple to identify an aspect of their lives that causes conflict—such as money, how to raise the kids, or who is doing more of the housework. Then they videotape the couple during a 15-minute discussion about that topic by themselves. Gottman and his colleagues have identified several emotional components of these conversations that predict the future of the couple's relationship.

You might think that anger would be the biggest risk factor for a relationship. Actually, Gottman and colleagues' research suggests that anger is not always a major problem. Obviously, it depends on how much anger and how people express it. Think back to our discussion of the constructive aspects of anger in Chapter 6. In some cases, mild anger (not screaming or throwing things) may help to let a partner know that you are serious about your concern and gives the partner an opportunity to make some change. However, Gottman has identified four emotional patterns that do predict serious problems for a relationship. He calls them "the four horsemen of the apocalypse":

1. *Criticism:* Suggesting changes in behavior can be constructive, but complaining about personal flaws is destructive. Criticism at its most destructive includes attacking the spouse (or the spouse's relatives), listing the spouse's flaws, and blaming the spouse for problems in the relationship ("You never help me with the housework! You're so lazy!").

2. *Defensiveness:* This is usually a response to criticism, in which one defends oneself by denying that the complaint is valid, giving an excuse for the behavior, or counter-criticizing the spouse ("You're such a perfectionist that you think I never do anything right, so why should I try?").

3. *Contempt:* This includes behaviors such as rolling one's eyes, being sarcastic, or insulting the spouse—any message suggesting that the spouse is incompetent or beneath the speaker.

4. *Stonewalling:* A spouse stonewalls when he or she ignores or shuts out the spouse who is trying to communicate something, sitting stone faced and not saying anything or actually looking away or closing his or her eyes.

So what communication patterns predicted happier marriages? For years, therapists have encouraged couples to empathize with each other, try to feel what the other is feeling, and to validate their spouses—to summarize the meaning of what a spouse has said and convey it back ("I hear you saying that . . ." or "so you feel that . . ."). Later, however, Gottman found that this pattern may not be as effective as researchers had thought and may be too much to expect from two people who are really invested in whatever they're arguing about (Gottman et al., 1998). It is difficult to listen sympathetically when one's partner is expressing hostility.

In couples who go on to more satisfying relationships, the pattern looks more like this: (1) The wife (often the one to raise a concern about the relationship) brings up the issue with, at most, mild levels of anger, expressing what she thinks is the problem, when the problem occurs, and what might be a solution. (2) The husband shows willingness to consider the wife's understanding of the problem and to accept her influence in figuring out a solution. (3) The husband remains fairly calm, rather than getting agitated. (4) The wife makes a joke. (5) The husband expresses affection or happiness. Among less happy couples, the wife is more likely to come in charging with high levels of anger, and the husband is more likely to deny his wife's power in the relationship and escalate the negative emotion in the conversation.

What does this mean for you? Well, if you are in a heterosexual relationship in which the woman is usually the one raising concerns, how you can help improve conflict depends on whether you are the man or the woman. Women might want to think about staying calm when they raise an issue, bringing it up when they are feeling relaxed, and trying not to frame the concern as a criticism or accusation. Men can bring a constructive frame of mind to

the conflict as well, trying to interpret their partners' concerns as an opportunity to develop the relationship, rather than a criticism or threat, and being open to solutions proposed by the partner. If you are not in this "typical" kind of relationship, you might find it more helpful to think about whether you or your partner is usually the one to raise concerns and act accordingly. For both partners, finding a natural way to introduce some positive emotion into the conversation is a big help. Don't make a joke at your partner's expense, or say something you don't mean, but you might look for something cheerful to say or some way to show signs of love and affection.

◻ **Attachment and Friendship**

Do people love their friends in the same way they love parents, children, and romantic partners? Well, not in exactly the same way, but studies suggest that people can develop attachments to their platonic friends as well. People begin to form friendship bonds early in childhood, and as children mature into their teens, friends become an increasingly important source of emotional and practical support (Furman & Buhrmester, 1992). Warm, secure friendships in adolescence may be crucial building blocks for healthy adult lives; in one study, researchers measured the number and quality of friendships in early adolescence and found that those with more and closer friends had higher self-esteem and fewer symptoms of psychological disorders (such as depression and anxiety) 12 years later (Bagwell, Newcomb, & Bukowski, 1998). As you can probably guess, this was a correlational study (after all, you can hardly randomly assign teenagers to have lots of friends or no friends), so it is difficult to know whether the friendships actually caused people to thrive emotionally in adulthood, or whether people who were already on track for healthy adult lives tended to form more friendships as teenagers. Certainly, happy people who feel good about themselves are more pleasant to be around than miserable people who hate themselves.

Some studies, however, suggest that healthy childhood and adolescent friendships do help buffer people from the effects of other negative influences. Theorists have proposed that the functions of attachment transfer from parents to peers during this time, so that as children grow up, they come to rely more on friends for a secure base and for support in times of danger or stress. If so, then close relationships with friends may even help compensate for troubled relationships with parents. In one study, researchers found that children from abusive home environments in early childhood were more likely than others to be the victims of bullying in third and fourth grade but that this correlation was weaker among children who reported having many friends (Schwartz, Dodge, Pettit, & Bates, 2000). In another study, researchers asked whether the security of relationships with parents or friends was the better predictor of adolescents' overall adjustment (Laible, Carlo, & Raffaelli, 2000). As expected, adolescents who reported secure relationships with both parents and peers were the best adjusted, and those reporting insecure relationships with both were the worst adjusted. However, teens who had secure relationships with peers, but insecure relationships with parents, were better adjusted than teens for whom the reverse was true. The buffering effect of friendships in adolescence is particularly strong for girls and is most associated with very close, warm, and supportive friendships rather than casual or activity-based friendships (Rubin et al., 2004). These findings suggest that close friendships do confer distinct benefits of their own and that attachment may be an important part of this process.

▢ Summary

John Bowlby once wrote: "Intimate attachments to other human beings are the hub around which a person's life revolves, not only when he is an infant or a toddler or a schoolchild, but throughout his adolescence and his years of maturity as well, and on into old age" (Bowlby, 1980, p. 422). As we have seen, our close relationships are fraught with emotion and can be a tremendous source of reward, a source of stress and pain, or both. Social contact can be rewarding even at the level of the brain's chemistry, increasing the activity of reward neurotransmitters like dopamine and opiates and promoting hormonal activity that can improve physical health. On the other hand, intimacy and closeness do entail risk. There are some things we'd prefer not to know about a partner's thoughts and feelings, and if we are so linked that we absorb a partner's good moods, we may absorb their bad moods as well.

Scientists are just beginning to understand the complex package of emotions that accompany emotional intimacy. Most research on close relationships has emphasized social, developmental, and biological processes rather than emotion. (No surprise there. Researchers naturally start with what is easiest to measure.) Psychologists have not agreed on a taxonomy of love, much less developed a complete understanding of love as an emotion or set of emotions. One reason is that emotion researchers have for so long thought of emotion purely as something within the individual. Of late, however, psychologists have begun to recognize the powerful role of emotion and its functions *between* people, so interest in love, compassion, and empathy is growing rapidly.

▢ Key Terms

adult attachments: relationships in which one or both people (1) prefer to be in close contact, experiencing distress during extended separation, (2) turn to the partner for support in times of stress or danger, and (3) derive security and confidence from the partner, facilitating an open and engaged approach to the rest of the world (p. 203)

attachment system: system that motivates infants and small children to stay near their parents or other caregivers (p. 190)

attitude: a combination of beliefs, feelings, and behaviors directed toward a person, object or category (p. 188)

caregiving system: according to John Bowlby, the system that motivates parents to nurture and protect their offspring (p. 192)

companionate love: strong attachment with an emphasis on security, mutual care, and protection (p. 201)

compassion: emotional desire to promote another's well-being (p. 192)

emotional empathy: actually feeling what another person is feeling (p. 198)

empathic accuracy: ability to figure out what another person is thinking and feeling (p. 198)

endorphins: naturally occurring brain chemicals with effects similar to those of heroin and morphine (p. 191)

interpersonal functions: activities that facilitate the development of relationships between people (p. 190)

intrapersonal functions: the way an emotion coordinates the cognitive, physiological, and behavioral impulses within an individual (p. 189)

maternal bonding: the attachment behaviors of a mother toward her baby (p. 196)

multimethod approach: research strategy of relying on several kinds of methods or measures and then comparing the results (p. 193)

oxytocin: a pituitary hormone released by female mammals while giving birth and while nursing and by both males and females during the sex act (p. 196)

passionate love: experience of frequent thoughts about the other person, intense desire to be together, and excitement from the partner's attention (p. 200)

personal distress: self-focused anxiety in the face of another's suffering (p. 193)

prototype: set of characteristics that describes the ideal example of some category but that may not be held by every member of that category (p. 189)

script: culturally learned set of expectations about events, thoughts, feelings, and behaviors (p. 188)

self-disclosure: sharing of personal, intimate, and confidential information (p. 208)

sex system: according to John Bowlby, the system designed to prompt sexual interest in people who are likely to be good reproductive partners (p. 194)

sympathy: concern, attention, and empathic sadness for another person who is suffering (p. 192)

☐ Thought Questions

1. During the stage of passionate love, early in a dating relationship, each person becomes more aware of the other's strengths than weaknesses. Why? (Think about it from the standpoint of both the perceiver and the person being perceived.)
2. The text distinguished sympathy, compassion, and personal distress. Under what circumstances might you experience one of these without the others—for example, distress without sympathy or compassion?

☐ Suggestion for Research Project

Psychologists know surprisingly little about the prevalence of love. You might survey people you know, asking with how many times they thought they were "in love" and, in retrospect, how many times they *now* believe they were really in love. Do the answers differ for men and women? For older and younger people? For people of different ethnic backgrounds?

☐ Suggestions for Further Reading

Hatfield, E., & Rapson, R. L. (1993). *Love, sex, and intimacy.* New York: Harper Collins.

Hrdy, S. B. (1999). *Mother Nature: Maternal instincts and how they shape the human species.* New York: Ballantine.

Swidler, A. (2001). *Talk of love: How culture matters.* Chicago: University of Chicago Press.

Tannen, D. (1990). *You just don't understand.* New York: Morrow.

10

Disgust and Contempt

Joy, sadness, fear, and anger are prototypical examples of what most people mean by "emotion." In this chapter and the next, we deal with experiences whose status is somewhat shakier. Are disgust and contempt separate emotions, variants of one emotion, variants of some other emotion such as anger, or perhaps not emotions at all? Is there more than one kind of disgust? Similar questions will arise for shame, pride, embarrassment, and guilt in the next chapter. Such questions are important because the research helps us refine our definition of the term *emotion*, and contributes to understanding of the states themselves.

In part because of these uncertainties, the experiences we will discuss in the next two chapters have received less research attention over the years than happiness, sadness, anxiety, and anger. Another reason pertains to prominence in clinical settings. Many people seek a therapist's help because they are too sad or too fearful and a smaller number because they are too angry or not happy enough. Fewer go to a therapist because of how often they feel disgusted or embarrassed.

The relative lack of research on these "other" emotions means that these next two chapters will present many unanswered questions, and you may

find yourself frustrated. However, you might also find the issues challenging. After all, an unanswered question implies the possibility of new insights awaiting discovery. Perhaps you will think of research you could contribute to the field.

◻ What Are Disgust and Contempt?

The term *disgust* is literally *dis,* meaning the opposite of, and *gust,* meaning taste or the pleasure of tasting. However, disgust is not simply "unpleasant taste." Many of us dislike the taste of one vegetable or another, but we do not call it disgusting. For example, even if you dislike spinach, you probably would not object to seeing someone else eating it, and if you found a tiny piece of spinach mixed into your stew, you might remove the spinach but you would continue eating the stew. In contrast, imagine how you would feel if you found a tiny but recognizable piece of rat fur, cockroach, or feces in your stew, or if you saw someone else eagerly eating such things. Your reaction would be stronger and more emotional.

Disgust has been defined as "revulsion at the prospect of oral incorporation of offensive objects"

(Rozin & Fallon, 1987). Disgust entails a desire to stay away from something, especially to keep it out of your mouth, but it is also a rejection of the mere thought of touching or tasting the object. Disgust is similar to fear and anger in that we are motivated to move ourselves away from something or drive it away from us. However, disgust does not provoke a vigorous fight-or-flight response. We neither flee nor attack, but simply turn away.

In previous chapters, we had to consider the question of how or why a given emotion might be useful—for example, why we had evolved an ability to feel sad or angry. In the case of disgust, the value is obvious: Disgust at the prospect of eating feces or rotten meat—what has been called "core disgust"—protects our health. However, people use the term *disgust* in broader, more abstract ways related to morality rather than eating. In one study of situations in which Americans and Japanese reported feeling disgust, participants were more likely to say that their feeling was elicited by another person's actions or beliefs than by an offensive object (Haidt, Rozin, McCauley, & Imada, 1997). This "moral disgust" has functions different from those of core disgust.

As just defined, disgust is an emotional response to something we find offensive or revolting. The object can be something like rotting meat or, in the case of moral disgust, someone else's behavior. Moreover, the English language distinguishes three types of emotional reactions to offensive behavior—anger, disgust, and contempt. According to one theoretical analysis, three distinct emotional reactions correspond to three kinds of moral offenses (Rozin, Lowery, Imada, & Haidt, 1999):

- *Anger* corresponds to a violation of *autonomy*—that is, individual rights. You are angry when someone has deprived you of something that you owned or to which you were entitled.
- **Contempt** corresponds to a violation of *community* standards. For example, we feel contempt toward someone who brags about doing

something we know he or she did not do or did poorly.
- *Disgust* corresponds to a violation of one's *divinity* in the sense of purity. To touch—or worse yet, taste—feces, cockroaches, or intestines would bring something impure into your body and therefore decrease your feeling of "divinity" (broadly defined). Similarly, associating with a person who is morally impure in some way might threaten your own feeling of purity or nobility.

Anger is easy to distinguish from contempt and disgust: You feel anger when someone hurts you, but you feel contempt or disgust when the actions do not affect you directly. The distinction between disgust and contempt is subtler and more ambiguous. According to anthropologists, most societies believe that humans are sacred or divine in some way, with a spiritual nature or soul that transcends our physical nature (Shweder, Much, Mahapatra, & Park, 1997). Using the classification system just listed, people feel disgust toward someone who has violated their soul, their spiritual nature. They feel contempt toward people who do something foolish or who behave in a way inappropriate for their social role.

Imagine seeing at a local bar another undergraduate who is clearly inebriated, making terrible jokes, and stumbling into people. Now imagine seeing one of your professors who is in the same state. If you consider this behavior tolerable for an undergraduate, but inappropriate in a faculty member, you would feel much stronger contempt toward the faculty member than toward the undergraduate, and you probably would not feel disgust toward either of them. On the other hand, if you consider intoxication to be a fundamental violation of someone's spiritual nature (as many religions do), you might feel disgust toward both people regardless of their status.

To test this distinction, researchers made a list of actions that seemed to violate autonomy, community standards, or divinity/purity. Then they asked college students in both the United States and Japan to label their reaction to each one as anger, contempt, or disgust and to choose the proper facial expression from choices like those shown in Figure 10.1. Most students chose an angry facial expression for the autonomy violations, a contemptuous expression for community violations, and a disgust expression for the divinity/purity violations (Rozin, Lowery, Imada, & Haidt, 1999). They chose these expressions more reliably than they applied the words *disgust, anger,* and *contempt.* For example, for violations of community standards they sometimes chose the contemptuous expression while saying they found the actions "disgusting."

That result is interesting. It suggests that these distinctions are less clearly reflected in people's language use than in our interpretation of others' expressions and social behavior. This idea will become important later in the chapter, for as we will see, much of the research challenging the classification of disgust as an emotion has examined the ways that people apply the word *disgust.* People don't always use words in a precise way, so the results based on facial expressions or other behaviors do not always match those from self-reports.

◻ Measuring Disgust and Contempt

As always, to study an emotion, we need to be able to measure it. Psychologists have devised a greater number and variety of ways to measure disgust than contempt. Disgust is measured regularly using facial expressions, self-reports, and several behaviors. Contempt is measured mainly with facial expressions (and even that is controversial) and by the question "how much contempt did/would you feel in this situation?" Consequently, we know more about disgust than contempt.

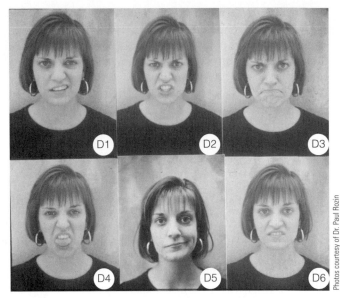

Photos courtesy of Dr. Paul Rozin

FIGURE 10.1 One set of facial expressions offered as choices for how to react to various types of offense. Faces D1 and D5 represent contempt, D2 and D3 represent anger, and D4 and D6 represent disgust. Some participants viewed these American faces, whereas others saw a set of Indian or Japanese faces. Source: Rozin et al. (1999).

Facial Expressions

Figure 10.1 contrasted the prototypical facial expressions associated with anger, disgust, and contempt. Faces D4 and D6 show typical expressions of disgust. In D4, the woman has stuck out her tongue, as if to spit out something offensive. In D6, note the slightly opened mouth, as if to spit something out or at least let it dribble out. Note also the curled upper lip, which partly covers the nostrils, as if to protect the nose from an offensive smell. The nose is wrinkled, as if one is trying to pull the nose up and away from the smell. Try to smell something near you (perhaps a cup of coffee or a flower) with your nose relaxed. Now try to smell it with your nose wrinkled, as in D6. The reflexive act of wrinkling your nose when you feel disgust slightly reduces your sense of smell. All aspects of the expression signal rejection and avoidance. People also signal disgust with their body postures and movements, which observers can also recognize as indicators of disgust, though less accurately than they can recognize the facial expressions (Rozin, Taylor, Ross, Bennett, & Hejmadi, 2005).

Note that the contempt expressions (D1 and D5) include some of the same movements but only on one side of the face. For example, the poser in D1 is showing the same lifting of the upper lip as in D6, but only on the left side of her face. The "smirk" in D5 is also only on one side. Is this really a "separate" display, or is it just a variant of the disgust display? People usually distinguish between the two when asked to apply the labels contempt and disgust, but they confuse these expressions more often than they do most other emotional expressions (Rozin, Taylor, Ross, Bennett, & Hejmadi, 2005). If people are asked to label the expressions without the specific suggestions of disgust and contempt, people frequently fail to identify the contempt expression. Furthermore, at some times people also show disgust on just one side of the face, especially if they are disgusted by something they see or smell on one side of the body. Many researchers therefore remain skeptical about how separate these expressions really are (Wagner, 2000).

To complicate things further, some evidence suggests that people associate different facial expressions with "core" and "moral" disgust. In one study, participants were asked to examine a set of photographs showing closely related expressions and choose the one that best reflected a particular situation (Rozin, Lowery, & Ebert, 1994). The face that "went with" bad tastes or smells, such as eating something bitter or sour, or smelling ammonia or rotten meat, was the nose wrinkle in Figure 10.1, D4. Participants said that the upper lip raise, as shown in D6 of Figure 10.1, applied to moral disgust, such as a reaction to looking at pictures of a concentration camp, thinking about a friend engaging in incest, or wearing a sweater previously owned and worn by Adolph Hitler. Do these results mean that "core" and "moral" disgust are separate emo-

tions, or are they just subtle variants of the same emotion? Participants who were asked which face went best with the situation "watching a body in a morgue being dissected" typically chose the upper lip raise (D6). Does this situation pertain to a moral violation? It seems ambiguous; it is not exactly a moral violation, but it isn't core disgust either, as no one is suggesting that you put anything into your mouth. In short, the distinction between core disgust and moral disgust is not always clear.

Self-Reports of Disgust

One way to measure disgust is through self-reports. In many studies, participants are simply asked "how much disgust do you feel right now on a scale from 0 to 8?" or something to that effect. Questionnaires about dispositional disgust sensitivity include items such as "how disgusted you would feel by seeing an accident victim whose intestines were exposed?" or "how disgusted you would feel to hear someone clear a throat full of mucus?" (Valentiner, Hood, & Hawkins, 2005).

How valid are self-reports of disgust? One way to answer this question is to look at the correlation between self-reports and behaviors that suggest disgust. Presumably, the more disgusting you consider something, the more you should show a disgust expression and the less willing you should be to touch it, smell it, or come near it. These three kinds of measurement are often in close agreement, although not always. For example, in one study, researchers first asked people to rate the disgust level they associated with various items and also asked how strongly they would avoid those items. One item was "You see a bowel movement left unflushed in a public toilet. (Rate how disgusted you would feel.)" Another was, "If I see someone vomit, it makes me sick to my stomach. (True or false?)" Later researchers asked the participants to approach and touch various items, if they were willing. As a rule, people who said they found something disgusting did in fact refuse to touch it (Rozin, Haidt, McCauley, Dunlop, &

Ashmore, 1999). That is, the self-reports correlated well with observable behaviors.

In another study, people who said they were highly disgusted by the sight of blood and gore had higher than average physiological responses to a film showing surgical procedures (Valentiner et al., 2005). So, again, self-reports correlated nicely with other kinds of responses.

However, in still another study, students completed questionnaires about their reactions toward spiders and other widely disliked items. Then the researchers observed the students' facial reactions toward a live tarantula spider. Nearly all students showed a disgust expression, including both those students who did and those who did not report strong fear or disgust concerning spiders (Vernon & Berenbaum, 2002). That is, in at least this one case, self-reports of disgust did not correlate well with facial expressions.

Implicit Measures of Disgust

Another method of measuring disgust and other emotions is still in the experimental stages. In an effort to measure emotions indirectly or implicitly—that is, without asking people to report them—researchers have used a variant form of the Stroop Test, a phenomenon commonly studied in cognitive psychology. The **Stroop Test** measures how quickly people can say the color of ink of a set of items. Typically, people can respond fairly quickly to a series of colored rectangles or nonsense words. In contrast, nearly everyone responds slower to saying the color of ink when an item is the name of a color that differs from the ink color itself.

The explanation is that when you look at the word BLUE written in green letters, your impulse to say "blue" powerfully interferes with the correct response "green." If the word is one that arouses your emotions, it also demands your attention and slows your reaction time. For example, researchers have found that people who are especially afraid of something (such as snakes) take longer than other people, on the average, to read the colors of words re-

lated to that fear (Williams, Mathews, & MacLeod, 1996). People with substance abuse disorders take longer with words related to alcohol or heroin (Franken, Kroon, Wiers, & Jansen, 2000; Stormark, Laberg, Nordby, & Hugdahl, 2000). This procedure is called the *Emotional Stroop Test*.

The Emotional Stroop Test has been applied to disgust words. The finding is that most people respond more slowly to reading the color of disgust-related words (such as *vomit, diarrhea,* and *feces*) than to neutral words (such as *pedal*) or fear-related words (such as *tumor*). Ordinarily, people who are highly prone to disgust (as measured by questionnaires) respond about the same as other people, but after being primed to disgust by reading a particularly disgusting story, the people prone to disgust become significantly slower than other people to read the colors of disgust-related words (Charash & McKay, 2002). However, the results so far show enough individual variability that they provide reliable information only for group averages, not for classifying individual people.

◘ Physiology of Disgust

Of the emotions we have studied so far, disgust has the most distinctive physiological profile. In contrast to fear and anger, which are associated with sympathetic nervous system arousal (the fight-or-flight response), some studies show that disgust is associated with *decreased* heart rate, a sign of parasympathetic nervous system activity. The strongest physiological symptom of disgust is nausea, usually to a mild degree, although extremely disgusted people occasionally do vomit. These findings make sense from a functional perspective. The pattern of sympathetic and parasympathetic nervous system activity observed in nausea (which includes decreased heart rate and blood pressure, increased salivation and sweating, and abrupt contraction of the stomach muscles) is clearly geared toward evacuating dangerous contents from the stomach. If you smell or taste something revolting, you try to get away from it. If it's too late and you've already consumed the offending substance, you should get it out fast.

Studies suggest that we can learn to feel disgust toward certain foods, just as we can learn new fears or new people to love, and that the experience of nausea and vomiting is part of this process. Even if a food tastes delicious, people develop a disgust response to it if they vomit after eating it, even once, especially if it was an unfamiliar food (Logue, 1985). It's as though our bodies immediately label a food "dangerous" after a single experience with contamination (Rozin & Kalat, 1971). If you are like many other college students, then at some point during your undergraduate career, you may become repulsed by the smell of tequila or some similar beverage as a result of this process. One of us (M.N.S.) used to love escargot, but after a single, miserable experience can no longer even be at a table where they are served.

The tendency to learn taste aversions is sometimes used to treat certain chemical dependencies. For example, a chemical marketed as "Antabuse" converts alcohol into a toxin that makes you throw up. Antabuse is sometimes effective in keeping alcoholics from drinking—they not only avoid alcohol to prevent initial nausea but also once they do imbibe, the resulting nausea causes an aversion to alcohol itself (Elkins, 1991). However, for a variety of reasons, Antabuse is only moderately effective as a treatment for alcoholism (Hughes & Cook, 1997).

The Neurobiology of Disgust

Does feeling disgust or watching someone else express disgust activate any specific brain areas? In one study, investigators asked people to look at various facial expressions while undergoing functional magnetic resonance imaging (fMRI). The researchers found that viewing expressions of disgust activated several brain areas but most strongly an area called the anterior insular cortex, or simply the insula (M. L. Phillips et al., 1997). Figure 10.2 shows the location of this area. Later studies have confirmed that viewing disgusting photos also activates the insular

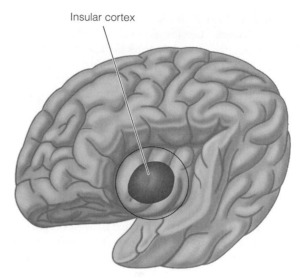

Insular cortex

FIGURE 10.2   The insular cortex is known to be important for taste; the experience of disgust also activates it.

cortex. In addition, the insular cortex responds when someone views pictures of other people's facial expressions of disgust (Wicker et al., 2003). That is, if you watch someone else acting disgusted, you feel disgusted, too.

The link between the insular cortex and disgust is interesting because the insular cortex is also the primary receptive area of the cortex for the sense of taste, and disgust is literally bad taste. A perfect relationship between experience of disgust and activation of the taste cortex would imply that disgust is independent of other emotions—a true "basic emotion."

Evidence on this issue is, however, mixed. One young man with damage limited to the insular cortex still described certain objects as "disgusting," such as a dirty toilet, suggesting that he could experience disgust without activity in that brain area. But using the term *disgust* is not necessarily the same as feeling disgust. After all, a blind person can learn to describe tomatoes as red and grass as green, without actually seeing the colors. When this patient looked at photographs of facial expressions of disgust, or listened to retching sounds, he did not recognize them as indications of disgust (Calder, Keane, Manes, Antoun, & Young, 2000). That impairment does suggest that the insular cortex is necessary for the full experience of disgust.

Nevertheless, another study using fMRI found that the insular cortex showed increased activity not only when people looked at disgusting pictures (vomit, maggots, dirty toilet, a man eating a grasshopper), but also when people looked at frightening pictures (lions, pistols, fire, car accidents). The amygdala also responded strongly to both kinds of pictures (Schienle et al., 2002). So the insular cortex is related to disgust but perhaps also to fear and other negative emotions. When disgust becomes more intense, it activates several additional brain areas as well as the insular cortex. For example, disgusting photos activate a larger circuit of the brain in people with obsessive-compulsive disorder (Shapira et al., 2003). Disgust feelings tend to be stronger among people with obsessive-compulsive disorder, as well as among people with strong obsessions that do not qualify as a disorder (Olatunji, Tolin, Huppert, & Lohr, 2005). The presumed explanation is that many obsessive people have a fear of contamination, and contamination is part of core disgust (Olatunji, Sawchuk, Arrindell, & Lohr, 2005).

As we have seen many times in this text, it is unclear whether specific aspects of emotion are associated with specific parts of the brain and, if so, how. Keep in mind that research on brain activation in emotion is at an early stage. Much more research needs to be done before we can say with any confidence that such-and-such brain area is responsible for such-and-such process. We may never be able to identify a "disgust area of the brain," or any other specific emotion area—the brain may not be set up that way. However, researchers hope that neuroimaging studies will help us refine emotion concepts with ever-greater precision, over time.

◻ Is Disgust an Emotion?

Up to now, we have been taking it for granted that disgust is a kind of emotion. In Chapter 2, we explored the definition of a "basic" emotion, or how one could decide which emotions, if any, are basic. How can we decide whether disgust is an emotion at all? Disgust undeniably is associated with strong, even intense, physical feelings. However, not all physiological feelings constitute emotions. Hunger produces strong feelings, as do thirst, sleepiness, and various other conditions that we do not ordinarily classify as emotions.

Unfortunately, as we discussed in Chapter 1, we have no definite criteria to distinguish emotions from motivations or drives (Solomon, 2002). As noted in Chapter 1, one criterion is that emotions tend to fade over time, whereas drives persist until they are satisfied. Another is that primary drives reflect body needs, whereas emotions arise in reaction to events around us. Although apparently no one has published research on this topic, we submit that disgust passes these criteria: If you have just seen something disgusting, your reaction ordinarily fades over time, unless you continue to see new disgusting images. And disgust is usually a reaction to an external event, not an internal need.

Other researchers feel, however, that disgust is not an emotion. To develop further the distinction between emotions and other kinds of experience, Edward Royzman and John Sabini (2001) took the approach of identifying anxiety and anger as prototypical examples of emotions. To decide whether disgust or any other candidate is also an emotion, they examined whether it shares basic features in common with anxiety and anger. They argued that disgust is substantially different. According to Royzman and Sabini, one important feature of anxiety and anger is that they generate many and varied responses. For example, if you are either frightened or angry, you will take many actions, depending on the circumstances. In contrast, the reaction to disgust is more limited: You make a facial expression, you turn away from the offending object, and you refuse to touch or taste it. If it is too late to avoid contact with it, you shake it off your hands or spit it out of your mouth. In short, disgust does not evoke the same wide range of responses that more prototypical emotions do. However, this criterion of varied responses does not convincingly apply to all emotions. Joy and sadness also lead to few actions. In fact, very sad people generally become inactive. Furthermore, hunger and thirst, which we classify as drives, do lead to flexible and varied actions.

Another criterion Royzman and Sabini suggested is that emotions are more "cognitively penetrable" than motivations. That is, you can sometimes talk someone out of anger, fear, joy, or sadness, just by getting the person to think about the situation differently. It is more difficult to say anything that would alter a motivation like hunger or thirst. (Pain is a debatable case here. Sometimes you can say something to decrease someone's pain, at least to a mild degree. Pain can be regarded as a sensation with both motivational and emotional aspects.) If we accept "cognitive penetrability" as a criterion, we can ask whether thinking differently about cockroaches, rats, feces, or other prototypical elicitors could increase or decrease the disgust one feels toward them. If not, then perhaps we should not consider disgust to be an emotion. However, not much research is available on this point.

Finally, Royzman and Sabini's main point is that "true" emotions can be triggered by abstract information. For example, a spot on a mammogram can evoke fear by suggesting possible breast cancer. An insulting word can evoke anger. A bit of good news or bad news can lead to joy or sadness. In these cases, one is responding to what the information *means,* not the event itself. In contrast, drives are triggered by specific stimuli: Stomach sensations or the presence of attractive food can provoke hunger. A burning pain produces a motivation to get away from whatever is causing the pain. The presence of an appealing and willing sexual partner increases sexual arousal. Disgust, Royzman and Sabini argue, is more like these motivations: It is provoked by a specific stimulus, not by an abstract representation.

Are they right or wrong? We need to distinguish two questions. First, do you agree that the ability to elicit a state through abstract information is a good criterion for calling it a "true emotion"? This issue might be a good topic for class discussion. To use this criterion, we need to agree that abstract information, such as something you read, can elicit anger

and anxiety, but that abstract information cannot elicit motivations such as hunger and sexual arousal. Second, is it true that abstract information cannot evoke disgust? We address this complicated question in the next section.

◘ Cognitive Aspects of Disgust

Although the "core" of disgust is bad taste or offensive smell, we extend our emphatic "bad taste" rejection to the sight or mere thought of such objects as insects, bloody body parts, and dead bodies. Although we react to them as if they would taste bad, most of us do not really care how they taste. The people who do eat insects say that many taste good. Consider this quote: "Served on toast points, stag beetle larvae are superb. They have a nutty flavor. The head capsules impart a subtle crunchy touch, while the thorax and abdomen have a delicately chewy texture" (Boyle, 1992, p. 101). Now that you know how good they taste, would you like to try them? Probably not. Most people find the idea of eating an insect repulsive, and they might gag if they actually chewed one regardless of how it actually tasted.

Similarly, our reactions to a smell depend mainly on what we think it is, not its sensory quality. Suppose someone asks you to close your eyes and smell a jar containing "a strong cheese." You rate the smell as moderately pleasant. Then you are told, "Oops, I'm sorry, that jar was mislabeled. I think that was feces, not cheese." Now you think it smells horrible. Then the person says, "Oh, no, I was right the first time. It really was cheese after all." Now you are not sure what to believe. Moreover, you don't know whether you like the smell or not (Rozin & Fallon, 1987).

Suppose a researcher dunked a cockroach in apple juice and asked you whether you would be willing to drink it. (See Figure 10.3.) Would you? If not, why not? Well, you answer, the cockroach might have had germs, so the juice would be unsafe to drink. But what if someone assures you that the

Photos courtesy of Dr. Paul Rozin

FIGURE 10.3 After you had seen a cockroach placed into a cup of apple juice, how thoroughly would you insist on washing the cup before you would drink from it?

© Michael Newman/Photo Edit

FIGURE 10.4 Although this object is shaped and colored to look like vomit, it is actually just rubber. Would you be willing to put it into your mouth?

cockroach was carefully sterilized and you can be sure it had no germs? Presumably you still don't want to drink the juice. Why not? No matter how sterile, it was still a cockroach. You are revolted by the very idea of eating or drinking anything that was once in contact with a cockroach (Rozin, Millman, & Nemeroff, 1986).

Similarly, many other disgust experiences depend on the thought of the object, not its sensory qualities. For example, suppose someone asks you to put a piece of rubber into your mouth. As you are about to agree to do it, you notice that the rubber is shaped and colored like vomit, from a novelty store (Figure 10.4). Would you still put it into your mouth? Second, someone offers you a piece of chocolate fudge but points out that it is shaped like dog feces. Would you still eat it? Would you eat soup after watching someone stir it with a brand new, unused fly swatter? Would you drink water from a new, never-been-used toilet bowl? Suppose you are eating something and someone asks you to spit it out onto a plate and look at it. Now could you put it back in your mouth and continue eating it? (If not, why not? It was already in your mouth and you were about to swallow it a moment ago. It is in no way unsafe.) In each of these cases, many people say they

would refuse. None of the items just described are dangerous; they are offensive because of the ideas associated with them (Rozin & Fallon, 1987).

Paul Rozin and his colleagues have noted that nearly everything that we find disgusting is animal in nature—specific animals such as cockroaches and spiders, body parts such as intestines, body excretions such as feces, dead bodies, and unsavory sexual acts such as incest. Nonanimal objects such as chocolate fudge or a piece of rubber can be disgusting if they remind us of some animal or animal part that we find disgusting. Rozin has suggested that an item becomes disgusting if and when it reminds us of our animal nature (Rozin & Fallon, 1987; Rozin, Lowery, et al., 1999). That is, we like to think of ourselves as noble, clean, and pure, and the sight of intestines, feces, or blood reminds us of the lowliest and most unclean aspects of our existence. Human hair can be disgusting, especially if at a beach you see a man with so much body hair that he looks like an ape. Animals in general evoke disgust when they urinate and defecate in public, have sex in public, and in other ways do the things that we like to hide about ourselves.

Others have argued that disgust is not simply a response to anything that reminds us of our animal nature (Royzman & Sabini, 2001). The animals we find most disgusting, such as rats, snakes, and cockroaches, are not the most human-like of animals, nor are they necessarily the least. Seeing a dog defecate might remind us of our animal nature, but dogs also resemble us when they walk, drink, scratch themselves, and engage in many other acts that we do not find disgusting. So, at least, we need to refine the idea that we feel disgust when something reminds us of our animal nature.

Core Versus Moral Disgust

As we noted at the beginning of this chapter, our revulsion at the thought of some unacceptable food is "primary" disgust, or what Haidt, McCauley, and Rozin (1994) have called the "core" of disgust. However, people certainly use the term *disgust* more broadly. To map the full meaning of the term, Haidt and colleagues began by asking 20 people to describe all the intensely disgusting experiences they could remember. The researchers then grouped those experiences into these categories:

- Bad-tasting foods
- Body products such as feces, urine, and nose mucus
- Unacceptable sexual acts, such as incest
- Gore, surgery, and other exposure of the inner body parts
- Socio-moral violations such as Nazis, drunk drivers, hypocrites, and ambulance-chasing lawyers
- Insects, spiders, snakes, and other repulsive animals
- Dirt and germs
- Contact with dead bodies

Certainly the socio-moral violations are more abstract than the body products and foods. Presumably most of the participants had never actually met a Nazi and many had not met a drunk driver, so their emotional responses must have been to the idea of these people. But then, is the emotional response to socio-moral violations "really" disgust? If disgust is a single kind of experience, people who get disgusted easily by one kind of item should also get disgusted easily by another. The researchers did find that pattern, with one exception: Disgust ratings about drunk drivers, hypocrites, and the other "socio-moral violations" did not correlate highly with any of the other events (Haidt et al., 1994). That is, someone who called drunk drivers "very disgusting" was neither more nor less likely than other people to consider insects, gore, dead bodies, or any of the other items highly disgusting. For that reason, the researchers deleted the socio-moral category from the list of disgust types. As many others have pointed out, English-speaking people use the term *disgust* rather loosely (Royzman & Sabini, 2001; Woody & Teachman, 2000). When you say you are "disgusted" by something, you might mean only that you disapprove of it. In such cases, your experience may include some element of core disgust, but you may also be describing anger and contempt, or sometimes fear and sadness (Marzillier & Davey, 2004).

Disgust and "Magical" or Superstitious Thinking

Disgust shows the fascinating property of **contagion,** the idea of "once in contact, always in contact." For example, if a cockroach crawls over your food, you might find the food disgusting, even after the cockroach is gone. That idea is part of a type of thinking called "sympathetic magic" (Rozin, Millman, & Nemeroff, 1986). Another example of contagion is that you probably would not want to wear a shirt that someone wore while committing a murder or a hat previously worn by Adolf Hitler or Osama bin Laden. Washing the shirt or hat repeatedly does not help; its history fouls it forever. The reverse also occurs to some extent: An object can be more valuable to you because it once belonged to one of your grandparents or some other beloved or famous person. Artworks provide a particularly powerful example of this principle: An original painting by a famous painter, such as Monet or van

Gogh, is worth a fortune, whereas a copy by some- one else is worth much less, no matter how high the quality of the copy. What matters is not just the quality of the art but also whose hand made it.

A second principle of sympathetic magic, also prominent in disgust, is **similarity,** the idea that if something looks similar, we treat it similarly. For ex- ample, recall that many people refused to put into their mouths a piece of rubber that looked like vomit, even though they knew it wasn't really vomit. Also recall that many people refuse to eat chocolate fudge shaped like dog feces. In both cases, people know they are behaving irrationally, but they feel an aversion to tasting something that reminds them of a disgusting object (Rozin, Millman, & Nemeroff, 1986). The ultimate example of magic similarity is voodoo dolls, in which people believe that hurting an image of someone will hurt the person himself or herself (Rozin & Nemeroff, 1990).

These tendencies relate to an idea prevalent in many "traditional" cultures—that is, cultures with little formal education. That idea is that "you are what you eat" in the literal sense that you take on characteristics of the objects you eat. That belief does contain a little truth: If you eat garlic, you tem- porarily smell of garlic. Some people say that if you eat enough carrots, your skin can turn somewhat orange, although it is hard to find a good example of an orange person to support this claim. People in many cultures go further, assuming that if you eat a plant that grew fast, you yourself will become quicker, and if you eat the meat of a hedgehog, you will become slow and timid.

We "educated" people have outgrown those su- perstitions, right? Maybe not. Nemeroff and Rozin (1989) asked two groups of college students to read descriptions of the "Chandoran" people. The de- scriptions were the same except that in one version the Chandorans ate wild boar and hunted marine turtles only for their shells; in the other version they ate marine turtles and hunted wild boar only for their tusks. The students were asked to describe their perceptions of the Chandorans. In comparison to students who thought the Chandorans ate turtles, those who thought they ate wild boar rated them as more irritable, excitable, loud, unreliable, fast- moving, bearded, and aggressive and less generous. Note an interesting point about survey methods here: If the researchers had asked whether eating wild boar makes people aggressive and irritable, presumably college students would say no. But with a different kind of question, students reveal that ap- parently they do hold such beliefs implicitly.

Recall from Chapter 1 the statement that emo- tions are closely linked to the concept of good and evil. What makes us happy is good; what makes us sad is evil. In many cases, the experience of disgust is also closely linked to the concept of morality and immorality. For example, people who become vege- tarians purely for reasons of health do not regard meat eating as disgusting, but those who become vegetarians for moral reasons do regard it as dis- gusting (Rozin, Markwith, & Stoess, 1997). Even they do not find eating meat disgusting at first, but they gradually come to feel more disgust at the idea (Fessler, Arguello, Mekdara, & Macias, 2003). Many find it repulsive simply to see someone else eat meat. Since about the 1970s, many people in the United States have begun to treat cigarette smoking as dis- gusting and somewhat immoral. One consequence of "moralizing" a choice or treating the unpleasant choice as disgusting is that the undesirable choice becomes much easier to resist. For example, vegetar- ians who regard meat as disgusting feel no tempta- tion to eat meat, regardless of the circumstances. Another consequence is that they become less toler- ant of people who do not share their feelings.

Given all of these findings, are Royzman and Sabini (2001) correct in saying that we cannot feel disgust in response to an abstract idea? It depends in part on what one means by "abstract." It appears that one can become disgusted by the idea of feces, or by a plastic representation of feces, but is that the same as seeing a spot on a mammogram and be- coming afraid? Certainly socio-moral violations have an abstract quality, but do they really elicit dis- gust, or do they elicit some other emotion or combi- nation of emotions? This may seem like splitting hairs, but such questions have significance for re- searchers studying emotion. We rely on words such as *emotion* and *disgust* to convey our ideas and research findings. Disagreements about what these and other words mean can cause tremendous confusion and slow down progress in understanding the human experience. Although these disagreements can be frustrating, they are important to hash out, and they usually resolve only with time and extensive research.

◘ Disgust: Development and Individual Differences

Virtually all people and other animals reject bad tastes. However, we have defined disgust as revulsion at the very idea of putting some offensive object into the mouth, regardless of its taste. Disgust in that sense develops gradually and becomes stronger in some people than others.

Very young children, up to about age 1 to $1\frac{1}{2}$ years, will put almost anything they can reach into their mouths, and unless it tastes bad, they will chew it and swallow it (Rozin, Hammer, Oster, Horowitz, & Marmora, 1986). Even if it tastes bad, the child may try it again. For this reason, parents of infants have to "child-proof" their house. Many children each year die by swallowing medicines, furniture polish, sharp objects, and so forth.

As children grow older, at first they reject foods only if they taste bad, but later they reject foods they believe might be dangerous, and still later reject foods because of the very idea that they are contaminated. Consider this scenario: Suppose you pour a fresh glass of apple juice. Before a child has a chance to drink it, you drop a small piece of dog feces into the apple juice. Will the child drink the apple juice? Even preschool children generally refuse; rejection of feces is probably the first real disgust. (How it develops is an interesting unresolved issue. Do toddlers learn the disgust on their own or from their parents?) But assuming the child refuses apple juice with dog feces in it, what happens after you spoon out the dog feces?

Children less than 7 years old generally agree to drink the juice. (Researchers don't actually let them drink it.) Slightly older children would not drink that apple juice, but they would accept it if you pour out the apple juice and refill the glass with new apple juice. Still older children insist that you first wash the glass before refilling it. Some adults will refuse no matter how many times you wash that glass, and insist on throwing the glass away (Rozin, Fallon, & Augustoni-Ziskind, 1985). Some adults go still further and say they have lost their taste for apple juice—even in a new container.

When adults are asked how disgusting they consider various items, women on the average express more disgust than men do (Haidt et al., 1994; Olatunji, Sawchuk, et al., 2005). That tendency fits a general pattern, where women also display stronger happiness, amusement, sadness, and anxiety. Of the emotions we have considered so far, the only one that men consistently express equally or more strongly than women is anger.

Expressions of disgust correlate fairly highly (+.45) with the personality trait *neuroticism* (Druschel & Sherman, 1999). That term, easily misunderstood, does not imply mental illness; it refers to a tendency to experience unpleasant emotions relatively easily. In other words, people prone to disgust are also prone to sadness and anxiety. Disgust also shows a weak negative correlation (−.28) with the personality trait *openness to experience* (Druschel & Sherman, 1999). Openness to experience is the tendency to explore new opportunities, such as trying new or unusual types of foods, art, music, literature, and so forth. It sounds reasonable that a tendency to get disgusted easily might get in the way of exploring a variety of new experiences.

◘ Relations Among Disgust, Fears, and Phobias

As mentioned, disgust almost always pertains to animals, animal parts, or animal products. Many phobias also relate to animals (such as spiders) and their parts or products (especially blood and gore). Several psychologists have suggested that some phobias may represent a combination of fear and disgust, not just fear alone. After all, various emotions blend and we almost always experience some combination of emotions, not just one by itself (Woody & Teachman, 2000).

People with phobias of spiders or blood do, in fact, report that they find them disgusting as well as frightening (Woody & Tolin, 2002), and their degree of avoidance correlates better with their disgust than with their fear (Woody, McLean, & Klassen, 2005). As a rule, when people report that they have become more afraid or less afraid of spiders, they also become more disgusted or less disgusted (Vernon & Berenbaum, 2004). Compared to people who report only fear, people who report both fear and disgust at the sight of blood, or at the thought of getting an injection, are more likely to faint when having blood drawn (Page, 2003). Similarly, women who rate high-calorie foods as both disgusting and frightening are more likely than other women to develop eating disorders (T. Harvey, Troop, Treasure, & Murphy, 2002).

Such results suggest that disgust adds to the intensity of a phobia. We should be cautious in the interpretation because most people use the term *disgust* loosely, referring to general dislike and not just revulsion. However, many people with phobias show the kind of magical thinking—"once in contact, always in contact"—that is characteristic of disgust. For example, people with a phobia of spiders avoid not only spiders but also even a pen or pencil that they saw a spider walk on (Woody et al., 2005). That observation sounds more like disgust than fear: You might well be afraid of a loaded gun, but you would not avoid everything that had touched the gun.

The role of disgust in phobia is an important point for clinicians to consider. If phobia includes disgust as well as fear (perhaps even more than fear), then overcoming a phobia requires overcoming the disgust.

"Unlearning" Disgusts

Little research has dealt with how we learn disgusts, but anecdotal reports suggest that we learn them easily and quickly. Many people say that they developed a feeling of disgust after a single experience, such as finding maggots in some kind of food (Rozin, 1986). Once something has become disgusting, the reaction tends to be very persistent. However, if you wanted to overcome some feeling of disgust, how could you do it? Research on this topic is slim, but here are a few suggestions (Rozin & Fallon, 1987):

- Inhibit yourself from making the facial expression of disgust.
- Change your concept of the object. For example, tell yourself, "This isn't what I thought it was."
- Expose yourself gradually and repeatedly to the disgusting object. Visitors to a foreign country sometimes find certain food items disgusting, but after necessarily eating them a few times, at first just in tiny amounts, they begin to find them acceptable. Plumbers and sewage disposal workers manage to overcome their disgust at human waste products.
- When appropriate, lower the psychological boundary between "self" and "other." We generally find our own body secretions and waste products less disgusting than those of others. Lovers come to accept each other's secretions and smells; parents change their infants' diapers, usually without feeling great offense. In effect, they treat the other person as an extension of the self.

◻ Summary

Disgust is a quick, sometimes powerful reaction we feel toward feces, rotting meat, and many types of animals, animal parts, and animal products. We also feel it toward anything that reminds us of disgusting objects, including (by sympathetic magic) anything that looks like or was ever in contact with something disgusting.

This description is not especially controversial. Once we move beyond that, however, the picture is less clear. Contempt has been defined as an emotional response to another's violation of social etiquette or of the role they are expected to take in the community. We can easily think of clear-cut examples that go into the "disgust" and "contempt" categories, but there is also much overlap—the boundaries between the two are fuzzy rather than distinct. Anger, the third "moral emotion," is easier to distinguish, but then Americans (on the whole, relative to people in other countries) are much more concerned about autonomy than about community or divinity. It may be that "anger" is a hypercognized concept in the United States (as discussed in Chapter 3), compared with disgust and contempt, even if the latter are distinct emotions. The fact that facial expressions match up more clearly with the hypothesized eliciting situations than do verbal labels is consistent with this possibility. However, there is not yet enough research to draw a firm conclusion.

The status of moral disgust is even more controversial. Is it disgust at all? Is it a combination of anger and contempt? Is it a different emotion entirely, and if so, what relationship does it have to "core" disgust? We leave you with many questions on this subject, but each is an opportunity for pioneering studies in this field.

◻ Key Terms

contagion: (as a principle of sympathetic magic) the idea of "once in contact, always in contact" (p. 221)

contempt: emotional reaction to a violation of community standards (p. 213)

disgust: revulsion at the prospect of oral incorporation of offensive objects (p. 212)

similarity: (as a principle of sympathetic magic) the idea that if something looks similar, we treat it similarly (p. 222)

Stroop Test: procedure that measures how fast people can name the color of ink of a set of items (p. 216)

◻ Thought Questions

1. Is "moral" disgust the same as contempt? If not, what difference do you see?
2. Do you agree with Royzman and Sabini that one criterion for an emotion is that an emotion can be elicited by abstract information?
3. What do you think of the proposal that we feel disgust when something reminds us of our animal nature?
4. Recall the discussion of "cognitive penetrability" of emotions. Can you think of anything you could say that would decrease someone's disgust at the idea of, say, eating a cockroach?

◻ Suggestions for Research Projects

1. Do any nonhuman animals experience disgust? You might see whether there is anything harmless that you could mix into your pet's food that would cause your pet to refuse to eat it.
2. Try overcoming disgust reactions toward some disturbing but harmless object, such as a plastic model of vomit. If you practice touching it, smelling it, and eventually putting it into your mouth, do you thereby decrease your disgust reactions toward real vomit or other disgusting objects?

◻ Suggestions for Further Reading

Rozin, P., & Fallon, A. (1987). A perspective on disgust. *Psychological Review, 94,* 23–41.

Rozin, P., Lowery, L., Imada, S., & Haidt, J. (1999). The CAD triad hypothesis: A mapping between three moral emotions (contempt, anger, disgust) and three moral codes (community, autonomy, divinity). *Journal of Personality and Social Psychology, 76,* 574–586.

Both of these articles review theory and research on disgust and related emotions.

The Self-Conscious Emotions: Embarrassment, Shame, Guilt, and Pride

In previous chapters, we considered the emotions of fear, anger, joy, love, sadness, disgust, and contempt. Each of these has been the subject of a considerable amount of research and appears on typical lists of emotions. What other emotions are there? The list of possible "other emotions" could go on for some time; various psychologists have nominated surprise, hope, jealousy, interest, confusion, contentment, awe, and others as likely candidates. If we include emotions considered "basic" in other cultures, the list grows even longer. On the other hand, psychologists caution against dividing the emotion domain into too many categories. In our eagerness to find subtle distinctions between one experience of emotion and another, it can be easy to overlook their shared characteristics, and "miss the forest for the trees." As we have noted repeatedly throughout this text, researchers have yet to agree on a definition of "emotion." Partly for this reason, researchers disagree on how many emotions there are, although they often agree about what states are *not* emotions.

In short, we must somewhat arbitrarily decide how many emotions to discuss. In this chapter, we wind up our "tour" with a cluster of emotions that are less prototypical than the other emotions discussed so far. The emotions we consider here have a common feature that distinguishes them from other emotions. When we are sad, frightened, angry, or loving, we feel those emotions toward some event or person outside ourselves. What pride, shame, embarrassment, and guilt have in common is that they all require self-evaluation. We feel these emotions when *we* have done something good or bad, something that will probably make others think better or worse of us, so our emotional reaction is actually in response to our own behavior. For this reason, pride, embarrassment, shame, and guilt are often called the "self-conscious emotions."

◻ Differentiating Among Embarrassment, Shame, and Guilt

Embarrassment, shame, and guilt have much in common. All three are unpleasant for the person feeling the emotion, all three include the belief that we have violated some moral code or social convention, and all three make us want to hide or withdraw in some way. In one study, investigators asked participants to read various sentences while having their brain activity monitored with fMRI. One block of sentences dealt with embarrassing experiences (such as "I was not dressed properly for the occasion"), another described experiences of guilt ("I left the restaurant without paying"), and others described unemotional events. As Figure C.7 shows (see inside back cover), the areas activated by the embarrassing sentences were almost the same as those activated by sentences about guilt (Takahashi et al., 2004).

In short, the experiences of embarrassment, shame, and guilt overlap heavily. Describing how they differ is more challenging, and researchers have conducted several studies trying to tease their causes and characteristics apart.

One way to do this is simply to ask people when they have felt each of these emotions and see whether different kinds of situations elicit them. In one study, investigators asked U.S. college students to recall a recent experience in which they felt embarrassment, shame, or guilt (Keltner & Buswell, 1996). The most common experiences associated with embarrassment were:

- Poor performance (doing something less well than others, or less well than expected)
- Physical clumsiness (such as tripping or spilling something)
- A cognitive error (such as forgetting an acquaintance's name or a friend's birthday)
- Inappropriate physical appearance (such as wearing casual clothes when everyone else was dressed formally or vice versa)
- Failure of privacy (such as accidentally being seen naked or intruding when someone else was naked)
- Being teased
- Conspicuousness (being the center of attention)

That final category, being the center of attention, deserves some comment. Having all eyes on you can

be embarrassing, even if it is for something positive. A familiar embarrassing event is having people sing "Happy Birthday" to you in a public place. For another example, suppose a professor in a large class is passing back a midterm and announces to the entire class that you got the highest score on the exam. She goes on to glow about how insightful and well-documented your answers were and says it was one of the most impressive exam performances she's ever seen. The whole class stares at you throughout her speech. The praise is nice, but most people would still want to crawl under their chair. Note that when you feel embarrassed, you have not done anything morally wrong. Even if you have made a mistake, it is an understandable, normal mistake; you just had the misfortune to do it in public.

The most common experiences associated with shame were:

- Poor performance (as with embarrassment)
- Hurting someone else's feelings
- Lying
- Failure to meet other people's expectations (such as getting poor grades in school and thereby disappointing one's parents)
- Failure to meet one's own expectations

The most common experiences associated with guilt were:

- Failure to perform one's duties (such as not studying hard enough, not following through on a commitment)
- Lying, cheating, or stealing
- Neglecting a friend or loved one
- Hurting someone else's feelings
- Infidelity to one's romantic partner
- Breaking a diet

As you can see, the kinds of experiences that elicit embarrassment, shame, and guilt overlap with one another. Poor performance is commonly cited as a cause for either embarrassment or shame; hurting others in some way is a common cause of either shame or guilt. A reasonable conclusion is that embarrassment, shame, and guilt overlap and shade into one another, much as the colors red, orange, and yellow do. However, when we look at all the events eliciting each emotion, some consistent themes emerge. Embarrassment seems most common when one is suddenly the focus of other people's attention, not because one has done something morally wrong, but because of a mistake, accident, or even a positive event. Shame seems most common when someone fails to live up to expectations. Guilt seems most common when one does something that hurts another person.

But these are subjective impressions, created by reading many descriptions of specific events and asking what they have in common. Another way to distinguish among emotions is for people to think of an experience in which they felt each emotion and then rate the accuracy of various statements in describing this experience. Then researchers see whether different emotions are characterized by different situations and interpretations of them. In one study, June Tangney and her colleagues (1996) asked participants to remember a time they felt embarrassment, shame, or guilt and then asked them to rate how intense the feeling was, how long it lasted, how much they expected the event that caused the emotion, and a number of aspects of the event itself.

Tangney and her colleagues found that people's rating patterns for the embarrassment experiences were quite different from their rating patterns for shame and guilt. Unlike shame and guilt, embarrassment was experienced briefly before fading. Embarrassment was also sudden and felt in response to an unexpected event; by contrast, the events that elicited shame and guilt were more expected, and the feelings themselves built up over a longer time. Participants reported being angry with themselves with regard to shame and guilt experiences but not angry with themselves (or only slightly) for times of embarrassment. We noted earlier that shame and guilt seemed to be associated, more so than embarrassment, with doing something morally wrong, and Tangney's results confirmed this point. Participants describing shame

and guilt experiences felt strongly that they had violated a moral standard, that the situation was serious, rather than funny, and that they were personally responsible for the event. Participants reporting embarrassment experiences felt less responsible for the event, thought it was as funny as it was serious, and did not think they had done anything morally wrong. Participants were also asked to infer what the people around them thought about the event. People describing embarrassment experiences felt strongly that other people were looking at them but that the onlookers felt amused by the event. People describing shame and guilt experiences felt less as though everybody was staring at them but more that other people were angry with them.

These studies, and others like them, allow psychologists to state somewhat more precisely what they mean by the terms *embarrassment, shame,* and *guilt.* Let's now consider each of these three emotions in turn.

□ **Embarrassment**

Of the three emotions we are discussing, embarrassment seems to be the most distinctive. We can tentatively define **embarrassment** as the emotion felt when one violates a social convention, thereby drawing unexpected social attention and motivating submissive, friendly behavior that should appease other people. We noted in Chapter 1 that emotions are presumed to have some kind of function—a way in which people benefit from feeling and/or displaying the emotion in certain kinds of situations. What function might embarrassment serve? Although the *experience* of embarrassment is unpleasant, your *display* of it lets other people know you care about their opinion, and may coax them into being nice to you after you have done something clumsy, awkward, or inappropriate (Keltner & Buswell, 1997).

To illustrate the usefulness of the embarrassment display, imagine this scenario. You are in a grocery store carrying a large, heavy box of kitty litter. As you walk through a crowded aisle, you manage to knock over a huge display of bottled salsa, causing a complete mess, breaking several bottles, spilling kitty litter, and even getting salsa and kitty litter on a couple of people's clothes. If you just walk away as though nothing had happened, how will other people react? There's a strong chance they'll be annoyed and think you are rude as well as clumsy. On the other hand, if you smile, blush, and look embarrassed, they might laugh and tell you not to worry—they might even start to like you a little bit (Semin & Manstead, 1982). Your embarrassment has transformed a potentially tense, aggressive situation into a polite and friendly one. From your perspective, as the person who caused the mess in the first place, you've just managed to avoid social ostracism, possibly even a physical attack.

Research evidence indicates that embarrassment helps to repair awkward social situations in just this way. Researchers in one study had participants watch videos of someone who knocked over a supermarket display and then either showed or did not show embarrassment; participants liked the embarrassed klutz more than the unconcerned one (Semin & Manstead, 1982). In a similar study, people said they would be more likely to forgive a person who broke a valuable item if he or she looked embarrassed (R. S. Miller, 2001b). Children who display embarrassment after breaking a rule are punished less severely by their parents than children who don't (Semin & Papadopoulou, 1990). People are also more likely to help a person who looks embarrassed and to feel liking and affection toward people who show embarrassment (Keltner, Young, & Buswell, 1997; Levin & Arluke, 1982).

One limitation of this effect is that embarrassment diverts people's anger only if they think your transgression was truly an accident (De Jong, Peters, De Cremer, & Vranken, 2002). That is, you are not appeased by hearing someone say "I'm sorry, I didn't mean to do it," if you think the person did mean it. Remember from the chapter on anger that people are more likely to become angry when they think another person's harmful actions were delib-

erate. Embarrassment sends the message that your actions were not deliberate, so other people should not be angry. If for some reason people don't believe you, they are likely to get mad anyway.

Experiences That Evoke Embarrassment

Let's explore the experiences that evoke embarrassment in more detail. After all, the definition we suggested earlier is vague: What does it mean to "violate a social convention"? Is all social attention embarrassing? Is it more embarrassing for some people than for others, and if so, why? To understand better the kinds of experiences that could cause embarrassment, John Sabini and his colleagues asked college students to read descriptions of several interpersonal scenarios and then asked how embarrassed the students thought they would feel in each situation (Sabini, Siepmann, Stein, & Meyerowitz, 2000). The situations fit into three categories: making a social mistake, being the center of attention, and being in a "sticky situation." Here are examples of each of these categories:

> *Mistake.* I had been working with Ellen for about six months on several projects. She was an excellent team member, and we got along well, but she seemed overly friendly, and it made me a bit uncomfortable. When she invited me over for dinner, I realized I would have to talk about it with her. So I accepted the invitation with the plan of clarifying our relationships as "friends only." Just as she let me into her apartment I suddenly felt so nervous that I blurted out, "Ellen, I just need to clarify that my coming here doesn't mean there's anything romantic between us," and just then a man walked into the entrance hall and introduced himself as Ellen's husband. (Sabini et al., 2000, p. 237)

> *Center of attention.* I was attending a cocktail party where I didn't know a lot of people. Just

as I started to enter I heard an announcement that the guest of honour was arriving, and a spotlight was turned on the door. It followed my entrance instead of that of the real guest of honour who was just behind me. (Sabini et al., p. 238)

Sticky situation. I had lent my friend a large sum of money, which he had not repaid. I suddenly found myself in a tight spot, and needed the money back in order to pay my rent, so I knew I was going to have to ask my friend to repay the loan. (Sabini et al., p. 238)

Sabini and colleagues' results suggest that all of these situations were considered embarrassing, but were they all embarrassing for the same reason? Put another way, if we want to understand what causes embarrassment, should we be looking for something all three kinds of situations have in common, or could the three kinds of situations cause embarrassment in different ways? One way to address this question is to ask whether the individuals who considered one kind of situation embarrassing also considered the other kinds equally embarrassing. If so, then presumably there is something that all three situations share. If not, then it may be that the features of the situations are different, and that different people actually become embarrassed for different reasons.

The results of this study supported the latter proposition. The ratings that students gave to "mistake" situations correlated highly with one another. That is, those who said they would be "highly embarrassed" in one mistake situation generally gave similarly high ratings to other mistake situations. Also, embarrassment ratings on "center of attention" situations correlated with one another, and ratings on "sticky situations" correlated with one another. However, ratings on different kinds of situations did not correlate highly with one another. In other words, people highly embarrassed by a mistake were not necessarily highly embarrassed by being the center of attention, and those embarrassed by being the center of attention were not necessarily embarrassed by a sticky situation.

One thing to keep in mind, when thinking about the implications of this study, is that participants said only how they *thought* they would feel in each situation. The researchers did not measure whether people *actually* felt embarrassed by each of these situations. Thus, these results may reflect people's expectations about embarrassment, rather than what "really" makes people feel embarrassed. To put it another way, people may have entered the study with different theories about what causes embarrassment, beliefs like "people feel embarrassed when everybody is looking at them" or "people feel embarrassed when they make a social mistake." If so, people with different theories would consider different kinds of situations embarrassing. There's no way to know, from this study alone, whether the differences in people's ratings reflect their beliefs about what causes embarrassment, or what would actually make them feel embarrassed.

Let's also consider a fourth scenario: **empathic embarrassment,** or being embarrassed in sympathy for someone else who we see is embarrassed or who we think *should* be embarrassed. Here is a study that demonstrated empathic embarrassment. Imagine yourself as one of the participants. First you come to a psychologist's laboratory, where, among other tasks, you are asked to sing *The Star Spangled Banner* (the U.S. national anthem). A week later, you are asked to return to the lab and to bring a friend with you. At this point, you have no idea what this study is about.

So you and the friend arrive, as does a third person unfamiliar to both of you. The researcher attaches electrodes to one cheek of each person. Again you don't know why, but in fact it is to measure blushing. Now the three of you are supposed to watch a video on the television screen. All goes smoothly for a while, and then suddenly the video shows *you—singing the national anthem*. How do you feel? Most people are embarrassed and blush immediately. After all, the *Star Spangled Banner* is a difficult song with a wide range of notes, and few people can sing it as a solo without sounding foolish. Figure 11.1 shows the mean amount of blushing by the singers,

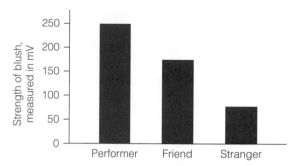

FIGURE 11.1   Mean amount of blushing by the participant watching him- or herself singing, by a friend, and by a stranger. Source: Based on the data of Shearn et al. (1999).

the singers' friends, and the strangers. Note that the singer blushes the most, but the friend blushes considerably too, presumably in sympathy with the friend, and the stranger blushes the least (Shearn, Spellman, Straley, Meirick, & Stryker, 1999).

A follow-up study was interesting also: If the stranger had to sing *The Star Spangled Banner* in the lab previously, then he or she blushed strongly also, about as much as the participant and friend (Shearn et al., 1999). One interpretation of this is that the stranger sympathizes, knowing what the poor participant is enduring. Another interpretation is that the stranger is thinking, "Uh oh! If they're showing a video of that person singing now, a video of me might be coming next!"

As you can see, researchers are still not certain exactly what, if anything, all experiences that cause embarrassment have in common. One possibility is that different people become embarrassed for somewhat different reasons. The functional definition proposed earlier may help to explain why. If the function of embarrassment is to appease people who might otherwise reject us, then we may feel embarrassed whenever we think other people's rejection is likely. Some people might expect rejection as a result of a social gaffe, others might expect rejection whenever they are the focus of other people's attention. Still, no one explanation accounts for all of the experiences in

which people say they experience embarrassment, and researchers are still trying to identify a "core" feature of embarrassing situations.

Facial Expression of Embarrassment

If you feel embarrassed, what is the first thing you ordinarily do? Most people avoid eye contact and hide their face, either by covering their eyes with their hands or by turning their head down and usually to the left. ("Why left?" We don't know. Good question.) The message is, "I don't want you to see me right now." (See Figure 11.2.) People who feel embarrassed often smile, although their lips also tense up as though they were trying to suppress the

FIGURE 11.2   The expression of embarrassment attempts to make the person smaller and less conspicuous. The message is, "I don't want you to see me."

smile. Researchers have noted that the display of embarrassment resembles the bashful behaviors of a child or subordinate, not like someone powerful or in charge (Keltner, 1995; R. S. Miller, 2001a). In addition, the most distinctive expression of embarrassment is the **blush,** a temporarily increased blood flow to the face, neck, and upper chest.

As we noted in Chapter 2, many emotion researchers assume that facial expressions of emotion are evolved characteristics, behaviors inherited from our primate ancestors because they serve some function. Psychologists have interpreted the embarrassment expression as an appeasement gesture, analogous to the way a weak, young animal deters an attack from a superior. The gesture says, "I know I made a mistake. I'm sorry. I feel lowly and inferior. Please don't be angry." Recall the function of embarrassment we proposed earlier—to deter aggression from another person you have accidentally offended, by letting them know your transgression was an accident and that you want to make amends.

This interpretation of embarrassment makes sense, given that people are more likely to forgive someone who looks embarrassed than someone who does not. However, it raises many questions as well. How did the experience and expression of embarrassment first arise? Are nonhuman animals ever embarrassed? Research on this topic is practically nonexistent, but many people will assure you that they have seen dogs or monkeys show embarrassment. How about a cat? A mouse? Unlike several other emotions we have discussed, it is difficult to imagine embarrassment except in a few, very social mammals. Even if dogs and perhaps a few other species are capable of embarrassment, no one has ever reported seeing a nonhuman animal blush. (Of course, fur covers a dog's face, so we might not notice.) So far as we can tell, blushing may have arisen specifically during human evolution (Edelmann, 2001). If we grant that humans evolved a tendency to blush to signal our apologies to others, a question remains: How visible or salient was that expression for our early human ancestors? Most anthropologists believe the original humans were Africans with dark skin, which makes the blush expression difficult to see.

Another issue: Why do we find blushing itself so unpleasant? Most people are embarrassed by the fact that they are blushing. Just telling someone "you are blushing" often causes them to blush or increases the intensity of a faint blush (Drummond et al., 2003).

We have mentioned in earlier chapters that different ways of measuring emotions have different strengths and weaknesses. This is true of self-reports and displays of embarrassment as well, because the two do not always go together. For example, people in one study were asked to watch a series of slides showing naked people of both sexes. Most of the observers later reported that they had felt embarrassed while looking at the slides, especially if other people were present. However, they had seldom looked away or turned their head aside—part of the prototypical embarrassment expression. If they were embarrassed, why hadn't they looked away? One explanation is obvious: They knew their task was to continue looking at the slides (Costa, Dinsbach, Manstead, & Bitti, 2001). So in a case like this, self-reports provide emotional information that objective facial expression measurements would not.

Individual Differences in Embarrassment

We can often learn about an emotion by asking whether some people feel that emotion more than others and what those people are like. Certainly, social experience suggests that some people are more easily embarrassed than others—teasing someone who is shy or blushes easily even becomes a game for many groups. But in doing research, we have to find a reliable way to measure dispositional embarrassment, or individual differences in how often and how intensely different people become embarrassed. Then we can ask what the people who are easily embarrassed have in common.

Objective behavioral measurements such as facial expressions are rarely used when we want to ask about people's "usual" behavior. Suppose we want to study differences between people who get embarrassed easily and those who do not. Embarrassment does not occur frequently in most people's lives, so it would not be practical to follow someone around waiting for spontaneous embarrassing situations. A researcher could set up a series of potentially embarrassing situations and record people's reactions to each of them. However, such a procedure would be questionable both ethically and scientifically. The scientific problem is this: Suppose you were in a laboratory experiment that exposed you to one embarrassing event after another. After the first two or three, you would get the idea, "Oh! They're trying to embarrass me." The later events might produce more annoyance and anger than embarrassment.

To measure dispositional experience of embarrassment, researchers often rely on self-reports. When people are embarrassed—such as when students have to give class presentations—their self-reports of embarrassment correlate moderately well (+.31) with observers' estimate of their embarrassment, so self-reports appear to be at least somewhat valid (Marcus & Miller, 1999). Several self-report scales of embarrassment are in widespread use, including the Embarrassability Scale (Modigliani, 1968) and the Susceptibility to Embarrassment Scale (Kelly & Jones, 1997). Each of these questionnaires briefly describes a variety of situations and asks people how embarrassed they think they would feel. One problem is that "how embarrassed you feel" implies a comparison to others, and people do not know exactly how they compare to others. Also, people are only moderately consistent in how they answer the questionnaire when they complete it multiple times (Maltby & Day, 2000).

Scores on embarrassment questionnaires correlate rather highly with scores on neuroticism questionnaires (Edelmann & McCusker, 1986; Maltby & Day, 2000). That relationship should not be surprising; as we have noted in earlier chapters, neuroticism is defined as a tendency toward easily experiencing "negative" emotions such as fear, anger, sadness, and . . . embarrassment. Susceptibility to embarrassment also correlates positively with social anxiety, shyness, and loneliness (Neto, 1996) and correlates negatively with extraversion and self-esteem (Edelmann & McCusker, 1986; Maltby & Day, 2000). People who feel confident about themselves in social situations do not become embarrassed often and handle their embarrassment well when they do. People who lack confidence frequently think they have made social mistakes even when they haven't.

One complication in interpreting these results is that many people misperceive how often they are embarrassed. People who particularly fear being embarrassed in public tend to overstate the frequency of these vividly remembered events (Mulkens, de Jong, Dobbelaar, & Bögels, 1999). Their fear of embarrassment is psychologically important and may even lead to social phobia, a condition of avoiding other people to decrease the risk of embarrassment (Leary, 2001; Miller, 2001a). However, because their reports are objectively inaccurate, they pose a problem for research in this field.

Who do you guess becomes embarrassed more strongly or more frequently, men or women? Most people's stereotype is that women are more easily embarrassed. A few reports confirm that view (e.g., Neto, 1996), but most indicate no significant difference (e.g., Maltby & Day, 2000). If there is a gender difference in susceptibility to embarrassment, it is not a strong one.

Age, however, does predict susceptibility to embarrassment more strongly and consistently. Infants and very young children don't really experience embarrassment (or shame, guilt, or pride, for that matter) at all. It is not until about age 2 that they show evidence of self-conscious emotion. This makes sense because until about age 2 they don't show much sign of self-consciousness—the ability to think about themselves as they think about other people. Signs of embarrassment become more intense and more frequent as children grow older, reaching a peak in the teenage years. Adolescents face many difficult and embarrassing situations, and they are acutely attentive to their social status.

Mutual ridicule can be merciless among teenagers. During adulthood, most people show embarrassment less and less often (Maltby & Day, 2000). We do not know to what extent that decline represents a weakening of the tendency to experience the emotion and to what extent it reflects increased self-confidence and prestige (and therefore decreased occasion to become embarrassed).

Shame and Guilt

Let's move on to other self-conscious emotions. In the studies discussed in the beginning of the chapter, embarrassment stood out as distinct in clear ways, but shame and guilt seemed more to overlap. Are shame and guilt different emotions, or just two varieties of the same emotion?

As is so often the case in emotion research, the answer depends on what measures are used and how each particular study is done. The facial expression of embarrassment is clearly distinct from the expressions of shame and guilt. When college students examine photos of people expressing embarrassment and shame, they correctly classify the expressions slightly more than half the time (Keltner, 1995). That is, they generally know which ones indicate embarrassment and which ones indicate shame. They do not, however, distinguish reliably between "ashamed" and "guilty" expressions (Keltner & Buswell, 1996). Researchers have not yet identified different facial expressions corresponding to the two terms. The expression of shame/guilt includes lowered eyes and a hunched posture, similar to the expression of embarrassment.

However, whereas an embarrassed person might have a little sheepish grin, someone who is ashamed does not smile and may even turn down the corners of the mouth. (See Figure 11.3.) In those regards, the expression resembles sadness.

As we saw earlier in the chapter, the *events* that elicit shame and guilt are not all that different. People tend to feel either shame or guilt when they think they have done something morally wrong or when they have failed to live up to their own or other people's expectations of them (Tangney, Miller, et al., 1996). The distinction between the two becomes more clear when researchers study how people *interpret* the negative event in question. Studies suggest that you are likely to feel shame when an event makes you think of yourself as bad or unworthy. You interpret the negative event as evidence that your entire self is defective or inadequate. Thus, we can tentatively define **shame** as the negative emotion felt when one fails or does something morally wrong and focuses on one's own global, stable inadequacies in explaining the transgression. By

FIGURE 11.3   The expression of shame implies a more serious violation than mere embarrassment.

© Corbis

contrast, you are more likely to feel guilt if you focus on the specific event and feel bad about your action but not about who you are as a person (Tangney, Wagner, Hill-Barlow, Marschall, & Gramzow, 1996). **Guilt** is the negative emotion felt when one fails or does something morally wrong but focuses on how to make amends and how to avoid repeating the transgression.

This distinction is observed mainly in people's descriptions of shame and guilt experiences. For example, when people think about times when they felt shame or guilt, and try to describe what would have made those situations turn out differently, people tend to focus on different aspects of the situation. People who felt shame say things like "If only I weren't so stupid," whereas people who felt guilt say things like "If only I hadn't done such-and-such" (Niedenthal, Tangney, & Gavanski, 1994). The distinction also emerges consistently in self-report measures of shame- and guilt-proneness, especially those in which you read a scenario and then rate the extent to which you would feel bad *about yourself* in that situation versus wishing you had *acted differently* (Tangney, 1996). When researchers examine the relationship between the "bad self" ratings and the "bad action" ratings, they are positively correlated, but not so strongly that shame- and guilt-proneness seem to be the same (e.g., Covert, Tangney, Maddux, & Heleno, 2003).

Dispositional shame-proneness and guilt-proneness are also differentially associated with people's approaches to social interaction. Shame-prone people tend to have more problems with interpersonal relationships than guilt-prone people. They tend to experience more anger and social anxiety and feel less empathy (O'Connor, Berry, & Weiss, 1999; Tangney, Burggraf, & Wagner, 1995; Tangney, Wagner et al., 1996). The correlation with anger is interesting and worth exploration. Why should shame-prone people, who presumably feel bad about themselves, tend to get angry with *others*? Why should guilt-prone people be immune to this effect? According to June Tangney and her colleagues (Tangney, Wagner, et al.,1996), shame-prone

people tend to attribute their own negative outcomes to global, stable personal inadequacies, over which they have little or no control. They may also feel a strong sense of other people's disapproval. At the same time, because shame-prone people do not feel that they have control over their outcomes, they may feel that this disapproval is unfair. As a result, they are more likely to be angered by the disapproving judgments they perceive in others. In contrast, says Tangney, guilt-prone people take more responsibility for their individual actions and feel more control over whether they will repeat those actions. As a result, defensive anger is unnecessary.

This explanation is supported by a study of the interpersonal problem-solving skills shown by shame-prone versus guilt-prone people (Covert et al., 2003). In this study, participants read scenarios involving some kind of interpersonal problem, such as the following:

> Your friend and co-worker has been getting behind in his/her work and asks you for help in catching up. You know that your friend needs this job to stay in school. This happens several times, and you notice that you are getting behind in your own work, in spite of putting in extra, unpaid hours. (Covert et al., 2003, p. 6)

After reading the scenario, participants described as many suggestions as they could for resolving the situation and stated how effectively they thought they could implement each solution themselves. Each participant's solution to each scenario was coded by the researchers as: (1) likely to make the situation worse, (2) not even trying to resolve the situation, (3) making a fair attempt to resolve the situation, (4) making a good attempt, or (5) making an excellent attempt to resolve the situation. The researchers found that shame-prone people tended to have a low quality of problem-solving attempts and a low belief in their ability to resolve the problems. In contrast, guilt-proneness had a *positive* relationship with quality of solutions and with sense of effectiveness at solving the problems. In other words, guilt-prone people seemed to be particularly good at solving interpersonal problems, whereas shame-prone people seemed to be particularly bad at it.

Consistent with earlier studies of shame and guilt, the researchers interpret this study as evidence that shame-proneness implies a low sense of control over one's own outcomes, combined with the feeling that one is a bad person. Guilt-proneness includes a high sense of control over outcomes and the feeling that if one has done something bad, one can make amends and avoid the negative action in the future.

So, are shame and guilt different emotions or not? Shame and guilt do not appear to fulfill at least one of the proposed criteria for separate, basic emotions—they do not have distinct, recognizable facial expressions. Also, the subjective feelings are similar, as are the actual events that elicit these emotions. On the other hand, shame and guilt appear to be associated with different appraisals, or interpretations of the eliciting situation. Researchers have not written much about possible evolutionary functions of shame and guilt, so it is difficult to compare the two on that criterion. Whether you think of shame and guilt as two different emotions depends on which criteria you emphasize in your definition of "emotion," but by most criteria, they appear to be variants of a single emotion.

In one way, it may not matter whether shame and guilt are separate, basic emotions, two variants of the same emotion, or not emotions at all. Research on how the two are related to each other, and on the clinical, social, and personality factors associated with guilt versus shame, has moved along just fine without a consensus on this issue. On the other hand, these questions continue to push researchers in refining their definitions of emotion and present new challenges to proposed definitions. In this way, the question remains useful.

▢ Pride

So far we have discussed the self-conscious emotions that feel bad. What about the one that feels good— pride? According to Jessica Tracy and Rick Robins (2004), **pride** is the emotion felt when some-one takes credit for causing a positive outcome that supports a positive aspect of his or her self-concept. Let's break this definition down a bit. We feel pride when something good happens. That's no big surprise because positive emotions should result from positive events. What makes pride special is (1) the proud person feels that he or she *caused* the good event, and can take the credit for it, and (2) the good event confirms the person's positive self-image.

For example, let's say you win an essay contest at your college. You will probably feel pride if you worked hard on your essay, if hundreds of people submitted essays, and if the judges used very strict standards in selecting the winner. You are also more likely to feel pride if being smart or being a good writer is important to your sense of self. You are less likely to feel pride if only a few essays were submitted, or if the judges selected the winning essay by folding all of the essays into paper airplanes and seeing which flew the farthest. In the latter scenario, you won the contest, but you can't really take credit for it. You might also feel less pride if, say, your music skills are more central to your sense of self than your writing skills.

Expressions of Pride

A few researchers have begun to study the aspects of pride that distinguish it from other kinds of positive emotion, and one of those aspects is expression. In many regards, the expression of pride is the opposite of embarrassment or shame: A person tilts the head back slightly, sits or stands tall, and puts the arms above the head or hands on the hips. (See Figure 11.4.) The message here is, "I want you to see me clearly right now." The prototypical pride expression does include a smile, but it is a small smile rather than a broad one. Most people—at least in the United States and Italy, the only countries tested so far—can easily identify this expression as meaning pride (Tracy & Robins, 2004).

Earlier in the chapter, we noted that the expression of embarrassment closely resembles the expressive behavior of a low-status animal. As you might

Reprinted from: Tracy, J. L., & Robins, R. W. (2004). Show your pride: Evidence for a discrete emotion expression. *Psychological Science, 15,* 194–197, with permission from Blackwell Publishing.

FIGURE 11.4   Although you can't clearly express pride from facial expression alone, you can from a combination of face and posture. The expression of pride makes you larger, helping others to see and admire you. Source: Tracy and Robins (2004).

expect, the expression of pride looks like the behavior of high-status people, and people who display pride are assumed to hold high-status positions in society (Cashdan, 1998; Tiedens, Ellsworth, & Mesquita, 2000).

Cultural Differences in Pride

Most research on the self-conscious emotions has been done in the United States, and we noted in Chapter 3 that the United States has some unusual cultural features. Americans are more individualistic—believing that individual rights, achievement, and expression take priority over group needs—than people in almost every other country in the world. On the other hand, American culture is horizontal, tending to downplay issues of social hierarchy. Because pride and the other self-conscious emotions reflect people's self-evaluations relative to group standards, and because the expressions of pride, embarrassment, and shame seem to reflect expectations about status, it may be that pride and the other self-conscious emotions present very differently in other cultures.

Experiences similar to embarrassment, shame, and pride do seem to be recognized in many cultures, so these emotions do not appear unique to the United States. What varies is the circumstances that

provoke these emotions. People feel embarrassed or ashamed when they fail to meet society's expectations, but society's expectations vary from one culture to another. For example, the Dusun Baguk of Malaysia say they experience *malu*, roughly corresponding to our embarrassment or shame, whenever they eat during a period set aside for fasting, dress too ostentatiously, or even walk too fast. They also feel *malu* just from being in the presence of a more prestigious person (Fessler, 1999). The Dusun Baguk also report an experience they call *bangga*, approximately translating as "pride," when they receive attention appropriately for something done well. For example, they feel *bangga* for a display of skill or wit or for hosting a fine feast for guests.

Some cultural differences in events that elicit pride may have to do with differences in the nature of "self." In the United States and many other Western countries, the self is a unique personality, defined by consistent traits that differentiate you from other people. Individuality is highly valued in the United States, and conformity is sneered at. In many East Asian countries, the self is defined more by your relationships with other people, and by the groups to which you belong. If self-conscious emotions involve an emotional reaction to the good or bad actions of the self, and the nature of "self" differs in the United States and in Asian cultures, then people may feel self-conscious emotions in very different situations. In Chapter 3 we discussed a study in which Chinese and American participants were asked how proud they would be if they themselves were accepted to a prestigious university and how proud they would be if their child were accepted to the university (Stipek, 1998). Recall from that discussion that Chinese participants (unlike Americans) said they would actually be prouder of their children's accomplishments than of their own. Does this mean that Chinese and American respondents are talking about two completely different experiences? Probably not—after all, the Chinese respondents said they would feel some pride for their own achievement, and Americans said they would feel some pride for their child's. This study does suggest that, even in terms of the events that elicit self-conscious emotions, the Chinese react to close relatives as though they were part of the self.

Pride is generally considered a good thing in the United States. In many societies, however, there is such a thing as too much pride. Among the Dusun Baguk it is considered rude and immoral to flaunt one's *bangga*. You can feel your pride, but don't show it too much. This is true in the West as well; a study of young German children found that, by about age 5 years, children would often hide their feelings of pride when they beat their younger siblings at a competitive game (Reissland & Harris, 1991). Calling someone "proud" in English is not always a compliment, but as a general rule, Americans are more comfortable with pride, and consider it more positive, than people in cultures that emphasize collectivism (valuing group harmony and efficiency) over individualism. For example, Chinese participants tend to agree far more strongly than Americans that expressing pride is generally a bad thing and that it is socially appropriate to show pride only for achievements that benefit other in-group members (Stipek, 1998). Americans may resist ideas of overall hierarchy but are not at all shy about celebrating their individual accomplishments.

◻ Summary

For happiness, the best amount to have may be "as much as possible," but for any other emotion, the best amount is some moderate quantity. Extreme fear is destructive, but total fearlessness would be hazardous to your health. Anger and sadness are unpleasant, but in small and appropriately timed doses they, too, have their benefits. Similarly, although excessive embarrassment and shame can be incapacitating, the capacity to feel these emotions helps guide our relationships with other people. It might be silly for people to be embarrassed for using the wrong fork at a formal dinner or violating some other trivial rule. In general, however, civilized societies depend on people to learn certain expectations and rules and show some sign of apology when they violate them. Pride may feel pleasant, but excessive displays of pride may offend people who are not as impressed with you as you are with yourself.

In a way, our discussion of the self-conscious emotions brings us back to the issues of universality versus cultural variability in emotion discussed in the beginning of this text. Embarrassment and pride are excellent examples of how emotions can be part of our shared evolutionary heritage *and* differ substantially from culture to culture. The building blocks of embarrassment and pride are similar in different cultures. When we have reason to think we have transgressed, we feel embarrassment or shame. When we have reason to think we have accomplished something valuable, we feel pride. Preliminary studies suggest that embarrassment, shame, and pride are displayed in similar ways wherever you go. But this leaves tremendous room for cultural differences in how these emotions actually play out in society. You may feel pride if your "self" has done something good, but that has very different implications depending on whether your "self" includes just you, or all of your family, close friends, teammates, and colleagues as well. Feeling pride also depends on interpreting some accomplishments as valuable, and different cultures value very different kinds of achievements. Once you do feel pride, the way in which you show it may vary dramatically depending on the kind of culture you come from—one that encourages displays of status and hierarchy or one that encourages modesty and equality.

The balance between evolutionary and cultural contributions to the self-conscious emotions is clear, largely because of strong earlier work on cultural differences in the self. We hope, however, that future research on other emotions can also treat evolution and culture as interacting forces, rather than competing ones.

Key Terms

blush: a temporarily increased blood flow to the face, neck, and upper chest (p. 232)

embarrassment: the emotion felt when one violates a social convention, thereby drawing unexpected social attention and motivating submissive, friendly behavior that should appease other people (p. 228)

empathic embarrassment: being embarrassed in sympathy for someone else who is embarrassed (p. 230)

guilt: the negative emotion felt when one fails or does something morally wrong but focuses on how to make amends and how to avoid repeating the transgression (p. 235)

pride: emotion felt when someone takes credit for causing a positive outcome that supports a positive aspect of his or her self-concept (p. 236)

shame: the negative emotion felt when one fails or does something morally wrong and then focuses on one's own global, stable inadequacies in explaining the transgression (p. 234)

☐ Thought Questions

1. Would it be easier to recognize expressions of embarrassment, shame, guilt, and pride from films than from still photos? Why or why not?
2. Would you be less likely to feel embarrassed by a mistake you made if you thought no one would recognize you personally? Imagine, for example, being on a visit far from home or attending a costume party. If so, what are the implications about embarrassment?
3. Researchers have found a moderate correlation between susceptibility to shame and susceptibility to guilt (Covert et al., 2003). What conclusion would we draw if the correlation had been close to 1? What if it had been close to zero?

☐ Suggestion for Research Project

We noted in passing that embarrassed people tend to look down and to the left. Why left? Is that tendency true for left-handers as well as right-handers? Children as well as adults? Does it matter where other people are standing? You might try collecting observations. It is possible to embarrass someone harmlessly by praising them publicly. You can also be alert to notice spontaneous occasions when people get embarrassed.

☐ Suggestion for Further Reading

Miller, R. S. (1996). *Embarrassment: Poise and peril in everyday life.* New York: Guilford. Excellent review of the issues and research by one of the very few who have specialized in the study of embarrassment.

PART THREE
Emotion in Relation to the Rest of Psychology

12

Emotion and Information Processing

You're in a good mood and you decide to walk instead of drive to a store a few blocks away. You notice the sunshine, the trees, the birds singing, the smiling faces of people you see along the way. Ah, what a glorious day!

A few days later, you're walking the same route but you're in a bad mood: You have to walk instead of drive because someone borrowed your car and wrecked it. Now you hardly notice the trees, birds, or smiling people. Instead you notice the litter on the street, the filthy smell of an uncovered trash can, and the sounds of the traffic. What a lousy day. Emotions influence what we notice, what we remember, and how we reason.

▢ Emotions and Attention

Almost any emotional stimulus captures attention, at least momentarily, at the expense of attention to other stimuli. Imagine yourself in this study: On each trial, the screen displays a pair of one-digit numbers separated by a word, like this:

5   chart   8

Your task is to press one key if both numbers are odd or both are even (such as 3 and 5, or 2 and 8), and a different key if one number is odd and the other even (such as 5 and 8). You are supposed to ignore the word between them. However, if that word is an emotional one, such as *kill,* it is hard to ignore, so it takes longer for you to press the correct key. Even though it is irrelevant to your task, that emotional word distracts your attention and slows your response to the numbers more than neutral words like *chart* (Harris & Pashler, 2004).

As discussed in Chapter 5, fear in particular focuses attention and, therefore, decreases attention to other items. Suppose a poisonous snake is near you and poised to strike. Many things that might have occupied your interest a few moments ago become trivial; your only interest is in how to escape.

To illustrate: Suppose we briefly display a series of complex pictures like those in Figure 12.1 and later test the viewers' memory. Ordinarily, when people look at an unemotional picture, they recall some mixture of central objects and background details. However, when they look at a picture with something frightening or distressing at the center, they remember the central object well and usually forget the details in the background (Adolphs, Denburg, & Tranel, 2001). In some ways, it is as if the person were looking at the emotional scene from a closer perspective and looking at the unemotional scene from a greater distance (Mathews & Mackintosh, 2004).

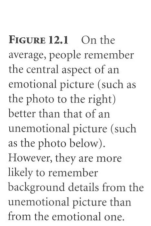

FIGURE 12.1 On the average, people remember the central aspect of an emotional picture (such as the photo to the right) better than that of an unemotional picture (such as the photo below). However, they are more likely to remember background details from the unemotional picture than from the emotional one.

Other kinds of emotional arousal also narrow the focus of attention. In one experiment, participants viewed a series of photographs of people and answered questions later about what they remembered about them. Among the series of otherwise ordinary photos was one photo of a nude. As you can imagine, participants remembered the nude well. However, they remembered almost nothing about the background details of that photo, and they also forgot almost entirely the next two or three photos after the nude. The nude captured their attention so thoroughly that for a while, they lost everything else (Schmidt, 2002).

In another kind of study, people sit in front of a screen that displays two or more pictures at once, which might include emotional content. Researchers record people's eye movements to identify which picture holds their attention at any given moment and sometimes also record their brain activity with EEG or fMRI methods. In these ways, researchers have found, for example, that pictures of angry faces usually attract more attention and evoke more cortical arousal than pictures of happy or neutral faces

(Schupp et al., 2004). Actively threatening pictures capture people's attention even if they are presented in the periphery of vision. For example, if a particular kind of picture previously has been paired with bursts of loud noise, then a viewer immediately attends to one of those pictures, even if it is far off to the side (Koster, Crombez, Van Damme, Verschuere, & De Houwer, 2004).

Studies of this type, however, have often reported conflicting data, and other researchers tried to discover why the results vary. ("It depends" is almost always true in psychology, but the challenge is to find out what it depends on.) One important reason for varying results is that different investigators measured people's eye movements for different durations. During the first half second after the presentation of two pictures, most people look first at the more emotionally arousing picture. However, after that first half second, many people look *away* from distressing pictures, such as a dead body or a starving child, and people who are prone to strong anxieties are especially likely to look away (Calvo & Avero, 2005). That is, a threatening image captures attention quickly, but people then try to avoid it.

Whereas a frightening stimulus captures attention and narrows its focus, the outcome is different for a positive emotions or affect. Barbara Fredrickson (2000) has proposed on theoretical grounds that positive emotions or affect should expand the focus of attention—the opposite of what unpleasant emotions do. According to her **broaden-and-build model** of positive emotions, positive emotions lead to no specific behavior, but to an increased readiness to explore new ideas and opportunities. That is, when we are joyful, we become flexible, creative, and playful. Instead of focusing on just the central facts, we attend also to the background and periphery that we usually overlook. We find positive meaning in daily events, we cope well and imaginatively with problems, and we do better than usual on tasks such as "see how many uses you can think of for a pencil" (Fredrickson & Joiner, 2002). These creative endeavors improve our chances for success and, therefore, can lead to still more positive emotions in the future.

In one test of this idea, college students first watched an amusing, pleasant, neutral, or unpleasant short film, and then were asked to concentrate on the emotion it aroused and then list "all the things you would like to do *right now.*" Those who had watched an amusing or pleasant film listed more actions than those who had watched a neutral or unpleasant film (Fredrickson & Branigan, 2005).

In another test of the broaden-and-build hypothesis, researchers presented young adults with three words at a time. Some of the three-word combinations were called "incoherent" because no other word related closely to all three. An example of an incoherent triplet is "town, root, car." Other combinations were "coherent," because each of them related to some fourth word. An example of a coherent triplet is "playing, credit, report," because all three relate to the word "card." In each case, the three words appeared on a screen for just four seconds. Participants had to state quickly whether or not they thought the words were a coherent group (even if they could not say which other word they related to). To manipulate participants' moods, the researchers asked some of them to think about a particularly happy experience before the start of this experiment and asked others to think about a particularly sad experience. A third, "neutral" group thought about neither happy nor sad events prior to the experiment. The results: People in a happy mood did significantly better than the neutral group, while those in a sad mood did significantly worse (Bolte, Goschke, & Kuhl, 2003). A happy mood had promoted the loose associations and divergent or creative thinking that this task requires.

◻ **Emotions and Memory**

Emotion affects memory in many ways, and at multiple stages of the memory process—encoding memories, storing them, and retrieving them. It is helpful to talk about each of these effects separately, because the effects of emotion on memory depend on which aspect of memory we are talking about. Let's start with the first step in the process— the initial formation of memory during some event.

Emotion and Memory Formation

One particularly robust effect of emotion is to enhance the formation and intensity of memories. Strong emotional arousal strengthens memories, even memories of events that were not themselves especially emotional but happened to occur during a time of heightened emotions. This effect breaks down at extreme levels of emotion. Occasionally, someone completely forgets an event that happened during a moment of absolute panic. But such instances are rare. As a general rule, a rousing emotion enhances the initial formation of memories.

In one classic study of this phenomenon, researchers showed participants 60 photographs of all kinds of objects and events, ranging from everyday pictures of hair dryers and umbrellas to emotionally intense pictures of mutilations and extreme sports (see Figure 12.2 for examples). Then they asked the

FIGURE 12.2 When people view large numbers of emotional and nonemotional images like these, they are more likely to remember the emotional ones—even as much as a year later. Source: Bradley et al. (1992).

participants to rate each picture on how pleasant or unpleasant it was and how calm or aroused it made them feel. After viewing all 60 pictures, each participant was asked to name or briefly describe as many pictures as possible. It turned out that people were more likely to remember slides that they had rated very arousing than slides they had rated as calming, regardless of whether the slides were pleasant or unpleasant. In short, the emotionality of some pictures seemed to promote encoding those pictures into memory. When the researchers contacted the same participants a year later and asked them to describe as many of the slides as they could, people were *still* more likely to remember the intense, arousal-producing ones than the more mundane ones (Bradley, Greenwald, Petry, & Lang, 1992). Research with word memory has produced similar results. Participants remember emotionally charged words better than neutral words and report remembering them more vividly (Kensinger & Corkin, 2003).

How do we know it was the emotionality of the arousal-producing pictures that made them more memorable? Maybe images of guns pointed at us are simply more unusual than images of trash cans, and they stick in our minds for that reason. However, physiological research supports a special role for emotion. Think back to our discussion about the nature of emotion, back in Chapter 1. The James-Lange theory argues that the feeling aspect of emotion is really about visceral, physiological experience—such things as a racing heart beat, heavy breathing, and sweaty palms. If so, and if strong emotions really do produce enhanced memory, then we should be able to strengthen or weaken memory encoding by increasing or decreasing emotional arousal.

Emotional arousal leads to increased release of the hormones epinephrine (adrenaline) and cortisol from the adrenal gland. Studies on both humans and laboratory animals have found that a direct injection of epinephrine or cortisol strengthens the memory of an event that was just experienced (Cahill & McGaugh, 1998). Epinephrine and cortisol stimulate the vagus nerve, which in turn excites the amygdala, a brain structure discussed in more detail in Chapters 2

and 5 (see Figure 2.9). Direct stimulation of either the vagus nerve or the amygdala in lab animals also strengthens memory storage (Akirav & Richter-Levin, 1999; K. B. Clark, Naritoku, Smith, Browning, & Jensen, 1999). Even events that arouse our stress response improve memory, if the stress is mild and doesn't last too long (Abercrombie, Kalin, Thurow, Rosenkranz, & Davidson, 2003).

On the other hand, weakening someone's emotional arousal weakens memory storage. One study examined this hypothesis by giving participants one of two pills—either a **beta-blocker**, a drug that temporarily disables the stress hormone system responsible for some types of emotional arousal, or a placebo with no physiological effects. Then participants viewed a slide show depicting some wrecked cars, an emergency room, a brain scan, and a surgery. While watching the slide show, participants heard one of two stories. In the "neutral" version a young boy walks by a junkyard and looks at some wrecked cars, then goes to the hospital where his Dad works, looks curiously at a brain scan, and watches a surgical team doing a practice drill. According to the "arousal" version, the boy is hit by a car on the way to visit his Dad, is rushed to the hospital, has a brain scan that shows his brain is bleeding badly, and undergoes intense surgery (Cahill, Prins, Weber, & McGaugh, 1994). Notice the clever design of this study—all participants watched exactly the same set of images, but their emotions were manipulated both by the content of the story that accompanied the pictures and by the pill that they took before the slide show.

One week later, participants were contacted and asked to answer 80 multiple-choice questions about the slides and the stories that had accompanied them. As expected, people who had heard the "neutral" version of the story had mediocre scores on the test—on average, they answered many of the questions incorrectly. For participants in the "arousal" version, memory depended on whether they had taken the beta-blocker pill or the placebo. Participants who had been given the beta-blocker (and who therefore would not have felt things like a racing heart or higher blood pressure, even if they recognized that the story was upsetting) performed no better on the memory test than participants in the "neutral" condition. Participants who had been given the placebo, however, did much better—on average answering a higher percentage of the questions correctly. (See Figure 12.3.)

Studies using functional magnetic resonance imaging, based on changes in blood flow in the brain, confirm that the amygdala is more active when people view emotionally intense slides than when they view neutral ones. These same studies show that, for more intense images, the greater the degree of amygdala activation, the more accurately participants remember those images later (Canli, Zhao, Brewer, Gabrieli, & Cahill, 2000). People with damage in the amygdala can still form memories, but the strength of their memory formation is no longer affected by emotion. For example, suppose you read a story containing some frightening or tragic events or read a list of words that included "taboo" words like *penis* and *bitch* mixed among more mundane words. You probably would remember the frightening events and the taboo words more than the rest of the material. In contrast, amygdala-damaged people remember those elements no better than anything else (LaBar & Phelps, 1998).

In summary, emotional information activates the amygdala, and anything that activates the amygdala—even artificial stimulation—enhances memory. Furthermore, blocking activity of the amygdala prevents emotional information from enhancing memory. So emotions enhance memory through a special route, not just by making the situation unusual.

But why should strong emotions strengthen memories? We have discussed the physiology, but why did we evolve in such a way that emotions enhance memory formation? One reasonable explanation is that the kinds of events that produce emotion are usually more important than most other events. After all, emotions accompany events that have serious implications for our lives—a time you were in danger, the day you were accepted into your dream college, a time when someone died, the time

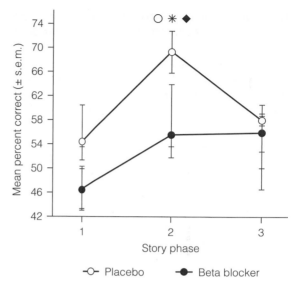

FIGURE 12.3   Memory results for the groups who listened to the arousing story. The emotionally distressing part of the story was phase 2. The placebo group remembered this phase well. The beta-blocker group, whose emotional responses in the brain were blunted, remembered the arousing phase no better than less arousing material. Source: From L. Cahill et al., "β-adrenergic activation and memory for emotional events," *Nature, 371,* pp. 702–704. © 1994 Nature Publishing.

someone cheated you out of hundreds of dollars, the day you fell in love. Maybe our survival depends particularly on our remembering these events—what led up to them, how they played out, which people were helpful or harmful, and what happened afterward. This kind of memory allows us to predict important events and improve the outcomes the next time you face a similar situation.

Emotion and Memory Storage

Emotion has a somewhat different, and considerably less clear, effect on the long-term storage of memories. To illustrate, consider the following. First, think about where you were and what you were doing on September 11, 2001, when you found out about the terrorist attacks on the World Trade Center and the Pentagon. If you were too young at the time for that event to make a big impression, or if you are from some other country where that event was not big news, substitute a personal memory of an extremely emotional nature. For example, you might recall the time when you heard that a close relative had died, or if you prefer a pleasant memory, perhaps the moment of your first kiss.

Whichever memory you have chosen, how vivid and detailed is it? Can you remember where you were, who else was around, what you were doing, how you felt, and what your first thoughts were? Can you remember what happened just before and after this moment? Can you remember the weather and the time of day? Now in contrast try to remember some unemotional event, like the last time you bought toothpaste. How long does it take to remember, specifically, the last time—do you remember immediately or do you have to think about it? Were you with someone or alone? What time of day was it, and what was the weather? What else did you buy? What did the person at the checkout counter say and do? Here are two other questions: How confident are you that your memory of September 11, 2001 (or whatever your emotional memory was) is accurate? How confident are you that your memory of your last trip to buy toothpaste is accurate?

For most people, highly emotional memories seem drastically different from those of everyday events. Psychologists refer to these emotion-laden, vivid, and highly detailed memories as **flashbulb memories** because they have such a clear, almost photographic quality. Flashbulb memories feel detailed and lifelike, and their vividness inspires us to feel confident of their accuracy. The "flashbulb" aspect is not entirely an illusion. In one of the first experimental (as opposed to observational) studies of this topic, students observed colored words displayed at various locations on a computer screen; their task was to ignore the words themselves and just say the color of the ink. (This procedure, discussed in Chapter 10, is known as the Stroop Test.) Half of the words were names of animals (such as

turtle) and half were profanities and ethnic insults. Each word appeared repeatedly, and some always occurred in the same computer location. At the end of this procedure, the students were asked (to their surprise) to identify which words occurred consistently in which locations. Even though they had no reason to pay attention to the meanings of the words, they were much more accurate at identifying the locations of the "taboo" words than the emotionally neutral words (MacKay & Ahmetzanov, 2005). The researchers suggest that the strong emotions led to the formation of image-like memories.

However, although flashbulb memories are vivid and image-like, research finds that they are sometimes inaccurate (Weaver, 1993). Shortly after the terrorist attacks of September 11, 2001, researchers asked U.S. students to recall details of what they were doing when they heard that news. At various later times, they asked the students to report their memories again. Over weeks and months, their memories gradually changed, presumably becoming less and less accurate (Talarico & Rubin, 2003). However, the students continued to insist that they were sure their vivid memories were right.

Similarly, Israeli students were interviewed 2 weeks after the assassination of Israel's Prime Minister, Yitzhak Rabin, and again 11 months later. Students reported their memories confidently at both times, but on the average more than one-third of what they said at the later time contradicted what they said the first time (Nachson & Zelig, 2003). The same general effect has been observed in studies of people's memories of Princess Diana's death in a car accident (Hornstein, Brown, & Mulligan, 2003). One laboratory study of people's memories for neutral and unpleasant photographs found that people remembered both kinds of photographs about equally well, but had greater confidence in their memory for the unpleasant, emotional photographs (Sharot, Delgado, & Phelps, 2004). In sum, flashbulb memories of highly emotional events are highly vivid and detailed, but sometimes wrong.

How can flashbulb memories be so vivid, yet inaccurate? If many of the details we remember are untrue, then where did they come from? One explanation for why highly emotional events produce such vivid memories is that we repeatedly discuss them with other people. This might also help explain why we sometimes misremember the details of these events. Most research on flashbulb memories has focused on highly publicized national or international events, such as deaths, assassinations, or terrorist attacks. These are the kind of events we sit around discussing with friends and family. Perhaps we confuse our own reports with what we have heard other people say when they describe their own experiences of the event. (Are flashbulb memories of personal emotional events, which we might not discuss with others, also sometimes inaccurate? Researchers have not addressed this question yet, but such a study could teach us more about the relationship between emotion and the storage of memory.)

Another implication: Suppose you were a witness or victim of a crime. Later you describe the event to the police, identify the guilty person from a lineup, and testify in court. You may say that you remember the event vividly, that you are sure of the facts, and that you can identify the guilty person confidently. Given your self-assurance, the jury is likely to convict. Unfortunately, DNA evidence or other physical evidence discovered years later has often demonstrated eyewitness reports to have been inaccurate. And researchers have found that eyewitnesses' confidence is not highly correlated with the accuracy of their memories (Wells, Olson, & Charman, 2002).

Memory Retrieval

When we remember our emotional experiences, we remember them selectively, and sometimes through rose-colored glasses. In one study, college students took personal data assistants (PDAs) with them on a spring-break trip. The PDAs beeped at seven unpredictable times each day, signaling the person to report his or her emotions at the moment. After returning home, students filled out a questionnaire about how much they enjoyed the trip. On the average, the remembered pleasantness of the trip was substantially greater than the average of all reports during the trip (Wirtz, Kruger, Scollon, & Diener, 2003). Evidently the pleasantness of an experience is not an average of emotions over the whole time but a reflection of a few highlight experiences.

Current emotions also modify what events we remember. To some extent, when you are in a good mood, you are more likely to remember events that previously happened when you were in a good mood, and when you are sad, you are more likely to recall events that happened to you in previous sad times. Similarly, when you are frightened, you tend to remember frightening information, and when you are angry, you remember information consistent with being angry (Levine & Pizarro, 2004). However, the key phrase a couple of sentences ago was "to some extent." Mood-specific memory is not a robust effect. Sometimes your mood helps you remember events related to the same mood, and sometimes it doesn't. You are most likely to strengthen one set of memories if your happy or sad mood is strong and stable over a fairly long time, and if you participate actively in events, as opposed to taking the passive role imposed in many laboratory studies (Eich, 1995).

◘ Emotions, Attributions, and Expectations

Emotions affect not only attention and memory but also how we evaluate ambiguous information. To illustrate: First, how are you feeling right now? If you had to choose, would you say you are feeling more angry or sad or neither? Second, consider the following situation:

> You and your housemates are having a party for about 10 people, one of whom you just met at a coffee house. This person was attractive and seemed interested in you and was excited by your invitation. You are really looking forward to getting to know this person and hope that a romantic relationship might develop.
>
> You tell your housemates about this person, hoping they will make him or her feel comfortable

and welcome. Your new friend arrives at the party after everyone else is there, and when you open the door, you see that this person has brought a date. To make things worse, the date is a good friend of your housemates.

The room suddenly becomes quiet, and you hear one of your housemates chuckle and say, "So there's the new love." Your new friend is silent, and the date seems upset. You try to create a more relaxed atmosphere, and your housemates attempt to keep everyone entertained, but as you go into the kitchen you hear your new friend and his or her date whispering to each other uncomfortably. (Adapted from Keltner, Ellsworth, & Edwards, 1993)

A pretty awful situation, certainly, but why was it so uncomfortable? Were your roommates to blame, or was it just the situation itself?

On the average, people who have recently imagined themselves in an anger-producing situation (in a supposed "warm-up" to the real study) are more likely to blame the roommates for the situation, whereas people who have just imagined themselves in a sad situation are more likely to blame it on bad luck. In fact, angry people blame most bad events on people (such as an inept cab driver) instead of blaming them on chance circumstances (heavy traffic), whereas the reverse is true for sad people (Keltner et al., 1993). In a similar study, participants who had just described several things that frightened them expressed more pessimistic beliefs about upcoming events than did participants who had just described something that made them angry (Lerner & Keltner, 2001).

Here's a similar experiment: Two months after the terrorist attacks on the U.S. Pentagon building and World Trade Center, more than 1,700 U.S. adults were randomly assigned to three groups who were asked to write different kinds of short essays. One group was asked to write about how the attacks made them feel angry. A second group was to write about how the attacks made them sad, and a third group was to write about how the attacks made them afraid. Then all were asked how much danger they foresaw for themselves personally and the United States in

general for the coming year. Those who had just finished writing about fear estimated greater probabilities of danger for both themselves and the country (Lerner, Gonzalez, Small, & Fischhoff, 2003).

How can we explain these effects of emotion on reasoning? Keep in mind that part of what causes an emotion in the first place is a particular interpretation, or appraisal, of an event. Maybe once the emotion gets going, that appraisal tendency carries on for a while, so that ensuing events are likely to be interpreted in the same way. According to the **Affect Infusion Model** of cognition, people use their emotional state as information in reaching a decision about some target, even if the target did not evoke the emotion (Forgas, 1995). For example, if you are feeling frightened, you interpret your situation as dangerous. Feeling either frightened or sad implies a lack of control. Feeling angry implies that someone else caused a bad situation, and it also implies that you have some control over what happens next (or there would be no point in getting angry). In each case, the appraisals that one situation evokes may carry over to the next.

If someone asks you on a sunny day to rate how well your life is going overall, you are likely to give a higher rating than if you are asked on a cloudy day (Cunningham, 1979). The current weather really isn't relevant to the question—after all, you're being asked how satisfied you are with your whole life, so the current cloud pattern shouldn't matter, but it does. Evidently people rely on their current mood to help answer broad questions about well-being.

One interesting aspect of this finding, however, is that the "cloudy day" effect disappears if participants pay explicit attention to the weather and recognize that it might be affecting them. When researchers in the previous study prefaced their question about life satisfaction by asking, "How's the weather down there?" (pretending they were calling from a survey company some distance away), the effect of weather disappeared and people answered the same on cloudy days as on sunny days. In a similar study, researchers found that participants who had just written about a sad experience reported lower life satisfaction than those who had just reported a happy experience, *unless* they had been told by the experimenter that the room they were sitting in (a soundproof room with a separate lighting system) often made people uncomfortable (Schwarz & Clore, 1983). These findings suggest the following interpretation: If you are feeling bad and you are not sure why, you report that you are generally unhappy with life. If you can easily blame your bad feelings on something in the situation, such as the weather or the room, then you discount your current mood when answering questions about your long-term satisfaction (Clore, 1992).

Psychologists sometimes refer to unconscious influences of emotion on judgment as **implicit attitudes**—that is, attitudes that influence us when we cannot or do not verbalize them. Sometimes people have an implicit emotional attitude that contradicts the attitude they express openly (T. D. Wilson, Lindsey, & Schooler, 2000). You might say that you are opposed to the death penalty, and even vote for candidates who want to abolish it, and yet part of you may involuntarily cheer when some particularly nasty murderer gets sentenced to death. You might say that you have no prejudices or stereotypes about other ethnic groups but, in fact, react differently to people of other ethnic groups, in ways that only subtle tests can detect (Dasgupta, McGhee, Greenwald, & Banaji, 2000; Phelps et al., 2000; Vanman, Saltz, Nathan, & Warren, 2004). Psychopathic murderers overtly state that they dislike violence, but if researchers test them in ways where it is hard to "fake" a response, they reveal attitudes favorable to, or at least not opposed to, violence (Gray, MacCulloch, Smith, Morris, & Snowden, 2003).

Sometimes our implicit emotional reactions to events contradict and betray even our deeply held values. Jesse Jackson, an African-American minister and powerful political figure, once said, "There is nothing more painful for me than to walk down the street and hear footsteps, and start to think about robbery, and then look around and see it's somebody white and feel relieved. How humiliating!" The point is that we can be influenced by emotions and attitudes that we do not admit to others, and perhaps not even to ourselves.

◻ Happiness, Sadness, and Reasoning

The examples we've discussed so far have focused mainly on anger and fear. What about happiness and sadness? Do we think differently when we're happy than when we're feeling sad or neutral?

As we discussed in previous chapters, we need to distinguish between short-term joy (an emotion) and long-term happiness (a mood or affect). It is also important to distinguish between sadness (an emotion) and depression (a mood). Those distinctions are especially important in relation to cognition, and apparently even different kinds of short-term positive emotions have different effects. In various studies, researchers have put participants in a "good mood" in several different ways: They asked participants to remember some pleasant experience, they praised participants for their performance of some task, they gave a bag of candy or some other present, or they showed a comedy film. These procedures led to different kinds of "positive" feelings and somewhat different effects on cognition.

For example, in one study, researchers wanted to study the effects of positive emotion on creativity. They gave candy to one group of participants and showed a funny film clip to those in another group. Then, to test creative thinking, they offered participants the items shown in Figure 12.4 and asked them to find a way to affix the candle to a corkboard

FIGURE 12.4   Using just the materials shown here, how could you affix the candle to the wall so that it would burn without dripping wax on the table or floor? Think creatively, and then check the answer at the end of this chapter.

on the wall in such a way that it would burn without dripping wax onto the table or the floor (Isen, Daubman, & Nowicki, 1987).

Can you figure out a solution? Here's a hint: To complete the task you need to think about using some of the objects in a way that's different from the way they are normally used—a classic aspect of creativity. Think about it and then check the solution given at the end of this chapter.

In this study, people who had watched the funny film clip were more likely to solve the problem (and solved it faster) than people in the neutral or negative conditions. This result suggests that amusement promotes creative thinking (Isen et al., 1987). After all, humor typically involves changing your perspective on some target and seeing it in a whole new light, just like creativity. However, those who had received the candy did no better than the neutral or negative groups. Although they said they were happy about receiving the candy, the effect may have been weaker than that of watching a funny film. Alternatively, perhaps amusement and happiness produce different effects in this situation.

"Depressive Realism"

As we saw in Chapter 8, optimistic people tend to be active, persistent, outgoing, and mentally and physically healthy. They believe they can control their situation, that they will succeed in most of their endeavors, and that in general things will turn out well for them and their loved ones. Those beliefs are encouraging and sustaining. But how often are they *true*? Might optimistic people *overestimate* their control and their likelihood of success?

In many situations, apparently they do. For example, optimistic people tend to assume incorrectly that most people agree with their opinions (Alicke & Largo, 1995), and they overestimate how much strangers like them and value their presence (Lewinsohn, Mischel, Chaplin, & Barton, 1980; Robins & Beer, 2001). Most people, especially in the United States, rate themselves above average on almost every desirable characteristic (Dunning, Heath, & Suls, 2004).

In other words, cheerful optimism is sometimes factually wrong, and pessimistic people are sometimes "sadder but wiser." According to the hypothesis of **depressive realism,** people who are mildly depressed, pessimistic, or at least neutral, are more realistic than highly optimistic people, and the pessimists are more likely to perceive themselves and their situation accurately and, therefore, to make careful and correct decisions. Although the usual term is "depressive" realism, few studies deal with people who are clinically depressed. Most participants in these studies are **dysthymic,** which means mildly depressed or even having a mixture of happy and depressed characteristics.

In one classic experiment, participants were told to try to find the best pattern of sometimes pressing and sometimes not pressing a key, to make a green light come on as frequently as possible. After a period of trying, they were asked how much control they had. When they had partial control of the light—for example, on 50 percent of the trials their response controlled the light and on the other 50 percent it was random—they generally perceived their control correctly. The interesting result occurred when people had no control at all. Normal, nondepressed students on the average estimated that they had about 40 percent control, whereas dysthymic students estimated only about 15 percent control (Alloy & Abramson, 1979). In other words, the dysthymic students more correctly recognized their lack of control.

The idea of depressive realism (or dysthymic realism) is surprising. Psychologists have long agreed that depressed people have cognitive distortions, sometimes to the point of being unable to function. Now we are told that depressed people are right and the rest of us are wrong. Partly because the idea is so surprising, psychologists have scrutinized the evidence carefully, and many find it to be less than compelling. Here's the problem (Ackermann & DeRubeis, 1991; Stone, Dodrill, & Johnson, 2001): You can't be sure how accurate a clock is if you have checked it only once or twice. If it said "9:35" when that was in fact the correct time, maybe the clock is accurate, or maybe it is stuck at 9:35. Similarly, if some dysphoric person is tested in some uncontrollable situation and correctly perceives, "I am doing badly and I have no control over my situation," we don't know whether the person is *accurate*, or consistently *negative*. Maybe he or she would say the same thing all the time. Some of the research has tested people in a variety of situations, but much of it has not. Let's consider a few research examples, and their strengths and weaknesses.

Dysthymia and Self-Confidence

Most people (at least in the prosperous countries from which most of the evidence comes) rate themselves as more happy than unhappy. They also tend to be more optimistic than pessimistic, and most people overestimate the accuracy of their own guesses and opinions. To illustrate, answer each of the following questions and next to each one estimate your confidence of being correct. For example, if you are certain you are right, put 100 percent; if you have no confidence at all, you could put 50 percent on a true-false item or 20 percent on a multiple-choice item with five choices. Of course, you could also put an intermediate number to indicate 70 percent confidence, 90 percent confidence, and so on.

Percent confidence
of answer

_____ 1. The actor John Wayne appeared in more than 100 movies. (true/false)

_____ 2. The largest giant redwood tree in the United States is more than 150 meters (492 feet) tall. (true/false)

_____ 3. The leaning tower of Pisa has more than 400 steps. (true/false)

_____ 4. In biology, rabbits are classified as (a) monotremes, (b) rodents, (c) lagomorphs, (d) artiodactyls, (e) pinnipeds.

_____ 5. The term "serendipity" originally came from (a) a story by Horace Walpole, (b) a society of musical composers in Austria, (c) a Greek word for lightning, (d) an American Indian word for treasure, (e) a contraction of "serene" and "disparity."

_____ 6. The word "absinthe" refers to (a) a precious stone, (b) a liqueur, (c) a point in the orbit of a moon, (d) a Caribbean island, (e) an exception to the rules of parliamentary procedure.

_____ 7. The most widely consumed fruit, worldwide, is the (a) apple, (b) banana, (c) grape, (d) mango, (e) orange.

Now add your numbers on percent confidence. For example, if you wrote 70, 60, 50, 50, 80, 70, and 100 percent, your total would be 480 percent, or 4.8. You would have estimated that you would get 4.8 answers correct. Now turn to the end of this chapter, and check your answers. Did you answer as many correctly as you predicted? Most people do not. When the questions are difficult, as they were here, most people overestimate how many questions they have answered correctly (Plous, 1993). In contrast, mildly depressed people express less confidence in their answers and therefore they estimate more accurately how many items they have answered correctly. Sometimes they even *under*estimate their percent correct (Stone, Dodrill, & Johnson, 2001). Note, however, that underestimating does not support the idea of depressive realism. Rather, it suggests that dysthymic people see themselves in a negative light. If the questions were easier, optimistic people's estimates of their percent correct would become accurate, while dysthymic people's lower estimates would be clearly inaccurate. Results like these confirm that dysthymic people are less likely than others to be overconfident, but they don't really indicate that dysthymic people are consistently accurate (Ackermann & DeRubeis, 1991).

Dysthymia and Self-Perception

Studies on self-perception also point to a difference in negativity, rather than accuracy. For example, college students in one study wrote predictions of what everyday events might happen to them in the next four or eight weeks, and then kept diaries that reported such events. Dysthymic students were slightly more accurate at predicting unpleasant events, such as how often they would cry, and happier students were more accurate at predicting pleasant events, such as how often they would laugh (Shrauger, Mariano, & Walter, 1988). In another study, students were given what they were told was their own individual personality profile, although everyone received the same printout. Then they were asked to rate how favorable it was. Although the profile itself was as close to neutral as the experimenters could make it, most dysthymic students rated it relatively unfavorable, whereas most other students saw it as favorable (McKendree-Smith & Scogin, 2000). In research of this type, dysthymic people are not necessarily more accurate; they are biased to see themselves in a negative light, whereas others see themselves in a positive light.

Happiness, Sadness, and Reasoning

Although most studies of "depressive realism" seem unconvincing, the evidence looks a little stronger that optimistic people make bold, sometimes risky decisions whereas pessimistic people are more cautious. Sometimes bold, decisive action is good, but if optimists underestimate the risk or cost of failure, their decisions can be disastrous. One oft-cited example is the Bay of Pigs fiasco. Shortly after his inauguration as U.S. President, John Kennedy and his administration had enormous self-confidence. They authorized an invasion of Cuba by a small group of ill-equipped Cuban refugees with only moderate U.S. support, confident that they were on the side of all that was right and good and, therefore, that the invasion was sure to succeed. This plan required many assumptions that the administration failed to question adequately. The invasion failed miserably, leading many people to wonder how so many smart people could make such a stupid decision. Part of the answer was overconfidence (Janis, 1972).

Should we as a rule prefer leaders who are optimists, pessimists, or those who see a balance of positives and negatives? Voters usually elect the candidate who seems more optimistic (Zullow, Oettingen, Peterson, & Seligman, 1988), and most corporations choose optimistic, bold, decisive people to lead them. Are those decisions wise or unwise? Do optimistic and pessimistic people evaluate the evidence differently?

One way to address this question is to ask how people respond to other people's attempts to persuade them of something. Do they carefully consider the strengths and weaknesses of the argument, or do they use mental shortcuts to make a decision? Psychologists distinguish between two major types of persuasion (Petty & Cacioppo, 1986): The **central route to persuasion** consists of providing facts and logic. The **peripheral route to persuasion** consists of superficial factors such as frequent repetition of a slogan or endorsements by celebrities. A classic example of the central route is a geometrical proof, which starts with explicit definitions and virtually self-evident assumptions and proceeds to show logically that if those assumptions are true, then certain other conclusions must also be true. For examples of the peripheral route, watch television advertisements for soft drinks, beer, or pet food. They will play cheerful music, entertain you, and show the product, but don't expect to hear a list of facts.

Political candidates typically aim for both the central and the peripheral routes to persuasion in their campaigns. A televised spot might show the candidate smiling, shaking hands with voters, and expressing nice-sounding generalities such as "I will fight for the citizens of this state." That approach is, of course, the peripheral route. The candidate might also say, "I am in favor of greater governmental efforts for environmental protection, and here is why. . . ." Statements of that sort qualify as the central route.

Both approaches can be effective, but their effectiveness depends on circumstances. It takes you almost no energy to watch an ad for cat food and say, "Oh, that was cute!" You need much more effort to understand and evaluate a geometrical proof. Consequently, when people think their decision is unimportant, they can be persuaded by the peripheral route, but if they think their decision will have major outcomes and is worth the effort, they respond better to the central route. That is, they examine the facts critically.

Several studies have indicated that when people are in a happy mood, they are *more* susceptible to peripheral route influences and *less* susceptible to the central route. That is, happy people are more apt to jump to conclusions without critically examining the evidence. Depressed people pay more attention to the quality of the evidence. If so, this tendency would be an example of depressive realism.

For example, students in one study were randomly assigned to writing for 15 minutes about either one of the most pleasant or one of the least pleasant events that ever happened to them, to induce a happy or a sad mood. Then they listened to either strong, factual arguments or weak, superficial arguments in favor of raising student fees at their university. As Figure 12.5 shows, the strong argument was more persuasive to those in a sad mood than to those in a happy mood. The weak argument was more persuasive to those in a happy mood. Said another way, the students in a happy mood were about equally persuaded by the strong or the weak argument, whereas those in a sad mood were persuaded by the strong argument but not by the weak one (Bless, Bohner, Schwarz, & Strack, 1990).

In another study, students were again randomly assigned to write about a pleasant or unpleasant life event and then asked to listen to a story titled "Going out for dinner." Later they were given a list of sentences and asked to identify which sentences had been part of the story. Some were part of the story and some were not; moreover, of those not in the story, some were typical going-out-for-dinner items that would have made sense (e.g., "He called a friend of his, who recommended several restaurants") and some were irrelevant or atypical (e.g., "Jack cleaned his glasses"). Students in a happy mood were more likely than the others to make the mistake of "remembering" the typical sentences that were not actually in the story (Bless et al., 1996). That is, they relied more on their "script" of what

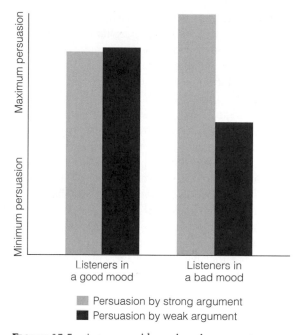

FIGURE 12.5   A strong, evidence-based argument was more persuasive to students in a sad mood, and a weak argument was more persuasive to students in a happy mood. Source: Based on data of Bless et al. (1990).

usually happens or what seems likely, instead of the information they had actually heard.

Another study concerned moral reasoning. A typical way of evaluating moral reasoning is by offering moral dilemmas. For example, imagine that your loved one has a life-threatening disease, and the only way you can get the extremely expensive medicine you need is by stealing it. What should you do? Even if we disagree about what is the right answer to that question, we can agree on what would be a better or worse explanation for a given answer. In one study, students who had just finished watching a sad movie tended to give more sophisticated and principled explanations, whereas those who had just finished watching a light comedy gave more superficial or casual explanations (Zarinpoush, Cooper, & Moylan, 2000).

Stereotypes offer another way to "shortcut" decision making and bypass careful analysis of the evidence. Suppose you are given a list of names and asked to identify which ones are famous basketball players, famous politicians, or infamous criminals. Some of the names (which are, in fact, neither famous nor infamous) sound like they are probably white people, such as John Olson or Daniel Stuart. Some are names that you would guess are probably black people, such as Leroy Washington or Karanja Jackson. If you resist the stereotypes and answer just on the basis of whether you have heard of these people, you will not classify any of them as famous or infamous, and people who have just watched a sad or neutral movie make few errors. However, people who have just watched a humorous movie make significantly more errors, identifying many of the black names as either basketball players or criminals and more of the white names as politicians (J. Park & Banaji, 2000). Several other studies have also found that happy people are more likely than others to apply stereotypes and to explain people's behavior in terms of personality traits rather than situational factors (Bodenhausen, Kramer, & Süsser, 1994; Forgas, 1998).

In each of these cases, it appears that sadder people rely more on facts and less on mental shortcuts, and indeed sadder people may make better decisions in some situations. One more study, however, suggests a limit to that conclusion. Instead of comparing average people who had been briefly saddened or entertained by a film clip, the researcher compared unselected college students to clinically depressed patients. Each participant had the task of choosing a partner for a tedious eight-hour task, and they could ask as many questions as they wanted about five potential partners before choosing one of them. The depressed patients asked more questions and collected more total information before deciding, and considered all candidates about equally instead of focusing mainly on one or two. In those regards, they would seem realistic and rational. However, they were no more satisfied with their final decisions than the college students, and they were just as likely as the college students to stick with whichever candidate they were leaning to-

ward at the start of the process. That is, all the additional evidence they collected did not apparently improve the quality of their decision. We might therefore characterize the depressed people as "indecisive" rather than "rational" (Lewicka, 1997).

The evidence presented so far suggests that sad people tend to examine the evidence more carefully, whereas happy people answer more impulsively, follow first impressions, rely on stereotypes, and yield to superficial "peripheral route" influences. Note that nearly all of this evidence comes from college students who are in a temporary happy or sad mood. Virtually no evidence points to realism or any other cognitive advantage in seriously depressed people . . . except for the anecdotal fact that certain famous philosophers, such as Immanuel Kant, were depressive ruminators.

If happiness turns people's brains to mush and they no longer examine the evidence carefully, why is that? One hypothesis is that happiness uses up a certain amount of attention or "mental energy" (whatever that means), leaving less available for other purposes, such as evaluating evidence. If so, we could predict that a happy mood would interfere with any and all kinds of intellectual activity. Research has refuted that prediction. People in a happy mood have performed better than those in a sad mood on some intellectual tasks, worse on others (Bless et al., 1996; Phillips, Bull, Adams, & Fraser, 2002). Earlier in the chapter, we saw that participants who had just watched a funny movie solved a creativity task faster than those who were in a neutral mood (Isen et al., 1987). In one study, older adults who were in *either* a happy mood or a sad mood performed worse on problem-solving tasks than those who were in a neutral mood (Phillips, Smith, & Gilhooly, 2002). In short, the evidence does not support the hypothesis that happiness uses up more mental energy than sadness does.

A second hypothesis is that sad people are motivated to decrease their sadness. They buy themselves presents and they become more motivated than usual to gain large rewards to cheer themselves up (Raghunathan & Pham, 1999). To avoid hurting themselves even further, they become more attentive than usual to details (Gasper & Clore, 2002) and the result is careful attention to evidence. This explanation is plausible, although it does not explain why happy people become *less* attentive than usual to details and evidence.

A third possibility is that sad people interpret their sadness as a signal that they are in a dangerous situation, which calls for attentiveness, whereas happy people infer from their mood that the situation is so safe that they can relax. Tiedens and Linton (2001) offered an interesting modification of this idea. According to their interpretation, the decisive factor is not really happiness versus sadness, but confidence versus uncertainty. Happy people are usually confident, and therefore prone to accept their first judgments quickly without challenging them. Sad people feel less certain about themselves (and everything else) and therefore question assertions, examine evidence carefully, and delay making a decision until they have enough facts.

To test this hypothesis, Tiedens and Linton (2001) induced two kinds of happy moods and two kinds of unhappy moods in their participants. Each participant was asked to write a short essay about a personal experience. Participants were randomly assigned to write about an experience that made them feel contented (a positive, confident mood), surprised (a positive but unconfident mood), angry (negative and confident), or worried (negative and unconfident). Then they were asked to read an essay and say whether they agreed with its conclusions. Some of them were told that a community-college student (lower prestige) wrote the essay, and others were told that a college professor (higher prestige) wrote it. Both groups actually read the same essay.

The students in the unconfident moods (surprised or worried) were about equally persuaded in both cases, suggesting that they evaluated the logic of the argument itself, regardless of the prestige of its author. The students in the confident moods (contented or angry) were more persuaded if they thought that a professor wrote the essay. Evidently, they were more vulnerable to "peripheral route"

persuasion. The overall results suggest that highly confident people are more likely than others to make quick decisions based on weak evidence. (Of course, a quick decision isn't always bad, if the evidence is good and the confidence is justified.) In short, happy and sad people differ in their decision making mainly because happy people tend to be more confident than sad people.

Are Optimistic Illusions Good or Bad?

Shelley Taylor and her associates have argued that although optimistic people tend to overestimate their probability of success, their illusions are usually helpful. For example, some patients with cancer or AIDS say that they expect to overcome their disease more successfully than average and to live longer than most other people with their disease. The people who express this belief do, in fact, tend to live longer than others (Taylor, Kemeny, Reed, Bower, & Gruenwald, 2000). Similarly, students who have average or below-average grades but rate their own academic ability as "above average" apparently have an illusion about themselves, but they are more likely to improve their grades next semester than are students who admit that they have average or below-average abilities (Wright, 2000).

Results showing that "unrealistic" expectations are associated with academic success or good health are interesting, but their implications are debatable. One interpretation is that positive beliefs about oneself provide encouragement that sustains action; the beliefs help people physically and psychologically. However, it is also possible that some of the cancer and AIDS patients who say they are going to do better than other patients have real evidence for their belief. Also, no doubt some of the students who say they have above-average abilities despite their below-average grades have good reasons to believe that they are better students than their grades indicate. So the data suggesting that people benefit from illusions are hard to evaluate. And high expectations do not always foreshadow a good outcome. One study identified college freshmen who predicted they would be much more successful than either their high-school grades or their SAT scores indicated. On the average, these students had high self-esteem, but did no better in college than similar students with more realistic predictions (Robins & Beer, 2001).

▢ Summary

You may have noticed a pattern of uncertain results and conflicting interpretations throughout this chapter. However, a few of the conclusions are reasonably clear. First, emotions influence our attention. Fear or anger narrows our attention to a particular disturbing object or event; happiness broadens our attention so that we consider a wider than usual range of possibilities.

Second, other things being equal, emotional arousal does improve memory. If you want to remember something that you read, try to be interested and aroused. If you are excited, especially if you are excited about what you are reading and its implications for your life, you are more likely to remember it.

Third, emotions influence how we interpret information. If you are already frightened, you tend to see new events as frightening, too. If you are angry, it doesn't take much to get you angry again. If you are in a good mood, you tend to make confident, even overconfident decisions and appraisals of your own likelihood for success. If you are in a sad mood, you tend to be more cautious, more likely to doubt that things will turn out well.

If one theme runs throughout this chapter, it is that emotion is part of our thinking, not something separate. Your thoughts influence your emotions, but in addition, your emotions alter what you remember, how intensely you remember it, what aspects of the environment you notice, whether you blame yourself or others for misfortunes, what events you consider likely in the future, and how much effort you put into making a careful decision. Your emotions to some degree change what kind of person you are and how others will perceive you.

▢ Key Terms

Affect Infusion Model: theory that people use their emotional state as information in reaching a decision about some target (p. 250)

beta-blocker: drug that temporarily disables the stress hormone system responsible for some types of emotional arousal (p. 246)

broaden-and-build model: theory that positive emotions lead to no specific behavior, but to an increased readiness to explore new ideas and opportunities (p. 244)

central route to persuasion: persuasion based on facts and logic (p. 254)

depressive realism: tendency for people who are mildly depressed or pessimistic, or at least neutral, to be more realistic than highly optimistic people, to perceive themselves and their situation accurately, and, therefore, to make careful and correct decisions (p. 252)

dysthymic: being mildly depressed or having a mixture of happy and depressed characteristics (p. 252)

flashbulb memories: recollections of highly emotional events that are vivid and detailed with a clear, almost photographic quality (p. 248)

implicit attitude: an attitude that influences behavior even when we cannot or do not verbalize it (p. 251)

peripheral route to persuasion: persuasion based on superficial factors such as frequent repetition of a slogan or endorsements by celebrities (p. 254)

▢ Thought Questions

1. Research has demonstrated that intense negative emotions such as fear focus attention more narrowly than usual. On the other hand, people report flashbulb memories including details of weather and setting concerning highly emotional events, such as hearing about some disaster. Do these two findings contra-

dict each other? If not, how might you explain the difference?

2. As reported earlier in this chapter, students' reported enjoyment of a spring break trip is usually higher than the average of how happy they reported being at various times during the trip. What result would you expect if we asked about a predominantly unpleasant experience, such as attending a funeral or a stay in a hospital? Would people report the total experience as happier, or less happy, than the average of individual moments within this experience? What leads you to this prediction? (To our knowledge, no one has done this study.)

Suggestions for Research Projects

1. Keep a diary of personal events, recording as much detail as possible and categorizing events as highly emotional or not emotional. A month or more later, test your own memory of each event. Do you remember the more emotional events more clearly than the others? Are your memories more accurate?

2. As an informal test of the Affect Infusion Model, ask some of your friends to make predictions about their grades for the current semester, their prospects of getting a good job, the direction of the national economy, or whatever else you wish to include. Ask some of them for their predictions just after your college team has won a big victory, and others just after a disappointing loss. Evaluate the predic-

tions and see whether people make more optimistic predictions when they are in a good mood than when in a sad mood.

Suggestion for Further Reading

Reisberg, D., & Hertel, P. (Eds.). (2004). *Memory and emotion*. New York: Oxford University Press.

Solution to the Problem Posed in Figure 12.4

Dump the matches out of the box, use tacks to pin the side of the box to the corkboard, light the candle, and use melted wax to stick the candle into the box.

Answers to Questions on Page 253

1. True. John Wayne was in 153 movies.

2. False. The tallest redwood was measured at 112 meters (367.5 feet).

3. False. The leaning tower of Pisa has 294 steps.

4. c. Rabbits are lagomorphs.

5. a. The term came from Walpole's story *The Three Princes of Serendip*.

6. b. Absinthe is a liqueur.

7. d. Mangoes are the world's most widely eaten fruits, thanks mainly to the people of India and Pakistan.

13

Emotional Decisions and Emotional Intelligence

When we are facing an important decision, people often advise us to think calmly and rationally, not to let our emotions get in the way of our logic. That advice implies that emotions lead to bad decisions. Sometimes they do. For example, during the first three months after the terrorist attacks of September 11, 2001, a great many Americans were afraid to get onto planes, so they drove to their destinations instead. During those three months, the number of people killed in U.S. traffic accidents increased enormously compared with similar periods of time. The increase in the number of traffic fatalities during those few months was greater than the number of people killed in the terrorist attacks themselves (Gigerenzer, 2004).

On the other hand, recall from the definition of emotion, presented in Chapter 1, that emotion is *functional*. That is, emotion should lead to productive, useful behavior more often than not. For example, fear of snakes, spiders, and grizzly bears keeps us away from unnecessary dangers. As it turned out, avoiding airplane flights after September 11, 2001, was a mistake, but no one could have known that at the time. Sometimes fear is exaggerated, but a total lack of fear would be disastrous. (Perhaps the lesson

from the increase in automobile fatalities during the months after 9/11 is not that we should fear airplanes less, but that we should fear cars more.) So, overall, do emotions help us make good decisions, or do they interfere?

The answer (of course) is "it depends." But "it depends" on what? One hypothesis is that mild or moderate emotion helps reasoning whereas higher amounts hurt. As we have seen in several earlier chapters, emotion is often accompanied by autonomic nervous system arousal. According to one of the oldest findings in psychological research, the **Yerkes-Dodson law,** learning is at its best when stimulation or arousal is intermediate (not too strong, not too weak). The original study of this law demonstrated that mice learned to enter one box instead of another faster if their errors were punished with medium-strength shocks than with very strong or very weak ones (Yerkes & Dodson, 1908). Moreover, the "best" shock level varied, depending on the difficulty of the task. Weak shocks were best when learning a difficult task, but stronger shocks were effective for an easy task. The original Yerkes-Dodson research used an experimental design that would not satisfy today's standards. Still, the idea

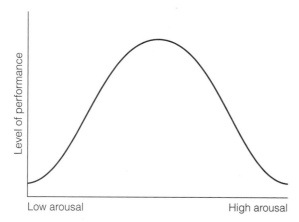

FIGURE 13.1 According to the Yerkes-Dodson law, performance is best at an intermediate level of stimulation or arousal.

caught on. Psychologists later broadened the idea to say that learning, memory, performance, and reasoning are most enhanced under medium levels of arousal, motivation, or emotion (Teigen, 1994). Figure 13.1 shows the idea.

The idea strikes most people as reasonable: "I do my best if I'm a little aroused, but not too much." Certainly at the extremes the principle is obvious: If your arousal is so low that you might fall asleep, you won't accomplish much, and if it reaches panic levels, you won't pause to choose a reasonable course of action. However, with arousal levels anywhere in the vast middle ground between utter boredom and absolute frenzy, the evidence does not clearly indicate a consistent "best" level of arousal (Bäumler, 1994). Support is even less clear for the idea that good performance requires intermediate levels of motivation or anxiety. In short, the Yerkes-Dodson law is probably too broad a generalization to be useful (Mendl, 1999).

There is another way to think about the benefits and harms of emotion. Maybe benefit or harm in making decisions depends not on the amount of emotion, but on the type of reasoning we are talking about. Let's consider some different kinds of reasoning.

Emotion and Logical Reasoning

Questions in formal logic are about as unemotional as one could imagine: "If A is true, then B is true. If B is true, then C is true. Therefore, if A, then C." This sequence seems ridiculously obvious when dealing with an unemotional topic. Does logic proceed as smoothly when the elements A, B, and C have emotional connotations?

To address this question, researchers posed to participants a series of logical questions of this kind, half of them emotional and half unemotional. Reasoning about an emotional situation is not the same as reasoning while experiencing an emotion, but the assumption is that while we read about an emotional situation, we identify with the person and therefore feel a bit of the emotion ourselves. Each question consisted of one if-then statement, four additional statements, and a question for each statement. Table 13.1 shows an emotional example and an unemotional example. Each case shows the correct answer.

Before proceeding, you should work out why the answers given are correct. For example, according to the first if-then statement, people in a tragic situation cry. It doesn't say anything about people in an untragic situation, so logically we can't draw a conclusion about Christine, who is happy.

In each case, items 3 and 4 (where the correct answer is that we can't draw a conclusion) tend to be more difficult. Many people answer "no" to item type 3, and they are more likely to make that error on emotional than on unemotional items. About 49 percent of people say that Christine, who is happy, will not cry, whereas only about 31 percent say that Daniel, who is not in a library, will not see books. Many also say "yes" on item type 4, and again the results depend on emotional content. About 30 percent say that Laura, who is crying, must be in a tragic situation, whereas only 21 percent say that Kareem, who sees books, must be in a library (Blanchette & Richards, 2004).

TABLE 13.1   Reasoning in emotional and unemotional situations

Emotional example

If-then statement: "If someone is in a tragic situation, then she cries."

Additional statement	Question	Correct Answer
1. Anne is in a tragic situation.	Does she cry?	Yes
2. Gayle is not crying.	Is she in a tragic situation?	No
3. Christine is in a happy situation.	Does she cry?	Maybe (We can't draw a conclusion.)
4. Laura is crying.	Is she in a tragic situation?	Maybe (We can't draw a conclusion.)

Unemotional example

If-then statement: "If one is in a library, then one sees books."

Additional statement	Question	Correct Answer
1. Scott is in a library.	Does he see books?	Yes
2. Max does not see books.	Is he in a library?	No
3. Daniel is not in a library.	Does he see books?	Maybe (We can't draw a conclusion.)
4. Kareem sees books.	Is he in a library?	Maybe (We can't draw a conclusion.)

The researchers properly worried that one set of questions might be more difficult than the other. Maybe it just seems less obvious that a person in a happy situation might cry than it does that a person outside a library could see books. So they did a second experiment in which they used only unemotional if-then sentences, such as "If a person is drinking juice, then she is getting vitamins." Some of their items included nonsense words, such as, "If someone looks like a clorious, then he is a cereful." However, before posing the logic problems, the researchers gave some of the words an emotional connotation. For example, they might present the made-up word *clorious* while showing a picture of a bloody, injured person. In this way, the researchers could use exactly the same sentences for all people but associate a given sentence with positive images for some people, neutral images for others, and unpleasant images for still others. As in the first experiment, people gave the logically correct answer more often to unemotional sentences than to those that had been associated with emotional pictures (Blanchette & Richards, 2004).

One way to take emotion completely out of the reasoning process, and see whether logic improves, is to use computers. In many situations, computers make better, more logical decisions than humans. If an insurance agent wants to figure out the fairest price to charge someone for health insurance, the best approach is to feed all known information about the person's age, activities, and health into a computer and let the computer use mathematical formulas to decide the right price. Similarly, computers outperform humans on a wide variety of other decisions, ranging from choosing the college admissions applicants with the best chance of success to choosing the right treatment for a medical patient and predicting the probable outcome (Swets, Dawes, & Monahan, 2000).

One thing all of these scenarios have in common is that they require someone to compute probabilities. To compute a fair price for insurance, you need to estimate the probability that a person will become ill or die. To choose among college applicants, you need to estimate the likelihood that a given individual will succeed, and so on. In this kind of task, computers have other advantages besides their lack of emotions. For example, they have huge memories and incredibly fast processing speeds. Still, many people have assumed that "clinical intuition" or "heart" would enable them to make better decisions than computers, despite the computers' advantages of speed and memory. The evidence, however, says that emotions don't help with this type of reasoning.

◻ Choices Based on Values

Although computers do an excellent job of figuring out the probability of various events, and thus can help us figure out how to reach certain goals, they don't *set* the goals. Suppose a computer tells us that some medical patient will probably survive longer with treatment A than treatment B, but will be more active and alert while undergoing treatment B. Can the computer tell us which treatment is "better?" Hardly. "Better" requires a value judgment, and a decision based on values is necessarily based on emotions. Remember the quote from Antonio Damasio (1999, p. 55) cited early in Chapter 1: "Emotions are inseparable from the idea of good and evil."

Decisions often depend on our expectations of future emotions. That is, you prefer the choice that will lead to an outcome that makes you and other people happiest. In addition, according to the **risk-as-feelings hypothesis,** people make different choices based on the emotions they feel at the time of making a decision (Loewenstein, Weber, Hsee, & Welch, 2001). Specifically, anything that enhances your fear makes you take precautions against danger, even if the objective probability of the danger is low. For example, people who are afraid of bats might avoid buying a house in a neighborhood known to have bats, even though the probability of getting any disease from bats is extremely low.

In one study, investigators asked people how much they would decrease their consumption of beef if they thought it had some small possibility of contamination with Mad Cow Disease. They asked

other people how much they would decrease consumption of beef if they thought it had some small possibility of contamination with bovine spongiform encephalopathy (BSE). People expressed a stronger avoidance based on Mad Cow Disease than of BSE, even though these well-educated participants knew that Mad Cow Disease and BSE are the same thing (Sinaceur, Heath, & Cole, 2005). "Mad Cow Disease" sounds scarier, so it leads to more avoidance.

In another study, people completed measures of fear-proneness and anger-proneness and then filled out a form in which they estimated how many people per year in the United States die from floods, brain cancer, and 10 other causes. People reporting much fear estimated higher than average numbers, whereas those reporting anger estimated lower numbers (Lerner & Keltner, 2000). Evidently, fear heightens your perception of danger. Anger implies more possibility of personal control and, therefore, lowers the perception of danger.

In yet another study, volunteers who had a cold were assigned to remember vividly an event that made them feel happy, sad, or neutral. When asked about their physical cold symptoms, participants in the "sad" condition reported more severe symptoms, and less confidence that they could do things to make themselves feel better, than participants in the other two conditions (Salovey & Birnbaum, 1989). The authors argued that mood influences people's decisions about whether to seek medical care when they're ill.

Decisions about buying and selling also yield to emotions. Suppose we ask you to estimate the value of some object, such as a set of highlighter pens. Perhaps you estimate a value of $10. Now we actually give you the pens to keep, but then we ask whether you would be willing to sell them back to us for $10, the price you said they were worth. Most people in a neutral or happy mood refuse, saying they would prefer to keep the pens. Sad people are more inclined to sell; they would prefer the money. People who are disgusted (because they just finished watching a disgusting film) estimate lower values for objects, and they don't seem to care whether they keep the object or the money. It's as if they don't want either one. They are in a mood to spit things out, to reject, to get rid of whatever they can (Lerner, Small, & Loewenstein, 2004). As we saw in Chapter 12, people actively use their current emotions as information when making decisions. If we feel good, then whatever we are currently contemplating (such as a set of pens) seems good and valuable. If we feel bad, then we assume the object is bad, too.

So emotions influence your choices. Do people ever use this idea for practical purposes? You bet they do! Stores arrange cheerful decorations and play happy music, hoping to entice you into a happy mood so you will be more likely to buy things. Television advertisers try to associate their product with happy scenes, especially if they are advertising something like cola beverages, where few facts separate one brand from another. The influences are quick and implicit. If you really thought it out, you wouldn't conclude that one kind of cola or potato chip will make you more fun or popular or attractive than another cola or potato chip. Political candidates want you to like them and dislike their opponents. In the constraints of a brief television advertisement, they can't explain the complexities of a difficult issue, so they try to associate themselves with smiles and cheerful music while associating their opponents with frightening, unpleasant images.

The Role of Emotions in Judgment: Evidence From Brain-Damaged Patients

Let's return to the point that computers can choose a good way to achieve a goal, but they cannot set the goals. People select goals based on values and, therefore, emotions. What kind of decisions would people make if they could not take emotion into consideration? Would they be highly logical or utterly clueless?

Certain kinds of brain damage greatly impair the use of emotion in decision making. The most promi-

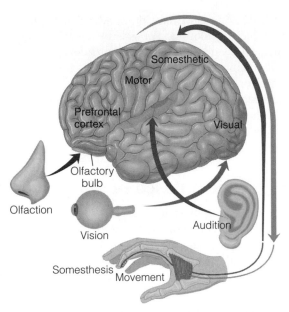

FIGURE 13.2   The prefrontal cortex is the most anterior portion of the human brain. Unlike many other cortical areas that receive a particular kind of sensation or control movement (as shown), the prefrontal cortex has functions that relate to working memory and other functions that are hard to summarize. People with damage in certain parts of the prefrontal cortex show decreased emotional expression and decreased understanding of other people's expressions.

nent example is damage to the prefrontal cortex (Figure 13.2). People who survive strokes in this area show diminished facial expressions of emotion, and an observer has trouble recognizing what emotion they are expressing. They are especially weak on expressing fear and disgust. If they are asked to imitate someone else's facial expression, they respond only weakly. They also have trouble recognizing other people's expressions or picking out the photo that best expresses the probable emotion someone would feel in a particular situation (Kolb & Taylor, 2000). In many ways, these results resemble those of damage to the amygdala, and the prefrontal cortex has rich interconnections with the amygdala (Hariri, Mattay, Tessitore, Fera, & Weinberger, 2003).

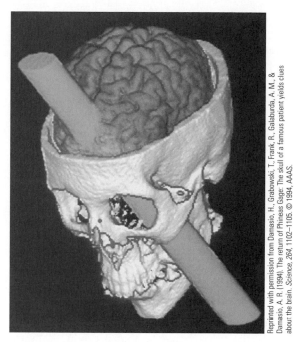

Reprinted with permission from Damasio, H., Grabowski, T., Frank, R., Galaburda, A. M., & Damasio, A. R. (1994). The return of Phineas Gage: The skull of a famous patient yields clues about the brain. *Science, 264,* 1102–1105. © 1994, AAAS.

FIGURE 13.3 A modern, computer-based reconstruction of the path the iron bar took through the brain of Phineas Gage in 1848. Gage survived, but he became unreliable, lost self-control, and made poor decisions. Source: H. Damasio et al. (1994).

A famous early case of someone with prefrontal-lobe damage was Phineas Gage, who in 1848 survived an explosion that sent an iron pole through his head. In the 1990s, researchers studied his skull (which is on exhibit in a Boston museum) and reconstructed the pole's probable route through his head, as shown in Figure 13.3 (H. Damasio, Grabowski, Frank, Galaburda, & Damasio, 1994). Gage's prefrontal cortex suffered severe damage, particularly to an area known as the orbitofrontal cortex. After the accident, Gage changed dramatically. Previously a conscientious worker, he could no longer keep a job. He became impulsive, often rude and vulgar, took no sense of responsibility toward others, and seemed unable to plan for the future.

In the 1990s, researchers reported extensive tests on a new patient with prefrontal damage (A. R.

Damasio, 1994; H. Damasio, 2002). This patient, known in the literature as "Elliot," suffered prefrontal damage from a surgical operation to remove a tumor. Afterward he seemed normal in many regards, but he consistently had trouble making decisions. He would deliberate endlessly about unimportant details, only to end with what appeared to be a haphazard (and often harmful) decision. He could neither plan for the future nor follow plans that others suggested. He would interrupt an important task to do something trivial or continue doing something unimportant when he should quit.

For example, at work, when he was supposed to be sorting documents, he once stopped to read one of the documents very carefully for the rest of the afternoon. All of us get distracted occasionally, but for Elliot this event was part of a pattern. As a result, he kept losing jobs. He divorced his first wife, married a woman who was clearly a bad choice, and then divorced her. He invested all his savings in a project that seemed sure to fail, and it did. Of course, many people make terrible decisions, even lots of them, without having brain damage. How do we know Elliot's problems with decisions are related to the surgery, and what does that mean for the relationship between emotion and decision making?

Part of the answer to this comes from the difference between Elliot's behavior before and after the surgery. Eventually these differences seemed serious enough to other people that he was brought to psychologists for testing (A. R. Damasio, 1994). He was about normal in tests of vision, memory, language, and intelligence. Even on memory tests that are sensitive to damage in certain parts of the prefrontal cortex, he performed surprisingly well. His only prominent abnormality was a lack of emotional reactivity. When he described terrible events from his own life, he was calm and relaxed. Even when he looked at photos of people injured in gory accidents, he showed none of the revulsion or distress that most people display.

The researchers tried to identify more precisely where Elliot's decision-making process went wrong. They presented him with a variety of hypothetical situations, such as "Imagine you went to a bank and the teller gave you too much change," or "Suppose you broke someone's flower pot," or "Suppose you owned stock in a company and you learned that it was doing badly." In each case, Elliot was asked to suggest various actions that he might take and then to predict the consequences of each. In another set of scenarios, he was also asked what was the morally right thing to do. To all these questions he gave normal answers; he seemed to understand the possible courses of action and their consequences as well as anyone else. There was no problem with Elliot's logic—he could reason through scenarios like these easily, as long as they weren't actually happening. The explanation of his problems with real-life decisions came from Elliot's own words. In one case, after describing all the possible actions he might take and all the probable consequences of each action, he remarked, "And after all this, I still wouldn't know what to do!" (A. R. Damasio, 1994, p. 49). It was as if he did not value one possible outcome more than another.

Researchers have tried to specify more precisely the ways in which the prefrontal cortex relates to decision making. According to some researchers, many decisions are based upon the magnitude of possible rewards and punishments, their likelihood, and how soon they will occur. For example, you might have to choose between a small reward now and a larger one later, or between a definite, small penalty and an uncertain but larger penalty. The prefrontal cortex is a large, complex area, but one part of it may be specialized for calculations about rewards and punishments. The orbitofrontal cortex and adjacent areas (located just above the "orbits" that hold the eyes) are activated by taste, smell, and touch stimuli (which are generally experienced as either "pleasant" or "unpleasant") as well as by rewards and punishments of all kinds, including winning or losing money and gaining or losing social approval (Clark, Cools, & Robbins, 2004; Krawczyk, 2002; Rolls, 2004). Antonio Damasio (1994) has described a dozen patients with prefrontal damage whose symptoms included flat emotions and poor decision making. People with damage in this area often act impulsively, taking the

first choice that looks reasonable instead of checking for a better one. They also express less empathy than average for other people in distress (Shamay-Tsoory, Tomer, Goldsher, Berger, & Aharon-Peretz, 2004). Two patients who suffered prefrontal damage during infancy never developed any sense of right and wrong; they frequently stole, lied, and hurt other people, without any signs of guilt (S. W. Anderson, Bechara, Damasio, Tranel, & Damasio, 1999).

One interpretation is that such patients are insensitive to the possible emotional consequences of their decisions (Berlin, Rolls, & Kischka, 2004). Several studies have documented a difficulty in shifting decision-making strategy based on rewards and punishments. For example, suppose your task is to choose button A or button B. Button A produces a monetary reward on 70 percent of trials and a loss on 30 percent; button B produces a reward on 40 percent and a loss on 60 percent. By trial and error, you learn to choose A. Then (without your being told), the rules change so that B produces reward more often than A. Every time you learn which button to choose, the rules switch to favor the other one. Most people learn to reverse their preferences quickly, but people with damage to the orbitofrontal cortex are slow to do so, and over the course of many trials, they choose the wrong stimulus more often than the right one (Berlin et al., 2004).

Also, suppose you had to choose between two decks of cards, each of which produces a gain or loss of money. At first you try both decks, and you discover that deck A has larger rewards than deck B. Soon, however, it becomes clear that deck A also has larger and more frequent losses, so in the long run you would do better with the slow, steady gains from deck B. Most people gradually shift their preference to deck B, but people with orbitofrontal damage continue choosing mostly from deck A (Bechara, 2004; Bechara, Damasio, Damasio, & Lee, 1999).

A plausible interpretation is that those with orbitofrontal damage do not anticipate the negative emotions associated with a loss and, therefore, do not adjust their preferences. According to this interpretation, the patient "Elliot" cannot make decisions because he has a difficult time anticipating how he might feel after various outcomes. Think of it this way: In response to the question about getting extra change at the bank, you could say that you could return the extra change and have the bank thank you, or you could try to walk away with it, probably get caught, and get a reputation for dishonesty. You prefer the first outcome because you anticipate feeling bad if you get caught running away with extra money. Your decision would be based in part on the emotions you anticipate feeling as a result of the consequences. Elliot doesn't know what to do because he does not anticipate his future emotions, especially the negative ones. Without the ability to imagine future feelings, one outcome seems as good as another.

The Down Side of Relying on Emotions

After discussing the benefits of emotions in decision making, let's consider some disadvantages. As we said earlier, people typically choose the course of action that they expect will bring them the greater happiness or the lesser distress. However, sometimes their estimates of future happiness or distress are seriously mistaken (Mellers & McGraw, 2001). Also, people can pay so much attention to the potential emotional payoff of some event that they overlook how likely or unlikely the event may be.

Consider gambling. Would you risk $1 on a 50 percent chance of winning $2? Most people would not. What about betting $1 on a 1 percent chance of winning $100? Statistically, this is the same as the first bet; you should come out even in the long run. But most people find this second bet more appealing, because winning $100 sounds like much more fun than winning $2. Would you bet $1 on a 0.0001 percent (that is, one in a million) chance of winning $1 million? Again, statistically this is a break-even bet in the long run; however, far more people are willing to make this bet than the 50 percent chance of winning a dollar.

In fact, almost half of U.S. college students say they would bet $10 on a one-in-a-million chance of winning $1 million (Rachlin, Siegel, & Cross, 1994). Statistically, this is a terrible bet. You would have to take a one-in-a-million bet about 700,000 times to have a 50 percent chance of winning at least once, and by that time you would have already lost close to $7 million. People in other countries show the same tendency to prefer bets with a very small chance of a very high payoff (Birnbaum, 1999). (See Figure 13.4.) The low-probability, high-payoff bet seems appealing because we anticipate enormous pleasure from the possible win, and the low probabilities do not weaken our emotions.

Curiously, people who are in a good mood become less interested in gambling, especially if they see some possibility of incurring large losses (Nygren, Isen, Taylor, & Dulin, 1996). One interpretation is that they try to protect their current happiness by avoiding something that might weaken it.

FIGURE 13.4   State lotteries entice many people by the lure of a very high (though very unlikely) win.

Scott Olson/AFP/Getty Images

Emotions and Moral Reasoning

Given the link between emotions and our understanding of good and bad, we should expect emotions to be particularly important in moral reasoning. Let's begin with two examples of difficult moral decisions, which have been of interest to both philosophers and psychological researchers.

Making Quick Decisions

The Trolley Dilemma. A trolley car's brakes have failed, and it is plunging toward five people who cannot move. You are standing at a switch that controls which track the trolley will enter at a junction.

If you leave the switch alone, the five people will be killed. If you pull the switch, you send the trolley onto another track, where only one person is standing. Then that person will be killed. Should you pull the switch? If so, your action will kill one person but save five, who are all strangers to you. (See Figure 13.5a.) Compare this dilemma to the next one.

The Footbridge Dilemma. An out-of-control trolley is, again, plunging downhill toward five people. Again, there is no hope that they will jump out of the way. This time there is no switch and only one track, but you are standing on a footbridge above the track. For a split second, you consider diving onto the trolley track to stop the trolley, sacrificing your life to save the other five. Unfortunately (or

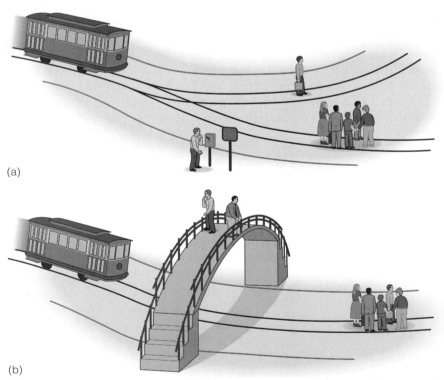

(a)

(b)

FIGURE 13.5   (a) Would it be right to flip a switch to divert the trolley to a different track in the trolley dilemma? (b) Would it be right to push a stranger off a bridge to block a trolley in the footbridge dilemma? In either case, your action would kill one person but save five others.

fortunately, depending on your point of view), you are not heavy enough to stop the trolley, so your sacrifice would accomplish nothing. However, standing right next to you is a very large wrestler, whose mass would surely stop the trolley. Should you push this person off the bridge to stop the trolley and save the five people's lives? (See Figure 13.5b.)

From a practical standpoint, these are the same dilemma, as you would be killing one person to save five, yet far more people say it is okay to pull the switch in the first example than to push the stranger off the bridge in the second. Even those who decide it is morally right to push the stranger in the footbridge dilemma are slow and hesitant about making that decision, as if they are fighting hard against an impulse to say no (Greene, Sommerville, Nystrom, Darley, & Cohen, 2001). Why is pulling the switch morally better than pushing the stranger? The idea of putting your hands on a stranger to push that person to a painful death is emotionally repugnant, even if the consequences seem good overall. (Of course, you may also hesitate to push a stranger off the bridge for other reasons, including being uncertain that doing so will save the others.)

The Lifeboat Dilemma. Consider a third situation: You are one of six people on a lifeboat in icy waters. The boat was built to hold only five, and it is beginning to sink. The only way to survive is to push someone overboard. Right now the person sitting next to you is precariously balanced on the edge of the boat and not paying attention. You could easily push this person overboard, saving yourself and four others. Should you do it?

Again, your action would kill one person but save five others. One big difference is that now *you* are one of those to be saved. You might decide to push, but even if you do, you will find it a difficult decision. And you will feel guilty afterward. Researchers have found that when people are even thinking about these decisions, as you are now, the process strongly activates the prefrontal cortex and other brain areas known to react to emotional arousal (Greene et al., 2001).

The Framing Effect

Researchers have found that they can shift people's choices in a two-choice situation just by reframing (rephrasing) the question. This observation is known as the **framing effect.** For example, consider the following choice: You are the health director in a small town where 600 people have contracted a potentially deadly illness. If you adopt Health Plan A, you will definitely save the lives of exactly 200 people. If you adopt Plan B, you have a 33 percent chance of saving all 600, but a 67 percent chance of saving no one. Which do you choose? (*Please decide before reading further.*)

Compare the following situation: Again you are the health director in a small town and 600 people are ill. You must choose between two plans. If you adopt Plan C, 400 of these people are sure to die. If you adopt Plan D, there is a 33 percent chance that no one will die, but a 67 percent chance that all 600 will die. Which do you choose? (*Again, please decide before reading on.*)

When these choices were offered to one group of people, 72 percent chose Plan A instead of B, guaranteeing that they would save 200 people. However, 78 percent chose D over C, taking a risk to try to save them all (Tversky & Kahneman, 1981). Note that Plan A is identical to Plan C (200 live and 400 die), whereas Plan B equals Plan D (33 percent chance that all live, 67 percent chance that all die). (See Figure 13.6.) Logically, anyone who prefers Plan A should also prefer Plan C. Why then do so many prefer A and D? The answer has to do with their emotions. In the first scenario, we imagine saving 200 people. That feels good, and the possible joy of saving even more wouldn't feel that much better, so we go with the choice certain to provide a good feeling. In the second situation, the framing of the question focuses on harm. Now we imagine causing the death of 400 people. That would feel terrible, and the thought of killing 600 wouldn't feel that much worse, so we take a gamble to try to avoid the bad feeling of killing anyone. It is emotionally painful to take an action that will kill even

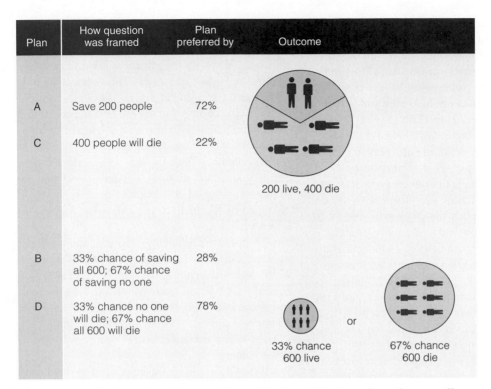

Plan	How question was framed	Plan preferred by	Outcome
A	Save 200 people	72%	
C	400 people will die	22%	

200 live, 400 die

Plan	How question was framed	Plan preferred by	Outcome
B	33% chance of saving all 600; 67% chance of saving no one	28%	
D	33% chance no one will die; 67% chance all 600 will die	78%	

33% chance 600 live   or   67% chance 600 die

FIGURE 13.6   Plan A produces the same effect as Plan C, and Plan B produces the same effect as Plan D. However, Amos Tversky and Daniel Kahneman (1981) found that most people preferred Plan A to Plan B and Plan D to Plan C. The framing of the question suggests different emotional outcomes and alters people's decisions.

one person, and multiplying the number of deaths does not multiply that emotional pain.

Judgments of Right and Wrong

Let's consider yet another moral decision. Here you don't have to decide what you should do, just whether other people have made an acceptable decision: Mark and Julie are brother and sister, college students, traveling together on a summer vacation. One night they are staying alone in a beach cabin, and they decide to have sex with each other. Julie is already taking birth control pills, but Mark uses a condom anyway. They both enjoy the experience, although they decide they will not do it again. They keep this night as their special secret, and neither

one feels hurt by the experience. In fact, they grow even closer together. So, what do you think? Was it okay for them to have sex?

Most people immediately scream, "Oh, no!!! Wrong, wrong, wrong!"

Well, okay, but *why* was it wrong? When asked, people begin searching for rational explanations of their reaction (Haidt, 2001). "It's wrong because if Julie got pregnant, that kind of inbreeding would probably produce a deformed child." But the scenario specified that they used two dependable forms of birth control, so pregnancy is not a realistic worry.

"But surely they would be emotionally scarred by the experience." This objection doesn't seem fair, either. The scenario explicitly stated that they both enjoyed it and neither was emotionally hurt. It is understandable that you might be skeptical, but if you accept what the scenario said, then Mark and Julie enjoyed the experience and were not hurt. Do you still think their act was wrong?

Even then, nearly everyone insists it was morally wrong. If you try long enough, you might propose some new, better explanation for why Mark and Julie were wrong. (For example, "Okay, you say they didn't get hurt, but the risk was huge, and people shouldn't do things with such a huge risk.") However, if you are honest, you will admit that the explanation you eventually thought of was not your reason for saying they were wrong. Your reason was that emotionally it *feels* wrong. The idea of sex between siblings is repulsive to most people in every culture, and some psychologists have even suggested that it is a built-in taboo that evolved in prehistoric times. What is striking is how hard people try to find a logical explanation for what is really an emotional decision.

Emotions also enter into many political attitudes. Consider the death penalty. Are you for it or against it? How much do you actually know about it? Is the murder rate lower in states that have the death penalty? Does the murder rate drop after a highly publicized execution? If a convicted murderer is sent to prison instead of being executed, how soon if ever would he or she be eligible for parole? How often have people been sentenced to death and later found to be innocent? How much more likely are poor people to get the death penalty than rich people, for similar crimes? On questions such as these, most people admit they "don't know" on many of the questions, and when they think they do know, they are almost as likely to be wrong as right. Moreover, most say that the facts do not matter; they could not imagine any fact that would change their attitude (Ellsworth & Ross, 1983). It is understandable that our emotions should be a major part of our attitudes here. What is striking is that facts seem almost irrelevant. Even when people do cite facts, it is as if they made up their minds first and then looked for facts to back up their opinion (Haidt, 2001).

Is it wrong to rely on emotions in decisions like these? That is really a philosophical question rather than a scientific one. If you think the "right" moral decision is the one that a computer would have reached (say, that it is morally right to save five lives by sacrificing one, even if it means shoving the wrestler off the bridge), then emotions are just getting in the way of the "right" decision. And, given people's questionable skills at estimating probabilities, our emotions sometimes push us toward some bad gambles or investments. Keep in mind, though, that scenarios like the footbridge dilemma describe unusual situations, designed so that carefully reasoned logic opposes our instincts. Presumably, emotions evolved because they provide benefits in *most* situations, and one major benefit is that they help us make quick decisions when we do not have time to analyze all the relevant data. These decisions help us to survive and produce healthy offspring. It *feels* wrong to push someone off a lifeboat or to have sex with your brother or sister, and almost all the time it really *is* a bad idea. Your emotions are not always right, but often enough they prepare you for a quick, probably useful response.

◘ Emotional Intelligence

Emotions have gotten something of a bad rap. People often think of emotions as disruptive or dangerous and pushing us toward undesirable behavior. They can certainly feel turbulent and overwhelming. Sometimes they push us toward an illogical course of action. But as we have seen, emotions also help us to make quick, generally useful decisions.

You may be wondering, "If emotions sometimes help me make decisions and sometimes interfere, how do I know when to follow my gut feelings and when to override them?" It's a good question to which there is no consistent answer, except to say that some people seem to know more often than others do. If you know when to follow your emotions, or when to show your emotions and when to suppress them, you are showing a kind of intelligence. Beginning in the 1990s, many psychologists began discussing **emotional intelligence,** the ability to recognize the meanings of emotions and their relationships and to use emotions effectively in reasoning and problem solving (Mayer, Caruso, & Salovey, 2000). The implication is that people's differences in this ability are consistent over time and situations and that emotional intelligence resembles academic intelligence in some ways but also differs in important ways.

Emotional intelligence might be important when dealing with situations like these:

- You are walking down the street when you notice a young woman sitting alone and crying on a park bench. You pause and look at her. She looks up briefly, curtly says, "Hello," and resumes crying. Should you go over and offer to help, or would she prefer to be left alone?
- You need to get to an appointment fast, and your roommate has promised to drive you. But your roommate is slow in getting ready, and you are starting to feel tense. Do you try to speed up your roommate or do you try to calm yourself down? In either case, how do you do it?
- Someone has just told you a joke that you find insulting. Do you say that the joke offends you or just fail to laugh and hope the person takes the hint?
- An attractive person smiles at you and says hello in a cheerful voice. Was this a flirtation and a signal of a potential romantic relationship? Or was it mere friendliness?
- You are sitting quietly with someone you have been dating for months. You are thinking romantic thoughts but you don't know what your partner is thinking. Would this be a good time to say for the first time, "I love you"? Or is the other person about to break up with you?

In each of these cases, the correct answer is obviously "it depends." In the first example, before you decide whether to offer help to the woman crying on the park bench, you might consider her facial expression, body language, tone of voice, any clues you can see about why she is crying, and so forth. The

right answer also depends on who you are. For example, she might be more willing to talk with a woman her own age than with a child or a middle-aged man. Similarly, in any of the other situations, you would assess the whole situation before deciding what to do. The point, however, is that you probably can think of people you know who usually make good decisions in cases like these. They look at someone and quickly discern that person's emotional state. They usually know the right thing to say or do. On the other hand, no doubt you also can think of people who make consistently bad decisions in emotional situations and invariably ignore or misread other people's emotional expressions.

The idea of emotional intelligence began attracting a good deal of attention in the 1990s, both among psychologists and in the popular press, and many people seem to agree that emotional intelligence is important, even though they are not exactly sure what it is. After all, emotions are important and intelligence is good, so emotional intelligence must be valuable too. The term has been used in many ways, however, so we need to work toward a clearer definition. Typically, researchers and theorists emphasize three major components (Mayer et al., 2000):

> *Perceiving* emotions in facial expressions, music, art, and so forth
>
> *Understanding* and reasoning about emotions
>
> *Managing* emotions, such as calming oneself down or relieving someone else's anxiety

◻ Measurements of Emotional Intelligence

As we have seen so often in this textbook, understanding and measurement of some concept support each other: The better we understand the concept, the better we know what to measure; and as we make better measurements, we increase our understanding. If we find that we cannot measure something effectively, then we have reason to question the concept itself. How has emotional intelligence been measured, and what do studies of these measures suggest about the concept?

Self-Report Measures

Psychologists have attempted to measure emotional intelligence in several ways (Ciarrochi, Chan, Caputi, & Roberts, 2001; Conte, 2005). One approach is to treat it like a personality trait and measure it with self-reports. For example, to measure the personality trait *extraversion*, psychologists ask people questions such as these:

> True or false: I have the time of my life at parties.
>
> or
>
> On a scale from 1 to 7, how much do you enjoy meeting new people?

Similarly, some psychologists have tried to measure emotional intelligence with self-report inventories. Here are a few true-false items from one such questionnaire (Austin, Saklofske, Huang, & McKenney, 2004):

> I sometimes can't tell whether someone is serious or joking.
>
> Other people find it easy to confide in me.
>
> I know what other people are feeling just by looking at them.
>
> I help other people feel better when they are down.

As you would guess, a "false" answer on the first of these items counts the same as a "true" on the next three. One problem with a test of this sort is the uncertain accuracy of people's answers. When psychologists measure extraversion, they generally trust people to report honestly how much they enjoy going to parties or meeting new people. But when someone claims to know people's feelings just by looking at them, how much should we trust that answer? Some people give themselves high ratings on

social sensitivity but get low ratings from their friends (Carney & Harrigan, 2003). It is possible to be socially insensitive and not realize it. In fact, the more insensitive you are, the less likely you are to notice your mistakes.

The best way to evaluate self-report tests of emotional intelligence is to check their predictive validity. That is, people's scores on a good test of emotional intelligence should predict how well they handle real emotional situations. Most of the research on self-reported emotional intelligence has measured its relationship to how well people *say* they handle emotional situations. That is, the studies compare one self-report to another. This approach is not ideal, but it is better than nothing. According to such studies, people with high self-reported emotional intelligence also rate themselves high on social adjustment (Engelberg & Sjöberg, 2004). They tend to be extraverted and agreeable (Warwick & Nettelbeck, 2004), and they recover better than most people do after a traumatic experience (Hunt & Evans, 2004). Workers with high self-reported emotional intelligence report higher work morale and lower job stress (Dulewicz, Higgs, & Slaski, 2003). Men with low emotional intelligence scores are more likely than others to have psychological disorders (Hemmati, Mills, & Kroner, 2004). Some studies find a significant relationship between overall emotional intelligence and overall positive mood (Schutte, Malouff, Simunek, McKenley, & Hollander, 2002), although other studies do not (Spence, Oades, & Caputi, 2004).

A few studies have related scores to actual (as opposed to self-reported) performance. In one study, people filled out an emotional intelligence questionnaire and also participated in tests of their ability to recognize as quickly as possible the emotional expressions in people's faces. People with higher emotional intelligence scores generally outperformed most other people on this task (Austin, 2004).

In short, the self-report measures do appear to be measuring something, and that something is beneficial. Problems remain, however. One is that, on the average, men in prison have higher self-reported emotional intelligence than men outside prison (Hemmati, Mills, & Kroner, 2004). The best guess is that some of the questions simply mean something different to prisoners than to others. For example, consider the item, "I know what other people are feeling just by looking at them." Maybe emotional expression in prisons is more intense and, therefore, easier to read. An alternative hypothesis is that prisoners are more confident in their ability to "read" other people, even though they are actually reading them incorrectly. Whatever the explanation, we need to worry about exactly what the test is measuring.

Another problem is that scores on self-report measures of emotional intelligence correlate fairly strongly with measurements of personality traits, such as agreeableness, extraversion, openness to new experiences, and lack of neuroticism (De Raad, 2005; Warwick & Nettelbeck, 2004). If emotional intelligence is to be a useful concept, it needs to be more than a new name for personality traits that psychologists were already measuring.

Ability Measures

The other approach to measuring emotional intelligence is to develop an ability test, comparable to IQ tests or other standardized tests. The best-known and most widely used test of this type is the **Mayer-Salovey-Caruso Emotional Intelligence Test (MS-CEIT**, pronounced "mes-keet"). Here are examples, reworded slightly from items in actual use (Mayer, Caruso, & Salovey, 2000):

1. On a scale from 1 to 5, rate the amount of each emotion in the photos you will see. For each emotion, 1 indicates "Definitely Not Present" and 5 indicates "Definitely Present."

   _____ Happiness

   _____ Anger

   _____ Fear

   _____ Sadness

   _____ Disgust

   _____ Surprise

2. A middle-aged man says his work has been piling up and he is falling behind. He works late at night and spends little time with his family. He feels guilty for spending so little time with his wife and daughter, and they feel left out. Recently a relative moved in with them after he got divorced and lost his job. After a while they told him he had to leave because they needed their privacy, but they felt bad about kicking him out.

   On a scale from 1 to 5, where 5 is highest, rate how much this man feels:

   _____ Depressed

   _____ Frustrated

   _____ Guilty

   _____ Energetic

   _____ Liking

   _____ Joyous

   _____ Happy

3. A dog runs into the street and gets hit by a car. The driver stops and the dog's owner hurries to check on the dog.

   On a scale from 1 to 5, where 5 means "extremely likely" and 1 means "extremely unlikely," how would the driver and the dog's owner probably feel?

   _____ The owner would feel angry at the driver

   _____ The owner would feel embarrassed at not training the dog better

   _____ The driver would feel guilty for not driving more carefully

   _____ The driver would feel relieved that it was dog and not a child

4. Someone you know at work looks upset. He asks you to have lunch with him, alone, in a quiet place. After a few minutes, he confides in you that he got his job by lying on his applica-

tion. Now he feels guilty and he is afraid of getting caught. What do you do?

The crucial question here is, *what are the correct answers?* On each item, you might like to answer, "It depends. I need more information!" However, you're not allowed that answer; you have to do your best with the meager information you have. We can imagine several ways of determining the right answers, but each faces serious problems (Roberts, Zeidner, & Matthews, 2001). One way is **expert scoring,** relying on the answers chosen by experts in the field, just as we would ask outstanding mathematicians to determine the correct answers on a mathematics test. However, we are not sure who are the "experts" at emotional intelligence. For want of any better choice, the psychologists doing research on emotional intelligence nominated themselves. But then something strange happened. According to their answer key, men showed slightly higher emotional intelligence than women did. That result gives us reason to scratch our heads. Most people agree that they can think of more women than men who seem to be good at emotional intelligence, given admittedly casual observations and unsystematic criteria. Also, a variety of studies show female superiority at such diverse tasks as identifying facial expressions of emotion from brief presentations (Hall & Matsumoto, 2004), interpreting other kinds of nonverbal communication (Hall, 1978; Hall & Halberstadt, 1994), foreseeing likely breakups in a dating relationship (Z. Rubin, Peplau, & Hill, 1981), and even guessing people's emotions from their smells (Chen & Haviland-Jones, 2000). On the average, women also score higher than men on self-report measures of emotional intelligence (Van Rooy, Alonso, & Viswesvaran, 2005).

What if the researchers' answers to the various questions were wrong? We shouldn't necessarily assume that researchers themselves have high emotional intelligence. After all, people who do research on vision or memory don't necessarily have outstanding vision or memory. Also, people who do research on marriage are not particularly good at identifying which couples have a happy marriage. In one study, people watched videotapes of married couples having short conversations and then guessed how happy the marriage was. The couples themselves had reported their own marital satisfaction, so there was a reasonably clear "right answer." Of all the groups tested, psychologists who had done research on marriage were *least* accurate in estimating the couples' marital satisfaction (Ebling & Levenson, 2003). People who had recently married or recently divorced did much better, on the average. The point is, if we want to use expert judgment as the criterion for some test, we have to be very careful in deciding who the experts are.

A related problem is that most people doing research on emotional intelligence have been men—mostly middle-aged white men. Therefore the "expert scoring" is based on the judgments by one kind of person. A big question is whether emotional intelligence items have any correct answer or whether the answers vary from one group to another. If we are going to rely on expert scoring, then we first need to get a diverse and representative group of "experts," and determine what kind of question, if any, has similar "correct" answers across cultures and subcultures.

A different way to determine the correct answers is **consensus-based scoring**—using the answer given by the largest number of people. That is, the most common answer is considered correct. In most cases, the consensus answer is the same as that chosen by the researchers (Mayer, Salovey, Caruso, & Sitarenios, 2003). (The emotion researchers aren't always wrong.) However, the consensus doesn't always agree with the researchers, and by consensus scoring, women consistently score higher than men do (Kafetsios, 2004). If men are motivated to "try harder," their scores improve, but on the average they still don't catch up with women (Ciarrochi, Hynes, & Crittenden, 2005).

The problem with the consensus method of scoring is that if the right answer is whatever the majority says, then the test can't include any difficult items that only "emotional geniuses" get right. For

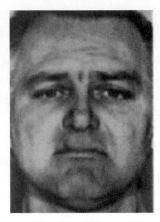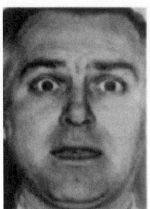

Reprinted from: Townshend, J. M. & Duka, T. (2003). Mixed emotions: Alcoholics' impairments in the recognition of specific emotional facial expressions. *Neuropsychologia, 41,* 773–782, with permission from Elsevier.

FIGURE 13.7   One way of testing people's ability to interpret facial expressions: Each of these faces is "morphed" (computer combined) between expressions of two emotions. How much happiness, sadness, anger, fear, surprise, and disgust do you see in each of these? Compare your ratings to the answer given at the end of this chapter. Source: Townshend and Duka (2003).

comparison, imagine a mathematics test in which we let people vote to determine the right answer. Because the test could not reward someone who was right when most people were wrong, it could not identify the best mathematicians. It could, however, identify the worst—those who consistently missed even easy questions that almost everyone else got right. Similarly, although the MSCEIT does not identify those with especially outstanding emotional intelligence, it does pick out those with the worst. Some have suggested that we rename it as a test of "emotional stupidity" (Roberts et al., 2001; Zeidner, Matthews, & Roberts, 2001).

In fact, there is merit in identifying people with low emotional intelligence. For example, if we ask people to identify other people's emotions from their facial expressions, as in Figure 13.7, or tone of voice, the people whose answers differ most strongly from the majority consist largely of people known to have problems with social relationships, such as:

- People with schizophrenia (Edwards, Jackson, & Pattison, 2002; Kohler et al., 2003)
- Psychopaths (Blair et al., 2004)
- People with brain damage in and near the amygdala (Adolphs, Baron-Cohen, & Tranel, 2002; H. J. Rosen et al., 2002)

- Alcoholics and recovering alcoholics (who tend to overstate the amount of fear they see in other people's faces) (Kornreich et al., 2001; Townshend & Duka, 2003)
- People who themselves have high anxiety levels (and who tend to overstate the fear they see in others) (Dowden & Allen, 1997; A. Richards et al., 2002)

It is possible to modify the consensus approach to make it a bit more flexible (McCann, Roberts, Matthews, & Zeidner, 2004). For example, suppose you read a paragraph about someone and then try to rate his depression on a 1-to-5 scale. The consensus answer is "5." The scoring system could give you full credit for an answer of 5, part credit for an answer of 4, less for 3, and so on. Another possibility: Suppose on some multiple-choice question, 55 percent choose answer C, 40 percent choose A, 4 percent choose B, and 1 percent choose D. One system would be to give .55 points to everyone who answers C, .4 points for A, and so on. In other words, the scoring system acknowledges that some "wrong" answers are better than others.

An alternative to either expert or consensus scoring is to base the correct answers on responses from **targets**—people who have had the experiences described in the test questions. For example, for the item about how a driver would feel after accidentally hitting someone's dog, we could find people who have had that experience and ask them. We could show videotapes of interviews with crime suspects, some of whom were later demonstrated to have been lying. The question then would be, "Can you identify who is lying?" We could show videotapes of discussions between married couples, some of whom later got divorced, and ask which couples appeared to be getting along better. We could show videotapes of psychiatric patients, some of whom attempted suicide a few days or weeks later, and ask what emotions each patient expressed. Target-based scoring has great potential, but so far it has not been used extensively.

Reliability and Validity of Emotional Intelligence Tests

Evaluating a test requires more than just being sure the answers are correct. Recall from Chapter 1 that psychologists evaluate tests in terms of reliability (the consistency of an individual's scores) and validity (the relationship between the scores and the behaviors we are trying to predict).

Tests of emotional intelligence, when graded according to consensus answers, yield reliabilities reported to be about .9, which is similar to other standardized psychological tests (Mayer, Salovey, Caruso, & Sitarenios, 2001). We can therefore accept that the test is measuring something, at least for the culture in which it has been used (the United States). Of course, demonstrating reliability indicates only that the test is measuring *something*, which may or may not be emotional intelligence. (For example, it might be measuring conformity.)

The issue of validity is a little different. A test has **predictive validity** if a test score accurately predicts people's behavior in another setting. In the case of emotional intelligence, valid test scores might predict how well people make decisions in emotional and social situations. One preliminary study identified teenagers with high or low scores on a test of emotional intelligence and then asked them

to describe an emotional situation in their own lives and how they handled it. First, here is an example from a 14-year-old girl with one of the lowest scores:

> "We were at a birthday party. A game was played. It was stupid, because it made me look like an idiot." [Question: How did you handle it?] "I cried and left." (Mayer, Perkins, Caruso, & Salovey, 2001, p. 135)

In contrast, here is an example from a 16-year-old girl with a very high score:

> "Once my friends wanted to sneak in someone's room and paint them while he slept. It began as joking around.... Then it slowly evolved into dares.... I felt like it was betraying the trust I had with the other person.... I know how little pranks like this could really hurt someone's feelings." [Question: How did you handle it?] "Told them straight out that it was a degrading thing to do and they shouldn't be so cruel." (Mayer, Perkins, Caruso, & Salovey, 2001, p. 136)

This result is promising because the person with the higher score certainly appears to be operating at a higher level. However, this was a preliminary study with just a few participants. Also, it is not obvious whether the test is specifically measuring emotional skills or just verbal skills.

Ideally, we would like to determine whether the emotional intelligence scores predict outcomes such as mental health, job performance, successful marriages, and overall life satisfaction. Studies of short-term outcomes are the easiest to complete, but in many ways the least satisfactory. For example, one study found that emotional intelligence scores did not correlate significantly with the impressions people made on others while working together in one brief session (Day & Carroll, 2004). Long-term studies have generally found positive but weak relationships between emotional intelligence and observed behaviors in work situations (Van Rooy & Viswesvaran, 2004). Several studies have found that people with high emotional intelligence scores have decreased probability of violence and criminal activity (Brackett, Mayer, & Warner, 2004; Mayer, 2001). These results are promising but hardly overwhelming. Psychologists disagree sharply with one another about whether emotional intelligence tests have enough validity to be useful (Daus & Ashkanasy, 2005; Locke, 2005).

An additional criterion for a good test, after reliability and validity, is that it should not overlap too much with existing tests, because if it does, it adds nothing. Self-report tests of emotional intelligence have a moderately high correlation with measurements of personality traits, such as extraversion, agreeableness, empathy, and lack of neuroticism (De Raad, 2005; Warwick & Nettelbeck, 2004) but only a low correlation with cognitive measures, such as IQ scores (Derksen, Kramer, & Katzko, 2002). Ability tests of emotional intelligence, such as the MSCEIT, correlate moderately well with cognitive measures and less strongly with personality measures (Mayer, Caruso, & Salovey, 2000; O'Connor & Little, 2003).

One study found that a combination of IQ and personality tests correlated .62 with scores on the MSCEIT—a result that becomes even more impressive when we consider the limited reliability of each of these measures (Schulte, Ree, & Caretta, 2004). Another study found that a self-report scale of emotional intelligence correlated .49 with life satisfaction, but it also correlated just as highly with extraversion and lack of neuroticism. In turn, extraversion and lack of neuroticism correlated significantly with life satisfaction. The researchers found that a combination of emotional intelligence and personality factors predicted life satisfaction just slightly better than the personality factors by themselves could (Gannon & Ranzijn, 2005).

In short, emotional intelligence, as currently measured, goes a little beyond measures of cognition and personality but only a little. Its predictive validity for long-term outcomes is positive but not high. However, those conclusions apply only to current measures. If emotional intelligence is a valuable concept, the key is to improve our measurements. Psychologists have a long history of measuring people's abilities, attitudes, and personalities with pencil-and-paper tests, and those procedures may not be well adapted for measuring emotional abilities. In a real-life emotional situation, you see, hear, and sometimes even smell information that a pencil-and-paper test cannot capture. Perhaps an adequate measure requires more realistic situations.

Is Emotional Intelligence Teachable?

It is certainly easy to point out the harm that results from poor emotional intelligence. A husband or wife says something, the other one incorrectly interprets it as hostile, and suddenly a fight erupts for no good reason (Flury & Ickes, 2001). A child on a playground misinterprets another child's facial expression or tone of voice and retreats from the playground in tears (Halberstadt, Denham, & Dunsmore, 2001). No doubt you can think of other examples.

As the concept of emotional intelligence became popular, many people set up programs to teach it or urged the schools to teach it (Elias, Hunter, & Kress, 2001). Given that we are not exactly sure what emotional intelligence is or how to measure it, you shouldn't be surprised that the early attempts to teach it produced no apparent benefits (Izard, 2001). Emotional intelligence is not something we can learn by reading about it or listening to lectures. We probably can learn it, however, in some other way. Measurements of emotional intelligence have found higher scores, on the average, for middle-aged people than for young adults (Derksen, Kramer, & Katzko, 2002; Hemmati, Mills, & Kroner, 2004; Kafetsios, 2004). The research used a cross-sectional design, so conceivably the results could represent a cohort effect. (That is, maybe people who were born in an earlier era developed more emotional intelligence than the current younger generation.) However, the more likely explanation is that as people grow older and more experienced, they learn more emotional intelligence. In contrast, general academic intelligence ("*g*") reaches its peak in the late teens and early 20s, and then starts a long, slow decline. If emotional intelligence increases over the years, it is more like expertise or "crystallized intelligence" (which can be learned) than like fluid intelligence (which is harder to increase).

If emotional intelligence can be learned, how do you learn it? One fascinating study assigned children randomly to receive drama lessons, keyboard lessons, singing lessons, or none. Afterward, the researchers tested the children's abilities to identify people's emotions from their tone of voice (which is one aspect of emotional intelligence). The children who had received either drama or keyboard lessons outperformed those with singing lessons or no lessons. The same researchers found that adults who have had musical training also excel, on the average, at recognizing emotion in other people's speech (Thompson, Schellenberg, & Husain, 2004). Presumably either drama or music lessons train people to listen carefully and attend to subtle aspects of intonation. Why keyboard lessons helped and singing lessons didn't, we don't know. We should be cautious until someone replicates this finding. The main point is that it does make sense to do research on ways of teaching emotional intelligence. Lecturing on "here's how to be emotionally intelligent" probably doesn't work, but indirect kinds of training might.

◻ Summary

When we are confronted with a sudden stimulus or when we have a decision to make, often our emotions respond quickly, before we have consciously identified the stimulus or cognitively pondered the decision. Our emotions are often a useful guide in such cases; they alert us to danger or urge us toward a quick response that is likely to be a good one. Presumably, emotions evolved precisely for this purpose, to prepare us for vigorous, usually correct responses when we have to act quickly.

The problem, of course, is that our quick emotional impulses sometimes differ from the decisions we would make if we thought out the situation logically and leisurely. The difficulty is to know when to follow our emotions and when to override them. Making that decision well is one aspect of emotional intelligence.

Most of us agree that it seems, at least to our unsystematic observations, that some people are better than others at understanding their own emotions and those of others. They control their emotions, judge when to follow their gut feelings and when not to, and so forth. As you have seen, things get tricky when we try to go beyond casual observations and specify exactly what we mean. We have dwelt on the measurement issues because they are critical. If emotional intelligence is real, there should be a reliable and valid way to measure it, and it should be something more than academic intelligence plus personality. At this point, the available measures of emotional intelligence are measuring something but not well enough to live up to the high expectations so many people still have. Future research will determine whether some better way of measuring emotional intelligence will prove to be more useful.

◻ Key Terms

consensus-based scoring: defining the correct answer to some question as the answer given by the largest number of people (p. 275)

emotional intelligence: ability to recognize the meanings of emotions and their relationships and to use emotions effectively in reasoning and problem solving (p. 272)

expert scoring: procedure of determining the correct answer by relying on the answers chosen by experts in the field (p. 275)

framing effect: tendency for people to change their decisions based on how a choice is phrased (p. 269)

Mayer-Salovey-Caruso Emotional Intelligence Test (MSCEIT): best-known and most widely used pencil-and-paper test to measure emotional intelligence (p. 274)

predictive validity: a test that accurately predicts people's behavior in another setting (p. 277)

risk-as-feelings hypothesis: proposal that people make different choices based on the emotions they feel while making a decision (p. 263)

targets: people who have had the experiences described in the test questions (p. 276)

Yerkes-Dodson law: generalization that learning is at its best when stimulation or arousal is intermediate (p. 260)

▢ Thought Questions

1. Happy people are less likely than others to gamble. One interpretation is that they are avoiding anything that might lower their happiness. Can you think of any other possible interpretation?

2. As discussed earlier regarding the framing effect, discussing a choice in terms of saving lives biases a decision maker toward choosing the sure success (which will feel good). Discussing the same choice in terms of people dying biases the decision maker toward taking a risk to avoid any deaths (which would feel bad). Can you imagine any way to phrase the question neutrally, so it does not favor one choice or the other?

▢ Suggestion for Research Project

Keep a diary of occasions when you observe examples of either good or poor emotional intelligence in those around you. Look for patterns. For example, do certain friends repeatedly show good examples while others show poor examples? Do some situations seem to encourage good emotional decisions more than others?

▢ Suggestion for Further Reading

Matthews, G., Zeidner, M., & Roberts, R. D. (2004). *Emotional intelligence: Science and myth.* Cambridge, MA: MIT Press. As the title implies, this book evaluates the evidence behind claims of emotional intelligence, separating those that the results support from those that appear unfounded.

Answers Concerning Figure 13.7

Left: Morphed to show equal parts of disgust and anger. Middle: Equal parts sadness and disgust. Right: Equal parts surprise and fear.

14

Stress and Its Health Consequences

Have you ever noticed how often people say they are "under stress?" We seem to be surrounded by stressed-out people, and sources of stress appear everywhere you look. Some stressors are blatant and extreme. Stress can be caused by a threatening world event, such as a terrorist attack, a natural disaster, such as an earthquake or flood, or the start of a war. Other stressors include serious personal and family events, such as an intense fight with a loved one, a divorce or other relationship break-up, a financial crisis, or having a relative who is seriously ill.

But not all stress comes from major events. When world events seem to be under control and no one in the family is having major problems, then people complain about the stress of meeting professional deadlines, conflict with co-workers or supervisors, keeping the house clean, getting the kids to soccer practice on time, and other day-to-day concerns. People even complain that some positive life events are stressful. For example, marriage and the birth of a child, two of the happiest times in many people's lives, are also considered stressful (Holmes & Rahe, 1977). No matter what's going on in the world, it seems people always find something to feel stressed about.

Stress can result from many kinds of events, and as Robert Sapolsky (1998) has pointed out, the prime stressors for humans today are different from those of our ancestors. Stressors for our remote ancestors tens of thousands of years ago were probably much like those of nonhuman animals today—immediate, life-and-death crises. If a fox is chasing a rabbit, the next few seconds will determine whether the rabbit lives or dies, and whether the fox eats today or not. As a result, this situation is stressful for both animals. It is a crisis, but at least when it's over, it's over.

For people today, the most common stressors are less immediate and life-threatening and more prolonged, such as difficulty paying the bills, dealing with a troubled romantic or family relationship, or taking care of a relative with a long-term health problem. Instead of resolving quickly (one way or the other), these problems can persist for weeks, months, or years, with few occasions for feeling relief. Because the human "fight-or-flight response" evolved to deal with scenarios like the fox-rabbit chase, rather than credit card bills, our bodies react to these prolonged, daily problems as if we were running or fighting for our lives. Our reactions are sometimes inappropriate, and our health suffers.

In this chapter, we will discuss what the various stressors have in common—what exactly is "stress"?—and will consider the research on the effect of stress on health. What are the biological effects of short-term stress? What happens when these effects add up over time? Are some kinds of stress worse for health than others? In Chapter 15, we will discuss emotion regulation, or the ways in which people deliberately try to change their emotions, including ways of avoiding, reducing, and recovering from stress.

◻ Stress and Emotion: Definition and Measurement

You might be wondering: "What is a chapter about stress doing in a textbook on emotion?" If we were to ask you whether fear, anger, sadness, and love are emotions, you would probably say "yes" with little hesitation—most people do (e.g., Shaver et al., 1987). Even though the status of contempt, pride, and shame is somewhat controversial among researchers, most laypeople agree that these are emotions as well. Is stress an emotion? Stress is not on any psychologist's list of emotions of which we are aware. Nevertheless, it has enormous impact on people's emotions, as well as on their well-being. In the medical field, the concept of stress has received a great deal of attention, with hundreds of studies asking whether stress is associated with greater susceptibility to various health problems.

Think of it this way: If stress is not a distinct emotion, is it *emotional*? Very! Working backward, is fear stressful? Yes. Is anger stressful? Yes. How about sadness? This is a somewhat less clear-cut example, but the death of a loved one is the prototypical elicitor of sadness in many studies, and it is also considered one of the greatest stressors a person can experience. The situations in which we feel these emotions overlap greatly with the situations that cause stress. Perhaps what we call "stress" really reflects some common features of emotions such as

fear, anger, and grief. To draw a conclusion about the role of emotion in stress, we must evaluate several definitions of the latter term—what do we really mean when we talk about "stress"?

Selye's Concept of Stress

Unlike the concept of emotion, the biological and psychological concept of stress is relatively recent. As with many advances in science, however, it was discovered largely by accident. The story is a great one, and it offers lessons about the importance of observation and ingenuity in science, as well as about stress (Sapolsky, 1998).

Hundreds of years ago, medical doctors treated most illnesses in the same way. When someone was ill, they would suggest bed rest, perhaps apply leeches to withdraw "excess" blood, and recommend herbs or "cure-all" tonics. The great progress of scientific medicine over the past century or so depended on distinguishing one disease from another, so that today the recommended treatment depends on which disease you have.

In spite of the differences among diseases, when Hans Selye (Figure 14.1) was in medical school, he noticed that almost all patients have many symptoms in common. Regardless of their specific symptoms, nearly all have a fever, loss of appetite, sleepiness, decreased activity levels, decreased sex drive, and various changes in their immune systems. Years later, Selye was doing research with laboratory rats, testing whether a particular kind of substance tended to cause cancer. As a good scientist, he administered the substance (by injection) into half of the rats on a regular basis and injected a saline solution into the remaining rats as a control group. He was expecting that, when he checked the rats for cancer after some months, the group given the experimental treatment would have an unusually high rate of cancer. He was right, but was surprised to find that his control rats *also* had a remarkably high rate of cancer!

It turns out that Selye, though a brilliant scientist, was not especially good at giving injections to

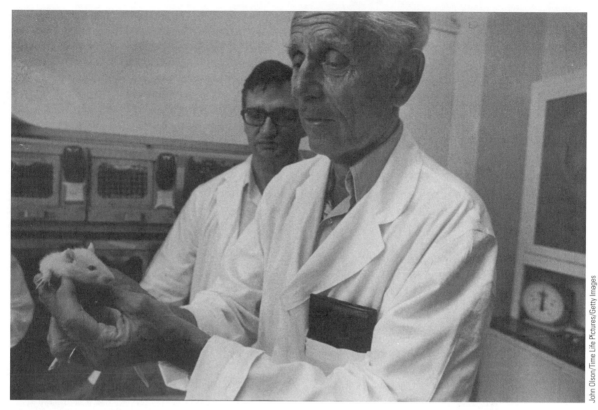

FIGURE 14.1   Hans Selye (1907–1982), an Austrian-born Canadian physician who became a great pioneer in the study of stress.

rats. When trying to administer the shots to both groups of rats, he would frequently miss the injection spot, get bitten, drop the rat, chase it around the room, and generally (though unintentionally) torment the poor creature. When he compared rats he had injected with the rats a more skilled research assistant had injected, it turned out that Selye's rats were more likely to have developed cancer. Presumably the way he had handled them caused stress, which increased their risk of cancer. In following up on this lead, Selye noticed that either prolonged heat or prolonged cold increased the rats' heart rate and breathing rate, enlarged their adrenal glands, weakened their immune system, and increased their risk of stomach ulcers and other illnesses. He found the same pattern after rats were exposed to pain, poisons, enforced activity (such as confinement to a motorized running wheel), or frightening stimuli (such as a cat or a larger, more aggressive rat).

Selye concluded that each kind of challenge to the body produced its own specific effects, but also produced more general effects, which were due to the body's efforts to fight the problem. He described the body's reaction to any threat as the **General Adaptation Syndrome,** which he said progressed through three stages—alarm, resistance, and exhaustion. **Alarm** is a brief period of high arousal of the sympathetic nervous system, readying the body for vigorous activity. **Resistance** is a stage of prolonged but moderate arousal. During resistance, the adrenal cortex secretes hormones that enable body cells to maintain high, steady levels of activity, heal wounds, and fight infections. With even more severe challenges, the body enters the stage of **exhaustion,** characterized by weakness, fatigue, loss of appetite, and lack of interest. The body's prolonged fight against its threats has weakened its ability to do anything else. For example, the immune system becomes less active and the individual becomes more vulnerable to illness. Exactly when someone moves from one stage of response to another is difficult to predict, and the transition between one stage and the next is gradual, but the data now strongly confirm the idea that short-term responses to stress differ from long-term responses.

Eventually Selye introduced the term *stress* to refer to the General Adaptation Syndrome. Selye was not the first to use the term stress, but he greatly popularized it and changed what people meant by it. **Stress,** according to Selye's definition, is the nonspecific response of the body to any demand made upon it. The analogy is to a metal: Every time you bend a metal, you weaken it. After you have bent it, bending it *back* also weakens it. Similarly, according to Selye, any major change in your life stresses you by demanding that *you* change, like bending a metal. Changing in any direction—pleasant or unpleasant—stresses you, and changing back stresses you also.

Is this the best definition of stress? To evaluate the definition, we follow its consequences and see what phenomena it explains, as well as what problems may arise.

The Social Readjustment Rating Scale

If Selye's definition is a useful one, then a good way to measure stress is to examine all the changes that have occurred in someone's life. Researchers have developed several questionnaires based on this assumption, each with its own strengths and weaknesses (Sarason, Johnson, & Siegel, 1979). We shall consider one of them in detail, as an example of the others.

An influential pioneering study devised a checklist to measure people's stress by how many life-change items they checked (T. H. Holmes & Rahe, 1967). The researchers began by assembling a list of major personal changes. Based on Selye's concept, the authors included both undesirable events (such as death of a loved one, divorce, or losing one's job) and desirable events that cause upheaval (such as marriage, birth of a child, or taking a vacation). They also included items such as "change in financial state" where *change* could refer to either an increase or a decrease. Again, the assumption was that changing something in life is like bending a metal—a movement in either direction is stressful.

Because various changes are not equally stressful, they should not count equally. The researchers asked more than 300 people to assign 100 points to "death of a spouse," and then to rate how stressful each of the other life changes would be in comparison. They computed the averages, developing the Social Readjustment Rating Scale (SRRS), as Table 14.1 shows. Note, for example, that divorce rates 73 points, indicating that on the average, people thought a divorce would be about 73 percent as stressful as death of a spouse. At the low end, a traffic ticket gets 11 points and surviving Christmas or a vacation gets 12 or 13 points.

Obviously these results are specific to a particular time and place. Christmas is irrelevant in cultures that do not celebrate it, and reference to a "mortgage over $10,000" sounds quaint today, when people can run up higher debts on their credit cards in a few months. In the 1970s, the life event "wife begins or stops work" sounded stressful to most people; today we gasp at the sexist implications of the item. Still, in its time and place, this questionnaire was certainly measuring some of the major changes people were likely to encounter. Anyone taking the questionnaire would check off all the events that happened within, say, the last 6 or 12 months, and a psychologist would total the points associated with all the checked events. For example, if you checked "begin or end school," "change in sleeping habits," "change in eating habits," and "va-

TABLE 14.1 The original Social Readjustment Rating Scale (T. H. Holmes & Rahe, 1967). To measure your stress level, check the events you have experienced recently and total their point values.

Rank	Life Event	Point Value	Rank	Life Event	Point Value
1.	Death of spouse	100	23.	Son or daughter leaving home	29
2.	Divorce	73	24.	Trouble with in-laws	29
3.	Marital separation	65	25.	Outstanding personal achievement	28
4.	Jail term	63	26.	Wife begins or stops work	26
5.	Death of close family member	63	27.	Begin or end school	26
6.	Personal injury or illness	53	28.	Change in living conditions	25
7.	Marriage	50	29.	Revision of personal habits	24
8.	Fired at work	47	30.	Trouble with boss	23
9.	Marital reconciliation	45	31.	Change in work hours or conditions	20
10.	Retirement	45	32.	Change in residence	20
11.	Change in health of family member	44	33.	Change in school	20
12.	Pregnancy	40	34.	Change in recreation	19
13.	Sex difficulties	39	35.	Change in church activities	19
14.	Gain of new family member	39	36.	Change in social activities	18
15.	Business readjustment	39	37.	Mortgage or loan less than $10,000	17
16.	Change in financial state	38	38.	Change in sleeping habits	16
17.	Death of close friend	37	39.	Change in number of family get-togethers	15
18.	Change to different line of work	36	40.	Change in eating habits	15
19.	Change in number of arguments with spouse	35	41.	Vacation	13
20.	Mortgage over $10,000	31	42.	Christmas	12
21.	Foreclosure of mortgage or loan	30	43.	Minor violations of the law	11
22.	Change in responsibilities at work	29			

Source: Reprinted from *Journal of Psychosomatic Research,* Vol. 11, pp. 213–218, "Social Readjustment Rating Scale" by Holmes & Rahe. © 1967, with permission from Elsevier.

cation," you would have 70 points, a low total. Many studies found that the higher someone's point total, the higher their probability of health problems.

However, before we draw any conclusion from such correlations, note a major problem: The questionnaire awards 53 points for "personal injury or illness" and additional points for changes in sleeping or eating habits, which are common symptoms of illness. Granted, being sick can be stressful, but if we give stress points for being sick, then it's hardly surprising that people with many stress points are more likely than other people to be sick.

A more fundamental problem: Selye defined stress in terms of life *changes.* So, according to that definition, suddenly *becoming* blind, deaf, or impov-

erished would be stressful, but a lifetime of blindness, deafness, or poverty would not be. Victims of racism or other kinds of prejudice describe their experience as stressful, and data suggest they suffer health problems as a result (R. Clark, Anderson, Clark, & Williams, 1999; Contrada et al., 2000). An unchanging pattern of unfair treatment does not count as stress under Selye's definition, however, and the original SRRS did not measure it.

Still another problem: In accord with Selye's concept of stress, the SRRS awards the same number of points for a change in either direction. For example, a family member becoming more healthy counts the same as one becoming more ill; fewer arguments with your spouse counts as much as more arguments; and having more money is considered just as stressful as having less. Surely something is wrong here. Also, the scale omits many issues that have become more widely recognized since the time of the original survey, such as becoming a single parent, employment discrimination, and sexual abuse.

The Revised Social Readjustment Rating Scale

Because of the limitations of the original questionnaire, later researchers developed a revised version (Hobson et al., 1998), which appears in Table 14.2. The instruction is to check the items you have experienced in the last 12 months and then add up the corresponding points. For a large representative sample of U.S. adults, the median total score was 145 (Hobson & Delunas, 2001). Therefore, if your total is above 145, you have had more stress in your recent life than most other people; if your score is below 145, you have had less. However, the distribution of scores is not a neat bell-shaped curve. About one-fourth of all people report scores of zero, and more than 5 percent report scores above a thousand. Although the median is 145, the mean is 278.

The revised scale is certainly an improvement over the original, although it continues to give points for "major injury/illness to self." It does not include every major stressor we could imagine—no questionnaire of reasonable length could—but it includes enough that it probably applies to most people. However, it still contains a number of problems. The instrument adds points for various minor stressors, but may weight them too heavily. Suppose you graduate from college (26 points), get some unexpected money (33), move to a new address (35), and then start a new job (43). Those events give you a total of 137 points—far more than you would get for a divorce (71) or the death of a husband or wife (87). Should a series of minor stressors count as much as or more than one major stressor? Probably not (Birbaum & Sotoodeh, 1991).

Another problem is the ambiguity of certain items. Consider, for example, the item "Major dis-agreement with boss/coworker." What you consider major may not be the same as someone else. Also consider "involved in auto accident." Would you count a mere fender-bender? Any questionnaire has some ambiguities, and the revised SRRS has fewer than the original, but the worry remains that people who are feeling bad—perhaps because they are ill—may be more likely than others to check some of the uncertain items. One study found that people with certain illnesses report experiencing more stressful events than average both before and after their illness (Kilpelainen, Koskenvuo, Helenius, & Terho, 2002). Although it is possible that they simply have a stressful life style, it is also possible that they tend to complain more or to list some slightly stressful events that other people would shrug off.

Yet another problem is inherent in almost any questionnaire of this type: The stressfulness of an event depends on individual circumstances. For example, the stressfulness of a pregnancy is surely different for a 27-year-old woman who wants a baby than for a 16-year-old who doesn't. Being laid off from work could be a catastrophe for a 50-year-old who loved the job and expects to have trouble finding another one; it means almost nothing to an 18-year-old who was planning to quit next week anyway to start college. You might have a strong stress response even when nothing objectively changes. For example, suppose you expect a promotion at work, you tell all your friends that you are about to get promoted, and then you don't get the promotion. Nothing has changed in your life, and you won't qualify for any check mark on this questionnaire, but you could still find the experience highly stressful. Thus, the SRRS is intended to measure stress, but it actually measures events, and the relationship between personal events and felt stress varies substantially from person to person and from situation to situation.

As Richard Lazarus (1977) pointed out, the stressfulness of an event depends on how people interpret the event and what they think they can do about it. Measuring the stressfulness of an event *to the individual* is obviously critical but virtually impossible with a brief questionnaire. One approach,

TABLE 14.2   The Revised Social Readjustment Rating Scale (Hobson et al., 1998).

Rank	Life Event	Point Value	Rank	Life Event	Point Value
1.	Death of spouse/mate	87	27.	Experiencing employment discrimination/sexual harassment	48
2.	Death of close family member	79	28.	Attempting to modify addictive behavior of self	47
3.	Major injury/illness to self	78	29.	Discovering/attempting to modify addictive behavior of close family member	46
4.	Detention in jail or other institution	76			
5.	Major injury/illness to close family member	72	30.	Employer reorganization/downsizing	45
6.	Foreclosure on loan/mortgage	71	31.	Dealing with infertility/miscarriage	44
7.	Divorce	71	32.	Getting married/remarried	43
8.	Being a victim of crime	70	33.	Changing employers/careers	43
9.	Being the victim of police brutality	69	34.	Failure to obtain/qualify for a mortgage	42
10.	Infidelity	69	35.	Pregnancy of self/spouse/mate	41
11.	Experiencing domestic violence/sexual abuse	69	36.	Experiencing discrimination/harassment outside the workplace	39
12.	Separation or reconciliation with spouse/mate	66	37.	Release from jail	39
13.	Being fired/laid off/unemployed	64	38.	Spouse/mate begins/ceases work outside the home	38
14.	Experiencing financial problems/difficulties	62	39.	Major disagreement with boss/co-worker	37
15.	Death of close friend	61	40.	Change in residence	35
16.	Surviving a disaster	59	41.	Finding appropriate child care/day care	34
17.	Becoming a single parent	59	42.	Experiencing a large unexpected monetary gain	33
18.	Assuming responsibility for sick or elderly loved one	56	43.	Changing positions (transfer, promotion)	33
19.	Loss of or major reduction in health insurance/benefits	56	44.	Gaining a new family member	33
20.	Self/close family member being arrested for violating the law	56	45.	Changing work responsibilities	32
21.	Major disagreement over child support/custody/visitation	53	46.	Child leaving home	30
22.	Experiencing/involved in auto accident	53	47.	Obtaining a home mortgage	30
23.	Being disciplined at work/demoted	53	48.	Obtaining a major loan other than home mortgage	30
24.	Dealing with unwanted pregnancy	51			
25.	Adult child moving in with parent/parent moving in with adult child	50	49.	Retirement	28
26.	Child develops behavior or learning problem	49	50.	Beginning/ceasing formal education	26
			51.	Receiving a ticket for violating the law	22

Source: From "Stressful Life Events" by Charles J. Hobson et al. in *International Journal of Stress Management*, 5 (1998), pp. 1–23. Reprinted with permission of the author.

which does not really get around that problem but at least helps, is to measure not only the difficulties in life, but also the good things—that is, both the "hassles" and the "uplifts." Examples of uplifts include good times with friends and family, feeling a sense of accomplishment from doing something well, and having a good meal (Kanner, Coyne, Schaefer, & Lazarus, 1981). Presumably, what matters in life is not just the stressful events but also the balance between the stressors and the positive experiences.

TABLE 14.3   An example of a checklist including both negative and positive events, which are assumed to compete against one another (Kanner et al., 1981)

Hassles	Uplifts
1. Concerns about weight	1. Relating well with your spouse or lover
2. Health of a family member	2. Relating well with friends
3. Rising prices of common goods	3. Completing a task
4. Home maintenance	4. Feeling healthy
5. Too many things to do	5. Getting enough sleep
6. Misplacing or losing things	6. Eating out
7. Yard work or outside home maintenance	7. Meeting your responsibilities
8. Property, investment, or taxes	8. Visiting, phoning, or writing someone
9. Crime	9. Spending time with family
10. Physical appearance	10. Home (inside) pleasing to you

Source: From "Comparison of 2 Models of Stress Management," by Kanner et al., in *Journal of Behavioral Medicine*, Vol. 4, pp. 1–39. © 1981. Reprinted with permission from Springer Science and Business Media.

Table 14.3 shows an example of a checklist including both stressors ("hassles") and positive events ("uplifts"). Note that this approach contradicts Selye's assumption that positive and negative events are equally stressful.

Because of all of the conceptual issues raised by these problems in measuring stress, contemporary theorists have been moving away from Selye's definition. According to Bruce McEwen (2000, p. 173), **stress** is "an event or events that are interpreted as threatening to an individual and which elicit physiological and behavioral responses." Note three key points about this definition: First, Selye defined stress in terms of the body's reaction to change in a person's life; McEwen defined it in terms of the event. This ambiguity in the meaning of the word *stress* sometimes causes problems. Second, Selye's definition included all kinds of changes in life, including pleasant ones. McEwen's definition is limited to threatening events. Third, McEwen's definition emphasizes that stress depends on how the individual *interprets* an event, not just the event itself. For example, not getting a promotion might or might not be stressful, depending on someone's expectations. Or suppose you see your professor sitting in the library grading term papers. On one pa-per, the professor scowls and writes lots of red marks to indicate errors. If you think the professor is reading *your* paper, you will be stressed. If you think it is someone else's, you won't be bothered at all.

▢ How Stress Can Affect Health

Selye's original definition of stress reflected the context in which he studied it—the effect of certain kinds of experiences on physical health. Much, if not most, of the later research on stress has also emphasized its role in illness. Researchers have often bypassed issues of the subjective aspects of stress and asked how stressful experiences affect physiology and health. In this way, researchers can identify stressful situations and then examine the mechanisms by which the stressors alter physiology and health. Some of these mechanisms relate to how people think about the situations they face, but researchers also sometimes focus purely on the body's reactions, regardless of what caused them.

There is little question that stress is associated with increased risks to health. People have long observed that if a couple has been together for many years, the death of one leaves the other vulnerable to a wide variety of illnesses, ranging from dental problems (Hugoson, Ljungquist, & Breivik, 2002) to cancer (Lillberg et al., 2003). After the death of one spouse, the other has a 40- to 50-percent higher than usual probability of also dying in the next six months, compared to other people of the same age (Manor & Eisenbach, 2003). People also tend to get sick after other, less severe changes. For example, many students describe their first year of college as a stressful time (Gall, Evans, & Bellerose, 2000), and many of them develop health problems (Fazio & Powell, 1997).

Over the years, many scientists and physicians have resisted the idea that a psychological state such as "stress" could significantly influence physical health. It sounded fuzzy, unscientific, and aligned with sloppy beliefs about "mind over matter." In some cases, people went to great lengths to explain the apparent effects of stress in terms of some feature of the material environment. For example, uninjured soldiers returning from war sometimes report a variety of emotional and physical problems that used to be called "battle fatigue" or "shell shock" and would now be called "post-traumatic stress disorder" (Lamprecht & Sack, 2002). Although we now accept that these symptoms are the result of extreme emotional strain, some physicians preferred the explanation that they were harmed by "ionized air caused by cannonballs whistling by" (McMahon, 1975). The skeptics wanted to know, if stress does affect health, then *how* does it have this effect? In what way could fleeting emotions, however unpleasant, actually cause damage to the body?

We hope to have convinced you by now that emotions are very physical. Fear is not just a feeling you have inside—it includes a racing heart, tense muscles, increased blood pressure, a distinct facial expression, and several other clearly physical reactions. People who cannot feel these reactions have very little sense of emotion, as we saw in Chapter 1. According to both Selye's and McEwen's definitions, stress is physical as well. The questions then are,

what are the physical aspects of stress, and what might be the long-term health effects?

Indirect Effects of Stress on Health

Given that people who report being under much stress have an increased risk of health problems, can we conclude that stress directly causes illness? Not exactly. Many of the people under the greatest levels of stress also suffer from poverty, substance abuse, or other problems that can impair health independently of the stress (Gallo & Matthews, 2003; Repetti, Taylor, & Seeman, 2002).

Furthermore, stress can correlate with health problems because stress alters behavior, and certain behaviors can lead to health problems. For example, consider the health problems of people whose husband or wife recently died. During that period of intense mourning, they eat little, don't enjoy their meals, and lose weight precipitously (Shahar, Schultz, Shahar, & Wing, 2001). They don't sleep much, either, and often awaken with bad dreams. They may forget to take their medications. If they start to feel sick, they don't go to the doctor, so a small problem grows into a big one. Many, especially males, try to escape by drinking alcohol excessively (Byrne, Raphael, & Arnold, 1999). True, the stressful experience led to the loss of appetite, sleeplessness, alcohol abuse, and so forth, yet the point is that the health problems were not exactly the result of the stress itself but instead the result of what the person did about the stress.

Consider also the health problems common among first-year college students. Yes, they report increased stress, but the relation between stress and illness could be partly coincidental. After entering college, students have a change of diet, change of sleeping habits, and exposure to hundreds of people who may be carrying contagious diseases. Many also start or increase their use of alcohol and other drugs. Each of these behavioral changes incurs health risks. In a case like this, researchers cannot easily separate the effects of stress from those of other simultaneous influences.

A fascinating study examined the long-term consequences of highly stressful childhood experiences. Researchers sent questionnaires to thousands of adults, asking them about childhood experiences, current behaviors, and current health. Slightly more than half of the respondents reported at least one such childhood experience as sexual abuse, physical abuse that resulted in injury, living with an alcoholic parent, or watching their father physically abuse their mother. The greater the variety of such experiences they reported, the greater the variety of high-risk adult behaviors they reported. That is, those with many abusive childhood experiences were more likely than others to smoke, drink alcohol excessively, use illegal drugs, become obese, and engage in unprotected sex with many partners—all behaviors that seriously threaten physical health. Not surprisingly, they were also more likely than most other people to be in poor health (Felitti et al., 1998). This study suggests that the intensely stressful experiences some people had during childhood had led to high-risk behaviors, which were the more immediate, or "proximal," causes of illness. In this model, the stress is referred to as a "distal" cause of the illness—a cause that has its effect through some other factor, rather than directly.

Direct Effects of Stress on Health

Aside from indirect effects, however, intense, prolonged, or repeated bouts of stress can also impair health more directly by inducing immediate physiological changes.

One difficulty in discussing the effects of stress on health is that the term *stress* has multiple meanings in the English language. According to McEwen's definition, it refers to an event, such as an insult or injury. According to Selye, stress is the body's reaction to an event. Sometimes people use the term to refer to the consequences of the body's reaction. To decrease this ambiguity, Bruce McEwen (2000, 2002) has introduced the words *allostasis* and *allostatic load*.

The term *allostasis* is related to *homeostasis,* a term long familiar in biology and medicine. **Homeostasis** (from Greek roots meaning "same" and "standing") refers to the tendency of many body variables to remain nearly constant over time. For example, the combined concentration of solutes within the body's fluids remains virtually constant under nearly all circumstances. However, as McEwen pointed out, the body adjusts many other variables depending on circumstances. Body temperature rises a fraction of a degree during the afternoon and falls at night. Insulin levels rise after a meal and fall during times of fasting. In some animal species, body weight increases during the fall to prepare for hibernation. **Allostasis** (from Greek roots meaning "variable" and "standing") refers to adaptive changes in the way the body regulates its levels of various chemicals and activities in the face of some threat or change in the environment.

The relevance to stress is that a stressful event changes many of the body's activities. Heart rate and breathing rate increase, the adrenal gland secretes more epinephrine, the immune system becomes more active, and so forth. In effect, the body resets all of these levels to prepare to fight an illness or injury of whatever type might develop. Allostasis is ordinarily a helpful response, and one advantage of the term is that *allostasis* doesn't have the mostly negative connotations of the term *stress*. However, if the allostatic response continues strongly for some time, it becomes less helpful and more costly. The aggregate cost from an excessive or prolonged response is called **allostatic load**. For the rest of this chapter, we shall use the term *stress* to refer to the event, *allostasis* to mean the body's adaptive response to a stressful event, and *allostatic load* to refer to the cost or damage from the body's prolonged response.

Short-Term Allostasis (Selye's Alarm and Resistance Stages)

A sudden emotional stimulus arouses the autonomic nervous system, especially the sympathetic nervous system (Figure C.1, see inside cover). You have already encountered sympathetic nervous system effects in previous chapters—increased heart rate,

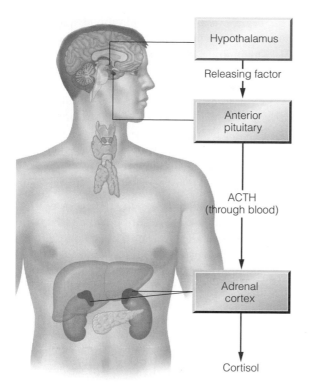

Cortisol

FIGURE 14.2   The hypothalamus-anterior pituitary-adrenal cortex axis. Stress leads to secretion of the hormone cortisol from the adrenal gland. Cortisol elevates blood sugar and increases metabolism.

breathing rate, sweating, and epinephrine secretions, as well as decreased digestive activity. That fight-or-flight response readies the body for vigorous, emergency actions, but the body cannot maintain emergency readiness for long. Even in an ongoing tense situation, sympathetic arousal gradually fades.

With continuing arousal needed to combat some challenge, a second system kicks in: the **HPA axis**, composed of the hypothalamus, pituitary gland, and adrenal cortex, as Figure 14.2 shows. The hypothalamus reacts to a stressful event by sending a releasing hormone to the anterior pituitary gland, which in turn secretes the hormone adrenocorticotropic hormone (ACTH). ACTH travels through the bloodstream to the adrenal cortex (part of the adrenal gland, located adjacent to each kidney). The adrenal cortex responds to ACTH by releasing the

hormone **cortisol,** which enhances metabolism and increases the availability of fuels. The body stores fuels in the form of carbohydrates, fats, and proteins; cortisol mobilizes all three types of fuel to come out of storage and enter the bloodstream. That activity is helpful up to a point, but muscles are the source of protein. That is, when cortisol provides your circulation with extra protein, it does so by breaking down your muscles. You don't want that process to continue for too long.

As with the sympathetic nervous system, the HPA axis readies the body for vigorous action, but it responds more slowly and lasts longer. That is, it readies the body for a more prolonged struggle, such as a difficult job, a tense relationship with someone you meet every day, living near a war zone, or simply worrying about everything that might go wrong. However, although the HPA axis prepares the body for a prolonged struggle, people fighting a prolonged struggle do not feel constantly vigorous. Frequently, they feel withdrawn or depressed, their performance is inconsistent, and they complain of decreased quality of life (Evans, Bullinger, & Hygge, 1998).

Cortisol is often described as a "stress hormone" because of its close relationship with the allostatic response to stress. In fact, researchers sometimes measure cortisol levels to gauge someone's stress level. That approach is reasonable, if we remember a few cautions. First, cortisol levels fluctuate substantially from one time of day to another, so we have to separate the effects of stress from changes due to the time of testing (Bremner et al., 2003). Second, we need to remember that cortisol measures a person's *reaction* to the stress and does not measure the stress itself. That is, some people react more strongly than others to a given event. Third, how strongly people react at first is no guarantee of how long their stress response will last. The ability to withstand stress or recover from it quickly has been referred to as **resilience** (Beasley, Thompson, & Davidson, 2003; Borella et al., 1999). Giving it a name is no explanation, of course, but a name at least calls attention to the fact that many people snap back from stress better than one might imagine. For years, most psychologists and psychiatrists assumed that anyone who suffered through severe emotional distress was on the way to post-traumatic stress disorder. Later research, however, indicated that most people recover well, even without therapy (Harvey & Bryant, 2002). The next chapter will discuss in more detail psychologists' attempts to explain why people differ so much in their reactions to stress.

A brief or moderate elevation of cortisol not only elevates blood sugar levels but also stimulates parts of the immune system, helping to fight off illnesses ranging from viruses to tumors (Benschop et al., 1995; F. Cohen et al., 1999; Connor & Leonard, 1998). Brief stressful events arouse the brain also, improving attention and memory formation (Diamond, Bennett, Fleshner, & Rose, 1992). A small dose of cortisol also improves memory (Abercrombie, Kalin, Thurow, Rosenkranz, & Davidson, 2003), and damage to the adrenal glands greatly impairs rats' performance on complex memory tasks (Mizoguchi, Ishige, Takeda, Aburada, & Tabira, 2004). The implication is that a mildly stressful event enhances memory partly by causing the adrenal glands to release cortisol and related hormones. However, more intense stress and higher levels of stress hormones impair memory (Kuhlmann, Piel, & Wolf, 2005).

Additionally, when the hypothalamus sends messages via the pituitary gland to stimulate cortisol release, it also sends messages to activate the locus coeruleus, a small area in the hindbrain (Jedema & Grace, 2004). The locus coeruleus sends axons that release norepinephrine diffusely throughout the brain, facilitating the storage of memories (Cirelli, Pompeiano, & Tononi, 1996). In other words, the best goal is not to aim for a stress-free life (even if this were possible). A small to moderate amount of stress is a good stimulant to your circulation, your immune system, and your memory.

An Overview of the Immune System

Although brief or moderate stress stimulates many helpful processes, a prolonged allostatic load gradually weakens many aspects of the immune system.

Let's begin by examining the immune system and then consider in more detail how stress affects it.

The **immune system** is a family of mechanisms that defend against bacteria, viruses, tumors, and other invaders (Kiecolt-Glaser & Glaser, 1993; O'Leary, 1990). A major part of the immune system consists of **leukocytes,** commonly known as white blood cells, which form in several parts of the body. The body has several kinds of leukocytes, including B cells, T cells, and natural killer cells:

- **B cells**, which mature mostly in the bone marrow, contribute to immunity mainly by producing antibodies. An **antibody** is a Y-shaped protein that attaches specifically to one kind of antigen, just as a key fits a lock, and an **antigen** (antibody-generating molecule) is a protein on the surface of a cell. Each individual has a characteristic set of antigens. That is, only an identical twin would have exactly the same set of antigens you do. B cells examine each cell they encounter, and if they find an antigen that they do not recognize as "self," they produce an antibody to attack it.
- **T cells** mature in the thymus gland. Several kinds of T cells attack intruders, and some help other T cells or B cells to multiply.
- **Natural killer cells**, another kind of leukocytes, attack tumor cells and cells that are infected with viruses. Unlike B and T cells, which attack a particular kind of intruder, natural killer cells unspecifically attack a wide variety of intruders.

Leukocytes and other cells secrete small proteins called **cytokines** in response to infection. Cytokines directly attack intruder cells but also serve other functions. They facilitate the production and activity of T cells, and they communicate with the brain (Kronfol & Remick, 2000). The cytokines produced by the organs stimulate the vagus nerve, one of the important nerves of the interior of the body, and the vagus nerve relays a message to stimulate release of cytokines in the brain. The process is like sending a fax; the paper you fax doesn't travel, but it initiates actions that produce a copy in the other location. In this case, the leukocytes send the fax, which the brain receives.

The cytokines released in the brain then produce a variety of responses that help fight disease. Among those responses are sleepiness (Ram et al., 1997), fever (Ek et al., 2001), inactivity, decreased appetite, and decreased sex drive—the very symptoms originally identified by Hans Selye as a medical student. These adaptations help to conserve energy, so the body can devote more of its resources to fighting the disease. Perhaps you have thought of fever as something a disease does to you, but in fact, it is something your body does to fight the disease. Many kinds of bacteria reproduce faster at normal body temperature than at feverish temperatures, and a mild fever (up to 39°C/103°F) actually increases someone's probability of surviving the infection (Kluger, 1991).

Prolonged Allostasis (Selye's Exhaustion Stage) and the Immune System

For a given individual, the levels of various kinds of immune cells and their activity are fairly consistent over long periods of time (Burleson et al., 2002), but they can fluctuate temporarily as a result of injury, illness, or stress. Stress affects the immune system in several ways. First, the body treats a sudden stressful experience like an illness and mobilizes the immune system. To be more precise, brief stress activates certain parts of the immune system, such as the natural killer cells, the leukocyte scavengers, and the secretion of cytokines (Segerstrom & Miller, 2004). Even brief bouts of fear or anger stimulate many aspects of immune system response (Mayne, 1999). Many college students have increased immune system activity during final exams, generally a stressful time (Liu et al., 2002). Rats subjected to inescapable shocks develop a fever, sleep much more than usual, and decrease their appetite and sex drive. People who feel much stress, such as those who are nervous about giving a public speech, show some of the same signs (Maier & Watkins, 1998). So, if you have been under a great deal of stress and start to feel ill, one possibility is that the only problem is the stress itself; the stress simply makes you feel sick.

Is the body "making a mistake" by acting sick when it is merely under stress? The response traces to our evolutionary history, so probably not: Most of the highly stressful events throughout the animal kingdom, including the stressors our own ancestors faced, have been situations in which an injury is likely. When your brain identifies some situation as intensely stressful, enough to activate your allostatic responses, in effect it tells the immune system, "Get ready for a probable injury!" For the next few minutes, all of your energy is mobilized for fast muscle movement. But after that, cytokines spring into action, you develop a fever, digestive and sex systems "turn off" to conserve your energy, your leukocytes proliferate, and in other ways you prepare for injuries and infections.

Although your initial allostatic response to a stressor activates your immune system, prolonged allostatic load weakens it (Segerstrom & Miller, 2004; Zorrilla et al., 2001). For example, production of natural killer cells is suppressed in women taking care of a husband with terminal cancer, women who became widows recently, survivors of a major earthquake, and medical students during final exams week (Glaser, Rice, Speicher, Stout, & Kiecholt-Glaser, 1986; Inoue-Sakurai, Maruyama, & Morimoto, 2000; Irwin, Daniels, Risch, Bloom, & Weiner, 1988).

The result? Increased chance of illness. In one study, volunteers reported their recent stressful experiences before being injected with a common cold virus. People who reported seriously stressful experiences lasting more than a month were more likely than others to become ill, presumably because their prolonged allostasis had weakened their immune response (S. Cohen et al., 1998). In a follow-up study, people answered personality questionnaires before being exposed to a cold virus. Those who reported higher levels of sociability (getting along well with others) had a lower probability of becoming ill

(S. Cohen, Doyle, Turner, Alper, & Skoner, 2003). Evidently, allostatic load increases the risk of illness, and sociability decreases it.

Because the evidence shows that allostatic load weakens the immune system and also impairs health, it seems natural to assume that it impairs health because it weakens the immune system. In fact, few studies have directly addressed the link between immune system functioning and health (Segerstrom & Miller, 2004), and of them, some have found only weak correlations between the two (Lindstrøm, 1997), except in elderly people, for whom the relationship becomes stronger (Kiecolt-Glaser & Glaser, 2001). As always, when we find a weak correlation, as we do here between immune activity and health, one possible explanation is a measurement problem. For example, if researchers measured either immune response or health inadequately, the correlation between them would suffer.

Given that stress impairs immune functions, how does it do so? One hypothesis relates to cortisol. As expected, short-term changes in stress levels or cortisol release do not impair immune responses (Bodner, Ho, & Kreek, 1998). However, because prolonged cortisol directs more energy toward blood sugar, theoretically it should leave less energy available for the synthesis of proteins that the immune system needs. Yet the data are mixed on this point. On one hand, many studies do find that prolonged high stress elevates cortisol levels, decreases immune function, and impairs health. That pattern has been reported for elderly people caring for a demented spouse (Vedhara et al., 1999), daughters of breast cancer patients (M. Cohen et al., 2002), and people traumatized by an earthquake (Fukuda, Morimoto, Mure, & Maruyama, 2000). On the other hand, two studies of medical students found that the stress of final exams increased the production of some cytokines while decreasing production of others (Marshall et al., 1998; Uchakin, Tobin, Cubbage, Marshall, & Sams, 2001). If some parts of the immune system strengthen while others weaken, the explanation must go beyond the fact that the body is running out of energy. The studies with medical students, of course, examined fairly brief periods of stress, not the exhaustion stage. More research is needed to track changes in immune response over various periods of stress.

People suffering from post-traumatic stress disorder—the ultimate in stress exhaustion—present a puzzling pattern. Because of their extreme stress, we would expect to find elevated cortisol levels, but many studies find that their cortisol levels are lower than average (Bremner et al., 2003; Glover & Poland, 2002; Yehuda, 1997). Nevertheless, their immune response is weakened, according to most studies (e.g., Kawamura, Kim, & Asukai, 2001). The results vary from one study to another, and several aspects of immune response are actually stronger than average in war veterans suffering from very long-term PTSD (Laudenslager et al., 1998; Spivak et al., 1997).

Although the relationship between prolonged cortisol and the immune system is unsettled, other harms from prolonged cortisol are better established. Prolonged cortisol elevation magnifies the effects of toxic chemicals on the hippocampus, a brain area essential for memory (Sapolsky, 1992). High cortisol levels lead to gradual damage to the hippocampus and, therefore, gradual decline of memory (Cameron & McKay, 1999). In one study, baby rats were separated from their mothers (very stressful for infant mammals) for three hours each day for the first two weeks of life. They were treated normally from then on. As adults, they showed less than the normal amount of production of new neurons in the hippocampus (Mirescu, Peters, & Gould, 2004). This is an interesting result because the stress was a social one rather than a physically painful one, and the effects lasted a lifetime. Other studies have found that a stressful experience in adulthood, such as placing rats in a location where they have previously received electrical shocks, also temporarily reduces their production of new hippocampal neurons (Pham, McEwen, LeDoux, & Nader, 2005). Apparently the cortisol damages the hippocampus by increasing excitation to the point of overstimulation, thereby shrinking dendrites and interfering with repair processes (McEwen, 2000). Even if hippocampal damage were the only cost of prolonged stress, it would be enough reason to make us try to avoid extreme stress.

◻ The Role of Stress in Specific Illnesses

Stress aggravates almost any illness. Here let's examine effects on heart disease and cancer, which have been topics of much research by psychologists studying health.

Heart Disease

A casual observation gave rise to a popular hypothesis about stress and heart disease: An upholsterer repairing chairs in a physician's waiting room noted that the fronts of the seats were worn out, but not the backs. The physician started watching the patients and reported that most of his heart patients sat on the front edges of the seats, impatiently waiting for their appointments. The hypothesis therefore arose that heart disease was linked to an impatient, high-achieving, success-driven personality (Friedman & Rosenman, 1974).

That type of personality became known as **Type A personality,** marked by competitiveness, impatience, and hostility. Since the mid-1970s, many studies have sought a link between Type A personality and heart disease, but the results have been unimpressive. A few studies have found a significant relationship (Kawachi et al., 1998), but most have not. As usual, part of the problem is measurement: Most studies rely on questionnaire results, which are not entirely valid. Some people with a Type A personality answer the questionnaires inaccurately because they do not realize how hostile or impatient they are, compared to other people (Kawachi et al., 1998).

Still, the fact is that most studies fail to find much of a relationship between heart disease and the competitive, success-seeking aspect of Type A personality. The results are stronger for the hostility aspect—the more emotional characteristic of Type

A people. With a few exceptions (O'Malley, Jones, Feuerstein, & Taylor, 2000; Sykes et al., 2002), most studies have found a significant link between self-reports of anger or hostility and the risk of either heart disease itself or heart conditions that are precursors to heart disease (Eaker, Sullivan, Kelly-Hayes, D'Agostino, & Benjamin, 2004; Iribarren et al., 2000; J. E. Williams et al., 2000; Yan et al., 2003). One hypothesis to explain this link is that anger increases heart rate, releases cortisol, and in other ways puts a strain on the system. However, remember our earlier discussions about not assuming a cause-and-effect relationship. Many people with high hostility also smoke, drink alcohol excessively, and engage in other high-risk activities. Also, high hostility is more common among people of low- than high-socioeconomic status. Because each of these other factors also predisposes to heart disease, it is difficult to isolate the direct effects of the emotions themselves (Krantz, Sheps, Carney, & Natelson, 2000).

Some of the better-designed research studies examine whether high levels of anger, anxiety, or depression predict *later* onset of high blood pressure. The results say they do, but with a correlation averaging only about .08 (Rutledge & Hogan, 2002). That correlation suggests a very weak relationship, yet the results fluctuate strongly from one study to another, so it may be that negative emotions contribute strongly under some circumstances and not others.

One promising study used behavioral observations to measure hostility, instead of questionnaires. The researchers videotaped people's facial expressions during an interview while recording their *transient myocardial ischemias*—brief periods of inadequate blood flow to the heart muscles. Transient myocardial ischemias are usually painless, but they can be precursors to heart attacks. People who showed many facial expressions of anger were more likely than others to have transient myocardial ischemia during the interview (Rosenberg et al., 2001).

Although the link between personality factors and heart disease remains unclear, social support does reduce the risk of heart disease. People with strong support from friends and family generally take better care of themselves and maintain good health, including a safe blood pressure (Uchino, Cacioppo, & Kiecolt-Glaser, 1996). Studies also show that teaching people good stress management techniques can significantly lower blood pressure, thereby decreasing the risk of heart disease (Linden, Lenz, & Con, 2001). Note the peculiarity of results: Personality factors, including stress-prone personality, appear to be poor predictors of heart disease, but learning to control stress is clearly helpful.

Cancer

Cancer is one of the most feared of all diseases. Its causes are poorly understood, and the treatments are unpleasant and often unsuccessful. People search for any hope of preventing the disease. Prolonged, severe stress suppresses the activity of natural killer cells, the part of the immune system that is most important for attacking tumors. Stress also impairs the process of repairing damaged DNA molecules, and DNA damage is believed to be a major cause of cancer. Theoretically, therefore, stress should increase the risk of certain kinds of cancer or at least increase the rate at which it spreads (Kiecolt-Glaser, Robles, Heffner, Loving, & Glaser, 2002).

Several studies have examined the correlation of stress with survival time in cancer patients. One of the most extensive studied 673 breast-cancer patients, and found no significant relationship between stressful events reported from the five years before disease diagnosis and the survival time after diagnosis of cancer (Maunsell, Brisson, Mondor, Verreault, & Deschênes, 2001). We cannot conclude from these data that stress is irrelevant to cancer. First, the research may not have measured stress adequately. Second, stress while fighting the disease may be more decisive than previous stress. People who receive steady support from their family, friends, or a self-help group of other patients improve their chance of recovery as well as increase

their quality of life while they are fighting the disease (Fawzy, Fawzy, Arndt, & Pasnau, 1995). Still, the results imply that stress is at most a minor contributor to the causes of cancer.

◻ Summary

"Everyone knows" that stress leads to health problems. And yet as you have reviewed the research described in this chapter, you have seen that the story is more complex. Mild to moderate levels of stress are either neutral or helpful to health, both mentally and physically. Evidently we are not biologically adapted for a stress-free way of life; we almost *need* occasional, moderate stress to function well. Cortisol, a "stress hormone," produces many helpful effects, in moderate amounts and moderate durations. However, coping with severe or prolonged stress weakens the immune system and impairs health. Our bodies are well adapted to deal with occasional stress, but not unending stress.

Unfortunately, modern life tends to present people with many long-term, non-life-threatening stressors where the short-term effects don't do us much good, and the long-term effects can do considerable harm. After all, you may want to run at lightning speed from an irritable boss, or pick a physical fight, and that is what your body is preparing you to do, but those are hardly constructive responses. If the conflict continues, your body may simply wear out waiting for the action. In some situations, the stress response is absolutely necessary, but too much stress over a long time starts to do physical damage.

What can we conclude about the relationship between stress and emotion? Certainly there are links between the two. Many of the kinds of events that elicit fear, anger, and grief are considered stressful. We have said that strong, negative emotions such as fear and anger include activation of the sympathetic nervous system, and sympathetic activation is also the first stage of the stress response. In studies of the relationship between Type A personality and heart disease, the emotional aspect of Type A—hostility, or frequent and intense anger—was the only one associated with heart trouble. However, the overlap between the two concepts is not perfect. The long-term stress response includes Selye's resistance and exhaustion stages, about which emotion theory has little to say. And not all emotions necessarily involve the initial stress response. For example, disgust is associated with *decreased* heart rate and blood pressure, and studies suggest that some positive emotions also reduce sympathetic arousal.

So why spend a chapter on stress in our text on emotion? First, in the process of studying the effects of stress on health, we've learned a bit about certain emotions. For example, studies of short-term anger emphasize immediate changes in blood pressure, heart rate, and so forth, but studies of dispositionally hostile people suggest that emotion researchers may be missing more subtle, long-term effects of the emotion. Also, the realization that stress depends on how people interpret events, not just on the events themselves, helped contribute to our understanding of the role of appraisal in emotion. Most important, however, is that if stress involves emotions (at least in the initial stages), then we may be able to reduce stress and its health effects by regulating our emotions. We turn to this topic in our final chapter.

◻ Key Terms

alarm: a brief period of high arousal of the sympathetic nervous system, readying the body for vigorous activity (p. 283)

allostasis: adaptive changes in the way the body regulates its levels of various chemicals and activities in the face of some threat (p. 290)

allostatic load: the cost from an excessive or prolonged response to a threat (p. 290)

antibody: a Y-shaped protein that attaches specifically to one kind of antigen (p. 292)

antigen: (antibody-generating molecules) proteins on the surface of the cells (p. 292)

B cells: leukocytes that contribute to immunity mostly by making antibodies (p. 292)

cortisol: adrenal gland hormone that enhances metabolism and increases the availability of fuels in the body (p. 291)

cytokines: small proteins secreted by leukocytes and many other cells in response to infection (p. 292)

exhaustion: final stage of reaction to a prolonged threat, characterized by weakness, fatigue, loss of appetite, and lack of interest (p. 284)

General Adaptation Syndrome: the body's reaction to any threat (p. 283)

homeostasis: tendency of many body variables to remain nearly constant over time (p. 290)

HPA axis: hypothalamus, pituitary gland, and adrenal cortex (p. 291)

immune system: family of mechanisms that defend against bacteria, viruses, tumors, and other invaders into the body (p. 292)

leukocytes: white blood cells, which are immune system cells that form in several parts of the body (p. 292)

natural killer cells: leukocytes that attack tumor cells and cells infected with viruses, but without any specificity to a particular target (p. 292)

resilience: ability to withstand stress or recover from it (p. 291)

resistance: stage of prolonged but moderate arousal in response to some threat (p. 283)

stress: (McEwen's definition) an event or events that are interpreted as threatening to an individual and which elicit physiological and behavioral responses (p. 288)

stress: (Selye's definition) the nonspecific response of the body to any demand made upon it (p. 284)

T cells: leukocytes that form in the bone marrow and mature in the thymus gland (p. 292)

Type A personality: personality marked by competitiveness, impatience, and hostility (p. 295)

◻ Thought Questions

1. Some students consistently become ill during one final exam period after another. Presuming that they have real symptoms and are not just pretending, what explanations can you offer based on material in this chapter?

2. Most cancer drugs act by preventing cells from dividing and sometimes by killing cells that are in the process of dividing. When a patient is given a large dose of such drugs, physicians sometimes surgically remove part of the bone marrow until after the treatment, and then return it. Why would they be particularly interested in saving the bone marrow?

3. Can you think of events in your own life that might be stressful if you give them one interpretation but not stressful under a different interpretation?

◻ Suggestions for Research Projects

1. Try writing a questionnaire or devising any other kind of measurement of what *you* consider to be the main dimensions of stress. See whether you can avoid the criticisms leveled against the Social Readjustment Rating Scale.

2. Survey people you know about what they consider the most stressful event they faced today. Do young people report different kinds of events from older people?

◻ Suggestions for Further Reading

McEwen, B. S. (with Lasley, E. N.). (2002). *The end of stress as we know it.* Washington, DC: Joseph Henry Press. Readable review by one of the leading researchers, with a biological emphasis.

Sapolsky, R. M. (1998). *Why zebras don't get ulcers: An updated guide to stress, stress-related diseases, and coping.* New York: W. H. Freeman. Another excellent review, written in a highly engaging style.

15

Emotion Regulation:
Coping With Stress

S tress happens. The challenges of earning a living, maintaining a household, and managing our relationships produce a certain amount of unavoidable stress for all of us. In some cases, these mundane challenges can build up into serious problems. For example, almost any family has at least occasional arguments, but in some families the conflicts develop into verbal or physical abuse. Many people face major, acute stressors at some point during their lives, such as a natural disaster, the serious illness or death of a loved one, being the victim of a crime, or bankruptcy.

Some of these stressors are, objectively speaking, worse than others. For example, losing your home and all your belongings in a fire is obviously more stressful than an argument with a co-worker. On the other hand, as we noted in Chapter 14, people interpret and react to stressors in very different ways. One person might lose everything in a fire, yet leave the experience feeling relieved that no one was hurt and competent to cope with the practical aspects of the tragedy. Another person might become hysterical and paralyzed after the professional argument. These people differ in their **emotion regulation**—the strategies we use to control which emotions we have, when we have them, and how strongly we experience

and express them (J. J. Gross, 2002). Another common term is **coping**, which refers to the ways that people reduce negative emotion after a stressful event. The distinction between the two is that coping is an attempt to reduce negative emotion caused by some stressor, whereas emotion regulation may include doing something pleasant just for the sake of feeling positive. It could also include *increasing* your display of anger, for example, if you thought that was a good strategy for responding to some situation.

People use a wide range of strategies to handle their own emotions. Some of these are more effective than others on the whole, and the most effective strategy depends on the situation. In this chapter, we will examine several kinds of emotion regulation strategies and evaluate their effectiveness.

▣ Freud's Ego Defense Mechanisms: An Early Taxonomy of Coping Strategies

Before we begin, try listing all the ways you can think of to cope with stress—talking with other people, getting away from other people, thinking about the problem, not thinking about the problem, and so on. Don't worry if some of your suggestions contradict one another; depending on the type of stress, sometimes one strategy helps the most, sometimes its opposite. If you compare lists with other people, you might find dozens of suggestions.

Perhaps the earliest formal taxonomy of coping mechanisms was constructed by Sigmund Freud, and elaborated by his daughter Anna, during the early twentieth century. According to Freud, humans by their very nature have fundamental drives and desires (the "id") that they cannot express in a

civilized society. The most famous of these, of course, is the supposed desire to have sex with your mother or father (whoever is the opposite-sex parent). The demands, rules, and societal expectations that limit the expression of the id are housed in a socially learned conscience, or "superego." Freud proposed a series of **ego defense mechanisms,** or psychological regulation strategies that serve to resolve the tension between the id and the superego and keep disturbing wishes and desires hidden from consciousness. Table 15.1 presents several of these mechanisms.

TABLE 15.1   Sigmund Freud believed that people use ego defense mechanisms, like those described here, to keep disturbing thoughts and desires out of consciousness. Freud's classification of defense mechanisms was an early taxonomy of emotion regulation strategies.

Defense Mechanism	Definition	Example
Denial	Refusing to acknowledge the reality of an unpleasant or threatening situation	Refusing to admit that your close friend has a serious, life-threatening illness
Repression	"Forgetting" or "blocking" memory of unpleasant or intolerable events; repression is automatic, rather than conscious and intentional	Blocking out memory of a car accident
Fantasy	Retreating to fantasy or daydreaming as a way to fulfill desires	Daydreaming about having a fling with a famous actor or actress
Reaction Formation	Adopting and expressing attitudes/ behaviors that are the extreme opposite of the underlying "real" attitudes and behaviors	Being excessively friendly toward a person you intensely dislike
Projection	Attributing one's own unacceptable desires, motives, or feelings to another person	Accusing your romantic partner of feeling bored with your relationship, when you are really the one feeling restless
Intellectualization	Focusing purely on the abstract, logical aspects of an issue or experience, rather than the personal or emotional aspects	Logically analyzing the motives and explanations for why a friend let you down, rather than feeling hurt
Displacement	Directing disturbing feelings toward an alternative target, rather than the person or event that really elicited them	Yelling at your dog after an argument with your supervisor at work
Suppression	Making a conscious, deliberate decision not to think about a disturbing topic at a particular time	Deciding not to worry about an upcoming deadline at work while you see a movie Friday night
Sublimation	Expressing socially unacceptable desires or impulses in a manner that is constructive and socially condoned	Writing a song or poem that captures your anger toward a parent, rather than arguing with the parent directly

The advantage of this system is that it offers a way to describe and categorize different coping strategies. Scientific progress requires clear categorization, so that different investigators can compare results. However, the specifics of Freud's system raise serious problems. Freud heavily emphasized the use of defense mechanisms to deal with inappropriate sexual and physical pleasure and the guilt and anxiety that they cause. This emphasis was based on Freud's interpretations of what his patients told him, but he never offered anything that would qualify as solid evidence to support his interpretations. When later researchers attempted to find a scientific basis for defense mechanisms such as repression and projection, their support for Freud's ideas was, to put it generously, "mixed" (Holmes, 1978, 1990).

Furthermore, as Freud's theory developed through one version after another, in many cases he used the same clinical example to support different and even contradictory conclusions (F. Crews, 1996; Esterson, 2001). That is, he did not develop theories to fit the data; he reinterpreted data to fit the theories.

Freud's theory has grown progressively less influential within psychology, although many scholars in literature and philosophy continue to follow his ideas.

Furthermore, Freud's views do not help explain the full range of ways we cope with emotional situations. The ego defense mechanisms he described were not intended to explain how people would cope with the loss of a job or a divorce, for example. Later researchers have renewed the search for a way to describe and categorize the various ways of dealing with stress.

◻ A Process Model of Emotion Regulation

James Gross (2002) has offered the **process model of emotion regulation**—a model that organizes emotion regulation strategies according to their place in the emotion process itself—as an alternative way of thinking about and classifying coping strategies (see Figure 15.1). Building upon earlier theories of emotion and emotion regulation by Lazarus (1991),

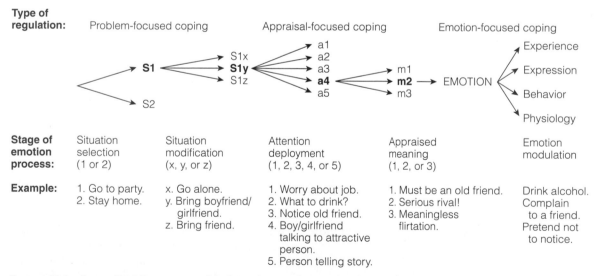

FIGURE 15.1   James Gross's process model of emotion regulation. According to this model, people enter a situation, attend to certain aspects of it, appraise those aspects in particular ways, and then experience an emotion as a result of the appraisal. Note that any decision at any stage in this model leads to different possible emotional outcomes. Regulation strategies can be classified according to where they occur within this process. Source: Adapted from Gross (2002).

Frijda (1986), and M. B. Arnold (1960), this model makes certain assumptions about the underlying emotion process: (1) we enter a particular situation; (2) we pay attention to certain aspects of the situation, rather than others; (3) we interpret, or appraise, those aspects of the situation in a way that facilitates an emotional response; and (4) we then experience a full-blown emotion, including physiological changes, behavior impulses, and subjective feelings. As we discussed in Chapter 1, this theory of emotion is far from conclusive: The order of events can vary, and sometimes we experience some aspects of emotion without others. However, the theory seems to explain enough of emotional experience that it has been helpful in understanding emotion regulation as well.

Using this model, we can classify emotion regulation strategies according to *when* they take place in the emotion process, and this classification helps us understand why some strategies are more effective than others. This model highlights three categories of strategies for regulating emotion. **Problem-focused coping** refers to controlling the situation, either by choosing to be in one situation rather than another or by changing the situation somehow. The second kind of strategy is **reappraisal,** or changing the way we think about the situation to deter some emotions and/or encourage others. The third kind of strategy is reducing emotions after they have already started, referred to as **emotion-focused coping,** or "blunting." Emotion-focused coping strategies presume that a person is already experiencing an emotion and wants it to change. These strategies may include "getting it out of your system" by talking about the emotion; attempting to turn off emotional experience, such as by sleeping or consuming drugs or alcohol; or attempting to suppress the expression of an emotion so that other people can't see what you are feeling. Let's look at each of these three categories in more detail.

◻ Problem-Focused Strategies

When possible, the ideal way to reduce stress is to improve the situation that's causing it (J. J. Gross,

2001). For example, if you are worried about a test next week, you could try to calm your emotions through breathing exercises, but you would do better to spend most of your time studying, so you have less reason for anxiety. If your job causes you great distress, you could learn ways to relax, but you might do better by looking for a different job. If it upsets you that your romantic partner never cleans the bathroom, you could be furious every time you have to do it, or you could tell your partner that sharing housework is important to you, and ask him or her to help out more often. If a friend repeatedly brings up an extremely distressing topic (an acrimonious political argument, detailed discussion of your worst romantic break-up, the time you accidentally sat on her hamster . . .), you can simply walk away when that topic comes up, or you could try to change the subject. If these strategies fail, you could actually tell your friend that you find the topic upsetting and would prefer not to discuss it. Whenever you manage to resolve or improve a situation, you can reduce the source of stress.

This point may seem so obvious that you wonder why we bother to make it. After all, why would somebody endure an unpleasant situation if they didn't have to? People don't always realize that they have some control over a situation. Recall from Chapter 5 the distinction between "threat" and "challenge" appraisals of some intimidating situation (Tomaka, Blascovich, Kibler, & Ernst, 1997). People feel threatened when they don't believe they have the personal resources to cope with some stressor; they feel challenged when they believe that they do have enough resources. People differ in the extent to which they typically feel a sense of control over situations, and these differences feed into dispositional tendencies toward threat or challenge appraisals (Lazarus, 1991). Put simply, some people tend not to realize that they may be able to do something about unpleasant situations, so they don't even try. Individuals who generally feel that they have little control over situations are at greater risk for depression than those with a stronger sense of personal control (Alloy et al., 1999).

Studies suggest that problem-focused coping strategies also promote emotion regulation in ways beyond their immediate effects on the situation. Even if something unpleasant is unavoidable, it will feel less disturbing if you can control some aspect of the situation or if you can at least predict what is going to happen and prepare for it. Suppose a professor in a large class calls on students at random to answer challenging questions. You would prefer not to be called on, but you have to be ready constantly because you could be called on next. Now change the situation: The professor still calls on students, but in alphabetical order. So, if your name is Zoë Zyzzlewicz, you can relax until late in the class; you can predict when you will be called. Change the situation one more time: The professor calls only on students who raise a hand to volunteer. Now you are in complete control. Even if you answer many questions, you feel less stressed because you can choose when to participate.

Even *thinking* you have some control over a situation makes it less stressful. Imagine yourself in this experiment: You are asked to do some difficult proofreading while seated next to a device that will make unpredictable, sudden, loud, annoying sounds. You are told that the point of the study is to examine the effects of that noise on your behavior. Right before you start, you are also shown an "escape button": If the noise becomes unbearable, you can simply press that button to turn it off. You are urged not to press the button unless necessary; after all, the point of the study is to determine the effects of the noise on your behavior. The button is there "just in case." When this study has been done, almost none of the participants actually pressed the button, so they did not learn whether it worked. But participants who had the button and believed they could turn off the noise if necessary performed better on the proofreading tasks than participants who were not offered an escape button (Glass, Singer, & Pennebaker, 1977; Sherrod, Hage, Halpern, & Moore, 1977).

In another study, people were given a series of painfully hot stimuli to their forearms. Participants in one group were told that they could decrease the duration of a stimulus from 5 seconds to 2 seconds if they manipulated a joystick quickly enough in the correct direction. In fact, they had no control; the duration of the stimulus varied randomly, but because they were trying hard with the joystick, they interpreted every short stimulus as a reward for a "quick enough" response. Participants in the control group were also asked to manipulate the joystick, but they knew they had no control of the outcome. The result was that participants who *thought* they had control experienced less pain. Measurements of brain activity using fMRI found less arousal in several pain-sensitive brain areas for these participants, in comparison to those who knew they had no control (Salomons, Johnstone, Backonja, & Davidson, 2004).

Consider this stressful situation: You are in a hospital for major surgery. The staff hasn't told you when the surgery will occur, how long it will last, what your chances for success are, or how long it will take to recover. You will feel helpless and frightened. Now change the situation: The staff tell you what to expect, in as much detail as you wish, and even give you some choices, such as when the surgery will begin and who will be present when you wake up from the anesthesia. When you have some sense of prediction and control, your anxiety is much less severe (Van Der Zee, Huet, Cazemier, & Evers, 2002), and chances are you will even have a better medical outcome (Shapiro, Schwartz, & Astin, 1996).

Hospitals now regularly allow patients to control the administration of painkillers after surgery, using a small button, rather than having a nurse administer the drugs on a fixed schedule. Naturally, there are restrictions; the device limits how often the patient can self-administer the drug. As a result, the patient receives no more of the drug, and frequently less, than if someone else had been controlling the delivery. However, patients who control the timing of their doses typically report more satisfaction with their pain management (Lehmann, 1995).

Self-help books often encourage people to "visualize success" as a way to gain control over their lives and cause desired outcomes. For example, you might be encouraged to visualize getting your dream job, meeting the perfect romantic partner, winning a contest, or driving a luxury automobile. This advice is a bit misleading. If you simply visualize glorious outcomes, you probably will enjoy the fantasy, but it will not improve your productivity. What *does* help is to visualize doing the work that would lead to the prizes and honors (Taylor, Pham, Rivkin, & Armor, 1998). If you want to succeed in athletics, visualize yourself practicing the movements of your sport. If you want to write a successful paper, visualize yourself in the library or organizing your notes.

Similarly, if you expect to face a challenge in the future, you can gain a sense of control by imagining what you will do when the challenge comes. For example, if you expect to have an unpleasant conversation with someone, you might imagine what you will say, how the other person will reply, and what you might say in return (Sanna, 2000). In one study, first-time pregnant women were asked to imagine and describe going through labor and arriving at the hospital. Those whose descriptions were rated as the most accurate and most detailed showed the least worry about the upcoming delivery (Brown, MacLeod, Tata, & Goddard, 2002).

You can also gain a sense of control through psychological "inoculation." To become immunized against a virus, you get inoculated with a weakened form of the virus. To gain **psychological inoculation** against a stressor, you can expose yourself to milder versions of the stressful events (Janis, 1983; Meichenbaum, 1985). For example, armies make soldiers practice combat skills under realistic but non-life-threatening conditions, and police departments ask trainees to practice arresting suspects, intervening in domestic quarrels, and so forth with actors playing the part of the other people. If you have to give a talk to a large audience, you might try giving it to a small group of friends or even to an imaginary audience. People who practice in this way develop a set of skills for handling the situation, which they can then apply to more serious and challenging versions of the situation.

☐ Appraisal-Focused Strategies

Unfortunately, we sometimes face unpleasant situations that offer little or no control. In some cases, the event has already taken place, and we no longer have any way to change it. For example, you applied for admission to several graduate schools, and all of them rejected you. In other cases, the event is still ongoing, but the outcome is uncontrollable or nearly so. For example, you might be caring for an aging relative with Alzheimer's disease or a loved one with cancer.

In such cases, if you think about the situation in a different way, you can sometimes find a better way to deal with it. By controlling your appraisal, or interpretation of a difficult situation, you may be able to reduce the negative emotion you feel and may even be able to find something to feel good about. When people change their interpretation of a particular situation, the process is known as reappraisal. This doesn't mean pretending the situation isn't happening or inventing some unrealistic story for how things will turn out. It does mean focusing on some real, but positive (or at least neutral) aspect or interpretation of the situation. For example, victims of automobile accidents, hurricanes, and all sorts of other misfortune frequently comfort themselves with the thought, "It could have been worse!" When people change the way they think about a larger emotional issue or frequently occurring situation, the process is called **cognitive restructuring**—a frequent goal in therapies for such mood disorders as depression and anxiety. For example, instead of reacting to every unfriendly comment as further evidence that "people don't like me," someone might learn to think, "Oh well, that person is just hard to please," or "I guess my boss is in another bad mood today."

What distinguishes reappraisal and cognitive restructuring from emotion-focused coping is that they *prevent* a negative emotion from being experienced at all, or at least reduce it. Look back at the model in Figure 15.1. Emotion-focused coping is an attempt to reduce or "turn off" an emotion that is already underway. Appraisal-focused coping happens earlier in the emotion process by altering the beliefs and interpretations that lead to the emotion in the first place.

Reappraisal can take many different forms. At the simplest level, one can ignore the emotional aspects of a situation and focus on trivial aspects such as the physical setting or what people are wearing. This approach does seem to reduce the experience of negative emotion. In one study, college students were asked to remember in as much detail as possible some experience in which they felt rejected or abandoned. Then some were told to focus on how they felt at the time while the others were told to try to describe the physical setting. Changing their focus to the physical setting decreased their self-reported anger, as well as their facial expressions of it (Ayduk, Mischel, & Downey, 2002).

Alternatively, one can pay attention to the negative event but try to interpret it in a more benign way. In another study, college students were asked to examine a series of 120 pictures, many of which were very unpleasant or disturbing, such as pictures of badly injured people, children crying, and displays of hatred. Participants in this study were asked to suppress their emotional expressions while they viewed the disturbing pictures—a process we will discuss in more detail later in the chapter. Of interest here is the strategy used by the people who were most successful at reducing their emotion displays. When asked how they managed, most said they tried to reinterpret the situation. For example, when they saw a wounded soldier, they told themselves the battle was over and the soldier was about to receive good medical care (Jackson, Malmstadt, Larson, & Davidson, 2000).

We can also consider forgiveness of others as a kind of cognitive restructuring. Forgiveness often includes finding some acceptable explanation for another person's hurtful behavior. You might decide, "We all have our weak moments, and sometimes I have hurt other people, too. Besides, I don't know everything going on in that other person's life. Maybe I should just give him [or her] the benefit of the doubt." Getting rid of a grudge releases tension and improves emotional stability (McCullough, 2001; Witvliet, Ludwig, & Vander Laan, 2001). That is, forgiveness helps not only the forgiven but also the forgiver.

◻ Positive Reappraisal in Emotion Regulation

Many studies of reappraisal as a coping strategy have focused on disengaging from the emotional implications of some event, or thinking about the event in an objective or disinterested way. Another reappraisal strategy, often referred to as **positive reappraisal**, consists of focusing on positive aspects of negative or challenging situations. For example, if every graduate school to which you applied rejected you, you might say, "Oh, well. I'll consider other career possibilities, and maybe I'll find something that will be an even better choice for me." If you have to care for an aging relative with Alzheimer's disease, you might say, "Here is an opportunity for me to rise to the occasion, to use my skills to help someone who really needs my help." Correlational studies suggest that positive reappraisal may be a particularly healthy emotion regulation strategy. For example, people who are resilient—those who recover relatively well or easily from negative events—report thinking about the potential positive effects of negative events more often than less resilient people (Tugade & Fredrickson, 2004). Positive emotions broaden one's attention and thereby help a person find solutions to problems (Fredrickson, 2000). They also help put the brakes on the cardiovascular response to a crisis, thus promoting a better health outcome (Fredrickson & Levenson, 1998).

Psychologists think of resilience mostly as a personality trait that is stable over time, but it can also vary with the situation. For example, most people react to a personal failure as a threat to their self-esteem, but if they are led to believe that they are capable of overcoming their weaknesses, they react with less distress—and more resilience (Niiya, Crocker, & Bartmess, 2004). That is, people tend to be resilient whenever they appraise their problem as an opportunity, not as a hopeless situation.

The utility of positive reappraisal strategies is also evident in research on clinical disorders. Researchers in one study compared the appraisal-focused emotion regulation strategies implemented by clinically depressed and anxious Dutch adults and by a comparable sample of emotionally healthy people (Garnefski et al., 2002). Both groups completed a self-report questionnaire measuring participants' typical frequency of using several reappraisal strategies: self-blame, other-blame, rumination, catastrophizing (emphasizing the terror of the experience), acceptance, planning, putting the negative event into perspective, thinking about other positive topics, and positive reappraisal. The one strategy used significantly more often by the healthy sample than by the clinical sample was positive reappraisal. Later studies also found that people who rely on positive reappraisal are less likely than others to report symptoms of depression (Garnefski, Teerds, Kraaij, Legerstee, & van den Kommer, 2004; Kraaij, Pruymboom, & Garnefski, 2002).

The Neurobiology of Reappraisal

Reappraisal is fundamentally a cognition-based way of regulating emotions. To reappraise an otherwise negative situation, a person may have to put some initial effort into concentrating on unemotional or positive aspects of the situation and may even need to generate some plans for interpreting future stimuli. Studies of the neural activation patterns associated with reappraisal are consistent with this view.

In one study, young men watched a series of short pornographic films while undergoing an fMRI scan. During some of the films, they were instructed to allow themselves to become aroused; during the others, they were told to inhibit their arousal. As Figure C.8 illustrates (see inside back cover), different brain areas became active under the two conditions (Beauregard, Lévesque, & Bourgouin, 2001). While the men were sexually aroused, activity increased in the hypothalamus, right amygdala, and part of the right temporal cortex—areas associated with sexuality and emotion. While they were inhibiting their arousal, activity was lower in the amygdala and hypothalamus but increased in part of the prefrontal cortex, presumably reflecting cognitive and language-based strategies that these men employed to distract themselves from sexual arousal.

In a similar study, participants looked at a series of disturbing photos while undergoing functional magnetic resonance imaging. Then they examined the same pictures while reappraising them to make them less disturbing. When participants examined the photos the first time, they showed extensive activity in the amygdala and the orbitofrontal part of the prefrontal cortex, areas that are often active during emotional experience; when they were reinterpreting the photos, those brain areas showed much less response, but other parts of the prefrontal cortex, related to cognitive processes, became more active (Ochsner, Bunge, Gross, & Gabrieli, 2002).

◻ Emotion-Focused Strategies

Suppose the worst has happened. For example, a close relative has died. Nothing you do can undo the loss, and no amount of reappraisal can improve the situation significantly. Once a full-blown emotion is underway, people rely on emotion-focused regulation strategies to dampen the emotion over time. There are many such strategies, and we will discuss several that have been subjected to good research. What they all have in common is that their goal is to change the feeling or expression of the emotion, rather than to change the situation or appraisals that led to the emotion.

Expressing Your Feelings

Popular psychology often recommends that you "let it all out"—deeply experience your feelings, and express them to their fullest. This strategy dates back to Freud's idea of **catharsis:** the "release" of strong emotions by experiencing and expressing them fully. The idea is that the emotions are "trapped" inside you, and they won't bother you after you release them. As with "visualizing success," the research on this strategy suggests that claims about the benefits of catharsis are partly accurate and partly bogus.

The bogus part is the idea that deeply feeling and expressing negative emotions will make you feel better. Contrary to the idea of catharsis, research finds that vigorously expressing fear or anger does not reliably reduce the emotion and often increases it. For example, people who deal with their negative emotions by venting them tend to have more anxiety than average in their interpersonal relationships (Jerome & Liss, 2005). When people are encouraged to cry during sad movies, they end up feeling worse, not better, than people who tried to restrain their tears (Kraemer & Hastrup, 1988).

Furthermore, although discussing an emotionally troubling situation does help, dwelling on it for too long can be harmful. (It's like medicine: The right amount can help you, but too much is harmful.) **Rumination** is thinking continuously about a problem for a long time, focusing on negative aspects of the situation instead of possible solutions. Excessive rumination is often a precursor to clinical depression and may be a contributing factor (Garnefski et al., 2004; Nolen-Hoeksema, 1991). Similarly, attempts to prevent suicide through extensive discussions sometimes lead to rumination that backfires and increases the risk of suicide (Moller, 1992).

We are *not* recommending that you try to suppress all thoughts or discussions about negative experiences. First, avoiding a topic implies that it is so bad or shameful that you *can't* talk about it. Second, because you don't talk about it, you never hear others' advice about how to handle the situation or prevent it from occurring again. Third, trying to suppress thoughts often makes them even more intrusive. Leo Tolstoy as a child belonged to a club for which the qualification for membership was to sit alone for 30 minutes *without thinking about a white bear*

(Simmons, 1949). Try it now, even for just a few minutes, before you read the next paragraph.

Ordinarily you might go weeks, even months, between one white-bear thought and the next, but when you are concentrating on *not* thinking about a bear, suddenly you are obsessed with it. Researchers have found that when people try to avoid all thoughts of something, soon everything in the room reminds them of it (Wegner, Schneider, Carter, & White, 1987). Soon the suppression effort takes so much energy that you can't pay attention to anything else. People who try not to think about recent unpleasant experiences perform more poorly than others on tests of working memory (K. Klein & Boals, 2001). Evidently, their efforts to block out unwanted thoughts use up resources that would have otherwise been available for other purposes.

So . . . we have cautioned against dwelling on unpleasant experiences and emotions but also against avoiding all thoughts about them. Somehow you need to find the happy medium between these extremes. One line of research suggests that you can derive substantial benefits from relatively brief explorations of your problems. In one experiment, college students in the treatment group spent half an hour a day for three to five days writing about their deepest thoughts and feelings concerning some intensely upsetting experience. Students who were randomly assigned to the control group spent the same time writing about an unemotional topic. Many in the treatment group wrote about traumatic events, such as the death of a friend or relative or experiences of physical or sexual abuse. At the end of the week, the students could either destroy their journals or hand them in, but no one discussed the content with them. So in these studies, the students were communicating only with themselves, in a way being their own therapists.

Afterward, the researchers asked the students for their reaction to the writing experience. In spite of becoming very upset while writing, sometimes even crying, nearly all said it was a valuable experience. Follow-up studies later in the semester revealed that, on the average, those in the treatment group had been ill less often, drank less alcohol, and got better grades than those in the control group (Pennebaker, 1997). People get some of the same benefits just by thinking about a stressful event and possible solutions, even if they do not put their thoughts on paper (Rivkin & Taylor, 1999).

Why did the writing task have such positive results, compared with pure emotional expression? According to further research with this same design, those most likely to profit from this experience were those who used their writing to try to understand the stressful event and their reactions to it. The more often people used such words as *because, reason, realize, know,* and *understand,* the greater their gains in health, academic performance, and overall adjustment (Pennebaker & Graybeal, 2001). That is, the writing helped not because people expressed their emotions but because they made decisions or came to terms with the situation while writing (Pennebaker & Graybeal, 2001).

On the other hand, another study found that a similar amount of writing about an intensely *positive* experience also improves mood and health over the next several months (Burton & King, 2004). Certainly we cannot attribute that benefit to problem solving because the positive experience poses no problems. If writing about negative and positive experiences produce similar benefits, perhaps the mechanism depends on the positive emotion. Writing about the positive emotion intensifies it. Writing about a negative experience enables one to solve the problem, feel relief, and substitute a more positive feeling.

Exercise

One of the most successful emotion-based coping strategies is physical exercise. Studies have shown repeatedly that exercise is a reliable way to prevent depression (Leppämäki, Partonen, & Lönnqvist, 2002). Over the long term, exercise also helps prevent anxiety (Salmon, 2001). One caveat here is that the benefits come from a consistent program of exercise, not from a single workout. Also, whereas a moderate amount of exercise improves mood, ex-

tremely strenuous exercise can actually make mood worse (Salmon, 2001).

Why does a steady program of moderate exercise help improve mood? No one is sure exactly, but several mechanisms are probably involved. First, exercise is a distraction from the actual source of stress. Any kind of distraction—such as listening to music or watching television—is one way of dealing with stress, although in most situations not a very powerful one (Fauerbach, Lawrence, Haythornthwaite, & Richter, 2002). Whether distraction makes sense or not really depends on the stressor. If the source of stress is completely out of your control, and reappraisal is not a reasonable strategy, then distraction may be a good idea. On the other hand, if you *do* have some control over a situation, then distracting yourself from it may interfere with resolving it and improving your situation in the long run.

Second, exercise improves overall health. People in good physical condition show less tension and autonomic arousal in response to stressful events compared to people in worse condition (Crews & Landers, 1987), and we know that muscle tension and autonomic arousal are part of the subjective feeling of stress.

Third, any stress readies the body for intense fight-or-flight activity, even if the particular stressful situation does not call for physical activity. Once the body has engaged in physical activity after stress, it tends to relax. Studies with laboratory rodents have found that wheel-running exercise, after a separate stressor, can even reduce adrenal stress responses (Mills & Ward, 1986).

Fourth, neurotransmitters called endorphins (see Chapter 9 for a definition) become substantially more active during intense physical exercise (Thoren, Floras, Hoffman, & Seals, 1990). These chemicals are part of the body's natural pain-killing system, and opiate activity is generally associated with a strong improvement in mood.

Relaxation

It may seem contradictory to list both exercise and relaxation as ways of controlling emotions, but they may be related. Both help the body reduce muscular tension and autonomic arousal. Having some trouble relaxing? Here is some advice (Benson, 1985):

- Find a place that is reasonably quiet.
- Begin by tensing all your muscles so you notice how they feel. Then systematically relax them one by one, starting with your feet and working upward.
- If at first you find it difficult to relax, don't worry about it. After all, the whole point of relaxation is to stop worrying!
- Shut out as much stimulation as possible by repeating a sound (such as "om") or repetitive prayer or focusing on some simple object or shape. Choose whatever seems comfortable to you. This practice is generally known as meditation. People who practice this technique daily report that they feel less stress. One study found that people who went through a 12-week meditation program had a long-lasting decrease in anxiety and depression compared with a control group who spent the same amount of time listening to lectures about how to reduce stress (Sheppard, Staggers, & John, 1997). Meditation produces its benefits by promoting relaxation; the research does not indicate it has any special benefits in comparison to other ways of relaxing (Holmes, 1987).

Suppressing Emotional Expression

In some situations, we may feel pressure to control our outward expressions of emotion, regardless of what we feel inside. Imagine receiving an unfair and rudely phrased criticism from a supervisor at work or a sarcastic comment from a professor. In these situations you might well feel offended, but you risk getting into trouble if you express your anger fully. When people try to hide their emotions, so that a person watching them would not know what they are feeling, most people are able to reduce their expressions (e.g., J. J. Gross, 1998; J. J. Gross, 2002; J. J. Gross & Levenson, 1997). However, this strategy re-

quires much effort and self-monitoring and may be costly in terms of cognitive resources (Richards & Gross, 1999).

Emotional Escape Strategies: Drugs, Alcohol, and Food

If recent events in your life have gone very badly, and you want to escape from the tension—fast—what options would you consider? Go on, be honest.

Many people try using alcohol or other drugs as a quick way to escape their problems, at least occasionally. Many men react to the death of their wife by increasing their consumption of alcohol, sometimes to a dangerous level (Byrne, Raphael, & Arnold, 1999). Many younger people use alcohol to escape from the stresses of work or school. Let's just say that we don't recommend this as a regular strategy. Alcohol by itself is not the problem—huge numbers of people drink alcohol in moderation almost every day without apparent harm—but relying on alcohol or other drugs to escape from problems can easily develop into being a problem itself. Aside from the obvious risks of addiction, and the problems that typically follow, someone who gets high to avoid feeling bad is probably *not* taking constructive actions to resolve the problematic situation.

Another quick way to make yourself feel good is overeating. However, most people who use overeating to escape from tension feel worse afterward (Solomon, 2001; Waters, Hill, & Waller, 2001). Also, as with alcohol and drugs, habitual "emotional eating" tends to crowd out more constructive, problem-focused approaches to negative events.

◻ Which Emotion Regulation Strategies Are Best?

Now that we have listed a broad range of emotion regulation strategies, which ones are best? Before we address this question, note that many are not easily classified as exclusively problem-focused, appraisal-focused, or emotion-focused strategies (Skinner, Edge, Altman, & Sherwood, 2003). For example, we listed "expressing your feelings" as an emotion-based strategy, but in some cases it promotes problem solving as well. Also, consider the many ways in which social support helps us deal with stressful situations. First, think of all the practical, problem-focused effects of social support: Your friends can give you advice about how to deal with the problem. If you have lost your job, they might help you find a new one. If you are sick, they can drive you to the doctor's office, get your medicine, warn you about side effects, bring your meals. Second, think of the ways social support provides emotional comfort. Loneliness hurts, and lonely people are at greater risk for suicide and a wide array of stress-related diseases (Cacioppo, Hawkley, & Berntson, 2003). Happily married people and others with close friendships report less stress, show a stronger immune response, and stay healthier than average (Kiecolt-Glaser, 1999; Kiecolt-Glaser & Newton, 2001). As with any correlational study, we cannot conclude that there is a cause-and-effect relationship, but some studies have addressed the issue by examining people shortly before and after they got married. For example, one study found that medical students who married during school reported decreased stress shortly after getting married. They said their spouse provided care, concern, and encouragement that helped them overcome fatigue and self-doubt (Coombs & Fawzy, 1982).

Although many emotional strategies are difficult to classify, some do fit clearly into one category or another, especially in a specific instance. Studies have observed consistent differences in the apparent effectiveness of the three kinds of strategies. As you might guess, the problem-based strategies, when successful, have major advantages. If you can actually reduce the problem, there is less reason for unpleasant emotions in the first place. One study of recently bereaved widows found that those who felt the most control over the events of their lives experienced the least anxiety (Ong, Bergeman, & Bisconti, 2005). Another study found that adults with attention-deficit hyperactivity disorder were less likely than average to use problem-solving approaches to their stressful situation and, therefore, were more likely to end up in aggressive confrontations (S. Young, 2005).

However, we cannot apply problem-solving approaches to every situation. Consider, for example, chronic illness, war, or the inevitable fact of human mortality. If you have little control over a problem, your choices are to reappraise the situation or to try to regulate your emotions. Ideally, people shift among problem-based, appraisal-based, and emotion-based strategies depending on the situation (Heszen-Niejodek, 1997).

Several studies have compared the effects of reappraisal strategies with those of suppressing emotional expressions. Note that here, "suppression" means something different from what Freud meant by the term (see Table 15.1). Freud used the term to refer to blocking a thought from consciousness, whereas here the term refers to blocking the behavioral *expression* of an emotion. Some individuals suppress their expressions of emotion habitually, as an overall regulation strategy (J. J. Gross & John, 2003). Researchers have consistently found that suppressing facial displays fails to reduce the experience of negative emotion and can actually increase physiological signs of stress (e.g., J. J. Gross, 1998; J. J. Gross, 2002; J. J. Gross & Levenson, 1997). For example, students who were told to suppress their emotional responses to a series of disturbing slides showed increased blood pressure compared with those given no instructions (Richards & Gross, 2000). In another series of studies, women watched a very upsetting film about the nuclear bombing of Hiroshima and Nagasaki during World War II. Then they were asked to discuss the film, either naturally or while suppressing their emotions. Those suppressing their emotions showed increased blood pressure, regardless of what method they used for emotional control (Butler et al., 2003).

Reappraisal and suppression strategies also have different effects on memory. Once people set a reappraisal strategy in motion, they deter the experience of negative emotion and attend to other aspects of the situation. Suppressing your emotion requires constant attention because you monitor your own behavior and think about the instruction to hide your feelings. The cognitive effort involved in the latter strategy leaves less room for other tasks. In studies of participants viewing negative film clips, watching unpleasant slides, and discussing conflicts with a romantic partner, those instructed to suppress their emotion displays consistently showed worse memory for verbal information than those instructed to reappraise or those given no regulation instructions (Richards, Butler, & Gross, 2003; Richards & Gross, 2000).

Studies also suggest that suppression has a negative impact on social relationships, compared with reappraisal. Individuals who report often suppressing their emotional displays rely less on close others for social support and are less well liked. By contrast, people who report more frequent use of reappraisal strategies are better liked by their peers (J. J. Gross & John, 2003). This trend is especially interesting because the most obvious reason for suppressing negative emotion is to avoid conflict with other people. It is unclear whether suppression has a negative impact on interpersonal relations in all situations. However, the effect is clear at the dispositional level. People who habitually hide their emotions from others are difficult to get close to—they may avoid conflict, but they also avoid liking and intimacy in the process.

So, a convergence of the research suggests that suppressing emotion displays is a far from ideal regulation strategy. What about the other emotion-focused strategies? As we noted earlier, talking or writing about a problem can have positive effects on emotional and physical health but only if the person emphasizes resolving the problem, rather than ruminating over negative aspects of the situation. Research on the long-term effects of exercise and meditation are promising, but because such studies typically use correlational designs rather than experimental designs, we are limited in what we can conclude about cause and effect. Certainly the habitual use of drugs, alcohol, and food is a poor method of coping with stress, especially in the long run.

◻ Summary

Although we expressed skepticism about Sigmund Freud's methods and theories, he was right on a basic point: People want to avoid anxiety or stress, and they will try one way after another until they succeed. Many people fall into a habit of relying mainly on one method or another, and some strategies work better than others. When possible, the best approach is almost always to try to solve the problem. Even if you cannot fully overcome the problem, exerting any control over it, or even thinking you are exerting some control, makes it seem less overwhelming.

When you have little or no control, a reappraisal is usually the next best idea. Consider the distressing situation from a different angle: Can anything good come from it? Can you make it an opportunity to do something worthwhile?

Finally, the emotion-focused approaches also have their place, either as a supplement to the others or as a final resort when the others fail. Here the research steers us away from a couple of popular ideas: Vigorously expressing your negative emotions does not, as a rule, help reduce them, and suppressing their expression often backfires, too. An intermediate approach is usually best—thinking about the problem and discussing it with others, but without dwelling or ruminating on it. Periodic exercise helps contain the emotions, as does relaxation.

◻ Key Terms

catharsis: the "release" of strong emotions by experiencing and expressing them fully (p. 307)

cognitive restructuring: changing how one thinks about a major emotional issue or frequently occurring situation—a frequent goal in therapies for mood disorders such as depression and anxiety (p. 304)

coping: the ways that people reduce negative emotion after a stressful event (p. 299)

ego defense mechanisms: psychological regulation strategies that, according to Sigmund Freud, serve to resolve the tension between the id and the super-ego and keep disturbing wishes and desires hidden from consciousness (p. 300)

emotion-focused coping: reducing negative emotions after they have already started (p. 302)

emotion regulation: the strategies we use to control which emotions we have, when we have them, and how strongly we experience and express them (p. 299)

positive reappraisal: focusing on positive aspects of negative or challenging situations (p. 305)

problem-focused coping: controlling the situation we are in, either by choosing to be in one situation rather than another or by changing the situation (p. 302)

process model of emotion regulation: a model that organizes emotion regulation strategies according to their place in the emotion process itself (p. 301)

psychological inoculation: dealing with a stressor by exposing yourself to milder versions of the stressful events (p. 304)

reappraisal: changing the way we think about a particular situation to deter a negative emotion and/or encourage a positive one (p. 302)

rumination: thinking continuously about a problem for a long time, focusing on negative aspects of the situation instead of possible solutions (p. 307)

◻ Thought Questions

1. Identify one or two problems or difficulties in your life. What would be a problem-based and an appraisal- or emotion-based approach to dealing with each problem?

2. Either by yourself or with others, make a list of ways to cope with stressful situations. Try to classify each as problem-focused, appraisal-focused, or emotion-focused strategies. How many of them fit into one category or another?

◻ Suggestion for Research Project

Ask several of your friends to keep a diary for one week, in which they describe the worst thing that happened to them each day and what they did during and after that event to make themselves feel better. Classify each emotion regulation strategy using the categories described in this chapter. At the end of the week, ask your friends to rate how happy they are, in general, with their lives. Do the happier people seem to use different regulation strategies than the less happy people?

◻ Suggestion for Further Reading

Snyder, C. R. (Ed.). *Coping with stress: Effective people and processes.* New York: Oxford University. A collection of chapters by noted researchers.

Epilogue

We've now reached the end of our journey through the scientific literature on emotion. On the one hand, we hope you are impressed with how much you learned from this textbook. After all, we wrote it. On the other hand, we also hope you are disappointed. If we answered all your questions about emotion, you didn't have many questions. Emotion research has come a long way in the past decade or two. It would be hard to appreciate that progress unless you looked at what introductory psychology texts said about emotion 20 years ago. (There weren't any textbooks on emotion.) However, in spite of that progress, many of the biggest questions remain unanswered and sometimes not even clearly stated.

At the beginning of this textbook, we posed several big questions, and although we offered tentative answers, we also noted that researchers still wrestle with those issues today. Now that you've had a chance to immerse yourself in emotion research, let's revisit those questions.

◻ What Is Emotion?

The first question we addressed was the most fundamental: What is emotion? After reviewing several elements of definitions, we offered the following, tentative answer: "An emotion is a universal, functional reaction to an external stimulus event, temporarily integrating physiological, cognitive, phenomenological, and behavioral channels to facilitate a fitness-enhancing, environment-shaping response to the current situation" (Keltner & Shiota, 2003, p. 89). We hope you find this definition easier to understand now than in Chapter 1. Emotions are not just subjective feelings—they reflect measurable changes in our bodies, they are often predictable responses to events in the environment (or at least our interpretations of those events), and they have meaningful effects on our thoughts and behavior. Although we often think of emotion as the most private part of our experience, emotions have a tremendous impact on how we interact with the world around us.

A core feature of this definition is its emphasis on function. According to our claim, emotions serve us well, on average, facilitating sensible, helpful responses to situations we face. Even more specifically, we argued that emotions served functions during our evolution, helping our ancestors to survive threats and to pass on their genes. For example, individuals who feared large, quickly moving objects—such as attacking tigers or stampeding elephants—did not have to think carefully about whether to hide from them or get out of their way.

In other cases, emotions may have increased our ancestors' reproductive success by cementing and smoothing interpersonal relationships. Most of our ancestors lived in small tribes and villages. A person living without such a group had a slim chance of surviving, much less passing on a thriving family. Emotions help motivate us to commit to these bonds, providing emotional rewards for staying close to certain people, and can also help heal the breach when relationships are threatened.

Of course, when we talk about evolutionary functions of emotion, we are talking about function in the hunter-gatherer environment our ancestors lived in tens or hundreds of thousands of years ago. Those of you reading this textbook live in a very different environment today. Our social networks are far larger, yet often more distant, and modern urban, and even suburban and rural ways of life present very different threats and opportunities. Are our emotional responses still functional? We addressed this question explicitly in the chapters on emotional reasoning and stress, but it's a valid question for other aspects of emotion as well. Are some emotions more functional than others? Are emotions more functional in some kinds of situations than others? If you could change anything about your emotions, what would it be, and what effect would it have on your overall life?

In Chapter 1, we also said that researchers disagree on the exact definition of "emotion." After everything you've read in this textbook, what do you think of the definition we proposed? Does it capture everything you think is important about emotion —either the way researchers have studied it, or the way you experience it in your life? If not, how would you change it?

◻ **What Causes Emotions?**

A second major question is: What causes emotions? In Chapter 1, we discussed three major theories of emotion. The James-Lange theory proposes a specific sequence to the emotion process: We interpret or "appraise" an event in a particular way, that ap-

praisal leads to specific patterns of physical changes, the physical changes facilitate certain behaviors, and the physical changes and behaviors in turn create our "feelings" of emotion. According to the Cannon-Bard theory, events lead to appraisals, physiological changes, actions, and feelings, but these components are all independent of each other. Finally, the Schachter-Singer theory proposes that events in the environment cause nonspecific physiological arousal, which is basically the emotion, but we only decide *which* emotion we feel based on all the information we have about a situation.

Of these three, most of the literature supports some version of the James-Lange theory. You had to take our word for this conclusion in Chapter 1, but by now you've seen for yourself how much this theory has influenced emotion research over the past couple of decades. Throughout the chapters on specific emotions, we saw how people's interpretations of situations determine their emotional responses. Several studies, such as the studies of physiological reactions to subliminal photos of spiders, snakes, and people's facial expressions, suggest that we sometimes appraise an event's emotional significance before we're even consciously aware of the event. In Chapter 15, we noted that *re*-appraisal is a particularly effective way for people to alter or change their emotions. In previous chapters, we also saw how physical emotions are. When people are incapable of detecting their own bodies' autonomic nervous system changes, they report feeling little emotion, and although research on central nervous system activation is still young, some studies do suggest that specific emotions activate certain brain areas more than others. And although we don't know for sure that different emotions are associated with different patterns of physiological responses (a feature that distinguishes some interpretations of the James-Lange theory from the Schachter-Singer theory), most researchers focus their attention on particular emotions.

We've also seen, however, some limitations of the James-Lange theory, if it is understood to imply that our physiological responses tell us *which* emotion we are feeling. Schachter and Singer were at least partly right in their claim that physical arousal can be interpreted as a number of different emotions, depending on the person's situation. It is difficult to distinguish among the physiological signs of different negative emotions, at least with current measurement techniques. In some cases, physical arousal associated with fear can even be interpreted as a positive emotion, such as attraction. Another problem with the James-Lange theory is that sometimes the direction of causation implied by the model seems to go *backward!* For example, people who are frightened are more likely to appraise a new event in the environment as a threat. That is, the physiological response influences the next appraisal. The appraisal, physical, behavioral, and feeling aspects of emotion are clearly related to each other (ruling out the Cannon-Bard theory), but the exact nature of these relationships is still something of a mystery. Thus, you can expect that the fundamental theories of emotion may themselves evolve over the next decades of research.

◻ How Many Emotions Are There?

This may be the most difficult question emotion researchers face. As we discussed in Chapter 2, several researchers believe there is no such thing as a "basic" emotion, but rather that emotional feelings range along a continuous spectrum from pleasant to unpleasant and from agitated to calm. Other researchers do believe that there are biologically distinct categories of emotion that should be considered emotional "elements." Who is right? Although we still can't answer that question with certainty, you should now be in a position to form an educated opinion. This is a little unfair because the textbook includes chapters on specific emotions, and we also argued in Chapter 2 that the "basic emotion" approach has generated more ideas for research than the dimensional and componential approaches. Nevertheless, you can re-examine various

studies: Which approach did the researchers apparently have in mind when they designed the study? Were the results consistent with that approach? Is it possible to explain the results in terms of the alternative approach?

Even researchers who do accept the "basic emotion" approach do not agree on the number of basic emotions. Largely because they were included in the groundbreaking cross-cultural studies of emotional expression, the "Ekman six"—happiness, surprise, fear, anger, sadness, and disgust—are what most people consider basic emotions. Although the vast majority of research has focused on these emotions, even Paul Ekman doesn't regard it as the final, definitive list. Researchers who study other emotions often describe them as a separate category—positive emotions, social bonding emotions, self-conscious emotions—suggesting something of a second-class status. Which of these, if any, qualify as "basic"? Possible criteria discussed in Chapter 2 included universal experience, functionality in the sense of enhancing survival and reproductive fitness, evidence early in life, universal expression, and unique central and/or autonomic nervous system physiology. Just demonstrating *one* of these criteria is challenging, much less demonstrating all of them. The truth is, it will take a great deal of time and effort to resolve these questions. Until then, we hope the research you've read about here sparks your interest in the kind of studies needed.

◻ How Do We Measure Emotion?

Measurement is an important and contentious issue in any area of science, and we have returned to this point repeatedly. Measurement is especially challenging for emotion researchers because emotion is something we have to *infer* in other people; we cannot observe it directly.

Each strategy for measuring emotion has strengths and weaknesses. A good study would use some of each kind of measure, but that's not always feasible. The "best" measures of emotion, such as they are, require observing research participants in a laboratory or other, very controlled situations. But strong emotions happen in real life—in the lab we elicit mild emotions, at best. After all, we can't measure people's heart rate and blood pressure when they have just escaped an automobile accident, at least not with current technologies. Self-report measures may be the least desirable in terms of validity, but they travel well.

When it is possible to take multiple measures of emotion, what if the different measures disagree? Which kind of measure should be the "gold standard"? In most studies presented in this textbook, self-reported emotion was the primary or only measurement, even though many researchers question the validity of self-reports. For the past several years, research on emotional brain activity has been hugely popular, suggesting that the ideal measure might be activation in some emotion-specific brain area. Even this claim, however, may be an oversimplification: Saying that some brain area becomes more active during an emotion is not the same as saying that the area becomes active *only* with emotion. Besides, how do we know it becomes active during emotion, except by correlating it with another measure—such as self-report?

Why do we care so much about measurement? First, scientific progress almost always depends on improved measurements. Second, results of emotion research vary with different measures. For example, researchers studying the causes of anger offer different explanations, depending on whether they are explaining self-reports of anger or aggressive behavior. Even different kinds of self-report measures may lead to different conclusions. For example, guilt and shame look somewhat similar when people are simply asked to describe experiences that made them feel ashamed or guilty, but dispositionally shame-prone people react to social situations quite differently from guilt-prone people.

When reading through the studies we've described in this textbook, did you ever find yourself questioning the methods used to elicit emotion, or the way in which emotion was measured? Which studies did you find most convincing, and what kinds of measures did they use?

◘ Connections to Other Topics in Psychology

Our final big question is: Where does emotion fit into the rest of psychology? After all, psychology departments don't typically have an "emotion" specialty the way they have social psychology, developmental psychology, and clinical psychology specialties. To what major areas of psychology is research on emotion relevant? The answer is, of course, all of them.

Perhaps the most obvious application is to social psychology, and many emotion researchers were trained primarily as social psychologists. This is increasingly true as researchers acknowledge that emotions have social functions, as well as intrapersonal ones. Three emotions that are widely accepted as "basic" (fear, anger, disgust) all have something in common: Their function is clearly to keep you alive and out of danger. But researchers are increasingly interested in another function of emotion, that of developing and maintaining relationships with other people. For the various kinds of love, and the self-conscious emotions, social functions are the main or only functions.

Social psychologists are also interested in the role of culture in emotion. The definition of emotion we offered in Chapter 1 emphasized universal aspects of emotion. In Chapter 3 and beyond, however, we've emphasized how people's day-to-day emotional experiences can differ, depending on their culture. Universality and cultural differences may seem like opposing claims, but they don't need to be. Even if the "foundation" of emotions consists of universal links among certain appraisals, physiological reactions, and behavior impulses, much room remains for cultural influences. People in different cultures can find different meanings in the same event. Cultures may use very different conceptual categories when thinking about emotion, and they can talk about emotion in different ways. Cultures may also have different rules for what emotions to express or conceal in various situations. Although the vast majority of research on emotion still emphasizes what is universal, or nearly so, researchers are becoming more interested in explaining the aspects of emotion that differ between cultures.

An understanding of emotion is also critical in developmental psychology. Some of the most carefully studied processes in early development— learning about the world, forming relationships with others—are driven largely by emotion. Because very young children can't tell us what they're thinking, we often use their emotional reactions to get a sense of how they interpret their world. Researchers also learn a lot about emotions by looking at how they develop in children. For example, the most illuminating research on the self-conscious emotions has come from psychologists interested in the development of self-awareness and the ability to guess what others are thinking and feeling.

Although Western philosophy often thinks of the heart and mind as mutually exclusive, research on emotion is important for cognitive psychology as well. Our emotional reactions closely relate to our attention and to our interpretations of events. Emotions influence what we notice about the environment, what we remember, and how we evaluate information.

Emotion has also emerged as a growing field of interest in biological psychology or neuroscience. Much of the research focuses on the amygdala. After damage to the amygdala, both people and laboratory animals show clear impairments in interpreting emotional situations. They frequently fail to show fear in situations where it seems appropriate (to everyone else). Understanding how the brain works requires understanding how emotion fits in with the other processes.

Clinical psychologists spend most of their time dealing with people's emotional difficulties. Many clinical diagnoses, such as depression, mania, and anxiety disorder, are based primarily on excessive amounts of one emotion or another. In learning about the biological characteristics of these disorders, and in finding effective ways to treat them, we also learn much about the emotions themselves. At the same time, knowing more about "normal" versions of these emotions may help guide treatment more effectively; in the past, treatments have often been identified through trial and error.

Finally, and perhaps most important, emotion is part of our everyday lives. Sometimes the emotions we feel contribute to our quality of life, and sometimes they interfere with it. We also deal with other people's emotions—pleasant and unpleasant ones—all the time. Emotions are not completely beyond our control. With practice, we can learn to manage our own emotions and to understand and respond to other people's emotions more effectively. We hope that you've learned some things from this text that improve your life, and we wish you a high ratio of positive to negative emotions.

References

Abbar, M., Courtet, P., Bellivier, F., Leboyer, M., Boulenger, J. P., Castelhau, D., et al. (2001). Suicide attempts and the tryptophan hydroxylase gene. *Molecular Psychiatry, 6,* 268–273.

Abbey, A. (1982). Sexual differences in attributions for friendly behavior: Do males misperceive females' friendliness? *Journal of Personality and Social Psychology, 42,* 830–838.

Abercrombie, H. C., Kalin, N. H., Thurow, M. E., Rosenkranz, M. A., & Davidson, R. J. (2003). Cortisol variation in humans affects memory for emotionally laden and neutral information. *Behavioral Neuroscience, 117,* 505–516.

Abramov, I., Gordon, J., Hendrickson, A., Hainline, L., Dobson, V., & LaBossiere, E. (1982). The retina of the newborn human infant. *Science, 217,* 265–267.

Abu-Lughod, L. (1986). *Veiled sentiments.* Berkeley: University of California Press.

Ackermann, R., & DeRubeis, R. J. (1991). Is depressive realism real? *Clinical Psychology Review, 11,* 565–584.

Adamec, R. E., Stark-Adamec, C., & Livingston, K. E. (1980). The development of predatory aggression and defense in the domestic cat (*Felis catus*): 3. Effects on development of hunger between 180 and 365 days of age. *Behavioral and Neural Biology, 30,* 435–447.

Adams, R. B., & Kleck, R. E. (2003). Perceived gaze direction and the processing of facial displays of emotion. *Psychological Science, 14,* 644–647.

Adams, R. B., & Kleck, R. E. (2005). Effects of direct and averted gaze on the perception of facially communicated emotion. *Emotion, 5,* 3–11.

Adler, A. (1927). *Understanding human nature.* New York: Greenberg.

Adolph, K. E. (2000). Specificity of learning: Why infants fall over a veritable cliff. *Psychological Science, 11,* 290–295.

Adolphs, R., Baron-Cohen, S., & Tranel, D. (2002). Impaired recognition of social emotions following amygdala damage. *Journal of Cognitive Neuroscience, 14,* 1264–1274.

Adolphs, R., Damasio, H., & Tranel, D. (2002). Neural systems for recognition of emotional prosody: A 3-D lesion study. *Emotion, 2,* 23–51.

Adolphs, R., Denburg, N. L., & Tranel, D. (2001). The amygdala's role in long-term declarative memory for gist and detail. *Behavioral Neuroscience, 115,* 983–992.

Adolphs, R., Gosselin, F., Buchanan, T. W., Tranel, D., Schyns, P., & Damasio, A. R. (2005). A mechanism for impaired fear recognition after amygdala damage. *Nature, 433,* 68–72.

Adolphs, R., Tranel, D., & Damasio, A. R. (1998). The human amygdala in social judgment. *Nature, 393,* 470–474.

Adolphs, R., Tranel, D., & Damasio, A. R. (2003). Dissociable neural systems for recognizing emotions. *Brain and Cognition, 52,* 61–69.

Adolphs, R., Tranel, D., Damasio, H., & Damasio, A. (1994). Impaired recognition of emotion in facial expressions following bilateral damage to the human amygdala. *Nature, 372,* 669–672.

Adolphs, R., Tranel, D., Damasio, H., & Damasio, A. R. (1995). Fear and the human amygdala. *Journal of Neuroscience, 15,* 5879–5891.

Ainsworth, M. D. S. (1989). Attachments beyond infancy. *American Psychologist, 44,* 709–716.

Akirav, I., & Richter-Levin, G. (1999). Biphasic modulation of hippocampal plasticity by behavioral stress and basolateral amygdala stimulation in the rat. *Journal of Neuroscience, 19,* 10530–10535.

Alicke, M. D., & Largo, E. (1995). The role of the self in the false consensus effect. *Journal of Experimental Social Psychology, 31,* 28–47.

Allen, N. B., & Badcock, P. B. T. (2003). The social risk hypothesis of depressed mood: Evolutionary, psychosocial, and neurobiological perspectives. *Psychological Bulletin, 129,* 887–913.

Alloy, L. B., & Abramson, L. Y. (1979). Judgment of contingency in depressed and nondepressed students: Sadder but wiser? *Journal of Experimental Psychology: General, 108*, 441–485.

Alloy, L. B., Abramson, L. Y., Whitehouse, W. G., Hogan, M. E., Tashman, N. A., Steinberg, D. L., et al. (1999). Depressogenic cognitive styles: Predictive validity, information processing and personality characteristics, and developmental origins. *Behaviour Research and Therapy, 37*, 503–531.

American Enterprise (1992, January/February). Women, men, marriages, and ministers (p. 106).

American Psychiatric Association. (1994). *Diagnostic and statistical manual of psychiatric disorders* (4th ed.). Washington, DC: Author.

Anderson, A. K., & Phelps, E. A. (2000). Expression without recognition: Contributions of the human amygdala to emotional communication. *Psychological Science, 11*, 106–111.

Anderson, A. K., & Phelps, E. A. (2001). Lesions of the human amygdala impair enhanced perception of emotionally salient events. *Nature, 411*, 305–309.

Anderson, A. K., & Phelps, E. A. (2002). Is the human amygdala critical for the subjective experience of emotion? Evidence of intact dispositional affect in patients with amygdala lesions. *Journal of Cognitive Neuroscience, 14*, 709–720.

Anderson, C., Keltner, D., & John, O. P. (2003). Emotional convergence between people over time. *Journal of Personality and Social Psychology, 84*, 1054–1068.

Anderson, C. A. (2001). Heat and violence. *Current Directions in Psychological Science, 10*, 33–38.

Anderson, C. A., & Bushman, B. J. (2001). Effects of violent video games on aggressive behavior, aggressive cognition, aggressive affect, physiological arousal, and prosocial behavior: A meta-analytic review of the scientific literature. *Psychological Science, 12*, 353–359.

Anderson, S. W., Bechara, A., Damasio, H., Tranel, D., & Damasio, A. R. (1999). Impairment of social and moral behavior related to early damage in human prefrontal cortex. *Nature Neuroscience, 2*, 1032–1037.

Angold, A., Costello, E. J., & Worthman, C. M. (1998). Puberty and depression: The role of age, pubertal status, and pubertal timing. *Psychological Medicine, 28*, 51–61.

Archer, J. (2000). Sex differences in aggression between heterosexual partners: A meta-analytic review. *Psychological Bulletin, 126*, 651–680.

Arnett, J. J. (1999). Adolescent storm and stress reconsidered: *American Psychologist, 54*, 317–326.

Arnett, J. J. (2000). Emerging adulthood: A theory of development from the late teens through the twenties. *American Psychologist, 55*, 469–480.

Arnold, M. B. (1960). *Emotion and personality* (Vols. 1–2). New York: Columbia University Press.

Arnold, M. J., & Reynolds, K. E. (2003). Hedonic shopping motivations. *Journal of Retailing, 79*, 77–95.

Aron, A., Melinat, E. Aron, E. N., Vallone, R. D., & Bator, R. J. (1997). The experimental generation of interpersonal closeness: A procedure and some preliminary findings. *Personality and Social Psychology Bulletin, 23*, 363–377.

Aron, A., Norman, C. C., Aron, E. N., McKenna, C., & Heyman, R. E. (2000). Couples' shared participation in novel and arousing activities and experienced relationship quality. *Journal of Personality and Social Psychology, 78*, 273–284.

Aron, A., Paris, M., & Aron, E. N. (1995). Falling in love: Prospective studies of self-concept change. *Journal of Personality and Social Psychology, 69*, 1102–1112.

Aspinwall, L. G., & Richter, L. (1999). Optimism and self-mastery predict more rapid disengagement from unsolvable tasks in the presence of alternatives. *Motivation and Emotion, 23*, 221–245.

Astington, J. W., & Gopnik, A. (1991). Theoretical explanations of children's understanding of the mind. *British Journal of Developmental Psychology. Special Perspectives on the Child's Theory of Mind: I. 9*(1), 7–31.

Augustine. (1955). *Confessions* (A. C. Outler, Trans.). (Original work written 397.) Retrieved Jan. 13, 2005, from http://www.ccel.org/a/augustine/confessions/confessions.html

Austin, E. J. (2004). An investigation of the relationship between trait emotional intelligence and emotional task performance. *Personality and Individual Differences, 36*, 1855–1864.

Austin, E. J., Saklofske, D. H., Huang, S. H. S., & McKenney, D. (2004). Measurement of trait emotional intelligence: Testing and cross-validating a modified version of Schutte et al.'s measure. *Personality and Individual Differences, 36*, 555–562.

Averill, J. R. (1983). Studies on anger and aggression: Implications for theories of emotion. *American Psychologist, 38,* 1145–1160.

Ayduk, O., Mischel, W., & Downey, G. (2002). Attentional mechanisms linking rejection to hostile reactivity: The role of "hot" versus "cool" focus. *Psychological Science, 13,* 443–448.

Bāccman, C., Folkesson, P., & Norlander, T. (1999). Expectations of romantic relationships: A comparison between homosexual and heterosexual men with regard to Baxter's criteria. *Social Behavior and Personality, 27,* 363–374.

Bachorowski, J.-A., & Owren, M. J. (2001). Not all laughs are alike: Voiced but not unvoiced laughter readily elicits positive affect. *Psychological Science, 12,* 252–257.

Bagwell, C. L., Newcomb, A. F., & Bukowski, W. M. (1998). Preadolescent friendship and peer rejection as predictors of adult adjustment. *Child Development, 69,* 140–153.

Baillargeon, R. (1986). Representing the existence and location of hidden objects: Object permanence in 6- and 8-month-old infants. *Cognition, 23,* 21–41.

Baillargeon, R. (1987). Object permanence in $3\frac{1}{2}$- and $4\frac{1}{2}$-month-old infants. *Developmental Psychology, 23,* 655–664.

Bair, M. J., Robinson, R. L., Katon, W., & Kroenke, K. (2003). Depression and pain comorbidity: A literature review. *Archives of Internal Medicine, 163,* 2433–2445.

Baker, K. B., & Kim, J. J. (2004). Amygdalar lateralization in fear conditioning: Evidence for greater involvement of the right amygdala. *Behavioral Neuroscience, 118,* 15–23.

Banks, M. S., & Salapatek, P. (1983). Infant visual perception. In P. H. Mussen (Series Ed.) & M. Haith & J. J. Campos (Vol. Eds.), *Handbook of child psychology: Vol 2. Infancy and developmental psychobiology* (4th ed., pp. 435–571). New York: Wiley.

Bard, K. A. (2000). Crying in infant primates: Insights into the development of crying in chimpanzees. In R. G. Barr, B. Hopkins, & J. A. Green (Eds.), *Crying as a sign, a symptom, & a signal* (pp. 157–175). London: MacKeith Press.

Bard, P. (1934). On emotional expression after decortication with some remarks on certain theoretical views. *Psychological Review, 41,* 309–329.

Bartels, A., & Zeki, S. (2000). The neural basis of romantic love. *Neuroreport, 11,* 3829–3834.

Bartholomew, K. (1990). Avoidance of intimacy: An attachment perspective. *Journal of Social and Personal Relationships, 7,* 147–178.

Bartholomew, K., & Horowitz, L. M. (1991). Attachment styles among young adults: A test of a four-category model. *Journal of Personality and Social Psychology, 61,* 226–244.

Basabe, N., Paez, D., Valencia, J., Gonzalez, J. L., Rimé, B., & Diener, E. (2002). Cultural dimensions, socioeconomic development, climate, and emotional hedonic level. *Cognition and Emotion, 16,* 103–125.

Batson, C. D., O'Quin, K., Fultz, J., Vandeplas, M., & Isen, A. (1983). Self-reported distress and empathy and egoistic versus altruistic motivation for helping. *Journal of Personality and Social Psychology, 45,* 706–718.

Battaglia, M., Bertella, S., Ogliari, A., Bellodi, L., & Smeraldi, E. (2001). Modulation by muscarinic antagonists of the response to carbon dioxide challenge in panic disorder. *Archives of General Psychiatry, 58,* 114–119.

Bauby, J.-D. (1997). *The diving bell and the butterfly* (J. Leggatt, Trans.). New York: Knopf.

Bauer, J. J., & Bonanno, G. A. (2001). Doing and being well (for the most part): Adaptive patterns of narrative self-evaluation during bereavement. *Journal of Personality, 69,* 451–482.

Baumeister, R. F., Smart, L., & Boden, J. M. (1996). Relation of threatened egotism to violence and aggression: The dark side of high self-esteem. *Psychological Review, 103,* 5–33.

Bäumler, G. (1994). On the validity of the Yerkes-Dodson law. *Studia Psychologica, 36,* 205–209.

Baxter, M. G., & Murray, E. A. (2002). The amygdala and reward. *Nature Reviews Neuroscience, 3,* 563–573.

Beasley, M., Thompson, T., & Davidson, J. (2003). Resilience in response to life stress: The effects of coping style and cognitive hardiness. *Personality and Individual Differences, 34,* 77–95.

Beauregard, M., Lévesque, J., & Bourgouin, P. (2001). Neural correlates of conscious self-regulation of emotion. *Journal of Neuroscience, 21* (RC165).

Bechara, A. (2004). The role of emotion in decision-making: Evidence from neurological patients with orbitofrontal damage. *Brain and Cognition, 55,* 30–40.

Bechara, A., Damasio, H., Damasio, A. R., & Lee, G. P. (1999). Different contributions of the human amygdala and ventromedial prefrontal cortex to decision-making. *Journal of Neuroscience, 19,* 5473–5481.

Becht, M. C., & Vingerhoets, A. J. J. M. (2002). Crying and mood change: A cross-cultural study. *Cognition and Emotion, 16,* 87–101.

Beck, A. T. (1973). *The diagnosis and management of depression.* Philadelphia: University of Pennsylvania Press.

Beck, A. T. (1987). Cognitive models of depression. *Journal of Cognitive Psychotherapy, 1,* 5–37.

Becker, C., Thiébot, M.-H., Touitou, Y., Hamon, M., Cesselin, F., & Benoliel, J.-J. (2001). Enhanced cortical extracellular levels of cholecystokinin-like material in a model of anticipation of social defeat in the rat. *Journal of Neuroscience, 21,* 262–269.

Beebe, B. (2003). Brief mother-infant treatment: Psychoanalytically informed video feedback. *Infant Mental Health Journal, 24,* 24–52.

Beebe, B., Jaffe, J., Lachman, F., Feldstein, S., Crown, C., & Jasnow, M. (2000). Systems models in development and psychoanalysis: The case of vocal rhythm coordination and attachment. *Infant Mental Health Journal, 21,* 99–122.

Benjamin, J., Li, L., Patterson, C., Greenberg, B. D., Murphy, D. L., & Hamer, D. H. (1996). Population and familial association between the D4 dopamine receptor gene and measures of novelty seeking. *Nature Genetics, 12,* 81–84.

Benschop, R. J., Godaert, G. L. R., Geenen, R., Brosschot, J. F., DeSmet, M. B. M., Olff, M., et al. (1995). Relationships between cardiovascular and immunologic changes in an experimental stress model. *Psychological Medicine, 25,* 323–327.

Benson, H. (1985). Stress, health, and the relaxation response. In W. D. Gentry, H. Benson, & C. J. de Wolff (Eds.), *Behavioral medicine: Work, stress and health* (pp. 15–32). Dordrecht, Netherlands: Martinus Nijhoff.

Bentham, J. (1970). *An introduction to the principles of morals and legislation.* London: Methuen. (Original work published 1780)

Berdoy, M., Webster, J. P., & Macdonald, D. W. (2000). Fatal attraction in rats infected with *Toxoplasma gondii. Proceedings of the Royal Society of London,* B, *267,* 1591–1594.

Berkowitz, L. (1990). On the formation and regulation of anger and aggression: A cognitive neo-associationistic analysis. *American Psychologist, 45,* 494–503.

Berkowitz, L., Cochran, S., & Embree, M. (1981). Physical pain and the goal of aversively stimulated aggression. *Journal of Personality and Social Psychology, 40,* 687–700.

Berkowitz, L., & Harmon-Jones, E. (2004). Toward an understanding of the determinants of anger. *Emotion, 4,* 107–130.

Berlin, H. A., Rolls, E. T., & Kischka, U. (2004). Impulsivity, time perception, emotion and reinforcement sensitivity in patients with orbitofrontal cortex lesions. *Brain, 127,* 1108–1126.

Berman, M., Gladue, B., & Taylor, S. (1993). The effects of hormones, Type A behavior pattern, and provocation on aggression in men. *Motivation and Emotion, 17,* 125–138.

Bernhardt, P. C. (1997). Influences of serotonin and testosterone in aggression and dominance: Convergence with social psychology. *Current Directions in Psychological Science, 6,* 44–48.

Berridge, K. C., & Robinson, T. E. (1995). The mind of an addicted brain: Neural sensitization of wanting versus liking. *Current Directions in Psychological Science, 4,* 71–76.

Bersheid, E. (1983). Emotion. In H. H. Kelley, E. Bersheid, A. Christensen, J. H. Harvey, T. L. Huston, G. Levinger, et al., *Close relationships* (pp. 110–168). New York: W. H. Freeman.

Best, M., Williams, J. M., & Coccaro, E. F. (2002). Evidence for a dysfunctional prefrontal circuit in patients with an impulsive aggressive disorder. *Proceedings of the National Academy of Sciences, (USA), 99,* 8448–8453.

Biben, M. (1979). Predation and predatory play behaviour of domestic cats. *Animal Behaviour, 27,* 81–94.

Bierut, L. J., Heath, A. C., Bucholz, K. K., Dinwiddie, S. H., Madden, P. A. F., Statham, D. J., et al. (1999). Major depressive disorder in a community-based twin sample. *Archives of General Psychiatry, 56,* 557–563.

Birditt, K. S., & Fingerman, K. L. (2003). Age and gender differences in adults' descriptions of emotional reactions to interpersonal problems. *Journal of Gerontology: Psychological Sciences, 58B,* P237–P245.

Birdwhistell, R. (1970). *Kinesics and context.* Philadelphia: University of Pennsylvania Press.

Birnbaum, M. H. (1999). Testing critical properties of decision making on the Internet. *Psychological Science, 10,* 399–407.

Birnbaum, M. H., & Sotoodeh, Y. (1991). Measurement of stress: Scaling the magnitudes of life changes. *Psychological Science, 2,* 236–243.

Bishop, S. J., Duncan, J., & Lawrence, A. D. (2004). State anxiety modulation of the amygdala response to unattended threat-related stimuli. *Journal of Neuroscience, 24,* 10364–10368.

Blackford, J. U., & Walden, T. A. (1998). Individual differences in social referencing. *Infant Behavior and Development, 21,* 89–102.

Blair, R. J. R., Mitchell, D. G. V., Peschardt, K. S., Colledge, E., Leonard, R. A., Shine, J. H., et al. (2004). Reduced sensitivity to others' fearful expressions in psychopathic individuals. *Personality and Individual Differences, 37,* 1111–1122.

Blanchette, I., & Richards, A. (2003). Anxiety and the interpretation of ambiguous information: Beyond the emotion-congruent effect. *Journal of Experimental Psychology: General, 132,* 294–309.

Blanchette, I., & Richards, A. (2004). Reasoning about emotional and neutral materials. *Psychological Science, 15,* 745–752.

Blascovich, J., & Tomaka, J. (1991). Measures of self-esteem. In J. P. Robinson, R. R. Shaver, & L. S. Wrightsman (Eds.), *Measures of personality and social psychological attitudes* (pp. 115–160). San Diego, CA: Academic Press.

Bless, H., Bohner, G., Schwarz, N., & Strack, F. (1990). Mood and persuasion: A cognitive response analysis. *Personality and Social Psychology Bulletin, 16,* 331–345.

Bless, H., Clore, G. L., Schwarz, N., Golisane, V., Rabe, C., & Wölk, M. (1996). Mood and the use of scripts: Does a happy mood really lead to mindlessness? *Journal of Personality and Social Psychology, 71,* 665–679.

Blood, A. J., & Zatorre, R. J. (2001). Intensely pleasurable responses to music correlate with activity in brain regions implicated in reward and emotion. *Proceedings of the National Academy of Sciences, 98,* 11818–11823.

Bodenhausen, G. V., Kramer, G. P., & Süsser, K. (1994). Happiness and stereotypic thinking in social judgment. *Journal of Personality and Social Psychology, 66,* 621–632.

Bodner, G., Ho, A., & Kreek, M. J. (1998). Effect of endogenous cortisol levels on natural killer cell activity in healthy humans. *Brain, Behavior, and Immunity, 12,* 285–296.

Bolles, R. C. (1970). Species-specific defense reactions and avoidance learning. *Psychological Review, 77,* 32–48.

Bolte, A., Goschke, T., & Kuhl, J. (2003). Emotion and intuition: Effects of positive and negative mood on implicit judgments of semantic coherence. *Psychological Science, 14,* 416–421.

Bonanno, G. A., & Keltner, D. (2004). The coherence of emotion systems: Comparing "on-line" measures of appraisal and facial expressions, and self-report. *Cognition and Emotion, 18,* 431–444.

Bond, A. J., Bauer, A., & Wingrove, J. (2004). Outcome of aggression affects processing and can legitimise subsequent aggression: Influence of trait aggressiveness. *Aggressive Behavior, 30,* 284–297.

Bond, M. H. (2002). Reclaiming the individual from Hofstede's ecological analysis—A 20-year odyssey: Comment on Oyserman et al. (2002). *Psychological Bulletin, 128,* 73–77.

Bongard, S., & al'Absi, M. (2003). Domain-specific anger expression assessment and blood pressure during rest and acute stress. *Personality and Individual Differences, 34,* 1383–1402.

Borella, P., Bargellini, A., Rovesti, S., Pinelli, M., Vivoli, R., Solfrini, V., et al. (1999). Emotional stability, anxiety, and natural killer activity under examination stress. *Psychoneuroendocrinology, 24,* 613–627.

Boucher, J. D. (1979). Culture and emotion. In A. J. Marsella, R. G. Tharp, & T. V. Ciborowski (Eds.), *Perspectives on cross-cultural psychology* (pp. 159–178). San Diego, CA: Academic Press.

Boucsein, K., Weniger, G., Mursch, K., Steinhoff, B. J., & Irle, E. (2001). Amygdala lesion in temporal lobe epilepsy subjects impairs associative learning of emotional facial expressions. *Neuropsychologia, 39,* 231–236.

Bouton, M. E., Mineka, S., & Barlow, D. H. (2001). A modern learning theory perspective on the etiology of panic disorder. *Psychological Review, 108,* 4–32.

Bower, T. G. R. (1977). *A primer of infant development.* San Francisco: W. H. Freeman.

Bowlby, J. (1969). *Attachment and loss: Vol. 1: Attachment.* New York: Basic Books.

Bowlby, J. (1979). *The making and breaking of affectional bonds.* London: Tavistock Publications.

Bowlby, J. (1980). *Attachment and loss: Vol. 3: Loss: Sadness and depression.* New York: Basic Books.

Boyatzis, C. J., Matillo, G. M., & Nesbitt, K. M. (1995). Effect of the "Mighty Morphin' Power Rangers" on children's aggression with peers. *Child Study Journal, 25*(1), 45–55.

Boyle, R. H. (1992, September–October). The joy of cooking insects. *Audubon, 94,* 100–103.

Brackett, M. A., Mayer, J. D., & Warner, R. M. (2004). Emotional intelligence and its relation to everyday behaviour. *Personality and Individual Differences, 36,* 1387–1402.

Bradley, M. M., Greenwald, M. K., Petry, M. C., & Lang, P. J. (1992). Remembering pictures: Pleasure and arousal in memory. *Journal of Experimental Psychology: Learning, Memory, and Cognition, 18,* 379–390.

Bradley, M. M., & Lang, O. J. (2000). Measuring emotion: Behavior, feeling, and physiology. In R. D. Lane & L. Nadel (Eds.), *Cognitive neuroscience of emotion* (pp. 242–276). New York: Oxford University Press.

Breiter, H. C., Aharon, I., Kahneman, D., Dale, A., & Shizgal, P. (2001). Functional imaging of neural responses to expectancy and experience of monetary gains and losses. *Neuron, 30,* 619–639.

Breiter, H. C., Etcoff, N. L., Whalen, P. J., Kennedy, W. A., Rauch, S. L., Buckner, R. L., et al. (1996). Response and habituation of the human amygdala during visual processing of facial expression. *Neuron, 17,* 875–887.

Bremner, J. D., Vythilingam, M., Anderson, G., Vermetten, E., McGlashan, T., Heninger, G., et al. (2003). Assessment of the hypothalamic-pituitary-adrenal axis over a 24-hour diurnal period and in response to neuroendocrine challenges in women with and without childhood sexual abuse and posttraumatic stress disorder. *Biological Psychiatry, 54,* 710–718.

Brennan, K. A., Clark, C. L., & Shaver, P. R. (1998). Self-report measurement of adult attachment: An integrative overview. In J. A. Simpson & W. S. Rholes (Eds.), *Attachment theory and close relationships* (pp. 46–76). New York: Guilford.

Brennan, P. A., Grekin, E. R., & Mednick, S. A. (1999). Maternal smoking during pregnancy and adult male criminal outcomes. *Archives of General Psychiatry, 56,* 215–219.

Brent, D. A., Oquendo, M., Birmaher, B., Greenhill, L., Kolko, D., Stanley, B., et al. (2002). Familial pathways to early onset sicide attempt: Risk for suicidal behavior in offspring of mood-disordered suicide attempters. *Archives of General Psychiatry, 59,* 801–807.

Bretherton, I., Fritz, J., Zahn-Waxler, C., & Ridgeway, D. (1986). Learning to talk about emotions: A functionalist perspective. *Child Development, 57,* 529–548.

Brooks, J., & Lewis, M. (1976). Infants' responses to strangers: Midget, adult, and child. *Child Development, 47,* 323–332.

Brooks, J. H., & Reddon, J. R. (1996). Serum testosterone in violent and nonviolent young offenders. *Journal of Clinical Psychology, 52,* 475–483.

Brown, G. P., MacLeod, A. K., Tata, P., & Goddard, L. (2002). Worry and the simulation of future outcomes. *Anxiety, Stress and Coping, 15,* 1–17.

Bruce, S. E., Machan, J. T., Dyck, I., & Keller, M. B. (2001). Infrequency of "pure" GAD: Impact of psychiatric comorbidity on clinical course. *Depression and Anxiety, 14,* 219–225.

Büchel, C., Morris, J., Dolan, R. J., & Friston, K. J. (1998). Brain systems mediating aversive conditioning: An event-related fMRI study. *Neuron, 20,* 947–957.

Burke, J. D., Loeber, R., & Birmaher, B. (2002). Oppositional defiant disorder and conduct disorder: A review of the past 10 years, part II. *Journal of the American Academy of Child and Adolescent Psychiatry, 41,* 1275–1293.

Burke, K. C., Burke, J. D., Jr., Regier, D. A., & Rae, D. S. (1990). Age at onset of selected mental disorders in five community populations. *Archives of General Psychiatry, 47,* 511–518.

Burleson, M. H., Poehlmann, K. M., Hawkley, L. C., Ernst, J. M., Berntson, G. G., Malarkey, W. B., et al. (2002). Stress-related immune changes in middle-aged and older women: 1-year consistency of individual differences. *Health Psychology, 21,* 321–331.

Burns, M. O., & Seligman, M. E. P. (1989). Explanatory style across the life span: Evidence for stability over 50 years. *Journal of Personality and Social Psychology, 56,* 471–477.

Burton, C. M., & King, L. A. (2004). The health benefits of writing about intensely positive experiences. *Journal of Research in Personality, 38,* 150–163.

Bushman, B. J., & Anderson, C. A. (2001). Media violence and the American public: Scientific facts versus media misinformation. *American Psychologist, 56,* 477–489.

Buss, D. M. (1989). Sex differences in human mate preferences: Evolutionary hypotheses tested in 37 cultures. *Behavioral and Brain Sciences, 12,* 1–49.

Buss, D. M. (2000). The evolution of happiness. *American Psychologist, 55,* 15–23.

Buss, K. A., Schumacher, J. R. M., Dolski, I., Kalin, N. H., Goldsmith, H. H., & Davidson, R. J. (2003). Right frontal brain activity, cortisol, and withdrawal behavior in 6-month-old infants. *Behavioral Neuroscience, 117,* 11–20.

Butler, E. A., Egloff, B., Wilhelm, F. H., Smith, N. C., Erickson, E. A., & Gross, J. J. (2003). The social consequences of expressive suppression. *Emotion, 3,* 48–67.

Buunk, B. P., & Van Yperen, N. W. (1991). Referential comparisons, relational comparisons, and exchange orientation: Their relation to marital satisfaction. *Personality and Social Psychology Bulletin, 17,* 709–717.

Byrne, G. J. A., Raphael, B., & Arnold, E. (1999). Alcohol consumption and psychological distress in recently widowed older men. *Australian and New Zealand Journal of Psychiatry, 33,* 740–747.

Cacioppo, J. T., Hawkley, L. C., & Berntson, G. G. (2003). The anatomy of loneliness. *Current Directions in Psychological Science, 12,* 71–74.

Cadoret, R. J., Yates, W. R., Troughton, E., Woodworth, G., & Steward, M. A. (1995). Genetic-environmental interaction in the genesis of aggressivity and conduct disorders. *Archives of General Psychiatry, 52,* 916–924.

Cahill, L., & McGaugh, J. L. (1998). Mechanisms of emotional arousal and lasting declarative memory. *Trends in Neurosciences, 21,* 294–299.

Cahill, L., Prins, B., Weber, M., & McGaugh, J. L. (1994). ß-Adrenergic activation and memory for emotional events. *Nature, 371,* 702–704.

Calder, A. J., Keane, J., Manes, F., Antoun, N., & Young, A. W. (2000). Impaired recognition and experience of disgust following brain injury. *Nature Neuroscience, 3,* 1077–1078.

Calvo, M. G., & Avero, P. (2002). Eye movement assessment of emotional processing in anxiety. *Emotion, 2,* 105–117.

Calvo, M. G., & Avero, P. (2005). Time course of attentional bias to emotional scenes in anxiety: Gaze direction and duration. *Cognition and Emotion, 19,* 433–451.

Camara, W. J. (1988). Reagan signs ban of polygraph testing for job applicants. *The Industrial-Organizational Psychologist, 26,* 39–41.

Cameron, H. A., & McKay, R. D. G. (1999). Restoring production of hippocampal neurons in old age. *Nature Neuroscience, 2,* 894–897.

Camodeca, M., Goossens, F. A., Schuengel, C., & Terwogt, M. M. (2003). Bullying and victimization among school-age children: Stability and links to proactive and reactive aggression. *Social Development, 11,* 332–345.

Campbell, A. (2002). *A mind of her own: The evolutionary psychology of women.* Oxford, England: Oxford University Press.

Campos, J. J., Bertenthal, B. I., & Kermoian, R. (1992). Early experience and emotional development: The emergence of wariness of heights. *Psychological Science, 3,* 61–64.

Camras, L. A. (1992). Expressive development and basic emotions. *Cognition and Emotion, 6,* 269–283.

Camras, L. A., Meng, Z., Ujiie, T., Dharamsi, S., Miyake, K., Oster, H., et al. (2002). Observing emotion in infants: Facial expression, body behavior, and rater judgments of responses to an expectancy-violating event. *Emotion, 2,* 179–193.

Canli, T., Sivers, H., Whitfield, S. L., Gotlib, I. H., & Gabrieli, J. D. E. (2002). Amygdala response to happy faces as a function of extraversion. *Science, 296,* 2191.

Canli, T., Zhao, Z., Brewer, J., Gabrieli, J. D. E., & Cahill, L. (2000). Event-related activation in the human amygdala associates with later memory for individual emotional experience. *The Journal of Neuroscience, 20* (RC99), 1–5.

Cannon, W. B. (1927). The James-Lange theory of emotion. *American Journal of Psychology, 39,* 106–124.

Carney, D. R., & Harrigan, J. A. (2003). It takes one to know one: Interpersonal sensitivity is related to accurate assessment of others' interpersonal sensitivity. *Emotion, 3,* 194–200.

Carpenter, S., & Halberstadt, A. G. (2000). Mothers' reports of events causing anger differ across family relationships. *Social Development, 9,* 458–477.

Carstensen, L. L. (1992). Social and emotional patterns in adulthood: Support for socioemotional selectivity theory. *Psychology and Aging, 7,* 331–338.

Carstensen, L. L., & Charles, S. T. (1998). Emotion in the second half of life. *Current Directions in Psychological Science, 7,* 144–149.

Carstensen, L. L., Fung, H. H., & Charles, S. T. (2003). Socioemotional selectivity theory and the regulation of emotion in the second half of life. *Motivation and Emotion, 27,* 103–123.

Carstensen, L. L., Gottman, J. M., & Levenson, R. W. (1995). Emotional behavior in long-term marriage. *Psychology and Aging, 10,* 140–149.

Carstensen, L. L., Isaacowitz, D. M., & Charles, S. T. (1999). Taking time seriously: A theory of socioemotional selectivity. *American Psychologist, 54,* 165–181.

Carstensen, L. L., Pasupathi, M., Mayr, U., & Nesselroade, J. R. (2000). Emotional experience in everyday life across the adult life span. *Journal of Personality and Social Psychology, 79,* 644–655.

Carstensen, L. L., & Turk-Charles, S. (1994). The salience of emotion across the life-span. *Psychology and Aging, 9,* 259–264.

Carter, C. S. (1998). Neuroendocrine perspectives on social attachment and love. *Psychoneuroendocrinology, 23,* 779–818.

Carver, C. S., Pozo, C., Harris, S. D., Noriega, V., Scheier, M. F., Robinson, D. S., et al. (1993). How coping mediates the effect of optimism on distress: A study of women with early stage breast cancer. *Journal of Personality and Social Psychology, 65,* 375–390.

Carver, C. S., & Scheier, M. F. (2002). Optimism. In C. R. Snyder & S. J. Lopez (Eds.), *Handbook of positive psychology* (pp. 231–243). New York: Oxford University Press.

Carver, C. S., & White, T. L. (1994). Behavioral inhibition, behavioral activation, and affective responses to impending reward and punishment: The BIS/BAS scales. *Journal of Personality and Social Psychology, 67*(2), 319–333.

Cashdan, E. (1998). Smiles, speech, and body posture: How women and men display sociometric status and power. *Journal of Nonverbal Behavior, 22,* 209–228.

Caspi, A., & Herbener, E. S. (1990). Continuity and change: Assortative marriage and the consistency of personality in adulthood. *Journal of Personality and Social Psychology, 58,* 250–258.

Cassia, V. M., Turati, C., & Simion, F. (2004). Can a nonspecific bias toward top-heavy patterns explain newborns' face preference? *Psychological Science, 15,* 379–383.

Chaplin, T. M., Cole, P. M., & Zahn-Waxler, C. (2005). Parental socialization of emotion expression: Gender differences and relations to child adjustment. *Emotion, 5,* 80–88.

Charash, M., & McKay, D. (2002). Attention bias for disgust. *Anxiety Disorders, 16,* 529–541.

Chen, D., & Haviland-Jones, J. (2000). Human olfactory communication of emotion. *Perceptual and Motor Skills, 91,* 771–781.

Chwalisz, K., Diener, E., & Gallagher, D. (1988). Autonomic arousal feedback and emotional experi-

ence: Evidence from the spinal cord injured. *Journal of Personality and Social Psychology, 54,* 820–828.

Ciarrochi, J., Chan, A., Caputi, P., & Roberts, R. (2001). Measuring emotional intelligence. In J. Ciarrochi, J. P. Forgas, & J. D. Mayer (Eds.), *Emotional intelligence in everyday life* (pp. 25–45). Philadelphia, PA: Psychology Press.

Ciarrochi, J., Hynes, K., & Crittenden, N. (2005). Can men do better if they try harder: Sex and motivational effects on emotional awareness. *Cognition and Emotion, 19,* 133–141.

Cirelli, C., Pompeiano, M., & Tononi, G. (1996). Neuronal gene expression in the waking state: A role for the locus coeruleus. *Science, 274,* 1211–1215.

Clark, C., Prior, M., & Kinsella, G. (2002). The relationship between executive function abilities, adaptive behaviour, and academic achievement in children with externalising behaviour problems. *Journal of Child Psychology and Psychiatry, 43,* 785–796.

Clark, K. B., Naritoku, D. K., Smith, D. C., Browning, R. A., & Jensen, R. A. (1999). Enhanced recognition memory following vagus nerve stimulation in human subjects. *Nature Neuroscience, 2,* 94–98.

Clark, L., Cools, R., & Robbins, T. W. (2004). The neuropsychology of ventral prefrontal cortex: Decision-making and reversal learning. *Brain and Cognition, 55,* 41–53.

Clark, R., Anderson, N. B., Clark, V. R., & Williams, D. R. (1999). Racism as a stressor for African Americans. *American Psychologist, 54,* 805–816.

Clohessy, A. B., Posner, M. I., Rothbart, M. K., & Veccra, S. P. (1991). The development of inhibition of

return in early infancy. *Journal of Cognitive Neuroscience, 3,* 345–350.

Clore, G. L. (1992). Cognitive phenomenology: Feelings and the construction of judgment. In L. L. Martin & A. Tesser (Eds.), *The construction of social judgments* (pp. 133–163). Hillsdale, NJ: Erlbaum.

Clore, G. L., & Centerbar, D. B. (2004). Analyzing anger: How to make people mad. *Emotion, 4,* 139–144.

Clore, G. L., Ortony, A., Dienes, B., & Fujita, F. (1993). Where does anger dwell? In R. S. Wyer & T. K. Srull (Eds.), *Advances in social cognition: Perspectives on anger and emotion* (Vol. 6, pp. 57–87). Hillsdale, NJ: Erlbaum.

Coan, J. A., & Allen, J. J. B. (2004). Frontal EEG asymmetry as a moderator and mediator of emotion. *Biological Psychology, 67,* 7–49.

Cobos, P., Sánchez, M., García, C., Vera, M. N., & Vila, J. (2002). Revisiting the James versus Cannon debate on emotion: Startle and autonomic modulation in patients with spinal cord injuries. *Biological Psychology, 61,* 251–269.

Cohen, D., & Gunz, A. (2002). As seen by the other . . . : Perspectives on the self in the memories and emotional perceptions of Easterners and Westerners. *Psychological Science, 13,* 55–59.

Cohen, F., Kearney, K. A., Zegans, L. S., Kemeny, M. E., Neuhaus, J. M., & Stites, D. P. (1999). Differential immune system changes with acute and persistent stress for optimists vs pessimists. *Brain, Behavior, and Immunity, 13,* 155–174.

Cohen, M., Klein, E., Kuten, A., Fried, G., Zinder, O., & Pollack, S. (2002). Increased emotional distress in daughters of breast cancer patients is associated with decreased natural cytotoxic activity, elevated levels of stress hormones and decreased secretion of Th1 cytokines. *International Journal of Cancer, 100,* 347–354.

Cohen, S., Doyle, W. J., Turner, R., Alper, C. M., & Skoner, D. P. (2003). Sociability and susceptibility to the common cold. *Psychological Science, 14,* 389–395.

Cohen, S., Frank, E., Doyle, W. J., Skoner, D. P., Rabin, B. S., & Swaltney, J. M., Jr. (1998). Types of stressors that increase susceptibility to the common cold in healthy adults. *Health Psychology, 17,* 214–223.

Cole, P. M., Bruschi, C. J., & Tamang, B. L. (2002). Cultural differences in children's emotional reactions to difficult situations. *Child Development, 73,* 983–996.

Cole, P. M., & Tamang, B. L. (1998). Nepali children's ideas about emotional displays in hypothetical challenges. *Developmental Psychology, 34,* 640–646.

Cole, P. M., Teti, L. O., & Zahn-Waxler, C. (2003). Mutual emotion regulation and the stability of conduct problems between preschool and early school age. *Development and Psychopathology, 15,* 1–18.

Collins, N. L., & Miller, L. C. (1994). Self-disclosure and liking: A meta-analytic review. *Psychological Bulletin, 116,* 457–475.

Compas, B. E., Ey, S., & Grant, K. E. (1993). Taxonomy, assessment, and diagnosis of depression during adolescence. *Psychological Bulletin, 114,* 323–344.

Conduct Problems Prevention Research Group. (2002). Evaluation of the first 3 years of the Fast Track prevention trial with children at high risk for adolescent conduct problems. *Journal of Abnormal Child Psychology, 30,* 19–35.

Connor, T. J., & Leonard, B. E. (1998). Depression, stress and immunological activation: The role of cytokines in depressive disorders. *Life Sciences, 62,* 583–606.

Conroy, M., Hess, R. D., Azuma, H., & Kashiwagi, K. (1980). Maternal strategies for regulating children's behavior: Japanese and American families. *Journal of Cross-Cultural Psychology, 11,* 153–172.

Consedine, N. S., Magai, C., & King, A. R. (2004). Deconstructing positive affect in later life: A differential functionalist analysis of joy and interest. *International Journal of Aging and Human Development, 58,* 49–68.

Conte, J. M. (2005). A review and critique of emotional intelligence measures. *Journal of Organizational Behavior, 26,* 433–440.

Contrada, R. J., Ashmore, R. D., Gary, M. L., Coups, E., Egeth, J. D., Sewell, A., et al. (2000). Ethnicity-related sources of stress and their effects on well-being. *Current Directions in Psychological Science, 9,* 136–139.

Coombs, R. H., & Fawzy, F. I. (1982). The effect of marital status on stress in medical school. *American Journal of Psychiatry, 139,* 1490–1493.

Costa, M., Dinsbach, W., Manstead, A. S. R., & Bitti, P. E. R. (2001). Social presence, embarrassment, and nonverbal behavior. *Journal of Nonverbal Behavior, 25,* 225–240.

Costa, P. T., & McCrae, R. R. (1980). Influence of extraversion and neuroticism on subjective well-being: Happy and unhappy people. *Journal of Personality and Social Psychology, 38,* 668–678.

Covert, M.. V., Tangney, J. P., Maddux, J. E., & Heleno, N. M. (2003). Shame-proneness, guilt-proneness, and interpersonal problem solving: A social cognitive analysis. *Journal of Social and Clinical Psychology, 22,* 1–12.

Cox, B. J., McWilliams, L. A., Clara, I. P., & Stein, M. B. (2003). The structure of feared situations in a nationally representative sample. *Journal of Anxiety Disorders, 17,* 89–101.

Crews, D. J., & Landers, D. M. (1987). A meta-analytic review of aerobic fitness and reactivity to psychological stressors. *Medicine & Science in Sports & Exercise, 19,* S144–S120.

Crews, F. (1996). The verdict on Freud. *Psychological Science, 7,* 63–68.

Crick, N. R., & Dodge, K. A. (1994). A review and reformulation of social information-processing mechanisms in children's social adjustment. *Psychological Bulletin, 115,* 74–101.

Crick, N. R., & Dodge, K. A. (1996). Social information-processing mechanisms in reactive and proactive aggression. *Child Development, 67,* 993–1002.

Critchley, H. D., Mathias, C. J., & Dolan, R. J. (2001). Neuroanatomical basis for first- and second-order representations of bodily states. *Nature Neuroscience, 4,* 207–212.

Critchley, H. D., Wiens, S., Rotshtein, P., Öhman, A., & Dolan, R. J. (2004). Neural systems supporting interoceptive awareness. *Nature Neuroscience, 7,* 189–195.

Crocker, J., & Park, L. E. (2004). The costly pursuit of self-esteem. *Psychological Bulletin, 130,* 392–414.

Crown, C. L., Feldstein, S., Jasnow, M. D., Beebe, B., & Jaffe, J. (2002).

The cross-modal coordination of interpersonal timing: Six-weeks-old infants' gaze with adults' vocal behavior. *Journal of Psycholinguistic Research, 31,* 1–23.

Crucian, G. P., Hughes, J. D., Barrett, A. M., Williamson, D. J. G., Bauer, R. M., Bowers, D., et al. (2000). Emotional and physiological responses to false feedback. *Cortex, 36,* 623–647.

Csikszentmihalyi, M. (1999). If we are so rich, why aren't we happy? *American Psychologist, 54,* 821–827.

Cunningham, M. R. (1979). Weather, mood, and helping behavior: Quasi experiments with the sunshine samaritan. *Journal of Personality and Social Psychology, 37,* 1947–1956.

Cunningham, M. R., Roberts, A. R., Barbee, A. P., Druen, P. B., & Wu, C. (1995). "Their ideas of beauty are, on the whole, the same as ours": Consistency and variability in the cross-cultural perception of female physical attractiveness. *Journal of Personality and Social Psychology, 68,* 261–279.

Cuthbert, B. N., Lang, P. J., Strauss, C., Drobes, D., Patrick, C. J., & Bradley, M. M. (2003). The psychophysiology of anxiety disorder: Fear memory imagery. *Psychophysiology, 40,* 407–422.

Dahlen, E. R., & Deffenbacher, J. L. (2001). Anger management. In W. J. Lyddon & J. V. Jones, Jr. (Eds.), *Empirically supported cognitive therapies* (pp. 163–181). New York: Springer Publishing.

Damasio, A. R. (1994). *Descartes' error: Emotion, reason, and the human brain.* New York: G. P. Putnam.

Damasio, A. R. (1999). *The feeling of what happens.* New York: Harcourt Brace.

Damasio, A. R., Grabowski, T. J., Bechara, A., Damasio, H., Ponto, L. L. B., Parvizi, J., et al. (2000). Subcortical and cortical brain activity during the feeling of self-generated emotions. *Nature Neuroscience, 3,* 1049–1056.

Damasio, H. (2002). Impairment of interpersonal social behavior caused by acquired brain damage. In S. G. Post, L. G. Underwood, J. P. Schloss, & W. B. Hurlbut (Eds.), *Altruism & altruistic love* (pp. 272–283). Oxford, England: Oxford University Press.

Damasio, H., Grabowski, T., Frank, R., Galaburda, A. M., & Damasio, A. R. (1994). The return of Phineas Gage: The skull of a famous patient yields clues about the brain. *Science, 264,* 1102–1105.

Danner, D. D., Snowdon, D. A., & Friesen, W. V. (2001). Positive emotions in early life and longevity: Findings from the nun study. *Journal of Personality and Social Psychology, 80,* 804–813.

Darwin, C. (1998). *The expression of the emotions in man and animals.* New York: Oxford University Press. (Original work published 1872)

Dasgupta, N., McGhee, D. E., Greenwald, A. G., & Banaji, M. (2000). Automatic preference for White Americans: Eliminating the familiarity explanation. *Journal of Experimental Social Psychology, 36,* 316–328.

Daus, C. S., & Ashkanasy, N. M. (2005). The case for the ability-based model of emotional intelligence in organizational behavior. *Journal of Organizational Behavior, 26,* 453–466.

David, C. F., & Kistner, J. A. (2000). Do positive self-perceptions have a "dark side"? Examination of the link between perceptual bias and

aggression. *Journal of Abnormal Child Psychology, 28,* 327–337.

Davidson, J. R. T., Hughes, D. C., George, L. K., & Blazer, D. G. (1996). The association of sexual assault and attempted suicide within the community. *Archives of General Psychiatry, 53,* 550–555.

Davidson, K., MacGregor, M. W., Stuhr, J., Dixon, K., & MacLean, D. (2000). Constructive anger verbal behavior predicts blood pressure in a population-based sample. *Health Psychology, 19,* 55–64.

Davidson, R. J., & Fox, N. A. (1982). Asymmetrical brain activity discriminates between positive and negative affective stimuli in human infants. *Science, 218,* 1235–1237.

Davidson, R. J., & Harrington, A. (Eds.). (2002). *Visions of compassion: Western scientists and Tibetan Buddhists examine human nature.* New York: Oxford University Press.

Davidson, R. J., & Henriques, J. (2000). Regional brain function in sadness and depression. In J. C. Borod (Ed.), *The neuropsychology of emotion* (pp. 269–297). Series in Affective Science. London: Oxford University Press.

Davidson, R. J., Putnam, K. M., & Larson, C. L. (2000). Dysfunction in the neural circuitry of emotion regulation: A possible prelude to violence. *Science, 289,* 591–594.

Davis, J. L., & Rusbult, C. E. (2001). Attitude alignment in close relationships. *Journal of Personality and Social Psychology, 81,* 65–84.

Dawson, D. A., & Grant, B. F. (1998). Family history of alcoholism and gender: Their combined effects on DSM-IV alcohol dependence and major depression. *Journal of Studies on Alcohol, 59,* 97–106.

Day, A. L., & Carroll, S. A. (2004). Using an ability-based measure of emotional intelligence to predict individual performance, group performance, and group citizenship behaviours. *Personality and Individual Differences, 36,* 1443–1458.

DeCasper, A. J., & Fifer, W. P. (1980). Of human bonding: Newborns prefer their mothers' voices. *Science, 208,* 1174–1177.

Deffenbacher, J. L. (in press). Psychosocial interventions: Anger disorders. In E. F. Coccaro (Ed.), *Aggression: Assessment and treatment.* New York: Marcel Dekker.

de Gelder, B. (2000). Recognizing emotions by ear and by eye. In R. D. Lane & L. Nadel (Eds.), *Cognitive neuroscience of emotion* (pp. 84–105). New York: Oxford University Press.

De Jong, P. J., Peters, M., De Cremer, D., & Vranken, C. (2002). Blushing after a moral transgression in a prisoner's dilemma game: Appeasing or revealing? *European Journal of Social Psychology, 32,* 627-644.

DeNeve, K. M. (1999). Happy as an extraverted clam? The role of personality for subjective well-being. *Current Directions in Psychological Science, 8,* 141–144.

DeNeve, K. M., & Cooper, H. (1998). The happy personality: A meta-analysis of 137 personality traits and subjective well-being. *Psychological Bulletin, 124,* 197–229.

Denham, S. A., Workman, E., Cole, P. M., Weissbrod, C., Kendziora, K. T., & Zahn-Waxler, C. (2000). Prediction of externalizing behavior problems from early to middle childhood: The role of parental socialization and emotion expression. *Development and Psychopathology, 12,* 23–45.

Dennis, P. M. (1998). Chills and thrills: Does radio harm our children? The controversy over program violence in the age of radio. *Journal of the History of the Behavioral Sciences, 34,* 33–50.

Dennis, T. A., Cole, P. M., Zahn-Waxler, C., & Mizuta, I. (2002). Self in context: Autonomy and relatedness in Japanese and U.S. mother-preschooler dyads. *Child Development, 73,* 1803–1817.

Depue, R. A., & Iacono, W. G. (1989). Neurobehavioral aspects of affective disorders. In M. R. Rosenzweig & L. W. Porter (Eds.), *Annual review of psychology, 40,* 457–492. Palo Alto, CA: Annual Reviews.

De Raad, B. (2005). The trait-coverage of emotional intelligence. *Personality and Individual Differences, 38,* 673–687.

Derksen, J., Kramer, I., & Katzko, M. (2002). Does a self-report measure for emotional intelligence assess something different than general intelligence? *Personality and Individual Differences, 32,* 37–48.

Detillion, C. E., Craft, T. K. S., Glasper, E. R., Prendergast, B. J., & DeVries, A. C. (2004). Social facilitation of wound healing. *Psychoneuroimmunology, 29,* 1004–1011.

Detre, J. A., & Floyd, T. F. (2001). Functional MRI and its applications to the clinical neurosciences. *Neuroscientist, 7,* 64–79.

Detterman, D. K. (1979). Detterman's laws of individual differences research. In R. J. Sternberg & D. K. Detterman (Eds.), *Human intelligence* (pp. 165–175). Norwood, NJ: Ablex.

de Waal, F. B. M. (2000). Primates—A natural heritage of conflict resolution. *Science, 289,* 586–590.

Diamond, D. M., Bennett, M. C., Fleshner, M., & Rose, G. M. (1992). Inverted-U relationship between the level of peripheral corticosterone and the magnitude of hippocampal primed burst potentiation. *Hippocampus, 2,* 421–430.

Diamond, L. M. (2004). Emerging perspectives on distinctions between romantic love and sexual desire. *Current Directions in Psychological Science, 13,* 116–119.

Diener, E., & Diener, C. (1996). Most people are happy. *Psychologcal Science, 7,* 181–185.

Diener, E., & Seligman, M. E. P. (2002). Very happy people. *Psychological Science, 13,* 81–84.

Diener, E., & Seligman, M. E. P. (2004). Beyond money: Toward an economy of well-being. *Psychological Science in the Public Interest, 5,* 1–31.

Diener, E., Suh, E. M., Lucas, R. E., & Smith, H. L. (1999). Subjective well-being: Three decades of progress. *Psychological Bulletin, 125,* 276–302.

Diener, M. L., & Lucas, R. E. (2004). Adults' desires for children's emotions across 48 countries. *Journal of Cross-Cultural Psychology, 35,* 525–547.

DiGiuseppe, R., & Tafrate, R. C. (in press). *The anger disorder scale manual.* Toronto: Multi-Health Systems.

Dimberg, U., & Thunberg, M. (1998). Rapid facial reactions to emotional facial expressions. *Scandinavian Journal of Psychology, 39,* 39–45.

Dinn, W. M., & Harris, C. L. (2000). Neurocognitive function in antisocial personality disorder. *Psychiatry Research, 97,* 173–190.

Dion, K. K., & Dion, K. L. (1993). Individualistic and collectivistic perspectives on gender and the cultural context of love and intimacy. *Journal of Social Issues, 49,* 53–69.

Dodge, K. A., & Coie, J. D. (1987). Social-information-processing factors in reactive and proactive aggression in children's peer groups. *Journal of Personality and Social Psychology, 53,* 1146–1158.

Doi, T. (1973). *The anatomy of dependence* (J. Beste,Trans.). Tokyo: Kodansha International.

Dollard, J., Miller, N. E., Doob, L. W., Mowrer, O. H., & Sears, R. R. (1939). *Frustration and aggression.* New Haven, CT: Yale University Press.

Dondi, M. Simion, F., & Caltran, G. (1999). Can newborns discriminate between their own cry and the cry of another newborn infant? *Developmental Psychology, 35,* 418–426.

Donnellan, M. B., Trzesniewski, K. H., Robins, R. W., Moffitt, T. E., & Caspi, A. (2005). Low self-esteem is related to aggression, antisocial behavior, and delinquency. *Psychological Science, 16,* 328–335.

Dowden, S. L., & Allen, G. J. (1997). Relationships between anxiety sensitivity, hyperventilation, and emotional reactivity to displays of facial emotion. *Journal of Anxiety Disorders, 11,* 63–75.

Drummond, P. D., Camacho, L., Formentin, N., Heffernan, T. D., Williams, F., & Zekas, T. E. (2003). The impact of verbal feedback about blushing on social discomfort and facial blood flow during embarrassing tasks. *Behaviour Research and Therapy, 41,* 413–425.

Druschel, B. A., & Sherman, M. F. (1999). Disgust sensitivity as a function of the Big Five and gender. *Personality and Individual Differences, 26,* 739–748.

Duclos, S. E., & Laird, J. D. (2001). The deliberate control of emotional experience through control of expressions. *Cognition and Emotion, 15,* 27–65.

Dulewicz, V., Higgs, M., & Slaski, M. (2003). Measuring emotional intelligence: Content, construct and criterion-related validity. *Journal of Managerial Psychology, 18,* 405–420.

Dunn, J., Bretherton, I., & Munn, P. (1987). Conversations about feeling states between mothers and their young children. *Developmental Psychology, 23,* 132–139.

Dunn, J., Brown, J. R., & Maguire, M. (1995). The development of children's moral sensibility: Indvidual differences and emotion understanding. *Developmental Psychology, 31,* 649–659.

Dunning, D., Heath, C., & Suls, J. M. (2004). Flawed self-assessment: Implications for health, education, and the workplace. *Psychological Science in the Public Interest, 5,* 69–106.

Durrett, M. E., Otaki, M., & Richards, P. (1984). Attachment and the mother's perception of support from the father. *International Journal of Behavioral Development, 7,* 167–176.

Dutton, D. G., & Aron, A. P. (1974). Some evidence for heightened sexual attraction under conditions of high anxiety. *Journal of Personality and Social Psychology, 30,* 510–517.

Dyregrov, A., Gjestad, R., & Raundalen, M. (2002). Children exposed to warfare: A longitudinal study. *Journal of Traumatic Stress, 15,* 59–68.

Eaker, E. D., Sullivan, L. M., Kelly-Hayes, M., D'Agostino, R. B., Sr., & Benjamin, E. J. (2004). Anger and hostility predict the development of atrial fibrillation in men in the Framingham Offspring Study. *Circulation, 109,* 1267–1271.

Ebling, R., & Levenson, R. W. (2003). Who are the marital experts? *Journal of Marriage and the Family, 65,* 130–142.

Ebstein, R. P., Novick, O., Umansky, R., Priel, B., Osher, Y., Blaine, D., et al. (1996). Dopamine D4 receptor (*D4DR*) exon III polymorphism associated with the personality trait of Novelty Seeking. *Nature Genetics, 12,* 78–80.

Edelmann, R. J. (2001). Blushing. In W. R. Crozier & L. E. Alden (Eds.), *International handbook of social anxiety* (pp. 301–323). Chichester, England: John Wiley.

Edelmann, R. J., & McCusker, G. (1986). Introversion, neuroticism, empathy, and embarrassibility. *Personality and Individual Differences, 7,* 133–140.

Edwards, J., Jackson, H. J., & Pattison, P. E. (2002). Emotion recognition via facial expression and affective prosody in schizophrenia: A methodological review. *Clinical Psychology Review, 22,* 789–832.

Edwards, K. (1998). The face of time: Temporal cues in facial expressions of emotion. *Psychological Science, 9,* 270–276.

Egloff, B., Wilhelm, F. H., Neubauer, D. H., Mauss, I. B., & Gross, J. J. (2002). Implicit anxiety measure predicts cardiovacular reactivity to an evaluated speaking task. *Emotion, 2,* 3–11.

Eibl-Eibesfeldt, I. (1973). *Der vorprogrammierte Mensch* [The preprogrammed human]. Vienna: Verlag Fritz Molden.

Eich, E. (1995). Searching for mood dependent memory. *Psychological Science, 6,* 67–75.

Eid, M., Riemann, R., Angleitner, A., & Borkenau, P. (2003). Sociability and positive emotionality: Genetic and environmental contributions to the covariation between different facets of extraversion. *Journal of Personality, 71,* 319–346.

Eisenberg, N., Fabes, R. A., Miller, P. A., Fultz, J., Shell, R., Mathy, R. M., et al. (1989). Relation of sympathy and personal distress to prosocial behavior: A multimethod study. *Journal of Personal-*

ity and Social Psychology, 57, 55–66.

Eisenberg, N., Fabes, R. A., Murphy, B., Karbon, M., Smith, M., & Maszk, P. (1996). The relations of children's dispositional empathy-related responding to their emotionality, regulation, and social functioning. *Developmental Psychology, 32,* 195–209.

Eisenberg, N., Liew, J., & Pidada, S. U. (2001). The relations of parental emotional expressivity with quality of Indonesian children's social functioning. *Emotion, 1,* 116–136.

Eisenberg, N., Pidada, S., & Liew, J. (2001). The relations of regulation and negative emotionality to Indonesian children's social functioning. *Child Development, 72,* 1747–1763.

Eisenberger, N. I., & Lieberman, M. D. (2004). Why rejection hurts: A common neural alarm system for physical and social pain. *Trends in Cognitive Sciences, 8*(7), 294–300.

Eisenberger, N. I., Lieberman, M. D., & Williams, K. D. (2003). Does rejection hurt? An fMRI study of social exclusion. *Science, 302,* 290–292.

Ek, M., Engblom, D., Saha, S., Blomqvist, A., Jakobsson, P.-J., & Ericsson-Dahlstrand, A. (2001). Pathway across the blood-brain barrier. *Nature, 410,* 430–431.

Ekman, P. (1972). Universals and cultural differences in facial expressions of emotion. In J. Cole (Ed.), *Nebraska Symposium on Motivation, 1971* (pp. 207–283). Lincoln: University of Nebraska Press.

Ekman, P. (1992). An argument for basic emotions. *Cognition and Emotion, 6,* 169–200.

Ekman, P. (1994a). All emotions are basic. In P. Ekman and R. J. Davidson (Eds.) *The nature of emotion: Fundamental questions* (pp.

15–19). New York: Oxford University Press.

Ekman, P. (1994b). Strong evidence for universals in facial expressions: A reply to Russell's misstaken critique. *Psychological Bulletin, 115,* 268–287.

Ekman, P. (2001). *Telling lies* (3rd ed.). New York: Norton.

Ekman, P., & Friesen, W. V. (1984). *Unmasking the face* (2nd ed.). Palo Alto, CA: Consulting Psychologists Press.

Ekman, P., Friesen, W. V., O'Sullivan, M., Chan, A., Diacoyanni-Tarlatzis, I., Heider, K., et al. (1987). Universals and cultural differences in the judgments of facial expressions of emotion. *Journal of Personality and Social Psychology, 51,* 712–717.

Ekman, P., Levenson, R. W., & Friesen, W. V. (1983). Autonomic nervous system activity distinguishes among emotions. *Science, 221,* 1208–1210.

Ekman, P., & O'Sullivan, M. (1991). Who can catch a liar? *American Psychologist, 46,* 913–920.

Ekman, P., O'Sullivan, M., & Frank, M. G. (1999). A few can catch a liar. *Psychological Science, 10,* 263–266.

Elfenbein, H. A., & Ambady, N. (2002a). On the universality and cultural specificity of emotion recognition: A meta-analysis. *Psychological Bulletin, 128,* 203–235.

Elfenbein, H. A., & Ambady, N. (2002b). Is there an in-group advantage in emotion recognition? *Psychological Bulletin, 128,* 243–249.

Elfenbein, H. A., & Ambady, N. (2003). Universals and cultural differences in recognizing emotions. *Current Directions in Psychological Science, 12,* 159–164.

Elias, M. J., Hunter, L., & Kress, J. S. (2001). Emotional intelligence and

education. In J. Ciarrochi, J. P. Forgas, & J. D. Mayer (Eds.), *Emotional intelligence in everyday life* (pp. 133–149). Philadelphia, PA: Psychology Press.

Elkins, R. L. (1991). An appraisal of chemical aversion (emetic therapy) approaches to alcoholism treatment. *Behaviour Research and Therapy, 29,* 387–413.

Ellsworth, P. C. (1994). William James and emotion: Is a century of fame worth a century of misunderstanding? *Psychological Review, 101,* 222–229.

Ellsworth, P. C., & Ross, L. (1983, January). Public opinion and capital punishment: A close examination of the views of abolitionists and retentionists. *Crime and Delinquency, 29,* 116–169.

Emde, R. N., Katz, E. L., & Thorpe, J. K. (1978). Emotional expression in infancy: II. Early deviations in Down's Syndrome. In M. Lewis & L. A. Rosenblum (Eds.), *The development of affect* (pp. 351–360). New York: Plenum.

Emde, R. N., & Koenig, K. (1969). Neonatal smiling and rapid eye movement states. *Journal of American Academic Child Psychiatry, 8,* 57–67.

Emery, N. J., Capitanio, J. P., Mason, W. A., Machado, C. J., Mendoza, S. P., & Amaral, D. G. (2001). The effects of bilateral lesions of the amygdala on dyadic social interactions in rhesus monkeys (*Macaca mulatta*). *Behavioral Neuroscience, 115,* 515–544.

Engelberg, E., & Sjöberg, L. (2004). Emotional intelligence, affect intensity, and social adjustment. *Personality and Individual Differences, 37,* 533–542.

Erlenmeyer-Kimling, L., Adamo, U. H., Rock, D., Roberts, S. A., Bassett, A. S., Squires-Wheeler, E., et al. (1997). The New York high-risk project. *Archives of General Psychiatry, 54,* 1096–1102.

Esslen, M., Pascual-Marqui, R. D., Hell, D., Kochi, K., & Lehmann, D. (2004). Brain areas and time course of emotional processing. *NeuroImage, 21,* 1189–1203.

Esterson, A. (2001). The mythologizing of psychoanalytic history: Deceptions and self-deception in Freud's accounts of the seduction theory episode. *History of Psychology, 12,* 329–352.

Etcoff, N. L., Ekman, P., Magee, J. J., & Frank, M. G. (2000). Lie detection and language comprehension. *Nature, 405,* 139.

Eugène, F., Lévesque, J., Mensour, B., Leroux, J-M., Beaudoin, G., Bourgouin, P., et al. (2003). The impact of individual differences on the neural circuitry underlying sadness. *NeuroImage, 19,* 354–364.

Evans, G. W., Bullinger, M., & Hygge, S. (1998). Chronic noise exposure and physiological response: A prospective study of children living under environmental stress. *Psychological Science, 9,* 75–77.

Fabes, R. A., Eisenberg, N., & Eisenbud, L. (1993). Behavioral and physiological correlates of children's reactions to others in distress. *Developmental Psychology, 29,* 655–663.

Fabes, R. A., Eisenberg, N., Nyman, M., & Michealieu, Q. (1991). Young children's appraisals of others' spontaneous emotional reactions. *Developmental Psychology, 27,* 858–866.

Fairbanks, L. A., Jorgensen, M. J., Huff, A., Blau, K., Hung, Y.-Y., & Mann, J. J. (2004). Adolescent impulsivity predicts adult dominance attainment in male vervet monkeys. *American Journal of Primatology, 64,* 1–17.

Farmer, E. M. Z., Compton, S. N., Burns, B. J., & Robertson, E. (2002). Review of the evidence base for treatment of childhood psychopathology: Externalizing disorders. *Journal of consulting and Clinical Psychology, 70,* 1267–1302.

Fauerbach, J. A., Lawrence, J. W., Haythornthwaite, J. A., & Richter, L. (2002). Coping with the stress of a painful medical procedure. *Behaviour Research and Therapy, 40,* 1003–1015.

Fawzy, F. I., Fawzy, N. W., Arndt, L. A., & Pasnau, R. O. (1995). Critical review of psychosocial interventions in cancer care. *Archives of General Psychiatry, 52,* 100–113.

Fazio, R. H., & Powell, M. C. (1997). On the value of knowing one's likes and dislikes: Attitude accessibility, stress, and health in college. *Psychological Science, 8,* 430–436.

Feeney, J., Peterson, C., & Noller, P. (1994). Equity and marital satisfaction over the family life cycle. *Personality Relationships, 1,* 83–99.

Fehr, B., & Russell, J. A. (1984). Concept of emotion viewed from a prototype perspective. *Journal of Experimental Psychology: General, 113,* 464–486.

Fehr, B., & Russell, J. A. (1991). The concept of love viewed from a prototype perspective. *Journal of Personality and Social Psychology, 60,* 425–438.

Feldman, R., Greenbaum, C. W., & Yirmiya, N. (1999). Mother-infant affect synchrony as an antecedent of the emergence of self-control. *Developmental Psychology, 35,* 223–231.

Felitti, V. J., Anda, R. F., Nordenberg, D., Williamson, D. F., Spitz, A. M., Edwards, V., et al. (1998). Relationship of childhood abuse and household dysfunction to many of the leading causes of death in

adults. *American Journal of Preventive Medicine, 14,* 245–258.

Fendt, M., Koch, M., & Schnitzler, H.-U. (1996). Lesions of the central gray block conditioned fear as measured with the potentiated startle paradigm. *Behavioral Brain Research, 74,* 127–134.

Fergusson, D. M., Woodward, L. J., & Horwood, J. (1998). Maternal smoking during pregnancy and psychiatric adjustment in late adolescence. *Archives of General Psychiatry, 55,* 721–727.

Fessler, D. M. T. (1999). Toward an understanding of the universality of second order emotions. In A. L. Hinton (Ed.), *Biocultural approaches to the emotions* (pp. 75–116). Cambridge, England: Cambridge University Press.

Fessler, D. M. T., Arguello, A. P., Mekdara, J. M., & Macias, R. (2003). Disgust sensitivity and meat consumption: A test of an emotivist account of moral vegetarianism. *Appetite, 41,* 31–41.

Fiedler, K., Schmid, J., & Stahl, T. (2002). What is the current truth about polygraph lie detection? *Basic and Applied Social Psychology, 24,* 313–324.

Field, T. M., Woodson, R. Greenberg, R., & Cohen, D. (1982). Discrimination and imitation of facial expressions by neonates. *Science, 218,* 179–181.

Fischer, A. H., Mosquera, P. M. R., van Vianen, A., & Manstead, A. S. R. (2004). Gender and culture differences in emotion. *Emotion, 4,* 87–94.

Fiske, A. P. (2002). Using individualism and collectivism to compare cultures—A critique of the validity and measurement of the constructs: Comment on Oyserman et al. (2002). *Psychological Bulletin, 128,* 78–88.

Fivush, R., Brotman, M. A., Buckner, J. P., & Goodman, S. H. (2000). Gender differences in parent-child emotion narratives. *Sex Roles, 42,* 233–253.

Flack, W. F., Jr., Laird, J. D., & Cavallaro, L. A. (1999). Separate and combined effects of facial expressions and bodily postures on emotional feelings. *European Journal of Social Psychology, 29,* 203–217.

Flannery, D. J., Torquati, J. C., & Lindemeier, L. (1994). The method and meaning of emotional expression and experience during adolescence. *Journal of Adolescent Research, 9*(1), 8–27.

Flury, J., & Ickes, W. (2001). Emotional intelligence and empathic accuracy. In J. Ciarrochi, J. P. Forgas, & J. D. Mayer (Eds.), *Emotional intelligence in everyday life* (pp. 113–132). Philadelphia, PA: Psychology Press.

Forgas, J. P. (1995). Mood and judgment: The affect infusion model (AIM). *Psychological Bulletin, 117,* 39–66.

Forgas, J. P. (1998). On being happy and mistaken: Mood effects on the fundamental attribution error. *Journal of Personality and Social Psychology, 75,* 318–331.

Fraiberg, S. (1974). Blind infants and their mothers: An examination of the sign system. In M. Lewis & L. A. Rosenblum (Eds.), *The effect of the infant on its caregiver.* Oxford, England: Wiley-Interscience.

Fraley, R. C., & Shaver, P. R. (1998). Airport separations: A naturalistic study of adult attachments dynamics in separating couples. *Journal of Personality and Social Psychology, 75*(5), 1198–1212.

Fraley, R. C., & Shaver, P. R. (2000). Adult romantic attachment: Theoretical developments, emerging controversies, and unanswered questions. *Review of General Psychology, 4,* 132–154.

Fraley, R. C., & Waller, N. G. (1998). Adult attachment patterns: A test of the typological model. In J. A. Simpson & W. S. Rholed (Eds.), *Attachment theory and close relationships* (pp. 77–114). New York: Guilford.

Frank, M. G., & Stennett, J. (2001). The forced-choice paradigm and the perception of facial expressions of emotion. *Journal of Personality and Social Psychology, 80,* 75–85.

Franken, I. H. A., Kroon, L. Y., Wiers, R. W., & Jansen, A. (2000). Selective cognitive processing of drug cues in heroin dependence. *Journal of Psychopharmacology, 14,* 395–400.

Frankland, P. W., Josselyn, S. A., Bradwejn, J., Vaccarino, F. J., & Yeomans, J. S. (1997). Activation of amygdala cholecystokinin B receptors potentiates the acoustic startle response in the rat. *Journal of Neuroscience, 17,* 1838–1847.

Fredrickson, B. L. (2000). Cultivating positive emotions to optimize health and well-being. *Prevention & Treatment, 3,* article 0001a. Retrieved October 20, 2004, from http://journals.apa.org/prevention/volume3/pre0030001a.html

Fredrickson, B. L. (2001). The role of positive emotion in psychology: The broaden-and-build theory of positive emotions. *American Psychologist, 56,* 218–226.

Fredrickson, B. L., & Branigan, C. (2005). Positive emotions broaden the scope of attention and thought-action repertoires. *Cognition and Emotion, 19,* 313–332.

Fredrickson, B. L., & Joiner, T. (2002). Positive emotions trigger upward spirals toward emotional well-being. *Psychological Science, 13,* 172–175.

Fredrickson, B. L., & Levenson, R. W. (1998). Positive emotions speed recovery from the cardiovascular sequelae of negative emotions. *Cognition and Emotion, 12,* 191–220.

Frey, W. H., II, DeSota-Johnson, D., Hoffman, C., & McCall, J. T. (1981). Effect of stimulus on the chemical composition of human tears. *American Journal of Ophthalmology, 92,* 559–567.

Friedman, M., & Rosenman, R. H. (1974). *Type-A behavior and your heart.* New York: Knopf.

Friedman, S., Smith, L., Fogel, D., Paradis, C., Viswanathan, R., Ackerman, R., et al. (2002). The incidence and influence of early traumatic life events in patients with panic disorder: A comparison with other psychiatric outpatients. *Journal of Anxiety Disorders, 16,* 259–272.

Friesen, W. V. (1972). *Cultural differences in facial expressions in a social situation: An experimental test of display rules.* Unpublished doctoral dissertation. University of California, San Francisco.

Frijda, N. H. (1986). *The emotions.* London: Cambridge University Press.

Fry, P. S. (1995). Perfectionism, humor, and optimism as moderators of health outcomes and determinants of coping styles of women executives. *Genetic, Social, and General Psychology Monographs, 121,* 213–245.

Fu, C. H. Y., Williams, S. C. R., Cleare, A. J., Brammer, M. J., Walsh, N. D., Kim, J., et al. (2004). Attenuation of the neural response to sad faces in major depression by antidepressant treatment. *Archives of General Psychiatry, 61,* 877–889.

Fu, Q., Heath, A. C., Bucholz, K. K., Nelson, E., Goldberg, J., Lyons, M. J., et al. (2002). Shared genetic risk of major depression, alcohol dependence, and marijuana dependence. *Archives of General Psychiatry, 59,* 1125–1132.

Fukuda, S., Morimoto, K., Mure, K., & Maruyama, S. (2000). Effect of the Hanshin-Awaji earthquake on posttraumatic stress, lifestyle changes, and cortisol levels of victims. *Archives of Environmental Health, 55,* 121–125.

Fultz, J., Batson, C. D., Fortenbach, V. A., McCarthy, P. M., & Varney, L. L. (1986). Social evaluation and the empathy-altruism hypothesis. *Journal of Personality and Social Psychology, 50,* 761–769.

Funayama, E. S., Grillon, C., Davis, M., & Phelps, E. A. (2001). A double dissociation in the affective modulation of startle in humans: Effects of unilateral temporal lobectomy. *Journal of Cognitive Neuroscience, 13,* 721–729.

Furman, W., & Burhmester, D. (1992). Age and sex differences in perceptions of networks and social relationships. *Child Development, 63,* 103–115.

Gable, S. L., Reis, H. T., & Downey, G. (2003). He said, she said: A quasi-signal detection analysis of daily interactions between close relationship partners. *Psychological Science, 14,* 100–105.

Gale, G. D., Anagnostaras, S. G., Godsil, B. P., Mitchell, S., Nozawa, T., Sage, J. R., et al. (2004). Role of the basolateral amygdala in the storage of fear memories across the adult lifetime of rats. *Journal of Neuroscience, 24,* 3810–3815.

Gall, T. L., Evans, D. R., & Bellerose, S. (2000). Transition to first-year university: Patterns of change in adjustment across live domains and time. *Journal of Social and Clinical Psychology, 19,* 544–567.

Gallo, L. C., & Matthews, K. A. (2003). Understanding the association between socioeconomic status and physical health: Do negative emotions play a role? *Psychological Bulletin, 129,* 10–51.

Gannon, N., & Ranzijn, R. (2005). Does emotional intelligence predict unique variance in life satisfaction beyond IQ and personality? *Personality and Individual Differences, 38,* 1353–1364.

Garcia, R., Vouimba, R.-M., Baudry, M., & Thompson, R. F. (1999). The amygdala modulates prefrontal cortex activity relative to conditioned fear. *Nature, 402,* 294–296.

Garnefski, N., Teerds, J., Kraaij, V., Legerstee, J., & van den Kommer, T. (2004). Cognitive emotion regulation strategies and depressive symptoms: Differences between males and females. *Personality and Individual Differences, 36,* 267–276.

Garnefski, N., van den Kommer, T., Kraaij, V., Teerds, J., Legerstee, J., & Onstein, E. (2002). The relationship between cognitive emotion regulation strategies and emotional problems: Comparison between a clinical and a non-clinical sample. *European Journal of Personality, 16,* 403–420.

Gasper, K., & Clore, G. L. (2002). Attending to the big picture: Mood and global versus local processing of visual information. *Psychological Science, 13,* 34–40.

Ge, X., Conger, R. D., & Elder, G. H. (2001). Pubertal transition, stressful life events, and the emergence of gender differences in adolescent depressive symptoms. *Developmental Psychology, 37*(3), 404–417.

Geen, R. G. (1978). Effects of attack and uncontrollable noise on aggression. *Journal of Research in Personality, 9,* 270–281.

Geertz, C. (1973). *Interpretation of cultures.* New York: Basic Books.

George, M. S., Ketter, T. A., Parekh, P. I., Horwitz, B., Herscovitch, P., & Post, R. M. (1995). Brain activity during transient sadness and happiness in healthy women. *American Journal of Psychiatry, 152,* 341–351.

Gifkins, A., Greba, Q., & Kokkinidis, L. (2002). Ventral tegmental area dopamine neurons mediate the shock sensitization of acoustic startle: A potential site of action for benzodiazepine anxiolytics. *Behavioral Neuroscience, 116,* 785–794.

Gigerenzer, G. (2004). Dread risk, September 11, and fatal traffic accidents. *Psychological Science, 15,* 286–287.

Gilbertson, M. W., Shenton, M. E., Ciszewski, A., Kasai, K., Lasko, N. B., Orr, S. P., et al. (2002). Smaller hippocampal volume predicts pathological vulnerability to psychological trauma. *Nature Neuroscience, 5,* 1242–1247.

Giuliani, D., & Ferrari, F. (1996). Differential behavioral response to dopamine D_2 agonists by sexually naïve, sexually active, and sexually inactive male rats. *Behavioral Neuroscience, 110,* 802–808.

Gjerde, P. J., & Block, J. (1991). Preadolescent antecedents of depressive symptomology at age 18: A prospective study. *Journal of Youth and Adolescence, 20*(2), 217–232.

Gläscher, J., & Adolphs, R. (2003). Processing of the arousal of subliminal and supraliminal emotional stimuli by the human amygdala. *Journal of Neuroscience, 23,* 10274–10282.

Glaser, R., Rice, J., Speicher, C. E., Stout, J. C., & Kiecolt-Glaser, J. K. (1986). Stress depresses interferon production by leukocytes concomitant with a decrease in natural killer cell activity. *Behavioral Neuroscience, 100,* 675–678.

Glass, D. C., Singer, J. E., & Pennebaker, J. W. (1977). Behavioral and physiological effects of uncontrollable environmental events. In D. Stokols (Ed.), *Perspectives on environment and behavior* (pp. 131–151). New York: Plenum.

Glover, D. A., & Poland, R. E. (2002). Urinary cortisol and catecholamines in mothers of child cancer survivors with and without PTSD. *Psychoneuroendocrinology, 27,* 805–819.

Gonzaga, G. C., Keltner, D., Londahl, E. A., & Smith, M. D. (2001). Love and the commitment problem in romantic relations and friendship. *Journal of Personality and Social Psychology, 81,* 247–262.

Gopnik, A., & Meltzoff, A. N. (1997). *Words, thoughts, and theories.* Cambridge, MA: MIT Press.

Gorman, J. M., Kent, J., Martinez, J., Browne, S., Coplan, J., & Papp, L. A. (2001). Physiological changes during carbon dioxide inhalation in patients with panic disorder, major depression, and premenstrual dysphoric disorder. *Archives of General Psychiatry, 58,* 125–131.

Gottman, J. M. (1994). *What predicts divorce?* Hillsdale, NJ: Erlbaum.

Gottman, J. M., Coan, J., Carrere, S., & Swanson, C. (1998). Predicting marital happiness and stability from newlywed interactions. *Journal of Marriage and the Family, 60,* 5–22.

Graber, J. A., & Brooks-Gunn, J. (1996). Transitions and turning points: Navigate the passage from childhood through adolescence. *Developmental Psychology, 32,* 768–776.

Grammer, K., Kruck, K., Jutte, A., & Fink, B. (2000). Non-verbal behavior as courtship signals: The role of control and choice in selecting partners. *Evolution and Human Behavior, 21,* 371–390.

Grammer, K., Kruck, K., & Magnusson, M. (1998). The courtship dance: Patterns of non-verbal synchronization in opposite sex encounters. *Journal of Non-Verbal Behavior, 22,* 3–29.

Gray, J. A. (1970). The psychophysiological basis of introversion-extraversion. *Behavioural Research Therapy, 8,* 249–266.

Gray, N. S., MacCulloch, M. J., Smith, J., Morris, M., & Snowden, R. J. (2003). Violence viewed by psychopathic murderers. *Nature, 423,* 497–498.

Green, D. P., & Salovey, P. (1999). In what sense are positive and negative affect independent? *Psychological Science, 10,* 304–306.

Greenberg, M. T., & Marvin, R. S. (1982). Reactions of preschool children to an adult stranger: A behavioral systems approach. *Child Development, 53,* 481–490.

Greene, J. D., Nystrom, L. E., Engell, A. D., Darley, J. M., & Cohen, J. D. (2004). The neural bases of cognitive conflict and control in moral judgment. *Neuron, 44,* 389–400.

Greene, J. D., Sommerville, R. B., Nystrom, L. E., Darley, J. M., & Cohen, J. D. (2001). An fMRI investigation of emotional engagement in moral judgment. *Science, 293,* 2105–2108.

Griffin, D. W., & Bartholomew, K. (1994). The metaphysics of measurement: The case of adult attachment. In K. Bartholomew & D. Perlman (Eds.), *Advances in personal relationships: Vol. 5. Attachment processes in adulthood* (pp. 17–52). London: Jessica Kingsley.

Grodnitzky, G. R., & Tafrate, R. C. (2000). Imaginal exposure for anger reduction in adult outpatients: A pilot study. *Journal of Behavior Therapy and Experimental Psychiatry, 31,* 259–279.

Gross, A. E., & Crofton, C. (1977). What is good is beautiful. *Sociometry, 40,* 85–90.

Gross, C., & Hen, R. (2004). The developmental origins of anxiety. *Nature Reviews Neuroscience, 5,* 545–552.

Gross, J. J. (1998). Antecedent- and response-focused emotion regulation: Divergent consequences for experience, expression, and physiology. *Journal of Personality and Social Psychology, 74,* 224–237.

Gross, J. J. (2001). Emotion regulation in adulthood: Timing is everything. *Current Directions in Psychological Science, 10,* 214–219.

Gross, J. J. (2002). Emotion regulation: Affective, cognitive, and social consequences. *Psychophysiology, 39,* 281–291.

Gross, J. J., Carstensen, L. L., Pasupathi, M., Tsai, J., Skorpen, C. G., & Hsu, A. Y. C. (1997). Emotion and aging: Experience, expression, and control. *Psychology and Aging, 12,* 590–599.

Gross, J. J., Fredrickson, B. L., & Levenson, R. W. (1994). The psychophysiology of crying. *Psychophysiology, 31,* 460–468.

Gross, J. J., & John, O. P. (2003). Individual differences in two emotion regulation processes: Implications for affect, relationships, and well-being. *Journal of Personality and Social Psychology, 85,* 348–362.

Gross, J. J., & Levenson, R. W. (1997). Hiding feelings: The acute effects of inhibiting positive and negative emotions. *Journal of Abnormal Psychology, 106,* 95–103.

Grossman, K., Grossman, K. E., Spangler, S., Suess, G., & Unzer, L. (1985). Maternal sensitivity and newborn responses as related to quality of attachment in Northern Germany. In I. Bretherton & E. Waters (Eds.), Growing points of attachment theory, *Monographs of the Society for Research in Child Development, 50* (1-2, Serial No. 209).

Gupta, U., & Singh, P. (1982). Exploratory study of love and liking and type of marriages. *Indian Journal of Applied Psychology, 19*, 92–97.

Haidt, J. (2001). The emotional dog and its rational tail: A social intuitionist approach to moral judgment. *Psychological Review, 108*, 814–834.

Haidt, J., & Keltner, D. (1999). Culture and facial expression: Open-ended methods find more faces and a gradient of recognition. *Cognition and Emotion, 13*, 225–266.

Haidt, J., McCauley, C., & Rozin, P. (1994). Individual differences in sensitivity to disgust: A scale sampling seven domains of disgust elicitors. *Personality and Individual Differences, 16*, 701–713.

Haidt, J., Rozin, P., McCauley, C. R., & Imada, S. (1997). Body, psyche, and culture: The relationship between disgust and morality. *Psychology and Developing Societies, 9*, 107–131.

Halberstadt, A. G., Denham, S. A., & Dunsmore, J. C. (2001). Affective social competence. *Social Development, 10*, 79–119.

Hall, J. A. (1978). Gender effects in decoding nonverbal cues. *Psychological Bulletin, 85*, 845–857.

Hall, J. A., & Halberstadt, A. G. (1986). Smiling and gazing. In J. S. Hyde & M. C. Linn (Eds.), *The psychology of gender: Advances through meta-analysis* (pp. 136–158). Baltimore, MD: Johns Hopkins University Press.

Hall, J. A., & Halberstadt, A. G. (1994). "Subordination" and sensitivity to nonverbal cues: A study of married working women. *Sex Roles, 31*, 149–165.

Hall, J. A., & Matsumoto, D. (2004). Gender differences in judgments of multiple emotions from facial expressions. *Emotion, 4*, 201–206.

Hama, Y. (2001). Shopping as a coping behavior for stress. *Japanese Psychological Research, 43*, 218–224.

Hamann, S. B., Ely, T. D., Hoffman, J. M., & Kilts, C. D. (2002). Ecstasy and agony: Activation of the human amygdala in positive and negative emotion. *Psychological Science, 13*, 135–141.

Hanish, L. D., Eisenberg, N., Fabes, R. A., Spinrad, T. L., Ryan, P., & Schmidt, S. (2004). The expression and regulation of negative emotions: Risk factors for young children's peer victimization. *Development and Psychopathology, 16*, 335–353.

Hansson, B., Bensch, S., & Hasselquist, D. (1997). Infanticide in great reed warblers: Secondary females destroy eggs of primary females. *Animal Behaviour, 54*, 297–304.

Hariri, A. R., Mattay, V. S., Tessitore, A., Fera, F., & Weinberger, D. R. (2003). Neocortical modulation of the amygdala response to fearful stimuli. *Biological Psychiatry, 53*, 494–501.

Hariri, A. R., Mattay, V. S., Tessitore, A., Kolachana, B., Fera, F., Goldman, D., et al. (2002). Serotonin transporter genetic variation and the response of the human amygdala. *Science, 297*, 400–403.

Harker, L. A., & Keltner, D. (2001). Expressions of positive emotion in women's college yearbook pictures and their relationship to personality and life outcomes across adulthood. *Journal of Personality and Social Psychology, 80*, 112–124.

Harris, C. R., & Pashler, H. (2004). Attention and the processing of emotional words and names. *Psychological Science, 15*, 171–178.

Harris, C. R., & Pashler, H. (2005). Enhanced memory for negatively emotionally changed pictures without rumination. *Emotion, 5*, 191–199.

Harris, R. A., Brodie, M. S., & Dunwiddie, T. V. (1992). Possible substrates of ethanol reinforcement: GABA and dopamine. *Annals of the New York Academy of Sciences, 654*, 61–69.

Harrison, A. O., Wilson, M. N., Pine, C. J., Chan, S. Q., & Buriel, R. (1990). Family ecologies of ethnic minority children. *Child Development, 61*, 347–362.

Harvey, A. G., & Bryant, R. A. (2002). Acute stress disorder: A synthesis and critique. *Psychological Bulletin, 128*, 886–902.

Harvey, T., Troop, N. A., Treasure, J. L., & Murphy, T. (2002). Fear, disgust, and abnormal eating attitudes: A preliminary study. *International Journal of Eating Disorders, 32*, 213–218.

Hatfield, E., & Rapson, R. L. (1993). *Love, sex, and intimacy.* New York: Harper Collins.

Hay, D. F., Nash, A., & Pedersen, J. (1981). Responses of six-month olds to the distress of their peers. *Child Development, 52*, 1071–1075.

Hayman, L. A., Rexer, J. L., Pavol, M. A., Strite, D., & Meyers, C. A. (1998). Klüver-Bucy syndrome after bilateral selective damage of amygdala and its cortical connections. *Journal of Neuropsychiatry, 10*, 354–358.

Hazan, C., & Shaver, P. (1987). Romantic love conceptualized as an attachment process. *Journal of Personality and Social Psychology, 52*, 511–524.

Hazebroek, J. F., Howells, K., & Day, A. (2000). Cognitive appraisals associated with high trait anger. *Personality and Individual Differences, 30,* 31–45.

Heath, A. C., Neale, M. C., Kessler, R. C., Eaves, L. J., & Kendler, K. S. (1992). Evidence for geetic influences on personality from self-reports and informant ratings. *Journal of Personality and Social Psychology, 63,* 85–96.

Heider, E. R. (1972). Universals in color naming and memory. *Journal of Experimental Psychology, 93,* 10–20.

Heine, S. J., Kitayama, S., & Lehman, D. R. (2001). Cultural differences in self-evaluation: Japanese readily accept negative self-relevant information. *Journal of Cross-Cultural Psychology, 32,* 434–443.

Heine, S. J., Lehman, D. R., Peng, K., & Greenholtz, J. (2002). What's wrong with cross-cultural comparisons of subjective Likert scales? The reference-group effect. *Journal of Personality and Social Psychology, 82,* 903–918.

Hejmadi, A., Davidson, R. J., & Rozin, P. (2000). Exploring Hindu Indian emotion expressions. *Psychological Science, 11,* 183–187.

Heldt, S., Sundin, V., Willott, J. F., & Falls, W. A. (2000). Posttraining lesions of the amygdala interfere with fear-potentiated startle to both visual and auditory conditioned stimuli in C56BL/6J mice. *Behavioral Neuroscience, 114,* 749–759.

Heller, D., Watson, D., & Ilies, R. (2004). The role of person versus situation in life satisfaction: A critical examination. *Psychological Bulletin, 130,* 574–600.

Helweg-Larsen, M., Sadeghian, P., & Webb, M. S. (2002). The stigma of being pessimistically biased. *Journal of Social and Clinical Psychology, 21,* 92–107.

Helzer, J. E., Robins, L. N., & McEnvoy, L. (1987). Posttraumatic stress disorder in the general population. *New England Journal of Medicine, 317,* 1630–1634.

Hemmati, T., Mills, J. F., & Kroner, D. G. (2004). The validity of the Bar-On emotional intelligence quotient in an offender population. *Personality and Individual Differences, 37,* 695–706.

Henderson, J. J. A., & Anglin, J. M. (2003). Facial attractiveness predicts longevity. *Evolution and Human Behavior, 24,* 351–356.

Hendrick, C., & Hendrick, S. S. (1986). A theory and method of love. *Journal of Personality and Social Psychology, 50,* 392–402.

Hendrick, S. S., Hendrick, C., & Adler, N. L. (1988). Romantic relationships: Love, satisfaction, and staying together. *Journal of Personality and Social Psychology, 54,* 980–988.

Henriques, J. B., & Davidson, R. J. (2000). Decreased responsiveness to reward in depression. *Cognition and Emotion, 14,* 711–724.

Herman, B. H., & Panksepp, J. (1978). Effects of morphine and naloxone on separation distress and approach attachment: Evidence for the opiate mediation of social affect. *Pharmacology, Biochemistry, and Behavior, 9,* 213–220.

Hertenstein, M. J. (2002). Touch: Its communicative functions in infancy. *Human Development, 45,* 70–94.

Hertenstein, M. J., & Campos, J. J. (2004). The retention effects of an adult's emotional displays on infant behavior. *Child Development, 75,* 595–613.

Hess, U., Kappas, A., McHugo, G. J., Lanzetta, J. T., & Kleck, R. E. (1992). The facilitative effect of facial expression on the self-generation of emotion. *International Journal of Psychophysiology, 12,* 251–265.

Heszen-Niejodek, I. (1997). Coping style and its role in coping with stressful encounters. *European Psychologist, 2,* 342–351.

Hettema, J. M., Neale, M. C., & Kendler, K. S. (2001). A review and meta-analysis of the genetic epidemiology of anxiety disorders. *American Journal of Psychiatry, 158,* 1568–1578.

Higley, J. D., Mehlman, P. T., Higley, S. B., Fernald, B., Vickers, J., Lindell, S. G., et al. (1996). Excessive mortality in young free-ranging male nonhuman primates with low cerebrospinal fluid 5-hydroxyindoleacetic acid concentrations. *Archives of General Psychiatry, 53,* 537–543.

Hitchcock, J. M., & Davis, M. (1991). Efferent pathway of the amygdala involved in conditioned fear as measured with the fear-potentiated startle paradigm. *Behavioral Neuroscience, 105,* 826–842.

Hobson, C. J., & Delunas, L. (2001). National norms and life-event frequencies for the revised social readjustment rating scale. *International Journal of Stress Management, 8,* 299–314.

Hobson, C. J., Kamen, J., Szostek, J., Neithercut, C. M., Tidemann, J. W., & Wojnarowicz, S. (1998). Stressful life events: A revision and update of the social readjustment rating scale. *International Journal of Stress Management, 5,* 1–23.

Hochschild, A. R. (2002). *The managed heart.* Berkeley: University of California Press.

Hodgins, S., Mednick, S. A., Brennan, P. A., Schulsinger, F., & Engberg,

M. (1996). Mental disorders and crime. *Archives of General Psychiatry, 53,* 489–496.

Holmes, D. S. (1978). Projection as a defense mechanism. *Psychological Bulletin, 85,* 677–688.

Holmes, D. S. (1987). The influence of meditation versus rest on physiological arousal: A second examination. In M. A. West (Ed.), *The psychology of meditation* (pp. 81–103). Oxford, England: Clarendon Press.

Holmes, D. S. (1990). The evidence for repression: An examination of sixty years of research. In J. L. Singer (Ed.), *Repression and dissociation* (pp. 85–102). New York: Wiley.

Holmes, T. H., & Rahe, R. H. (1977). The social readjustment rating scale. *Journal of Psychosomatic Research, 11,* 213–218.

Hong, Y., Morris, M. W., Chiu, C., & Benet-Martinez, V. (2000). Multicultural minds: A dynamic constructivist approach to culture and cognition. *American Psychologist, 55,* 709–720.

Horley, K., Williams, L. M., Gonsalvez, C., & Gordon, E. (2003). Social phobics do not see eye to eye: A visual scanpath study of emotional expression processing. *Journal of Anxiety Disorders, 17,* 33–44.

Hornstein, S. L., Brown, A. S., & Mulligan, N. W. (2003). Long-term flashbulb memory for learning of Princess Diana's death. *Memory, 11,* 293–206.

Howard, J. W., & Dawes, R. M. (1976). Linear prediction of marital happiness. *Personality and Social Psychology Bulletin, 2,* 478–480.

Howell, S. (1981). Rules not words. In P. Heelas & A. Lock (Eds.), *Indigenous psychologies: The anthropologies of the self* (pp. 133–143). San Diego, CA: Academic Press.

Huber, R., Orzeszyna, M., Pokorny, N., & Kravitz, E. A. (1997). Biogenic amines and aggression: Experimental approaches in crustaceans. *Brain, Behavior and Evolution, 50*(Suppl. 1), 60–68.

Hudson, J. I., Mangweth, B., Pope, H. G., Jr., De Col, C., Hausmann, A., Gutweniger, S., et al. (2003). Family study of affective spectrum disorder. *Archives of General Psychiatry, 60,* 170–177.

Hughes, J. C., & Cook, C. C. H. (1997). The efficacy of disulfiram: A review of outcome studies. *Addiction, 92,* 381–395.

Hugoson, A., Ljungquist, B., & Breivik, T. (2002). The relationship of some negative events and psychological factors to periodontal disease in an adult Swedish population 50 to 80 years of age. *Journal of Clinical Periodontology, 29,* 247–253.

Hull, E. M., Eaton, R. C., Markowski, V. P., Moses, J., Lumley, L. A., & Loucks, J. A. (1992). Opposite influence of medial preoptic D_1 and D_2 receptors on genital reflexes: Implications for copulation. *Life Sciences, 51,* 1705–1713.

Hupka, R. B., Lenton, A. P., & Hutchison, K. A. (1999). Universal development of emotion categories in natural language. *Journal of Personality and Social Psychology, 77,* 247–278.

Huston, T. L., Niehuis, S., & Smith, S. E. (2001). The early marital roots of conjugal distress and divorce. *Current Directions in Psychological Science, 10,* 116–119.

Iacono, W. G., & Patrick, C. J. (1999). Polygraph ("lie detector") testing: The state of the art. In A. K. Hess & I. B. Weiner (Eds.), *Handbook of forensic psychology* (pp. 440–473). New York: Wiley.

Ickes, W., Stinson, L., Bissonnette, V., & Garcia, S. (1990). Naturalistic social cognition: Empathic accuracy in mixed-sex dyads. *Journal of Personality and Social Psychology, 59,* 730–742.

Iidaka, T., Omori, M., Murata, T., Kosaka, H., Yonekura, Y., Okada, T., et al. (2001). Neural interaction of the amygdala with the prefrontal and temporal cortices in the processing of facial expressions as revealed by fMRI. *Journal of Cognitive Neuroscience, 13,* 1035–1047.

Inglehart, R. (1997). *Modernization and postmodernization.* Princeton, NJ: Princeton University Press.

Inoue-Sakurai, C., Maruyama, S., & Morimoto, K. (2000). Posttraumatic stress and lifestyles are associated with natural killer cell activity in victims of the Hanshin-Awaji earthquake in Japan. *Preventive Medicine, 31,* 467–473.

Insel, T. R., O'Brien, D. J., & Leckman, J. F. (2002). Oxytocin, vasopressin, and autism: Is there a connection? In J. T. Cacioppo et al. (Eds.), *Foundations of social neuroscience* (pp. 695–711). Cambridge, MA: MIT Press.

Ireland, J. L. (2004). Anger management therapy with young male offenders: An evaluation of treatment outcome. *Aggressive Behavior, 30,* 174–185.

Iribarren, C., Signey, S., Bild, D. E., Liu, K., Markovitz, J. H., Roseman, J. M., et al. (2000). Association of hostility with coronary artery calcification in young adults. *Journal of the American Medical Association, 283,* 2546–2551.

Irwin, M., Daniels, M., Risch, S. C., Bloom, E., & Weiner, H. (1988).

Plasma cortisol and natural killer cell activity during bereavement. *Biological Psychology, 24,* 173–178.

Isabella, R. A., & Belsky, J. (1991). Interactional synchrony and the origins of infant-mother attachment. *Child Development, 62,* 373–384.

Isen, A. M., Daubman, K. A., & Nowicki, G. P. (1987). Positive affect facilitates creative problem solving. *Journal of Personality and Social Psychology, 52,* 1122–1131.

Ito, T. A., Larsen, J. T., Smith, K., & Cacioppo, J. T. (2002). Negative information weighs more heavily on the brain: The negativity bias in evaluative categorizations. In J. T. Cacioppo et al. (Eds.), *Foundations in social neuroscience* (pp. 575–597). Cambridge, MA: MIT Press.

Izard, C. E. (1994). Innate and universal facial expressions: Evidence from developmental and cross-cultural research. *Psychological Bulletin, 115,* 288–299.

Izard, C. E. (2001). Emotional intelligence or adaptive emotions? *Emotion, 1,* 249–257.

Izard, C. E., & Abe, J. A. A. (2004). Developmental changes in facial expressions of emotions in the Strange Situation during the second year of life. *Emotion, 4,* 251–265.

Jackson, D. C., Malmstadt, J. R., Larson, C. L., & Davidson, R. J. (2000). Suppression and enhancement of emotional responses to unpleasant pictures. *Psychophysiology, 37,* 515–522.

Jackson, R. W., Treiber, F. A., Turner, J. R., Davis, H., & Strong, W. B. (1999). Effects of race, sex, and socioeconomic status upon cardiovascular stress responsivity and recovery in youth. *International Journal of Psychophysiology, 31,* 111–119.

James, W. (1884). What is an emotion? *Mind, 9,* 188–205.

James, W. (1894). The physical basis of emotion. *Psychological Review, 1,* 516–529.

James, W. (1961). *Psychology: The briefer course.* New York: Harper. (Original work published 1892)

Janis, I. L. (1972). *Victims of groupthink.* Boston: Houghton Mifflin.

Janis, I. L. (1983). Stress inoculation in health care. In D. Meichenbaum & M. E. Jaremko (Eds.), *Stress reduction and prevention* (pp. 67–99). New York: Plenum.

Jankowiak, W. R., & Fischer, E. F. (1992). A cross-cultural perspective on romantic love. *Ethnology, 31,* 149–155.

Jedema, H. P., & Grace, A. A. (2004). Corticotropin-releasing hormone directly activates noradrenergic neurons of the locus ceruleus recorded *in vitro. Journal of Neuroscience, 24,* 9703–9713.

Jerome, E. M., & Liss, M. (2005). Relationships between sensory processing style, adult attachment, and coping. *Personality and Individual Differences, 38,* 1341–1352.

Jewell, J. D., & Stark, K. D. (2003). Comparing the family environments of adolescents with conduct disorder or depression. *Journal of Child and Family Studies, 12,* 77–89.

Johnson, J. G., Cohen, P., Smailes, E. M., Kasen, S., & Brook, J. S. (2002). Television viewing and aggressive behavior during adolescence and adulthood. *Science, 295,* 2468–2471.

Johnson, M. H., Posner, M. I., & Rothbart, M. K. (1991). Components of visual orienting in early infancy: Contingency learning, anticipatory looking, and disengaging. *Journal of Cognitive Neuroscience, 3,* 335–344.

Johnson-Laird, P. N., & Oatley, K. (1989). The language of emotions: An analysis of a semantic field. *Cognition and Emotion, 3,* 81–123.

Jonsson, C.-O., Clinton, D. N., Fahrman, M., Mazzaglia, G., Novak, S., & Sörhus, K. (2001). How do mothers signal share feeling-states to their infants? An investigation of affect attunement and imitation during the first year of life. *Scandinavian Journal of Psychology, 42,* 377–381.

Juslin, P. N., & Laukka, P. (2003). Communication of emotions in vocal expression and music performance: Different channels, same code? *Psychological Bulletin, 129,* 770–814.

Kafetsios, K. (2004). Attachment and emotional intelligence abilities across the life course. *Personality and Individual Differences, 37,* 129–145.

Kagan, J. (1984). *The Nature of the Child.* New York: Basic Books.

Kagan, J., Reznick, J. S., & Snidman, N. (1988). Biological bases of childhood shyness. *Science, 240,* 167–171.

Kalick, S. M., Zebrowitz, L. A., Langlois, J. H., & Johnson, R. M. (1998). Does human facial attractiveness honestly advertise health? *Psychological Science, 9,* 8–13.

Kalin, N. H., Shelton, S. E., & Barksdale, C. M. (1988). Opiate modulation of separation-induced distress in non-human primates. *Brain Research, 440,* 285–292.

Kalin, N. H., Shelton, S. E., & Davidson, R. J. (2004). The role of the central nucleus of the amygdala in mediating fear and anxiety in the primate. *Journal of Neuroscience, 24,* 5506–5515.

Kampe, K. K., Frith, C. D., Dolan, R. J., & Frith, U. (2002). Reward value of attractiveness and gaze. *Nature, 413,* 589–590.

Kanner, A. D., Coyne, J. C., Schaefer, C., & Lazarus, R. S. (1981). Comparison of two modes of stress management: Daily hassles and uplifts versus major life events. *Journal of Behavioral Medicine, 4,* 1–39.

Karney, B. R., & Bradbury, T. N. (1995). The longitudinal course of marital quality and stability: A review of theory, method, and research. *Psychological Review, 118,* 3–34.

Kassinove, H., Sudholdolsky, D. G., Tsytsarev, S. V., & Solovyova, S. (1997). Self-reported constructions of anger episodes in Russia and America. *Journal of Social Behavior and Personality, 12,* 301–324.

Katkin, E. S., Wiens, S., & Öhman, A. (2001). Nonconscious fear conditioning, visceral perception, and the development of gut feelings. *Psychological Science, 12,* 366–370.

Kawachi, I., Sparrow, D., Kubzansky, L. D., Spiro, A., Vokonas, P. S., & Weiss, S. T. (1998). Prospective study of a self-report Type A scale and risk of coronary heart disease. *Circulation, 98,* 405–412.

Kawamura, N., Kim, Y., & Asukai, N. (2001). Suppression of cellular immunity in men with a past history of posttraumatic stress disorder. *American Journal of Psychiatry, 158,* 484–486.

Kawasaki, H., Adolphs, R., Kaufman, O., Damasio, H., Damasio, A. R., Granner, M., et al. (2001). Single-neuron responses to emotional visual stimuli recorded in human ventral prefrontal cortex. *Nature Neuroscience, 4,* 15–16.

Keillor, J. M., Barrett, A. M., Crucian, G. P., Kortenkamp, S., & Heilman, K. M. (2002). Emotional experience and perception in the absence of facial feedback. *Journal of the International Neuropsychological Society, 8,* 130–135.

Keith-Lucas, T., & Guttman, N. (1975). Robust single-trial delayed backward conditioning. *Journal of Comparative and Physiological Psychology, 88,* 468–476.

Keller, M. C. Fredrickson, B. L., Ybarra, O., Côté, S., Johnson, K., Mikels, J., et al. (2005). A warm heart and a clear head. *Psychological Science, 16,* 724–731.

Kelly, K. M., & Jones, W. H. (1997). Assessment of dispositional embarrassibility. *Anxiety, Stress, and Coping, 10,* 307–333.

Keltner, D. (1995). Signs of appeasement: Evidence for the distinct displays of embarrassment, amusement, and shame. *Journal of Personality and Social Psychology, 68,* 441–454.

Keltner, D., & Buswell, B. N. (1996). Evidence for the distinctness of embarrassment, shame, and guilt: A study of recalled antecedents and facial expressions of emotion. *Cognition and Emotion, 10,* 155–171.

Keltner, D., & Buswell, B. N. (1997). Embarrassment: Its distinct form and appeasement functions. *Psychological Bulletin, 122,* 250–270.

Keltner, D., Ellsworth, P. C., & Edwards, K. (1993). Beyond simple pessimism: Effects of sadness and anger on social perception. *Journal of Personality and Social Psychology, 64,* 740–752.

Keltner, D., & Gross, J. J. (1999). Functional accounts of emotions. *Cognition and Emotion, 13,* 467–480.

Keltner, D., Gruenfeld, D. H., & Anderson, C. (2003). Power, approach, and inhibition. *Psychological Review, 110,* 265–284.

Keltner, D., & Haidt, J. (1999). Social functions of emotions at four levels of analysis. *Cognition and Emotion, 13,* 505–521.

Keltner, D., & Shiota, M. N. (2003). New displays and new emotions: A commentary on Rozin and Cohen (2003). *Emotion, 3,* 86–91.

Keltner, D., Young, R. C., & Buswell, B. N. (1997). Appeasement in human emotion, social practice, and personality. *Aggressive Behavior, Special Issue: Appeasement and Reconciliation, 23*(5), 359–374.

Kendler, K. S., Gardner, C. O., & Prescott, C. A. (1999). Clinical characteristics of major depression that predict risk of depression in relatives. *Archives of General Psychiatry, 56,* 322–327.

Kendler, K. S., Myers, J., & Prescott, C. A. (2002). The etiology of phobias. *Archives of General Psychiaty, 59,* 242–248.

Kendler, K. S., Myers, J., Prescott, C. A., & Neale, M. C. (2001). The genetic epidemiology of irrational fears and phobias in men. *Archives of General Psychiatry, 58,* 257–265.

Kendler, K. S., Walters, E. E., Neale, M. C., Kessler, R. C., Heath, A. C., & Eaves, L. J. (1995). The structure of the genetic and environmental risk factors for six major psychiatric disorders in women. *Archives of General Psychiatry, 52,* 374–383.

Kensinger, E. A., & Corkin, S. (2003). Memory enhancement for emotional words: Are emotional words more vividly remembered than neutral words? *Memory & Cognition, 31,* 1169–1180.

Keverne, E. B., & Kendrick, K. M. (1992). Oxytocin facilitation of maternal behavior in sheep. *Annals of the New York Academy of Science, 807,* 455–468.

Kiecolt-Glaser, J. K. (1999). Stress, personal relationships, and immune function: Health implications. *Brain, Behavior, and Immunity, 13,* 61–72.

Kiecolt-Glaser, J. K., & Glaser, R. (1993). Mind and immunity. In D. Goleman & J. Gurin (Eds.), *Mind body medicine* (pp. 39–61). Yonkers, NY: Consumer Reports Books.

Kiecolt-Glaser, J. K., & Glaser, R. (2001). Stress and immunity: Age enhances the risks. *Current Directions in Psychological Science, 10,* 18–21.

Kiecolt-Glaser, J. K., McGuire, L., Robles, T. F., & Glaser, R. (2002). Psychoneuroimmunology: Psychological influences on immune function and health. *Journal of Consulting and Clinical Psychology, 70,* 537–547.

Kiecolt-Glaser, J. K., & Newton, T. L. (2001). Marriage and health: His and hers. *Psychological Bulletin, 127,* 472–503.

Kiecolt-Glaser, J. K., Robles, T. F., Heffner, K. L., Loving, T. J., & Glaser, R. (2002). Psycho-oncology and cancer: Psychoneuroimmunology and cancer. *Annals of Oncology, 13*(Suppl. 4), 165–169.

Kilpelainen, M., Koskenvuo, M., Helenius, H., & Terho, E. O. (2002). Stressful life events promote the manifestation of asthma and atopic diseases. *Clinical & Experimental Allergy, 32,* 256–263.

Kim, J., & Hatfield, E. (2004). Love types and subjective well-being: A cross cultural study. *Social Behavior and Personality, 32,* 173–182.

King, J. E., & Landau, V. I. (2003). Can chimpanzees (*Pan troglodytes*) happiness be estimated by human raters? *Journal of Research in Personality, 37,* 1–15.

Kitayama, S., Markus, H. R., & Kurokawa, M. (2000). Culture, emotion, and well-being: Good feelings in Japan and the United States. *Cognition and Emotion, 14,* 93–124.

Klaus, M. H., & Kennell, J. H. (1976). *Maternal-infant bonding.* St. Louis, MO: Mosby.

Klein, K., & Boals, A. (2001). The relationship of life event stress and working memory capacity. *Applied Cognitive Psychology, 15,* 565–579.

Kleinmuntz, B., & Szucko, J. J. (1984). A field study of the fallibility of polygraphic lie detection. *Nature, 308,* 449–450.

Klineberg, O. (1938). Emotional expression in Chinese literature. *Journal of Abnormal and Social Psychology, 31,* 517–520.

Klinnnert, M. D., Emde, R. N., Butterfield, P., & Campos, J. J. (1986). Social referencing: The infant's use of emotional signals from a friendly adult with mother present. *Developmental Psychology, 22,* 427–432.

Klohnen, E. C., & Mendelsohn, G. A. (1998). Partner selection for personality characteristics: A person-centered approach. *Personality and Social Psychology Bulletin, 24,* 268–278.

Kluger, M. J. (1991). Fever: Role of pyrogens and cryogens. *Phsyiological Reviews, 71,* 93–127.

Klüver, H., & Bucy, P. C. (1939). Preliminary analysis of functions of the temporal lobes in monkeys. *Archives of Neurological Psychiatry, 42,* 979–1000.

Kniffin, K. M., & Wilson, D. S. (2004). The effect of nonphysical traits on the perception of physical attractiveness. *Evolution and Human Behavior, 25,* 88–101.

Knight, G. P., Guthrie, I. K., Page, M. C., & Fabes, R. A. (2002). Emotional arousal and gender differences in aggression: A meta-analysis. *Aggressive Behavior, 28,* 366–393.

Knutson, B., Burgdorf, J., & Panksepp, J. (2002). Ultrasonic vocalizations as indices of affective states in rats. *Psychological Bulletin, 128,* 961–977.

Knyazev, C. G., Slobodskaya, H. R., & Wilson, G. D. (2002). Psychophysiological correlates of behavioural inhibition and activation. *Personality and Individual Differences, 33,* 647–660.

Koepp, M. J., Gunn, R. N., Lawrence, A. D., Cunningham, V. J., Dagher, A., Jones, T., et al. (1998). Evidence for striatal dopamine release during a video game. *Nature, 393,* 266–268.

Kohler, C. G., Turner, T. H., Bilker, W. B., Brensinger, C. M., Siegel, S. J., Kanes, S. J., et al. (2003). Facial emotion recognition in schizophrenia: Intensity effects and error pattern. *American Journal of Psychiatry, 160,* 1768–1774.

Kokkinaki, T. (2003). A longitudinal, naturalistic and cross-cultural study on emotions in early infant-parent imitative interactions. *British Journal of Developmental Psychology, 21,* 243–258.

Kolb, B., & Taylor, L. (2000). Facial expression, emotion, and hemispheric organization. In R. D. Lane & L. Nadel (Eds.), *Cognitive neuroscience of emotion* (pp. 62–83). New York: Oxford University Press.

Kontsevich, L. L., & Tyler, C. W. (2004). What makes Mona Lisa smile? *Vision Research, 44,* 1493–1498.

Kornreich, C., Blairy, S., Philippot, P., Hess, U., Noel, X., Streel, E., et al. (2001). Deficits in recognition of emotional facial expression are still present in alcoholics after mid- to long-term abstinence. *Journal of Studies on Alcohol, 62,* 533–542.

Kosfeld, M., Heinrichs, M., Zak, P. J., Fischbacher, U., & Fehr, E. (2005).

Oxytocin increases trust in humans. *Nature, 435,* 673–676.

Koster, E. H. W., Crombez, G., Van Damme, S., Verschuere, B., & De Houwer, J. (2004). Does imminent threat capture and hold attention? *Emotion, 4,* 312–317.

Kottler, J. A. (1996). *The language of tears.* San Francisco: Jossey-Bass.

Kraaij, V., Pruymboom, E., & Garnefski, N. (2002). Cognitive coping and depressive symptoms in the elderly: A longitudinal study. *Aging & Mental Health, 6,* 275–281.

Kraemer, D. L., & Hastrup, J. L. (1988). Crying in adults: Self-control and autonomic correlates. *Journal of Social and Clinical Psychology, 6,* 53–68.

Krantz, D. S., Sheps, D. S., Carney, R. M., & Natelson, B. H. (2000). Effects of mental stress in patients with coronary artery disease. *Journal of the American Medical Association, 283,* 1800–1802.

Krawczyk, D. C. (2002). Contributions of the prefrontal cortex to the neural basis of human decision making. *Neuroscience and Biobehavioral Reviews, 26,* 631–664.

Krohne, H. W., Schmukle, S. C., Spaderna, H., & Spielberger, C. D. (2002). The state-trait depression scales: An international comparison. *Anxiety, Stress and Coping, 15,* 105–122.

Kronfol, Z., & Remick, D. G. (2000). Cytokines and the brain: Implications for clinical psychiatry. *American Journal of Psychiatry, 157,* 683–694.

Kruesi, M. J. P., Hibbs, E. D., Zahn, T. P., Keysor, C. S., Hamburger, S. D., Bartko, J. J., et al. (1992). A 2-year prospective follow-up of children and adolescents with disruptive behavior disorders. *Archives of General Psychiatry, 49,* 429–435.

Kruk, M. R., Halász, J., Meelis, W., & Haller, J. (2004). Fast positive feedback between the adrenocortical stress response and a brain mechanism involved in aggressive behavior. *Behavioral Neuroscience, 118,* 1062–1070.

Kübler, A., Kotchoubey, B., Kaiser, J., Wolpaw, J. R., & Birbaumer, N. (2001). Brain-computer communication: Unlocking the locked-in. *Psychological Bulletin, 127,* 358–375.

Kubota, Y., Sato, W., Murai, T., Toichi, M., Ikeda, A., & Sengoku, A. (2000). Emotional cognition without awareness after unilateral temporal lobectomy in humans. *Journal of Neuroscience, 20* (RC97), 1–5.

Kubzhansky, L. D., Martin, L. T., & Buka, S. L. (2004). Early manifestations of personality and adult emotional functioning. *Emotion, 4,* 364–377.

Kuhlmann, S., Piel, M., & Wolf, O. T. (2005). Impaired memory retrieval after psychosocial stress in healthy young men. *Journal of Neuroscience, 25,* 2977–2982.

Kundera, M. (1980). *The book of laughter and forgetting* (M. H. Heim, Trans.). New York: Knopf. (Original work published 1979)

Kuppens, P. P., Van Mechelen, I., Smits, D. J. M., & De Boeck, P. (2003). The appraisal basis of anger: Specificity, necessity, and sufficiency of components. *Emotion, 3,* 254–269.

LaBar, K. S., Cook, C. A., Torpey, D. C., & Welsh-Bohmer, K. A. (2004). Impact of healthy aging on awareness and fear conditioning. *Behavioral Neuroscience, 118,* 905–915.

LaBar, K. S., & Phelps, E. A. (1998). Arousal-mediated memory consolidation: Role of the medial temporal lobe in humans. *Psychological Science, 9,* 490–493.

LaBarre, W. (1947). The cultural basis of emotions and gestures. *Journal of Personality, 16,* 49–68.

Labouvie-Vief, G., Lumley, M. A., Jain, E., & Heinze, H. (2003). Age and gender differences in cardiac reactivity and subjective emotion responses to emotional autobiographical memories. *Emotion, 3,* 115–126.

Lachman, M. E., & Firth, K. M. P. (2004). The adaptive value of feeling in control during midlife. In O. G. Brim, C. D. Ryff, & R. C. Kessler (Eds.), *How healthy are we?* (pp. 320–349). Chicago: University of Chicago Press.

Lacroix, L., Spinelli, S., Heidbreder, C. A., & Feldon, J. (2000). Differential role of the medial and lateral prefrontal cortices in fear and anxiety. *Behavioral Neuroscience, 114,* 1119–1130.

LaFramboise, T., Coleman, H. L. K., & Gerton, J. (1993). Psychological impact of biculturalism: Evidence and theory. *Psychological Bulletin, 114,* 395–412.

LaFrance, M., Hecht, M. A., & Paluck, E. L. (2003). The contingent smile: A meta-analysis of sex differences in smiling. *Psychological Bulletin, 129,* 305–334.

Laible, D. J., Carlo, G., & Raffaelli, M. (2000). The differential relations of parent and peer attachment to adolescent adjustment. *Journal of Youth and Adolescence, 29,* 45–59.

Lake, R. I. E., Eaves, L. J., Maes, H. H. M., Heath, A. C., & Martin, N. G. (2000). Further evidence against the environmental transmission of individual differences in neuroticism from a collaborative study of 45,850 twins and relatives on two continents. *Behavior Genetics, 30,* 223–233.

Lakin, J. L., & Chartrand, T. L. (2003). Using nonconscious behavioral mimicry to create affiliation and rapport. *Psychological Science, 14,* 334–339.

Lambie, J. A., & Marcel, A. J. (2002). Consciousness and the varieties of emotion experience: A theoretical framework. *Psychological Review, 109,* 219–259.

Lamprecht, F., & Sack, M. (2002). Posttraumatic stress disorder revisited. *Psychosomatic Medicine, 64,* 222–237.

Lang, P. J. (1994). The varieties of emotional experience: A meditation on James-Lange theory. *Psychological Bulletin, 101,* 211–221.

Lang, P. J., Bradley, M. M., & Cuthbert, B. N. (2002). A motivational analysis of emotion: Reflex-cortex connections. In J. T. Cacioppo et al. (Eds.), *Foundations in social neuroscience* (pp. 461–471). Cambridge, MA: MIT Press.

Lange, C. G. (1922). The emotions: A psychological study. (I. A. Haupt, Trans.) In C. G. Lange & W. James, *The emotions* (pp. 33–90). Baltimore, MD: Williams & Wilkins. (Original work published 1885)

Langer, E. J. (1975). The illusion of control. *Journal of Personality and Social Psychology, 32,* 311–328.

Langlois, J. H., & Roggman, L. A. (1990). Attractive faces are only average. *Psychological Science, 1,* 115–121.

Langlois, J. H., Roggman, L. A., & Musselman, L. (1994). What is average and what is not average about average faces? *Psychological Science, 5,* 214–220.

Larsen, J. T., McGraw, A. P., & Cacioppo, J. T. (2001). Can people feel happy and sad at the same time? *Journal of Personality and Social Psychology, 81,* 684–696.

Larsen, J. T., McGraw, A. P., Mellers, B. A., & Cacioppo, J. T. (2004). The agony of victory and thrill of defeat. *Psychological Science, 15,* 325–330.

Larsen, R. J., Kasimatis, M., & Frey, K. (1992). Facilitating the furrowed brow—An unobtrusive test of the facial feedback hypothesis applied to unpleasant affect. *Cognition & Emotion, 6,* 321–338.

Larsen, R. J., & Ketelaar, T. (1989). Extraversion, neuroticism, and susceptibility to positive and negative mood induction procedures. *Personality and Individual Differences, 10,* 1221–1228.

Larson, R., & Lampman-Petraitis, C. (1989). Daily emotional states as reported by children and adolescents. *Child Development, 60,* 1250–1260.

Larson, R., & Richards, M. (1991). Daily companionship in late childhood and early adolescence: Changing developmental contexts. *Child Development, 62,* 284–300.

Latta, R. L. (1999). *The basic humor process: A cognitive-shift theory and the case against incongruity.* New York: Mouton de Gruyter.

Laudenslager, M. L., Aasal, R., Adler, L., Berger, C. L., Montgomery, P. T., Sandberg, E., et al. (1998). Elevated cytotoxicity in combat veterans with long-term posttraumatic stress disorder: Preliminary observations. *Brain, Behavior, and Immunity, 12,* 74–79.

Lawton, M. P. (2001). Emotion in later life. *Current Directions in Psychological Science, 10,* 120–123.

Lazarus, R. S. (1977). Cognitive and coping responses in emotion. In A. Monat & R. S. Lazarus (Eds.), *Stress and coping* (pp. 145–158). New York: Columbia University Press.

Lazarus, R. S. (1991). *Emotion and adaptation.* New York: Oxford University Press.

Lazarus, R. S. (2001). Relational meaning and discrete emotions. In K. R. Scherer, A. Schorr, & T. Johnstone (Eds.), *Appraisal processes in emotion* (pp. 37–67). New York: Oxford University Press.

Leach, C. W., Spears, R., Branscombe, N. R., & Doosje, B. (2003). Malicious pleasure: Schadenfreude at the suffering of another group. *Journal of Personality and Social Psychology, 84,* 932–943.

Leary, M. R. (2001). Shyness and the self: Attentional, motivational, and cognitive self-processes in social anxiety and inhibition. In W. R. Crozier & L. E. Alden (Eds.), *International handbook of social anxiety* (pp. 218–234). Chichester, England: John Wiley.

LeDoux, J. (1996). *The emotional brain.* New York: Simon & Schuster.

Lefcourt, H. M. (2002). Humor. In C. R. Snyder & S. J. Lopez (Eds.), *Handbook of positive psychology* (pp. 619–631). New York: Oxford University Press.

Lehmann, K. A. (1995). New developments in patient-controlled postoperative analgesia. *Annals of Medicine, 27,* 271–282.

Lensvelt-Mulders, G., & Hettema, J. (2001). Genetic analysis of autonomic reactivity to psychologically stressful situations. *Biological Psychiatry, 58,* 25–40.

Leonard, B. E. (2000). Peripheral markers of depression. *Current Opinion in Psychiatry, 13,* 61–68.

Leppämäki, S., Partonen, T., & Lönnqvist, J. (2002). Bright-light exposure combined with physical exercise elevates mood. *Journal of Affective Disorders, 72,* 139–144.

Leppänen, J. M., & Hietanen, J. K. (2003). Affect and face perception: Odors modulate the recognition advantage of happy faces. *Emotion, 3,* 315–326.

Lerner, J. S., Gonzalez, R. M., Small, D. A., & Fischhoff, B. (2003). Effects of fear and anger on perceived risks of terrorism: A national field experiment. *Psychological Science, 14,* 144–150.

Lerner, J. S., & Keltner, D. (2000). Beyond valence: Toward a model of emotion-specific influences on judgement and choice. *Cognition and Emotion, 14,* 473–493.

Lerner, J. S., & Keltner, D. (2001). Fear, anger, and risk. *Journal of Personality and Social Psychology, 81,* 146–159.

Lerner, J. S., Small, D. A., & Loewenstein, G. (2004). Heart strings and purse strings. *Psychological Science, 15,* 337–341.

Levenson, R. W. (1992). Autonomic nervous system differences among emotions. *Psychological Science, 3,* 23–27.

Levenson, R. W. (1999). The intrapersonal functions of emotion. *Cognition & Emotion, 13,* 481–504.

Levenson, R. W., Carstensen, L. L., & Gottman, J. M. (1994). The influence of age and gender on affect, physiology, and their interrelations: A study of long-term marriages. *Journal of Personality and Social Psychology, 67,* 56–68.

Levenson, R. W., Ekman, P., & Friesen, W. V. (1990). Voluntary facial action generates emotion-specific autonomic nervous system activity. *Psychophysiology, 27,* 363–383.

Levenson, R. W., Ekman, P., Heider, K., & Friesen, W. V. (1992). Emotion and autonomic nervous system activity in the Minangkabau of West Sumatra. *Journal of Personality and Social Psychology, 62,* 972–988.

Levenson, R. W., & Gottman, J. M. (1983). Marital interaction: Physiological linkage and affective exchange. *Journal of Personality and Social Psychology, 45,* 587–597.

Levenson, R. W., & Ruef, A. M. (1992). Empathy: A physiological substrate. *Journal of Personality and Social Psychology, 63,* 234–246.

Lévesque, J., Joanette, Y., Mensour, B., Beaudoin, G., Leroux, J.-M., Bourgouin, P., et al. (2003). Neural correlates of sad feelings in healthy girls. *Neuroscience, 121,* 545–551.

Levin, J., & Arluke, A. (1982). Embarrassment and helping behavior. *Psychological Reports, 51,* 999–1002.

Levine, L. J., & Pizarro, D. A. (2004). Emotion and memory research: A grumpy overview. *Social Cognition, 22,* 530–554.

LeVine, R. A. (1997). Mother-infant interaction in cross-cultural perspective. In N. L. Segal, G. E. Weisfeld, & C. C. Weisfeld (Eds.), *Uniting psychology and biology* (pp. 339–354). Washington, DC: American Psychological Association.

Levinger, G. (1980). Toward the analysis of close relationships. *Journal of Experimental Social Psychology, 16,* 510–544.

Levinger, G. (1983). Development and change. In H. H. Kelley, E. Bersheid, A. Christensen, J. H. Harvey, T. L. Huston, G. Levinger et al. (Eds.), *Close relationships* (pp. 315–359). New York: W. H. Freeman.

Levy, R. (1973). *The Tahitians.* Chicago: University of Chicago Press.

Levy, R. I. (1984). The emotions in comparative perspective. In K. R. Scherer & P. Ekman (Eds.), *Approaches to emotion* (pp. 397–412). Hillsdale, NJ: Erlbaum.

Lewicka, M. (1997). Rational or uncommitted? Depression and indecisiveness in interpersonal decision making. *Scandinavian Journal of Psychology, 38,* 227–236.

Lewinsohn, P. M., Mischel, W., Chaplin, W., & Barton, R. (1980). Social competence and depression: The role of illusory self-impressions. *Journal of Abnormal Psychology, 89,* 203–212.

Lewis, M. (1993). The development of anger and rage. In R. A. Glick & S. P. Roose (Eds.), *Rage, power, and aggression* (pp. 148–168). New Haven, CT: Yale University Press.

Lewis, M. (1992). *Shame: The exposed self.* New York: Free Press.

Lewis, M. (2000). The emergence of human emotions. In M. Lewis & J. M. Haviland (Eds.), *Handbook of emotions* (2nd ed., pp. 265–280). New York: Guilford.

Lewis, M., & Brooks-Gunn, J. (1979). *Social cognition and the acquisition of self.* New York: Plenum Press.

Lewis, M., & Feiring, C. (1981). Direct and indirect interactions in social relationships. *Advances in Infancy Research, 1,* 129–161.

Lewis, M., Stanger, S., & Sullivan, M. W. (1989). Deception in 3-year-olds. *Developmental Psychology, 25,* 439–443.

Lewis, M., Sullivan, M. W., Stanger, C., & Weiss, M. (1989). Self-development and self-conscious emotions. *Child Development, 60,* 146–156.

Liew, J., Eisenberg, N., & Reiser, M. (2004). Preschoolers' effortful control and negative emotionality, immediate reactions to disappointment, and quality of social functioning. *Journal of Experimental Child Psychology, 89,* 298–319.

Lillberg, K., Verkasalo, P. K., Kaprio, J., Teppo., L., Helenius, H., & Koskenvuo, M. (2003). Stressful life events and risk of breast cancer in 10,808 women: A cohort study. *American Journal of Epidemiology, 157,* 415–423.

Lilly, R., Cummings, J. L., Benson, F., & Frankel, M. (1983). The human

Klüver-Bucy syndrome. *Neurology, 33,* 1141–1145.

Lim, M. M., Wang, Z., Olazábel, D. E., Ren, X., Terwilliger, E. F., & Young, L. J. (2004). Enhanced partner preference in a promiscuous species by manipulating the expression of a single gene. *Nature, 429,* 754–757.

Linden, W., Lenz, J. W., & Con, A. H. (2001). Individualized stress management for primary hypertension: A randomized trial. *Archives of Internal Medicine, 161,* 1071–1080.

Lindstrøm, T. C. (1997). Immunity and somatic health in bereavement: A prospective study of 39 Norwegian widows. *Omega, 35,* 231–241.

Liu, L. Y., Coe, C. L., Swenson, C. A., Kelly, E. A., Kita, H., & Busse, W. W. (2002). School examinations enhance airway inflammation to antigen challenge. *American Journal of Respiratory and Critical Care Medicine, 165,* 1062–1067.

Locke, E. A. (2005). Why emotional intelligence is an invalid concept. *Journal of Organizational Behavior, 26,* 425–431.

Loeber, R., Burke, J. D., Lahey, B. B., Winters, A., & Zera, M. (2000). Oppositional defiant and conduct disorder: A review of the past 10 years, part I. *Journal of the American Academy of Child and Adolescent Psychiatry, 39,* 1468–1484.

Loehlin, J. C. (1992). *Genes and environment in personality development.* Newbury Park, CA: Sage.

Loewenstein, G. (1987). Anticipation and the valuation of delayed consumption. *The Economic Journal, 97,* 666–684.

Loewenstein, G. F., Weber, E. U., Hsee, C. K., & Welch, N. (2001). Risk as feelings. *Psychological Bulletin, 127,* 267–286.

Logue, A. W. (1985). Conditioned food aversion learning in humans. *Annals of the New York Academy of Sciences, 443,* 316–329.

Lorber, M. F. (2004). Psychophysiology of aggression, psychopathy, and conduct problems: A meta-analysis. *Psychological Bulletin, 130,* 531–532.

Lovallo, D., & Kahneman, D. (2000). Living with uncertainty: Attractiveness and resolution timing. *Journal of Behavioral Decision Making, 13,* 179–190.

Lowe, J., & Carroll, D. (1985). The effects of spinal injury on the intensity of emotional experience. *British Journal of Clinical Psychology, 24,* 135–136.

Lu, L. (2001). Understanding happiness: A look into the Chinese folk psychology. *Journal of Happiness Studies, 2,* 407–432.

Lucas, R. E., Clark, A. E., Georgellis, Y., & Diener, E. (2003). Reexamining adaptation and the set point model of happiness: Reactions to changes in marital status. *Journal of Personality and Social Psychology, 84,* 527–539.

Lucas, R. E., Clark, A. E., Georgellis, Y., & Diener, E. (2004). Unemployment alters the set point for life satisfaction. *Psychological Science, 15,* 8–13.

Ludwig, D., Goetz, P., Balgemann, D., & Roschke, T. (1972). Language and color perception: A cross-cultural study. *International Journal of Symbology, 3,* 25–29.

Lutz, C. (1982). The domain of emotion words in Ifaluk. *American Ethnologist, 9,* 113–128.

Lykken, D., & Tellegen, A. (1996). Happiness is a stochastic process. *Psychological Science, 7,* 186–189.

Lyons, M. J., Eisen, S. A., Goldberg, J., True, W., Lin, N., Meyer, J. M., et al. (1998). A registry-based twin study of depression in men. *Archives of General Psychiatry, 55,* 468–472.

Lyons, M. J., True, W. R., Eisen, S. A., Goldberg, J., Meyer, J. M., Faraone, S. V., et al. (1995). Differential heritability of adult and juvenile antisocial traits. *Archives of General Psychiatry, 52,* 906–915.

Maas, J. W. (1975). Biogenic amines and depression: Biochemical and pharmacological separation of two types of depression. *Archives of General Psychiatry, 32,* 1357–1361.

MacKay, D. G., & Ahmetzanov, M. V. (2005). Emotion, memory, and attention in the taboo Stroop phenomenon. *Psychological Science, 16,* 25–32.

Madsen, K. B. (1959). *Theories of motivation.* Copenhagen: Munksgaard.

Magnussen, D. (1988). *Individual development from an interactional perspective: A longitudinal study.* Hillsdale, NJ: Erlbaum.

Mahler, M. S., Pine, F., & Bergman, A. (1975). *The psychological birth of the infant.* New York: Basic Books.

Maier, S. F., & Watkins, L. R. (1998). Cytokines for psychologists: Implications of bidirectional immune-to-brain communication for understanding behavior, mood, and cognition. *Psychological Review, 105,* 83–107.

Malatesta, C. Z., Grigoryev, P., Lamb, C., Albin, M., & Culver, C. (1986). Emotion socialization and expressive development in preterm and full-term infants. *Child Development, 57,* 316–330.

Malatesta, C. Z., & Haviland, J. M. (1982). Learning display rules: The socialization of emotion expression in infancy. *Child Development, 53,* 991–1003.

Malinosky-Rummell, R., & Hansen, D. J. (1993). Long-term consequences of childhood physical abuse. *Psychological Bulletin, 114,* 68–79.

Malt, B. C., Sloman, S. A., Gennari, S., Shi, M, & Wang, Y. (1999). Knowing versus naming: Similarity and the linguistic categorization of artifacts. *Journal of Memory and Language, 40,* 230–262.

Maltby, J., & Day, L. (2000). The reliability and validity of a susceptibility to embarrassment scale among adults. *Personality and Individual Differences, 29,* 749–756.

Mann, J. J., McBride, P. A., Anderson, G. M., & Mieczkowski, T. A. (1992). Platelet and whole-blood serotonin content in depressed inpatients: Correlations with acute and lifetime psychopathology. *Biological Psychiatry, 32,* 243–257.

Manor, O., & Eisenbach, Z. (2003). Mortality after spousal loss: Are there socio-demographic differences? *Social Science & Medicine, 56,* 405–413.

Manuck, S. B., Flory, J. D., Ferrell, R. E., Dent, K. M., Mann, J. J., & Muldoon, M. F. (1999). Aggression and anger-related traits associated with a polymorphism of the tryptophan hydroxylase gene. *Biological Psychiatry, 45,* 603–614.

Marcus, D. K., & Miller, R. S. (1999). The perception of "live" embarrassment: A social relations analysis of class presentations. *Cognition and Emotion, 13,* 105–117.

Markus, H. R., & Kitayama, S. (1991). Culture and the self: Implications for cognition, emotion, and motivation. *Psychological Bulletin, 98,* 224–253.

Markus, H. R., Ryff, C. D., Curhan, K. B., & Palmersheim, K. A. (2004). In their own words: Well-being at midlife among high school-educated and college-educated adults. In O. G. Brim,

C. D. Ryff, & R. C. Kessler (Eds.), *How healthy are we?* (pp. 273–319). Chicago: University of Chicago Press.

Marlowe, F., & Wetsman, A. (2001). Preferred waist-to-hip ratio and ecology. *Personality and Individual Differences, 30,* 481–489.

Marsh, A. A., Elfenbein, H. A., & Ambady, N. (2003). Nonverbal "accents": Cultural differences in facial expressions of emotion. *Psychological Science, 14,* 373–376.

Marshall, G. D., Jr., Agarwal, S. K., Lloyd, C., Cohen, L., Henninger, E. M., & Morris, G. J. (1998). Cytokine dysregulation associated with exam stress in healthy medical students. *Brain, Behavior, and Immunity, 12,* 297–307.

Marshall, G. D., & Zimbardo, P. G. (1979). Affective consequences of inadequately explained physiological arousal. *Journal of Personality and Social Psychology, 37,* 970–988.

Martin, G. B., & Clark, R. D. (1982). Distress crying in neonates: Species and peer specificity. *Developmental Psychology, 18,* 3–9.

Martin, R., Watson, D., & Wan, C. K. (2000). A three-factor model of trait anger: Dimensions of affect, behavior, and cognition. *Journal of Personality, 68,* 869–897.

Martin, R. A. (2001). Humor, laughter, and physical health: Methodological issues and research findings. *Psychological Bulletin, 127,* 504–519.

Marzillier, S. L., & Davey, G. C. L. (2004). The emotional profiling of disgust-eliciting stimuli: Evidence for primary and complex disgusts. *Cognition and Emotion, 18,* 313–336.

Maslach, C. (1979). Negative emotional biasing of unexplained arousal. *Journal of Personality and Social Psychology, 37,* 953–969.

Maslow, A. H. (1971). *The farther reaches of human nature.* New York: Viking.

Masters, W. H., & Johnson, V. E. (1966). *Human sexual response.* Boston: Little, Brown.

Mastropieri, D., & Turkewitz, G. (1999). Prenatal experience and neonatal responsiveness to vocal expressions of emotion. *Developmental Psychobiology, 35,* 204–214.

Mather, M., Canli, T., English, T., Whitfield, S., Wais, P., Ochsner, K., et al. (2004). Amygdala responses to emotionally valenced stimuli in older and younger adults. *Psychological Science, 15,* 259–263.

Mather, M., & Carstensen, L. L. (2003). Aging and attentional biases for emotional faces. *Psychological Science, 14,* 409–415.

Mathews, A., & Mackintosh, B. (2004). Take a closer look: Emotion modifies the boundary extension effect. *Emotion, 4,* 36–45.

Matsumoto, D. (1990). Cultural similarities and differences in display rules. *Motivation and Emotion, 14,* 195–214.

Matsumoto, D. (1996). *Unmasking Japan: Myths and realities about the emotions of the Japanese.* Stanford, CA: Stanford University Press.

Matsumoto, D. (2002). Methodological requirements to test a possible in-group advantage in judging emotions across cultures: Comment on Elfenbein and Ambady (2002) and evidence. *Psychological Bulletin, 128,* 236–242.

Matsumoto, D., Consolacion, T., Yamada, H., Suzuki, R., Franklin, B., Paul, S., et al. (2002). American-Japanese cultural differences in judgements of emotional expressions of different intensities. *Cognition and Emotion, 16,* 721–747.

Matsumoto, D., & Ekman, P. (1989). American-Japanese cultural differences in intensity ratings of facial expressions of emotion. *Motivation and Emotion, 13,* 143–157.

Matsumoto, D., Yoo, S. H., Hirayama, S., & Petrova, G. (2005). Development and validation of a measure of display rule knowledge: The display rule assessment inventory. *Emotion, 5,* 23–40.

Matsuyama, Y., Hama., H., Kawamura, Y., & Mine, H. (1978). An analysis of emotional words. *The Japanese Journal of Psychology, 49,* 229–232.

Maughan, B., Pickles, A., Rowe, R., Costello, E. J., & Angold, A. (2000). Developmental trajectories of aggressive and non-aggressive conduct problems. *Journal of Quantitative Criminology, 16,* 199–221.

Maunsell, E., Brisson, J., Mondor, M., Verreault, R., & Deschênes, L. (2001). Stressful life events and survival after breast cancer. *Psychosomatic Medicine, 63,* 306–315.

Mauro, R., Sato, K., & Tucker, J. (1992). The role of appraisal in human emotions: A cross-cultural study. *Journal of Personality and Social Psychology, 62,* 301–317.

Mauss, I. B., Levenson, R. W., McCarter, L, Wilhelm, F. W., & Gross, J. J. (2005). The tie that binds?: Coherence among emotion experience, behavior, and physiology. *Emotion, 5,* 175–190.

Mayer, J. D. (2001). A field guide to emotional intelligence. In J. Ciarrochi, J. P. Forgas, & J. D. Mayer (Eds.), *Emotional intelligence in everyday life* (pp. 3–24). Philadelphia, PA: Psychology Press.

Mayer, J. D., Caruso, D. R., & Salovey, P. (2000). Emotional intelligence meets traditional standards for an intelligence. *Intelligence, 27,* 267–298.

Mayer, J. D., Perkins, D. M., Caruso, D. R., & Salovey, P. (2001). Emo-

tional intelligence and giftedness. *Roeper Review, 23,* 131–137.

Mayer, J. D., Salovey, P., Caruso, D. R., & Sitarenios, G. (2001). Emotional intelligence as a standard intelligence. *Emotion, 1,* 232–242.

Mayer, J. D., Salovey, P., Caruso, D. R., & Sitarenios, G. (2003). Measuring emotional intelligence with the MSCEIT V2.0. *Emotion, 3,* 97–105.

Mayne, T. J. (1999). Negative affect and health: The importance of being earnest. *Cognition and Emotion, 13,* 601–635.

McCall, W. A. (1939). *Measurement.* New York: Macmillan.

McCann, C., Roberts, R. D., Matthews, G., & Zeidner, M. (2004). Consensus scoring and empirical option weighting of performance-based Emotional Intelligence (EI) tests. *Personality and Individual Differences, 36,* 645–662.

McCullough, M. E. (2001). Forgiveness: Who does it and how do they do it? *Current Directions in Psychological Science, 10,* 194–197.

McDougall, W. (1932). *The energies of men.* New York: Scribner.

McElheny, V. (2004). Three Nobelists ask: Are we ready for the next frontier? *Cerebrum, 5,* 69–81.

McEwen, B. S. (2000). The neurobiology of stress: From serendipity to clinical relevance. *Brain Research, 886,* 172–189.

McEwen, B. S. (with Lasley, E. N.) (2002). *The end of stress as we know it.* Washington, DC: Joseph Henry Press.

McGregor, I. S., Hargreaves, G. A., Apfelbach, R., & Hunt, G. E. (2004). Neural correlates of cat odor-induced anxiety in rats: Region-specific effects of the benzodiazepine midazolam. *Journal of Neuroscience, 24,* 4134–4144.

McKendree-Smith, N., & Scogin, F. (2000). Depressive realism: Effects

of depression severity and interpretation time. *Journal of Clinical Psychology, 56,* 1601–1608.

McMahon, C. E. (1975). The wind of the cannonball: An informative anecdote from medical history. *Psychotherapy and Psychosomatics, 26,* 125–131.

McNally, R. J. (2002). Anxiety sensitivity and panic disorder. *Biological Psychiatry, 52,* 938–946.

McNaughton, N., & Corr, P. J. (2004). A two-dimensional neuropsychology of defense: Fear/anxiety and defensive distance. *Neuroscience and Biobehavioral Reviews, 28,* 285–305.

Medver, V. H., Madey, S. F., & Gilovich, T. (1995). When less is more: Counterfactual thinking and satisfaction among Olympic athletes. *Journal of Personality and Social Psychology, 69,* 603–610.

Meichenbaum, D. (1985). *Stress inoculation training.* New York: Pergamon.

Mellers, B. A., & McGraw, A. P. (2001). Anticipated emotions as guides to choice. *Current Directions in Psychological Science, 10,* 210–214.

Meltzoff, A. N., & Moore, M. K. (1977). Imitation of facial and manual gestures by human neonates. *Science, 198,* 75–78.

Meltzoff, A. N., & Moore, M. K. (2002). Imitation, memory, and the representation of persons. *Infant Behavior and Development, 25*(1), 39–61.

Mendl, M. (1999). Performing under pressure: Stress and cognitive function. *Applied Animal Behaviour Science, 65,* 221–244.

Menon, U., & Shweder, R. A. (1994). Kali's tongue: Cultural psychology, cultural consensus and the meaning of "shame" in Orissa, India. In H. Markus & S. Kitayama (Eds.),

Emotion and culture: Empirical studies of mutual influence (pp. 241–284). Washington, DC: American Psychological Association.

Messinger, D. S. (2002). Positive and negative: Infant facial expressions and emotions. *Current Directions in Psychological Science, 11,* 1–6.

Meyer, B., Olivier, L., & Roth, D. A. (2005). Please don't leave me! BIS/BAS, attachment styles, and responses to a relationship threat. *Personality and Individual Differences, 38,* 151–162.

Mikulincer, M., Birnbaum, G., Woddis, D., & Nachmias, O. (2000). Stress and accessibility of proximity-related thoughts: Exploring the normative and intraindividual components of attachment theory. *Journal of Personality and Social Psychology, 78,* 509–523.

Mikulincer, M., Gillath, O., & Shaver, P. (2002). Activation of the attachment system in adulthood: Threat-related primes increase the accessibility of mental representations of attachment figures. *Journal of Personality and Social Psychology, 83,* 881–895.

Milgram, S. (1974). *Obedience to authority.* New York: Harper & Row.

Miller, R. S. (1996). *Embarrassment: Poise and peril in everyday life.* New York: Guilford Press.

Miller, R. S. (2001a). Embarrassment and social phobia: Distant cousins or close kin? In S. G. Hofmann & P. M. DiBartolo (Eds.), *From social anxiety to social phobia* (pp. 65–85). Needham Heights, MA: Allyn & Bacon.

Miller, R. S. (2001b). Shyness and embarrassment compared: Siblings in the service of social evaluation. In W. R. Crozier & L. E. Alden (Eds.), *International Handbook of Social Anxiety* (pp. 281–300). Chichester, England: John Wiley.

Mills, D. W., & Ward, R. P. (1986). Attenuation of stress-induced hypertension by exercise independent of training effects: An animal model. *Journal of Behavioral Medicine, 9,* 599–605.

Miltner, W. H. R., Krieschel, S., Hecht, H., Trippe, R., & Weiss, T. (2004). Eye movements and behavioral responses to threatening and nonthreatening stimuli during visual search in phobic and nonphoic subjects *Emotion, 4,* 323–339.

Mineka, S. (1987). A primate model of phobic fears. In H. Eysenck & I. Martin (Eds.), *Theoretical foundations of behavior therapy* (pp. 81–111). New York: Plenum.

Mineka, S., Davidson, M., Cook, M., & Keir, R. (1984). Observational conditioning of snake fear in rhesus monkeys. *Journal of Abnormal Psychology, 93,* 355–372.

Mirescu, C., Peters, J. D., & Gould, E. (2004). Early life experience alters response of adult neurogenesis to stress. *Nature Neuroscience, 7,* 841–846.

Miyake, K., Campos, J. J., Kagan, J., & Bradshaw, D. L. (1986). Issues in socioemotional development. In H. Azuma, K. Hakuta, & H. Stevenson (Eds.), *Kodomo: Child development and education in Japan.* San Francisco: W. H. Freeman.

Miyake, K., Chen, S. J., & Campos, J. J. (1985). Infant temperament, mother's mode of interaction, and attachment in Japan: An interim report. In I. Bretherton & E. Waters (Eds.), Growing points of attachment theory and research. *Monographs of the Society for Research in Child Development, 50* (1–2, Serial No. 209).

Mizoguchi, K., Ishige, A., Takeda, S., Aburada, M., & Tabira, T. (2004). Endogenous glucocorticoids are essential for maintaining pre-

frontal cortical cognitive function. *Journal of Neuroscience, 24,* 5492–5499.

Mobbs, D., Grecius, M. D., Abdel-Azim, E., Menon, V., & Reiss, A. L. (2003). Humor modulates the mesolimbic reward centers. *Neuron, 40,* 1041–1048.

Modigliani, A. (1968). Embarrassment and embarrassibility. *Sociometry, 31,* 313–326.

Moe, B. K., King, A. R., & Bailly, M. D. (2004). Retrospective accounts of recurrent parental physical abuse as a predictor of adult laboratory-induced aggression. *Aggressive Behavior, 30,* 217–228.

Moles, A., Kieffer, B. L., & D'Amato, F. R. (2004). Deficit in attachment behavior in mice lacking the μ-opioid receptor gene. *Science, 304,* 1983–1986.

Moller, H. J. (1992). Attempted suicide: Efficacy of different aftercare strategies. *International Clinical Psychopharmacology, 6*(Suppl. 6), 58–59.

Moore, M. M. (1985). Nonverbal courtship patterns in women: Context and consequences. *Ethology and Sociobiology, 6,* 237–247.

Moore, T. M., Scarpa, A., & Raine, A. (2002). A meta-analysis of serotonin metabolite 5-HIAA and antisocial behavior. *Aggressive Behavior, 28,* 299–316.

Morgan, C. A., III, Grillon, C., Southwick, S. M., Davis, M., & Charney, D. S. (1995). Fear-potentiated startle in posttraumatic stress disorder. *Biological Psychology, 38,* 378–385.

Morgan, C. A., III, Grillon, C., Southwick, S. M., Davis, M., & Charney, D. S. (1996). Exaggerated acoustic startle reflex in Gulf War veterans with posttraumatic stress disorder. *American Journal of Psychiatry, 153,* 64–68.

Morling, B., Kitayama, S., & Miyamoto, Y. (2003). American and Japanese women use different coping strategies during normal pregnancy. *Personality and Social Psychology Bulletin, 29,* 1533–1546.

Morris, J. S., deBonis, M., & Dolan, R. J. (2002). Human amygdala responses to fearful eyes. *NeuroImage, 17,* 214–222.

Morrow, J., & Nolen-Hoeksema, S. (1990). Effects of responses to depression on the remediation of depressive affect. *Journal of Personality and Social Psychology, 58,* 518–527.

Morsbach, H., & Tyler, W. J. (1986). A Japanese emotion: Amae. In R. Harre (Ed.), *The social construction of emotions* (pp. 289–307). New York: Blackwell.

Morse, S. J., & Gruzen, J. (1976). The eye of the beholder: A neglected variable in the study of physical attractiveness. *Journal of Psychology, 44,* 209–225.

Moses, L. J., Baldwin, D. A., Rosicky, J. G., & Tidball, G. (2001). Evidence for referential understanding in the emotions domain at twelve and eighteen months. *Child Development, 72,* 718–735.

Mroczek, D. K. (2004). Positive and negative affect at midlife. In O. G. Brim, C. D. Ryff, & R. C. Kessler (Eds.), *How healthy are we?* (pp. 205–226). Chicago: University of Chicago Press.

Mroczek, D. K., & Spiro, A. (2005). Change in life satisfaction during adulthood: Findings from the veterans affairs normative aging study. *Journal of Personality and Social Psychology, 88,* 189–202.

Much, N. C. (1997). A semiotic view of socialization, lifespan development and cultural psychology: With vignettes from the moral culture of traditional Hindu households. *Psychology and Developing Societies, 9,* 65–105.

Mulkens, S., de Jong, P. J., Dobbelaar, A., & Bögels, S. M. (1999). Fear of blushing: Fearful preoccupation irrespective of facial coloration. *Behaviour Research and Therapy, 37,* 1119–1128.

Mulvey, E. P., & Cauffman, E. (2001). The inherent limits of predicting school violence. *American Psychologist, 56,* 797–802.

Mumme, D. L., Fernald, A., & Herrera, C. (1996). Infants' responses to facial and vocal emotional signals in a social referencing paradigm. *Child Development, 67,* 3219–3237.

Murphy, F. A. C., Nimmo-Smith, I., & Lawrence, A. D. (2003). Functional neuroanatomy of emotions: A meta-analysis. *Cognitive, Affective, & Behavioral Neuroscience, 3,* 207–233.

Murphy, J. M., Laird, N. M., Monson, R. R., Sobol, A. M., & Leighton, A. H. (2000). A 40-year perspective on the prevalence of depression. *Archives of General Psychiatry, 57,* 209–215.

Murray, H. A. (1938). *Explorations in personality.* New York: Oxford University Press.

Murray, J. P. (1998). Studying television violence. A research agenda for the 21st century. In J. K. Asamen & G. L. Berry (Eds.), *Research paradigms, television, and social behavior* (pp. 369–410). Thousand Oaks, CA: Sage.

Murray, S. L., & Holmes, J. G. (1999). The (mental) ties that bind: Cognitive structures that predict relationship resilience. *Journal of Personality and Social Psychology, 77,* 1228–1244.

Murray, S. L., Holmes, J. G., Gellavia, G., Griffin, D. W., & Dolderman, D. (2002). Kindred spirits? The benefits of egocentrism on close relationships. *Journal of Personality and Social Psychology, 82,* 563–581.

Murube, J., Murube, L., & Murube, A. (1999). Origin and types of emotional tearing. *European Journal of Ophthalmology, 9,* 77–84.

Myers, D. G. (2000a). The funds, friends, and faith of happy people. *American Psychologist, 55,* 56–67.

Myers, D. G. (2000b). *The American paradox: Spiritual hunger in an age of plenty.* New Haven, CT: Yale University Press.

Nachson, I., & Zelig, A. (2003). Flashbulb and factual memories: The case of Rabin's assassination. *Applied Cognitive Psychology, 17,* 519–531.

Nakamura, J., & Csikszentmihalyi, M. (2002). The concept of flow. In C. R. Snyder & S. J. Lopez (Eds.), *Handbook of positive psychology* (pp. 89–105). New York: Oxford University Press.

Neimeyer, R. A. (1995). An invitation to constructivist psychotherapies. In R. A. Neimeyer & M. J. Mahoney (Eds.), *Constructivism in psychology* (pp. 1–8). Washington, DC: American Psychological Association.

Nelson, E. C., Heath, A. C., Madden, P. A. F., Cooper, L., Dinwiddie, S. H., Bucholz, K. K., et al. (2002). Association between self-reported childhood sexual abuse and adverse psychosocial outcomes: Results from a twin study. *Archives of General Psychiatry, 59,* 139–145.

Nelson, E. E., & Panksepp, J. (1996). Oxytocin mediates acquisition of maternally associated odor preferences in preweaning rat pups. *Behavioral Neuroscience, 110,* 583–592.

Nelson, E. E., & Panksepp, J. (1998). Brain substrates of infant-mother attachment: contributions of opioids, oxytocin, and norepinephrine. *Neuroscience Biobehavioral Review, 22,* 437–452.

Nelson, E. E., Shelton, S. E., & Kalin, N. H. (2003). Individual differences in the responses of naive rhesus monkeys to snakes. *Emotion, 3,* 3–11.

Nemeroff, C., & Rozin, P. (1989). "You are what you eat": Applying the demand-free "impressions" technique to an unacknowledged belief. *Ethos, 17,* 50–69.

Neto, F. (1996). Correlates of social blushing. *Personality and Individual Differences, 20,* 365–373.

Nettle, D. (2004). Evolutionary origins of depression: A review and reformulation. *Journal of Affective Disorders, 81,* 91–102.

Neumeister, A., Nugent, A. C., Waldeck, T., Geraci, M., Schwarz, M., Bonne, O., et al. (2004). Neural and behavioral responses to tryptophan depletion in unmediated patients with remitted major depressive disorder and controls. *Archives of General Psychiatry, 61,* 765–773.

Nezlek, J. B., & Zebrowski, B. D. (2001). Implications of the dimensionality of unrealistic optimism for the study of perceived health risks. *Journal of Social and Clinical Psychology, 20,* 521–537.

Nickerson, C., Schwarz, N., Diener, E., & Kahneman, D. (2003). Zeroing in on the dark side of the American dream: A closer look at the negative consequences of the goal for financial success. *Psychological Science, 14,* 531–536.

Nie, Z., Schweitzer, P., Roberts, A. J., Madamba, S. G., Moore, S. D., & Siggins, G. R. (2004). Ethanol augments GABAergic transmission in the central amygdala via CRF1 receptors. *Science, 303,* 1512–1514.

Niedenthal, P. M., Auxiette, C., Nugier, A., Dalle, N., Bonin, P., & Fayol, M. (2004). A prototype analysis of the French category "émotion." *Cognition and Emotion, 18,* 289–312.

Niedenthal, P. M., Tangney, J. P., & Gavanski, I. (1994). "If only I weren't" versus "If only I hadn't": Distinguishing shame and guilt in conterfactual thinking. *Journal of Personality and Social Psychology, 67,* 585–595.

Niiya, Y., Crocker, J., & Bartmess, E. N. (2004). From vulnerability to resilience. *Psychological Science, 15,* 801–805.

Nolen-Hoeksema, S. (1991). Responses to depression and their effects on the duration of depressive episodes. *Journal of Abnormal Psychology, 100,* 569–582.

Nolen-Hoeksema, S., Larsen, J., & Grayson, C. (1999). Explaining the gender difference in depressive symptoms. *Journal of Personality and Social Psychology, 77,* 1061–1072.

Nolen-Hoeksema, S., & Morrow, J. (1991). A prospective study of depression and post-traumatic stress symptoms after a natural disaster: The Loma Prieta earthquake. *Journal of Personality and Social Psychology, 61,* 115–121.

Nygren, T. E., Isen, A. M., Taylor, P. J., & Dulin, J. (1996). The influence of positive affect on the decision rule in risk situations: Focus on outcome (and especially avoidance of loss) rather than probability. *Organizational Behavior and Human Decision Processes, 66,* 59–72.

Ochsner, K. N., Bunge, S. A., Gross, J. J., & Gabrieli, J. D. E. (2002). Rethinking feelings: An fMRI study of the cognitive regulation of emotion. *Journal of Cognitive Neuroscience, 14,* 1215–1229.

O'Connor, L. E., Berry, J. W., & Weiss, J. (1999). Interpersonal guilt, shame, and psychological problems. *Journal of Social and Clinical Psychology, 18,* 181–203.

O'Connor, R. M., Jr., & Little, I. S. (2003). Revisiting the predictive validity of emotional intelligence: Self-report versus ability-based measures. *Personality and Individual Differences, 35,* 1893–1902.

Ohbuchi, K. O., Tamura, T., Quigley, B. M., Tedeschi, J. T., Madi, N., Bond, M. H., & Mummendey, A. (2004). Anger, blame, and dimensions of perceived norm violations: Culture, gender, and relationships. *Journal of Applied Social Psychology, 34,* 1587–1603.

Öhman, A., Eriksson, A., & Olofsson, C. (1975). One-trial learning and superior resistance to extinction of autonomic responses conditioned to potentially phobic objects. *Journal of Comparative and Physiological Psychology, 88,* 619–627.

Olatunji, B. O., Sawchuk, C. N., Arrindell, W. A., & Lohr, J. M. (2005). Disgust sensitivity as a mediator of the sex differences in contamination fears. *Personality and Individual Differences, 38,* 713–722.

Olatunji, B. O., Tolin, D. F., Huppert, J. D., & Lohr, J. M. (2005). The relation between fearfulness, disgust sensitivity and religious obsessions in a non-clinical sample. *Personality and Individual Differences, 38,* 891–902.

Olweus, D. (1995). Bullying or peer abuse at school: Facts and intervention. *Current Directions in Psychological Science, 4,* 196–200.

O'Malley, P. G., Jones, D. L., Feuerstein, I. M., & Taylor, A. J. (2000). Lack of correlation between psychological factors and subclinical coronary artery disease. *New England Journal of Medicine, 343,* 1298–1304.

Ong, A. D., Bergeman, C. S., & Bisconti, T. L. (2005). Unique effects of daily perceived control on anxiety symptomatology during conjugal bereavement. *Personality and Individual Differences, 38,* 1057–1067.

Ortony, A., & Turner, T. J. (1990). What's basic about basic emotions? *Psychological Review, 97,* 315–331.

Oster, H., Hegley, D., & Nagel, L. (1992). Adult judgments and fine-grained analysis of infant facial expressions. *Developmental Psychology, 28,* 1115–1131.

Otto, M. W., Pollack, M. H., Maki, K. M., Gould, R. A., Worthington, J. J., III, Smoller, J. W., et al. (2001). Childhood history of anxiety disorders among adults with social phobia: Rates, correlates, and comparisons with patients with panic disorder. *Depression and Anxiety, 14,* 209–213.

Oyserman, D., Coon, H. M., & Kemmelmeier, M. (2002). Rethinking individualism and collectivism: Evaluation of theoretical assumptions and meta-analysis. *Psychological Bulletin, 128,* 3–72.

Özgen, E. (2004). Language, learning, and color perception. *Current Directions in Psychological Science, 13,* 95–98.

Page, A. C. (2003). The role of disgust in faintness elicited by blood and injection stimuli. *Journal of Anxiety Disorders, 17,* 45–58.

Panksepp, J. (2003). At the interface of the affective, behavioral, and cognitive neurosciences: Decoding the emotional feelings of the brain. *Brain and Cognition, 52,* 4–14.

Park, C. L., Moore, P. J., Turner, R. A., & Adler, N. E. (1997). The roles of constructive thinking and optimism in psychological and behavioral adjustment during pregnancy. *Journal of Personality and Social Psychology, 73,* 584–592.

Park, J., & Banaji, M. R. (2000). Mood and heuristics: The influence of happy and sad states on sensitivity and bias in stereotyping. *Journal of Personality and Social Psychology, 78,* 1005–1023.

Pavlidis, I., Eberhardt, N. I., & Levine, J. A. (2002). Seeing through the face of deception. *Nature, 415,* 35.

Pavot, W., & Diener, E. (1993). Review of the satisfaction with life scale. *Psychological Assessment, 5,* 164–172.

Pellis, S. M., O'Brien, D. P., Pellis, V. C., Teitelbaum, P., Wolgin, D. L., & Kennedy, S. (1988). Escalation of feline predation along a gradient from avoidance through "play" to killing. *Behavioral Neuroscience, 102,* 760–777.

Pennebaker, J. W. (1997). Writing about emotional experiences as a therapeutic process. *Psychological Science, 8,* 162–166.

Pennebaker, J. W., & Graybeal, A. (2001). Patterns of natural language use: Disclosure, personality, and social integration. *Current Directions in Psychological Science, 10,* 90–93.

Persson, M.-L., Wasserman, D., Geijer, T., Frisch, A., Rockah, R., Michaelovsky, E., et al. (2000). Dopamine D$_4$ receptor gene polymorphism and personality traits in healthy volunteers. *European Archives of Psychiatry and Clinical Neuroscience, 250,* 203–206.

Peters, F., Nicolson, N. A., Berkhof, J., Delespaul, P., & deVries, M. (2003). Effects of daily events on mood states in major depressive disorder. *Journal of Abnormal Psychology, 112,* 203–211.

Petersen, A., Kennedy, R., & Sullivan, P. A. (1991). Coping with adolescence. In S. Gore & M. E. Colton (Eds.), *Adolescent stress: Causes and consequences* (pp. 93–110).

Hawthorne, NY: Aldine de Gruyter.

Peterson, C. (2000). The future of optimism. *American Psychologist, 55,* 44–55.

Peterson, C., & Steen, T. A. (2002). Optimistic explanatory style. In C. R. Snyder & S. J. Lopez (Eds.), *Handbook of positive psychology* (pp. 244–256). New York: Oxford University Press.

Petty, R. E., & Cacioppo, J. T. (1986). *Communication and persuasion: Central and peripheral routes to attitude change.* New York: Springer Verlag.

Pezze, M. A., Bast, T., & Feldon, J. (2003). Significance of dopamine transmission in the rat medial prefrontal cortex for conditioned fear. *Cerebral Cortex, 13,* 371–380.

Pham, K., McEwen, B. S., LeDoux, J. E., & Nader, K. (2005). Fear learning transiently impairs hippocampal cell proliferation. *Neuroscience, 130,* 17–24.

Phan, K. L., Wager, T., Taylor, S. F., & Liberzon, I. (2002). Functional neuroanatomy of emotion: A meta-analysis of emotion activation studies in PET and fMRI. *NeuroImage, 16,* 331–348.

Phelps, E. A., O'Connor, K. J., Gatenby, J. C., Gore, J. C., Grillon, C., & Davis, M. (2001). Activation of the left amygdala to a cognitive representation of fear. *Nature Neuroscience, 4,* 437–441.

Philippot, P., Chapelle, G., & Blairy, S. (2002). Respiratory feedback in the generation of emotions. *Cognition and Emotion, 16,* 605–627.

Phillips, L. H., Bull, R., Adams, E., & Fraser, L. (2002). Positive mood and executive function: Evidence from Stroop and fluency tasks. *Emotion, 2,* 12–22.

Phillips, L. H., Smith, L., & Gilhooly, K. J. (2002). The effects of adult aging and induced positive and negative mood on planning. *Emotion, 2,* 263–272.

Phillips, M. L., Young, A. W., Senior, C., Brammer, M., Andrew, C., Calder, A. J., et al. (1997). A specific neural substrate for perceiving facial expressions of disgust. *Nature, 389,* 495–498.

Phillips, R. G., & LeDoux, J. E. (1992). Differential contribution of amygdala and hippocampus to cued and contextual fear conditioning. *Behavioral Neuroscience, 106,* 274–285.

Piaget, J. (1954). *The construction of reality in the child* (M. Cook, Trans.). New York: Basic books. (Original work published 1937)

Pitman, R. K., van der Kolk, B. A., Orr, S. P., & Greenberg, M. S. (1990). Naloxone-reversible analgesic response to combat-related stimuli in posttraumatic stress disorder. *Archives of General Psychiatry, 47,* 541–544.

Plous, S. (1993). *The psychology of judgment and decision making.* Philadelphia, PA: Temple University Press.

Plutchik, R. (1982). A psychoevolutionary theory of emotions. *Social Science Information, 21,* 529–553.

Popenoe, D. (2002). *The top ten myths of divorce.* Unpublished manuscript, National Marriage Project, Rutgers University.

Posternak, M. A., & Zimmerman, M. (2002). Partial validation of the atypical features of major depressive disorder. *Archives of General Psychiatry, 59,* 70–76.

Poulin, F., Dishion, T. J., & Burraston, B. (2001). Three-year iatrogenic effects associated with aggregating high-risk adolescents in cognitive-behavioral preventive interventions. *Applied Developmental Science, 5,* 214–224.

Preti, A., Miotto, P., De Coppi, M., Petretto, D., & Carmelo, M. (2002). Psychiatric chrono-epidemiology: Its relevance for the study of aggression. *Aggressive Behavior, 28,* 477–490.

Provine, R. R. (2000). *Laughter.* New York: Viking.

Quadrel, M. J., Fischhoff, B., & Davis, W. (1993). Adolescent (in)vulnerability. *American Psychologist, 48,* 102–116.

Rachlin, H., Siegel, E., & Cross, D. (1994). Lotteries and the time horizon. *Psychological Science, 5,* 390–393.

Raghunathan, R., & Pham, M. T. (1999). All negative moods are not equal: Motivational influences of anxiety and sadness on decision making. *Organizational Behavior and Human Decision Processes, 79,* 56–77.

Raine, A., Reynolds, C., Venables, P. H., Mednick, S. A., & Farrington, D. P. (1998). Fearlessness, stimulation-seeking, and large body size at age 3 as early predispositions to childhood aggression at age 11 years. *Archives of General Psychiatry, 55,* 745–751.

Raleigh, M. J., McGuire, M. T., Brammer, G. L., Pollack, D. B., & Yuwiler, A. (1991). Serotonergic mechanisms promote dominance acquisition in adult male verbet monkeys. *Brain Research, 559,* 181–190.

Ram, A., Pandey, H. P., Matsumura, H., Kasahara-Orita, K., Nakajima, T., Takahata, R., et al. (1997). CSF levels of prostaglandins, especially the level of prostaglandin D_2 are correlated with increasing propensity towards sleep in rats. *Brain Research, 751,* 81–89.

Ramirez, J. M., Santisteban, C., Fujihara, T., & Van Goozen, S. (2002). Differences between experience of anger and readiness to angry action: A study of Japanese and Spanish students. *Aggressive Behavior, 28,* 429–438.

Reddy, P. L., Khanna, S., Subhash, M. N., Channabasavanna, S. M., & Rao, B. S. S. R. (1992). CSF amine metabolites in depression. *Biological Psychiatry, 31,* 112–118.

Reisenzein, R. (1983). The Schachter theory of emotions: Two decades later. *Psychological Bulletin, 94,* 239–264.

Reissland, N., & Harris, P. (1991). Children's use of display rules in pride-eliciting situations. *British Journal of Developmental Psychology, 9,* 431–435.

Remington, N. A., Fabrigar, L. R., & Visser, P. S. (2000). Reexamining the circumplex model of affect. *Journal of Personality and Social Psychology, 79,* 286–300.

Repetti, R. L., Taylor, S. E., & Seeman, T. E. (2002). Risky families: Family social environments and the mental and physical health of offspring. *Psychological Bulletin, 128,* 330–366.

Reuter-Lorenz, P., & Davidson, R. J. (1981). Differential contributions of the two cerebral hemispheres to the perception of happy and sad faces. *Neuropsychologia, 19,* 609–613.

Rhee, S. H., & Waldman, I. D. (2002). Genetic and environmental influences on antisocial behavior: A meta-analysis of twin and adoption studies. *Psychological Bulletin, 128,* 490–529.

Richards, A., French, C. C., Calder, A. J., Webb, B., Fox, R., & Young, A. W. (2002). Anxiety-related bias in the classification of emotionally ambiguous facial expressions. *Emotion, 2,* 273–287.

Richards, J. M., Butler, E. A., & Gross, J. J. (2003). Emotion regulation in romantic relationships: The cognitive consequences of concealing feelings. *Journal of Social and Personal Relationships, 20,* 599–620.

Richards, J. M., & Gross, J. J. (1999). Composure at any cost? The cognitive consequences of emotion suppression. *Personality and Social Psychology Bulletin, 25,* 1033–1044.

Riesman, P. (1977). *Freedom in Fulani social life: An introspective ethnography* (M. Fuller, Trans.). Chicago: University of Chicago Press.

Rind, B., Tromovitch, B., & Bauserman, R. (1998). A meta-analytic examination of assumed properties of child sexual abuse using college samples. *Psychological Bulletin, 124,* 22–53.

Ritter, D., & Eslea, M. (2005). Hot sauce, toy guns, and graffiti: A critical account of current laboratory aggression paradigms. *Aggressive Behavior, 31,* 407–419.

Rivkin, I. D., & Taylor, S. E. (1999). The effects of mental stimulation on coping with controllable stressful events. *Personality and Social Psychology Bulletin, 25,* 1451–1462.

Roberson, D., Davies, I., & Davidoff, J. (2000). Color categories are not universal: Replications and new evidence from a Stone-Age culture. *Journal of Experimental Psychology: General, 129,* 369–398.

Roberts, R. D., Zeidner, M., & Matthews, G. (2001). Does emotional intelligence meet traditional standards for an intelligence? Some new data and conclusions. *Emotion, 1,* 196–231.

Robins, R. W., & Beer, J. S. (2001). Positive illusions about the self: Short-term benefits and long-term costs. *Journal of Personality and Social Psychology, 80,* 340–352.

Robinson, M. D. (1998). Running from William James' bear: A review of preattentive mechanisms and their contributions to emotional experience. *Cognition and Emotion, 12,* 667–696.

Robinson, M. D., & Clore, G. L. (2002). Belief and feeling: Evidence for an accessibility model of emotional self-report. *Psychological Bulletin, 128,* 934–960.

Robinson, M. D., Vargas, P. T., Tamir, M., & Solberg, E. C. (2004). Using and being used by categories. *Psychological Science, 15,* 521–526.

Rochat, P., & Striano, T. (1999). Social-cognitive development in the first year. In P. Rochat (Ed.), *Early social cognition: Understanding others in the first months of life* (pp. 3–34). Mahwah, NJ: Erlbaum.

Rogers, S. J., & Puchalski, C. B. (1986). Social smiles of visually impaired infants. *Journal of Visual Impairment & Blindness, 80,* 863–865.

Rohan, M., Parow, A., Stoll, A. L., Demopulos, C., Friedman, S., Dager, S., et al. (2004). Low-field magnetic stimulation in bipolar depression using an MRI-based stimulator. *American Journal of Psychiatry, 161,* 93–98

Rolls, E. T. (2004). The functions of the orbitofrontal cortex. *Brain and Cognition, 55,* 11–29.

Rosaldo, M. Z. (1980). *Knowledge and passion: Ilongot notions of self and social life.* Cambridge, England: Cambridge University Press.

Rosen, H. J., Perry, R. J., Murphy, J., Kramer, J. H., Mychack, P., Schuff, N., et al. (2002). Emotion comprehension in the temporal variant of frontotemporal dementia. *Brain, 125,* 2286–2295.

Rosen, J. B., & Schulkin, J. (1998). From normal fear to pathological anxiety. *Psychological Review, 105,* 325–350.

Rosen, J. B., & Schulkin, J. (2004). Adaptive fear, allostasis, and the pathology of anxiety and depression. In J. Schulkin (Ed.), *Allostasis, homeostasis, and the costs of physiological adaptation* (pp. 164–227). Cambridge, England: Cambridge University Press.

Rosenberg, E. L., Ekman, P., Jiang, W., Babyak, M., Coleman, R. E., Hanson, M., et al. (2001). Linkages between facial expressions of anger and transient myocardial ischemia in men with coronary artery disease. *Emotion, 1,* 107–115.

Rosenstein, D., & Oster, H. (1988). Differential facial responses to four basic tastes in newborns. *Child Development, 59,* 1555–1568.

Rosvold, H. E., Mirsky, A. F., & Pribram, K. H. (1954). Influence of amygdalectomy on social behavior in monkeys. *Journal of Comparative and Physiological Psychology, 47,* 173–178.

Rothbaum, F., Weisz, J., Pott, M., Miyake, K., & Morelli, G. (2000). Attachment and culture: Security in the United States and Japan. *American Psychologist, 55,* 1093–1104.

Rotshtein, P., Malach, R., Hadar, U., Graif, M., & Hendler, T. (2001). Feeling or features: Different sensitivity to emotion in high-order visual cortex and amygdala. *Neuron, 32,* 747–757.

Rottenberg, J., Gross, J. J., Wilhelm, F. H., Najmi, S., & Gotlib, I. H. (2002). Crying threshold and intensity in major depressive disorder. *Journal of Abnormal Psychology, 111,* 302–312.

Rottenberg, J., Kasch, K. L., Gross, J. J., & Gotlib, I. H. (2002). Sadness and amusement reactivity differentially predict concurrent and prospective functioning in major depressive disorder. *Emotion, 2,* 135–146.

Roy, A., DeJong, J., & Linnoila, M. (1989). Cerebrospinal fluid monoamine metabolites and suicidal behavior in depressed patients. *Archives of General Psychiatry, 46,* 609–612.

Royet, J.-P., Zald, D., Versace, R., Costes, N., Lavenne, F., Koenig, O., et al. (2000). Emotional responses to pleasant and unpleasant olfactory, visual, and auditory stimuli: A positron emission tomography study. *Journal of Neuroscience, 20,* 7752–7759.

Røysamb, E., Harris, J. R., Magnus, P., Vittersø, J., & Tambs, K. (2002). Subjective well-being: Sex-specific effects of genetic and environmental factors. *Personality and Individual Differences, 32,* 211–223.

Royzman, E. B., & Sabini, J. (2001). Something it takes to be an emotion: The interesting case of disgust. *Journal for the Theory of Social Behavior, 31,* 29–59.

Rozenblit, L., & Keil, F. (2002). The misunderstood limits of folk science: An illusion of explanatory depth. *Cognitive Science, 26,* 521–562.

Rozin, P. (1986). One-trial acquired likes and dislikes in humans: Disgust as a US, food predominance, and negative learning predominance. *Learning and Motivation, 17,* 180–189.

Rozin, P., & Cohen, A. B. (2003). High frequency of facial expressions corresponding to confusion, concentration, and worry in an analysis of naturally occurring facial expressions of Americans. *Emotion, 3,* 68–75.

Rozin, P., & Fallon, A. (1987). A perspective on disgust. *Psychological Review, 94,* 23–41.

Rozin, P., Fallon, A., & Augustoni-Ziskind, M. L. (1985). The child's conception of food: The development of contamination sensitivity to "disgusting" substances. *Developmental Psychology, 21,* 1075–1079.

Rozin, P., Haidt, J., McCauley, C., Dunlop, L., & Ashmore, M. (1999). Individual differences in disgust sensitivity: Comparisons and evaluations of paper-and-pencil versus behavioral measures. *Journal of Research in Personality, 33,* 330–351.

Rozin, P., Hammer, L., Oster, H., Horowitz, T., & Marmora, V. (1986). The child's conception of food: Differentiation of categories of rejected substances in the 16 months to 5 year age range. *Appetite, 7,* 141–151.

Rozin, P., & Kalat, J. W. (1971). Specific hungers and poison avoidance as adaptive specializations of learning. *Psychological Review, 78,* 459–486.

Rozin, P., Lowery, L., & Ebert, R. (1994). Varieties of disgust faces and the structure of disgust. *Journal of Personality and Social Psychology, 66,* 870–881.

Rozin, P., Lowery, L., Imada, S., & Haidt, J. (1999). The CAD triad hypothesis: A mapping between three moral emotions (contempt, anger, disgust) and three moral codes (community, autonomy, divinity). *Journal of Personality and Social Psychology, 76,* 574–586.

Rozin, P., Markwith, M., & Stoess, C. (1997). Moralization and becoming a vegetarian: The transformation of preferences into values and the recruitment of disgust. *Psychological Science, 8,* 67–73.

Rozin, P., Millman, L., & Nemeroff, C. (1986). Operation of the laws of sympathetic magic in disgust and other domains. *Journal of Personality and SocialPsychology, 50,* 703–712.

Rozin, P., & Nemeroff, C. (1990). The laws of sympathetic magic. In J. W. Stigler, R. A. Shweder, & G. Herdt (Eds.), *Cultural psychology* (pp. 205–232). Cambridge, England: Cambridge University Press.

Rozin, P., Taylor, C., Ross, L., Bennett, G., & Hejmadi, A. (2005). General and specific abilities to recognise negative emotions, especially disgust, as portrayed in the face and the body. *Cognition and Emotion, 19,* 397–412.

Rubin, K. H., Dwyer, K. M., Booth-LaForce, C., Kim, A. H., Burgess, K. B., & Rose-Krasnor, L. (2004). Attachment, friendship, and psychosocial functioning in early adolescence. *Journal of Early Adolescence, 24,* 326–356.

Rubin, Z. (1970). Measurement of romantic love. *Journal of Personality and Social Psychology, 16,* 265 273.

Rubin, Z., Peplau, L. A., & Hill, C. T. (1981). Loving and leaving: Sex differences in romantic attachments. *Sex Roles, 7,* 821–835.

Rujescu, D., Giegling, I., Bondy, B., Gieti, A., Zill, P., & Möller, H.-J. (2002). Association of anger-related traits with SNPs in the TPH gene. *Molecular Psychiatry, 7,* 1023–1029.

Rushton, D. H. (2002). Nutritional factors and hair loss. *Clinical and experimental dermatology, 27,* 396–404.

Russell, J. A. (1980). A circumplex model of affect. *Journal of Personality and Social Psychology, 39,* 1161–1178.

Russell, J. A. (1991). Culture and the categorization of emotions. *Psychological Bulletin, 110,* 426–450.

Russell, J. A. (1994). Is there a universal recognition of emotion from facial expression? A review of the cross-cultural studies. *Psychological Bulletin, 115,* 102–141.

Russell, J. A. (1997). Reading emotions from and into faces: Resurrecting a dimensional-contextual perspective. In J. A. Russell & J. M. Fernández-Dols (Eds.), *The psychology of facial expression* (pp. 295–320). Cambridge, England: Cambridge University Press.

Russell, J. A. (2003). Core affect and the psychological construction of emotion. *Psychological Review, 110,* 145–172.

Russell, J. A., & Carroll, J. M. (1999). On the bipolarity of positive and negative affect. *Psychological Bulletin, 125,* 3–30.

Rutledge, T., & Hogan, B. E. (2002). A quantitative review of prospective evidence linking psychological factors with hypertension development. *Psychosomatic Medicine, 64,* 758–766.

Rutter, M. (1986). The developmental psychopathology of depression: Issues and perspectives. In M. Rutter, C. E. Izard, & P. B. Read (Eds.), *Depression in young people: Developmental and clinical perspectives* (pp. 3–32). New York: Guilford.

Ryff, C. D., Keyes, C. L. M., & Hughes, D. L. (2004). Psychological well-being in MIDUS: Profiles of ethnic/racial diversity and life-course uniformity. In O. G. Brim, C. D. Ryff, & R. C. Kessler (Eds.), *How healthy are we?* (pp. 398–422). Chicago: University of Chicago Press.

Ryff, C. D., & Singer, B. (2003). Thriving in the face of challenge. In F. Kessel, P. L. Rosenfield, & N. B. Anderson (Eds.), *Expanding the boundaries of health and social science* (pp. 181–205). Oxford, England: Oxford University Press.

Sabini, J., Siepmann, M., Stein, J., & Meyerowitz, M. (2000). Who is embarrassed by what? *Cognition and Emotion, 14,* 213–240.

Salmivalli, C., & Kaukiainen, A. (2004). "Female aggression" revis-

ited: Variable and person-centered approaches to studying gender differences in different types of aggression. *Aggressive Behavior, 30,* 158–163.

Salmon, P. (2001). Effects of physical exercise on anxiety, depression, and sensitivity to stress: A unifying theory. *Clinical Psychology Review, 21,* 33–61.

Salomons, T. V., Johnstone, T., Backonja, M.-M., & Davidson, R. J. (2004). Perceived controllability modulates the neural response to pain. *Journal of Neuroscience, 24,* 7199–7203.

Salovey, P., & Birnbaum, D. (1989). Influence of mood on health-relevant cognitions. *Journal of Personality and Social Psychology, 57,* 539–551.

Sanderson, C. A., & Cantor, N. (2001). The association of intimacy goals and marital satisfaction: A test of four mediational hypotheses. *Personality and Social Psychology Bulletin, 27,* 1567–1577.

Sanna, L. J. (2000). Mental simulation, affect, and personality: A conceptual framework. *Current Directions in Psychological Science, 9,* 168–173.

Sapir, E. (1921). *Language: An introduction to the study of speech.* New York: Harcourt, Brace.

Sapolsky, R. M. (1992). *Stress, the aging brain, and the mechanisms of neuron death.* Cambridge, MA: MIT Press.

Sapolsky, R. M. (1998). *Why zebras don't get ulcers.* New York: W. H. Freeman.

Sarason, I. G., Johnson, J. H., & Siegel, J. M. (1979). Assessing the impact of life changes: Development of the life experiences survey. *Journal of Consulting and Clinical Psychology, 46,* 932–946.

Sarlo, M., Palomba, D., Angrilli, A., & Stegagno, L. (2002). Blood phobia and spider phobia: Two specific phobias with different autonomic cardiac modulations. *Biological Psychology, 60,* 91–108.

Sato, W., Yoshikawa, S., Kochiyama, T., & Matsumura, M. (2004). The amygdala processes the emotional significance of facial expressions: An fMRI investigation using the interaction between expression and face direction. *NeuroImage, 22,* 1006–1013.

Saudou, F., Amara, D. A., Dierich, A., LeMeur, M., Ramboz, S., Segu, L., et al. (1994). Enhanced aggressive behavior in mice lacking 5-HT$_{1B}$ receptor. *Science, 265,* 1875–1878.

Saxe, L., & Ben-Shakhar, G. (1999). Admissibility of polygraph tests: The applicability of scientific standards post-Daubert. *Psychology, Public Policy and Law, 5,* 203–223.

Schachter, S., & Singer, J. (1962). Cognitive, social, and physiological determinants of emotional state. *Psychological Review, 69,* 379–399.

Schafe, G. E., Atkins, C. M., Swank, M. W., Bauer, E. P., Sweatt, J. D., & LeDoux, J. E. (2000). Activation of ERK/MAP kinase in the amygdala is required for memory consolidation of Pavlovian fear conditioning. *Journal of Neuroscience, 20,* 8177–8187.

Schaffer, H. R. (1971). *The growth of sociability.* Baltimore, MD: Penguin.

Scheier, M. F., Carver, C. S., & Bridges, M. W. (1994). Distinguishing optimism from neuroticism (and trait anxiety, self-mastery, and self-esteem): A reevaluation of the Life Orientation Test. *Journal of Personality and Social Psychology, 67,* 1063–1078.

Scheier, M. F., Matthews, K. A., Owens, J. F., Magovern, G. J., Sr.,

Lefebvre, R. C., Abbott, R. A., et al. (1989). Dispositional optimism and recovery from coronary artery bypass surgery: The beneficial effects on physical and psychological well-being. *Journal of Personality and Social Psychology, 57,* 1024–1040.

Scherer, K. R. (1992). What does facial expression express? In K. T. Strongman (Ed.), *International review of studies on emotion* (Vol. 2, pp. 139–165). Chichester, England: Wiley.

Scherer, K. R. (1997). The role of culture in emotion-antecedent appraisal. *Journal of Personality and Social Psychology, 73,* 902–922.

Scherer, K. R., & Wallbott, H. G. (1994). Evidence for universality and cultural variation of differential emotion response patterning. *Journal of Personality and Social Psychology, 66,* 310–328.

Scherer, K. R., & Zentner, M. R. (2001). Emotional effects of music: Production rules. In J. A. Sloboda & P. W. Juslin (Eds.), *Music and emotion: Theory and research* (pp. 361–392). London: Oxford University Press.

Scherer, K. R., Zentner, M. R., & Stern, D. (2004). Beyond surprise: The puzzle of infants' expressive reactions to expectancy violation. *Emotion, 4,* 389–402.

Schienle, A., Stark, R., Walter, B., Blecker, C., Ott, U., Kirsch, P., et al. (2002). The insula is not specifically involved in disgust processing: An fMRI study. *NeuroReport, 13,* 2023–2026.

Schimmack, U., Oishi, S., & Diener, E. (2002). Cultural influences on the relation between pleasant emotions and unpleasant emotions: Asian dialectic philosophies or individualism-collectivism? *Cognition and Emotion, 16,* 705–719.

Schkade, D. A., & Kahneman, D. (1998). Does living in California make people happy? *Psychological Science, 9,* 340–346.

Schmid, A., Koch, M., & Schnitzler, H.-U. (1995). Conditioned pleasure attenuates the startle response in rats. *Neurobiology of Learning and Memory, 64,* 1–3.

Schmidt, L. A. (1999). Frontal brain electrical activity in shyness and sociability. *Psychological Science, 10,* 316–320.

Schmidt, L. A., Fox, N. A., Schulkin, J., & Gold, P. W. (1999). Behavioral and psychophysiological correlates of self-presentation in temperamentally shy children. *Developmental Psychobiology, 35,* 119–135.

Schmidt, S. R. (2002). Outstanding memories: The positive and negative effects of nudes on memory. *Journal of Experimental Psychology: Learning Memory and Cognition, 28,* 353–361.

Schulman, P., Keith, D., & Seligman, M. E. P. (1993). Is optimism heritable? A study of twins. *Behaviour Research and Therapy, 31,* 569–574.

Schulte, M. J., Ree, M. J., & Caretta, T. R. (2004). Emotional intelligence: Not much more than *g* and personality. *Personality and Individual Differences, 37,* 1059–1068.

Schupp, H. T., Öhman, A., Junghöfer, M., Weike, A. I., Stockburger, J., & Hamm, A. O. (2004). The facilitated processing of threatening faces; An ERP analysis. *Emotion, 4,* 189–200.

Schutte, N. S., Malouff, J. M., Simunek, M., McKenley, J., & Hollander, S. (2002). Characteristic emotional intelligence and emotional well-being. *Cognition and Emotion, 16,* 769–785.

Schwartz, C. E., Wright, C. I., Shin, L. M., Kagan, J., & Rauch, S. L. (2003). Inhibited and uninhibited infants "grown up": Adult amygdalar response to novelty. *Science, 300,* 1952–1953.

Schwartz, D., Dodge, K. A., Pettit, G. S., & Bates, J. E. (2000). Friendship as a moderating factor in the pathway between early harsh home environment and later victimization in the peer group. *Developmental Psychology, 36,* 646–662.

Schwarz, N., & Clore, G. L. (1983). Mood, misattribution, and judgments of well-being: Informative and directive functions of affective states. *Journal of Personality and Social Psychology, 45,* 513–523.

Scott, S. K., Young, A. W., Calder, A. J., Hellawell, D. J., Aggleton, J. P., & Johnson, M. (1997). Impaired auditory recognition of fear and anger following bilateral amygdala lesions. *Nature, 385,* 254–257.

Segerstrom, S. C., & Miller, G. E. (2004). Psychological stress and the human immune system: A meta-analytic study of 30 years of inquiry. *Psychological Bulletin, 130,* 601–630.

Seidner, L. B., Stipek, D. J., & Feshbach, N. D. (1988). A developmental analysis of elementary school-aged children's concepts of pride and embarrassment. *Child Development, 59,* 367–377.

Seligman, M. E. P. (1971). Phobias and preparedness. *Behavior Therapy, 2,* 307–320.

Seligman, M. E. P., & Csikszentmihalyi, M. (2000). Positive psychology. *American Psychologist, 55,* 5–14.

Seligman, M. E. P., Schulman, P., DeRubeis, R. J., & Hollon, S. D. (1999). The prevention of depression and anxiety. *Prevention and Treatment, 2,* article 8.

Semin, G. R., & Manstead, A. S. (1982). The social implications of embarrassment displays and restitution behavior. *European Journal of Social Psychology, 12*, 367–377.

Semin, G. R., & Papadopoulou, K. (1990). The acquisition of reflexive social emotions: The transmission and reproduction of social control through joint action. In G. Duveen & B. Lloyd (Eds.), *Social representations and the development of knowledge* (pp. 107–125). New York: Cambridge University Press.

Shackelford, T. K., & Larsen, R. J. (1999). Facial attractiveness and physical health. *Evolution and Human Behavior, 20*, 71–76.

Shahar, D. R., Schultz, R., Shahar, A., & Wing, R. R. (2001). The effect of widowhood on weight change, dietary intake, and eating behavior in the elderly population. *Journal of Aging and Health, 13*, 18–199.

Shair, H. N., Brunelli, S. A., Masmela, J. R., Boone, E., & Hofer, M. A. (2003). Social, thermal, and temporal influences on isolation-induced and maternally potentiated ultrasonic vocalizations of rat pups. *Developmental Psychobiology, 42*, 206–222.

Shalev, A. Y., Peri, T., Brandes, D., Freedman, S., Orr, S. P., & Pitman, R. K. (2000). Auditory startle response in trauma survivors with posttraumatic stress disorder: A prospective study. *American Journal of Psychiatry, 157*, 255–261.

Shamay-Tsoory, S. G., Tomer, R., Goldsher, D., Berger, B. D., & Aharon-Peretz, J. (2004). Impairment in cognitive and affective empathy in patients with brain lesions: Anatomical and cognitive correlates. *Journal of Clinical and Experimental Neuropsychology, 26*, 1113–1127.

Shapira, N. A., Liu, Y., He, A. G., Bradley, M. M., Lessig, M. C.,

James, G. A., et al. (2003). Brain activation by disgust-inducing pictures in obsessive-compulsive disorder. *Biological Psychiatry, 54*, 751–756.

Shapiro, D. H., Jr., Schwartz, E. D., & Astin, J. A. (1996). Controlling ourselves, controlling our world. *American Psychologist, 51*, 1213–1230.

Sharot, T., Delgado, M. R., & Phelps, E. A. (2004). How emotion enhances the feeling of remembering. *Nature Neuroscience, 7*, 1376–1380.

Shaver, P., Morgan, H. J., & Wu, S. (1996). Is love a "basic" emotion? *Personal Relationships, 3*, 81–96.

Shaver, P., Schwartz, J., Kirson, D., & O'Connor, C. (1987). Emotion knowledge: Further exploration of a prototype approach. *Journal of Personality and Social Psychology, 52*, 1061–1086.

Shearn, D., Spellman, L., Straley, B., Meirick, J., & Stryker, K. (1999). Empathic blushing in friends and strangers. *Motivation and Emotion, 23*, 307–316.

Shen, B. J., Stroud, L. R., & Niaura, R. (2004). Ethnic differences in cardiovascular responses to laboratory stress: A comparison between Asian and white Americans. *International Journal of Behavioral Medicine, 11*, 181–186.

Sheppard, W. D., II, Staggers, F. J., Jr., & John, L. (1997). The effects of a stress management program in a high security government agency. *Anxiety, Stress, and Coping, 10*, 341–350.

Sherrod, D. R., Hage, J. N., Halpern, P. L., & Moore, B. S. (1977). Effects of personal causation and perceived control on responses to an aversive environment: The more control, the better. *Journal of Ex-*

perimental Social Psychology, 13, 14–27.

Shiota, M. N., Campos, B., & Keltner, D. (2003). The faces of positive emotion: prototype displays of awe, amusement, and pride. *Annals of the New York Academy of Sciences, 1000*, 296–299.

Shiota, M. N., Campos, B., Keltner, D., & Hertenstein, M. J. (2004). Positive emotion and the regulation of interpersonal relationships. In P. Philippot & R. S. Feldman (Eds.), *The regulation of emotion.* Mahwah, NJ: Erlbaum.

Shrauger, J. S., Mariano, E., & Walter, T. J. (1988). Depressive symptoms and accuracy in the prediction of future events. *Personality and Social Psychology Bulletin, 24*, 880–892.

Shweder, R. A. (1993). The cultural psychology of the emotions. In M. Lewis & J. A. Haviland (Eds.), *Handbook of emotions* (pp. 417–434). New York: Guilford.

Shweder, R. A., Much, N. C., Mahapatra, M., & Park, L. (1997). The "big three" of morality (autonomy, community, divinity), and the "big three" explanations of suffering. In A. Brandt & P. Rozin (Eds.), *Morality and health* (pp. 119–169). New York: Routledge.

Siegel, J. M. (1986). The multidimensional anger inventory. *Journal of Personality and Social Psychology, 51*, 191–200.

Siegman, A. W. (1994). From Type A to hostility to anger: Reflections on the history of coronary-prone behavior. In A. W. Siegman & T. W. Smith (Eds.), *Anger, hostility, and the heart* (pp. 1–21). Hillsdale, NJ: Erlbaum.

Silberg, J. L., Parr, T., Neale, M. C., Rutter, M., Angold, A., & Eaves, L. J. (2003). Maternal smoking during pregnancy and risk to boys' conduct disturbance: An examination of the causal hypothesis. *Biological Psychiatry, 53,* 130–135.

Simmons, E. J. (1949). *Leo Tolstoy.* London: Lehmann.

Simpson, J. A., Ickes, W., & Blackstone, T. (1995). When the head protects the heart: Empathic accuracy in dating relationships. *Journal of Personality and Social Psychology, 69,* 629–641.

Simpson, J. A., Oriña, M. M., & Ickes, W. (2003). When accuracy hurts, and when it helps: A test of the empathic accuracy model in marital interactions. *Journal of Personality and Social Psychology, 85,* 881–893.

Sinaceur, M., Heath, C., & Cole, S. (2005). Emotional and deliberative reactions to a public crisis: Mad cow disease in France. *Psychological Science, 16,* 247–254.

Singer, T., Seymour, B., O'Doherty, J., Kaube, H., Dolan, R. J., & Frith, C. D. (2004). Empathy for pain involves the affective but not sensory components of pain. *Science, 303,* 1157–1162.

Singh, D. (1993). Adaptive significance of female physical attractiveness: Role of waist to hip ratio. *Journal of Personality and Social Psychology, 65,* 293–307.

Sivak, M., & Flannagan, M. J. (2003, January-February). Flying and driving after the September 11 attacks. *American Scientist, 91*(1), 6–8.

Skinner, E. A., Edge, K., Altman, J., & Sherwood, H. (2003). Searching for the structure of coping: A review and critique of category systems for classifying ways of coping. *Psychological Bulletin, 129,* 216–269.

Skolnick, A. (1978). *The intimate environment: Exploring marriage and the family* (2nd ed.). Boston: Little, Brown.

Skre, I., Onstad, S., Torgerson, S., Lygren, S., & Kringlen, E. (2000). The heritability of common phobic fear: A twin study of a clinical sample. *Journal of Anxiety Disorders, 14,* 549–562.

Sloan, D. M., Strauss, M. E., & Wisner, K. L. (2001). Diminished response to pleasant stimuli by depressed women. *Journal of Abnormal Psychology, 110,* 488–493.

Small, D. M., Zatorre, R. J., Dagher, A., Evans, A. C., & Jones-Gotman, M. (2001). Changes in brain activity related to eating chocolate: From pleasure to aversion. *Brain, 124,* 1720–1733.

Smith, A. D. (1996). Memory. In J. Birren & W. Schaie (Eds.), *Handbook of the psychology of aging* (pp. 236–250). San Diego, CA: Academic Press.

Smith, C. A., & Kirby, L. D. (2004). Appraisal as a pervasive determinant of anger. *Emotion, 4,* 133–138.

Smith, D. M., Langa, K. M., Kabeto, M. U., & Ubel, P. A. (2005). Health, wealth, and happiness. *Psychological Science, 16,* 663–666.

Smith, P., & Waterman, M. (2004). Role of experience in processing bias for aggressive words in forensic and non-forensic populations. *Aggressive Behavior, 30,* 105–122.

Snyder, C. R., Sympson, S. C., Michael, S. T., & Cheavens, J. (2001). Optimism and hope constructs: Variants on a ositive expectancy theme. In E. C. Chang (Ed.), *Optimism & pessimism: Implications for theory, research, and practice* (pp. 101–125). Washington, DC: American Psychological Association.

Solomon, M. R. (2001). Eating as both coping and stressor in overweight control. *Journal of Advanced Nursing, 36,* 563–572.

Solomon, R. C. (2002). Back to basics: On the very idea of "basic emotions." *Journal for the Theory of Social Behavior, 32,* 115–144.

Somerville, L. H., Kim, H., Johnstone, T., Alexander, A. L., & Whalen, P. J. (2004). Human amygdala responses during presentation of happy and neutral faces: Correlations with state anxiety. *Biological Psychiatry, 55,* 897–903.

Sorce, J. F., Emde, R. N., Campos, J. J., & Klinnert, M. D. (1985). Maternal emotional signaling: Its effect on the visual cliff behavior of 1-year-olds. *Developmental Psychology, 21,* 195–200.

Soussignan, R. (2002). Duchenne smile, emotional experience, and autonomic reactivity. A test of the facial feedback hypothesis. *Emotion, 2,* 52–74.

Sowell, E. R., Thompson, P. M., Holmes, C. J., Jernigan, T. L., & Toga, A. W. (1999). In vivo evidence for post-adolescent brain maturation in frontal and striatal regions. *Nature Neuroscience, 2,* 859–861.

Sowell, E. R., Thompson, P. M., Tessner, K. D., & Toga, A. W. (2001). Mapping continued brain growth and gray matter density reduction in dorsal frontal cortex: Inverse relationships during postadolescent brain maturation. *Journal of Neuroscience, 21,* 8819–8829.

Soyka, M., Preuss, U. W., Koller, G., Zill, P., & Bondy, B. (2002). Dopamine D_4 receptor gene polymorphism and extraversion revisited: Results from the Munich gene bank project for alcoholism. *Journal of Psychiatric Research, 36,* 429–435.

Spangler, D. L., & Burns, D. D. (1999). Are dysfunctional attitudes and attributional style the same or different? *Behavior Therapy, 30,* 239–252.

Spence, G., Oades, L. G., & Caputi, P. (2004). Trait emotional intelligence and goal self-integration: Important predictors of emotional well-being? *Personality and Individual Differences, 37,* 449–461.

Spielberger, C. D. (1991). *State-trait anger expression inventory revised research edition, professional manual.* Odessa, FL: Psychological Assessment Resources.

Spielberger, C. D., Jacobs, G., Russell, S., & Crane, R. S. (1983). Assessment of anger: The state-trait scale. *Advances in Personality Assessment, 2,* 161–189.

Spitz, R. (1965). *The first year of life.* New York: International Universities Press.

Spivak, B., Shohat, B., Mester, R., Avraham, S., Gil-Ad, I., Bleich, A., Vet al. (1997). *Biological Psychiatry, 42,* 345–348.

Spreux-Varoquaux, O., Alvarez, J.-C., Berlin, I., Batista, G., Despierre, P.-G., Gilton, A., et al. (2001). Differential abnormalities in plasma 5-HIAA and platelet serotonin concentrations in violent suicide attempters. Relationships with impulsivity and depression. *Life Science, 69,* 647–657.

Sroufe, L. A. (1977). Wariness of strangers and the study of infant development. *Child Development, 48,* 1184–1199.

Sroufe, L. A. (1996). *Emotional development: The organization of emotional life in the early years.* Cambridge, England: Cambridge University Press.

Stein, M. B., Hanna, C., Koverola, C., Torchia, M., & McClarty, B. (1997). Structural brain changes in PTSD. *Annals of the New York Academy of Sciences, 821,* 76–82.

Stein, M. B., Goldin, P. R., Sareen, J., Zorrilla, L. T. E., & Brown, G. G. (2002). Increased amygdala activation to angry and contemptuous faces in generalized socialized phobia. *Archives of General Psychiatry, 59,* 1027–1034.

Sternberg, C. R., & Campos, J. J. (1990). The development of anger expressions in infancy. In N. L. Stein, B. Leventhal, & T. Trabasso (Eds.), *Psychological and biological approaches to emotion* (pp. 297–310). Hillsdale, NJ: Erlbaum.

Sternberg, C. R., Campos, J. J., & Emde, R. N. (1983). The facial expression of anger in seven-month infants. *Child Development, 54,* 178–184.

Stewart, M. E., Ebmeier, K. P., & Deary, I. J. (2005). Personality correlates of happiness and sadness: EPQ-R and TPQ compared. *Personality and Individual Differences, 38,* 1085–1096.

Steuer, F. B., Applefield, J. M., & Smith, R. (1971). Televised aggression and the interpersonal aggression of preschool children. *Journal of Experimental Child Psychology, 11,* 442–447.

Stipek, D. (1998). Differences between Americans and Chinese in the circumstances evoking pride, shame, and guilt. *Journal of Cross-Cultural Psychology, 29,* 616–629.

Stone, E. R., Dodrill, C. L., & Johnson, N. (2001). Depressive cognition: A test of depressive realism versus negativity using general knowledge items. *Journal of Psychology, 135,* 583–602.

Stormark, K. M., Laberg, J. C., Nordby, H., & Hugdahl, K. (2000). Alcoholics' selective attention to alcohol stimuli: Automated processing? *Journal of Studies on Alcohol, 61,* 18–23.

Strack, F., Martin, L. L., & Stepper, S. (1988). Inhibiting and facilitating

conditions of the human smile: A nonobtrusive test of the facial feedback hypothesis. *Journal of Personality and Social Psychology, 54,* 768–777.

Streeter, S. A., & McBurney, D. H. (2003). Waist-hip ratio and attractiveness: New evidence and critique of "a critical test." *Evolution and Human Behavior, 24,* 88–98.

Strzelczuk, M., & Romaniuk, A. (1996). Fear induced by the blockade of $GABA_A$-ergic transmission in the hypothalamus of the cat: Behavioral and neurochemical study. *Behavioural Brain Research, 72,* 63–71.

Swann, W. B., Jr., & Gill, M. J. (1997). Confidence and accuracy in person perception: Do we know what we think we know about our relationship partners? *Journal of Personality and Social Psychology, 73,* 747–757.

Swets, J. A., Dawes, R. M., & Monahan, J. (2000). Psychological science can improve diagnostic decisions. *Psychological Science in the Public Interest, 1,* 1–26.

Swidler, A. (2001). *Talk of love: How culture matters.* Chicago: University of Chicago Press.

Sykes, D. H., Arveiler, D., Salters, C. P., Ferrieres, J., McCrum, E., Amouyel, P., et al. (2002). Psychosocial risk factors for heart disease in France and Northern Ireland: The Prospective Epidemiological Study of Myocardial Infarction (PRIME). *International Journal of Epidemiology, 31,* 1227–1234.

Tafrate, R. C., Kassinove, H., & Dundin, L. (2002). Anger episodes in high- and low-trait anger community adults. *Journal of Clinical Psychology, 58,* 1573–1590.

Takahashi, H., Yahata, N., Koeda, M., Matsuda, T., Asai, K., & Okubo, Y. (2004). Brain activation associated with evaluative processes of guilt and embarrassment: An fMRI study. *NeuroImage, 23,* 967–974.

Takano, Y., & Osaka, E. (1999). An unsupported common view: Comparing Japan and the U.S. on individualism/collectivism. *Asian Journal of Social Psychology, 2,* 311–341.

Talarico, J. M., & Rubin, D. C. (2003). Confidence, not consistency, characterizes flashbulb memories. *Psychological Science, 14,* 455–461.

Tangney, J. P. (1996). Conceptual and methodological issues in the assessment of shame and guilt. *Behaviour Research and Therapy, 34,* 741–754.

Tangney, J. P., Burggraf, S. A., & Wagner, P. E. (1995). Shame-proneness, guilt-pronness, and psychological symptoms. In J. P. Tangney & K. W. Fischer (Eds.), *Self-conscious emotions: The psychology of shame, guilt, embarrassment, and pride* (pp. 343–367), New York: Guilford Press.

Tangney, J. P., Miller, R. S., Flicker, L., & Barlow, D. H. (1996). Are shame, guilt, and embarrassment distinct emotions? *Journal of Personality and Social Psychology, 70,* 1256–1264.

Tangney, J. P., Wagner, P. E., Hill-Barlow, D., Marschall, D. E., & Gramzow, R. (1996). Relation of shame and guilt to constructive versus destructive responses to anger across the lifespan. *Journal of Personality and Social Psychology, 70,* 797–809.

Tassinary, L. G., & Hansen, K. A. (1998). A critical test of the waist-to-hip ratio hypothesis of female attractiveness. *Psychological Science, 9,* 150–155.

Taylor, S. E., & Brown, J. D. (1988). Illusion and well-being: A social psychological perspective on men-

tal health. *Psychological Bulletin, 103,* 193–210.

Taylor, S. E., Kemeny, M. E., Reed, G. M., Bower, J. E., & Gruenwald, T. L. (2000). Psychological resources, positive illusions, and health. *American Psychologist, 55,* 99–109.

Taylor, S. E., Pham, L. B., Rivkin, I. D., & Armor, D. A. (1998). Harnessing the imagination: Mental simulation, self-regulation, and coping. *American Psychologist, 53,* 429–439.

Teigen, K.-H. (1994). Yerkes-Dodson: A law for all seasons. *Theory and Psychology, 4,* 525–547.

Tellegen, A., Watson, D., & Clark, L. A. (1999). On the dimensional and hierarchical structure of affect. *Psychological Science, 10,* 297–303.

Thomas, S. P. (1993). *Women and anger.* New York: Springer.

Thompson, W. F., Schellenberg, E. G., & Husain, G. (2004). Decoding speech prosody: Do music lessons help? *Emotion, 4,* 46–64.

Thoren, P., Floras, J. S., Hoffman, P., & Seals, D. R. (1990). Endorphins and exercise: Physiological mechanisms and clinical implications. *Medicine and Science in Sports and Exercise, 22,* 417–428.

Thorndike, E. (1918). The nature, purposes, and general methods of measurements of educational products. In E. J. Ashbaugh, W. A. Averill, L. P. Ayres, F. W. Ballou, E. Bryner, B. R. Buckingham, et al. (Eds.), *The seventeenth yearbook of the National Society for the Study of Education, Part II: The measurement of educational products* (pp. 16–24). Bloomington, IN: Public School Publishing.

Thornton, B. (1977). Toward a linear prediction model of marital happiness. *Personality and Social Psychology Bulletin, 3,* 674–676.

Tiedens, L. Z. (2001). Anger and advancement versus sadness and subjugation: The effect of negative emotion expressions on social status conferral. *Journal of Personality and Social Psychology, 80,* 86–94.

Tiedens, L. Z., Ellsworth, P. C., & Mesquita, B. (2000). Stereotypes about sentiments and status: Emotional expectations for high- and low-status group members. *Personality and Social Psychology Bulletin, 26,* 560–574.

Tiedens, L. Z., & Linton, S. (2001). Judgment under emotional certainty and uncertainty: The effects of specific emotions on information processing. *Journal of Personality and Social Psychology, 81,* 973–988.

Tomaka, J., Blascovich, J., Kibler, J, & Ernst, J. M. (1997). Cognitive and physiological antecedents of threat and challenge appraisal. *Journal of Personality and Social Psychology, 73,* 63–72.

Tooby, J., & Cosmides, L. (1990). The past explains the present: Emotional adaptations and the structure of ancestral environments. *Ethology and Sociobiology, 11,* 375–424.

Townshend, J. M., & Duka, T. (2003). Mixed emotions: Alcoholics' impairments in the recognition of specific emotional facial expressions. *Neuropsychologia, 41,* 773–782.

Tracy, J. L., & Robins, R. W. (2004). Show your pride: Evidence for a discrete emotion expression. *Psychological Science, 15,* 194–197.

Trevarthen, C., & Hubley, P. (1978). Secondary intersubjectivity: Confidence, confiders, and acts of meaning in the first year of life. In A. Lock (Ed.), *Action, gesture, and symbol: The emergence of language* (pp. 183–229). New York: Academic Press.

Triandis, H., McCusker, C., & Hui, C. (1990). Multimethod probes of individualism and collectivism. *Journal of Personality and Social Psychology, 59,* 1006–1020.

Tsai, J. L., & Chentsova-Dutton, Y. (2003). Variation among European Americans in emotional facial expression. *Journal of Cross-Cultural Psychology, 34,* 650–657.

Tsai, J. L., Chentsova-Dutton, Y., Freire-Bebeau, L., & Przymus, D. E. (2002). Emotional expression and physiology in European Americans and Hmong Americans. *Emotion, 2,* 380–397.

Tsai, J. L., Simeonova, D. I., & Watanabe, J. T. (2004). Somatic and social: Chinese Americans talk about emotion. *Personality and Social Psychology Bulletin, 30,* 1226–1238.

Tse, W. S., & Bond, A. J. (2002). Serotonergic intervention affects both social dominance and affiliative behaviour. *Psychopharmacology, 161,* 324–330.

Tugade, M. M., & Fredrickson, B. L. (2004). Resilient individuals use positive emotions to bounce back from negative emotional experiences. *Journal of Personality and Social Psychology, 86,* 320–333.

Tversky, A., & Kahneman, D. (1981). The framing of decisions and the psychology of choice. *Science, 211,* 453–458.

Twenge, J. M. (2002). Birth cohort, social change, and personality. In D. Cervone & W. Mischel (Eds.), *Advances in personality science* (pp. 196–218). New York: Guilford.

Tzeng, M. (1992). The effects of socioeconomic heterogamy and changes on marital dissolution for first marriages. *Journal of Marriage and the Family, 54,* 609–619.

Uchakin, P. N., Tobin, B., Cubbage, M., Marshall, G., Jr., & Sams, C. (2001). Immune responsiveness following academic stress in first-year medical students. *Journal of Interferon and Cytokine Research, 21,* 687–694.

Uchida, Y., Norasakkunkit, V., & Kitayama, S. (2004). Cultural constructions of happiness: Theory and empirical evidence. *Journal of Happiness Studies, 5,* 223–239.

Uchino, B. N., Cacioppo, J. T., & Kiecolt-Glaser, J. K. (1996). The relationship between social support and physiological processes: A review with emphasis on underlying mechanisms and implications for health. *Psychological Bulletin, 119,* 488–531.

Urry, H. L., Nitschke, J. B., Dolski, I., Jackson, D. C., Dalton, K. M., Mueller, C. J., et al. (2004). Making a life worth living: Neural correlates of well-being. *Psychological Science, 15,* 367–372.

Uvnäs-Moberg, K., Johansson, B., Lupoli, B., & Svennersten-Sjaunja, K. (2001). Oxytocin facilitates behavioural, metabolic, and physiological adaptations during lactation. *Applied Animal Behavioural Science, 72,* 225–234.

Uwano, T., Nishijo, H., Ono, T., & Tamura, R. (1995). Neuronal responsiveness to various sensory stimuli, and associative learning in the rat amygdala. *Neuroscience, 68,* 339–361.

Valentiner, D. P., Hood, J., & Hawkins, A. (2005). Fainting history, disgust sensitivity, and reactions to disgust-eliciting film stimuli. *Personality and Individual Differences, 38,* 1329–1339.

Valiente, C., Eisenberg, N., Shepard, S. A., Fabes, R. A., Cumberland, A. J., Losoya, S. H., et al. (2004). The relations of mothers' negative expressivity to children's experience and expression of negative emotion. *Applied Developmental Psychology, 25,* 215–235.

Valzelli, L. (1973). The "isolation syndrome" in mice. *Psychopharmacologia, 31,* 305–320.

Valzelli, L. (1979). Effect of sedatives and anxiolytics on aggressivity. *Modern Problems in Pharmacopsychiatry, 14,* 143–156.

Valzelli, L. (1980). *An approach to neuroanatomical and neurochemical psychophysiology.* Torino, Italy: Edizioni Saint Vincent.

Valzelli, L., & Bernasconi, S. (1979). Aggressiveness by isolation and brain serotonin turnover changes in different strains of mice. *Neuropsychobiology, 5,* 129–135.

Van der Does, A. J. W. (2001). The effects of tryptophan depletion on mood and psychiatric symptoms. *Journal of Affective Disorders, 64,* 107–119.

van der Vegt, B. J., Lieuwes, N., van de Wall, E. H. E. M., Kato, K., Moya-Albiol, L., Martínez-Sanchez, S., et al. (2003). Activation of serotonergic neurotransmission during the performance of aggressive behavior in rats. *Behavioral Neuroscience, 117,* 667–674.

Van Der Zee, K. I., Huet, R. C. G., Cazemier, C., & Evers, K. (2002). The influence of the premedication consult and preparatory information about anesthesia on anxiety among patients undergoing cardiac surgery. *Anxiety, Stress, and Coping, 15,* 123–133.

van Honk, J., Tuiten, A., Hermans, E., Putman, P., Koppenschaar, H., Thijssen, J., et al. (2001). A single administration of testosterone induces cardiac accelerative responses to angry faces in healthy young women. *Behavioral Neuroscience, 115,* 238–242.

Van Kleef, G. A., De Dreu, C. K. W., & Manstead, A. S. R. (2004). The interpersonal effects of anger and happiness in negotiations. *Journal of Personality and Social Psychology, 86,* 57–76.

Vanman, E. J., Saltz, J. L., Nathan, L. R., & Warren, J. A. (2004). Racial discrimination by low-prejudiced whites: Facial movements as implicit measures of attitudes related to behavior. *Psychological Science, 15,* 711–714.

Van Rooy, D. L., Alonso, A., & Viswesvaran, C. (2005). Group differences in emotional intelligence scores: Theoretical and practical implications. *Personality and Individual Differences, 38,* 689–700.

Van Rooy, D. L., & Viswesvaran, C. (2004). Emotional intelligence: A meta-analytic investigation of predictive validity and nomological net. *Journal of Vocational Behavior, 65,* 71–95.

Van Tilburg, M. A. L., Unterberg, M. L., & Vingerhoets, A. J. J. M. (2002). Crying during adolescence: The role of gender, menarche, and empathy. *British Journal of Developmental Psychology, 20,* 77–87.

Van Yperen, N. W., & Buunk,. B. P. (1990). A longitudinal study of equity and satisfaction in intimate relationships. *European Journal of Social Psychology, 20,* 287–309.

Vedhara, K., Cox, N. K. M., Wilcock, G. K., Perks, P., Hunt, M., Anderson, S., et al. (1999). Chronic stress in elderly carers of dementia patients and antibody response to influenza vaccination. *Lancet, 353,* 627–631.

Vernon, L. L., & Berenbaum, H. (2002). Disgust and fear in response to spiders. *Cognition and Emotion, 16,* 809–830.

Vernon, L. L., & Berenbaum, H. (2004). A naturalistic examination of positive expectations, time course, and disgust in the origins

and reduction of spider and insect distress. *Journal of Anxiety Disorders, 18,* 707–718.

Viken, R. J., Rose, R. J., Kaprio, J., & Koskenvuo, M. (1994). A developmental genetic analysis of adult personality: Extraversion and neuroticism from 18 to 59 years of age. *Journal of Personality and Social Psychology, 66,* 722–730.

Virkkunen, M., DeJong, J., Bartko, J., Goodwin, F. K., & Linnoila, M. (1989). Relationship of psychobiological variables to recidivism in violent offenders and impulsive fire setters. *Archives of General Psychiatry, 46,* 600–603.

Virkkunen, M., Eggert, M., Rawlings, R., & Linnoila, M. (1996). A prospective follow-up study of alcoholic violent offenders and fire setters. *Archives of General Psychiatry, 53,* 523–529.

Virkkunen, M., Nuutila, A., Goodwin, F. K., & Linnoila, M. (1987). Cerebrospinal fluid monoamine metabolite levels in male arsonists. *Archives of General Psychiatry, 44,* 241–247.

von der Pahlen, B., Lindman, R., Sarkola, T., Mäkisalo, H., & Eriksson, C. J. P. (2002). An exploratory study on self-evaluated aggression and androgens in women. *Aggressive Behavior, 28,* 273–280.

Vuilleumier, P. (2005). Cognitive science: Staring fear in the face. *Nature, 433,* 22–23.

Vuilleumier, P., Armony, J. L., Driver, J., & Dolan, R. J. (2001). Effects of attention and emotion on face processing in the human brain: An event-related fMRI study. *Neuron, 30,* 829–841.

Wagner, H. L. (2000). The accessibility of the term "contempt" and the meaning of the unilateral lip curl. *Cognition and Emotion, 14,* 689–710.

Wakely, A., Rivera, S., & Langer, J. (2000). Can young infants add and subtract? *Child Development, 71,* 1525–1534.

Walden, T. A., & Baxter, A. (1989). The effect of context and age on social referencing. *Child Development, 60,* 1511–1518.

Wallace, A. F. C., & Carson, M. T. (1973). Sharing and diversity in emotion terminology. *Ethos, 1,* 1–29.

Wang, L., McCarthy, G., Song, A. W., & LaBar, K. S. (2005). Amygdala activation to sad pictures during high-field (4 Tesla) functional magnetic resonance imaging. *Emotion, 5,* 12–22.

Warwick, J., & Nettelbeck, T. (2004). Emotional intelligence is . . . ? *Personality and Individual Differences, 37,* 1091–1100.

Waters, A., Hill, A., & Waller, G. (2001). Bulimics' responses to food cravings: Is binge-eating a product of hunger or emotional state? *Behaviour Research and Therapy, 39,* 877–886.

Watson, D. (2002). Positive affectivity. In C. R. Snyder & S. J. Lopez (Eds.), *Handbook of positive psychology* (pp. 106–119). New York: Oxford University Press.

Watson, D., Clark, L. A., & Tellegen, A. (1984). Cross-cultural convergence in the structure of mood: A Japanese replication and a comparison with U.S. findings. *Journal of Personality and Social Psychology, 47,* 127–144.

Watson, D., Clark, L. A., & Tellegen, A. (1988). Development and validation of brief measures of positive and negative affect: The PANAS scales. *Journal of Personality and Social Psychology, 54,* 1063–1070.

Watson, D., & Tellegen, A. (1985). Toward a consensual structure of mood. *Psychological Bulletin, 98,* 219–235.

Watson, J. B., & Rayner, R. (1920). Conditioned emotional reactions. *Journal of Experimental Psychology, 3,* 1–14.

Watson, P. J., & Andrews, P. W. (2002). Towards a revised evolutionary adaptationist analysis of depression: The social navigation hypothesis. *Journal of Affective Disorders, 72,* 1–14.

Weaver, C. A., III (1993). Do you need a "flash" to form a flashbulb memory? *Journal of Experimental Psychology: General, 122,* 39–46.

Wegner, D. M., Schneider, D. J., Carter, S. R., III, & White, T. L. (1987). Paradoxical effects of thought suppression. *Journal of Personality and Social Psychology, 53,* 5–13.

Wehr, T. A., Turner, E. H., Shimada, J. M., Lowe, C. H., Barker, C., & Leinbenluft, E. (1998). Treatment of a rapidly cycling bipolar patient by using extended bed rest and darkness to stabilize the timing and duration of sleep. *Biological Psychiatry, 43,* 822–828.

Weinberg, M. K., Tronick, E. Z., Cohn, J. F., & Olson, K. L. (1999). Gender differences in emotional expressivity and self-regulation during early infancy. *Developmental Psychology, 35,* 175–188.

Weissman, M. M., Bland, R. C., Canino, G. J., Faravelli, C., Greenwald, S., Hwu, H.-G., et al. (1997). The cross-national epidemiology of panic disorder. *Archives of General Psychiatry, 54,* 305–309.

Wellman, H. M., Harris, P. L., Banerjee, M., & Sinclair, A. (1995). Early understanding of emotion: Evidence from natural language. *Cognition and Emotion, 9,* 117–149.

Wells, G. L., Olson, E. A., & Charman, S. D. (2002). The confidence of eyewitnesses in their identifications from lineups. *Current Directions in Psychological Science, 11,* 151–154.

Wender, P. H., Kety, S. S., Rosenthal, D., Schulsinger, F., Ortmann, J., & Lunde, I. (1986). Psychiatric disorders in the biological and adoptive families of adopted individuals with affective disorders. *Archives of General Psychiatry, 43,* 923–929.

Westergaard, G. C., Cleveland, A., Trenkle, M. K., Lussier, I. D., & Higley, J. D. (2003). CSF 5-HIAA concentration as an early screening tool for predicting significant life history outcomes in female specific-pathogen-free (SPF) rhesus macaques (*Macaca mulatta*) maintained in captive breeding groups. *Journal of Medical Primatology, 32,* 95–104.

Whalen, P. J. (1998). Fear, vigilance, and ambiguity: Initial neuroimaging studies of the human amygdala. *Current Directions in Psychological Science, 7,* 177–188.

Whalen, P. J., Kagan, J., Cook, R. G., Davis, F. C., Kim, H., Polis, S., et al. (2004). Human amygdala responsivity to masked fearful eye whites. *Science, 306,* 2061.

Whorf, B. L. (1956). *Language, thought, and reality.* Cambridge, MA: Technology Press of the Massachusetts Institute of Technology.

Wicker, B., Keysers, C., Plailly, J., Royet, J.-P., Gallese, V., & Rizzolatti, G. (2003). Both of us disgusted in my insula: The common neural basis of seeing and feeling disgust. *Neuron, 40,* 655–664.

Widom, C. S. (1989). Does violence beget violence? A critical examination of the literature. *Psychological Bulletin, 106,* 3–28.

Wieselquist, J., Rusbult, C. E., Foster, C. A., & Agnew, C. R. (1999). Commitment, pro-relationship behavior, and trust in close relationships. *Journal of Personality and Social Psychology, 77,* 942–966.

Wilde, J. (2001). Interventions for children with anger problems. *Journal of Rational-Emotive & Cognitive-Behavior Therapy, 19,* 191–197.

Williams, J. E., Paton, C. C., Siegler, I. C., Eigenbrodt, M. L., Nieto, F. J., & Tyroler, H. A. (2000). Anger proneness predicts coronary heart disease risk. *Circulation, 101,* 2034–2039.

Williams, J. M. G., Mathews, A., & MacLeod, C. (1996). The emotional Stroop task and psychopathology. *Psychological Bulletin, 120,* 3–24.

Williams, J. R., Insel, T. R., Harbaugh, C. R., & Carter, C. S. (1994). Oxytocin centrally administered facilitates formation of a partner preference in female prairie voles. *Journal of Neuroendocrinology, 6,* 247–250.

Williams, M. A., Morris, A. P., McGlone, F., Abbott, D. F., & Mattingley, J. B. (2004). Amygdala responses to fearful and happy facial expressions under conditions of binocular suppression. *Journal of Neuroscience, 24,* 2898–2904.

Wilson, G. S., Raglin, J. S., & Pritchard, M. E. (2002). Optimism, pessimism, and precompetition anxiety in college athletes. *Personality and Individual Differences, 32,* 893–902.

Wilson, K. A., & Hayward, C. (2005). A prospective evaluation of agoraphobia and depression symptoms following panic attacks in a community of adolescents. *Journal of Anxiety Disorders, 19,* 87–103.

Wilson, T. D., Lindsey, S., & Schooler, T. Y. (2000). A model of dual attitudes. *Psychological Review, 107,* 101–126.

Wirtz, D., Kruger, J., Scollon, C. N., & Diener, E. (2003). What to do on spring break? The role of predicted, on-line, and remembered experience in future choice. *Psychological Science, 14,* 520–524.

Wiseman, R. (1995). The megalab truth test. *Nature, 373,* 391.

Witherington, D. C., Campos, J. J., & Hertenstein, M. J. (2001). Principles of emotion and its development in infancy. In G. Bremner & A. Fogel (Eds.), *Blackwell handbook of infant development. Handbooks of developmental psychology* (pp. 427–464). Malden, MA: Blackwell.

Wittchen, H.-U., Reed, V., & Kessler, R. C. (1998). The relationship of agoraphobia and panic in a community sample of adolescents and young adults. *Archives of General Psychiatry, 55,* 1017–1024.

Wittchen, H.-U., Zhao, S., Kessler, R. C., & Eaton, W. W. (1994). *DSM-III-R* generalized anxiety disorder in the National Comorbidity Survey. *Archives of General Psychiatry, 51,* 355–364.

Witvliet, C. V. O., Ludwig, T. E., & Vander Laan, K. L. (2001). Granting forgiveness or harboring grudges: Implications for emotion, physiology, and health. *Psychological Science, 12,* 117–123.

Wolf, S. (1995). Dogmas that have hindered understanding. *Integrative Physiological and Behavioral Science, 30,* 3–4.

Wolff, P. H. (1987). *The development of behavioral states and the expression of emotions in early infancy.* Chicago: University of Chicago Press.

Woody, S. R., McLean, C., & Klassen, T. (2005). Disgust as a motivator of avoidance of spiders. *Journal of Anxiety Disorders, 19,* 461–475.

Woody, S. R., & Teachman, B. A. (2000). Intersection of disgust and fear: Normative and pathological views. *Clinical Psychology: Science and Practice, 7,* 291–311.

Woody, S. R., & Tolin, D. F. (2002). The relationship between disgust sensitivity and avoidant behavior: Studies of clinical and nonclinical samples. *Journal of Anxiety Disorders, 16,* 543–559.

Wright, S. S. (2000). Looking at the self in a rose-colored mirror: Unrealistically positive self-views and academic performance. *Journal of Social and Clinical Psychology, 19,* 451–462.

Wynn, K., & Chiang, W.-C. (1998). Limits to infants' knowledge of objects: The case of magical appearance. *Psychological Science, 9,* 448–455.

Xie, H., Cairns, R. B., & Cairns, B. D. (2002). The development of social aggression and physical aggression: A narrative analysis of interpersonal conflicts. *Aggressive Behavior, 28,* 341–355.

Xu, X., & Whyte, M. (1990). Love matches and arranged marriages: A Chinese replication. *Journal of Marriage and the Family, 52,* 709–722.

Yan, L. L., Liu, K., Matthews, K. A., Daviglus, M. L., Ferguson, T. F., & Kiefe, C. I. (2003). Psychosocial factors and risk of hypertension. *Journal of the American Medical Association, 290,* 2138–2148.

Yehuda, R. (1997). Sensitization of the hypothalamic-pituitary-adrenal axis in posttraumatic stress disorder. *Annals of the New York Academy of Sciences, 821,* 57–75.

Yehuda, R. (2002). Post-traumatic stress disorder. *New England Journal of Medicine, 346,* 108–114.

Yeomans, J. S., & Frankland, P. W. (1996). The acoustic startle reflex: Neurons and connections. *Brain Research Reviews, 21,* 301–314.

Yerkes, R. M., & Dodson, J. D. (1908). The relation of strength of stimulus to rapidity of habit formation. *Journal of Comparative Neurology and Psychology, 18,* 459–482.

Yik, M. S. M., & Russell, J. A. (2003). Chinese affect circumplex: I. Structure of recalled momentary affect. *Asian Journal of Social Psychology, 6,* 185–200.

Young, L. J. (2002). The neurobiology of social recognition, approach, and avoidance. *Biological Psychiatry, 51,* 18–26.

Young, P. T. (1936). *Motivation of behavior.* New York: Wiley.

Young, S. (2005). Coping strategies used by adults with ADHD. *Personality and Individual Differences, 38,* 809–816.

Young, S. N., & Leyton, M. (2002). The role of serotonin in human mood and social interaction: Insight from altered tryptophan levels. *Pharmacology, Biochemistry and Behavior, 71,* 857–865.

Yu, D. W., & Shepard, G. H., Jr. (1998). Is beauty in the eye of the beholder? *Nature, 396,* 321–322.

Zangara, A., Blair, R. J. R., & Curran, H. V. (2002). A comparison of the effects of a b-adrenergic blocker and a benzodiazepine upon the recognition of human facial expressions. *Psychopharmacology, 163,* 36–41.

Zarinpoush, F., Cooper, M., & Moylan, S. (2000). The effects of happiness and sadness on moral reasoning. *Journal of Moral Education, 29,* 397–412.

Zeidner, M., Matthews, G., & Roberts, R. D. (2001). Slow down, you move too fast: Emotional intelligence remains an "elusive" intelligence. *Emotion, 1,* 265–275.

Zillmann, D., Baron, R. A., & Tamborini, R. (1981). Social costs of smoking: Effects of tobacco smoke on hostile behavior. *Journal of Applied Social Psychology, 11,* 548–561.

Zillman, D., & Weaver, J. B. III (1999). Effects of prolonged exposure to gratuitous media violence on provoked and unprovoked hostile behavior. *Journal of Applied Social Psychology, 29,* 145–165.

Zorrilla, E. P., Luborsky, L., McKay, J. R., Rosenthal, R., Houldin, A., Tax, A., et al. (2001). The relationship of depression and stressors to immunological assays: A meta-analytic review. *Brain, Behavior, and Immunity, 15,* 199–226.

Zubieta, J.-K., Ketter, T. A., Bueller, J. A., Xu, Y., Kilbourn, M. R., Young, E. A., et al. (2003). Regulation of human affective responses by anterior cingulate and limbic μ-opiod neurotransmission. *Archives of General Psychiatry, 60,* 1145–1153.

Zullow, H. M., Oettingen, G., Peterson, C., & Seligman, M. E. P. (1988). Pessimistic explanatory style in the historical record: CAVing LBJ, presidential candidates, and East versus West Berlin. *American Psychologist, 43,* 673–682.

Photo Credits

This page constitutes an extension of the copyright page. We have made every effort to trace the ownership of all copyrighted material and to secure permission from copyright holders. In the event of any question arising as to the use of any material, we will be pleased to make the necessary corrections in future printings. Thanks are due to the following authors, publishers, and agents for permission to use the material indicated.

Inside front cover, bottom: Reprinted from Pavlidis, I., Eberhardt, N. L., and Levine, J. A., Seeing through the face of deception. *Nature, 415,* 35. Reproduced with permission of NATURE PUB. GROUP via Copyright Clearance Center. **Inside front cover, center:** Reprinted from Phan, K. L., Wager, T., Taylor, S. F., & Liberzon, I. (2002). Functional neuroanatomy of emotion: A meta-analysis of emotion activation studies in PET and fMRI. *NeuroImage, 16,* 331–348, with permission from Elsevier.

Chapter 1. Page 8: top left, Adam Pretty/Getty Images. **Page 8:** top right, © Peter Turnley/Corbis. **Page 11:** bottom right, © Lester Lefkowitz/Corbis. **Page 12:** top right, WDCN / Univ. College London / Photo Researchers, Inc. **Page 13:** bottom left, © P. Ekman & W. Friesen, *Unmasking the Face,* 2nd edition 1984. Used by permission of P. Ekman. **Page 14:** bottom right, Paul Thompson/FPG/Getty Images. **Page 23:** bottom left, Kathleen Olson. **Page 24:** top right, Philippe Marchand/Getty Images. **Page 24:** top left, © Cut and Deal Ltd/Alamy.

Chapter 2. Page 34: top left, Joseph Van Os/Getty Images. **Page 34:** top right, Stuart Westmorland/Corbis.

Page 34: top center, Tom McHugh / Photo Researchers, Inc. **Page 35:** Source: Darwin, Charles, *The Expression of the Emotions in Man and Animals (1872/1998),* with permission from Oxford University Press. **Page 36:** top left, © Eibl-Eibesfeldt. **Page 37:** top, © P. Ekman & W. Friesen, *Unmasking the Face,* 2nd edition 1984. Used by permission of P. Ekman. **Page 40:** Reprinted from Adams, R. B., & Kleck, R. E. (2003). Perceived gaze direction and the processing of facial displays of emotion. *Psychological Science, 14,* 644–647, with permission from Blackwell Publishing. **Page 41:** center left, photo courtesy of Dr. Paul Rozin. **Page 46:** top right, reprinted from: Scherer, K. R. (1992). What does facial expression express? In K. T. Strongman (Ed.), *International Review of Studies on Emotion,* Vol. 2 (p.139–165). Chichester: Wiley.

Chapter 3. Page 53: top right, Warner Bros. TV/Bright/Kauffman/Crane Pro/The Kobal Collection. **Page 53:** top left, © Corbis Sygma. **Page 61:** center, © Antoine Gyori/AGP/Corbis. **Page 61:** top center, © Mark Richards/PhotoEdit.

Chapter 4. Page 77: top right, Kristin I. Stith/Getty Images. **Page 77:** top left, Niki Mareschal/Getty Images. **Page 78:** top left, © Blend Images / Alamy. **Page 83:** top right, © Anne Dowie. **Page 85:** top left, © Mark Richards/PhotoEdit. **Page 86:** top left, © LWA-Dann Tardif/Corbis. **Page 87:** top left, from A. N. Meltzoff & M. K. Moore, Imitation of facial and manual gestures by human neonates. *Science, 198* (1977), pp. 75–78. **Page 95:** center right, Jonathan Kirn/Getty Images. **Page 95:** center left, © Patrik Giardino/Corbis.

Chapter 5. Page 103: bottom center, from Bishop, S. J., Duncan, J., & Lawrence, A. D. (2004). State anxiety modulation of the amygdala response to unattended threat-related stimuli. *Journal of Neuroscience, 24,* 10364–10368. © 2004 Society for Neuroscience. **Page 105:** bottom right, Source: Darwin, Charles, *The Expression of the Emotions in Man and Animals* (1872/1998), with permission from Oxford University Press. **Page 106:** bottom right, Michelle Shiota. **Page 111:** top left, Robert E. Daemmrich/Getty Images. **Page 116:** top left, reprinted from Vuilleumier, P. (2005). Cognitive science: Staring fear in the face. *Nature, 433,* 22–23. Reproduced with permission of NATURE PUB. GROUP via Copyright

Clearance Center. **Page 116:** top right, reprinted with permission from Whalen, P. J., Kagan, J., Cook, R. G., Davis, F. C., Kim, H., Polis, S., McLaren, D. G., Somerville, L. H., McLean, A. A., Maxwell, J. S., & Johnstone, T. (2004). Human amygdala responsivity to masked fearful eye whites. *Science, 306,* 2061. © 2003, AAAS.

Chapter 6. Page 127: top right, Sean Murphy/Getty Images. **Page 132:** top center, Akhtar Soomro/Deanpictures/The Image Works. **Page 132:** top right, © Corbis. **Page 132:** top left, © Emely/zefa/Corbis. **Page 140:** top left, © Mike Lane/Alamy.

Chapter 7. Page 153: bottom, Source: Darwin, Charles, *The Expression of the Emotions in Man and Animals* (1872/1998), with permission from Oxford University Press. **Page 154:** top left, © David Young-Wolff/PhotoEdit.

Chapter 8. Page 167: top, © Paul Ekman. **Page 178:** top left, Al Bello/Getty Images. **Page 183:** top right, © Bettmann/Corbis.

Chapter 9. Page 195: top right, Jurgen Reisch/Getty Images. **Page 197:** top right, Gary Meszaros / Photo Researchers, Inc.

Chapter 10. Page 214: top right, Photos courtesy of Dr. Paul Rozin. **Page 220:** top left, Photo courtesy of Dr.

Paul Rozin. **Page 220:** top right, © Michael Newman/Photo Edit.

Chapter 11. Page 231: bottom right, © Corbis. **Page 234:** bottom right, © Corbis. **Page 237:** top left, Reprinted from Tracy, J. L., & Robins, R. W. (2004). Show your pride: Evidence for a discrete emotion expression. *Psychological Science, 15,* 194–197, with permission from Blackwell Publishing.

Chapter 12. Page 243: bottom, © Dmitry Azarov/ITAR-TASS/Corbis. **Page 243:** top, © Reuters/Corbis. **Page 245:** bottom left, © Adrian Burke/Corbis. **Page 245:** bottom right, © Frans Lanting/Corbis. **Page 245:** top right, © Josh Westrich/zefa/Corbis.

Chapter 13. Page 265: top left, reprinted with permission from Damasio, H., Grabowski, T., Frank, R., Galaburda, A. M., & Damasio, A. R. (1994). The return of Phineas Gage: The skull of a famous patient yields clues about the brain. *Science, 264,* 1102–1105. © 1994, AAAS. **Page 267:** bottom right, Scott Olson/AFP/Getty Images. **Page 276:** top left, reprinted from Townshend, J. M., & Duka, T. (2003). Mixed emotions: Alcoholics impairments in the recognition of specific emotional facial expressions. *Neuropsychologia, 41,* 773–782, with permission from Elsevier.

Chapter 14. Page 283: top, John Olson/Time Life Pictures/Getty Images.

Inside back cover, top left: From Williams, M. A., Morris, A. P., McGlone, F., Abbott, D. F., & Mattingley, J. B. (2004). Amygdala responses to fearful and happy facial expressions under conditions of binocular suppression. *Journal of Neuroscience, 24,* 2898–2904. © 2004. Society for Neuroscience. **Inside back cover, center right:** Reprinted from Kontsevich, L. L., & Tyler, C. W. (2004). What makes Mona Lisa smile? *Vision Research, 44,* 1493–1498, with permission from Elsevier. **Inside back cover, center left:** Reprinted from Takahashi, H., Yahata, N., Koeda, M., Matsuda, T., Asai, K., & Okubo, Y. (2004). Brain activation associated with evaluative processes of guilt and embarrassment: An fMRI study. *NeuroImage, 23,* 967–974, with permission from Elsevier. **Inside back cover, bottom right:** Reprinted with permission from Beauregard, M., Lévesque, J., & Bourgouin, P. (2001). Neural correlates of conscious self-regulation of emotion. *Journal of Neuroscience, 21,* RC165. © 2001, Society for Neuroscience. **Inside back cover, top right:** Reprinted with permission from Eisenberger, N. I., Lieberman, M. D., & Williams, K. D. (2003). Does rejection hurt? An fMRI study of social exclusion. *Science, 302,* 290–292. © 2003, AAAS.

Name Index

A

Abbar, M., 138
Abbey, A., 195
Abbott, D. F., 115
Abdel-Azim, E., 179
Abe, J. A. A., 89
Abercrombie, H. C., 246, 292
Abramov, I., 82
Abramson, L. Y., 159, 252
Abu-Lughod, L., 67
Aburada, M., 292
Ackermann, R., 119, 252, 253
Adamec, R. E., 127
Adamo, U. H., 160
Adams, E., 256
Adams, R. B., 40, 153
Adler, A., 176, 208
Adler, N. E., 181
Adolph, K. E., 79
Adolphs, R., 40, 42, 43, 114, 115, 116,
    242, 276
Agnew, C. R., 208
Aharon, I., 180
Aharon-Peretz, J., 266
Ahmetzanov, M. V., 248
Ainsworth, M. D. S., 88, 196, 203
Akirav, I., 246
al'Absi, M., 146
Albin, M., 91
Alexander, A. L., 114
Alicke, M. D., 252
Allen, D. J., 276
Allen, J. J. B., 168
Allen, N. B., 151
Alloy, L. B., 159, 252, 302
Alonso, A., 275
Alper, C. M., 294

Altman, J., 309
Alvarez, J. -C., 158–159
Amara, D. A., 135
Amaral, D. G., 113
Ambady, N., 38, 39, 60
American Psychiatric Association,
    118, 144, 145, 148
Anagnostaras, S. G., 113
Anderson, A. K., 42, 115, 116
Anderson, C., 102, 126, 128, 141, 142,
    202
Anderson, G., 158–159, 291
Anderson, N. B., 285
Anderson, S. W., 266
Andrews, P. W., 152
Angleitner, A., 174
Anglin, J. M., 194
Angold, A., 93, 145
Angrilli, A., 119
Antoun, N., 43, 218
Apfelbach, R., 113
Applefield, J. M., 141–142
Archer, J., 139
Arguello, A. P., 222
Arluke, A., 229
Armony, J. L., 20, 114
Armor, D. A., 304
Arndt, L. A., 296
Arnett, J. J., 92, 93
Arnold, E., 289
Arnold, M. B., 302, 309
Arnold, M. J, 166
Aron, A., 200–201, 202, 208
Aron, A. P., 19
Aron, E. N., 200–201, 208
Arrindell, W. A., 218
Ashkanasy, N. M., 278

Ashmore, M., 215–216
Ashmore, R. D., 285
Aspinwall, L. G., 166
Astin, J. A., 303
Astington, J. W., 84
Asukai, N., 294
Atkins, C. M., 113
Augustine, 3
Augustoni-Ziskind, M. L., 223
Austin, E. J., 273
Averill, J. R., 138, 139
Avero, P., 108, 244
Ayduk, O., 144, 305
Azuma, H., 92

B

Baccman, C., 200
Bachorowski, J.-A., 182
Backonja, M.-M, 303
Badcock, P. B. T., 151
Bagwell, C. L., 209
Baillargeon, R., 88
Bailly, M. D., 133
Bair, M. J., 151
Baker, K. B., 113
Baldwin, D. A., 85
Balgemann, D., 55
Banaji, M., 251, 256
Banerjee, M., 87
Barbee, A. P., 194
Bard, K. A., 154
Bard, P., 15–16
Bargellini, A., 291
Barker, C., 161
Barlow, D. H., 66, 118
Baron-Cohen, S., 276
Baron, R. A., 129

Subject Index

A

ability tests, 274–278
abuse
  friendship and, 209–210
  personality disorders and, 145
  sexual, 161
  Stroop Test for substance, 216
  violence and, 140–141
academic intelligence, 278
ACTH (adrenocorticotropic hormone), 291
action of the nervous system hypothesis, Darwin, 33–34, 60
action tendencies
  Cannon-Bard theory of, 15–16
  defining emotion in terms of, 4
  James-Lange theory of, 15
  physiological measurements of, 9–13
  usefulness of, 4–5
adaptive mechanism, depression as, 152
adolescents
  cognitive maturation in, 83
  embarrassment in, 233–234
  emotions in, 93
  friendship and, 209–210
  happiness and, 174–175
adoption, violence and, 140–141
adrenal cortex
  continuing arousal stimulating, 291
  resistance stage, General Adaptation Syndrome, 283–284
adrenal glands
  anger measurement and, 137
  memory tasks and, 292
adrenaline, memory and, 246
adrenocorticotropic hormone (ACTH), 291
adult attachments
  attraction and, 203–206
  defined, 210

oxytocin and, 196–198
  romantic love and, 202–206
adulthood, emotional development in, 93–96
advertising, 264
Affect Infusion Model, 250, 258
Africans
  bodily signs of stress in, 60
  negative emotions and, 57
age
  embarrassment and, 233–234
  emotional intelligence and, 278
  emotional intensity and, 93–95
  emotional regulation and, 96
  emotional salience and, 96
  happiness and, 174–176
aggression
  frustration-aggression hypothesis, 127–128
  hostile and instrumental, 124–125
  individual and situational differences in, 137–142
  measurement of, 130–134
  neurochemistry of, 135–137
agoraphobia, 118, 122
alarm stage
  defined, 297
  in General Adaptation Syndrome, 283–284
  short-term allostasis and, 290–292
alcohol
  amygdala and, 117
  emotional escape through, 289, 309
allostasis
  defined, 297
  immune system and prolonged, 293–295
  overview of, 290
  short-term, 290–292
allostatic load, 290, 297
amae
  defined, 73

love/attachment and, 190–191
  not acknowledged by Americans, 55
  not encouraged in some cultures, 31
  overview of, 54–55
American Enterprise, 207
Americans
  emotional display rules of, 61–63
  gestures and expressions of, 36–37
  horizontal society of, 66–67
  individualism vs. collectivism and, 64–65
  interpreting facial displays of, 63–64
  self-conscious emotions and, 65–66
  shame and, 67
  socialization of emotional expression, 90
  style of training children, 92
amusement. *See also* positive emotion
  causes of, 181–184
  creativity and, 252
  function of, 184–185
amygdala
  defined, 122
  disgust and, 218
  effect of tranquilizers on, 117
  emotional information processed in, 12
  enthusiasm and, 179–180
  facial expressions and, 113–115
  fear and, 42, 104
  impairment in emotions after damage to, 42–43, 115–117, 317
  memory and, 246–247
  prefrontal cortex connection to, 264
  reappraisal and, 306
  response of older people to positive events and, 94
  startle response and, 112–113

TO THE OWNER OF THIS BOOK:

I hope that you have found *Emotion* useful. So that this book can be improved in a future edition, would you take the time to complete this sheet and return it? Thank you.

School and address:_____

Department:_____

Instructor's name:_____

1. What I like most about this book is:_____

_____

_____

2. What I like least about this book is:

_____

_____

3. My general reaction to this book is:

_____

_____

4. The name of the course in which I used this book is:

_____

5. Were all of the chapters of the book assigned for you to read?_____

   If not, which ones weren't?_____

6. In the space below, or on a separate sheet of paper, please write specific suggestions for improving this book and anything else you'd care to share about your experience in using this book.

_____

_____

_____

_____

THOMSON

WADSWORTH

BUSINESS REPLY MAIL
FIRST-CLASS MAIL   PERMIT NO. 102   MONTEREY CA

POSTAGE WILL BE PAID BY ADDRESSEE

Attn: *Vicki Knight, Psychology Publisher*

Wadsworth/Thomson Learning
60 Garden Ct Ste 205
Monterey CA 93940-9967

OPTIONAL:

Your name: _____ Date: _____

May we quote you, either in promotion for *Emotion*, or in future publishing ventures?

Yes: _____   No: _____

Sincerely yours,

James W. Kalat and Michelle N. Shiota